HUMOR OF THE OLD SOUTHWEST

Humor
of the
Old Southwest

EDITED WITH AN INTRODUCTION BY

HENNIG COHEN

AND

WILLIAM B. DILLINGHAM

Second Edition

Donated by
The Flock Family

THE UNIVERSITY OF GEORGIA PRESS

ATHENS

Library of Congress Catalog Card Number: 74-13512
International Standard Book Number: 0-8203-0358-5

The University of Georgia Press, Athens 30602

Originally published by the Houghton Mifflin Company

Printed in the United States of America

PREFACE
TO THE SECOND EDITION

Among the more pleasant opportunities that knock at a scholar's door is the opportunity to revise. This is thrice a pleasure because it flatters his vanity, it allows him to correct his mistakes and update his findings, and it gives him a chance to look at his handiwork with a soul-satisfying sense of detachment, for his viewpoint has shifted to that cooler region of time and distance.

The first pleasure is personal, and it would be impertinent to remark on it here except for the fact that *Humor of the Old Southwest* was, upon publication, unique. It was—and still is—the most complete collection devoted exclusively to this body of material. A decade has made it something of a historical object in its own right. It can now be seen as marking a few miles along a fascinating bypath of American literary history first explored in the 1930's by such trailblazers as Franklin J. Meine in *Tall Tales of the Southwest* (1930), Constance Rourke in *American Humor* (1931), Bernard DeVoto in *Mark Twain's America* (1932), and Walter Blair in *Native American Humor* (1937). These pioneering anthologies and cultural commentaries date almost exactly a century from the Indian removals that opened to settlement the backcountry known as the "Old Southwest," and from the publication of Longstreet's *Georgia Scenes* (1835), conventionally considered the place where the genre called "Southwestern humor" begins.

Mark Twain was born the year Longstreet's newspaper sketches were gathered into a book. Longstreet was born during Washington's first term as president and he survived the 1860's, which the large majority of Southwestern humorists did not. In short, the 1930's literary historians of Southwestern humor were defining a genre that, in its original form, had lived out its life. By the 1930's it was part of a historical record, one especially interesting to critics concerned with discovering the origins of American culture, the nature of the American experience, and the particular usefulness of the usable past. They did not recognize its existence in the revitalized form that Faulkner, for example, was giving it.

Regarding the reviser's second pleasure, typographical errors have been quietly corrected. One of the two "Anonymous" contributions, selections uneasily included though their quality seemed to demand it, has been identified through the kindness of an expert (see p. 376). The most important updating is bibliographical. The "Bibliography" has been completely revised. Toward this end the serial bibliographies in *American Literature, PMLA,* and *American Literary Scholarship* have been searched, as have such general compilations as *A Bibliographical Guide to the Study of Southern Literature* (1968) and the recent specialized checklist, "Humor of the Old Southwest" in *Mississippi Quarterly* (1974). Its enhanced size and quality indicate the growth of scholarship and have demanded a corresponding degree of selectivity. Harris, the writer who has consistently attracted the most critical interest, provides a case in point. The original bibliography has fifteen entries following his name, including, in anticipation of publication, Milton Rickels' biography of 1965. The list now has forty entries, among them such important contributions as the corrected text of *Sut Lovingood's Yarns* (1966) and his uncollected sketches, *High Times and Hard Times* (1967), edited by M. Thomas Inge.

The "Introduction" has not been altered because its basic statements appear to have lasted out the years, and the revised, expanded bibliography facilitates access to supplementary and modifying information. Yet ten years *have* passed and re-examination of the book *does* evoke second thoughts. For instance, it was once considered discerning to distinguish between the teller and the protagonist of the tale. Proper attention paid to the structure often revealed an elite raconteur who described the doings of a lowlife character while holding himself above and apart. This procedure emphasized social and political distinctions which are significant. But it occasionally blurred those moments when lowlife is not simply something quaint, extravagant, clownish, perhaps grotesque, those vital moments when vernacular style and high style, lowlife and highlife converge. In "The Big Bear of Arkansas" the frame structure and the division between narrator and bear hunter are important, but the power of the story of the "unhuntable bear" that "died when his time come" is dramatized in the "grave silence" that follows the telling. In this moment of insight, the distinctions between backwoods hunter, genteel narrator, and the diverse audience aboard the Mississippi steamboat have somehow disappeared. And if, in the process of the drama, the hunter slips at the crucial moment and almost falls into his own excrement, then so do we all.

The social hierarchy, moreover, may be subtly inverted, even in a spare, apparently unpretentious anecdote. Sol Smith describes "The

Consolate Widow" whose worthless husband has met a grisly death in "a quarter race for a gallon of whisky." An outsider and a man of sensibility, he is aghast when the widow voices more sorrow that her husband lost the gallon of whiskey than that he lost his life. "I reckon you ain't acquainted about these parts," she says to Smith, softly mocking his fundamental ignorance and conventionality. Uncouth and heartless she might first appear to be, and on this surface the anecdote produces a comic shock, but she has a Hobbesian grasp of the brutishness and brevity of human existence and the joke is on Sol Smith who does not. Sut Lovingood would have seen the point.

Edmund Wilson stirred up the animals when he pronounced *Sut Lovingood's Yarns* "by far the most repellent book of any literary merit in American literature." In a superficial way he is right, and his verdict might be applied, superficially at least, to Southwestern humor as a whole. The genre contains much that is repellent. To apply currently fashionable terms, Southwestern humor is often racist and sexist. It battens on brutality and squalor. Yet Wilson missed the lust for life it reveals, its firm grip on reality, its basic compassion. It is not always easy to see these qualities in a character like Lige Benadix, the costive glutton who survived heroic medical attentions, or Ransy Sniffle, dirt-eater and trouble-maker, or Sut. But they are there.

"Marse Henry" Watterson, one of the first and best students of Southwestern humor, preserves a fragment of the eulogy said at the graveside of Sut Lovingood by Parson Bullen: "We air met, my brethering, to bury this ornery cuss. He had hosses, an' he run 'em; he had chickens, an' he fit 'em; he had kiards, an' he played 'em. Let us try an' ricollect his virtues—ef he had any—an' forgit his vices— ef we can. *For of sich air the kingdom of heaven!*" As usual Parson Bullen came through with a pretty good performance, but here he seems to have caught something of the ambivalence that characterizes Sut and Southwestern humor as a whole. But ambivalence or not, and likely because of it, we can be sure that Sut and his "brethering" and his progeny will not submit quietly to anybody's burial service.

CONTENTS

INTRODUCTION

The Southern frontier in the first half of the nineteenth century was an elusive, ever-changing line. What was wilderness in the 1820's became a settlement by the 1830's. The frontier moved rapidly from the interior of North Carolina, South Carolina, and Georgia westward through Alabama, Tennessee, Mississippi, and across the great river through Missouri, Arkansas, and Louisiana. William Byrd, a Virginia aristocrat, and numerous other early travelers in this region wrote about the peculiar specimens of humanity to be seen in the backwoods. In 1728 Byrd portrayed comically the squatters of backcountry North Carolina. They were so lazy that they imposed all the work on their poor wives, he said, while they would "lye and Snore, till the sun has risen one-third of his course." Many of the travelers commented upon the strange, comic ritual the frontiersmen performed before they indulged in fighting. James Kirke Paulding wrote in *Letters from the South* (1817) of a batteauxman and a wagoner who worked themselves up to a fight by exaggerated bragging: "The wagoner flapped his hands against his hips, and crowed like a cock; the batteauxman curved his neck and neighed like a horse." Then they argued which man had the finest horse, the handsomest sweetheart, and the best rifle. Their anger mounted at each new brag, and they finally fought it out with a loss of much blood and many teeth. Roving preachers, Timothy Flint and Mason L. Weems, who were both traveling the Southwest in the early years of the nineteenth century, described their meetings with braggarts or ring-tailed roarers. Weems recorded a fight in which one of the combatants swore that he could "flog any Son of a B-tch on the whole ground." His opponent answered: "Here I come, gentlemen! . . . Half Horse Half Alligator, and with a little touch of the snapping Turtle."

When these odd frontier hybrids, these half-alligators, half-horses, were not bragging and fighting, they might have been heard spinning yarns of superhuman hunters and describing animals that possessed a fantastic understanding of human beings. The loud-talking, wildly imaginative storytellers provided the origins of Old Southwest humor.

By the 1830's the region was saturated with tall tales and comic stories that were laughed at over campfires, aboard rafts floating slowly under the stars, or in villages wherever men gathered. Then all over the South men, many of whom never thought of themselves principally as writers, began to compose humorous sketches for publication. Before the 1860's dozens of them sent their accounts of ring-tailed roarers or of comic manners to newspapers and sporting journals. This brand of American comedy flourished from the publication of Augustus Baldwin Longstreet's *Georgia Scenes* (1835) until the Civil War. There were forerunners, Weems, Paulding, and others; and Southwestern humor can also be found later in the writings of such authors as Mark Twain and even William Faulkner and Robert Penn Warren. But the overwhelming concentration was in that period of some twenty-six years from 1835 to 1861.

Not all of Longstreet's sketches in *Georgia Scenes* dealt with rustic Southern types, but there was enough Southwestern humor in the book to influence other writers. Numerous collections of humor did follow: William Tappan Thompson's *Major Jones's Courtship* (1843), Johnson Jones Hooper's *Some Adventures of Simon Suggs* (1845), Thomas Bangs Thorpe's *Mysteries of the Backwoods* (1846), John S. Robb's *Streaks of Squatter Life* (1847), Joseph M. Field's *The Drama in Pokerville* (1847), Henry Clay Lewis's *Odd Leaves from the Life of a Louisiana "Swamp Doctor"* (1850), Joseph B. Cobb's *Mississippi Scenes* (1851), Joseph G. Baldwin's *The Flush Times of Alabama and Mississippi* (1853), George Washington Harris's *Sut Lovingood's Yarns* (1867), and several more.

Many of the stories in these collections were first printed in a humor and sporting magazine called the New York *Spirit of the Times*. The editor of this journal, William T. Porter, was sympathetic to the Southern humorists, sought their sketches, and helped them get their books published. Although he did not himself write humorous material, he was extremely influential among those who did. The *Spirit of the Times* was their principal medium of publication, serving not only as a ready means for countless new humorists to break into print but also setting a standard of form and quality. During his editorship (1831-1856) Porter's paper was, as its subtitle indicates, "A Chronicle of the Turf, Agriculture, Field Sports, Literature, and the Stage." Its humor "correspondents" were not paid but were lavishly thanked and praised for their contributions. By 1856 Porter claimed (an exaggeration, no doubt) 40,000 subscribers and extensive international circulation. Readers and contributors in the North and in the South were usually gentlemen of some means with a leisurely interest in masculine pursuits. They were, Porter said, "country gentle-

men, planters, lawyers, etc. 'who live at home at ease.' " Racing news
and humorous anecdotes constituted the chief appeal of the journal.
The success of the *Spirit* prompted other papers to include humorous
sketches — sometimes original, sometimes reprintings — in their col-
umns. By the early 1850's such newspapers as the New Orleans
Delta and the *Picayune,* the St. Louis *Reveille,* and the Cincinnati
News rivaled the *Spirit of the Times* in this respect.

The writers who sent their brief anecdotes to these papers often
went on to publish one or more collections of stories. But they were
not professional authors. They wanted to do something in the writing
line, did not expect to be paid for it, liked to publish under a
pseudonym, and sometimes regretted at a later date having indulged
in such a trivial pastime. They had their own professions and were
writers only by avocation. What is surprising is that there were so
many of them and that they were producing such similar results.
They hid behind such pseudonyms as "Pete Whetstone" and "The
Turkey Runner" to enjoy the amateurish thrill of writing surreptitiously. Others no doubt felt that their tales were relatively unim-
portant and would injure their professional status. After all, some of
these stories were earthy, shocking to the gentle reader. The gap
between the genteel literature which was being enjoyed by pale young
ladies in New England drawing rooms and the masculine humor which
filled the pages of the *Spirit of the Times* was immense. The use of
pseudonyms also suggests the extent to which basic materials were
common property, a part of the folk heritage of the region.

So similar were these writers that a composite portrait is possible.
The typical Southwestern humorist smiled easily but was no clown.
He was a man of education and breeding who felt deeply and spoke
with conviction. Usually he wanted to talk about politics. Often a
devoted Whig, he was convinced that if the nation was to be saved
from chaos and degradation, only the honor, reasonableness, and
sense of responsibility of gentlemen — Whig gentlemen — could save
it. Usually he was a lawyer and often also a judge, a state legislator,
a congressman, or even a governor, but he might have been a
physician, a planter, or, rarely, an actor, artist, or army officer.
Frequently he was also a newspaper editor. For the South he felt a
protective and defensive love, though he might have been born elsewhere. He was keenly angered by the North, which seemed to show
little understanding of the South and its institutions. He defended
slavery and, when the time came, secession, with passion. He was
a relatively young man, but already he had known frustration, and he
was to know a good deal more of it before his life was over.
Ambitious and hot-tempered, he endured defeat only with great per-

sonal pain. This is a rigid mold, perhaps, but the Southwestern writers who do not fit into it are few. Seldom has a literary movement or school of writers of any time or place reflected more unanimity in background, temperament, literary productions, aims, and beliefs.

For subjects to write about, the Southwestern frontier humorist had simply to open his ears and his eyes. The oral tale passed from one generation to another and remained a rich reservoir of materials. As important as the oral tradition was, however, the influence of literary sources should not be underestimated. Even though the Southwestern writers were not professionals, they were educated men, self-taught or otherwise, who especially admired the style and wit of such eighteenth-century essayists as Addison, Steele, and Goldsmith and who were acquainted with some of the best of classical and modern literature. If they used folk tales from their Southern environment, they frequently also made use of stories they had read. They knew, for example, *The Travels of Baron Munchausen,* and situations in that book appear repeatedly in their writings. The subtitle of Paulding's *John Bull in America* (1825) is "The New Munchausen," and one of Francis James Robinson's sketches about "the Texas Traveller" is entitled, in part, "Baron Munchausen Revived." Washington Irving exerted a strong influence on Southern humor. The *Sketch Book* (1819) achieved immediate popularity. "The Legend of Sleepy Hollow" has most of the ingredients of a typical sketch of Southwestern humor: the physically awkward, ugly, and avaricious Ichabod; the good-natured but rowdy Brom Bones and his friends, who love a practical joke; the desirable plum, Katrina Van Tassel. All that is missing is the Southern backwoods vernacular. It would be difficult to estimate the number of Southern tales directly influenced by "Sleepy Hollow." Some were obviously and openly based on it: Joseph B. Cobb's "The Legend of Black Creek," William Tappan Thompson's "The Runaway Match" and "Adventure of a Sabbath-Breaker," and Francis James Robinson's "The Frightened Serenaders." Others show the influence indirectly but unmistakably in their use of characters modeled after Ichabod Crane, Brom Bones, and Katrina Van Tassel.

Folk and literary elements were combined by the Southwestern humorists with local and personal materials and emerged in the form of hundreds of sketches ranging from mythic tales of gigantic men and animals to more comic treatments of rogues, practical jokers, and eccentrics. The backwoodsman, the squatter, or the villager is shown enjoying his favorite sport or social event — hunting, fighting, politicking, party-going, or yarn spinning. The nature and variety of Southwestern frontier humor may be suggested by the following list of subjects:

(1) The hunt
(2) Fights, mock fights, and animal fights
(3) Courtings, weddings, and honeymoons
(4) Frolics and dances
(5) Games, horse races, and other contests
(6) Militia drills
(7) Elections and electioneering
(8) The legislature and the courtroom
(9) Sermons, camp meetings, and religious experiences
(10) The visitor in a humble home
(11) The country boy in the city
(12) The riverboat
(13) Adventures of the rogue
(14) Pranks and tricks of the practical joker
(15) Gambling
(16) Trades and swindles
(17) Cures, sickness and bodily discomfort, medical treatments
(18) Drunks and drinking
(19) Dandies, foreigners, and city slickers
(20) Oddities and local eccentrics

Besides amusing himself and others, the Southwestern frontier humorist was attempting to record realistically local customs and manners and to provide a chronicle of the times. He generally dealt with scenes and customs out of the immediate past, striving, as he often explained, to preserve the picture of an era which was quickly passing away. Longstreet subtitled *Georgia Scenes* "Characters, Incidents, etc., in the First Half Century of the Republic" and stressed in his preface the basis in real life for the incidents and the people he wrote about. In the preface to *The Big Bear of Arkansas and Other Sketches* (1845), one of two anthologies of humor which he edited, William T. Porter commented on the new school of humorous writers in the South whose objective was to describe "thrilling scenes and adventures in that then comparatively unknown region, and the extraordinary characters occasionally met with — their strange language and habitudes, and the peculiar and sometimes fearful characteristics of the 'squatters' and early settlers." John S. Robb wrote in *Streaks of Squatter Life* (1847) that "every step of the pioneer's progress has been marked wtih incidents, humorous and thrilling, which wait but the wizard spell of a bright mind and able pen to call them from misty tradition, and clothe them with speaking life."

To some extent these pronouncements resulted from a desire to give an aura of reality. The widespread objection to fiction as untrue was still an obstacle to the writer. Thus authors like Longstreet may have been protecting themselves in the same fashion as the early novelists Hannah Foster and Susanna Rowson, whose works were always "founded on fact." But this must have been a slight motive. They did not have to please the fastidious hairsplitters of moral principle. Their audience was far different from that which swooned over *The Coquette* (1797) and *Charlotte Temple* (1791). They had a genuine interest in local color and in history, and filled their pages with vivid pictures of the times. Hooper, for example, portrays a segment of the chaos in Alabama which resulted from the rumor of approaching Indians in the Creek War:

> There goes old man Simmons, with his wife and three daughters, together with two feather beds, a few chairs, and a small assortment of pots and ovens, in a cart drawn by a bob-tail, gray pony. On the topmost bed, and forming the apex of this pile of animate and inanimate "luggage," sits the old tom-cat, whom the youngest daughter would not suffer to remain lest he might come to harm. "Who knows," she exclaims, *"what* they might do to the poor old fellow?" On they toil! the old man's head, ever and anon, turned back to see if they are pursued by the remorseless foe; while the wife and daughters scream direfully, every ten minutes, discerning in the distance a cow or a hog— "Oh, they'll kill us! they'll skelp us; they'll tar us all *to* pieces! Oh, Lord! daddy! oh, Lord!" But the old tom-cat sits there, gravely and quietly; the very incarnation of tom philosophy!

Baldwin's *The Flush Times of Alabama and Mississippi* is virtually a social history of "that halcyon period, ranging from the year of Grace, 1835, to 1837; that golden era, when shinplasters were the sole currency; when bank-bills were 'as thick as Autumn leaves in Vallambrosa,' and credit was a franchise." The inordinate love of oysters, the popularity of the bustle, the flush times and hard times, wars and rumors of wars, the great excitement centering on the Millerites and their frenzied belief in the end of the world — all emerge clearly from the pages of the Southwestern humorists.

In a sense, then, these writers were local colorists, the immediate ancestors of that group of regional authors who flourished from a few years after the Civil War to the turn of the century. But the Southwestern humorists were vastly different from the later local colorists in several ways, one of which was their lack of respect for delicate sensibilities. A writer like Longstreet who felt the need to apologize for putting "damn" in the mouth of some of his characters was capable of having another character say to the coins he has just won in a gander pulling: "Oh you little shining sons o' bitches! walk into your Mas' Johnny's pocket." The writings of Bret Harte, Joel Chandler Harris, Thomas Nelson Page, and the other local colorists would hardly have offended the taste of young women in nineteenth-century seminaries. Even the earliest documents of the Southern frontier, on the other hand, are often characterized by stark, realistic details and off-color, bawdy comments. For example, in *The Drunkard's Looking Glass* (1812) Parson Weems describes with unpleasant clarity a drunkard who rides his horse into a tree: "There was not a sign of a nose remaining on his face, the violence of the blow had crushed it flat, miserably battering his mouth and teeth, and completely scalping the right side of his face and head — the flesh, skin, and ear, torn off to the back of his skull. One of his eyes, meeting a snag on the trunk of a tree, was clearly knocked out of its socket; and, held only by a string of skin, there it lay naked on his bloody cheek."

The Southwestern humorist portrayed relationships between the sexes as directly as he described gory accidents and fights. In numerous stories visitors in one-room cabins have to undress for bed before the young ladies of the house — all to the great embarrassment of the visitor. Courtings and honeymoons also provoke racy humor. Joseph B. Cobb's "The Bride of Lick-the-Skillet" favors the reader with a bawdy account of a wild, prank-filled wedding night, during which an old suitor of the bride, posing as a ghost, frightens the bridegroom away and takes his place in the bed. Cobb's description of the bride's nude bath in a spring adds to the earthiness of this uninhibited story. Another sketch, John Winslow's "Mr. Warrick in Distress," is representative of a number of pieces which deal openly with some of the distressing hardships of a young man in love. Not the least of Billy Warrick's troubles is his fiancée's mother, old Mrs. Bass, who embarrasses him by criticizing pants that button down the front (he had forgotten to button his) and ladies' bustles, which she says make them look like "an 'oman was sorter in a curious way behind." After the old lady retires for the night Billy begins kissing his beloved Barbry in earnest, only to be mortified by Mrs. Bass's sudden cry: "My lord! — Barbry, old Troup [the dog] is in the milk-pan! — I heerd him smackin his lips a lickin of the milk." At the furthest extreme from the genteel tradition in almost every way are Harris's yarns of Sut Lovingood. Whether lusting after sensuous Sicily Burns or making love to fat Sal Yardley, Sut is one of literature's most unabashed spokesmen on the subject of sex. About young widows, for instance, he says:

> But then, George, gals an' ole maids haint the things tu fool time away on. Hits widders, by golly, what am the rale sensibil, steady-goin, never-skeerin, never-kickin, willin, sperrited, smoof pacers. They cum clost up tu the hoss-block, standin still wif thar purty silky years playin, an' the naik-veins a-throbbin, an' waits fur the word, which ove course

yu gives, arter yu finds yer feet well in the stirrup, an' away they moves like a cradil on cushioned rockers, ur a spring buggy runnin in damp san'.

The form which Southern humorists preferred was much more conventional than their subject matter. It ranges from the semi-literate epistles of Thompson, C. F. M. Noland, and Phillip B. January to the literary essays of Joseph G. Baldwin. Most sketches, however, employ a framework. In such stories, the author takes the superior vantage point of a cultured gentleman observing and describing the doings of rougher folk. The typical sketch opens and closes with the author's own words, reasoned and dignified. Often he speaks in the first person and relates an occurrence which he says he personally witnessed. Hooper's "Col. Hawkins and the Court" begins: "Some years ago, I knew an individual whose *sobriquet* was 'Col. Hawkins,' and who was the most perfect specimen of the dare-devil frontier-man, that I ever saw, at least in Alabama." After telling of Hawkins's escapade, frequently allowing the characters to speak in their own dialect, Hooper himself closes the sketch: "Satisfied — almost — with his victory, our hero charged back to town — putting to flight everything equine, of which he came in view. . . ." Part of the motivation for using this envelope was that the flawless grammar and flowery rhetoric of the narrator contrast comically with the vernacular speech used by the backwoodsmen and country folk of the sketch. But the frequent recurrence of the framework suggests another reason. This technique created an aesthetic distance between the author and his characters not unlike that of the American naturalists. Stephen Crane and Frank Norris wrote about people moved by forces over which they had no control. Crane's Maggie and Norris's McTeague are described, watched, studied, and sometimes laughed at by their authors. Likewise, Southwest humorists often separated themselves from their characters. It is as hard to identify Longstreet with the lowly characters of *Georgia Scenes* as it is to link Norris with his brute dentist. In both cases the authors place themselves in positions above and apart. The Southwest humorist wanted to laugh at the earthy life around him and to enjoy it, but he did not want to be identified with it. Like the romantics, he recognized the existence of the more humble aspects of life; but he had no desire to cast his lot with the yokels. The framework was thus an effective method of setting off the narrator, who liked to consider himself a gentleman of self-control, taste, and reason, from the oddities he presented in his story.

The framework was also used for other reasons. Though many narrators were patronizing, others respected the backwoodsmen. The attitude of the narrator toward the yarn-spinning hunter, Jim Doggett, in "The Big Bear of Arkansas" is a case in point. Instead of viewing him with superiority, the narrator seems to set himself apart from Doggett's audience and to share with him a sense of the profound mystery of the great bear. If most of the humorists looked upon their characters with amused condescension, others envied them their freedom and manliness. But sometimes the frame was used simply because it had become a convenient tradition; this was the way most stories were told and had been told for years. The Southwestern writers were rarely sophisticated craftsmen, much less innovators of structural techniques.

They were innovators, however, in language. When the narrator abandoned his gentlemanly pose and made the characters themselves speak, he was laying the foundation for a new style in American writing. Rich in similes and metaphors and in exaggerations, this backwoods language is characterized by concreteness, freshness, and color. It was effective, too, because it rang true where the pale or pompous dialogues of the genteel novels were contrived and unrealistic. The difference between the language of Old Southwest humor and that employed in most contemporary novels is expressed in the following sentence from Henry Clay Lewis's "The City Physician *versus* the Swamp Doctor": "The city physician . . . requires a patient to 'inflate his lungs to their utmost capacity;' the swamp doctor tells his to 'draw a long breath, or swell your d — dest:' one calls an individual's physical peculiarities, 'idiosyncrasy;' the other terms it 'a fellow's nater.' "

Vernacular speech was being employed in Down East humor in such writings as Seba Smith's letters of Major Jack Downing, which began to appear in 1830, but it blossomed in the work of the Southern humorists. The use of the vernacular in Southern tales was more widespread, bolder, more surprising in its metaphorical richness. Constance Rourke sums up this basic difference in her treatment of American humor: "It was always possible to see where the Yankee left off and the backwoodsman began. The low key of the Yankee was maintained against the rhapsody of the backwoodsman. Yankee humor was gradual in its approaches, pervasive rather than explicit in its quality, subtle in its range. Backwoods drawing was broad, with a distinct bias toward the grotesque, or the macabre. Backwoods profusion was set against Yankee spareness. The Yankee might compare himself or another with a weasel or a blacksnake, but he never was the weasel or the blacksnake as the backwoodsman was the alligator or the raccoon or the tornado."

The most striking feature of vernacular language as it was used by the Southwestern writers is the earthy vividness of its comic similes.

Having become captain of the local militia, Simon Suggs says in his acceptance speech: "Let who will run, gentle*men*, Simon Suggs will allers be found sticking thar, like a tick onder a cow's belly." The simile is remarkably visual, and it also is supremely appropriate to Simon, who does resemble a blood-sucking tick. Characters frequently compare themselves to animals and insects. In the big brags the speaker is half-man, half-horse or alligator. Harris's Sut Lovingood complained: "I ladles out my words at randum, like a calf kickin at yaller-jackids; yu ["George"] jis' rolls em out tu the pint, like a feller a-layin bricks — every one fits." Such comparisons are effective not only because they are comically incongruous but because they are also strikingly accurate. Rich figurativeness is accompanied by unrestrained exaggeration. William C. Hall's Mike Hooter says that he has known some men in Mississippi "what war so hungry for er fight that they fell away an' got so poor an' thin that they had to lean up agin er saplin' to cuss!" Mike knew one man so mean "he was cotch one day stealin' acorns from a blind hog." Although the use of local dialects was not new, this kind of language was. It combined the wild imagination of the frontiersman with the concreteness of poetry.

The humor of these sketches derives only in part from the exuberance and exaggeration of the language. The Southwest humorist was also adept at creating incongruous and ridiculously comic situations. His stories abound in slapstick comedy. In Harris's "Mrs. Yardley's Quilting" Sut Lovingood describes a wild-eyed horse and how it romped over the guests and through the quilts at Mrs. Yardley's party. Much of the humor at the beginning of the story comes from Sut's figures of speech, his extraordinary exaggerations, and his bold treatment of sex. He says Mrs. Yardley's stockings hanging on the clothes line to dry "looked like a par ove sabre scabbards, an' her naik looked like a dry beef shank smoked." Of fat Sal, Mrs. Yardley's daughter, he says: "I'd 'bout es lief be shet up in a steam biler wif a three hundred pound bag ove lard, es to make a bisiness ove sleepin wif that gal — 'twould kill a glass-blower." With this same vigorous language he then tells what happened at the party. Always ready to play a practical joke, Sut scares a horse in Mrs. Yardley's yard while the quilting party is in full swing. The results are depicted in incredibly clear, well-defined images: the horse running over and under the lines of quilts in the yard, popping ropes and carrying quilts and lines and people along with him, approaching the front door of the house, encountering Mrs. Yardley and her neighbor as they admire a quilt on the ground, running over the old lady, carrying the quilt along on his foot, the corners of it cracking like a whip in the wind. Then the horse's mad rush away from the house, its owner trying to stop him and being run over, and the chaos which generally follows in the wake of the horse's wild run. Not content to end there, Sut goes on to tell how he is kicked by old man Yardley while making love to Sal.

Few of the Southwestern writers were equal to Harris in the creation of physical comedy, but many of them strove for the same basic effect. In that time and place and to those writers, life was action and movement, and comedy was largely the result of things that happened. The fundamental and lasting appeal of this kind of unsophisticated humor, of which the Old Southwest humorists were early masters, is attested by its continued vitality in literature as well as in motion pictures, on the stage, and on television. William Faulkner's "Spotted Horses," one of his funniest stories, is the modern counterpart of "Mrs. Yardley's Quilting." The ingredients are essentially the same: the homey, comic similes, the uninhibited backwoods discussion of sexual matters, and the hilarious situations flashed swiftly before the reader's eyes as he watches the movements of those wild Texas ponies. Faulkner owned a copy of *Sut Lovingood's Yarns.*

Character, language, and comic physical movement are all essential considerations in the Southwestern sketches, but underlying the most successful is a tension which the reader senses. Stories of practical jokes, of country boys in town, of rogues swindling their prey, of misunderstandings and mistakes, of contests and militia drills, of mock fights, and of many other subjects all depend upon the absence of information. If all knew what the reader knows, naive country boys in the stories would not make fools of themselves; would-be victims of practical jokes and swindles and deceptions of all kinds would not fall into the traps set for them; fighters would seldom have cause to fight; and characters generally would avoid misunderstandings and mistakes which are often the basis of comedy. But the world of Southwestern humor is populated with those who do not know all they need to know, and the tension between knowledge and ignorance acts as the essential stimulant to laughter. This tension often functions in language and character as well as in situation. For example, one feels the difference between the illiterate language Sut Lovingood speaks and the wisdom embodied in his words, or the difference between the lowly characters of the sketch and the sane, reasonable gentleman who is the narrator. Whatever form it takes, this tension underlies Southwestern humor.

Some sketches, however, are not funny, nor were they intended to be. The most obvious example is the tall tale. While there is a decidedly comic effect in "The Big Bear of Arkansas," it is not

humorous in the same sense as Robb's "Swallowing an Oyster Alive."
No one really laughs when the powerful conclusion of Thorpe's story
is reached. Instead, the reader is left with a feeling of almost sad
comic wonder. A like reaction may result from reading the legends of
Davy Crockett's superhuman accomplishments or from merely hearing fishermen tell of extraordinary catches. One smiles and at the
same time feels something akin to nostalgia. This mixed effect derives
chiefly from another tension, the head-on meeting of the humorous
and the serious. To put it another way, the effect of the tall tale
comes from the reader's delighted appreciation of the exaggerations
and of the comic character and his language in juxtaposition with
the sad realization that the events of the tale, the accomplishments
of the protagonist, could never really happen. In real life one never
encounters "creation bears" or giants who can wake up the sun. And
it is regrettable that this is so. The reader knows how ridiculous such
exaggerations are, and yet he half wishes that such wild and illogical
and unbounded wonders could be true.

Some elements of Southwestern humor were more amusing when the
sketches were written than now. It is something of a shock to see
pranksters playing practical jokes at funerals, making fun of the
disappointed, the sick, and the deformed, or glorying in the bodily
discomforts of their fellows. It is amazing how much of this unhealthy
humor there is in Southwestern tales. Lapses in decorum occur in
the middle of otherwise conventional comic sketches, and the author
apparently makes no distinction between the quality or kinds of
humor he is dealing with. Longstreet's "The Character of a Native
Georgian" portrays one Ned Brace, who indulges in a series of practical jokes. Most of them are relatively harmless pranks which take
advantage of others' pomposity, foolish curiosity, and gullibility. But
one jest seems astonishing in its bad taste. Ned joins a solemn funeral
procession, makes a bad pun on the name of the dead man, and
causes great laughter among some of those present. The head of
the procession was in "mourning and in tears, and the foot of it convulsed with laughter."

The prankster has thus attempted to bring laughter into a realm of
the reader's experience where it is ordinarily forbidden. Longstreet's
sketch is one of many which reveal a preoccupation with death and
graveyard humor. A long parade of corpses passes through the work
of Hooper, Lewis, Harris, and others. Henry Clay Lewis's *Odd Leaves
from the Life of a Louisiana "Swamp Doctor"* was a popular success
in the 1850's; yet much of it seems macabre to the modern reader.
It is as much an experience in Gothic horror to read Lewis as it is to

read Poe. In "The Curious Widow," for example, a young medical student tells of a cadaver he has been dissecting:

> The *subject* that we were engaged upon was one of the most hideous specimens of humanity that ever horrified the sight. . . . Just emaciated sufficiently to remove the fatty tissue, and leave the muscles and blood vessels finely developed, still he was so hideous that nothing but my devotion to anatomy, and the fineness of the subject, could reconcile me to dissection; and even after working a week upon him, I never caught a glimpse of his countenance but what I had the nightmare in consequence. He was one of that peculiar class called Albinoes, or white negroes. Every feature was deformed and unnatural; a horrible hare-lip, the cleft extending half way up his nose externally, and a pair of tushes projecting from his upper jaw, completed his bill of horrors.

By way of a practical joke, the student cuts this hideous face from the cadaver and hides it in oilcloth among his belongings so that his curious landlady will find it as she snoops about.

Other stories in the *Swamp Doctor* attest to a morbid fascination for cadavers. Since Lewis was a physician, these sketches are understandably less inhibited on matters of dead bodies, diseases, and suffering than they might otherwise have been. Young Dr. Lewis wanted to be funny, but he also wanted to shock, to demonstrate superiority. Much of his writing is extreme if not disgusting, but he was not unusual in his humorous treatment of death. To cite one more example, Harris has Sut Lovingood explain his whereabouts by saying he has been "helpin tu salt ole Missis Yardley down. . . . Fixin her fur rotten cumfurtably, kiverin her up wif sile, tu keep the buzzards frum cheatin the wurms." In other words, he has been preparing her corpse for burial and feels pretty lighthearted about it.

In his comic treatment of death and bodily decay, the Southern writer was not without precedent. For example, macabre jokes are common in Elizabethan literature. Shakespeare furnished the clown in *Hamlet* with a tall tale about the rate of decay in dead bodies. In answer to an inquiry regarding the length of time a man will "lie i' th' earth ere he rot," the clown replies: "Faith, if 'a be not rotten before 'a die (as we have many pocky corpses now-a-days that will scarce hold the laying in), 'a will last you some eight year or nine year. A tanner will last you nine year." When asked why a tanner's body will last longer, he answers: "Why, sir, his hide is so tanned with his trade that 'a will keep out water a great while, and your water is a sore decayer of your whoreson dead body." Similar jests appear in writings after the Southwest humorists. In Twain's *Life on the Mississippi* (1883), a raftsman discusses with his fellows the relative merits of water from the Mississippi and the Ohio rivers: "The Child of Calamity said that was so; he said there was nutritiousness in the mud, and a man that drunk Mississippi water could grow corn in his stomach if he wanted to. He says: 'You look at the graveyards; that tells the tale. Trees won't grow worth shucks in a Cincinnati graveyard, but in a Sent Louis graveyard they grow upwards of eight hundred foot high. It's all on account of the water the people drunk before they laid up. A Cincinnati corpse don't richen a soil any.' " Although humor may not be the predominant intent of Faulkner's *As I Lay Dying* (1930), the comic undeniably plays a large part in the novel, and some of it results indirectly from the situations involving Addie Bundren's corpse and the troubles her family has in getting it to the burial ground.

While the Southwestern writers cannot be viewed as unique in their graveyard humor, they were unusual in the consistency with which they employed it. To understand this one has to realize that death has always held man's attention and stimulated his deepest curiosity. The writers of the Old Southwest knew death intimately. It pervaded their lives and their folklore. From childhood they witnessed its ravages and were forced to think of its terrors and mystery. They sought through humor to reduce this fearful spectre to less awful proportions. They also pursued the possibilities of the grotesque to the extreme point of comic incongruity — to the grin on the face of the skull.

Since the Southwestern humorists frequently distorted the surfaces of reality in order to picture a somewhat different world, the term "realists" must be used with care and qualification when describing them. They were realistic, often nakedly so, in that they endeavored to capture the flavor of the times in scene and language. In this sense, they were the first American realists in fiction. In another sense, however, the world of such characters as Simon Suggs and Sut Lovingood is anything but the real world. The reader is taken into a real-unreal place where suffering and ugliness and death do not clash with horseplay so much as they become part of it. Exaggeration is the quality which prevails in this world from the tall tales about Davy Crockett and Mike Fink to the adventures of Billy Fishback. To accept this exaggeration and to view the universe comically requires suspension of some of the judgments and restraints that ordinarily apply.

To understand what stimulated the beginnings of Old Southwest humor one would have to probe deeply into the psychology of laughter as well as into the history of the westward movement of the frontier. Under the almost savage conditions of a wild new land, laughter was one of the means by which the frontiersman could for a time forget his hardship, preserve his courage, and retain his balance and his humanity. Through his tall tales and his exaggerated, at times almost bestial, behavior, he could laugh at himself and know at the same time that he was playing a role, that his civilized self remained intact beneath the half-man, half-alligator comic façade he created. It was a self-imposed mask, assumed for the purpose of contrasting the true self with the mask. He had attracted the attention of the outside world, too, and he was acting for it as well as for himself. Ring-tailed roarers furnished much of the folklore upon which the authors of Southwestern humor based their sketches. However, the writers were not themselves the rugged, illiterate but imaginative hearties who told their yarns but never wrote them down. They were educated men who seldom broke the wilderness, although they were close to it. From the roarers, from literary sources such as eighteenth-century essayists, from the tales of Baron Munchausen, and even from such contemporaries as Washington Irving, these men formed a new kind of literature, chiefly anecdotal in nature but with a freshness in language and a boldness in detail which stands as a foundation for modern American writing.

The motives of doctors, lawyers, judges, editors, actors, preachers, and politicians who wrote humorous sketches were not precisely the same as those of the keelboatmen and the frontiersmen or the backwoods hunters who spun their yarns and bragged comically of their prowess. The conditions which produced Old Southwest humor are numerous and complex, but at least four interrelated ones are clearly apparent.

(1) As the youngest and most untutored region of the country, the Southwest was keenly self-conscious. In addition, its institutions, especially slavery, began to come under heavy fire from the North in the 1830's and 1840's. Accused of both crudity and cruelty, Southerners felt the need to let the world know that they were proud enough of their colorful, rustic homeland to want to write about it with the express purpose of preserving in literature its scenes and customs. But at the same time, these men, more than they themselves perhaps realized, wanted to be recognized as gentlemen. Therefore from their detached position as narrators, they contrasted themselves with the common folk they observed and wrote about. They liked the folk but maintained a proper distance.

(2) Political undertones are discernible in the work of nearly all of the Southwestern authors. Many were staunch members of the Whig Party, and their plainly stated views occur in their sketches. But even where the political is not an obvious factor, it is a real, if slightly obscured one. The writers' amused observations on the outspoken, crude, and often illiterate democratic man reveal a per-

sistent if sometimes only half-conscious feeling that while these ring-tailed roarers had their virtues, they could not be trusted to run the country.

(3) The Southern frontier was a man's world. The essentially masculine emphasis of the frontier allowed and even encouraged the kind of writing which this group produced. In more settled and effeminate New England, Sut Lovingood could not have been created. The Southwest humorists wrote for a specific audience of men, and this fact alone accounts for many of the qualities of form and content. If they wanted to be accepted as gentlemen, they wished to be known as good fellows who knew how to tell a first-rate story. Horseplay is inevitable when men with a sense of humor get together.

(4) It was easy in this time and place to become a storehouse of tall tales and comic stories. Through oral transmission, sketches like those of Longstreet, Thorpe, Hooper, and Robb were well known before they were written down. These writers, Arthur Palmer Hudson says, "had the wit to realize that something old in talking might look new in writing." Not before the Southwest humorists nor after them has there been a richer opportunity to take advantage of folklore. To this they added a knowledge of ancient and modern comedy and produced sketches which show the influence of both.

The Civil War, which radically altered the South's way of life, and the disappearance of the Southern frontier combined to erase most of the conditions necessary for the widespread creation of humor of the kind that the antebellum authors produced. Those professional writers who owed their livelihood to humor, the literary comedians, followed the war with loud voices and entertaining stage mannerisms. A new age and a new kind of comedy had arrived, and those who had joyed in the humorists of the vanished Southwest could only look about them and say with Thorpe's old and sadly reminiscing Mike Fink: "Where's the fun, the frolicking, the fighting? Gone! Gone!"

The times changed and so did the mode of comedy, but Southwestern humor did not entirely disappear. Its vitality was recognized by young Samuel Clemens, who as a Southern youth had known the era and the ways which the frontier humorists wrote about. He used the lore and the language, giving them new dimensions. From Twain on into the twentieth century, Southwestern humor has remained live in writers like Erskine Caldwell, Robert Penn Warren, and, more recently, William Price Fox. In the work of William Faulkner, who read Southwest humor with great pleasure, it shows signs of living forever.

HUMOR OF THE OLD SOUTHWEST

Mason Locke Weems

(1759-1825)

A native of Arundel County, Maryland, Parson Weems was the first American to be ordained as a priest of the Anglican Church after the interruption of the Revolutionary War. He also studied medicine and was a skillful performer on the violin. By 1794 he was selling books for Carey and Hart, Philadelphia publishers, and by 1797 he was traveling for them as far south as the Georgia frontier. He spent most of the remainder of his life in the South, hawking books, preaching, and playing the fiddle. He died in Beaufort, South Carolina.

Weems is best known for his immensely popular life of Washington, but he also wrote biographies of Franklin, William Penn, and General Francis Marion and a host of bestselling religious pamphlets with such titles as *Hymen's Recruiting Sergeant* (1805), *The Drunkard's Looking Glass* (1812), *God's Revenge Against Adultery* (1815), *God's Revenge Against Duelling* (1820). His letters to Carey show that he kept his ears open for pungent anecdotes to spice up his writings. He knew a good story when he heard one, and he did not hesitate to improve on it in the retelling or, as the cherry tree legend attests, to fabricate a suitable illustration if the occasion required it.

Parson Weems's purpose — to sell books and save souls — was different from that of the Southwestern humorists who followed him a generation later. Nevertheless, he shows a close kinship to them in his illustrative anecdotes about the bragging, hard-drinking, fighting rustics of the Southern frontier. His keen sense of what would hold the attention of his readers, his knowledge of the South, and the interest he took in country dances, quarter races, and tall talk are responsible for the vernacular strain in his religious chapbooks. Weems once wrote to Carey that to be effective and marketable they should contain a proper degree of the "melodramatical-comical-etc." The skill with which he used lurid stories to play upon his readers' superior feeling of self-righteousness and their itch for the sensational suggests comparison with another accomplished preacher, Chaucer's Pardoner.

TEXT: "Awful History of Young Dred Drake" from *The Drunkard's Looking Glass* (6th ed.; n.p., 1818).

3

Awful History of Young Dred Drake

.   .   .   .

But few are the citizens of Greene county, Georgia, who have not heard of Noyle Nelms's *race paths.* Many a precious hour has been murdered there; and often has the silence of its pine groves been disturbed by the horrid oaths of noisy crowds celebrating their horse-races. But *idleness* and *profanity* are not the only concomitants of such *cruel sports.* No! for when young men, heated with whiskey, and mounted on fiery steeds, are bounding over the turf, who can tell how soon their rosy cheeks may become the food of devouring worms?

Dred Drake was a young man, naturally warm hearted and gay; and had it been his lot to have received the early light of education, 'tis probable he would have lived many years, a useful member of society. But, alas! it was his misfortune to have been neglected in his education; and hence sprung all his vices and misfortunes: for, in his rage after pleasure, *"which is Nature's Law,"* instead of rising to the pleasures of the MIND, he sunk to those of *sense,* particularly to that of *strong drink,* in which he indulged to such excess, that the friends of humanity were always sad, whenever they saw him. But the days of his folly were but few. He was soon snatched away to bear awful witness to that *general truth, "the wicked shall not live out half their days."*

A match is made in Greene county, and the purse is to be run for over Noyle Nelms's race-paths. Notice of the same is given by plentiful advertisements stuck up, as usual, at blacksmiths' shops, taverns, and cross roads. At length the *eventful day* arrives; and the neighbourhood, for miles around, quitting their spinning-wheels and ploughs, are all in motion to see the *races!* By an early hour the piny wood, which surrounds the race-paths, is filled with a motley crowd — *yonder,* the delicate daughters of wealth, lolling at ease in their silks and chariots, waiting for the starting of the horses; and *here* the sturdier daughters of poverty, standing together in giggling groups, shining in health and homespun. On *this side,* a gang of smirky-faced negroes, each with a whiskey bottle sticking out of his pocket — and on *that* a troop of broad grinning Indians, with their brandy kegs and children strapped over their shoulders — while in rows, along the course, stand the whiskey wagons and cyder carts, surrounded by thirsty topers, thick as bees, all *sipping away as hard* as the smiling tapsters can fill, and hand their tin pots and noggins. Presently the fiery draughts begin to operate; dull care unbends from every brow; and all tongues are loosened to chatter; for honest Nature, now unmuzzled by the whiskey, throws off restraint, and bids every man appear in his proper character. Some are singing — and some are dancing; *here,* they hug and fondle like brothers — *there* they curse and quarrel like enemies. The negroes laugh — the Indians whoop — and all the wood resounds with uproar. No flock of black-birds lighting on an autumnal cornfield, ever raised such a chorus of ear distracting discords.

But hark! what dreadful noise is that? *"A fight! a fight!"* is the general cry. Instantly the people from all sides are running towards the crowded spot, but with widely different looks: some with pleasure in their eyes, like negro boys running to a dog-fight; but others, and particularly the young women, with faces pale with fright and calling on the names of their brothers supposed to be in the fray.

The uproar is all created by a couple of big-limbed young boobies, rushing into furious combat. It had often been a question among their *vulgar* neighbours which of them was the *best man.* The poor blockheads knowing no better, and mistaking their shame for their glory, have long wished to try each other. And now, accidentally meeting at the *horse-race,* (the proper theatre for such work) and being put up to it partly by vanity, but more by whiskey, they have grappled each other.

"Part 'em! part 'em!" — is the cry of some. But others of the more savage sort bawl out — *"No touch! no touch! Hands off, gentlemen, hands off! — Hurra! — Now, then, crack away again my little game cocks! At it again, my Heroes!"*

Rid now of all restraint, forward they pitch at each other like bull-dogs. The contest, however, is but of short duration; for, one of the fools, in taking his dose of Dutch courage, had gone so deep into the whiskey bottle, that h. was quite on the staggers, when the fight began; so that on the first or second thump he was tumbled over sprawling and helpless as a cotton bag. Whereat his antagonist, charmed with so glorious a victory, leaped into the air, and snapping his fingers, roared out, *"Hurra, for me! a hard horse I am gentlemen, a proper hard horse, depend! may-be I an't a* Roarer!*"*

O the GLORY! the GLORY! the GLORY, of such an exploit as this! what young man of six foot by three over the shoulders, but must covet an equal fame? yes, they will covet it. See them now leaping out from the crowd, binding up their heads, and throwing off their clothes! Some strip to the shirt — others throw off shirt and all to the bare pantaloons and suspenders. Then boldly stepping forward, and striking their right-hand fists into the hollow of the left, with a noise loud as a pistol's crack, crossing their arms like boxers, and bawling out to each in his own *blackguard phrases.*

One swears by his Maker, that, "HE IS THE CLEVEREST FELLOW IN ALL GREENE COUNTY."

Another *d—ns himself to h—ll,* "IF HE CAN'T FLOG ANY SON OF A B — TCH ON THE WHOLE GROUND."

"Here I come, gentlemen!" roars a third, *"Here I come! a screamer! yes, d—n me, if I an't a proper screamer;* JUST FROM BENGAL! HALF HORSE HALF ALLIGATOR, AND WITH A LITTLE TOUCH OF THE SNAPPING TURTLE."

Up comes a fourth and more beastly still, rips out, *"Hurra for little* BONAPARTE, the Stud! yes, *I'll be d—n'd if I an't a* TRUE STUD. *O! may be I an't a* ROARER."

A fifth now pushes forward, and like one ready for battle, thunders out — *"Don't fight for nothing! d—n you, don't fight for nothing! fight for a horse."*

Into the midst of this drunken crew, up dashes poor *Dred Drake* with red eyes and whiskey bloated face, bearing hard in hand a high mettled Tacky, and screaming out, *"Clear the track! clear the track! d—n you, clear the track."*

Though fit only for the pillory or prison, he fancies himself the greatest man on the ground. He can hardly sit on his horse, and yet hear how he roars, *"Hurra for young Fulker! against horse, mare, or gelding, the best Tacky on the turf, d—n me!"* That's a whaler! replies another young sot, *half-shaved,* for here's little READY MONEY can beat him high or low, the best day he ever *see'd,* for a hundred dollars all down upon the nail.

Dred's friends all gathered around him — *"For God's sake, Dred, don't think of running! you have drank too much; my dear boy, you have drank too much. And, besides, only look how thick the pine trees stand around the course, you'll get your brains dash'd out, as sure as ever you were born."*

"D—n the pine trees," he replied, "who cares for the pine trees! I'll stave through 'em like a hurricane! — I'll sweep 'em all to h—ll!"

In the same moment, the other horse by his side, and the word *"go,"* given, he applies his whip, and off he drives, in the proper garb of a piney-wood sot — no hat — no jacket — and his uncombed locks flying in every direction on the wind.

He had not gone above an hundred yards, when his horse under the lash, as hard as he could crack it, rather flying than running, started a little from the path, and in full lightening speed, dash'd his rider against the body of a pine tree. Knocked backwards, high above his horse's rump, he fell dead, without a groan, to the earth. Instantly in tumultuous crowds, the people all gathered around him, and were presented with as sad a spectacle, as mortal eyes ever beheld. He whom they had but this moment seen so brisk and gay, now lay there before them a lifeless lump, and so mangled that no friend on earth could have recognized a feature. There was not a sign of a nose remaining on his face, the violence of the blow had crushed it flat, miserably battering his mouth and teeth, and completely scalping the right side of his face and head — the flesh, skin, and ear, torn off to the back of his skull. One of his eyes, meeting a snag on the trunk of a tree, was clearly knocked out of its socket; and, held only by a string of skin, there it lay naked on his bloody cheek.

The next day the mangled remains of poor Dred Drake were buried. They were buried by his weeping brothers in a field belonging to his father. To this day the place where he sleeps is beheld at a distance with secret awe. The children, when they run to the door, before the hour of bed, listen with terror to the voice of the Whip-poor-will mourning from the oak that bends in darkness over his grave. The negro boys, too, as they seek their horses through the field, carefully shun the haunted spot. For often, in dead of night, a noise, they say, is heard, as of cracking whips, and the sound of horses' feet loud galloping over the race paths. . . .

James Kirke Paulding

(1770-1860)

✣ Though a native of New York and associated with Washington Irving and the Knickerbocker group, Paulding was among the first American writers to make extended use of the half-horse, half-alligator type of frontier humor. His work reveals a lifelong interest in the South and the West. In addition to his satires against the British such as *The Diverting History of John Bull and Brother Jonathan* (1812) and tales of the Dutch pioneers such as *The Dutchman's Fireside* (1831), he made use of Southern and Western materials. *Letters from the South* (1817) is a leisurely account of his travels in Virginia during the previous year. His narrative poem, *The Backwoodsman* (1818), and *Westward Ho!* (1832), a melodramatic novel in which a Virginia cavalier learns to cherish the frontier virtues, feature Western settings. In 1842, accompanying Martin Van Buren under whom he had served as Secretary of the Navy, Paulding made an extensive tour of the South and West. Together they visited South Carolina, then went overland to New Orleans, and by river to Tennessee where they called on Andrew Jackson at the Hermitage. For Paulding, who was a loyal Democrat and long an admirer of the Southwestern hero, this was the high point of the tour.

Letters from the South, as the name suggests, consists of epistolary essays describing the manners, history, and customs of Virginia as well as Paulding's own experiences as he rambled about the countryside. The inhabitants and living conditions of the Virginia back country were somewhat like those of Kentucky and Tennessee of a slightly later date. Therefore Paulding could appropriately incorporate episodes like the fight between the boatman and the wagoner into his farce, *The Lion of the West* (1830), which features the frontier character called Colonel Nimrod Wildfire. In addition to his Virginia experiences, Paulding had the living example of Congressman David Crockett, though the Crockett biographies had not yet been written nor had the publication of the Crockett almanacs begun. In 1830 Paulding wrote to John Wesley Jarvis, the widely traveled portrait painter, asking him to supply "a few sketches, short stories and incidents, of Kentucky or Tennessee manners, especially some of their peculiar phrases and comparisons" and "a few ludicrous Scenes of Col. Crockett at Washington." When the newspapers suggested that Wildfire was a caricature of Crockett, Paulding conveyed a tactful denial through a common friend, the Georgia congressman and poet, Richard Henry Wilde. Crockett wrote Paulding politely accepting this explanation. However, when the play opened in Washington Crockett's appearance in the front row was greeted with applause which redoubled when James H. Hackett, coming onto the stage in the role of Nimrod Wildfire, bowed ostentatiously to him and he arose from his seat and returned the compliment.

Paulding's play was revised by the dramatist John A. Stone after the initial production in New York in 1831. In 1833, when Hackett took the play to England, it was again revised, this time by the English playwright William Bayle Bernard. Bernard added Mrs. Wollope, a caricature of Frances Trollope whose *Domestic Manners of the Americans* (1832) had been published after Paulding's farce was first performed. Despite its great popularity *The Lion of the West* (or *The Kentuckian; or a Trip to New York* as it was called in England) was lost for many years and the only surviving text is the Bernard version, a copy of which was filed with the Lord Chamberlain's Office in order to obtain official permission for performance. Hence a curious and interesting situation prevails: a British dramatist as well as a Northern man of letters is in part responsible for providing the first important example on the stage of a Southwestern frontier archetype.

TEXT: Letter 29 from *Letters from the South* (New York, 1817); "The Lion of the West" from *The Lion of the West,* ed. James N. Tidwell (Stanford, 1954).

Letter from the South

DEAR FRANK,

Yesterday we laid by at the little town of W——. It was court time, and two lawyers, the pick of the whole country round, were to take the field against each other, in a suit between a wagoner and a batteauxman, in a case of assault and battery. You are to understand, the beautiful river Shenandoah passes not far from this town, and is navigable for batteaux; while at no great distance runs the great western road, which is travelled by the west country wagoners — some of whom, you know, are "half horse, half alligator"; others "part earthquake, and a little of the steamboat"; and others compounded, according to their own accounts, of ingredients altogether different from the common constituent parts of the rest of mankind. The batteauxmen are for the most part composed of materials equally combustible; and the consequence is, that occasionally, when they meet, they strike fire, and blow up the powder magazine each carries about him in the form of a heart.

The history of the present contest, as detailed by the Counsel for the plaintiff, is as follows: One summer evening, when the mild air, the purple light, the green earth, and the blue sky, all seemed to invite to peace and repose, the batteauxman fastened his boat to the stump of a tree, lighted his fire to broil his bacon, and began to sing that famous song of "The opossum up the gum-tree." By and by a west country wagoner chanced to come jingling his bells that way, and stopping his wagon, unhooked his horses, carried them round to the little trough at the back of his vehicle, gave them some *shorts*, sat himself down at the top of the bank, below which the batteauxman was sitting in his boat, and began to whistle "The batteauxman robb'd the old woman's hen-roost." The batteauxman cocked up his eye at the wagoner, and the wagoner looking askance down on the batteauxman, took a chew of tobacco with a leer that was particularly irritating. The batteauxman drew out his whiskey-bottle, took a drink, and put the cork in again, at the same time thrusting his tongue in his cheek in a manner not to be borne. The wagoner flapped his hands against his hips, and crowed like a cock; the batteauxman curved his neck, and neighed like a horse. Being, however, men of rather phlegmatic habits, they kept their tempers so far as not to come to blows just then. In a few minutes the wagoner swore "he had the handsomest sweetheart of any man in all Greenbriar." The batteauxman jumped up in a passion, but sat down again, and took a drink. In a few minutes the wagoner swore "he had the finest horse of any man in a hundred miles." The batteauxman bounced up, pulled the waistband of his trowsers, took another drink, and bounced down again. A minute after the wagoner swore "he had a better rifle than any man that ever wore a blue jacket." This was too much — for the batteauxman wore a jacket of that colour, and of course this amounted to a personal insult. Besides, to attack a man's rifle! He could have borne any reflection on his sweetheart, or his horse; but to touch his rifle, was to touch his honour. Off went the blue jacket; the batteauxman scrambled up the bank, and a set to commenced, that ended in the total discomfiture of the wagoner, with the loss of three of his grinders, and a gain of "divers black and bloody bruises," as honest Lithgow says. The batteauxman waited till the moon rose, when he went whistling down the stream to carry the news of his victory to Old Potomac; and the poor wagoner went "to take the law," as a man says, when the law is about to take him.

The honest batteauxman was arrested on his return for assault and battery on the west country wagoner. It being you know the great object of the law to find out which party is in the wrong, the lawyer of each side of course labours to throw the imputation on his adversary's client. It appeared clearly enough that the batteauxman made the first assault, but it also appeared in evidence that crowing like a cock was a direct challenge, according to the understanding of these people; that to undervalue a batteauxman's sweetheart or horse, whether he had any or not, was a mortal insult; and that to insinuate any inferiority in his rifle, was an offence which no one could put up with without dishonour. That such points of honour constituted the chivalry of these people, that no class of mankind is without something of this nature — that however low a man may be, there are insults he cannot submit to, without being disgraced among his equals, who constitute his world — and that to oblige him, in any situation, to put up with disgrace, was to debase his nature, and to destroy every manly principle within him. Trifling as this case may appear, it called forth a display of talent, and a depth of investigation as to how far it was possible, and if possible, how far it was salutary to attempt to repress the operation of those feelings which spur men in all situations to avoid disgrace at the risk of every thing, that gave me a high idea of the two advocates. They were both young men, new to the bar, &c. yet they spoke with a degree of fluency as well as self-possession which is seldom exhibited by our young lawyers of the cities, whose genius is too frequently rebuked by the presence of an audience they can hardly hope to please, disheartened by the supercilious airs of the elder counsel, or overpowered by the deadening sense of inferiority. . . .

The Lion of the West *

(from Act I, Scene 1)

. . . .

(*Enter Nimrod Wildfire*)

WILDFIRE. Madam, your most obedient.

MRS. WOLLOPE. Sir.

WILDFIRE. I believe your name is Mrs. Wollope.

MRS. WOLLOPE. It is.

WILDFIRE. Then you know my uncle, Peter Freeman. He tells me you have come among us to take a squint at things in general on this here side of the big pond.

*Reprinted from *The Lion of the West* by James Kirke Paulding, edited by James N. Tidwell, with the permission of the publishers, Stanford University Press. Copyright 1954 by the Board of Trustees of the Leland Stanford Junior University.

MRS. WOLLOPE. The big pond! Oh, the Atlantic. That, sir, is my object.

WILDFIRE. Then I mean to say, madam, on that subject, I can out-talk any fellar in this country — and give him half an hour's start.

MRS. WOLLOPE. A man of intelligence. Pray be seated.

WILDFIRE. (*brings forward two chairs, sits on one and as Mrs. Wollope is about to sink into the other, he throws his legs on it*) Now, Mrs. Wollope.

MRS. WOLLOPE. The soldier tired. Perhaps, sir, you would prefer an arm chair?

WILDFIRE. No, madam. If it was just after dinner, I should like to put my legs out of [the] winder.

MRS. WOLLOPE. His legs out of the window — a very cool proceeding certainly. May I offer you a cup of tea?

WILDFIRE. Much objected to you, madam. I never raise the steam with hot water — always go on the high pressure principle — all whiskey.

MRS. WOLLOPE. A man of spirit! Are you stationed in New York, sir?

WILDFIRE. Stationed — yes! but don't mean to stop long. Old Kaintuck's the spot. There the world's made upon a large scale.

MRS. WOLLOPE. A region of superior cultivation — in what branch of science do its gentlemen excel?

WILDFIRE. Why, madam, of all the fellers either side the Alleghany hills, I myself can jump higher — squat lower — dive deeper — stay longer under and come out drier.

MRS. WOLLOPE. Here's amelioration! And your ladies, sir?

WILDFIRE. The galls! Oh, they go it on the big figure too — no mistake in them. There's my late sweetheart, Patty Snaggs. At nine year old she shot a bear, and now she can whip her weight in wild cats. There's the skin of one of 'em. (*Takes off his cap.*)

MRS. WOLLOPE. Feminine accomplishments! Doubtless your soil and people correspond.

WILDFIRE. The soil — oh, the soil's so rich you may travel under it.

MRS. WOLLOPE. Travel under ground, sir? I must put this down.

WILDFIRE. Yes, madam, particularly after the spring rains. Look you here now, tother day, I was a horseback paddling away pretty comfortably through Nobottom swamp, when suddenly — I wish I may be currycomb'd to death by 50,000 tom cats, if I didn't see a white hat getting along in mighty considerable style all alone by itself on the top of the mud — so up I rid, and being a bit jubus, I lifted it with the butt end of my whip when a feller sung out from under it, Hallo, stranger, who told you to knock my hat off?

Why, says I, what sort of a sample of a white man are you? What's come of the rest of you? Oh, says he, I'm not far off — only in the next county. I'm doing beautifully — got one of the best horses under me that ever burrowed — claws like a mole — no stop in him — but here's a waggon and horses right under me in a mighty bad fix, I reckon, for I heard the driver say a spell ago one of the team was getting a leetel tired.

MRS. WOLLOPE. What a geological novelty.

WILDFIRE. So, says I, you must be a pretty considerable feller on your own, but you had better keep your mouth shut or you'll get your teeth sunburnt. So, says I, good bye, stranger. I wish you a pleasant ride, but I prognosticate afore you get through the next sandbank you'll burst your biler.

MRS. WOLLOPE. This shall be the first well authenticated anecdote in my perusal. . . .

(from Act II, Scene 2)

.   .   .   .

WILDFIRE. A gentleman? Oh, I'll put it to him *like* a *gentleman,* but if this had happened about ten years ago — when I was chock full of fun and fight — I wouldn't have minded going it in Old Mississippi style.

PERCIVAL. Some mode once peculiar to the wildness of the region?

WILDFIRE. Why, I'll tell you how it was. I was riding along the Mississippi one day when I came across a fellow floating down the stream sitting cock'd up in the starn of his boat fast asleep. Well, I hadn't had a fight for as much as ten days — felt as though I must kiver myself up in a salt bin to keep — "so wolfy" about the head and shoulders. So, says I, hullo, stranger, if you don't take keer your boat will run away wi' you. So he looked up at me "slantindickular," and I looked down on him "slanchwise." He took out a chaw of tobacco from his mouth and, says he, I don't value you tantamount to that, and then he flopp'd his wings and crowed like a cock. I ris up, shook my mane, crooked my neck, and neighed like a horse. Well, he run his boat foremost ashore. I stopped my waggon and set my triggers. Mister, says he, I'm the best man — if I ain't, I wish I may be tetotaciously exflunctified! I can whip my weight in wild cats and ride strait through a crab apple orchard on a flash of lightning — clear meat axe disposition! And what's more, I once back'd a bull off a bridge. Poh, says I, what do I keer for that? I can tote a steam boat up the Mississippi and over the Alleghany mountains. My father can whip the best man in old Kaintuck, and I can whip my father. When I'm good natured I weigh about a hundred and seventy, but when I'm mad, I weigh a *ton*. With that I fetched him the regular Ingen warwhoop. Out he jumped from his boat, and down I tumbled from my waggon — and, I say, we came together like two steam boats going sixty mile an hour. He was a pretty severe colt, but no part of a priming to such a feller as me. I put it to him mighty droll — tickled the varmint till he squealed like a young colt, bellowed "enough" and swore I was a "rip staver." Says I, *ain't* I a horse? Says he, stranger, you're a *beauty* anyhow, and if you'd stand for Congress I'd vote for you next *lection*. Says I, would you? My name's Nimrod Wildfire. Why, I'm the yaller flower of the forest. I'm all *brimstone but* the *head*, and that's *aky fortis.*

PERCIVAL. A renowned achievement. Well, Colonel, I feel it my duty before I leave New York to disclose the rumor I have heard to your uncle. Proceed in this affair as you think best, but remember, if you do meet his Lordship, it must be with the weapons of a gentleman. (*Exit.*)

WILDFIRE. A gentleman's weapons? Oh, of course, he means rifles. May be that Lord has heard of mine. She's a noisy varmint made of Powder house lightning-rod steel and twisted like our Kentucky widow. She's got but one peeper, but if she blinks that at him, his head will hum like a hornet's nest — he'll see the stars dance in the day time. He'll come off as badly as a feller I once hit a sledge hammer lick over the head — a rale "sogdolloger." He disappeared altogether; all they could ever find of him was a little grease spot in one corner. (*Exit.*)

David Crockett

(1786-1836)

Nine years before David Crockett was born in Eastern Tennessee, his grandparents were murdered by Creek and Cherokee Indians. By the time of his birth, most of the Indians had been pushed farther westward, but the severity of frontier life remained. It was still difficult just to survive. To the people of the frontier, formal education was irrelevant in a life where a man was measured by his skill in hunting and in taming the wilderness and by his hard common sense. David Crockett developed these talents early. To them he added an ardent desire for freedom and independence. In his autobiography he tells of how as a youth he walked seven miles in a snowstorm to escape a cattle drover who wanted to retain him by force. Schooling and family interfered with his independence; so after only a few months he ran away from the classroom and from home to make his way in the world. In 1813 he left Tennessee to fight under General Andrew Jackson in the Creek War. He returned to find himself something of a popular hero, with a reputation as a shrewd frontiersman and Indian fighter. First elected justice of the peace, he was soon made a colonel in the state militia. Beginning in 1821, he served two terms in the Tennessee legislature. Three times elected to Congress, Davy Crockett came to represent all the courage, level-headedness, and vitality of the frontier. After an abrupt break with Jackson in 1828, he became a devoted Whig, that party's counterpart to the vigorous Jacksonian man. His death at the Alamo, where he had joined the Texans in their fight for independence, confirmed his heroism in the public mind. In his lifetime tall tales about him were told, and after his death Crockett "almanacs" were published by the dozens. He entered the realm of myth, a folk hero who could tie a knot in the tail of a comet or wake up the sun to thaw out the frozen earth.

Just how much of the writing attributed to Crockett is actually his is not easy to determine. Since he lacked formal education, he required assistance in almost everything prepared for publication. The one book which he had a large part in producing is the "autobiography," *A Narrative of the Life of David Crockett* (1834). Probably edited by Thomas Chilton, it nevertheless contains Crockett's own stories and reflects his spirit and wit. The content is his even though the actual words are not. The earlier *Sketches and Eccentricities of Colonel David Crockett* (1833) was probably the work of Matthew St. Clair Clarke, written with Crockett's knowledge and for the purpose of getting him elected to Congress. Three later books appeared under Crockett's name: *An Account of Colonel Crockett's Tour to the North and Down East* (1835), *The Life of Martin Van Buren* (1835), and *Colonel Crockett's Exploits and Adventures in Texas* (1836). With the exception of a few passages in the *Tour* and the *Exploits,* Crockett had little part in writing these books. The "Useful Coon Skin" sketch published here appears in very brief form in the 1833 *Sketches and Eccentricities* and in expanded form in Chapter One of the *Exploits.* Although most of the latter book was written by Richard Penn Smith at the request of publishers Carey and Hart, it is likely that the first chapter was based on notes supplied by Crockett.

TEXT: Chapters 14 and 15 of the *Narrative of the Life of David Crockett of the State of Tennessee* (Philadelphia, 1834); "A Useful Coon Skin" from *Colonel Crockett's Exploits and Adventures in Texas* (Philadelphia, 1836).

Bear Hunting in Tennessee

But the reader, I expect, would have no objection to know a little about my employment during the two years while my competitor was in Congress. In this space I had some pretty tuff times, and will relate some few things that happened to me. So here goes, as the boy said when he run by himself.

In the fall of 1825, I concluded I would build two large boats, and load them with pipe staves for market. So I went down to the lake, which was about twenty-five miles from where I lived, and hired some hands to assist me, and went to work; some at boat building, and others to getting staves. I worked on with my hands till the bears got fat, and then I turned out to hunting, to lay in a supply of meat. I soon killed and salted down as many as were necessary for my family; but about this time one of my old neighbours, who had settled down on the lake about twenty-five miles from me, came to my house and told me he wanted me to go down and kill some bears about in his parts. He said they were extremely fat, and very plenty. I know'd that when they were fat, they were easily taken, for a fat bear can't run fast or long. But I asked a bear no favours, no way, further than civility, for I now had *eight* large dogs, and as fierce as painters; so that a bear stood no chance at all to get away from them. So I went home with him, and then went on down towards the Mississippi, and commenced hunting.

We were out two weeks, and in that time killed fifteen bears. Having now supplied my friend with plenty of meat, I engaged occasionally again with my hands in our boat building, and getting staves. But I at length couldn't stand it any longer without another hunt. So I concluded to take my little son, and cross over the lake, and take a hunt there. We got over, and that evening turned out and killed three bears, in little or no time. The next morning we drove up four forks, and made a sort of scaffold, on which we salted up our meat, so as to have it out of the reach of the wolves, for as soon as we would leave our camp, they would take possession. We had just eat our breakfast, when a company of hunters came to our camp, who had fourteen dogs, but all so poor, that when they would bark they would almost have to lean up against a tree and take a rest. I told them their dogs couldn't run in smell of a bear, and they had better stay at my camp, and feed them on the bones I had cut out of my meat. I left them there, and cut out; but I hadn't gone far, when my dogs took a first-rate start after a very large fat old *he-bear,* which run right plump towards my camp. I pursued on, but my other hunters had heard my dogs coming, and met them, and killed the bear before I got up with him. I gave him to them, and cut out again for a creek called Big Clover, which wa'n't very far off. Just as I got there, and was entering a cane brake, my dogs all broke and went ahead, and, in a little time, they raised a fuss in the cane, and seemed to be going every way. I listened a while, and found my dogs was in two companies, and that both was in a snorting fight. I sent my little son to one, and I broke for t'other. I got to mine first, and found my dogs had a two-year-old bear down, a-wooling away on him; so I just took out my big butcher, and went up and slap'd it into him, and killed him without shooting. There was five of the dogs in my company. In a short time, I heard my little son fire at his bear; when I went to him he had killed it too. He had two dogs in his team. Just at this moment we heard my other dog barking a short distance off, and all the rest immediately broke to him. We pushed on too, and when we got there, we found he had still a larger bear than either of them we had killed, treed by himself. We killed that one also, which made three we had killed in less than half an hour. We turned in and butchered them, and then started to hunt for water, and a good place to camp. But we had no sooner started, than our dogs took a start after another one, and away they went like a thunder-gust, and was out of hearing in a minute. We followed the way they had gone for some time, but at length we gave up the hope of finding them, and turned back. As we were going back, I came to where a poor fellow was grubbing, and he looked like the very picture of hard times. I asked him what he was doing away there in the woods by himself? He said he was grubbing for a man who intended to settle there; and the reason why he did it was, that he had no meat for his family, and he was working for a little.

I was mighty sorry for the poor fellow, for it was not only a hard, but a very slow way to get meat for a hungry family; so I told him if he would go with me, I would give him more meat than he could get by grubbing in a month. I intended to supply him with meat, and also to get him to assist my little boy in packing in and salting up my bears. He had never seen a bear killed in his life. I told him I had six killed then, and my dogs were hard after another. He went off to his little cabin, which was a short distance in the brush, and his wife was very anxious he should go with me. So we started and went to where I had left my three bears, and made a camp. We then gathered my meat and salted, and scaffled it, as I had done the other. Night now came on, but no word from my dogs yet. I afterwards found they had treed the bear about five miles off, near to a man's house, and had barked at it the whole enduring night. Poor fellows! many a time they looked for me, and wondered why I didn't come, for they knowed there was no mistake in me, and I know'd they were as good as ever fluttered. In the morning, as soon as it was light enough to see, the man took his gun and went to them, and shot the bear, and killed it. My dogs, however, wouldn't have anything to say to this stranger; so they left him, and came early in the morning back to me.

We got our breakfast, and cut out again; and we killed four large and very fat bears that day. We hunted out the week, and in that time we killed seventeen, all of them first-rate. When we closed our hunt, I gave the man over a thousand weight of fine fat bear-meat, which pleased him mightily, and made him feel as rich as a Jew. I saw him the next fall, and he told me he had plenty of meat to do him the whole year from his week's hunt. My son and me now went home. This was the week between Christmas and New-year that we made this hunt.

When I got home, one of my neighbours was out of meat, and wanted me to go back, and let him go with me, to take another hunt. I couldn't refuse; but I told him I was afraid the bear had taken to house by that time, for after they get very fat in the fall and early part of the winter, they go into their holes, in large hollow trees, or into hollow logs, or their cane-houses, or the harricanes; and lie there till spring, like frozen snakes. And one thing about this will seem mighty strange to many people. From about the first of January to about the last of April, these varments lie in their holes altogether. In all that time they have no food to eat; and yet when they come out, they are not an ounce lighter than when they went to house. I don't know the cause of this, and still I know it is a fact; and I leave it for others who have more learning than myself to account for it. They have not a particle of food with them, but they just lie and suck the bottom of their paw all the time. I have killed many of them in their trees, which enables me to speak positively on this subject. However, my neighbour, whose name was McDaniel, and my little son and me, went on down to the lake to my second camp, where I had killed my seventeen bears the week before, and turned out to hunting. But we hunted hard all day without getting a single start. We had carried but little provisions with us, and the next morning was entirely out of meat. I sent my son about three miles off, to the house of an old friend, to get some. The old gentleman was much pleased to hear I was hunting in those parts, for the year before the bears had killed a great many of his hogs. He was that day killing his bacon hogs, and so he gave my son some meat, and sent word to me that I must come in to his house that evening, that he would have plenty of feed for my dogs, and some accommodations for ourselves; but before my son got back, we had gone out hunting, and in a large cane brake my dogs found a big bear in a cane-house, which he had fixed for his winter-quarters, as they sometimes do.

When my lead dog found him, and raised the yell, all the rest broke to him, but none of them entered his house until we got up. I encouraged my dogs, and they knowed me so well, that I could have made them seize the old serpent himself, with all his horns and heads, and cloven foot and ugliness into the bargain, if he would only have come to light, so that they could have seen him. They bulged in, and in an instant the bear followed them out, and I told my friend to shoot him, as he was mighty wrathy to kill a bear. He did so, and killed him prime. We carried him to our camp, by which time my son had returned; and after we got our dinners we packed up, and cut for the house of my old friend, whose name was Davidson.

We got there, and staid with him that night; and the next morning, having salted up our meat, we left it with him, and started to take a hunt between the Obion lake and the Red-foot lake; as there had been a dreadful harricane, which passed between them, and I was sure there must be a heap of bears in the fallen timber. We had gone about five miles without seeing any sign at all; but at length we got on some high cany ridges, and, as we rode along, I saw a hole in a large black oak, and on examining more closely, I discovered that a bear had clomb the tree. I could see his tracks going up, but none coming down, and so I was sure he was in there. A person who is acquainted with bear-hunting, can tell easy enough when the varment is in the hollow; for as they go up they don't slip a bit, but as they come down they make long scratches with their nails.

My friend was a little ahead of me, but I called him back, and told him there was a bear in that tree, and I must have him out. So we lit from our horses, and I found a small tree which I thought I could fall so as to lodge against my bear tree, and we fell to work chopping it with our tomahawks. I intended, when we lodged the tree against the other, to let my little son go up, and look into the hole, for he could climb like a squirrel. We had chop'd on a little time and stop'd to rest, when I heard my dogs barking mighty severe at some distance from us, and I told my friend I knowed they had a bear; for it is the nature of a dog, when he finds you are hunting bears, to hunt for nothing else; he becomes fond of the meat, and considers other game as "not worth a notice," as old Johnson said of the devil.

We concluded to leave our tree a bit, and went to my dogs, and when we got there, sure enough they had an eternal great big fat bear up a tree, just ready for shooting. My friend again petitioned me for liberty to shoot this one also. I had a little rather not, as the bear was so big, but I couldn't refuse; and so he blazed away, and down came the old fellow like some great log had fell. I now missed one of my dogs, the same that I before spoke of as having treed the bear by himself sometime before, when I had started the three in the cane break. I told my friend that my missing dog had a bear somewhere, just as sure as fate; so I left them to butcher the one we had just killed, and I went up on a piece of high ground to listen for my dog. I heard him barking with all his might some distance off, and I pushed ahead for him. My other dogs hearing him broke to him, and when I got there, sure enough again he had another bear ready treed; if he hadn't, I wish I may be shot. I fired on him, and brought him down; and then went back, and help'd finish butchering the one at which I had left my friend. We then packed both to our tree where we had left my boy. By this time, the little fellow had cut the tree down that we intended to lodge, but it fell the wrong way; he had then feather'd in on the big tree, to cut that, and had found that it was nothing but a shell on the outside, and all doted in the middle, as too many of our big men are in these days, having only an outside appearance. My friend and my son cut away on it, and I went off about a hundred yards with my dogs to keep them from running under the tree when it should fall. On looking back at the hole, I saw the bear's head out of it, looking down at them as they were cutting. I hollered to them to look up, and they did so; and McDaniel catched up his gun, but by this time the bear was out, and coming down the tree. He fired at it, and as soon as it touch'd ground the dogs were all round it, and they had a roll-and-tumble fight to the foot of the hill, where they stop'd him. I ran up, and putting my gun against the bear, fired and killed him. We now had three, and so we made our scaffold and salted them up.

In the morning I left my son at the camp, and we started on towards the harricane; and when we had went about a mile, we started a very large bear, but we got along mighty slow on account of the cracks in the earth occasioned by the earthquakes. We, however, made out to keep in hearing of the dogs for about three miles, and then we came to the harricane. Here we had to quit our horses, as old Nick himself couldn't have got through it without sneaking it along in the form that he put on, to make a fool of our old grandmother Eve. By this time several of my dogs had got tired and come back; but we went ahead on foot for some little time in the harricane, when we met a bear coming straight to us, and not more than twenty or thirty yards off. I started my tired dogs after him, and McDaniel pursued them, and I went on to where my other dogs were. I had seen the track of the bear they were after, and I knowed he was a screamer. I followed on to about the middle of the harricane; but my dogs pursued him so close, that they made him climb an old stump about twenty feet high. I got in shooting distance of him and fired, but I was all over in such a flutter from fatigue and running, that I couldn't hold steady; but, however, I broke his shoulder, and he fell. I run up and loaded my gun as quick as possible, and shot him again and killed him. When I went to take out my knife to butcher him, I found I had lost it in coming through the harricane. The vines and briers was so thick that I would sometimes have to get down and crawl like a varment to get through at all; and a vine had, as I supposed, caught in the handle and pulled it out. While I was standing and studying what to do, my friend came to me. He had followed my trail through the harricane, and had found my knife, which was mighty good news to me; as a hunter hates the worst in the world to lose a good dog, or any part of his hunting-tools. I now left McDaniel to butcher the bear, and I went after our horses, and brought them as near as the nature of case would allow. I then took our bags, and went back to where he was; and when we had skin'd the bear, we fleeced off the fat and carried it to our horses at several loads. We then packed it up on our horses, and had a heavy pack of it on each one. We now started and went on till about sunset, when I concluded we must be near our camp; so I hollered and my son answered me, and we moved on in the direction to the camp. We had gone but a little way when I heard my dogs make a warm start again; and I jumped down from my horse and gave him up to my friend, and told him I would follow them. He went on to the camp, and I went ahead after my dogs with all my might for a considerable distance, till at last night came on. The woods were very rough and hilly, and all covered over with cane.

I now was compel'd to move on more slowly; and was frequently falling over logs, and into the cracks made by the earthquakes, so that I was very much afraid I would break my gun. However I went on about three miles, when I came to a good big creek, which I waded. It was very cold, and the creek was about knee-deep; but I felt no great inconvenience from it just then, as I was all over wet with sweat from running, and I felt hot enough. After I got over this creek and out of the cane, which was very thick on all our creeks, I listened for my dogs. I found they had either treed or brought the bear to a stop, as they continued barking in the same place. I pushed on as near in the direction to the noise as I could, till I found the hill was too steep for me to climb, and so I backed and went down the creek some distance till I came to a hollow, and then took up that, till I come to a place where I could climb up the hill. It was mighty dark, and was difficult to see my way or anything else. When I got up the hill, I found I had passed the dogs; and so I turned and went to them. I found, when I got there, they had treed the bear in a large forked poplar, and it was setting in the fork.

I could see the lump, but not plain enough to shoot with any certainty, as there was no moonlight; and so I set in to hunting for some dry brush to make me a light; but I could find none, though I could find that the ground was torn mightily to pieces by the cracks.

At last I thought I could shoot by guess, and kill him; so I pointed as near the lump as I could, and fired away. But the bear didn't come, he only clomb up higher, and got out on a limb, which helped me to see him better. I now loaded up again and fired, but this time he didn't move at all. I commenced loading for a third fire, but the first thing I knowed, the bear was down among my dogs, and they were fighting all around me. I had my big butcher in my belt, and I had a pair of dressed buckskin breeches on. So I took out my knife, and stood, determined, if he should get hold of me, to defend myself in the best way I could. I stood there for some time, and could now and then see a white dog I had, but the rest of them, and the bear, which were dark coloured, I couldn't see at all, it was so miserable dark. They still fought around me, and sometimes within three feet of me; but, at last, the bear got down into one of the cracks, that the earthquakes had made in the ground, about four feet deep, and

I could tell the biting end of him by the hollering of my dogs. So I took my gun and pushed the muzzle of it about, till I thought I had it against the main part of his body, and fired; but it happened to be only the fleshy part of his foreleg. With this, he jumped out of the crack, and he and the dogs had another hard fight around me, as before. At last, however, they forced him back into the crack again, as he was when I had shot.

I had laid down my gun in the dark, and I now began to hunt for it; and, while hunting, I got hold of a pole, and I concluded I would punch him awhile with that. I did so, and when I would punch him, the dogs would jump in on him, when he would bite them badly, and they would jump out again. I concluded, as he would take punching so patiently, it might be that he would lie still enough for me to get down in the crack, and feel slowly along till I could find the right place to give him a dig with my butcher. So I got down, and my dogs got in before him and kept his head towards them, till I got along easily up to him; and placing my hand on his rump, felt for his shoulder, just behind which I intended to stick him. I made a lounge with my long knife, and fortunately stuck him right through the heart; at which he just sank down, and I crawled out in a hurry. In a little time my dogs all come out too, and seemed satisfied, which was the way they always had of telling me that they had finished him.

I suffered very much that night with cold, as my leather breeches, and every thing else I had on, was wet and frozen. But I managed to get my bear out of this crack after several hard trials, and so I butchered him, and laid down to try to sleep. But my fire was very bad, and I couldn't find any thing that would burn well to make it any better; and I concluded I should freeze, if I didn't warm myself in some way by exercise. So I got up, and hollered a while, and then I would just jump up and down with all my might, and throw myself into all sorts of motions. But all this wouldn't do; for my blood was now getting cold, and the chills coming all over me. I was so tired, too, that I could hardly walk; but I thought I would do the best I could to save my life, and then, if I died, nobody would be to blame. So I went to a tree about two feet through, and not a limb on it for thirty feet, and I would climb up it to the limbs, and then lock my arms together around it, and slide down to the bottom again. This would make the insides of my legs and arms feel mighty warm and good. I continued this till daylight in the morning, and how often I clomb up my tree and slid down I don't know, but I reckon at least a hundred times.

In the morning I got my bear hung up so as to be safe, and then set out to hunt for my camp. I found it after a while, and McDaniel and my son were very much rejoiced to see me get back, for they were about to give me up for lost. We got our breakfasts, and then secured our meat by building a high scaffold, and covering it over. We had no fear of its spoiling, for the weather was so cold that it couldn't.

We now started after my other bear, which had caused me so much trouble and suffering; and before we got him, we got a start after another, and took him also. We went on to the creek I had crossed the night before and camped, and then went to where my bear was, that I had killed in the crack. When we examined the place, McDaniel said he wouldn't have gone into it, as I did, for all the bears in the woods.

We took the meat down to our camp and salted it, and also the last one we had killed; intending, in the morning, to make a hunt in the harricane again.

We prepared for resting that night, and I can assure the reader I was in need of it. We had laid down by our fire, and about ten o'clock there came a most terrible earthquake, which shook the earth so, that we were rocked about like we had been in a cradle. We were very much alarmed; for though we were accustomed to feel earthquakes, we were now right in the region which had been torn to pieces by them in 1812, and we thought it might take a notion and swallow us up, like the big fish did Jonah.

In the morning we packed up and moved to the harricane, where we made another camp, and turned out that evening and killed a very large bear, which made *eight* we had now killed in this hunt.

The next morning we entered the harricane again, and in little or no time my dogs were in full cry. We pursued them, and soon came to a thick cane brake, in which they had stop'd their bear. We got up close to him, as the cane was so thick that we couldn't see more than a few feet. Here I made my friend hold the cane a little open with his gun till I shot the bear, which was a mighty large one. I killed him dead in his tracks. We got him out and butchered him, and in a little time started another and killed him, which now made *ten* we had killed; and we know'd we couldn't pack any more home, as we had only five horses along; therefore we returned to the camp and salted up all our meat, to be ready for a start homeward next morning.

The morning came, and we packed our horses with the meat, and had as much as they could possibly carry, and sure enough cut out for home. It was about thirty miles, and we reached home the second day. I had now accommodated my neighbour with meat enough to do him, and had killed in all, up to that time, fifty-eight bears, during the fall and winter.

As soon as the time come for them to quit their houses and come out again in the spring, I took a notion to hunt a little more, and in about one month I killed forty-seven more, which made one hundred and five bears I had killed in less than one year from that time.

A Useful Coon Skin

.   .   .   .

While on the subject of election matters, I will just relate a little anecdote, about myself, which will show the people to the east, how we manage these things on the frontiers. It was when I first run for Congress; I was then in favour of the Hero, for he had chalked out his course so sleek in his letter to the Tennessee legislature that, like Sam Patch, says I, "there can be no mistake in him," and so I went ahead. No one dreamt about the monster and the deposites at that time, and so, as I afterward found, many, like myself, were taken in by these fair promises, which were worth about as much as a flash in the pan when you have a fair shot at a fat bear.

But I am losing sight of my story. — Well, I started off to the Cross Roads, dressed in my hunting shirt, and my rifle on my shoulder. Many of our constituents had assembled there to get a taste of the quality of the candidates at orating. Job Snelling, a gander-shanked Yankee, who had been caught somewhere about Plymouth Bay, and been shipped to the west with a cargo of cod fish and rum, erected a large shantee, and set up shop for the occasion. A large posse of the voters had assembled before I arrived, and my opponent had already made considerable headway with his speechifying and his treating, when they spied me about a rifle shot from the camp, sauntering along as if I was not a party in the business. "There comes Crockett," cried one. "Let us hear the colonel," cried another, and so I mounted the stump that had been cut down for the occasion, and began to bushwhack in the most approved style.

I had not been up long before there was such an uproar in the crowd that I could not hear my own voice, and some of my constituents let me know, that they could not listen to me on such a dry subject as the welfare of the nation, until they had something to drink, and that I must treat 'em. Accordingly I jumped down from the rostrum, and led the way to the shantee, followed by my constituents, shouting, "Huzza for Crockett," and "Crocket forever!"

When we entered the shantee, Job was busy dealing out his rum in a style that showed he was making a good day's work of it, and I called for a quart of the best, but the crooked critur returned no other answer than by pointing at a board over the bar, on which he had chalked in large letters, *"Pay to-day and trust to-morrow."* Now that idea brought me all up standing; it was a sort of cornering in which there was no back out, for ready money in the west, in those times, was the shyest thing in all natur, and it was most particularly shy with me on that occasion.

The voters, seeing my predicament, fell off to the other side, and I was left deserted and alone, as the Government will be, when he no longer has any offices to bestow. I saw, plain as day, that the tide of popular opinion was against me, and that, unless I got some rum speedily, I should lose my election as sure as there are snakes in Virginny, — and it must be done soon, or even burnt brandy wouldn't save me. So I walked away from the shantee, but in another guess sort from the way I entered it, for on this occasion I had no train after me, and not a voice shouted "Huzza for Crockett." Popularity sometimes depends on a very small matter indeed; in this particular it was worth a quart of New England rum, and no more.

Well, knowing that a crisis was at hand, I struck into the woods with my rifle on my shoulder, my best friend in time of need, and as good fortune would have it, I had not been out more than a quarter of an hour before I treed a fat coon, and in the pulling of a trigger he lay dead at the root of the tree. I soon whipped his hairy jacket off his back, and again bent my way towards the shantee, and walked up to the bar, but not alone, for this time I had half a dozen of my constituents at my heels. I threw down the coon skin upon the counter, and called for a quart, and Job, though busy in dealing out rum, forgot to point at his chalked rules and regulations, for he knew that a coon was as good a legal tender for a quart, in the west, as a New York shilling, any day in the year.

My constituents now flocked about me, and cried "Huzza for Crockett," "Crockett forever," and finding that the tide had taken a turn, I told them several yarns, to get them in a good humour, and having soon despatched the value of the coon, I went out and mounted the stump, without opposition, and a clear majority of the voters followed me to hear what I had to offer for the good of the nation. Before I was half through, one of my constituents moved that they would hear the balance of my speech, after they had washed down the first part with some more of Job Snelling's extract of cornstalk and molasses, and the question being put, it was carried unanimously. It wasn't considered necessary to call the yeas and nays, so we adjourned to the shantee, and on the way I began to reckon that the fate of the nation pretty much depended upon my shooting another coon.

While standing at the bar, feeling sort of bashful while Job's rules and regulations stared me in the face, I cast down my eyes, and discovered one end of the coon skin sticking between the logs that supported the bar. Job had slung it there in the hurry of business. I gave it a sort of quick jerk, and it followed my hand as natural as if I had been the rightful owner. I slapped it on the counter, and Job, little dreaming that he was barking up the wrong tree, shoved along another bottle, which my constituents quickly disposed of with great good humour, for some of them saw the trick, and then we withdrew to the rostrum to discuss the affairs of the nation.

I don't know how it was, but the voters soon became dry again, and nothing would do, but we must adjourn to the shantee, and as luck would have it, the coon skin was still sticking between the logs, as if Job had flung it there on purpose to tempt me. I was not slow in raising it to the counter, the rum followed of course, and I wish I may be shot, if I didn't, before the day was over, get ten quarts for the same identical skin, and from a fellow too, who in those parts was considered as sharp as a steel trap, and as bright as a pewter button. . . .

Augustus Baldwin Longstreet

(1790-1870)

✢ *Georgia Scenes* by Augustus Baldwin Longstreet was the first of a seemingly endless number of stories and books of Southern humor that poured from the presses until the Civil War. Born in Augusta, Georgia, the author was educated first at Moses Waddel's famous Academy in South Carolina, and then attended Yale College. After two years of law school at Litchfield, Connecticut, he returned to Georgia, married a wealthy young woman of Greensboro, and settled down to a life of gentlemanly comfort.

Settled comfort, however, was not to the liking of this energetic young attorney. His life was marked by changes. He was a member of the state legislature for a year and judge of the superior court for three. When his son died, he withdrew from politics, joined the Methodist church, and became a minister in 1838. In the next few years he was in succession the president of four Southern colleges: Emory, Centenary, and the state universities of Mississippi and South Carolina. During his years as a minister and an educator, he remained actively interested in politics. A strong advocate of states' rights, he spent much of his life angrily preaching nullification and then secession.

Although Longstreet wrote several books and pamphlets, only *Georgia Scenes* is still of interest. The nineteen sketches which it includes were first published in 1833 and 1834 in the Milledgeville, Georgia, *Southern Recorder* and Longstreet's own newspaper, the Augusta *State Rights Sentinel*. When the collected sketches appeared in 1835, Edgar Allan Poe, who reviewed the book for the *Southern Literary Messenger,* praised it highly. "Perhaps never," he said, had he "laughed as immoderately over any book" as over this one. After quoting profusely from Longstreet, Poe concluded his review by calling *Georgia Scenes* "a sure omen of better days of the literature of the South." The fame of *Georgia Scenes* spread quickly, gaining for Longstreet a large audience and leading to an honorary LL.D. degree from Yale in 1841.

To account for the appeal of *Georgia Scenes* is to see it as a remarkably varied collection. There was something in it for almost every class of American reader in the 1830's. For the gentle reader, there was sentimentalism and didacticism in the serious narrative "The Charming Creature as a Wife" and in the genteelly humorous "The Mother and Her Child." Less domestic and sentimental and more urbanely humorous is Poe's favorite, "The Debating Society."

From there the stories run the gamut of taste and appeal down to the vivid description of the horse's enormous sore in "The Horse Swap" and the details of the gory encounter in "The Fight." But even in these two stories, the gentleman could safely indulge in unrestrained laughter, for the narrator is an aristocrat, describing from a superior social and moral viewpoint the antics of these peculiar specimens. Longstreet was talented in the writing of Addisonian humor and in the invention of humorous incident, but he is most likely to be remembered for the creation of such clearly drawn frontier characters as the troublemaker Ransy Sniffle in "The Fight" and the horse traders in "The Horse Swap." Adept at describing places and events with sharp outlines, he was also an early master at realistic characterization.

TEXT: "The Horse Swap," "The Character of a Native Georgian," and "The Fight" from *Georgia Scenes* (Augusta, Ga., 1835).

The Horse Swap

During the session of the Superior Court, in the village of ——, about three weeks ago, when a number of people were collected in the principal street of the village, I observed a young man riding up and down the street, as I supposed, in a violent passion. He galloped this way, then that, and then the other. Spurred his horse to one group of citizens, then to another. Then dashed off at half speed, as if fleeing from danger; and suddenly checking his horse, returned — first in a pace, then in a trot, and then in a canter. While he was performing these various evolutions, he cursed, swore, whooped, screamed, and tossed himself in every attitude which man could assume on horse back. In short, he *cavorted* most magnanimously, (a term which, in our tongue, expresses all that I have described, and a little more) and seemed to be setting all creation at defiance. As I like to see all that is passing, I determined to take a position a little nearer to him, and to ascertain if possible, what it was that affected him so sensibly. Accordingly I approached a crowd before which he had stopt for a moment, and examined it with the strictest scrutiny. — But I could see nothing in it, that seemed to have anything to do with the cavorter. Every man appeared to be in a good humor, and all minding their own business. Not one so much as noticed the principal figure. Still he went on. After a semicolon pause, which my appearance seemed to produce, (for he eyed me closely as I approached) he fetched a whoop, and swore that "he could out-swap any live man, woman or child, that ever walked these hills, or that

ever straddled horse flesh since the days of old daddy Adam."
"Stranger," said he to me, "did you ever see the *Yellow* Blossom
from Jasper?"

"No," said I, "but I have often heard of him."

"I'm the boy," continued he; "perhaps a *leetle* — jist a *leetle* of
the best man, at a horse swap, that ever trod shoe-leather."

I began to feel my situation a little awkward, when I was relieved
by a man somewhat advanced in years, who stept up and began to
survey the *"Yallow Blossom's"* horse with much apparent interest.
This drew the rider's attention, and he turned the conversation from
me to the stranger.

"Well, my old coon," said he, "do you want to swap *hosses?"*

"Why, I don't know," replied the stranger; "I believe I've got a
beast I'd trade with you for that one, if you like him."

"Well, fetch up your nag, my old cock; you're jist the lark I wanted
to get hold of. I am perhaps a *leetle,* jist a *leetle,* of the best man at
a horse swap, that ever stole *cracklins* out of his mammy's fat gourd.
Where's your *hoss?"*

"I'll bring him presently; but I want to examine your horse a little."

"Oh! look at him," said the Blossom, alighting and hitting him a
cut — "look at him. He's the best piece of *hoss* flesh in the thirteen
united universal worlds. There's no sort o' mistake in little Bullet.
He can pick up miles on his feet and fling 'em behind him as fast as
the next man's *hoss,* I don't care where he comes from. — And he can
keep at it as long as the Sun can shine without resting."

During this harangue, little Bullet looked as if he understood it all,
believed it, and was ready at any moment to verify it. He was a
horse of goodly countenance, rather expressive of vigilance than fire;
though an unnatural appearance of fierceness was thrown into it, by
the loss of his ears, which had been cropt pretty close to his head.
Nature had done but little for Bullet's head and neck; but he managed, in a great measure, to hide their defects, by bowing perpetually.
He had obviously suffered severely for corn; but if his ribs and hip
bones had not disclosed the fact, *he* never would have done it; for
he was in all respects, as cheerful and happy, as if he commanded all
the corn-cribs and fodder stacks in Georgia. His height was about
twelve hands; but as his shape partook somewhat of that of the
Giraffe, his haunches stood much lower. They were short, strait,
peaked and concave. Bullet's tail, however, made amends for all his
defects. All that the artist could do to beautify it, had been done; and
all that horse could do to compliment the artist, Bullet did. His tail
was nicked in superior style, and exhibited the line of beauty in so
many directions, that it could not fail to hit the most fastidious taste

in some of them. From the root it dropt into a graceful festoon; then rose in a handsome curve; then resumed its first direction; and then mounted suddenly upwards like a cypress knee to a perpendicular of about two and a half inches. The whole had a careless and bewitching inclination to the right. Bullet obviously knew where his beauty lay, and took all occasions to display it to the best advantage. If a stick cracked, or if any one moved suddenly about him, or coughed, or hawked, or spoke a little louder than common, up went Bullet's tail like lightning; and if the *going up* did not please, the *coming down* must of necessity, for it was as different from the other movement, as was its direction. The first, was a bold and rapid flight upward; usually to an angle of forty-five degrees. In this position he kept his interesting appendage, until he satisfied himself that nothing in particular was to be done; when he commenced dropping it by half inches, in second beats — then in triple time — then faster and shorter, and faster and shorter still; until it finally died away imperceptibly into its natural position. If I might compare sights to sounds, I should say, its *settling,* was more like the note of a locust than anything else in nature.

Either from native sprightliness of disposition, from uncontrolable activity, or from an unconquerable habit of removing flies by the stamping of the feet, Bullet never stood still; but always kept up a gentle fly-scaring movement of his limbs, which was peculiarly interesting.

"I tell you, man," proceeded the Yellow Blossom, "he's the best live hoss that ever trod the grit of Georgia. Bob Smart knows the hoss. Come here, Bob, and mount this hoss and show Bullet's motions." Here, Bullet bristled up, and looked as if he had been hunting for Bob all day long, and had just found him. Bob sprang on his back. "Boo-oo-oo,!" said Bob, with a fluttering noise of the lips; and away went Bullet, as if in a quarter race, with all his beauties spread in handsome style.

"Now fetch him back," said Blossom. Bullet turned and came in pretty much as he went out.

"Now trot him by." Bullet reduced his tail to *"customary"* — sidled to the right and left airily, and exhibited at least three varieties of trot, in the short space of fifty yards.

"Make him pace!" Bob commenced twitching the bridle and kicking at the same time. These inconsistent movements obviously (and most naturally) disconcerted Bullet; for it was impossible for him to learn, from them, whether he was to proceed or stand still. He started to trot — and was told that wouldn't do. He attempted a canter — and was checked again. He stopt — and was urged to go on. Bullet now rushed into the wide field of experiment, and struck out a gait of his own, that completely turned the tables upon his rider, and certainly deserved a patent. It seemed to have derived its elements from the jig, the minuet and the cotillion. If it was not a pace, it certainly had *pace* in it; and no man would venture to call it anything else; so it passed off to the satisfaction of the owner.

"Walk him!" Bullet was now at home again; and he walked as if money was staked on him.

The stranger, whose name I afterwards learned was Peter Ketch, having examined Bullet to his heart's content, ordered his son Neddy to go and bring up Kit. Neddy soon appeared upon Kit; a well formed sorrel of the middle size, and in good order. His *tout ensemble* threw Bullet entirely in the shade; though a glance was sufficient to satisfy anyone, that Bullet had the decided advantage of him in point of intellect.

"Why man," said Blossom, "'do you bring such a hoss as that to trade for Bullet? Oh, I see you're no notion of trading."

"Ride him off, Neddy!" said Peter. Kit put off at a handsome lope.

"Trot him back!" Kit came in at a long, sweeping trot, and stopt suddenly at the crowd.

"Well," said Blossom, "let me look at him; may be he'll do to plough."

"Examine him!" said Peter, taking hold of the bridle close to the mouth; "He's nothing but a tacky. He an't as *pretty* a horse as Bullet, I know; but he'll do. Start 'em together for a hundred and fifty *mile;* and if Kit an't twenty mile ahead of him at the coming out, any man may take Kit for nothing. But he's a monstrous mean horse, gentlemen; any man may see that. He's the scariest horse, too, you ever saw. He won't do to hunt on, no how. Stranger, will you let Neddy have your rifle to shoot off him? Lay the rifle between his ears, Neddy, and shoot at the blaze in that stump. Tell me when his head is high enough."

Ned fired, and hit the blaze; and Kit did not move a hair's breadth.

"Neddy, take a couple of sticks and beat on that hogshead at Kit's tail."

Ned made a tremendous rattling; at which *Bullet* took fright, broke his bridle and dashed off in grand style; and would have stopt all farther negotiations, by going home in disgust, had not a traveller arrested him and brought him back; but Kit did not move.

"I tell you, gentlemen," continued Peter, "he's the scariest horse you ever saw. He an't as gentle as Bullet; but he won't do any harm if you watch him. Shall I put him in a cart, gig, or wagon for you, stranger? He'll cut the same capers there he does here. He's a monstrous mean horse."

During all this time, Blossom was examining him with the nicest scrutiny. Having examined his frame and limbs, he now looked at his eyes.

"He's got a curious look out of his eyes," said Blossom.

"Oh yes, sir," said Peter, "just as blind as a bat. Blind horses always have clear eyes. Make a motion at his eyes, if you please, sir."

Blossom did so, and Kit threw up his head rather as if something pricked him under the chin, than as if fearing a blow. Blossom repeated the experiment, and Kit jirked back in considerable astonishment.

"Stone blind, you see, gentlemen," proceeded Peter; "but he's just as good to travel of a dark night as if he had eyes."

"Blame my buttons," said Blossom, "if I like them eyes."

"No," said Peter, "nor I neither. I'd rather have 'em made of diamonds; but they'll do, if they don't show as much white as Bullet's."

"Well," said Blossom, "make a pass at me."

"No," said Peter, "you made the banter; now make your pass."

"Well I'm never afraid to price my hosses. You must give me twenty-five dollars boot."

"Oh certainly; say fifty, and my saddle and bridle in. Here, Neddy, my son, take away daddy's horse."

"Well," said Blossom, "I've made my pass; now you make yours."

"I'm for short talk in a horse swap; and therefore always tell a gentleman, at once, what I mean to do. You must give me ten dollars."

Blossom swore absolutely, roundly and profanely, that he never would give boot.

"Well," said Peter, "I didn't care about trading; but you cut such high shines, that I thought I'd like to back you out; and I've done it. Gentlemen, you see I've brought him to a hack."

"Come, old man," said Blossom, "I've been joking with you. I begin to think you do want to trade; therefore, give me five dollars and take Bullet. I'd rather lose ten dollars, any time, than not make a trade; though I hate to fling away a good hoss."

"Well," said Peter, "I'll be as clever as you are. Just put the five dollars on Bullet's back and hand him over, it's a trade."

Blossom swore again, as roundly as before, that he would not give boot; and, said he, "Bullet wouldn't hold five dollars on his back, no how. But as I bantered you, if you say an even swap, here's at you."

"I told you," said Peter, "I'd be as clever as you; therefore, here goes two dollars more, just for trade sake. Give me three dollars, and it's a bargain."

Blossom repeated his former assertion; and here the parties stood for a long time, and the by-standers (for many were now collected,) began to taunt both parties. After some time, however, it was pretty unanimously decided that the old man had backed Blossom out.

At length Blossom swore he "never would be backed out, for three dollars, after bantering a man;" and accordingly they closed the trade.

"Now," said Blossom, as he handed Peter the three dollars, "I'm a man, that when he makes a bad trade, makes the most of it until he can make a better. I'm for no rues and after-claps."

"That's just my way," said Peter; "I never goes to law to mend my bargains."

"Ah, you're the kind of boy I love to trade with. Here's your hoss, old man. Take the saddle and bridle off him, and I'll strip yours; but lift up the blanket easy from Bullet's back, for he's a mighty tender-backed hoss."

The old man removed the saddle, but the blanket stuck fast. He attempted to raise it, and Bullet bowed himself, switched his tail, danced a little, and gave signs of biting.

"Don't hurt him, old man," said Blossom archly; "take it off easy. I am, perhaps, a leetle of the best man at a horse-swap that ever catched a coon."

Peter continued to pull at the blanket more and more roughly; and Bullet became more and more *cavortish:* in so much, that when the blanket came off, he had reached the *kicking* point in good earnest.

The removal of the blanket, disclosed a sore on Bullet's back-bone, that seemed to have defied all medical skill. It measured six full inches in length, and four in breadth; and had as many features as Bullet had motions. My heart sickened at the sight; and I felt that the brute who had been riding him in that situation, deserved the halter.

The prevailing feeling, however, was that of mirth. The laugh became loud and general, at the old man's expense; and rustic witticisms were liberally bestowed upon him and his late purchase. These, Blossom continued to provoke by various remarks. He asked the old man, "if he thought Bullet would let five dollars lie on his back." He declared most seriously, that he had owned that horse three months, and had never discovered before, that he had a sore back, "or he never should have thought of trading him," &c. &c.

The old man bore it all with the most philosophic composure. He evinced no astonishment at his late discovery, and made no replies. But his son, Neddy, had not disciplined his feelings quite so well. His eyes opened, wider and wider, from the first to the last pull of the blanket; and when the whole sore burst upon his view, astonishment and fright seemed to contend for the mastery of his countenance. As the blanket disappeared, he stuck his hands in his breeches pockets, heaved a deep sigh, and lapsed into a profound reverie; from which he was only roused by the cuts at his father. He bore them as long as he could; and when he could contain himself no longer, he began, with a certain wildness of expression, which gave a peculiar interest to what he uttered: "His back's mighty bad off; but dod drot my soul, if he's put it to daddy as bad as he thinks he has, for old Kit's both blind and *deef,* I'll be dod drot if he eint."

"The devil he is," said Blossom. "Yes, dod drot my soul if he *eint.* You walk him and see if he *eint.* His eyes don't look like it; but he *jist as live go agin* the house with you, or in a ditch, as any how. Now you go try him." The laugh was now turned on Blossom; and many rushed to test the fidelity of the little boy's report. A few experiments established its truth, beyond controversy.

"Neddy," said the old man, "you oughtn't to try and make people discontented with their things." "Stranger, don't mind what the little boy says. If you can only get Kit rid of them little failings, you'll find him all sorts of a horse. You are a *leetle* the best man, at a horse swap, that ever I got hold of; but don't fool away Kit. Come, Neddy, my son, let's be moving; the stranger seems to be getting snappish."

The Character of a Native Georgian

There are some yet living, who knew the man whose character I am about to delineate; and these will unanimously bear testimony, that if it be not faithfully drawn, it is not overdrawn. They cannot avouch for the truth of the anecdotes which I am about to relate of him, because of these they know nothing; but they will unhesitatingly declare, that there is nothing herein ascribed to him, of which he was incapable, and of which he would not readily have been the author, supposing the scenes in which I have placed him to be real, and the thoughts and actions attributed to him, to have actually suggested themselves to him. They will further testify, that the thoughts and actions, are in perfect harmony with his general character.

I do not feel at liberty as yet to give the name of the person in question, and therefore, he shall be designated for the present, by the appellation of Ned Brace.

This man seemed to live only to amuse himself with his fellow-beings, and he possessed the rare faculty, of deriving some gratification of his favorite propensity, from almost every person with whom he met, no matter what his temper, standing or disposition. Of course he had opportunities enough of exercising his uncommon gift, and he rarely suffered an opportunity to pass unimproved. The beau in the presence of his mistress, the fop, the pedant, the purse-proud, the over-fastidious and sensitive, were Ned's favorite game. These never passed him uninjured; and against such, he directed his severest shafts. With these he commonly amused himself, by exciting in them every variety of emotion, under circumstances peculiarly ridiculous. He was admirably fitted to his vocation. He could assume any character which his humor required him to personate, and he could sustain it to perfection. His knowledge of the character of others, seemed to be intuitive.

It may seem remarkable, but it is true, that though he lived his own peculiar life for about sixteen years, after he reached the age of manhood, he never involved himself in a personal recounter with anyone. This was owing in part to his muscular frame, which few would be willing to engage; but more particularly to his adroitness in the management of his projects of fun. He generally conducted them in such a way, as to render it impossible for anyone to call him to account, without violating all the rules of decency, politeness and chivalry at once. But a few anecdotes of him, will give the reader a much better idea of his character, than he can possibly derive from a general description. If these fulfil the description which I have given of my hero, all will agree that he is no imaginary being: if they do not, it will only be, because I am unfortunate in my selection. Having known him from his earliest manhood to his grave — for he was a native Georgian — I confess, that I am greatly perplexed, in determining what portions of his singular history, to lay before the reader, as a proper specimen of the whole. A three days' visit, which I once made with him to Savannah, placed him in a greater variety of scenes, and among a greater diversity of characters, than perhaps any other period of his life, embracing no longer time; and therefore, I will choose this for my purpose.

We reached Savannah just at night-fall, of a cold December's evening. As we approached the tavern of Mr. Blank, at which we designed to stop, Ned proposed to me, that we should drop our acquaintance, until *he* should choose to renew it. To this proposition I most cordially assented, for I knew, that so doing, I should be saved some mortifications, and avoid a thousand questions, which I would not know how to answer. According to this understanding, Ned lingered behind, in order that I might reach the tavern alone.

On alighting at the public house, I was led into a large dining-room, at the entrance of which, to the right, stood the bar, opening into the dining-room. On the left, and rather nearer to the centre of the room, was a fire-place, surrounded by gentlemen. Upon entering the room, my name was demanded at the bar: it was given, and I took my seat in the circle around the fire. I had been seated just long enough for the company to survey me to their satisfaction, and resume their conversation, when Ned's heavy footstep at the door, turned the eyes of the company to the approaching stranger.

"Your name, sir, if you please?" said the restless little bar-keeper, as he entered.

Ned stared at the question with apparent alarm — cast a fearful glance at the company — frowned and shook his head in token of caution to the bar-keeper — looked confused for a moment — then, as if suddenly recollecting himself, jirked a piece of paper out of his pocket — turned from the company — wrote on it with his pencil — handed it to the bar-keeper — walked to the left of the fire-place, and took the most conspicuous seat in the circle. He looked at no one, spoke to no one; but fixing his eyes on the fire, lapsed into a profound reverie.

The conversation, which had been pretty general before, stopped as short, as if every man in the room had been shot dead. Every eye was fixed on Ned, and every variety of expression was to be seen on the countenances of the persons present. The landlord came in — the bar-keeper whispered to him and looked at Ned. The landlord looked at him too with astonishment and alarm — the bar-keeper produced a piece of paper, and both of them examined it, as if searching for a fig-mite with the naked eye. They rose from the examination unsatisfied, and looked at Ned again. Those of the company who recovered first from their astonishment, tried to revive the conversation; but the effort was awkward, met with no support, and failed. The bar-keeper, for the first time in his life, became dignified and solemn, and left the bar to take care of itself. The landlord had a world of foolish questions to ask the gentlemen directly opposite to Ned, for which purpose he passed round to them every two minutes, and the answer to none did he hear.

Three or four boarders coming in, who were unapprized of what had happened, at length revived the conversation; not however, until they had created some confusion, by enquiring of their friends, the cause of their sober looks. As soon as the conversation began to become easy and natural, Ned rose, and walked out into the entry. With the first movement, all were as hush as death; but when he had cleared the door, another Babel scene ensued. Some enquired, others suspected, and all wondered. Some were engaged in telling the strangers what had happened, others were making towards the bar, and all were becoming clamorous, when Ned returned and took his seat. His re-entry was as fatal to conversation, as was the first movement of his exit; but it soon recovered from the shock — with the difference, however, that those who *led* before, were now mute, and wholly absorbed in the contemplation of Ned's person.

After retaining his seat for about ten minutes, Ned rose again, enquired the way to the stable, and left the house. As soon as he passed the outer door, the bar-keeper hastened to the company with Ned's paper in his hand. "Gentlemen," said he, "can any of you tell me what name this is?" All rushed to the paper in an instant — one or two pair of heads met over it with considerable force. After pondering over it to their heart's content, they all agreed that the first letter was an "E" and the second a "B" or an "R," and the d—l himself could not make out the balance. While they were thus engaged, to the astonishment of everybody, Ned interrupted their deliberations with "gentlemen, if you have satisfied yourselves with that paper, I'll thank you for it." It is easy to imagine, but impossible to describe the looks and actions of the company, under their surprise and mortification. They dropt off and left the bar-keeper to his appropriate duty, of handing the paper to Ned. He reached it forth, but Ned moved not a hand to receive it, for about the space of three seconds; during which time he kept his eyes fixed upon the arch-offender in awfully solemn rebuke. He then took it gravely and put it in his pocket, and left the bar-keeper, with a shaking ague upon him. From this moment he became Ned's most obsequious and willing slave.

Supper was announced; Mrs. Blank, the landlady, took the head of the table, and Ned seated himself next to her. Her looks denoted some alarm at finding him so near to her; and plainly showed, that he had been fully described to her by her husband, or some one else.

"Will you take tea or coffee, sir?" said she.

"Why madam," said Ned, in a tone as courteous as Chesterfield himself could have used, "I am really ashamed to acknowledge and to expose my very singular appetite; but habitual indulgence of it, has made it necessary to my comfort, if not to my health, that I should still favor it when I can. If you will pardon me, I will take both at the same time."

This respectful reply, (which, by the way, she alone was permitted to hear,) had its natural effect. It won for him her unqualified indulgence, raised doubts whether he could be the suspicious character which had been described to her, and begat in her a desire to cultivate a further acquaintance with him. She handed to him the two cups, and accompanied them with some remarks drawn from her own observation in the line of her business, calculated to reconcile him to his whimsical appetite; but she could extract from Ned nothing but monosyllables, and sometimes not even that much. Consequently, the good lady began very soon to relapse into her former feelings.

Ned placed a cup on either side of him, and commenced stirring both at the same time very deliberately. This done, he sipped a little tea, and asked Mrs. B. for a drop more milk in it. Then he tasted his coffee, and desired a little more sugar in it. Then he tasted his tea again and requested a small lump more sugar in it. — Lastly he tasted his coffee, and desired a few drops more milk in that. It was easy to discover, that before he got suited, the landlady had solemnly resolved, never to offer any more encouragements to such an appetite. She waxed exceedingly petulant, and having nothing else to scold, she scolded the servants of course.

Waffles were handed to Ned, and he took one: batter-cakes were handed, and he took one; and so on of muffins, rolls, and corn bread. Having laid in these provisions, he turned into his plate, upon his waffle and batter-cake, some of the crums of the several kinds of bread which he had taken, in different proportions, and commenced mashing all together with his knife. During this operation the landlady frowned and pouted, — the servants giggled, — and the boarders were variously affected.

Having reduced his mess to the consistency of a hard poultice, he packed it all up to one side of his plate in the form of a terrapin, and smoothed it all over nicely with his knife. Nearly opposite to Ned, but a little below him, sat a waspish little gentleman, who had been watching him with increasing torments, from the first to the last movement of Ned's knife. His tortures were visible to blinder eyes than Ned's, and doubtless had been seen by him in their earliest paroxysms. This gentleman occupied a seat nearest to a dish of steak, and was in the act of muttering something about 'brutes' to his next neighbor, when Ned beckoned a servant to him, and requested him "to ask that gentleman for a small bit of steak." The servant obeyed, and planting Ned's plate directly between the gentleman's and the steak-dish, delivered his message. The testy gentleman turned his head, and the first thing he saw was Ned's party-coloured terrapin, right under his nose. He started as if he had been struck by a snapping-turtle — reddened to scarlet — looked at Ned, (who appeared as innocent as a lamb) — looked at the servant, (who appeared as innocent as Ned) and then fell to work on the steak, as if he were amputating all Ned's limbs at once.

Ned now commenced his repast. He ate his meat and *breads* in the usual way; but he drank his liquids in all ways. First a sip of tea, then of coffee; then two of the first and one of the last; then three of the last, and one of the first, and so on.

His steak was soon consumed, and his plate was a second time returned to the mettlesome gentleman "for another *very* small bit of steak." The plate paid its second visit, precisely as it had its first; and as soon as the fiery gentlman saw the half-demolished terrapin again under his nose, he seized a fork, drove it into the largest slice of steak in the dish, dashed it into Ned's plate, rose from the table, and left the room; cursing Ned from the very inmost chamber of his soul. Every person at the table, except Ned, laughed outright at the little man's fury; but Ned did not even smile — nay, he looked for all the world, as if he thought the laugh was at him.

The boarders, one after another, retired, until Ned and the landlady were left alone at the table.

"Will you have another cup of tea and coffee sir?" said she, by the way of convincing him that he ought to retire, seeing that he had finished his supper.

"No I thank you madam," returned Ned.

"Will you have a glass of milk and a cup of tea or coffee, or all three together?"

"No ma'am," said Ned. "I am not blind madam," continued he, "to the effects which my unfortunate eccentricities have produced upon yourself and your company; nor have I witnessed them without those feelings which they are well calculated to inspire in a man of ordinary sensibilities. I am aware, too, that I am prolonging and aggravating your uneasiness, by detaining you beyond the hour which demands your presence at the table; but I could not permit you to retire, without again bespeaking your indulgence of the strange, unnatural appetite, which has just caused you so much astonishment and mortification. The story of its beginning might be interesting, and certainly would be instructing to you if you are a mother: but I am indisposed at this time to obtrude it upon your patience, and I presume you are still less disposed to hear it. My principal object, however, in claiming your attention for a moment at this time, is to assure you, that out of respect to your feelings, I will surrender the enjoyment of my meals for the few days that I have to remain in Savannah, and conform to the customs of your table. The sudden change of my habits will expose me to some inconvenience, and may perhaps affect my health; but I willingly incur these hazards, rather than to renew your mortification, or to impose upon your family the trouble of giving me my meals at my room."

The good lady, whose bitter feelings had given place to the kinder emotion of pity and benevolence, before Ned had half concluded his apology, (for it was delivered in a tone of the most melting eloquence,) caught at this last hint, and insisted upon sending his meals to his room. Ned reluctantly consented, after extorting a pledge from her, that *she* would assume the responsibilities of the trouble that he was about to give the family.

"As to your *boarders,* madam," said Ned, in conclusion, "I have no apology to make to them. I grant them the privilege of eating what they please, and as they please; and so far as they are concerned I shall exercise the same privileges, reckless of their feelings or opinions; and I shall take it as a singular favor if you will say nothing to them or to anyone else, which may lead them to the discovery, that I am acquainted with my own peculiarities."

The good lady promised obedience to his wishes, and Ned, requesting to be conducted to the room, retired.

A group of gentlemen at the fire-place had sent many significant "hems" and smiles to Mrs. Blank, during her *tete a tete* with Ned; and as she approached them, on her way out of the room, they began to taunt her playfully, upon the impression which she seemed to have made upon the remarkable stranger.

"Really," said one, "I thought the *impression* was on the other side."

"And in truth, so it was," said Mrs. B. At this moment her husband stept in.

"I'll tell you what it is, Mr. Blank," said one of the company, "you'd better keep a sharp look out on that stranger; our landlady is wonderfully taken with him."

"I'll be bound," said Mr. B., "for my wife; the less like anybody else in the world he is, the better will she like him."

"Well I assure you," said Mrs. B., "I never had my feelings so deeply interested in a stranger in my life. I'd give the world to know his history."

"Why, then," rejoined the landlord; "I suppose he has been quizzing us all this time."

"No," said she, "he is incapable of quizzing. All that you have seen of him is unaffected, and perfectly natural to him."

"Then, really," continued the husband, "he is a very interesting object, and I congratulate you upon getting so early into his confidence; but as I am not quite as much captivated with his unaffected graces as you seem to be, I shall take the liberty, in charity to the rest of my boarders, of requesting him to-morrow, to seek other lodgings."

"Oh," exclaimed Mrs. B. in the goodness of her heart, and with a countenance evincive of the deepest feeling, "I would not have you do such a thing for the world. He's only going to stay a few days."

"How do you know?"

"He told me so, and do let's bear with him that short time. He shan't trouble you or the boarders any more."

"Why Sarah," said the landlord, "I do believe you are out of your senses!"

"Gone case!" said one boarder. "Terrible affair!" said another. "Bewitching *little* fellow," said a third. "Come, Mrs. Blank, tell us all he said to you? We young men wish to know how to please the ladies, so that we may get wives easily. I'm determined the next party I go to, to make a soup of every thing on the waiters, and eat all at once. I shall then become irresistible to the ladies."

"Get along with your nonsense," said Mrs. B. smiling as she left the room.

At 8 o'clock, I retired to my room, which happened (probably from the circumstance of our reaching the hotel within a few minutes of each other,) to be adjoining Ned's. I had no sooner entered my room, than Ned followed me, where we interchanged the particulars which make up the foregoing story. He now expended freely the laughter which he had been collecting during the evening. He stated that his last interview with Mrs. Blank, was the result of necessity — That he found he had committed himself in making up and disposing of his odd supper; for that he should have to eat in the same way, during his whole stay in Savannah, unless he could manage to get his meals in private; and though he was willing to do penance for one meal, in order to purchase the amusement which he had enjoyed, he had no idea of tormenting himself three or four days for the same purpose. To tell you the honest truth, said he, nothing but an appetite whetted by fasting and travelling, could have borne me through the table scene. As it was, my stomach several times threatened to expose my tricks to the whole company, by downright open rebellion. I feel that I must make it some atonement for the liberty I have taken with it; and therefore, propose that we go out and get an oyster supper before we retire to rest. I assented: we set out, going separately, until we reached the street.

We were received by the oyster-vender, in a small shop, which fronted upon the street, and were conducted through it to a back door, and thence, by a flight of steps, to a convenient room, on a second floor of an adjoining building. We had been seated about three minutes, when we heard footsteps on the stairs, and distinctly caught this sentence from the ascending stranger: "Aha, Monsieur Middletong! you say you hab de bes oystar in de cittee? Well, me shall soon see."

The sentence was hardly uttered, before the door opened, and in stept a gay, smerky little Frenchman. He made us a low bow, and as soon as he rose from his obeisance, Ned rushed to him in transports of joy — seized him by the hand, and shaking it with friendship's warmest grasp, exclaimed, "How do you do my old friend — I had no idea of meeting you here — how do you do Mr. Squeezelfanter? how have you been this long time?"

"Sair," said the Frenchman, "me tank you ver' much to lub me so hard; but you mistake de gentleman — my name is not de Squeezilfaunter."

"Come, come John," continued Ned, "quit your old tricks before strangers. Mr. Hall, let me introduce you to my particular friend, John Squeezelfanter, from Paris."

"Perhaps, sir" said I — not knowing well what to say, or how to act in such an emergency — "perhaps you have mistaken the gentleman."

"Begar, sair," said Monsieur, "he is mistake ebery ting at once. My name is not *Zhaun*, me play no *treek*, me is not de gentilmong fren', me did not come from *Paree*, but from Bordeaux — and me did not suppose dare was one man in all France, dat was name de Squeezilfaunter."

"If I am mistaken," said Ned, "I humbly ask your pardon; but really, you look so much like my old friend *Jack*, and talk so much like him, that I would have sworn you were he."

"Vel sair," said Monsieur, looking at Ned as though he might be an acquaintance after all — "vell sair, dis time you tell my name right — my name is Jacques* — *Jacques Sancric*."

"There," proceeded Ned, "I knew it was impossible I could be mistaken — your whole family settled on *Sandy Creek* — I knew your father and mother, your sister Patsy and Dilsy, your brother Ichabod, your aunt Bridget, your ———."

"Oh mon Dieu, mon Dieu!" exclaimed the Frenchman, no longer able to contain his surprise; "dat is von 'Mericane familee. Dare vas not one French familee hab all dat name since dis vorl' vas make."

"Now look at me good Jack," said Ned, "and see if you don't recollect your old friend Obadiah Snoddleburg, who used to play with you when a boy, in Sandy Creek."

"Vel, Monsieur Snotborg, me look at you ver' well; and begar me neber see you in de creek, nor out de creek — 'Tis ver' surprise, you not know one *name*, from one *creek*."

"Oh, very well sir, very well, I forgot where I was — I understand you now perfectly. You are not the first gentleman I have met with in Savannah, who knew me well in the country, and forgot me in town. I ask your pardon sir, and hope you'll excuse me."

"Me is ver' will to know you *now*, sair; but begar me will not tell you one lie, to know you *twenty-five and tirty years ago*."

"It makes no difference sir," said Ned, looking thoughtfully and chagrined. "I beg leave, however, before we close our acquaintance; to correct one mistake which I made. — I said you were from Paris —

---

* This name is pronounced very nearly like "Jack," in English. [Author's note]

I believe on reflection, I was wrong — I think your sister Dilsy told me you *were* from Bordeaux."

"Foutre, de sist, Dils! — Here Monsieur Middletong! My oystar ready?"

"Yes sir."

'Vel, if my oystar ready, you give dem to my fren' Monsieur Snotborg; and ask him to be so good to carry dem to my sist' Dils and my brodder Ichbod on Sand' Creek." — So saying, he vanished like lightning.

The next morning at breakfast, I occupied Ned's seat. Mrs. Blank had no sooner taken her place, than she ordered a servant to bring her a waiter; upon which she placed a cup of tea, and another of coffee — then ordering three plates, she placed them on it; sent one servant for one kind of bread, and another for another, and so on through all the varieties that were on the table, from which she made selections for plate No. 1. In the same way did she collect meats for plate No. 2 — No. 3 she left blank. She had nearly completed her operations, when her husband came to know why every servant was engaged, and no gentleman helped to anything, when the oddly furnished waiter met his eye, and fully explained the wonder.

"In God's name, Sarah," said he, "who are you mixing up those messes for?"

"For that strange gentleman we were speaking of last night," was the reply.

"Why doesn't he come to the table?"

"He was very anxious to come, but I would not let him."

"*You* would not let him! Why not?"

"Because I did not wish to see a man of his delicate sensibilities ridiculed and insulted at my table."

"Delicate devilabilities! Then why didn't you send a *servant* to collect his mixtures?"

"Because I preferred doing it myself, to troubling the boarders. I knew that wherever his plates went, the gentlemen would be making merry over them, and I couldn't bear to see it."

The landlord looked at her for a moment, with commingled astonishment, doubt, and alarm; and then upon the breath of a deep drawn sigh proceeded. —

"Well, d—n* the man! He hasn't been in the house more than

---

* I should certainly omit such expressions as this, could I do so with historic fidelity; but the peculiarities of the times of which I am writing, cannot be faithfully represented without them. In recording things *as they are,* truth requires me sometimes to put profane language into the mouths of my characters. [Author's note]

two hours, except when he was asleep, and he has insulted one half my boarders, made fools of the other half, turned the head of my bar-keeper, crazed all my servants, and run my wife right stark, staring, raving mad — A man who is a perfect clown in his manners, and who, I have no doubt, will, in the end, prove to be a horse thief."

Much occurred between the landlord and his lady in relation to Ned, which we must of necessity omit. Suffice it to say, that her assiduities to Ned, her unexplained sympathies for him, her often repeated desires to become better acquainted with him, conspiring with one or two short interviews which her husband saw between her and Ned, (and which consisted of nothing more than expressions of regret on his part, at the trouble he was giving the family, and assurance on hers, that it was no trouble at all,) began to bring upon the landlord, the husband's worst calamity. This she soon observed, and considering her duty to her husband as of paramount obligation, she gave him an explanation that was entirely satisfactory. She told him that Ned was a man of refined feelings and high cultivated mind, but that in his infancy his mother had forced him to eat different kinds of diet together, until she had produced in him a vitiated and unconquerable appetite, which he was now constrained to indulge, as the drunkard does his, or be miserable. As the good man was prepared to believe any story of *woman's* folly, he was satisfied.

This being the Sabbath, at the usual hour, Ned went to Church, and selected for his morning's service, one of those Churches in which the pews are free, and in which the hymn is given out, and sung by the congregation, a half recitative.

Ned entered the Church, in as fast a walk as he could possibly assume — proceeded about half down the aisle, and popt himself down in his seat as quick as if he had been shot. The more thoughtless of the congregation began to titter, and the graver peeped up slyly, but solemnly at him.

The Pastor rose, and before giving out the hymn, observed, that *singing* was a part of the service, in which he thought the whole congregation ought to join. Thus saying, he gave out the first lines of the hymn. As soon as the tune was raised, Ned struck in, with one of the loudest, hoarsest, most discordant voices, that ever annoyed a solemn assembly.

"I would observe," said the preacher, before giving out the next two lines, "that there are some persons who have not the gift of singing; such of course are not expected to sing." Ned took the hint, and sang no more; but his entrance into church, and his entrance into the hymn, had already dispersed the solemnity of three fifths of the congregation.

As soon as the Pastor commenced his sermon, Ned opened his

eyes, threw back his head, dropt his underjaw, and surrendered himself to the most intense interest. The preacher was an indifferent one, and by as much as he became dull and insipid, by so much did Ned become absorbed in the discourse. And yet it was impossible for the nicest observer to detect anything in his looks or manner, short of the most solemn devotion. The effect which his conduct had upon the congregation, and their subsequent remarks must be left to the imagination of the reader. I give but one remark — "Bless that good man who came in the Church so quick," said a venerable matron as she left the church door, "how he was affected by the *sarment.*"

Ned went to church no more that day. About four o'clock in the afternoon, while he was standing at the tavern door, a funeral procession passed by, at the foot of which, and singly, walked one of the smallest men I ever saw. As soon as he came opposite the door, Ned stept out and joined him with great solemnity. The contrast between the two was ludicrously striking, and the little man's looks and uneasiness, plainly showed that he felt it. However, he soon became reconciled to it. They proceeded but a little way before Ned enquired of his companion, who was dead?

"Mr. Noah Bills," said the little man.

"Nan?" said Ned, raising his hand to his ear in token of deafness, and bending his head to the speaker.

"Mr. Noah Bills," repeated the little man loud enough to disturb the two couple immediately before him.

"Mrs. Noel's Bill!" said Ned, with mortification and astonishment. "Do the white persons pay such respect to niggers in Savannah? *I* shan't do it" — So saying he left the procession.

The little man was at first considerably nettled; but upon being left to his own reflections, he got into an uncontrollable fit of laughter, as did the couple immediately in advance of him, who overheard Ned's remark. The procession now exhibited a most mortifying spectacle — The head of it in mourning and in tears, and the foot of it convulsed with laughter.

On Monday, Ned employed himself in disposing of the business which brought him to Savannah, and I saw but little of him; but I could not step into the street without hearing of him. All talked about him, and hardly any two agreed about his character.

On Tuesday he visited the Market, and set it all in astonishment or laughter. He wanted to buy something of everybody, and some of everything; but could not agree upon the terms of a trade, because he always wanted his articles in such portions and numbers, as no one would sell, or upon conditions to which no one would submit. To give a single example — He beset an old negro woman to sell him the half of a living chicken.

"Do my good mauma, sell it to me," said he, "my wife is very sick, and is longing for chicken pie, and this is all the money I have," (holding out twelve and a half cents in silver,) "and it's just what a half chicken comes to at your own price."

"Ki, massa! How gwine cut live chicken in two?"

"I don't want you to cut it in two alive — kill it, clean it, and then divide it."

"Name o' God! What sort o' chance got to clean chicken in de market-house! — Whay de water for scall um, and wash um?"

"Don't scald it at all; just pick it so."

"Ech-ech! Fedder fly all ober de buckera-man meat, he come bang me fo' true — No massa, I mighty sorry for your wife, but I no cutty chicken open."

In the afternoon, Ned entered the dining room of the tavern, and who should he find there but Monsieur Sancric, of oyster-house memory. He and the tavern-keeper were alone. With the first glimpse of Ned, "La diable," exclaimed the Frenchman, "here my broder Ichbod gain!" — and away he went.

"Mr. Sancric!" said the landlord, calling to him as if to tell him something just thought of, and following him out, "What did you say that man's name is?"

"He name Monsieur Snotborg."

"Why that can't be his name, for it begins with a B. or an R. Where is he from?"

"From Sand Creek."

"Where did you know him?"

"Begar, me neber did know him." Here Ned sauntered in sight of the Frenchman, and he vanished.

"Well," said the landlord, as we returned, "it does seem to me, that everybody who has anything to do with that man, runs crazy forthwith."

When he entered the dining room he found Ned deeply engaged reading a child's primer, with which he seemed wonderfully delighted. The landlord sat for a moment, smiled, and then hastily left the room. As soon as he disappeared, Ned laid down his book, and took his station behind some cloaks in the bar, which at the moment was deserted. He had just reached his place, when the landlord returned with his lady.

"Oh," said the first, "he's gone! I brought you in to show you what kind of books your man of 'refined feelings and highly cultivated mind' delights in — But he has left his book, and here it is, opened at the place where he left off — and do let's see what's in it?"

They examined, and found that he had been reading the interesting poem of "Little Jack Horner."

"Now," continued the landlord, "if you'll believe me, he was just as much delighted with that story, as you or I would be with the best written number of the *Spectator*."

"Well, it's very strange," said Mrs. Blank — "I reckon he must be *flighty*, for no man could have made a more gentlemanly apology than he did to me, for his peculiarities; and no one could have urged it more feelingly."

"One thing is very certain," said the husband, "if he be not flighty himself, he has a wonderful knack of making everybody else so. Sancric ran away from him just now, as if he had seen the devil — called him by one name when he left the room, by another at the door, told me where he came from, and finally swore he did not know him at all."

Ned having slipt softly from the bar into the entry, during this interview, entered the dining room, as if from the street.

"I am happy," said he, smiling, to meet you together and alone, upon the eve of my departure from Savannah, that I may explain to you my singular conduct, and ask your forgiveness of it. I will do so if you will not expose my true character until I shall have left the city."

This they promised — "My name then," continued he, "is Edward Brace, of Richmond County. Humor has been my besetting sin from my youth, up. It has sunk me far below the station to which my native gifts entitled me. It has robbed me of the respect of all my acquaintances; and what is much more to be regretted, the esteem of some of my best and most indulgent friends. All this I have long known, and I have a thousand times deplored, and as often resolved to conquer, my self-destroying propensity. But so deeply is it wrought into my very nature — so completely and indissolubly interwoven is it, with every fibre and filament of my being, that I have found it impossible for me to subdue it. Being on my first visit to Savannah, unknowing and unknown, I could not forego the opportunity which it furnished, of gratifying my ungovernable proclivity. All the extravagancies which you have seen, have been in subservience to it."

He then explained the cause of his troubling the kind lady before him, to give him his meals at his room, and the strange conduct of Monsieur Sancric; at which they both laughed heartily. He referred them to me for confirmation of what he had told them. Having gone thus far, continued he, "I must sustain my character until to-morrow, when I shall leave Savannah."

Having now two more to enjoy his humor with him and myself, he let himself loose that night among the boarders, with all his strength, and never did I see two mortals laugh, as did Mr. and Mrs. Blank.

Far as I have extended this sketch, I cannot close, without exhibiting Ned in one new scene, in which accident placed him before he left Savannah.

About 2 o'clock on the morning of our departure, the town was alarmed by the cry of fire. Ned got up before me, and taking one of my boots from the door, and putting one of his in its place, he marched down to the front door with odd boots. On coming out and finding what had been done, I knew that Ned could not have left the house, for it was impossible for him to wear my boot. I was about descending the stairs, when he called to me from the front door, and said the servant had mixed our boots, and that he had brought down one of mine. When I reached the front door, I found Ned and Mr. and Mrs. Blank there; all the inmates of the house having left it, who designed to leave it, but Ned and myself.

"Don't go and leave me Hall," said he, holding my boot in his hand, and having his own on his leg.

"How can I leave you," said I, "unless you'll give me my boot?" This he did not seem to hear.

"Do run gentlemen," said Mrs. Blank greatly alarmed — "Mr. Brace, you've got Mr. Hall's boot, give it to him."

"In a minute madam," said he, seeming to be beside himself. A second after, however, all was explained to me. He designed to have my company to the fire, and his own fun before he went.

A man came posting along in great alarm, and crying "fire" loudly. "Mister, Mister," said Ned, jumping out of the house.

"Sir," said the man, stopping and puffing awfully.

"Have you seen Mr. Peleg Q. C. Stone, along where you've been?" enquired Ned, with anxious solicitude.

"D—n Mr. Peleg Q. C. Stone," said the stranger, — "What chance have I of seeing anybody, hopping up at two o'clock in the morning, and the town a fire!" and on he went.

Thus did he amuse himself with various questions and remarks, to four or five passengers, until even Mrs. Blank forgot for a while, that the town was in flames. The last object of his sport, was a woman who came along, exclaiming, "Oh, its Mr. Dalby's house — I'm sure it is Mr. Dalby's house!" Two gentlemen assured her, that the fire was far beyond Mr. Dalby's house; but still she went on with her exclamations. When she had passed the door about ten steps, Ned permitted me to cover my frozen foot with my boot, and we moved on towards the fire. We soon overtook the woman just mentioned, who had become somewhat pacified. As Ned came along side of her, without seeming to notice her, he observed "Poor Dalby, I see his house is gone."

"I said so," she screamed out — "I knew it!" — and on she went, screaming ten times louder than before.

As soon as we reached the fire, a gentleman in military dress rode up and ordered Ned into the line, to hand buckets. Ned stept in, and the first bucket that was handed to him, he raised it very deliberately to his mouth, and began to drink. In a few seconds, all on Ned's. right, were overburdened with buckets, and calling loudly for relief, while those on his left were unemployed. Terrible was the cursing and clamor, and twenty voices at once ordered Ned out of the line. Ned stept out, and along came the man on horse back, and ordered him in again.

"Captain," said Ned, "I am so thirsty that I can do nothing until I can get some water, and they will not let me drink in the line."

"Well," said the Captain, "step in, and I'll see that you get a drink."

Ned stept in again, and receiving the first bucket, began to raise it to his lips very slowly, when some one halloed to him to pass on the bucket, and he brought it down again, and handed it on.

"Why didn't you drink?" said the Captain.

"Why don't you see they won't let me?" said Ned.

"Don't mind what they say — drink, and then go on with your work."

Ned took the next bucket, and commenced raising it as before, when some one again ordered him to pass on the bucket.

"There," said Ned, turning to the Captain, with the bucket half-raised, "you hear that?"

"Why, blast your eyes," said the Captain, "what do you stop for? Drink on and have done with it."

Ned raised the bucket to his lips and drank, or pretended to drink, until a horse might have been satisfied.

"Ain't you done?" said the Captain, general mutiny and complaint beginning to prevail in the line.

"Why ha'nt you drank enough?" said the Captain, becoming extremely impatient.

"Most," said Ned, letting out a long breath, and still holding the bucket near his lips.

"Zounds and blood!" cried the Captain, "clear yourself — you'll drink an engine full of water."

Ned left the ranks, and went to his lodgings; and the rising sun found us on our way homeward.

The Fight

In the younger days of the Republic, there lived in the county of ——, two men, who were admitted on all hands to be the very *best men* in the county — which, in the Georgia vocabulary, means they could flog any other two men in the county. Each, through many a hard fought battle, had acquired the mastery of his own battalion; but they lived on opposite sides of the Court House, and in different battalions; consequently they were but seldom thrown together. When they met, however, they were always very friendly; indeed, at their first interview, they seemed to conceive a wonderful attachment to each other, which rather increased than diminished, as they became better acquainted; so that, but for the circumstance which I am about to mention, the question which had been a thousand times asked "Which is the best man, Billy Stallions, (Stallings,) or Bob Durham?" would probably never have been answered.

Billy ruled the upper battalion, and Bob the lower. The former measured six feet and an inch, in his stockings, and without a single pound of cumbrous flesh about him weighed a hundred and eighty. The latter, was an inch shorter than his rival, and ten pounds lighter; but he was much the most active of the two. In running and jumping, he had but few equals in the county; and in wrestling, not one. In other respects they were nearly equal. Both were admirable specimens of human nature in its finest form. Billy's victories had generally been achieved by the tremendous power of his blows; one of which had often proved decisive of his battles; Bob's, by his adroitness in bringing his adversary to the ground. This advantage he had never failed to gain, at the onset, and when gained, he never failed to improve it to the defeat of his adversary. These points of difference, have involved the reader in a doubt, as to the probable issue of a contest between them. It was not so, however, with the two battalions. Neither had the least difficulty in determining the point by the most natural and irresistible deductions *a priori:* and though, by the same course of reasoning, they arrived at directly opposite conclusions, neither felt its confidence in the least shaken by this circumstance. The upper battalion swore "that Billy only wanted one lick at him to knock his heart, liver and lights out of him; and if he got two at him, he'd knock him into a cocked hat." The lower battalion retorted, "that he wouldn't have time to double his fist, before Bob would put his head where his feet ought to be; and that, by the time he hit the ground, the meat would fly off his face so quick, that people would think it was shook off by the fall." These disputes often led to the *argumentum ad hominem;* but with such equality of success on both sides, as to leave the main question just where they found it. They usually ended, however, in the common way, with a bet; and many a quart of old Jamaica, (whiskey had not then supplanted rum,) were staked upon the issue. Still, greatly to the annoyance of the curious, Billy and Bob continued to be good friends.

Now there happened to reside in the county, just alluded to, a little fellow, by the name of Ransy Sniffle: a sprout of Richmond, who, in his earlier days, had fed copiously upon red clay and blackberries. This diet had given to Ransy a complexion that a corpse would have disdained to own, and an abdominal rotundity that was quite unprepossessing. Long spells of the fever and ague, too, in Ransy's youth, had conspired with clay and blackberries, to throw him quite out of the order of nature. His shoulders were fleshless and elevated; his head large and flat; his neck slim and translucent; and his arms, hands, fingers and feet, were lengthened out of all proportion to the rest of his frame. His joints were large, and his limbs small; and as for flesh, he could not with propriety be said to have any. Those parts which nature usually supplies with the most of this article — the calves of the legs for example — presented in him the appearance of so many well drawn blisters. His height was just five feet nothing; and his average weight in blackberry season, ninety-five. I have been thus particular in describing him, for the purpose of showing what a great matter a little fire sometimes kindleth. There was nothing on this earth which delighted Ransy so much as a fight. He never seemed fairly alive, except when he was witnessing, fomenting, or talking about a fight. Then, indeed, his deep sunken grey eye, assumed something of a living fire; and his tongue acquired a volubility that bordered upon eloquence. Ransy had been kept for more than a year in the most torturing suspense, as to the comparative manhood of Billy Stallings and Bob Durham. He had resorted to all his usual expedients to bring them in collision, and had entirely failed. He had faithfully reported to Bob all that had been said by the people in the upper battalion "agin him," and "he was sure Billy Stallings started it. He heard Bill say himself to Jim Brown, that he could whip him, *or any other man in his battalion;*" and this he told to Bob — adding, "Dod burn his soul, if he was a little bigger, if he'd let any man *put upon* his battalion in such a way." Bob replied, "If he (Stallings) thought so, he'd better come and try it." This Ransy carried to Billy, and delivered it with a spirit becoming his own dignity, and the character of his battalion, and with a coloring well calculated to give it effect. These, and many other schemes which Ransy laid, for the gratification of his curiosity, entirely failed of their object. Billy and Bob continued friends, and Ransy had began to lapse into the most tantalizing and hopeless despair, when a circumstance occurred, which led to a settlement of the long disputed question.

It is said that a hundred game cocks will live in perfect harmony together, if you will not put a hen with them: and so it would have been with Billy and Bob, had there been no women in the world. But there were women in the world, and from them, each of our heroes had taken to himself a wife. The good ladies were no strangers to the prowess of their husbands, and strange as it may seem, they presumed a little upon it.

The two battalions had met at the Court House, upon a regimental parade. The two champions were there, and their wives had accompanied them. Neither knew the other's lady, nor were the ladies known to each other. The exercises of the day were just over, when Mrs. Stallings and Mrs. Durham stept simultaneously into the store of Zepheniah Atwater, from "down east."

"Have you any Turkey-red?" said Mrs. S.

"Have you any curtain calico?" said Mrs. D. at the same moment.

"Yes, ladies," said Mr. Atwood, "I have both."

"Then help me first," said Mrs. D., "for I'm in a hurry."

"I'm in as great a hurry as she is," said Mrs. S., "and I'll thank you to help me first."

"And pray, who are you, madam!" continued the other.

"Your betters, madam," was the reply.

At this moment Billy Stallings stept in. "Come," said he, "Nancy, let's be going; it's getting late."

"I'd o' been gone half an hour ago," she replied, "if it hadn't been for that impudent huzzy."

"Who do you call an impudent huzzy? you nasty, good-for-nothing, snaggle-toothed gaub of fat, you," returned Mrs. D.

"Look here woman," said Billy, "have you got a husband here? If you have, I'll *lick* him till he learns to teach you better manners, you *sassy* heifer you." At this moment something was seen to rush out of the store, as if ten thousand hornets were stinging it; crying "Take care — let me go — don't hold me — where's Bob Durham?" It was Ransy Sniffle, who had been listening in breathless delight, to all that had passed.

"Yonder's Bob, setting on the Court-house steps," cried one. "What's the matter?"

"Don't talk to me!" said Ransy. "Bob Durham, you'd better go long yonder, and take care of your wife. They're playing h—l with her there, in Zeph. Atwater's store. Dod deternally durn my soul, if any man was to talk to my wife as Bill Stallions is talking to yours, if I didn't drive blue blazes through him in less than no time."

Bob sprang to the store in a minute, followed by a hundred friends; for the bully of a county never wants friends.

"Bill Stallions," said Bob, as he entered, "what have you been saying to my wife?"

"Is that your wife?" inquired Billy, obviously much surprised, and a little disconcerted.

"Yes, she is, and no man shall abuse her, I don't care who he is."

"Well," rejoined Billy, "it an't worth while to go over it — I've said enough for a fight: and if you'll step out, we'll settle it!"

"Billy," said Bob, "are you for a fair fight?"

"I am," said Billy. "I've heard much of your manhood, and I believe I'm a better man than you are. If you will go into a ring with me, we can soon settle the dispute."

"Choose your friends," said Bob; "make your ring, and I'll be in it with mine, as soon as you will."

They both stept out, and began to strip very deliberately; each battalion gathering round its champion — except Ransy, who kept himself busy, in a most honest endeavor to hear and see all that transpired in both groups, at the same time. He ran from one to the other, in quick succession — peeped here, and listened there — talked to this one — then to that one — and then to himself — squatted under one's legs, and another's arms; and in the short interval between stripping and stepping into the ring, managed to get himself trod on by half of both battalions. But Ransy was not the only one interested upon this occasion: — the most intense interest prevailed every where. Many were the conjectures, doubts, oaths and imprecations uttered, while the parties were preparing for the combat. All the knowing ones were consulted as to the issue; and they all agreed to a man, in one of two opinions: either that Bob would flog Billy, or Billy would flog Bob. We must be permitted, however, to dwell for a moment upon the opinion of 'Squire Thomas Loggins; a man, who it was said, had never failed to predict the issue of a fight, in all his life. Indeed, so unerring had he always proved, in this regard, that it would have been counted the most obstinate infidelity, to doubt for a moment, after he had delivered himself. 'Squire Loggins was a man who said but little; but that little was always delivered with the most imposing solemnity of look and cadence. He always wore the aspect of profound thought, and you could not look at him without coming to the conclusion, that he was elaborating truth from its most intricate combinations.

"Uncle Tommy," said Sam Reynolds, "you can tell us all about it, if you will — how will the fight go?"

The question immediately drew an anxious group around the 'Squire. He raised his teeth slowly from the head of his walking cane, on which they had been resting — pressed his lips closely and thoughtfully together — threw down his eye brows — dropped his chin — raised his eyes to an angle of twenty three degrees — paused about half a minute, and replied: "Sammy, watch Robert Durham close in the beginning of the fight — take care of William Stallions in the middle of it — and see who has the wind at the end." As he utttered the last member of the sentence, he looked slyly at Bob's friends, and winked very significantly; whereupon they rushed, with one accord, to tell Bob what Uncle Tommy had said. As they retired, the "Squire turned to Billy's friends, and said, with a smile: "Them boys think I mean that Bob will whip."

Here the other party kindled into joy, and hastened to inform Billy how Bob's friends had deceived themselves as to Uncle Tommy's opinion. In the meantime, the principals and seconds, were busily employed in preparing themselves for the combat. The plan of attack and defence, the manner of improving the various turns of the conflict, "the best mode of saving wind," &c. &c. were all discussed and settled. At length, Billy announced himself ready, and his crowd were seen moving to the centre of the Court House Square; he and his five seconds in the rear. At the same time, Bob's party moved to the same point, and in the same order. The ring was now formed, and for a moment the silence of death reigned through both battalions. It was soon interrupted, however, by the cry of "clear the way!" from Billy's seconds; when the ring opened in the centre of the upper battalion, (for the order of march had arranged the centre of the two battalions on opposite sides of the circle,) and Billy stept into the ring from the east, foll⌐ ⸴d by his friends. He was stript to the trowsers, and exhibited an arm, breast and shoulders, of the most tremendous portent. His step was firm, daring and martial; and as he bore his fine form a little in advance of his friends, an involuntary burst of triumph broke from his side of the ring; and at the same moment, an uncontrollable thrill of awe, ran along the whole curve of the lower battalion.

"Look at him!" was heard from his friends — "just look at him."

"Ben, how much you ask to stand before that man two seconds?"

"Pshaw, don't talk about it! Just thinkin' about it's broke three o' my ribs a'ready!"

"What's Bob Durham going to do, when Billy lets that arm loose upon him?"

"God bless your soul, he'll think thunder and lightning a mint julip to it."

"Oh, look here men, go take Bill Stallions out o' that ring, and bring in Phil Johnson's stud horse, so that Durham may have some chance! I don't want to see the man killed right away."

These and many other like expressions, interspersed thickly with oaths of the most modern coinage, were coming from all points of the upper battalion, while Bob was adjusting the girth of his pantaloons, which walking had discovered, not to be exactly right. It was just fixed to his mind, his foes becoming a little noisy, and his friends a little uneasy at his delay, when Billy called out, with a smile of some meaning, "Where's the bully of the lower battalion? I'm getting tired of waiting."

"Here he is," said Bob, lighting, as it seemed from the clouds in the ring, for he had actually bounded clear of the head of Ransy Sniffle, into the circle. His descent was quite as imposing as Billy's entry, and excited the same feelings, but in opposite bosoms.

Voices of exultation now rose on his side.

"Where did he come from?"

"Why," said one of the seconds, (all having just entered,) "we were girting him up, about a hundred yards out yonder, when he heard Billy ask for the bully; and he fetched a leap over the Court House, and went out of sight; but I told them to come on, they'd find him here."

Here the lower battalion burst into a peal of laughter, mingled with a look of admiration, which seemed to denote their entire belief of what they had heard.

"Boys widen the ring, so as to give him room to jump."

"Oh, my little flying wild cat, hold him if you can! and when you get him fast, hold lightning next."

"Ned what you think he's made of?"

"Steel-springs and chicken-hawk, God bless you!"

"Gentlemen," said one of Bob's seconds, "I understand it is to be a fair fight; catch as catch can, rough and tumble: — no man touch 'till one or the other hollos."

"That's the rule," was the reply from the other side.

"Are you ready?"

"We are ready."

"Then blaze away my game cocks."

At the word, Bob dashed at his antagonist at full speed; and Bill squared himself to receive him with one of his most fatal blows. Making his calculation from Bob's velocity, of the time when he would come within striking distance, he let drive with tremendous force. But Bob's onset was obviously planned to avoid this blow; for contrary to all expectations, he stopt short just out of arms reach; and before Billy could recover his balance — Bob had him "all under-hold." The next second, sure enough, "found Billy's head where his feet ought to be." How it was done, no one could tell; but as if by supernatural power, both Billy's feet were thrown full half his own height in the air, and he came down with a force that seemed to shake the earth. As he struck the ground, commingled shouts, screams and yells burst from the lower battalion, loud enough to be heard for miles. "Hurra my little hornet!" — "Save him!" — "Feed him! — Give him the Durham physic till his stomach turns!" Billy was no sooner down than Bob was on him, and lending him awful blows about the face and breast. Billy made two efforts to rise by main strength, but failed. "Lord bless you man, don't try to get up! — *Lay* still and take it! — you *bleege* to have it."

Billy now turned his face suddenly to the ground, and rose upon his hands and knees. Bob jerked up both his hands and threw him on his face. He again recovered his late position, of which Bob endeavored to deprive him as before; but missing one arm, he failed, and Billy rose. But he had scarcely resumed his feet before they flew up as before, and he came again to the ground. "No fight gentlemen!" cried Bob's friends, "the man can't stand up! — Bouncing feet are bad things to fight in." His fall, however, was this time comparatively light; for having thrown his right arm round Bob's neck, he carried his head down with him. This grasp, which was obstinately maintained, prevented Bob from getting on him, and they lay head to head, seeming, for a time, to do nothing. Presently they rose, as if by mutual consent; and as they rose, a shout broke from both battalions. "Oh, my lark!" cried the east, "has he foxed you? Do you begin to feel him! He's only beginning to fight — He ain't got warm yet."

"Look yonder!" cried the west — "didn't I tell you so! He hit the ground so hard, it jarred his nose off. Now ain't he a pretty man as he stands! He shall have my sister Sall just for his pretty looks. I want to get in the breed of them sort o' men, to drive ugly out of my kin folks."

I looked and saw that Bob had entirely lost his left ear, and a large piece from his left cheek. His right eye was a little discolored, and the blood flowed profusely from his wounds.

Bill presented a hideous spectacle. About a third of his nose, at the lower extremity, was bit off, and his face so swelled and bruised, that it was difficult to discover in it any thing of the human visage — much more the fine features which he carried into the ring.

They were up only long enough for me to make the foregoing discoveries, when down they went again, precisely as before. They no sooner touched the ground than Bill relinquished his hold upon Bob's neck. In this, he seemed to all, to have forfeited the only advantage which put him upon an equality with his adversary. But the movement was soon explained. Bill wanted this arm for other purposes than defence; and he had made arrangements whereby he knew that he could make it answer these purposes; for when they rose again, he had the middle finger of Bob's left hand in his mouth. He was now secure from Bob's annoying trips; and he began to lend his adversary most tremendous blows, every one of which was hailed by a shout from his friends. "Bullets! — *Hoss* kicking! — Thunder!" — "That'll do for the face — now feel his short ribs, Billy!"

I now considered the contest settled. I deemed it impossible for any human being to withstand for five seconds, the loss of blood which issued from Bob's ear, cheek, nose and finger, accompanied with such blows as he was receiving. Still he maintained the conflict, and gave blow for blow with considerable effect. But the blows of each became slower and weaker, after the first three or four; and it became obvious, that Bill wanted the room, which Bob's finger occupied, for breathing. He would therefore, probably, in a short time, have let it go, had not Bob anticipated his politeness, by jerking away his hand, and making him a present of the finger. He now seized Bill again, and brought him to his knees — but he recovered. He again brought him to his knees; and he again recovered. A third effort, however, brought him down, and Bob on top of him. These efforts seemed to exhaust the little remaining strength of both; and they lay, Bill undermost, and Bob across his breast, motionless, and panting for breath. After a short pause, Bob gathered his hand full of dirt and sand, and was in the act of grinding it in his adversary's eyes, when Bill cried "ENOUGH!" — Language cannot describe the scene which followed — the shouts, oaths, frantic jestures, taunts, replies and little fights; and therefore I shall not attempt it. The champions were borne off by their seconds, and washed: when many a bleeding wound, and ugly bruise, was discovered on each, which no eye had seen before.

Many had gathered round Bob, and were in various ways congratulating and applauding him, when a voice from the centre of the circle cried out: "Boys, hush and listen to me!" It proceeded from 'Squire Loggins, who had made his way to Bob's side, and had gathered his face into one of its most flattering and intelligible expressions. All were obedient to the 'Squire's command. "Gentlemen," continued he, with a most knowing smile, "is — Sammy — Reynold — in — this — company — of — gentlemen." "Yes," said Sam, "here I am." "Sammy," said the 'Squire, winking to the company, and drawing the head of his cane to his mouth with an arch smile, as he closed, "I —

wish — you — to tell — cousin — Bobby — and — these — gentlemen here present — what — your — uncle — Tommy — said —
before — the — fight — began." "Oh! get away, Uncle Tom," says
Sam, smiling, (the 'Squire winked,) "you don't know nothing about
fighting." (The 'Squire winked again.) "All you know about it, is
how it'll begin; how it'll go on; how it'll end; that's all. Cousin Bob,
when you going to fight again, just go to the old man, and let him tell
you all about it. If he can't, don't ask nobody else nothing about it,
I tell you." The 'Squire's foresight was complimented in many ways
by the by-standers; and he retired, advising "the boys to be at peace,
as fighting was a bad business."

Durham and Stallings kept their beds for several weeks, and did
not meet again for two months. When they met, Billy stepped up to
Bob and offered his hand, saying: "Bobby you've *licked* me a fair
fight; but you wouldn't have done it, if I hadn't been in the wrong. I
oughtn't to have treated your wife as I did; and I felt so through the
whole fight; and it sort o' cowed me."

"Well Billy," said Bob, "let's be friends. Once in the fight, when you
had my finger in your mouth, and was pealing me in the face and
breast, I was going to hollo; but I thought of Betsy, and knew the
house would be too hot for me, if I got whipt, when fighting for her,
after always whipping when I fought for myself."

"Now, that's what I always love to see," said a by-stander: "It's
true, I brought about the fight; but I wouldn't have done it, if it
hadn't o' been on account of *Miss*, (Mrs.) Durham. But dod eternally
durn my soul, if I ever could stand by and see any woman put upon
— much less *Miss* Durham. If Bobby hadn't been there, I'd o' took it
up myself, be durned if I wouldn't, even if I'd o' got whipt for it —
But we're all friends now." The reader need hardly be told, this was
Ransy Sniffle.

Thanks to the Christian religion, to schools, colleges, and benevolent associations, such scenes of barbarism and cruelty, as that which
I have been just describing, are now of rare occurrence: though
they may still be occasionally met with in some of the new counties.
Wherever they prevail, they are a disgrace to that community. The
peace officers who countenance them, deserve a place in the Penitentiary.

Thomas Kirkman

(1800-1864)

✄ An Irishman by birth, Thomas Kirkman spent his youth in Nashville, Tennessee, where his father established a thriving mercantile business. After his marriage Kirkman moved in 1821 to Florence, Alabama, to begin his own business, probably much like his father's. As his wealth grew he acquired other interests, including a plantation in Mississippi, iron works in Tennessee, and a stable of race horses. Kirkman imported expensive thoroughbreds from England, and his stable produced some of the finest race horses of the era. His horse Peytona is said to have won in 1844 a purse of one hundred thousand dollars in a race on Long Island.

This wealthy merchant, planter, and sportsman published anonymously two sketches in the New York *Spirit of the Times* which became widely known. William T. Porter, editor of the *Spirit*, thought so well of one of them, "A Quarter Race in Kentucky," that he selected it as the title story of an anthology of Southwestern humor. "Jones' Fight" first appeared in the *Spirit* in 1840 and then in Porter's *The Big Bear of Arkansas and Other Tales*. Its hero is one of the first in a long line of Kentucky colonels to serve as an object of satire. Colonel Dick Jones is "true Virginian bred and Kentucky raised." Charming the ladies with his dress and manners and impressing the men with his knowledge, wit, and swagger, he is the town hero until he is called upon to demonstrate his courage and skill. His fight with Bill Patterson takes place in another village; therefore the townspeople (and the reader) hear only Jones's account of it. In telling the story the Colonel gradually characterizes himself through his language and behavior until the final sentence reveals his full portrait.

TEXT: "Jones' Fight" from *The Big Bear of Arkansas*, ed. W. T. Porter (Philadelphia, 1845).

Jones' Fight

Col. Dick Jones was decidedly the great man of the village of Summerville. He was colonel of the regiment — he had represented his district in congress — he had been spoken of as candidate for governor — he was at the head of the bar in Hawkins county, Kentucky, and figured otherwise largely in public life. His legal opinion and advice were highly valued by the senior part of the population — his dress and taste were law to the juniors — his easy, affable, and attentive manner charmed all the matrons — his dignified politeness captivated the young ladies — and his suavity and condescension delighted the little boarding-school misses. He possessed a universal smattering of information — his manners were the most popular; extremely friendly and obliging, lively and witty; and, in short, he was a very agreeable companion.

Yet truth requires it to be admitted, that Col. Dick Jones was professionally more specious than deep, and that his political advancement was owing to personal partiality more than superior merit — that his taste and dress were of questionable propriety: for instance, he occasionally wore a hunting-shirt white fringed, or a red waistcoat, or a fawn-skin one, or a calico morning gown of a small yellow pattern, and he indulged in other similar vagaries in clothing. And in manners and deportment, there was an air of harmless (true Virginian bred and Kentucky raised) self-conceit and swagger, which, though not to be admired, yet it gave piquancy and individuality to his character.

If further particulars are required, I can only state that the colonel boarded at the Eagle hotel — his office, in the square, fronted the court-house — he was a manager of all the balls — he was vice-president of the Summerville Jockey Club — he was trustee of the Female Academy — he gallanted the old ladies to church, holding his umbrella over them in the sun, and escorted the young ladies, at night, to the dances or parties, always bringing out the smallest ones. He rode a high headed, proud-looking sorrel horse, with a streak down his face; and he was a general referee and umpire, whether it was a horse swap, a race, a rifle match, or a cock fight.

It so chanced, on a time, though Col. Jones was one of the best-natured of men, that he took umbrage at some report circulated about him in an adjoining county and one of his districts, to the effect that he had been a federalist during the last war; and, instead of relying on the fact of his being a school-boy on Mill Creek at that time, he proclaimed, at the tavern table, that the next time he went over the mountain to court, Bill Patterson, the reputed author of the slander, should either sign a *liebill,* fight, or run.

This became narrated through the town, — the case and argument of the difference was discussed among the patriarchs of the place, who generally came to the conclusion that the colonel had good cause of quarrel, as more had been said of him than an honorable man could stand. The young store boys of the village became greatly interested, conjectured how the fight would go, and gave their opinions what they would do under similar circumstances. The young lawyers, and young M.D.'s, as often as they were in the colonel's company, introduced the subject of the expected fight. On such occasions, the colonel spoke carelessly and banteringly. Some good old ladies spoke deprecatingly, in the general and in the particular, that so good and clever a young man as Colonel Dick should set so bad an example; and the young ladies, and little misses, bless their dear little innocent souls, they only consulted their own kind hearts, and were satisfied that he must be a wicked and bad man that Colonel Jones would fight.

Spring term of the courts came on, and the lawyers all started on their circuit, and, with them, Col. Jones went over the mountain. The whole town was alive to the consequences of this trip, and without much communion or understanding on the subject, most of the population either gathered at the tavern at his departure, or noticed it from a distance, and he rode off, gaily saluting his acquaintances, and raising his hat to the ladies, on both sides of the street, as he passed out of town.

From that time, only one subject engaged the thoughts of the good people of Summerville; and on the third day the common salutation was, "Any news from over the mountain?" "Has any one come down the road?" The fourth, fifth, and sixth came, and still the public anxiety was unappeased: it had, with the delay, become insufferable, quite agonizing; business and occupation was at a stand still; a doctor or a constable would not ride to the country lest news of the fight might arrive in their absence. People in crossing the square, or entering or coming out of their houses, all had their heads turned up that road. And many, though ashamed to confess it, sat up an hour or two past their usual bed-time, hoping some one would return from court. Still all was doubt and uncertainty. There is an unaccountable perversity in these things that bothers conjecture. I watched the road from Louisville two days, to hear of Grey Eagle beating Wagner, on which I had one hundred dollars staked, of borrowed money, and no one came; though before that, some person passed every hour.

On the seventh morning, the uneasy public were consoled by the certainty that the lawyers must be home that day, as court seldom held a week, and the universal resolve seemed to be that nothing was to be attended to until they were satisfied about the fight. Storekeepers and their clerks, saddlers, hatters, cabinet-makers, and their apprentices, all stood out at the doors. The hammer ceased to ring on the anvil, and the barkeeper would scarcely walk in to put away the stranger's saddle-bags, who had called for breakfast; when suddenly a young man, that had been walking from one side of the street to the other, in a state of feverish anxiety, thought he saw dust away up the road, and stopped. I have been told a man won a wager in Philadelphia, on his collecting a crowd by staring, without speaking, at an opposite chimney. So no sooner was this young man's *point* noticed, than there was a general reconnoissance of the road made, and before long, doubt became certainty, when one of the company declared he knew the colonel's old sorrel riding-horse, "General Jackson," by the blaze on his face.

In the excited state of the public mind it required no ringing of the court-house bell to convene the people; those down street walked up, and those across the square came over, and all gathered gradually at the Eagle hotel, and nearly all were present by the time Col. Jones alighted. He had a pair of dark green specks on, his right hand in a sling, with brown paper bound round his wrist; his left hand held the bridle, and the forefinger of it wrapped with a linen rag "with care." One of his ears was covered with a muslin scrap, that looked much like the countrywomen's plan of covering their butter when coming to market; his face was clawed all over, as if he had had it raked by a cat held fast by the tail; his head was unshorn, it being "too delicate an affair," as * * * said about his wife's character. His complexion suggested an idea to a philosophical young man present, on which he wrote a treatise, dedicated to Arthur Tappan, proving that the negro was only a white well pummelled; and his general swelled appearance would induce a belief he had led the forlorn hope in the storming of a beehive.

The colonel's manner did not exactly proclaim "the conquering hero," but his affability was undiminished, and he addressed them with, "Happy to see you, gents; how are you all?" and then attempted to enter the tavern; but Buck Daily arrested him with, "Why, Colonel, I see you have had a skrimmage. How did you make it! You didn't come out at the little *eend* of the horn, did you?" "No, not exactly, I had a tight fit of it, though. You know Bill Patterson; he weighs one hundred and seventy-five pounds, has not an ounce of superfluous flesh, is as straight as an Indian, and as active as a wildcat, and as quick as powder, and very much of a man, I assure you. Well, my word was out to lick him; so I hardly put up my horse before I found him at the court-house door, and, to give him a white man's chance, I proposed alternatives to him. He said his daddy, long ago, told him never to give a *liebill,* and he was not good at running, so he thought he had best fight. By the time the word was fairly out, I hauled off, and took him in the burr of the ear that raised a singing in his head, that made him think he was in Mosquitoe town. At it we went, like killing snakes, so good a man, so good a boy; we had it round and round, and about and about, as dead a yoke as ever pulled at a log chain. Judge Mitchell was on the bench, and as soon as the cry of 'fight' was raised, the bar and jury ran off and left him. He shouted, 'I command the peace,' within the court-house, and then ran out to see the fight, and cried out, 'I can't prevent you!' 'fair fight!' 'stand back!' and he caught Parson Benefield by the collar of the coat, who, he thought, was about to interfere, and slung him on his back at least fifteen feet.

"It was the evenest and longest fight ever fought: everybody was tired of it, and I must admit, in truth, that I was" (*here he made an effort to enter the tavern.*) But several voices called out, "Which whipped? How did you come out?" "Why, much as I tell you; we had it round and round, about and about, over and under. I could throw him at rastle, but he would manage some way to turn me. Old Sparrowhawk was there, who had seen all the best fighting at Natchez, under the hill, in the days of Dad Girty and Jim Snodgrass, and he says my gouging was beautiful; one of Bill's eyes is like the mouth of an old ink bottle, only, as the fellow said, describing the jackass by the mule, it is more so. But, in fact, there was no great choice between us, as you see. I look like having ran into a brush fence of a dark night. So we made it round and round, and about and about" (*here again he attempted a retreat into the tavern.*) But many voices demanded, "Who hollored?" "Which gave up?" "How did you hurt your hand?" "Oh! I forgot to tell you, that as I aimed a sockdollager at him he ducked his head, and he can dodge like a diedapper, and hitting him awkwardly, I sprained my wrist; so, being like the fellow who, when it rained mush, had no spoon, I changed the suit and made a trump — and went in for eating. In the scuffle we fell, cross and pile, and, while he was chawing my finger, my head was between his legs; his woollen jean britches did not taste well, but I found a bare place, where the seat had worn out, and meat in abundance; so I laid hold of a good mouthful, but the bit came out; and finding his appetite still good for my finger, I adopted Doctor Bones', the toothsmith's, patent method of removing teeth with-out the aid of instruments, and I extracted two of his incisors, and then I could put my finger in or out at pleasure. However, I shall, for some time, have an excuse for wearing gloves without being thought proud." (*He now tried to escape under cover of a laugh.*) But vox populi again. "So you tanned him, did you?" "How did the fight finish?" "You were not parted?" "You fought it out, did you?" The colonel resumed, "Why, there is no telling how the fight might have gone; an old Virginian, who had seen Francesco, and Otey, and Lewis, and Blevins, and all the best men of the day, said he had never seen any one stand up to their fodder better than we did. We had fought round and round, and about and about, all over the court-yard, and, at last, just to end the fight, every body was getting tired of it; so, at l—a—a—st, I hollered. — (*Exit colonel.*)

Solomon Franklin Smith

(1801-1869)

❧ Sol Smith grew up in a log cabin in Cortlandt County, New York, where his father, a goldsmith, had received a land grant for Revolutionary War service. He was put to work on a farm when he was eight and in a store run by his brothers in Boston when he was twelve. In 1814 the brothers moved to Albany, again as storekeepers. Here Sol read Shakespeare, attended the theater for the first time, met some of the actors, and surreptitiously obtained a job as a supernumerary. There followed several years of playing small parts in Ohio River valley towns; a period of apprenticeship to a printer in Louisville, Kentucky; work as a press foreman in Vincennes, Indiana; study of the law; and in 1822 the editorship of the *Independent Press,* a Jacksonian newspaper in Cincinnati, where the family was then living. Meanwhile, he continued to study law and became a proprietor and occasional actor at a local theater. In 1823 he formed his own company, and for the next thirty years was a theatrical manager and actor.

Smith took his various companies down through the cities and hamlets of the Ohio and Mississippi river valleys, into the Old Southwest, and east to Georgia and South Carolina. In the 1840's he dominated the theater in St. Louis and Mobile and invaded New Orleans. He also acted in New York and Philadelphia, but he was most successful in the West and South. As an actor he was best known for his comic roles. In 1853 he retired from the theater to practice law in St. Louis. By this time many of his sketches and anecdotes, based largely on his experiences as an actor-manager, had appeared in the *Spirit of the Times* and in such collections as Porter's *The Big Bear of Arkansas* (1845) and *A Quarter Race in Kentucky* (1846), and stories about his comic exploits were being circulated. His first book, *Sol Smith's Theatrical Apprenticeship* (1845), was reprinted in paperback in 1849, initiating the popular Carey and Hart series, "Library of American Humorous Works." It was followed by *Sol Smith's Theatrical Journey Work* (1854). The year before he died Smith combined and expanded the two books into *Theatrical Management in the West and South.* Instead of chapters, he divided his last book into five "acts." For an afterpiece he presented an inscription for his gravestone with suitable lines from Shakespeare and the stage directions, "Exit Sol."

When he died he was almost as legendary in the theater as was Mike Fink on the river or Davy Crockett along the frontier.

TEXT: "Slow Traveling by Steam," "A Tennessee Door-Keeper," "The Consolate Widow," and "Breaking a Bank" from *Theatrical Management in the West and South* (New York, 1868).

Slow Traveling by Steam

Does any one remember the Caravan? She was what would now be considered a slow boat; *then* she was regularly advertised as the "fast-running" etc. Her regular trips from New Orleans to Natchez were usually made in from six to eight days; a trip made by her in five days was considered remarkable. A voyage from New Orleans to Vicksburg and back, including stoppages, generally entitled the officers and crew to a month's wages. Whether the Caravan ever achieved the feat of a voyage to the Falls (Louisville) I have never learned; if she did, she must have "had a *time* of it!"

It was my fate to take passage in this boat. The captain was a good-natured, easy-going man, careful of the comfort of his passengers, and exceedingly fond of the *game of brag.*

We had been out a little more than five days, and were in hopes of seeing the bluffs of Natchez on the next day. Our wood was getting low, and night coming on. The pilot on duty *above* (the other pilot held three aces at the time, and was just calling out the captain, who "went it strong" on three kings) sent down word that the mate had reported the stock of wood reduced to half a cord. The worthy captain excused himself to the pilot whose watch was below and the two passengers who made up the party, and hurried to the deck, where he soon discovered by the landmarks that we were about half a mile from a wood-yard, which, he said, was situated "right round yonder point." "But," muttered the captain, "I don't much like to take wood of the yellow-faced old scoundrel who owns it; he always charges a quarter of a dollar more than any one else; however, there's no other chance." The boat was pushed to her utmost, and in little less than an hour, when our fuel was about giving out, we made the point, and our cables were out and fastened to trees alongside of a good-sized wood-pile.

"Halloo, colonel! how do you sell your wood *this* time?"

A yellow-faced old countryman, with a two-weeks' beard, strings over his shoulders holding up to his armpits a pair of copperas-colored linsey-woolsey pants, the legs of which reached a very little below the knee, shoes without stockings, a faded broad-brimmed hat which had once been black, and a pipe in his mouth, casting a glance at the empty guards of our boat, and uttering a grunt as he rose from fastening our "spring-line," answered,

"Why, capting, we must charge you *three and a quarter* THIS time."

"The d—l!" replied the captain (captains did swear a little in those days). "What's the odd *quarter* for, I should like to know? You only charged me *three* as I went down."

"Why, capting," drawled out the wood merchant, with a sort of leer on his yellow countenance, which clearly indicated that his wood was as good as sold, "wood's riz since you went down two weeks ago; besides, you are awar' that you very seldom stop going *down;* when you're going *up* you're sometimes obleeged to give me a call, becaze the current's against you, and there's no other wood-yard for nine miles ahead; and if you happen to be nearly out of fooel, why —"

"Well, well," interrupted the captain, "we'll take a few cords under the circumstances," and he returned to his game of brag.

In about half an hour we felt the Caravan commence paddling again. Supper was over, and I retired to my upper berth, situated alongside and overlooking the brag table, where the captain was deeply engaged, having now the *other* pilot as his principal opponent. We jogged on quietly, and seemed to be going at a good rate.

"How does that wood burn?" inquired the captain of the mate, who was looking on at the game.

" 'Tisn't of much account, I reckon," answered the mate; "it's cottonwood, and most of it green at that."

"Well, Thompson — (three aces again, stranger — I'll take that X and the small change, if you please — it's your deal) — Thompson, I say, we'd better take three or four cords at the next wood-yard; it can't be more than six miles from here — (two aces and a bragger, with the age! hand over those V's").

The game went on and the paddles kept moving. At eleven o'clock it was reported to the captain that we were nearing the wood-yard, the light being distinctly seen by the pilot on duty.

"Head her in shore, then, and take in six cords, if it's good. See to it, Thompson; I can't very well leave the game now — it's getting right warm. This pilot's beating us all to smash."

The wooding completed, we paddled on again. The captain seemed somewhat vexed when the mate informed him that the price was the same as at the last wood-yard — *three and a quarter,* but soon again became interested in the game.

From my upper berth (there were no staterooms then) I could observe the movements of the players. All the contention appeared to be between the captain and the pilots (the latter personages took it turn and turn about, steering and playing brag), *one* of them almost invariably winning, while the two passengers merely went through the ceremony of dealing, cutting, and paying up their *"anties."* They were anxious to *learn the game* — and they *did* learn it! Once in a while, indeed, seeing they had two aces and a bragger, they would venture a bet of five or ten dollars, but they were always compelled to back out before the tremendous bragging of the captain *or* pilot; or, if they *did* venture to "call out" on "two bullits and a bragger," they had the mortification to find one of the officers had the same kind of a hand, and was *more venerable!* Still, with all these disadvantages, they continued playing — they wanted to learn the game.

At two o'clock the captain asked the mate how we were getting on.

"Oh, pretty glibly, sir," replied the mate. "We can scarcely tell what headway we *are* making, for we are obliged to keep the middle of the river, and there is the shadow of a fog rising. This wood seems rather better than that we took in at old Yellow Face's, but we're nearly out again, and must be looking out for more. I saw a light just ahead on the right — shall we hail?"

"Yes, yes," replied the captain: "ring the bell, and ask 'em what's the price of wood up here. I've got you again — here's double kings."

I heard the bell and the pilot's hail: "What's *your* price for wood?"

A youthful voice on the shore answered, "Three *and* a quarter!"

"D—n it!" ejaculated the captain, who had just lost the price of two cords to the pilot — the strangers suffering *some* at the same time — "three and a quarter again! Are we *never* to get to a cheaper country? Deal, sir, if you please — better luck next time." The other pilot's voice was again heard on deck —

"How much *have* you?"

"Only about ten cords, sir," was the reply of the youthful salesman.

The captain here told Thompson to take six cords, which would last till daylight, and again turned his attention to the game.

The pilots here changed places. *When did they sleep?*

Wood taken in, the Caravan again took her place in the middle of the stream, paddling on as usual.

Day at length dawned. The brag party broke up, and settlements were being made, during which operation the captain's bragging propensities were exercised in cracking up the speed of his boat, which, by his reckoning, must have made at least sixty miles, and *would* have made many more if he could have procured good wood. It appeared the two passengers, in their first lesson, had incidentally lost one hundred and twenty dollars. The captain, as he rose to see about taking in some *good* wood, which he felt sure of obtaining, now he had got above the level country, winked at his opponent, the pilot, with whom he had been on very bad terms during the progress of the game, and said, in an under tone, "Forty apiece for you, and I, and Jemes (the other pilot) is not bad for one night."

I had risen, and went out with the captain to enjoy a view of the bluffs. There was just fog enough to prevent the vision taking in more than sixty yards, so I was disappointed in *my* expectation. We were nearing the shore for the purpose of looking for wood, the banks being invisible from the middle of the river.

"There it is!" exclaimed the captain: "stop her!" Ding, ding, ding! went the big bell, and the captain hailed:

"Halloo! the wood-yard!"

"Halloo yourself!" answered a squeaking female voice, which came from a woman with a petticoat over her shoulders in place of a shawl.

"What's the price of wood?"

"I think you ought to know the price by this time," answered the old lady in the petticoat — "it's three and a qua-a-rter! and now you know it."

"Three and the d—l!" broke in the captain: "what! have you raised on *your* wood too? I'll give you *three,* and not a cent more."

"Well," replied the petticoat, "here comes the old man; *he'll* talk to you!" And, sure enough, out crept from the cottage the veritable faded hat, copperas-colored pants, yellow countenance, and two weeks' beard we had seen the night before, and the same voice we had heard regulating the price of cottonwood, squeaked out the following sentence, accompanied by the same leer of the same yellow countenance:

"Why, darn it all, capting, there is but three or four cords left, and *since it's you,* I don't care if I *do* let you have it for THREE — *as you're a good customer!*"

After a quick glance at the landmarks around, the captain bolted, and turned in to take some rest.

The fact became apparent — the reader will probably have discovered it some time since — that WE HAD BEEN WOODING ALL NIGHT AT THE SAME WOOD-YARD!

A Tennessee Door-Keeper

At Greenville, East Tennessee, we made a halt, and determined to treat the inhabitants of that beautiful village with three representations of the "legitimate drama," in a carpenter's shop, hastily, but tastefully fitted up for the occasion.

The first representation was attended by just *six people*, making the total receipts of the evening THREE DOLLARS!

My landlord, the carpenter, attributed the slim attendance to a *camp-meeting* that was in successful operation about two miles from town, and "reckoned" that if I would "hold on" until that broke up, we should have full *shops* every night.

Thus urged, we did "hold on," and our next performance was rewarded with a receipt of TWO DOLLARS AND A HALF!

I proposed to decamp next morning, but the printer of the Green-ville Expositor (who was on the *free-list* as a matter of course) remonstrated against so sudden a move, urging that a *third* performance must be successful, as it was quite certain the camp-meeting would break up that morning, and the young folk would all return to their homes.

I yielded and advertised for "positively the last performance" the play of WILLIAM TELL, a favorite afterpiece, and a lot of comic songs.

At the time of beginning I was glad to find a crowded audience in waiting — the shop, work-bench and all, was literally crammed. One of the carpenter's apprentices, whom I had transformed into a citizen of Altorf for the occasion, told me that all but five or six of the people in front were *religious folks,* who had attended the camp-meeting faithfully to its conclusion.

The performance proceeded — the actors were in high spirits. Lyne bullied Governor *Gesler* with great fierceness; *Sarnem* whacked the carpenter's apprentice with a hearty good-will, while the latter was making a bow to the governor's cap, on a pole five feet and a half high — the arrow, aimed at the apple on *Albert's* head, flew, with remarkable exactness, into the horse-blanket held up as a target to receive it behind the scenes, and the play was received with shouts of satisfaction by the Greenvillians. The farce was honored by peal on peal of laughter, while the comic songs were doubly encored, every one of them.

The entertainment over, I observed there was a reluctance in the audience to depart — *they wanted another song.* I gave them one. Still they remained as if glued to their seats. I went before the curtain and thanked the people for their patronage, and informed them the performance had concluded. They did not move — they wanted yet *another song.* I gave them another, and again told them the entertainment of the evening was over, intimating, at the same time, that the stage-carpenter was waiting to take down the scenery. A gentleman in the gallery (the work-bench) here arose and addressed me as follows: "Mr. Sol. Smith: Sir, — I have been requested to express to you the unanimous wish of this meeting that you will *prolong your season.* The liberal patronage bestowed upon you this evening must have convinced you that we *can* make something of a turn-out here, and I feel authorized to say that, if you will give us a performance to-morrow night, you will have another house *as crowded as this.*"

A murmur of applause confirmed the opinion of the speaker, and I was greatly tempted to yield to their wishes; but, bethinking me of certain announcements for performances in towns farther south, I was obliged to decline the invitation of my kind auditors, and content myself with the eighty or ninety dollars which I supposed had been contributed that night to my ways and means. Finding me determined, the audience gradually dispersed, each individual casting wishful and sidelong glances toward the stage, which by this time was beginning to be dismantled.

Motioning the door-keeper to follow me into a sort of shed adjoining the theatre, I proceeded to open the ticket-box in his presence, while he sat down on a bench in the corner to wait for his wages. I found SEVEN TICKETS in the box, and, turning to the waiting door-keeper, who was busily engaged chewing tobacco and spitting, I asked him what he had done with the rest.

"They are all *thar,*" he replied, with great composure, looking intently on a beam of the shed, and rocking his right knee, which he held in his clenched hands, and raised about half way from the floor to his chin.

"All *there* — where?" was the very natural question that I next propounded.

"*In the box* whar you *told* me to put 'em," he answered, still eying the beam or rafter.

"I find but seven here," I remarked: "I want to know where are the tickets for the one hundred and sixty or one hundred and eighty people that were in the house to-night."

"I tell you again they are all *thar,* sir," he answered, sturdily; "and I allow 'twon't be safe for any man to insinuate anything agin my character," he continued, releasing his knee, and taking a large quid of tobacco from a rusty steel box and ramming it into his mouth.

"I do not wish to insinuate anything against your character," I said, soothingly, "but I want to know what you have done with the tickets."

"They are *thar,*" he again alleged — "every one of 'em thar; no one passed *me* without giving me a ticket, and the tickets are all *thar.*"

I began to get a little pettish, and asked the tobacco-chewer to explain himself. "There were nearly two hundred people in the house," I urged.

"There war full that," he admitted.

"Well, then," I asked, finally, "where are the tickets? Will you explain this mystery?"

My friend, the tobacco-chewing door-keeper, here renewed his grasp on his raised knee, deliberately withdrew his eyes from the rafter, and fixing them, half closed, on mine, at length afforded me the desired *explanation,* thus:

"You engaged me to *keep your door;* and I performed my dooties to the best of my abilities, for which you are indebted to me three dollars, and I want my money. No person has passed me without a ticket. My char*a*cter is above suspicion, and no one must say nothin' agin it."

"My good friend," I ventured to say, "I don't wish to say any thing against —"

"No, I should think *not —* you'd *better* not," he continued, "for I'm too well known here; well, as I was a sayin', you employed me as *door-keeper* — mark the distinction — I had nothin' at all to do with the WINDERS — *and thar's where your hundred and eighty people came in,* you 'tarnal fool to leave 'em open when there was sich a crowd comin' from camp-meetin'!"

I paid the fellow his three dollars, and next day was far on my road to the Warm Springs, in the famous county of Buncombe, where they raise the largest peaches and the yellowest children in all creation.

The Consolate Widow

Between Caleba Swamp and Lime Creek, in the "Nation," we saw considerable of a crowd gathered near a drinking-house, most of them seated and smoking. We stopped to see what was the matter. It was Sunday, and there had been a quarter race for a gallon of whisky. The first thing I noticed on alighting was the singular position of one of the horses of the party. He was kneeling down and standing on his hinder feet, his head wedged in between the ends of two logs of the grocery, and was stone dead, having evidently ran directly against the building at full speed, causing the house partially to fall. About five paces from the body of the horse lay the rider, quite senseless, with a gash in his throat which might have let out a thousand lives. As I said, most of the crowd were seated and smoking.

"What is all this?" I inquired. "What is the matter here?"

"Matter?" after a while answered one in a drawling voice, giving a good spit, and refilling his mouth with a new cud. "Matter enough; there's been a quarter race."

"But how came this man and horse killed?" I asked.

"Well," answered the chewing and spitting gentleman, "the man was considerably in liquor, I reckon, and he run his hoss chuck agin the house, and that's the whole on it."

"Has a doctor been sent for?" inquired one of our party.

"I reckon there ain't much use of doctors *here*," replied another of the crowd. "Burnt brandy couldn't save either of 'em, man or hoss."

"Has this man a wife and children?" inquired I.

"No children, that I knows on," answered a female, who was sitting on the ground a short distance from the dead man, smoking composedly.

"He has a wife, then?" I remarked. "What will be her feelings when she learns the fatal termination of this most unfortunate race?"

"Yes," sighed the female, "it *was* an unfortunate race. Poor man! he lost the whisky."

"Did you happen to know his wife? Has she been informed of the untimely death of her husband?" were my next inquiries.

"Do I *know* her? Has she been informed of his death?" said the woman. "Well, I reckon you ain't acquainted about these parts. *I* am the unfortunate widder."

"*You,* madam! *You* the wife of this man who has been so untimely cut off?" I exclaimed, in astonishment.

"Yes, and what about it?" said she. "Untimely cut off? His throat's cut, that's all, by that 'tarnal sharp end of a log; and as for it's being *untimely,* I don't know but it's as well now as any time — *he warn't of much account, no how!"*

She resumed her smoking, and we resumed our journey.

Breaking a Bank

Captain Summons was a very clever fellow, and the "Dr. Franklin" was a very superb boat, albeit inclined to rock about a good deal, and nearly turn over on her side when visited by a breath of air in the least resembling a gale. Captain Summons was a clever fellow. All steamboat captains are clever fellows, or *nearly* all; but what I mean to say is, Captain Summons was a *particularly* clever fellow; a clever fellow in the widest sense of the term; a fellow that is clever in every way — anxious that his passengers shall be comfortably bestowed, well fed and well attended to, and *determined* that they shall amuse themselves "just as they d—n please," as the saying is. If he happened to have preachers on board, he put on a serious countenance of a Sunday morning, consented that there should be preaching, ordered the chairs to be set out, and provided Bibles and hymn-books for the occasion, himself and his officers, whose watch was below, taking front seats and listening attentively to the discourse. Likely as not, at the close of the service, he would ask the reverend gentleman who had been officiating, with his back in close proximity to a hot fire in a Franklin furnace, to accompany him to the bar and join him in some refreshments! If there were passengers on board who desired to pass away the time in playing poker, euchre, brag, or whist, tables and chairs were ready for *them* too — poker, brag, euchre, and whist be it! All sorts of passengers were accommodated on the Dr. Franklin; the rights of none were suffered to be infringed; all were free to follow such employments as should please themselves. A *dance* in the evening was a very common occurrence on this boat and when cotillons were *on the carpet* the captain was sure to be *thar.*

It sometimes happened that, at the commencement of a voyage, it was found somewhat difficult to reconcile *all* the passengers to the system of Captain Summons, which was founded on the broad principle of equal rights to all.

On the occasion of my voyage in the "Doctor," in December, 1844, I found myself surrounded by a crowd of passengers who were *entire strangers* to me — a very rare occurrence to one who travels so often on the Western rivers as I do. I wished my absence from New Orleans to be as brief as possible, and the "Doctor" was the fastest boat in port at the time of my leaving the Crescent City; so I resolved to secure a berth in her, and trust to luck to find a St. Louis boat at the Mouth.

I don't know how it is or *why* it is, but by strangers I am almost always taken for a PREACHER. It was so on this voyage. There were two Methodist *circuit* riders on board, and it happened that we got acquainted and were a good deal together, from which circumstance I was supposed to be *one of them*, which supposition was the means of bringing me into an acquaintance with the female passengers, who, for the most part, were very pious, religiously-inclined souls. We had preaching every day, and sometimes at night; and I must say, in justice to Brothers Twitchell and Switchell, that their sermons were highly edifying and instructive.

In the mean time a portion of the passengers "at the other end of the hall" continued to play sundry games with cards, notwithstanding the remonstrances of the worthy followers of Wesley, who frequently requested the captain to interfere and break up such unholy doings. The captain had but one answer — it was something like this: "Gentle*men*, amuse yourselves as you like; preach and pray to your hearts' content — none shall interfere with your pious purposes; some like that sort of thing — *I* have no objection to it. These men prefer to amuse themselves with cards; let them; they pay their passages as well as you, gentle*men*, and have as much right to *their* amuse*ments* as you have to *yours,* and they shall not be disturbed. Preach, play cards, dance cotillons, do what you like, *I* am agreeable; only understand that *all games* (preaching among the rest) *must cease at* 10 *o'clock.*" So *we* preachers got very little comfort from Captain Summons.

Up, up, up, up we went. Christmas day arrived. All the *other* preachers had holden forth on divers occasions, and it being ascertained that it was my intention to leave the boat on her arrival at Cairo, a formal request was preferred that *I should preach the Christmas sermon!* The women (God bless them all!) were *very* urgent in their applications to me. "Oh do, Brother Smith; we want to hear *you* preach. All the others have contributed their share to our spiritual comfort — you *must* oblige us — indeed you must." I endeavored to excuse myself the best way I could, alleging the necessity of my leaving the boat in less than an hour — my baggage was not ready — I had a terrible cold, and many other good and substantial reasons were given, but all in vain; preach I must. "Well," thinks I, "if I must, I must." At this crisis, casting my eyes down toward the Social Hall, and seeing an unusual crowd assembled around a table, I asked one of the brethren what might be going on down there. The fattest of the preaching gentlemen replied, "The poor miserable sinners have filled the measure of their iniquity by opening a FARO BANK!" "Horrible!" exclaimed I, holding up my hands, and "horrible!" echoed the women and missionaries in full chorus. "Can not such doings be put a stop to?" asked an elderly female, addressing the pious travelers. "I fear not," groaned my Methodist colleague (the fat one). "We have been trying to convince the captain that some dreadful accident will inevitably befall the boat if such proceedings are permitted, and what do you think he answered?" "What?" we all asked, of course. "Why, he just said that, inasmuch as he permitted *us* to preach and pray, he should let other passengers dance and play, if they chose to do so; and that, if I didn't like the 'proceedings' complained of, *I might leave the boat!* Yes, he did; and, moreover, he

mentioned that it was 11 o'clock, and asked me if I wouldn't 'liquor!' "
This announcement of the captain's stubbornness and impiety was met
with a general groan of pity and sorrow, and we resumed the conversation respecting the unhallowed faro bank. "It is much to be
regretted," remarked the gentlewoman who had spoken before, "that
something can't be done. Brother Smith," she continued, appealing
directly to me, and laying her forefinger impressively upon my arm,
"can not *you* break up that bank?" "Dear madam," I answered, "you
know not the difficulty of the task you impose upon me; FARO BANKS
ARE NOT SO EASILY BROKEN UP as you may imagine; however, as you
all appear so anxious about it, if you'll excuse me from preaching the
sermon I'll see what can be done." "Ah, that's a dear soul!" "I knew
he would try!" "He'll be sure to succeed!" "Our prayers shall not be
wanting!" Such were the exclamations that greeted me as I moved
off toward the faro bank. Elbowing my way into the crowd, I got
near the table in front of the dealer, and was for a time completely
concealed from the view of my pious friends near the door of the
ladies' cabin. I found the bank was a small affair. The betters were
risking trifling sums, ranging from six to twenty-five cents.

"Mr. Dealer," I remarked, "I have come to break up this bank."
"The deuce you have!" replied the banker; "let's see you do it."
"What amount have you in bank?" I inquired. "Eleven dollars," was
his answer. "What is your limit?" asked I. "A dollar," he replied.
"Very well," said I, placing a ragged Indiana dollar behind the
queen — "turn on." He turned, and the king won for me. I took
the two dollars up and let him make another turn, when I replaced
the bet, and the queen came up in my favor. I had now four dollars,
which I placed in the square, taking in the 5, 6, 7, and 8, and it won
again! Here were seven dollars of the banker's money. I pocketed
three of them, and bet four dollars behind the queen again; the
jack won, and the BANK WAS BROKEN! The crowd dispersed in all
directions, laughing at the breaking up of the petty bank, and I made
my way toward the ladies' cabin, where my new friends were anxiously
awaiting the result of my bold attempt. "Well, well, well," they all
exclaimed, "what success? Have you done it? Do let us hear all about
it!" I wiped the perspiration from my brow, and, putting on a very
serious face, I said solemnly, "I HAVE BROKEN THAT BANK!" "You
have?" they all exclaimed. "Yes, I'll be d—d if he hasn't!" muttered
the disappointed gamester, the keeper of the late bank, who was
just going into his state-room. In the midst of the congratulations
which were showered upon me, I received a *summons* from the captain to come forward with my baggage — we were at Cairo.

Alexander G. McNutt

(1802-1848)

A native of Virginia, Alexander Gallatin McNutt received a classical education at Washington and Lee. After studying law, he moved to Vicksburg, Mississippi, where he soon established himself as a prosperous lawyer and cotton planter. Like most of the authors of Southwestern humor, he was well educated and active in politics. He served in the state senate and was Governor of Mississippi for two terms (1838-1842). His political career has been the subject of controversy, some historians declaring that he was intemperate, cowardly, and even murderous; and others praising him as capable, moral, and courageous.

During his lifetime McNutt was acclaimed a witty teller of stories, but his abilities as a humorous writer were little known. The sketches and stories which he sent to the New York *Spirit of the Times* were signed "The Turkey Runner," and probably only the editor, William T. Porter, and perhaps a few others knew for sure that this was McNutt's pseudonym. Most of these sketches concern the adventures of Jim and Chunkey, two backwoods hearties in the employ of a wealthy cotton planter called "the Captain." When he is not killing deer or wrestling bears, Jim likes to spin yarns, especially about his friend Chunkey: "You know what kind of man Chunkey is when he gits started — if he commences talkin, singin, or whistlin, no matter which, you'd just as well try and stop the Mississippi as him. Why I have knoed him to whistle three days and three nights on a stretch." Jim and Chunkey are representative of the exaggerated but convincing characterizations and the bold masculine humor which mark the best of Southwestern writing.

TEXT: "A Swim for a Deer" and "Chunkey's Fight with the Panthers" from *The Big Bear of Arkansas,* ed. W. T. Porter (Philadelphia, 1845).

A Swim for a Deer

"Yes, Capting, they war *lower,* I tell *you* — why, God bless your soul, honey, they war not only powerful thick, but some on 'em war as big as common-sized horses, I *do* reckon; 'cause why, nobody ever had hunted 'em, you see. In the winter time the overflow, and in the summer time the lakes and snakes, bayous and alligators, musketoes and gallinippers, buffalo gnats and sand flies, with a small sprinkle of the agur and a *perfect cord* of congestive, prevented the Ingins from gwine through the country! Oh no; the red skins would rather hunt the fat turkey and deer in the Azoo hills and pine lands t'other side of the Pearl river, to killin' fat bar on the Creek or Sunflower."

"Well, Jim, I think they were right; you must then have been among the first hunters in the country."

"Yes, I *do* reckon when I first went into that country, from the Azoo Hills to the Mississippi, there never had been but *mighty few* hunters. Why thar ar places thar now whar the deer ar tame as sheep, and whar the bar don't care a dam for *nobody!* Fact! ask Chunkey!"

"That is very remarkable; what is the cause?"

" 'Cause they've never been hunted; no, sir; never hearn the crack of a rifle nor the yelp of a dog; why thar ar more nor a hundred lakes and brakes in them diggins, that hain't never been pressed by no mortal 'ceptin' varmints. You know more nor half the country is overflowed in the winter, and t'other half, which is a darned sight the biggest, is covered with cane, palmetto and other fixins; — why it stands to reason, and in course no man ever *had* hunted 'em. — Why, sir, when I first went to the Creek" —

"Let the Creek run, Jim; tell us about the bear!"

"Well, sir, the bar war *very* promiscuous indeed, and some of the old hees war mighty mellifluous, I tell *you.* I had no sens about bar *then,* but thar warn't no cabin or camp in the whole settlement, and in course I soon larnt thar natur by livin' 'mongst 'em. A bar, Capting, an old *he* bar, ain't no candidate or other good-natured greenhorn to stand gougin' and treating. Oh no, *he* ain't, but he's as ramstugenous an animal as a log-cabin loafer in the dog days, jist about, and if a stranger fools with him he'll get sarved like that white gal what come into my settlement."

"How was that, Jim?"

"Why *perfectly* ruinated, as Buck Brien says."

"You don't mean to say Jim, that you" —

"Yes, dam'd if I diddent. Ask Chunkey, or" —

"Oh, I am satisfied with the girl. Go on with the bear."

"Well, let's licker — (after drinking) — a bar is a *consaity* animal, but as far as his sens do go he's about as smart as any other animal; arter that, the balance is clear fat and fool. I have lived 'mongst 'em, and know ther natur. I have killed as many as seven in a day, and *smartly* to the rise of sixty in a season. Arter I'd been on the Creek about two months, *up* comes the Governor *and* Chunkey; the Governor 'tended like he wanted to see how I come on with the clearin'; but sir, he were arter a spree, and I knoe'd it, or *why* did he bring Chunkey? Every thing looked *mighty* well; the negers looked fat and slick as old Belcher in catfish season. I'd done cut more nor two hundred acres of cane, and had the rails on the ground. I'd done" —

"Come, Jim, keep the track!"

"Well, Capting, they war mighty savagerous arter likker; they'd been fightin' the stranger* mightly comin' up, and war perfectly wolfish arter some har of the dog, and dam'd the drop did I have; so I started two negers with mules and jugs to the pint (Princeton, Washington county,) and the ox team arter a barrel. Well, sir, the day arter, the jugs come, and we *darted* on 'em, (giving a sigh) but lord, what war two jugs in *sich* a crowd? They jist kept Chunkey from dyin', as he was so dry he had the rattles; next day the barrel come, and then we *krack*-ovienned up to it in airnest. *You* know what kind of man Chunkey is when he gits started — if he commences talkin', singin', or whistlin', no matter which, you'd jist as well try and stop the Mississippi as him. Why I've knoed him to whistle three days and three nights on a stretch, — the Governor couldent eat nor drink for Chunkey's whistlin', and at last he gits mad, and that's the last thing he does with any body what *he* likes, and, says he to Chunkey —

" 'Chunkey, you have kept me awake two nights a whistlin, and you must stop it to night, or *you* or *me* must quit the plantation.' "

"Chunkey said, 'Governor I don't want to put you to no trouble, but I *can't* stop in the middle of a chune, and as you have known the plantation longer than me, I expect you can leave it with lest trouble.'

"The Governor jist roar'd, and gin Chunkey a new gun and" —

"Stop, Jim, you have forgot the bear."

"Well, whar was I, Capting — oh, I remember, now! Well, when the barrel come we *did* lumber; Chunkey he soon commenced singin', and I to thinkin' about that white gal. We went on that way nigh a week, and then cooled off. One mornin', I and Chunkey had gone down to the creek to git a bait of water, and I knoed the bar would be thar, as it war waterin' time with them."

"Why Jim, have they a particular time to water?"

* A barrel of whiskey is called a "stranger," from the fact that it is brought from a distance, there being none made in the country. [Author's note]

"In course they has; they come to water at a certain place, and jist as reglar as a parson to his eatin'; every bar has his waterin' place, and he comes and goes in the same path and in *the same foot tracks,* always, until he moves his settlement: and jist you break a cane, or limb, or move a chunk or stick near his trail, and see how quick he'll move his cabin! Oh yes, a bar is mighty particlar about sich things — that's his *sens* — that's his *trap* to find out if you are in his settlement. Why, Capting, I have watched 'em" —

"Jim, you have left yourself and Chunkey on the bank of the creek, 'a waterin'.' Are you going to stay there?"

"Well, we set down on the bank and took our stand opposite the *biggest kind* of sign, and sure enough, presently *down* he come; a bar don't lap water like a dog; no, they sucks it like a hog. You jist ought to see him rais his nose and smell the wind. Well, he seed us, and with that he *ris!* He war a whopper, I *tell you!* He looked like a big burn, and he throw'd them arms about awful, honey. It war about one hundred and twenty yards to him, but I knoed he were *my* meat without an accident, so I let drive, and he took the creek — then out he went and scampered up the bank *mighty quick,* and then sich a ratlin' among cane, sich a growlin' and a snortin', sich a breakin' of saplins and vines, I reckon you never *did* hear! I knoed, in course, I had him. I throwed a log in and paddled across — found his trail, and lots of har and fat, but no blood!"

"That was very strange, Jim; how did you account for that?"

"Why he were too fat to bleed! Oh, you think I am foolin' you, but you ask Chunkey. It is frequently the case. I follered his trail about a quarter and a half a quarter, and *thar* he lay; so I jist hollered to Chunkey to git two negers and a yoke of steers to take him to the house. How much do you reckon he weighed?"

"I have no idea, Jim."

"Now, sir, he weighed, without head, skin, or entrails, four hundred and ninety-three pounds, and his head sixty pounds! You don't believe me! Well, just ask Chunkey if I haint killed 'em smartly over seven hundred pounds! Killin' him sorter got my blood up, and I determined to have another. Chunkey had been jerkin' it to the licker gourd mighty smart, and was jest right. 'Chunkey,' says I, 'let's gin it to another.' 'Good as ——,' says Chunkey. 'Who cars for expenses? a hundred dollar bill aint no more in my pocket nor a cord of wood!' With that we started down to the Bend; we haddent been thar long when *in* comes an old buck; he was a smasher, and one horn were broke off. I telled Chunkey now's his time, as I skorn'd to toch him arter killin' a bar. Chunkey lathered away, and *ca chunk!* he went into the creek; he then gin him a turn with t'other barrel; the buck wabbled about a time or two and sunk, jist at the head of the little raft at the lower end of the clearin'. I know'd he'd lodged agin the drift, and determined to have him, and if you'll believe me, I'd been workin' at the gourd since I'd killed the bar. I pulled off my coat and jest throwed myself in; I swimd out to the place and *div* — you know the current are might rapid thar. Well, I found him, yes, —— if I diddent. But, Moses! warn't I in a tight place *that* time? Well, I reckon I were. I'd been willin' to fite the biggest *he* on the creek, and gin him the fust bite, to have been out!"

"Why, Jim, what was the matter?"

"Arter I'd got in, I couldent get out — *that* was the matter! You see the drift were a homogification of old cyprus logs, vines, and drift-wood of evry description, for nigh three hundred yards long, and the creek runs under thar like it was arter somebody; the trees and vines, and prognostics of all sorts, ar sorter nit together like a sock, and you couldent begin to get through 'em. Well, Capting, I thought my time had come, and I knowed it war for killin' that cub what I telled you about. And, sir, it would have come if it haddent been for the sorritude I felt arterwards. You see, the young cub was standin' in the corner of the fence eatin' roastin' ears, and I was goin' to the" —

"But, Jim, you have told that once, and I don't want to hear it again."

"Well, I tried to rise, but I'd as well tried to rise down'ard. I then tried to swim up 'bove the raft, but I found from the way the logs and vines ware tearin' the extras off me, that I were goin' further under, and I was gettin' out of wind very fast. I knowed thar was but one chance, and that was *to go clean through!* So I busted loose and set my paddles to goin' mightily; presently my head bumped agin the drift! I div agin, and kept my paddles a lumberin'! Chunk! my head went agin a log, and then I knowed the thing were *irrefrangably out,* but I div agin, still workin' on my oars smartly, until I hung agin! 'Good bye, Chunkey! — farewell, Governor,' says I. But, Capting, I were all the time tryin' to do *something.* Things had begun to look speckled, green, and then *omniferous;* but findin' I were not gone yet, by the way I were kickin' and pawin', and knowin' I were goin' *somewhere,* and expectin' to the devil, there ain't *no* tellin' how long or powerful I *did* work! The fust thing I recollect arter that, was gittin' a mouthful of wind! *Fact!* I'd done, gone clean through, and were hangin' on to a tree below the raft! But, sir, I were *mighty* weak, and couldent tell a stump from an old he, and 'spected smartly for some time that I were in the yother world, and commenced an excuse for comin' so onexpectedly! However, presently I got sorter right, and when I found I were safe, I reckon you never *did* see a man feel so *unanimous* in your life, and I made the water fly for joy."

"Well, Jim, what had become of Chunkey! He did not leave you!"

"Yes, — if he diddent! He'd commenced gittin' dry afore he shot the deer; and when Chunkey wants a drink, if his daddy was drounin', Chunkey would go to the licker gourd afore he'd go to his daddy. I went to the house, and *thar* he was settin' at the table, jist a rattlin' his teeth agin the bar's ribs; the greese war runnin' off his chin; he held a tin cup in one hand 'bout half full of licker; his head were sorter throwd back; he was breathin' sorter hard, his eye set on the Governor, humpin' himself on politics. 'Dam the specie kurrency,' says Chunkey, 'it aint no account, and I'm agin it. When we had good times, I drank five-dollar-a-gallon brandy, and had pockets full of money.' 'But,' says the Governor, 'you bought the brandy on a credit, and never paid for it!' 'What's the difference?' asks Chunkey! 'Them what I bought it from never paid for it; they bought it on a credit from them fureigners, and never paid for it, and them fureigners, you say, are a pack of scoundrels, and I go in for ruinin' 'em, so far as good licker is concarned.' 'You are drunk,' says the Governor, and then — but, Capting, you look sleepy; let's licker and go to bed."

"No, I am not sleepy, Jim."

"Well, then, I'll tell you how I sarved Chunkey for leavin' me under the raft. Moses! diddent I pay him back? Did I ever tell you 'bout takin' Chunkey out on Sky Lake, makin' him drunk, takin' his gun and knife away from him, and a puttin' him to sleep in a panter's nest?"

"No, you never did; but was you not apprehensive they would kill him?"

"Apple — hell! No! If they'd commenced bitin' Chunkey, they'd have been looed, as that's a game Chunkey *invented*. But here he comes; and if you mention it afore him, it puts the devil in him. Let's licker."

Chunkey's Fight with the Panthers

Co chunk! went Jem into the middle of the floor, jest at the crack off day — (Jem is a labor savin' man, and don't pull off his socks or britches when he goes to bed.) He commenced chunkin' the fire, then "ah!" says he, feelin' for the tin cup — *"gluck, gluck, gluck,"*

went the licker — then "ah!" agin; presently he went to the door
and shouted to the foreman — "Sound that horn, Hembry; tell the niggers in the kitchen to holler to the niggers in the quarter to lumber
the holler back agin to the kitchen, for hell has *surely* broke loose!"
then "ah!" says he agin, and in he comes.

"Chunkey?" says he.

"What's busted, Jem?"

"Hell *has* busted and no mistake! *the ground is kivered with snow!*"

I sprung up, and sure enough *thar* was the snow, the first that ever
fell in the Creek, jest follerin' civilization. I *knowed* thar'd be howlin',
smashin' of teeth, burnin' of brimstone, and a worryin' of the "stranger"
on the Creek to-day, and so I reckon did the dogs, cause when Hembry
blowed the horn they come a shoutin', like so many devils. Jest imagin',
Captin', thirty full grown dogs, a cross of the blood on the old Virginny
fox hound, keen as a bowyer, and adzactly of Jem's opinion that hell
had busted, and signifyin' as plain as they could if huntin's goin' on
they'd take a chance.

Well, we splurged about till breakfast time, gettin' up and cleanin'
guns, countin' balls, and dividin' powder. "Bring out them bar sassage
and deer melts; I'll take a little jaw-exercise," says Jem; "and then,
Chunkey, we'll locomotion," his eyes all the time lookin' like a live
coal of fire, and every muscle jumpin' for joy.

"Look out bar!" says he.

"Lay low and keep dark, panter," says I.

"Deer, *don't* you come nigh me," says Jem, and then he commenced singin'—

> "Oh, rain, come wet me, sun, come dry me,
> Take car, white man, don't come nigh me!"

and strikin' a few licks of the goin'-and-comin' double shuffle.

"Hurrah for Sky Lake," says I.

"Hurrah for the Forkin Cypress drive," says Jem, takin' a drink and
cuttin' a few pigeon wings with his left leg — "Them's the licks,
Chunkey, what makes a gal say 'yes.' Now mind, Chunkey, no deer
or wild turkey, no wild hogs or cub, nothin' but bar or panter!"

"Agreed," says I, and then we bugled. Capting, you've hearn Jem
say he's hard of hearin'? Well, he is, sometimes, 'specially when he
don't want to hear; but *that* mornin' he was wide awake all over, and
could have hearn an old he grunt in a thunder storm! "I'll carry the
horn, Chunkey; if you blow I can't hear you and when I want you
I'll blow, and you can."

I dident 'spect anything then, but you'll see.

Well, we had our big guns, them the Governor gin us; they throw twelve to the pound, and war made by that man what lives in Louis-ville — what's his name? He promised to send me a deer gun gratis for two young panters, but he aint done it. Jem's gun were in bar order that mornin', and if you'd jest say *varmint*, above your breath, *click* it would go, cockin' itself. We haddint crossed the creek two hundred yards afore yelp, yelp, went old Rambler. "Cuss them dogs!" says Jem, "that's a deer?" Big Solomon went to examin' the sign. "No it aint, massa Jem — it's a panter *sure!* — look at her long foot and sharp nail, and see hear whar he's been ridin' pigs! Cuss his saitful countenance!" "It's a wolf," says Jem, "or a dog! Run down to the hossin-gum tree, Chunkey, and I'll go to the Cypress crossin' log; he's bound to go one way or the yether, to git out." Well, I husseled off to the hossin-gum and Jem to the foot log, and afore we got to our stands the dogs had him gwine like a streak; away he went down to the Pint, and I knowed that's no place for him, and presently I heard 'em comin' back — nearer and nearer — here they is! — don't they make the snow fly, and jest look at him! Look at them yaller eyes! — them ears laid back, and them meat hooks a shinin'! Aint he stretchin' himself? Aint them dogs talkin' to him with "tears in their eyes!" Yes they is, hoss, and now I'll git him! — *Bang!* Oh, dam you! you've got it! I *know* you is! you aint shakin' that tail for nothin'! Yes, thar's blood on the snow! But aint he "gittin' out de way?" "Never mind; them dogs will suck him afore he's much older, and if they don't Jem's yager will" — *Bang*, went Jem's gun, and then all were still. "Howdy, wolf! how do you rise?" says I, and started. When I got up Jem were shakin him. He were a smasher, but too full to run.

Arter lickerin and cussin a spell, we took a "bee line" for Sky Lake. Goin along we lickered freely, and arter awhile Jem said, "Chunkey, I can slash you, shootin at that knot?" "Well, I reckun you can, Jem," says I, but *you* know he couldent, Capting. I wouldent shoot cause we haddent any amminition to spare. "Keep them dogs in, and break for the Forkin-Cypress, Sol," says I, "and make a cain camp; and Sol, do you hear, jest let them dogs loose, and I'll swaller you, wrong end foremost!" "Massa Chunkey *is* risin," said Sal, and then he busted.

Lots of deer war 'tinually passin; some on 'em stood feedin jist as careless as a loafer with a full belly — they kno'ed they war safe. The day was mighty clear and yaller; it warn't very cold, but still the snow diddent melt, but floated sorter like turkey feathers in the wind, and in the tall cane it fell round us like a fog. When we got to the Forkin-Cypress, Sol soon had a camp done, and I and Jem started to look for sign.

We haddent been gone long when I hearn Jem's horn, and made

to him; thar war a sign at the foot of a tree, and *thar* was his track in the snow. "Shall we nail him, Chunkey?" *"In course,"* says I. Well, he hollered to Sol to turn the dogs loose, and *hear* they come; they jest fell onto the trail like a starved dog on a bloody bone. They circled about among the switchcane and priscimmon bushes a long time afore they could make it out. Presently I hearn 'em give some short licks, and I knowed he war up. "That's a cry for you!" Away they go, further and further; presently you can jest hear 'em, and then they are clean gone. I hearn Jem shoutin awhile, and then *his* mouth is lost too. I started on, spectin to meet em comin back, and in about an hour I hearn Jem's voice — *who-whoop.* "Ah, *bar,"* says I, "whar's your friends?" I soon hearn Jem agin, and presently I hearn the dogs, like the ringin' of a cowbell, a long way off. They come up the ridge, and then bore off to the thick cane on my right; then they hushed awhile, and I kno'ed they's a fightin. Look out dogs; — *thar*, they are gwine agin; no, hear they comes! Lay low and keep dark! I put down another ball and stood for him. I heard the cane crackin, and cocked my gun! Here he comes — here he is! I hearn him snortin; wake snakes! *Aint that lumberin?* Thar, they've got him agin, and now the fur flies. I crawled through the cane trying to get a shot afore the dogs seen me. *Thar they is,* but which is *he?* Dam that dog's head! *Bang!* Whiff, whiff, said the bar, and with that every dog jumped him. The cane's a crackin, and the dogs a hollerin. I jerked my bowyer and plunged in, and thar they war, hung together like a swarm of bees! Thar lay "Singer" on the ground, and limber as a rag, and he had the "Constitutional" down. I felt the har risin on my head, and the blood ticklin the end of my fingers. I crept up behind him, and *zip, zip, zip,* I took him jest behind the shoulder-blade, and *he war done fightin.* He sot down, and sorter rolled his head from side to side, the blood runnin off his tongue, and his eyes full of dirt. He haddent got a hundred yards from the place whar I'd shot him. It war a death shot, and blinded him, and thar side of him lay "Singer" and the "Constitutional," two of the best dogs in Jem's pack.

H—l! I gin a shout and Jem answered. Presently I hearn him cummin, *blowin* like a steamboat, and mad as hell; he always gits mad when he's tired, and when he seen them dogs he commenced breathen mighty hard, and the blood filled the veins in his neck big as your fingers. Presently he commenced cussin, and then he got sorter easy. Arter a while he turned in and cleaned him; we warn't more than a quarter and a half from the camp, whar we soon got, both mighty hungry and tired. Sol cooked the liver jest to the right pint, and we giv it Jessy. We spent the balance of the evenin in drinkin, braggin, and eatin spar ribs roasted brown. Jim made Sol sing

"Oh, she waked me in the mornin, and its broad day,
    I looked for my *canu*, and its done gone away" —

till we went to sleep.

Next mornin' when we waked it war sorter cloudy and warm, and I
and Jem were cloudy and warm too. The wind war blowin' mightily.
"Now, Chunkey, let's have a panter to-day, or *nothin'*."
"All *sot*," says I.

Well, arter breakfast Jem says, "Chunkey, you must take the right
side the Lake, and I'll take the 'yether, till we meet — and, Chunkey,
you must *rush;* it aint more nor eight miles round, but your side *may*
seem long, as you aint usen to the ground. Let's licker out of *my*
gourd, you aint got more nor you'll want. Keep your eye skinned
for sign, and listen for my horn!"

"Hump yourself," says I, and we both darted — *well*, I worked my
passage through cane, palmetto and vines, until I war tired — I haddent
hearn Jem's horn, and pushed on the harder to meet him; every
once and a while I'd think *hears the turn of the Lake,* but when I'd
git to the place, *thar it was* stretchin out big as ever. Once I thought
I hearn Jem's horn, but couldent quite make it out. I kept movin'; hours
passed and no Jem or end of the Lake; I'd seen lots of bar and panter
sign, lots of deer, and more swan, wild goose, and duck, than you
ever will see; but I paid no attention to 'em, as I 'spected I'd taken
some wrong arm of the Lake and war lost. It war gettin' towards
night, and I 'spected I'd have to sleep by myself, but you know I
diddent mind that, as I war used to it. But it war the first time in my
life that I'd bin lost, and that *did* pester me mightily. Well, sir, after
studyin awhile, I thought I'd better put back towards the camp, mighty
tired and disc raged. I then throw'd my gourd round to take a drink
of licker, an_ _ were *filled with water!* fact! — Thinks I, Chunkey, you
must have been *mighty* drunk last night; that made me sorter low
spirited like a 'oman, and my heart war weak as water. It had commenced gittin sorter dark; the wind were blowin' and groanin' through
the trees, and the black clouds were flyin', and I war goin' along sorter
oneasy and cussin', when *a panter yelled out, close to me!* I turned
with my gun cocked, but couldent see it; presently I hearn it agin, and
out it come, and then another! "Here's hell!" said I, takin' a crack
and missin' to a sartainty; and away they darted through the cane. I
drap'd my gun to load, and by the great Jackson, there warn't a full
load of powder in my gourd! — I loaded *mighty* carefully, and started
on to pick out some holler tree to sleep in. Every once and awhile I'd
git a glimpse of the panters on my trail. "Panters," says I, "I'll make a
child's bargain with you; if you will let *me* alone, *you* may *golong;* —

and if you don't here's a ball into the head of one of ye'er, and this knife! — *hush, if my knife warn't gone, I wish I may never taste bar's meat!* I raised my arm, trimblin' like a leaf, and says I, "Jem! — *I'll have your melt!"* Well, I *war* in trouble sure! — I thought I war on the *Tchule a Leta Lake,* and *witched!*

Well I did! Oh, you may larph, but jist imagin' *yourself* lost in the cane on Sky Lake, (the cane on Sky Lake *is some* — thirty miles long, from one to three miles wide, thick as the har on a dog's back, and about thirty feet high!) out of licker, out of powder, your knife gone, the ground kivered with snow, you very hungry and tired, *and two panters follerin' your trail,* and you'd think you was bewitched too!

Well, here they come, never lettin' on, but makin' arrangements to have my skalp that night; I never lettin' on, but detarmin'd they shouldent. The har had been standin' on my head for more nor an hour, and the sweat were gist *rollin'* off me, and that satisfied me a fight war a brewin' atween me and the panters! I stopped two or three times, thinkin' they's gone, but presently hear they'd come, creepin' along through the cane, and soon as they'd see me they stop, lay down, roll over and twirl their tails about like kittens playin'; I'd then shout, shake the cane, and away they'd go. Oh, they thought they had me! *In course they did,* and I detarmined with myself, if they *did let me go,* if they diddent attack an onarmed man, alone and lost, without licker, dogs, powder or knife, that the very fust time I got a panter up a tree, with my whole pack at the root, my licker gourd full, and I half full, my twelve-to-the-pound-yager loaded, and my knife in shavin' order, I'd let *him* go! Yes, *dam'd if I diddent!*

But what did *they* care? They'd no more feelin' than the devil! I know'd it woulddent do to risk a fight in the cane, and pushed on to find an open place whar I could make sure of my one load, and rely on my gun barrel arter. I soon found a place whar the cane drifted, and *thar* I determined to stand and fight it out! Presently here they come; and if a stranger had seen 'em, he'd a thought they were playin'! They'd jump and squat, and bend their backs, lay down and roll, and grin like puppys; — *they kept gittin' nearer and nearer,* and it wer gettin' dark, and I know'd I must let drive at the old *he,* 'afore it got so dark I coulddent see my sights; so I jist dropped on one knee to make sure, and when I raised my gun, I were all in a trimble! I know'd *that* woulddent do, and *ris!*

"You are witched, Chunkey, sure and sartin'," said I. Arter bracin' myself, I raised up agin and *fired!* One on 'em sprung into the air and gin a yell, and the other bounded towards me like a streak! Lightin' close to me, it squatted to the ground and commenced creepin' towards me — its years laid back, its eyes turnin' green, and sorter swimmin' round like, and the end of its tail twistin' like a snake. I felt light as a cork, and strong as a buffalo. I seen her commence slippin' her legs under her, and knew she were gwine to spring. I throw'd back my gun to gin it to her, as she come; the lick I aimed at her head struck across the shoulders and back, without doing any harm, *and she had me!* — Rip, rip, rip — and 'way went my blanket, coat, and britches. She sunk her teeth into my shoulder, her green eyes were close to mine, and the froth from her mouth were flyin' in my face!! *Moses!* how fast she *did* fight! I felt the warm blood runnin' down my side — I seen she were arter *my* throat! and with that I grabbed *hern,* and commenced pourin' it into her side with my fist, like cats-a-fightin! — Rip, rip, she'd take me, — diff, slam, bang, I'd gin it to her — she fightin' for her *supper,* I fightin' for my *life!* Why, in course it war an onequal fight, but she ris it! Well, we had it round and round, sometimes one, and then yother on top, she a growlin' and I a gruntin'! We had both commenced gittin' mighty tired, and presently she made a spring, *tryin' to git away!* Arter *that* thar warn't no mortal chance for her! Cause why she were whipped. I'd sorter been thinkin' about sayin'

"Now I lay me down to sleep,"

but I knowd if I commenced it would put her in heart, and she'd riddle me in a minit, and when *she* hollered *nuff,* I were glad to my shoe soles, and had sich confidence in whippin' the fight, that *I offered two to one on Chunkey,* but no takers!

"Oh, dam you," says I, a hittin' her a lick every time I spoke, "you are willin' to quit even and divide stakes, are you?" and then round and round we went agin! You could have hearn us blow a quarter, but presently she made a *big struggle* and broke my hold! I fell one way, and she the other! She darted into the cane, and that's the last time I ever hearn of *that* panter!!!

When I sorter come to myself, I war struttin' and *thunderin'* like a big he-gobler, and then I commenced examinin' to see what harm she'd done me; I war bit powerful bad in the shoulder and arm — *jist look at them scars!* — and I were cut into solid whip strings; but when I found thar warn't no danger of its *killin'* me, I set in to cussin'. "Oh, you ain't dead yet, Chunkey!" says I, "if you are sorter wusted, and have whipped a panter in a fair fight, and *no* gougin';" and then I *cock a doodle dood* a spell, for joy!

When I looked around, *thar* sot the old he, a lickin' the blood from his breast! I'd shot him right through the breast, but sorter slantin-dickler, breakin' his shoulder blade into a perfect smash. I walked up to him —

"Howdy, panter? how do you do? how *is* missis panter, and the little panters? how is your consarns in gineral? Did you ever hearn tell of the man they calls 'Chunkey'? born in Kaintuck and raised in Missississippi? death on a bar, and *smartly* in a panter fight? If you diddent, look, for *I'm he!* I kills bar, whips panters in a fair fight; I walks the water, I out-bellars the thunder, and when I gets hot, the Mississippi hides itself! I — I — Oh, you thought you *had* me, did you? — *dam you!* But *you* are a gone sucker, now. I'll have your melt, if I never gits home, so" —

Look out, Capting! here's the place! make the skift fast to that cyprus log. Take care them oars, Abe! Spring out and oncupple the dogs, and take car they don't knock them guns overboard. Now, Capting, we will have a deer movin' afore you can tell who's your daddy.

George Wilkins Kendall

(1809-1867)

❧❧ A serious and skillful newspaper man, George Kendall was never so serious that he could forgo the occasion for a laugh. He was born near Amherst, New Hampshire, into a family of New England Puritan ancestry, apprenticed to a printer, and employed by Horace Greeley on the *New Yorker,* a weekly literary miscellany, before he began his journalistic career in the Southwest. By 1835 he was in New Orleans on the *True American;* and on January 25, 1837, in partnership with Francis A. Lumsden, he brought out the first issue of the New Orleans *Picayune.*

The *Picayune* aimed at a mass circulation. To make it acceptable to the largest possible number of readers, the editors avoided political controversy and sought what would be called at a later date "human interest stories" and "local color." For example, Kendall's reports of the police courts were more often bantering than grim. His audacity and irreverence irritated some readers but the *Picayune* circulation mounted. Nor did he neglect factual reporting, another attraction in an age when a newspaper article was likely to be more effusive than substantial.

In 1841 Kendall joined an expedition organized by General Mirabeau B. Lamar, president of Texas, ostensibly to improve commercial relations between Texas and the territories to the west but also with an eye to extending Texas sovereignty. Uneasy Mexican authorities captured the some three hundred soldiers and civilians who made up the party and marched them to Mexico City. After seven months as a prisoner, during which Kendall underwent privations including confinement in a "Black Hole" and a lazaretto, he returned to New Orleans, his energy and sense of humor intact. His *Narrative of the Texan Santa Fé Expedition* was a popular success.

The *Picayune* had long agitated against Mexico. When war broke out in May 1846, Kendall immediately went overland to Point Isabel near the mouth of the Rio Grande where General Zachary Taylor was encamped. He arrived well ahead of the other journalists and set up a courier service which utilized horsemen and steamboats to outstrip his rivals and often official dispatches as well. His reports and his military exploits made him the best-known newspaper correspondent in the country. In 1848 Kendall went to Europe where he wrote *The War between the United States and Mexico* (1851). Though he retained an interest in the *Picayune,* he moved to Texas and grew rich from the sheep ranch he established there.

Kendall was regarded as witty and convivial in his early newspaper days in New York, and even his account of the Santa Fé disaster has so many light moments and so much prankishness that he felt the need to apologize in the preface. To a great extent his success as a journalist stemmed from his ability to deal graphically with the facts, his eye for the "peculiar" which imparted the flavor of region and individual alike, and his sense of the ridiculous.

TEXT: "A Superb Wild Horse" from *Narrative of the Texan Santa Fé Expedition* (New York, 1844); "Bill Dean, the Texan Ranger" from *Spirit of the Times,* July 11, 1846.

A Superb Wild Horse

. . . .

There were two great advantages in marching with the spies: one was the opportunity of meeting with more exciting adventure, while the other was the brisk pace at which we travelled, being a steady trot, instead of the snail-like movement of the wagons. On the day when I joined them, after a pleasant ride of some ten miles, we arrived at a small creek of fresh and running water, a delicious treat on a hot prairie march. It was a beautiful stream, overhung with grape and other vines now in the full richness of summer verdure. In many places the vines had completely crossed the creek, thus forming a delightful natural arbour, and under this cool shade the restless waters swept along to mingle with the hot and brackish river, now some two or three miles to the south. After finding an easy crossing-place, a man was sent back to the command as a guide, while we unsaddled and turned our horses loose to graze, and then threw ourselves upon the green carpeting of grass under the shade-trees, to enjoy a quiet noonday siesta.

We scarcely had time to establish ourselves comfortably before three or four mustangs were seen approaching at a rapid gallop. Ever and anon they would halt for a moment, throw up their heads as if to scan us more closely, and then, as though not satisfied with the scrutiny, would again approach at the same rapid pace. It may be that they could not see us while reclining under the shade-trees, or mistook our animals for some of their own wild companions; be this as it may, they approached within a few hundred yards, wheeling and dashing about with all the joyousness of unrestrained freedom, and occasionally stopping to examine our encampment more closely. The leader was a bright bay, with long and glossy black tail and mane.

With the most dashing and buoyant action he would trot around our camp, and throw aloft his beautifully-formed head, as if, after the manner of some ringleted school-girl, to toss the truant hair from his eyes. Then he would lash his silken tail, shake his flowing mane in pride, and eye us with looks that plainly told his confidence in his powers of flight should danger or treachery be lurking in our vicinity. I had formed a strong attachment for my own powerful bay, for he was gentle as a house-dog, and would run all day if necessity required it; yet I would instantly have "swapped" even him for this wild horse of the prairies, with no other knowledge of his qualities than what I could discover at the distance of a hundred and fifty or two hundred yards.

After gambolling about us for some little time, his bright eyes apparently gleaming with satisfaction, as if conscious that we were watching and admiring his showy points, he suddenly wheeled, and, in a canter, placed himself at a more prudent distance. Then he turned again to take another look, curved his beautiful neck, once more tossed his head, half timidly, half in sport, pawed the ground playfully, and again dashed off. Several times he turned to take still another look at our encampment, and even in the far distance we could distinguish his proud and expanded nostrils, his bright, flashing eyes, and the elastic movements of his symmetrical limbs as he playfully pranced and curvetted about. I watched him until he was but a speck upon the prairie, and then turned from gazing with regret that he was not mine.

The Indians and Mexicans have a way of capturing mustangs by running up on their fleetest and most untiring horses and noosing them with the *lariat*. The white hunters have also a method, which is often successful, of taking the wild horses. It is called *creasing,* and is done by shooting them with a rifle-ball upon a particular cord or tendon in the neck, immediately under the mane. If the ball takes effect precisely in the right spot the animal falls benumbed, and without the power to move for several minutes, when he is easily secured. Should it strike too low, the horse is still able to run off, but eventually dies. An attempt was made to *crease* the magnificent steed I have mentioned; but it was impossible to approach near enough to shoot with accuracy, and to endanger his life would have been a wanton act, which the most eager hunter among us would not have committed. When our provisions became scarce several of these animals were shot for their flesh. It seems repugnant to the feelings to eat horseflesh; but the meat is tender and finely flavoured, and a three-year-old mustang is really better food than either buffalo or common beef. . . .

Bill Dean, the Texan Ranger

Rare wags may be found among the Texas Volunteers, yet the funniest fellow of all is a happy-go-lucky chap named Bill Dean, one of Chevallier's spy company, and said to be one of the best "seven up" players in all Texas. While at Corpus Christi, a lot of us were sitting out on the stoop of the Kinney House, early one morning, when along came Bill Dean. He did not know a single soul in the crowd, although he knew we were all bound for the Rio Grande; yet the fact that the regular formalities of an introduction had not been gone through with, did not prevent his stopping short in his walk and accosting us. His speech, or harangue, or whatever it may be termed, will lose much in the telling, yet I will endeavor to put it upon paper in as good shape as possible.

"Oh, yes," said he, with a knowing leer of the eye: "oh, yes; all going down among the robbers on the Rio Grande, are you? Fine time *you'll* have, over the left. I've been there, myself, and done what a great many of you won't do — I come back: but if I didn't see nateral h—ll — in August at that — I *am* a teapot. Lived eight days on one poor hawk and three blackberries — couldn't kill a prairie rat on the whole route to save us from starvation. The ninth day come, and we struck a small streak of good luck — a horse give out and broke down, plumb in the centre of an open prairie — not a stick big enough to tickle a rattlesnake with, let alone killing him. Just had time to save the critter by shootin' him, and that was all, for in three minutes longer he'd have died a nateral death. It didn't take us long to butcher him, nor cut off some chunks of meat and stick 'em on our ramrods; but the cookin' was another matter. I piled up a heap of prairie grass, for it was high and dry, and sot it on fire; but it flashed up like powder, and went out as quick. But —"

"But," put in one of his hearers, "but how did you cook your horse-meat after that?"

"How?"

"Yes, how?"

"Why, the fire caught the high grass close by, and the wind carried the flames streakin' across the prairie. I followed up the fire, holding my chunk of meat directly over the blaze, and the way we went it was a caution to anything short of locomotive doin's. Once in a while a little flurry of wind would come along, and the fire would get a few yards the start; but I'd brush upon her, lap her with my chunk, and then we'd have it again, nip and chuck. You never seed such a tight race — it was beautiful."

"Very, we've no doubt," ejaculated one of the listeners, interrupting the mad wag just in season to give him a little breath: "but did you cook your meat in the end?"

"Not bad I didn't. I chased that d——d fire a mile and a half, the almightiest hardest race you ever heer'd tell of, and never give it up until I run right plumb into a wet marsh: there the fire and chunk of horsemeat came out even — a dead heat, especially the meat."

"But wasn't it cooked?" put in another of the listeners.

"Cooked! — no — just crusted over a little. You don't cook broken down horse flesh very easy no how, but when it come to chasing up a prairie fire with a chunk of it, I don't know which is the toughest, the meat or the job. You'd have laughed to split yourself to have seen me in that race — to see the fire leave me at times, and then to see me brushin' up on her agin, humpin' and movin' myself as though I was runnin' agin some of those big ten mile an hour Gildersleeves in the old States. But I'm a goin' over to Jack Haynes's to get a cocktail and some breakfast — I'll see you all down among the robbers on the Rio Grande."

And so saying, Bill Dean stalked off. I saw the chap this morning in front of a Mexican *fonda* trying his Spanish with a *Greaser*, and endeavoring to convince him that he was a "d——d robber." Such is one of Bill Dean's stories — if I could only make it as effective on paper as he did in the telling, it would draw a laugh from those fond of the ludicrous.

Joseph M. Field

(1810-1856)

✿ Admiring contemporaries of Joseph M. Field thought that he spread himself too widely for his own good. A successful actor, playwright, and journalist, he divided his talents between the stage and the newspaper office.

Field was born in Dublin, Ireland, and was brought to Baltimore and later New York by his family when he was a small child. He studied law briefly but by 1827 was acting at the Tremont Theater in Boston; he may have been the "Mr. Field . . . from the Tremont" who, with several other young Boston actors, was with the Caldwell Company in New Orleans in 1829. In 1830 he made his New York debut at the Park Theater. By 1832 he was filling a successful engagement at the American Theater in New Orleans. Under the management of Sol Smith, he traveled the Southwestern circuit, playing in Cincinnati, St. Louis, Mobile, Montgomery, and smaller cities. According to the theatrical manager, Noah Miller Ludlow, with whom he once toured, Field originally thought of himself as a tragedian and favored Shakespearian roles but found that he was best at "eccentric comedy."

After his marriage to Eliza Riddle, Sol Smith's leading lady, the two played the Southwestern theaters together. In 1839 they were once more in New Orleans. Field wrote a number of humorous sketches and versified comments on current affairs for the New Orleans *Picayune,* on which his brother, Matthew, a former actor, was a reporter. A year later he went to Europe as special correspondent for the *Picayune.* In 1844 Field was associated in the founding and editing of the St. Louis *Reveille,* a newspaper notable for its sprightliness and originality. When the *Reveille* ceased publication after six years, Field returned to the stage, managing theaters in Mobile and St. Louis.

Among Field's plays are *Victoria* (1838), which features the British queen and James Gordon Bennett; *Such As It Is* (1842), a social satire; *Family Ties* (1846), a comedy which won a $500 prize; *Oregon, or the Disputed Territory* (1846), a topical play on the Northwestern boundary dispute with Great Britain; and *Job and His Children* (1852), a religious drama. As a literary figure he is best remembered for the sketches he wrote for the *Reveille,* some of which were collected in *The Drama in Pokerville; the Bench and Bar of Jurytown, and Other Stories.* Field also made a contribution to the growth of the Mike Fink legend, though he asserted that he sought to dispel some of the *"mythic* haze" already gathering about the historic figure. His story "The Death of Mike Fink," first printed in the *Reveille* of October 21, 1844, challenges the account of Morgan Neville, published in a gift book in 1829, on the basis of information supplied by Colonel Charles Keemle, co-editor of the *Reveille.* Fink was killed on the Yellowstone River in 1823, and Keemle had visited the area the same year. Field expanded his original tale into a melodramatic and at times sentimental novel, *Mike Fink, the Last of the Boatmen,* which was printed serially in the *Reveille* in June 1847.

TEXT: "Honey Run," "Stopping to Wood," and "Death of Mike Fink" from *The Drama in Pokerville* (Philadelphia, 1847); "Kicking a Yankee" from *A Quarter Race in Kentucky,* ed. W. T. Porter (Philadelphia, 1854).

Honey Run

"Mr. Douglass, you've a mighty small chance of legs, there, any how!"
Judge Douglass's Story.

The "gentleman from Illinois" is not the only gentleman whose *legs* have led him into embarrassment! A political friend of ours, equally happy in his manners, if not in his party, among the Missouri constituency, found himself, while canvassing the state one summer for Congress, in even a *more* peculiarly perplexing predicament than the Illinois judge.

There is a spot, in the south-western part of this state, known as the *Fiery Fork of Honey Run* — a delicious locality, no doubt, as the *run* of "honey" is, of course, accompanied by a corresponding flow of "milk," and a mixture of milk and honey, or, at any rate, honey and "Peach" is the evidence of sublunary contentment, every place where they have preaching!

"Honey Run" is further christianized by the presence of an extremely hospitable family, whose mansion, comprising *one apartment* — neither more nor less — is renowned for being never shut against the traveller, and so our friend found it during the chill morning air, at the expense of a rheumatism in his shoulder — its numerous unaffected cracks and spaces clearly showing that dropping the latch was a useless formality. The venerable host and hostess, in their one apartment, usually enjoy the society of two sons, four daughters, sundry dogs and "niggers," and as many lodgers as may deem it prudent to risk the somewhat equivocal allotment of sleeping partners. On the night in question, our friend, after a hearty supper of ham and eggs, and a canvass of the *Fiery Forkers* — the old lady having pointed out his bed — felt very weary, and only looked for an opportunity to "turn in," though the mosquitoes were trumping all sorts of wrath, and no net appeared to *bar* them. The dogs flung themselves along the floor, or again rose, restlessly, and sought the door-step; the "niggers" stuck their feet in the yet warm ashes; the old man stripped, unscrupulously, and sought his share of the one collapsed-looking pillow, and the sons cavalierly followed his example, leaving the old woman, "gals," and "stranger," to settle any question of delicacy that might arise.

The candidate yawned, looked at his bed, went to the door, looked at the daughters; finally, in downright recklessness, seating himself upon "the downy," and pulling off his coat. Well, he *pulled* off his coat, and he folded his coat, and then he yawned, and then he whistled, and then he called the old lady's attention to the fact, that it would *never* do to sleep in his muddy trowsers; and then he "undid" his vest, and then he whistled again, and then, suddenly, an idea of her lodger's possible embarrassment seemed to flash upon the old woman, and she cried —

"*Gals,* jest turn your backs round 'till the *stranger* gits into bed."

The backs were turned, and the stranger *did* get into bed in "less than no time," when the hostess again spoke:

"Reckon, stranger, as you ain't used to us, you'd better *kiver up* till the *gals* undress, hadn't you?"

By this time our friend's sleepy fit was over, and, though he did "kiver up," as desired, some how or other the old counterpane was equally kind in hiding his blushes, and favoring his sly glances. The nymphs were soon stowed away, for there were neither bustles to unhitch nor corsets to unlace, when their mamma, evidently anxious not to smother her guest, considerately relieved him.

"You can un*kiver* now, stranger; I'm *married folks,* and you ain't afeard o' *me,* I reckon!"

The stranger happened to be "married folks" himself; he un*kivered* and turned his back with true connubial indifference, as far as the ancient lady was concerned; but, with regard to the "*gals*," he declares that his half-raised curiosity inspired the most tormenting dreams of *mermaids* that ever he experienced.

Stopping to Wood

In spite of the magic changes which have been wrought in the "way of doing things" upon the western waters, the primitive mode of "wooding" from the bank remains unaltered — as a sort of vagabond Indian in the midst of a settlement — as the gallows does in the light of civilization. The same rude plank is "shoved" ashore, the same string of black and white straggle through the mud to the "pile," the same weary waste of time exists as was the case twenty years ago. Steamers have grown from pigmies to giants, speed has increased from a struggle to a "rush," yet the conception of a ready loaded truck, or a burden-swinging crane — despatching a "cord" for every shoulder load, appears not to have entered the head of either wood dealer or captain.

At the same time, though the present mode is to be condemned as "behind the time;" as tedious, slovenly, and unnecessary, there are occasions when "stopping to wood" is an event of positive interest and excitement. Passed over be the fine sun-shiney morning when, jogging along — nothing behind — nothing before, the passengers lounging about — heels up, or heads down — the unnoticed bell gives the signal for "wood," and the boat draws listlessly alongside of the "pile." Equally unregarded be the rainy day, when, mud to the knees and drenched to the skin, the steaming throng, slipping and plashing, drop their backloads, with a *"whew!"* and fail to find, even in the whisky barrel, a laugh or a "break down." But *not* so the star-lit evening in June, when, the water at a "good stage," and out for a "brag trip," with a rival boat behind, and the furnaces roaring for "more" the more they are fed, the signal is given and a faint flicker on the distant bank beacons the hungry monster towards its further supply of fuel. From New Orleans thus far on the trip up, the two boats, of nearly equal speed, have alternately passed each other during the stop to "wood," showing no gain of consequence on the part of either, and the grand struggle has been as it at present is, to "rush" the operation so as to get a start before being overtaken. The bank is reached — the boat made fast — gangways are formed — "Lively! men, lively!" cries the mate, and while the upper cabins pour out their crowds upon the boiler deck, the "hands," and the swarms of wild-looking passengers below (obliged by contract) dash ashore among the brush. Now ensues a scene that tasks description! The fire, augmented by piles of the driest wood, crimsons the tangled forest! Black and white, many of them stripped to their waist, though others, more careful, protect their skins by ripping and form-ing *cowls* of empty salt sacks, attack the lengthened pile, and amid laugh, shout, curse, and the scarcely intermitting scream of the iron chimneys, (tortured by the still making steam,) remove it to the boat.

"Lively, men, lively!" rings the cry, and lively, lively is the impulse inspired by it! See that swart, gigantic negro, his huge shoulder hidden beneath a pyramid of wood, hurl to the deck his load, cut a caper along the plank, and, leaping back, seize a flaming brand to whirl it round his head in downright enjoyment! "Lively! lively!" Laugh, shout, whoop, and the pile is rapidly disappearing, when a cry is heard from the "hurricane deck" —

"Here she comes, round the point!"

'Tis the rival steamer, sure enough; and once more she will pass during this detention. Now dash both mate and captain ashore to "rush" the matter. The bell is struck for starting, as if to compel impossibility; the accumulated steam is let off in brief, impatient screams, and the passengers, sharing the wild excitement, add their cries.

"Passed again, by thunder!" "We've got enough wood!" "Leave the rest!" &c. In the meantime, round the point below, sweeps the up-comer — all lights and sparks — moving over the water like a rushing fire-palace! Now her "blow" is heard, like a suppressed curse of struggle and defiance, and now, nearing the bank where lies her rival, a sort of frenzy seizes on the latter —

"Tumble it in!" "Rush her!" "D—n the rest!" "You've got enough!" *Ra-a-a-s-h!* goes the steam; the engine, "working off," thunders below; — again, the bell rings, and the hurly burly on shore is almost savage. At length, as the coming boat is hard on astern, the signal tap is given, "all hands aboard!" The lines are let go, the planks are shoved in by the negroes who are themselves drawn from the water with them, and amid a chaos of timber, a whirl of steam, and a crash of machinery, once more she is under weigh. The struggle is to leave the bank before she can be passed, and fuel, flame, and phrensy, seemingly unite to secure the object; barrels of com-bustibles are thrust into the furnaces, while, before the doors, the "firemen," naked and screaming, urge their wild efforts!

"Here she is, along-side!" and now the struggle indeed is startling; the one endeavouring to shoot out from the bank across the bows of the other, and *she,* authorized by river custom, holding her way, the consequences of collision resting alone on her imprudent competitor. Roar for roar — scream for scream — huzza for huzza — but now, the inner boat apparently gaining, a turn of her antagonist's wheel leaves her no option but to be *run into* or turn again towards the bank! A hundred oaths and screams reply to this manœuvre, but *on she comes* — on, on, — a moment more and she strikes! With a shout of rage the defeated pilot turns her head — at the same moment snatching down his rifle and discharging it into the pilot-house of his opponent! Fury has now seized the thoughts of all, and the iron throats of the steamers are less hideous than the human ones beneath them. The wheel for a moment neglected, the thwarted monster has now "taken a sheer in the wild current," and, beyond the possibility of prevention, is driving on to the bank! A cry of terror rises aloft — the throng rush aft — the steam, every valve set free — makes the whole forest shiver, and, amid the fright, the tall chimneys, caught by the giant trees, are wrenched and torn out like tusks from a recoiling mastadon.

"That's a stretcher," will cry out some readers, and such a scene is not likely to be witnessed *now,* but the writer will not soon forget that such he bore a part in, some ten years ago, and that the captain, when asked what he thought of it, replied, "Well, I think we've got h—ll, any how!"

Death of Mike Fink

"The Last of the Boatmen" has not become altogether a *mythic* personage. There be around us those who still remember him as one of flesh and blood, as well as of proportions simply human, albeit he lacked not somewhat of the *heroic* in stature, as well as in being a "perfect terror" to people!

As regards Mike, it has not yet become that favourite question of doubt — "Did such a being really live?" Nor have we heard the skeptic inquiry — "Did such a being really die?" But his death in half a dozen different ways and places has been asserted, and this, we take it, is the first gathering of the *mythic* haze — that shadowy and indistinct enlargement of outline, which, deepening through long ages, invests distinguished mortality with the sublimer attributes of the hero and the demi-god. Had Mike lived in "early Greece," his flat-boat feats would, doubtless, in poetry, have rivalled those of Jason, in his ship; while in Scandinavian legends, he would have been a river-god, to a certainty! The Sea-kings would have sacrificed to him every time they "crossed the bar," on their return; and as for Odin, himself, he would be duly advised, as far as any interference went, to "lay low and keep dark, or, *pre*-haps," &c.

The story of Mike Fink, including *a* death, has been beautifully told by the late Morgan Neville, of Cincinnati, a gentleman of the highest literary taste, as well as of the most amiable and polished manners. "The Last of the Boatmen," as his sketch is entitled, is unexceptionable in style, and, we believe, in *fact,* with one exception, and that is, the statement as to the manner and place of Fink's death. He did *not die* on the Arkansas, but at Fort Henry, near the mouth of the Yellow Stone. Our informant is Mr. Chas. Keemle of this paper,* who held a command in the neighbourhood, at the time, and to whom every circumstance connected with the affair is most familiar. We give the story as it is told by himself.

In the year 1822, steamboats having left the "keels" and "broad-horns" entirely "out of sight," and Mike having, in consequence, fallen from his high estate — that of being "a little bit the almightiest man on the river, *any* how" — after a term of idleness, frolic and desperate rowdyism, along the different towns, he, at St. Louis, entered the service of the Mountain Fur Company, raised by our late fellow-citizen Gen. W. H. Ashley, as a trapper and hunter; and in that capacity was he employed by Major Henry, in command of the fort at the mouth of Yellow Stone river, when the occurrence took place of which we write.

Mike, with many generous qualities, was always a reckless dare-devil; but, at this time, advancing in years and decayed in influence, above all become a victim of whisky, he was morose and desperate in the extreme. There was a government regulation which forbade the free use of alcohol at the trading posts on the Missouri river, and this was a continual source of quarrel between the men and the commandant, Major Henry, — on the part of Fink, particularly. One of his freaks was to march with his rifle into the fort, and demand a supply of spirits. Argument was fruitless, force not to be thought of, and when, on being positively denied, Mike drew up his rifle and sent a ball through the cask, deliberately walked up and filled his can, while his particular "boys" followed his example, all that could be done was to look upon the matter as one of his "queer ways," and that was the end of it.

This state of things continued for some time; Mike's temper and exactions growing more unbearable every day, until, finally, a "split" took place, not only between himself and the commandant, but many others in the fort, and the unruly boatman swore he would not live among them. Followed only by a youth named Carpenter, whom he had brought up, and for whom he felt a rude but strong attachment, he prepared a sort of cave in the river's bank, furnished it with a supply of whisky, and, with his companion, *turned in* to pass the winter, which was then closing upon them. In this place he buried himself, sometimes unseen for weeks, his *protege* providing what else was *necessary* beyond the whisky. At length attempts were used, on the part of those in the fort, to withdraw Carpenter from Fink; foul

* St. Louis Reveille. [Author's note]

insinuations were made as to the nature of their connection; the youth was twitted with being a mere slave, &c., all which (Fink heard of it in spite of his retirement) served to breed distrust between the two, and though they did not separate, much of their cordiality ceased. The winter wore away in this sullen state of torpor; spring came with its reviving influences, and to celebrate the season, a supply of alcohol was procured, and a number of his acquaintances from the fort coming to "rouse out" Mike, a desperate "frolic," of course, ensued.

There were river yarns, and boatmen songs, and "nigger breakdowns," interspersed with wrestling-matches, jumping, laugh, and yell, the can circulating freely, until Mike became somewhat mollified.

"I tell you what it is, boys," he cried, "the fort's a skunk-hole, and I rather live with the *bars* than stay in it. Some on ye's bin trying to part me and my boy, that I love like my own cub — but no matter. Maybe he's *pi*soned against me; but, Carpenter, (striking the youth heavily on the shoulder,) I took you by the hand when it had forgotten the touch of a father's or a mother's — you know me to be a man, and you ain't a going to turn out a dog!"

Whether it was that the youth fancied something insulting in the manner of the appeal, or not, we can't say; but it was not responded to very warmly, and a reproach followed from Mike. However, they drank together, and the frolic went on, until Mike, filling his can, walked off some forty yards, placed it upon his head, and called to Carpenter to take his rifle.

This wild feat of shooting cans off each other's head was a favourite one with Mike — himself and "boy" generally winding up a hard frolic with this savage, but deeply-meaning proof of continued confidence; — as for risk, their eagle eyes and iron nerves defied the might of whisky. After their recent alienation, a doubly generous impulse, without doubt, had induced Fink to propose and subject himself to the test.

Carpenter had been drinking wildly, and with a boisterous laugh snatched up his rifle. All present had seen the parties "shoot," and this desperate aim, instead of alarming, was merely made a matter of wild jest.

"Your grog is spilt, for ever, Mike!"

"Kill the old varmint, young 'un!"

"What'll his skin bring in St. Louis?" &c. &c.

Amid a loud laugh, Carpenter raised his piece — even the jesters remarked that he was unsteady, — crack!" — the can fell, — a loud shout, — but, instead of a smile of pleasure, a dark frown settled upon the face of Fink! He made no motion except to clutch his rifle as though he would have crushed it, and there he stood, gazing at the youth strangely! Various shades of passion crossed his features — surprise, rage, suspicion — but at length they composed themselves into a sad expression; the ball had grazed the top of his head, cutting the scalp, and the thought of treachery had set his heart on fire.

There was a loud call upon Mike to know what he was waiting for, in which Carpenter joined, pointing to the can upon his head and bidding him fire, if he knew how!

"Carpenter, my son," said the boatman, "I taught you to shoot differently from that *last* shot! You've *missed* once, but you won't again!"

He fired, and his ball, crashing through the forehead of the youth, laid him a corpse amid his, as suddenly hushed, companions!

Time wore on — many at the fort spoke darkly of the deed. Mike Fink had never been known to miss his aim — he had grown afraid of Carpenter — he had murdered him! While this feeling was gathering against him, the unhappy boatman lay in his cave, shunning both sympathy and sustenance. He spoke to none — when he did come forth, 'twas as a spectre, and only to haunt the grave of his "boy," or, if he did break silence, 'twas to burst into a paroxysm of rage against the enemies who had "turned his boy's heart from him!"

At the fort was a man by the name of Talbott, the gunsmith of the station: he was very loud and bitter in his denunciations of the "murderer," as he called Fink, which, finally, reaching the ears of the latter, filled him with the most violent passion, and he swore that he would take the life of his defamer. This threat was almost forgotten, when one day, Talbott, who was at work in his shop, saw Fink enter the fort, his first visit since the death of Carpenter. Fink approached; he was careworn, sick, and wasted; there was no anger in his bearing, but he carried his rifle, (had he ever gone without it?) and the gunsmith was not a coolly brave man; moreover, his life had been threatened.

"Fink," cried he, snatching up a pair of pistols from his bench, "don't approach me — if you do, you're a dead man!"

"Talbott," said the boatman, in a sad voice, "you needn't be afraid; you've done me wrong — I'm come to talk to you about — Carpenter — my boy!"

He continued to advance, and the gunsmith again called to him:

"Fink! I know you; if you come three steps nearer, I'll fire, by —!"

Mike carried his rifle across his arm, and made no hostile demonstration, except in gradually getting nearer — *if* hostile his aim was.

"Talbott, you've accused me of murdering — my boy — Carpenter — that I raised from a child — that I loved like a son — that I can't live without! I'm not mad with you *now*, but you must let me show you that I *couldn't* do it — that I'd rather died than done it — that you've wronged me —"

By this time he was within a few steps of the door, and Talbott's agitation became extreme. Both pistols were pointed at Fink's breast, in expectation of a spring from the latter.

"By the Almighty above us, Fink, I'll fire — I don't want to speak to you now — don't put your foot on that step — don't."

Fink did put his foot on the step, and the same moment fell heavily within it, receiving the contents of both barrels in his breast! His last and only words were,

"I didn't mean to kill my boy!"

Poor Mike! we are satisfied with our senior's conviction that you did *not* mean to kill him. Suspicion of treachery, doubtless, entered his mind, but cowardice and murder never dwelt there.

A few weeks after this event, Talbott himself perished in an attempt to cross the Missouri river in a skiff.

Kicking a Yankee

A very handsome friend of ours, who a few weeks ago was *poked* out of a comfortable office up the river, has betaken himself to Bangor, for a time, to recover from the wound inflicted upon his feelings by our "unprincipled and immolating administration."

Change of air must have had an instantaneous effect upon his spirits, for, from Galena, he writes us an amusing letter, which, among other things, tells us of a desperate quarrel that took place on board of the boat between a real live dandy tourist, and a real live Yankee settler. The latter trod on the toes of the former; whereupon the former threatened to "Kick out of the cabin" the latter.

"You'll kick me out of this cabing?"

"Yes, sir, I'll kick you out of this cabin!"

"You'll kick *me*, Mr. *Hitchcock*, out of this cabing?"

"Yes, sir, I'll kick *you*, Mr. Hitchcock!"

"Wal, I guess," said the Yankee, very coolly, after being perfectly satisfied that it was himself who stood in such imminent peril of assault — "I guess, since you talk of kicking, you've never heard me tell about old Bradley and my mare, there, to hum?"

"No, sir, nor do I wish —"

"Wal, guess it won't set you back much, any how, as kicking's generally best to be considered on. You see old Bradley is one of these sanctimonious, long-faced hypocrites, who put on a religious suit every Sabbath morning, and with a good deal of screwing, manage to keep it on till after sermon in the afternoon; and as I was a Universalist, he allers picked me out as a subject for religious conversation — and the darned hypocrite would talk about heaven, hell, and the devil — the crucifixion and prayer, without ever winking. Wal, he had an old roan mare that would jump over any fourteen-rail fence in Illinois, and open any door in my barn that hadn't a padlock on it. Tu or three times I found her in my stable, and I told Bradley about it, and he was 'very sorry' — 'an unruly animal' — 'would watch her,' and a hull lot of such things, all said in a very serious manner, with a face twice as long as old Deacon Farrar's on Sacrament day. I knew all the time he was lying, and so I watched him and his old roan tu; and for three nights regular, old roan came to my stable about bedtime, and just at daylight Bradley would come, bridle her, and ride off. I then just took my old mare down to a blacksmith's shop, and had some shoes made with 'corks' about four inches long, and had 'em nailed on to her hind feet. Your heels, mister, ain't nuthing tu 'em. I took her home, give her about ten feet halter, and tied her right in the centre of the stable, fed her well with oats about nine o'clock, and after taking a good smoke, went to bed, knowing that my old mare was a truth-telling animal, and that she'd give a good report of herself in the morning. I hadn't got fairly to sleep before the old 'oman hunched me and wanted to know what on airth was the matter out at the stable. Says I, 'Go tu sleep, Peggy, it is nothing but Kate — she is kicking off flies, I guess!' Purty soon she hunched me agin, and says she, 'Mr. Hitchcock, du git up and see what in the world is the matter with Kate, for she is kicking most powerfully.' 'Lay still, Peggy, Kate will take care of herself, I guess.' Wal, the next morning, about daylight, Bradley, with bridle in hand, cum to the stable, as true as the book of Genesis; when he saw the old roan's sides, starn, and head, he cursed and swore worse than you did, mister, when I came down on your toes. Arter breakfast that morning Joe Davis cum to my house, and says he, 'Bradley's old roan is nearly dead — she's cut all to pieces and can scarcely move.' 'I want to know,' says I, 'how on airth did it happen?' Now Joe Davis was a member of the same church with Bradley, and whilst we were talking, up cum that everlastin' hypocrite, and says he, 'Mr. Hitchcock, my old roan is ruined!' 'Du tell,' says I. 'She is cut all to pieces,' says he; 'do you know whether she was in your stable, Mr. Hitchcock, last night?' Wal, mister, with this I let out: 'Do I *know* it?' — (the Yankee here, in illustration, made a sudden advance upon the dandy, who made way for him unconsciously, as it were) — 'Do I know it, you no-souled, shad-bellied, squash-headed, old night-owl you! — you hay-hookin', corn-cribbin', fodder-fudgin', cent-shavin', whitlin'-of-nuthin' you! — Kate kicks like a mere dumb beast, but I've reduced the thing to a *science!'* " The Yankee had not ceased to advance, or the dandy, in his astonishment, to retreat; and now, the motion of the latter being accelerated by an apparent demonstration on the part of the former to "suit the action to the word," he found himself in the "social hall," tumbling backwards over a pile of baggage, and tearing the knees of his pants as he scrambled up, a perfect scream of laughter stunning him from all sides. The defeat was total: — a few moments afterwards he was seen dragging his own trunk ashore, while Mr. *Hitch*cock finished his story on the boiler deck.

Charles F. M. Noland

(1810-1858)

🐾 As "Pete Whetstone of Devil's Fork" and "N. of Arkansas,"
Colonel Charles Fenton Mercer Noland wrote more than two hundred Southwestern sketches for the New York *Spirit of the Times*.
After his discharge from the United States Military Academy for aca-
demic deficiency, Noland joined his father, who had moved from
Virginia to Arkansas, and was put to reading law in the office of
another Virginian, a judge at Batesville. He made rapid progress in
his studies and in acclimating himself to his new surroundings, particularly the woods, streams, and race tracks. By 1829 he was prac-
ticing law, trying his hand at land speculation, and contributing travel
sketches to the Little Rock *Arkansas Advocate*. He also became involved in politics and attacked Governor John Pope in a newspaper
article. The governor's nephew responded by publicly insulting Noland, who reluctantly challenged him to a duel and killed him.

Restless and unsettled, Noland considered an offer from Sam Hous-
ton who required "a companion of intelligence, of honor, and of first
rate moral and physical courage" for a mysterious enterprise in Texas.
He was diverted from this scheme by the possibility of a political
appointment. An Indian uprising in the Northwest led to his obtaining a commission as a first lieutenant in the United States Mounted
Rangers, recruited for service in the Black Hawk War. His assign-
ments in Illinois, the Michigan Territory, and St. Louis proved less
exciting than he had hoped, though he sent lively reports to the *Arkansas Advocate*. Disappointed by his failure to be promoted and
suffering from an attack of consumption, he requested a furlough in
1834. Except for intermittent recruiting duty and a commission as a
lieutenant colonel in the Arkansas militia, his military career was
over. He continued his interest in politics, breaking with the Democratic Party though retaining his personal admiration for Andrew
Jackson. As a member of the minority Whig Party, he was elected to
the first Arkansas legislature in 1836 and was returned for three subsequent terms; he edited and contributed editorials to several Whig
newspapers; and he held various appointive offices. For the duration
of his life he bred horses and followed the races, raised cotton, specu-
lated in land, and enjoyed the friendship of such politicians, sports-
men, and journalists as Henry Clay, Robert Y. Hayne, Wade Hamp-
ton, George W. Kendall, and Thomas Bangs Thorpe.

Noland was one of the earliest and most prolific writers for William T. Porter's *Spirit of the Times*. His first letter, written in 1836,

is a general survey of horse breeding and training in the South. Five others that year deal with racing and hunting. But as his contributions increased, they became more complex. He included picturesque detail which interested others than hunters and horsemen, added bits of local color and tongue-in-cheek exaggeration, sketched in his characters more fully, and extended his use of dialect. The first of the forty-five Pete Whetstone letters was published early in 1837. They are flawed by careless composition and repetition, but Pete Whetstone was a fresh creation, a Southwestern character who spoke in his own language, without a cultivated gentleman standing on the sidelines to interpret or to serve implicitly as a basis of comparison. The name Noland borrowed from a historic Pete Whetstone — a commercial hunter in Arkansas as early as 1816, who later became something of a legendary figure in Texas — but the rest he himself supplied.

TEXT: "Pete Whetstone's Bear Hunt," "Race between 'Worm-Eater' and 'Apple Sas,' " "Pete Whetstone's Last Frolic," and "Dan Looney's Big Fight in Illinois" from *Spirit of the Times*, Mar. 25, 1837; Mar. 10, 1838; Mar. 16, 1839; and *Porter's Spirit of the Times*, Nov. 8, 1856.

Pete Whetstone's Bear Hunt

DEVIL'S FORK OF LITTLE RED RIVER (ARK.) *Feb. 15th*, 1837

Dear Mr. Editor, — Being that this is a rainy day, I thought I would write you about the bear hunt. Well, next morning after the fight with Dan Looney, I started out. I was mighty sore I tell you, for Dan had thumped me in the sides till I was as blue as indigo. I saddled my horse, got my wallet, and fetched a whoop, that started my dogs; they knew what I was after, and seemed mightily pleased. I took six with me, as good dogs as ever fought a bear. *Sharp-tooth* and *General Jackson,* if there was any difference, were a little the best. I struck for the Big Lick, where Sam Jones and Bill Stout were to meet me. I found them there — they had a good team of dogs. We had heard of great *sign* up the Dry Fork, and there we determined to go. It was about thirty miles off, and as we did not wish to fatigue our dogs, it took us until the middle of next day to reach it; we rested that evening, and put out by day-break next morning.

In about half an hour, old General raised a cry: I knew then we were good for a bear — the other dogs joined him. The track was cold; we worked with him till about ten, when they bounced him. Bill Stout was ahead, and raised the yell — such music, oh lord, and such fighting. I got the first shot; my gun made long fire, and I only slightly wounded him. At the crack of the gun the dogs gathered; he knocked two of my young dogs into the middle of next week before you could say Jack Robinson — the others kept him at bay until Bill Stout could shoot; his ball struck him too far back. He was a tremendous bear, and just lean enough to make a good fight. He made two other dogs hear it thunder, shook off the whole pack, and got into a thicket, and the next moment plunged down a steep cliff. I listened only for an instant, to hear the clear shrill note of Sharp-tooth, as he plunged in after him, and then socked the spurs into *Dry-bones,* and with Bill Stout on *Fire-tail,* and Sam Jones on *Hard-times,* dashed round the hill. We rode for our lives, for we knew that many of our dogs would suffer if we did not relieve them. When we overtook them, they had him at bay; two dead, and three crippled dogs told of the bloody fight they had had. Sam Jones fired; the wound was that time mortal. At the crack of the gun, the dogs again clamped him; with a powerful reach of his paw, he grabbed the old General, and the next moment fastened his big jaws on him; this was more than flesh and blood could stand: I sprung at him with a butcher-knife, and the first lick sent it to the handle. He loosened his jaws and Sam Jones caught the old General by the hind legs and pulled him away. I gave him one more stab, and he fell dead.

I examined the old General, and found that he was not much injured. We lost seven dogs that day, and many of the others were so badly crippled, as to render it necessary for us to lay by a few days. Sam found a bee tree, and I killed some fat turkies; with them, and the ribs of the old *he,* we had fine times. It has stopped raining, so I must stop for the present.

Ever yours,
PETE WHETSTONE.

Race between "Worm-Eater" and "Apple Sas"

Devil's Fork of Little Red, (*Arkansas*) Jan. 28, 1838

My dear Mr. Editor — So you have been all the way to the Big Orleans and woulden't pay us chaps on the Devil's Fork a visit. I reckon, may be, you haden't time. Well, we will be glad to see you, come when you will.

The way there has been all sorts of fighting over on *Cravat-Stuffing Creek,* is a sin to Crockett. Here is just about the way it was: Dan Looney bet a feller two chunks of second rate cows and calves, that the *Worm-Eater* could beat Bill Stone's pony, *Apple-Sas*, one quarter of a mile, with put up and put up on both. Well, Jim Cole, Bill Spence, and me, went over the day of the race. Going along, says I, "boys, *they* will be hell here to-day." Bill Spence asked me what made me think so: "why," says I, *"Ruby Honey* is going to turn *Apple-Sas."* — "Is he," said Jim; "well, just let me turn the *Worm-Eater* and I'll show him sights, for since Giles Scroggins died I can out turn any man on the face of the earth, and I would bet more money on it than I would on 4 aces." "Well now," says I, "Jim, don't you have anything to do with it, for I believe *Apple-Sas* can slam him." "Why, Pete, you are crazy," says he, "for I can prove by Bill Spence that *Worm-Eater* ain't more than 17 feet behind *Old Swayback* in a quarter." "Well," says I, "are you sure of that?" They said they were. — "Well, then," says I, "we can knock the fur off Rube, and you know he is a monstrous thief" — so on we went. Well, when we got to the *paths,* there was a heap of people gathered, so I slips in the crowd and shook hands with first this one and then that one. "Well, Col. Whetstone, how do you think the race is gwine?" said one fellow. I knew he was on *Apple-Sas,* so says I *"Apple-Sas* is the horse for my money" — "Good as hell," says he, "and I lay my pile on him."

Up comes Dan Looney. Well, Dan and me ain't been mighty friendly since I had the big fight with him — so says he, "good morning, Col. Whetstone," "good morning, *Mister* Looney," says I. "How are you going on the race," says he; "I haven't bet yet," says I, "but if the *Worm-Eater* is in good fix, and Hiram rides him, I'll go a forty dollar horse on him." "Good as the thing you set on!" said *Zacky Stones* — "done, and done," was the word. At that Dan winked to me, and out we went. "Now, Pete," says he, "without talking the thing over, let us just wipe out that fight we had, and be good friends;" "agreed," says I; "well," says he, "it is going to be a foul race — I see the thing working, and *Rube has wrung* in *Piney-woods Smith."* "Who judges for you?" says I — "why, I ain't picked my judges yet," says he. "Well, you pick Sam Jones and Bill Spence — put Bill at the start, and let Jim Cole turn the *Worm-Eater,* and if you win the word and get the *bulge,* it will be twenty feet clear day light." At that up comes Bill Stones. "Are you ready, Dan?" says he; "I will be as soon as my horse is cupped," says Dan: — "here let us fling up for the track; toss, and I'll call," says Dan. *"I have nothing but shin plasters,"* says *Stones:* "spit on a chip and fling it up," says I. Up went the chip. "Wet or dry?" says Stones — "wet," says Dan. It was dry, and Stones won the path — he took the left hand path. "Toss her up for the word" — up she went again. Dan cried wet: she came down dry side up, and Stones had the word. By this time the crowd was thick; I looked up the track and saw Jim Cole leading the *Worm-Eater.* Jim was stripped to his pantaloons and shirt — his sleeves were rolled above his elbows, and his *red head* was tied up in a striped *cotting handkerchief.* — *Worm-Eater* looked slick, I tell you; he is a strawberry roan, about 14 hands 3 inches high, with heavy muscles and big bony legs. Jim stopped, and Looney's friends gathered round him. "There is a hind leg for you," said one — "that shoulder beats them all," said another; "give him hell, Hiram, and pay him down," said a third; while a fourth continued, "Jim against Rube." Presently up they led *Apple-Sas.* He is a light sorrel, with white face and legs, and one glass eye, great back and shoulders. Stones' friends gathered round. "There is a *picter,*" says one: "made like *Old Vol,*" says another: "*Champion's* shoulder," said a third: "a *panther's* hind parts," said a fourth. "A likely cow and calf on *Apple-Sas,*" cried a fifth — "Dick Wilson knows the cow, and she runs on the Corny Fork." "I'll bet you my spotted steer that runs over on the Dry *Fork,* if you'll give me 10 feet," cried a lame fellow from the Raccoon Fork. "Give you what you can git." "No harm done," said the lame fellow. The fellow with the cow and calf begin to cavort. "*Apple-Sas* can make a perfect smash of all your d—d ticky tail horses; you daresn't bet; Dan Looney nor Dan Looney's horse haint no friends." "You darsen't give me 10 feet, any how," said the lame fellow. "D—n my soul, if I don't give you ten, and risk it, as Paddy did his soul." "Good," said the lame fellow, and called up the witnesses. "Let us drink," said *Apple-Sas's* friend, and over he went to a little old cart standing under a tree, with a barrel of whiskey in it. "Give us half a pint," says he, "and damn the difference — come up fellows and take a horn." "Well, I don't care, Hightower, if I do take a slug with you," said a long, crane-built, fellow. "Well, they say you bet *dot-and-carry-one, Nelson,* a cow and calf on *Apple-Sas,* and give 10 feet." "Yes, I did." "Well, I'm afear'd you are picked up." "What? why Rube turns, and Piney-woods Smith judges at the start." "You don't say so?" "It is a fact." "Then you are in town, — yes, it is just as good as the thing you set on."

The riders are up, was the cry. I went up to the head of the paths; Piney-woods Smith, and Bill Spencer were judging the start, Tom Brown and Sam Jones were at the out come. The Worm-Eater was quiet as a lamb, while the way Apple-Sas fretted was agreeable to Dan and his friends. "Come up," says Rube, "and let us git a fair start, I know I don't want the advantage of you, and you look like a man that wouldn't take advantage of me." But Jim was wide awake, and never asked the word unless he had the advantage. Rube saw that

Jim was no fool at turning a horse, and after about forty minutes spent in trying, let go when Jim asked. Away they went; the timber was poured on Apple-sas with a perfect looseness. I saw the Worm-eater had him at the out come, and the start was about a foot in his favor, for I stood right behind Piney-woods Smith. Well, down I went. I meets Hiram. — "How was it, Hiram?" "I beat him out about three lengths," said Hiram. I raised the shout. Dan Looney's friends roared. "Wait for the judges," says one fellow. "No use of judging," says I. "Why, the Worm-eater got twenty feet start," said Bill Hightower. *"Fight! fight!"*

I looked up the track. Rube and Jim Cole had yoked. The crowd gathered round them. — "Go it, Jim!" — "Go it, Rube!" — "stand back and don't crowd them." "Hurrah, Jim!" — "Hurrah, Rube!" broke from fifty voices. I knew there would be hell to pay. "Close on him, Jim," says I; and Jim grabbed him and flung him. At that I saw Stones grab Jim's leg; I pitched right into him. "Give them hell!" shouted Dan Looney, and the fight became general.

"I am stabbed!" was shouted by Bill Spencer. I rushed to him and found him cut down. I saw who did it, for he still had the knife in his hand.

"You d—d coward, set to me," says I, as I drew my knife. The first lick I made slashed him right across the face, cutting his nose in two. I fended off his lick, and the next moment Dan Looney was betwixt us.

"Come, men, this won't do — put up your knives," "I'll have his heart's blood for his killing Bill Spencer," says I. "Oh, he aint hurt much," says Dan. Well, I agreed to drop it. By this time the fight was over; we had licked them from *a-b—ab to crucifix.*

"What do the judges say?" says I. "They can't agree," says Dan. "Why not?" says I. "Piney-woods Smith holds out for a *draw,"* says Dan. "Swear them," says I.

Well, it was agreed we should all go up to Squire Burns and have the judges sworn. Up we went; when we got there, Piney-woods Smith said he wouldn't swear. That made me mad, sure enough. Says I — "Piney, you are, perhaps, the d—dest rascal unhung." "You are a liar, Whetstone," says he. Cherow I took him; he staggered, and Dan Looney jumped betwen us; he rared and pitched. Rube came up and talked with him and that quieted him. "Well," says Rube, "inasmuch as the judges can't agree, we are willing to *give up half the bet* and drop the thing, or else run it right over." Dan agreed to take half.

Well, then, they begin to drink; I had a quart set out, and told the crowd to come up. By this time I had got over my passion, and begin to look around and notice the boys; such a banged-up set I never saw before; but they soaked the liquor and commenced cavorting. Rube and Piney-woods gathered their friends and soon put out, not before they had flung out some mighty big bouters. Jim told Rube he wasn't cut the right way of the leather, and that he couldn't shine among gentlemen. Rube looked mighty mad, but said nothing, for Jim had used him up in their fight.

It began to get late, and we gathered our horses and started home with Dan Looney. On the way we talked it all over. Says Dan — "What chance would a stranger have in that crowd?" "None," says I. "Well, after all, we came out pretty well," says Jim. "I reckon I did," says *Dot-and-carry-one,* who was tolerable tight with liquor, I tell you. "A cow and a calf aint made every day," says he, and at that he broke out in a sorter hiccupping laugh. "Sing, Dot," says Bill. "I can't," says Dot. "I know better," says Bill; "give us raccoon on a rail." "Well, I'll try:" —

"Oh raccoon on a rail, raccoon on a rail —

Ladies and gentlemen, I wish I may be squeezed to death in a cider press if here wasn't the same identical raccoon —

"A setting on a rail, a setting on a rail."

"Oh, I can't think of it." "No wonder, Dot, for you are as full as a tick," said Dan. Well, we staid all night at Dan's, and next morning Jim and me went home.

I start back to the Rock next week. More legislating, though that are small pox will run them off again, I reckon.

Ever yours,
PETE WHETSTONE.

Pete Whetstone's Last Frolic

DEVIL'S FORK OF LITTLE RED, *Jan.* 9, 1839

My dear Mr. Editor, — Since the last time I writ you, I have had all sorts of times; I took a trip away out South. Well, when I got to the Rock, I was in a big hurry to keep on, so I walked up early in the morning to Goodrich and Loomis, thinking I would rig out in a suit of their best, but they hadn't opened their store; so I steps into another, and bought me a pair of red broadcloth britches. The fellow measured me, and put up a pair that he said would fit me to a shaving. So I stuffs them into my saddle-bags, and put out South.

Well, when I gets out, I was asked to a party, and I rigged myself up; but oh, lordy! my britches were big enough for the fat man what was blowed up in the steamboat. I had my gallowses up to the last notch, but it wouldn't all do, for I could have carried a grist of corn in them without stretching the cloth. I hardly knew what to do; my old britches couldn't do at all, and my new ones hung like a shirt on a bean-pole. Thinks I, there is no frolic for Pete; but just right at this time in pops Major Greene. "Well," says he, "Kurnel, ain't you ready to go?" Says I, "I am thinking I won't go." — "Why?" says he. "Look at my britches," says I. Well, he commenced laughing; says he, "Them britches were made for Daniel Lambert." — "Well," says I, "Daniel Lambert is a stranger to me, but I know they are a pretty loose fit." — "Oh, never mind them," says he; "come, go, and nobody will notice them." So I went. I found lots of people, and an abundance of pretty gals. Well, there was no dancing, and the folks were all sitting round the room; so I slips in a corner, thinking I would hide my britches. Presently some gentleman asked a lady to sing; so up she gits, and he leads her to something in the corner, that looked like the nicest kind of a chest. Well, she opened the lid, and it was right chuck full of horseteeth; she just run her hand across them, and I never heard such a noise in all my life. I whispered to the next fellow to me, and asked what sort of a varmint that was? "Why, Kurnel," says he, "that is a pe-anny." Well, the young lady commenced, and I never heard such singing. I forgot my britches, and started to walk close up to the pe-anny, when I heard them tittering. "Daniel Lambert," says one — then I knew they were laughing at my britches. So I feels my dander rising, and began to get mad; I walked right up, bold as a sheep. There was a sort of a dandy looking genius standing by the pe-anny. — Says he "Now do, Miss, favor us with that delightful little ditty — my favorite — you know it." Then she commenced.

"When the Belly-aker is hearn over the sea,
I'll dance the Ronny-aker by moonlight with thee."

That is all I recollect. When she got through, up steps Maj. Greene, and introduces me to her. Says she, (and I tell you she looked pretty), "Col. Whetstone, what is your favorite?" Says I, "Suit yourself, and you suit me." And that made her laugh. Well, right at that, up steps a fellow that looked as if he had been sent for and couldn't go. Says he, "Miss, will you give me 'the last link is broken'?" — "Why," says she, "indeed, sir, I have the most wretched cold in the world." — "Why, Miss," says I, "you wouldn't call yours a bad cold if you had seen Jim Cole arter he lay out in the swamp and catched cold."

"Why," says she, (and lord, but she looked killing), "how bad was his cold?" "Why, Miss," says I, "he didn't quit spitting ice till the middle of August." That made her laugh. "Well," says she, "Kurnel Whetstone, that cures my cold." So she commenced —

"The last link is broken that binds you to me,
The words you have spoken is sorry to I."

Well, arter the lady was over, they all went into supper; lots of good things. I sat next to a young lady, and I heard them saying, "Miss, with your permission, I'll take a piece of the turkey," and so on. I sees a plate of nice little pickles. — "Miss, with your permission, I'll take a pickle," and she said I might do so. I reached over and dipped up one on my fork — it was small, and I put the whole of it in my mouth. Oh, lordy! but it burnt; — well, the more I chawed the worse it was. Thinks I, if I swallow, I am a burnt koon. Well, it got too hot for human nater to stand; so says I, "Miss, with your permission, I'll lay the pickle back," and I spit it out. Oh, lordy! what laughing. "Excuse me, ladies, if I have done wrong," says I, "but that pickle is too hot for the Devil's fork." Everybody seemed to take the thing in good part, but one chap; says he, "I never seed such rude behavior in all my life." At this I turns round to him; says I, "Look here, Mister, if you don't like the smell of freshbread, you had better quit the bakery." Well, I tell you, that shot up his fly-trap quicker. Arter supper the party broke up. Oh, confound the britches! I wish the fellow that made them could be fed on cloth for twelve months. Even the little boys made fun of them, for I heard one singing —

"Mister, Mister, who made your britches?
Daddy cut them out, and mammy sowed the stitches."

Ever yours,
PETE WHETSTONE.

Dan Looney's Big Fight in Illinois

DEVIL'S FORK OF LITTLE RED RIVER, *October* 10, 1856

MY DEAR MISTER EDITOR:

I writ you a few days since, and I told you I would try and send you an account of Dan Looney's big fight in Illinois. Well, it is a sorter of a dull day; and here goes, in Dan's own words:

I tuck a steam-boat at Louisville — one of your real jam-up boats. Lots of passengers; and as I had old Uncle Tommy Price's ligacy, and felt rich, and as old Bill Montgomery used to say, I cared no more for a silver dollar than a Pennsylvanian would for a yoke of steers, so I told them to book me for the cabin. I tied the pups way up on top of the boat, and agreed with one of the servants to pay him for feeding them. We started out jist before dark; and when supper came on, I tell you, there was nicer doings than there was at Squire Sim's Infar. After supper I went forward to take a smoke, and soon made two acquaintances; one of 'em a great big raw-boned fellow from old Kentuck, with about 20 head of the likeliest mules I ever did see, that he was carrying to New Orleans; the other a monstrous pale-looking little fellow, that had the chills so long that he had an ager-coke nigh on to as big as a smallsize sifter — he was from old Virginny — from what, he said, they called the *Pan-handle.* He was little, and sickly, but had a craw chock full of sand, as I afterwards found out. I tuck a mighty liking to them, and we three kept mighty close together. When all the supper fixings was cleared away, in we went to the cabin and tuck our seats. Pan-handle was full of fun, and oncommon smart. Says he, "Mr. Looney, if you will jist skin your eye close, you can see all sorts of people, on a big boat like this." Well, I did look round; for I had heard old Giles Scroggins say, mankind was divided into five sorts — viz., quality, bob-quality, and commonality, rubbish, and trash. Says I, "There is three sorts of people here, but two kinds are missing — I can see quality, bob-quality, and commonality, but no rubbish and trash." "Ah, Mr. Looney," said Old Kentuck, who was a mighty plain matter-of-fact man, "when you have traded mules to Orleans seventeen seasons in succession, you will be a better judge of rubbish and trash than you are now; for I would be willing to take $200 for the best pair of mules I have got on this boat, if them hairy-lip fellows over there, cutting up such shines, ain't trash, and the meanest sort." Well, there was a pe-anny on board, and some of the nicest ladies; but I tell you, Pete, if you was buying them by weight, unless you put the stilyards to them, you would be a ruined man. Why, there was one standing up by the pe-anny, and I hearn one feller say, "Well, if these hoop-dresses don't alter a gal faster than anything I ever seed — for there stands Miss Sally Spinel, that I have seen every day, for weeks and months at a time, and I hardly know her." "An oncommon hearty and robust gal," said a big Yankee, that was standing by the fellow who knowed her, "what do you think she would weigh?" said he to the Yankee. "Well," said the Yankee, without hefting her, "at a rough guess, I would say, not less than 215 pounds." At this, the first fellow broke out laughing: "Why, she don't weigh 115 without her rigging."

Bime-by they be gone to play on the pe-anny and sing songs, some of 'em mighty high falutin; but there was one young gal, I tell you, could make a mocking-bird ashamed of himself; she sung "Old Folks at Home" and "Master is in the cold, cold Ground"; and I tell you, I found the tears coming down my face. "Well," says Pan-handle, "I'd rather hear her sing, than go to the Circus — there." "My sentiments," said Old Kentuck; "and gentlemen, let us take a drink and go to bed." "Agreed," says I. But Pan-handle left mighty unwilling. I tell you, that gal had charmed him.

Next day, about two hours before sun-down, the boat landed at a little town on the Illinois side; and as the captain said he would be kept till dark, I thought I would take the pups ashore, and give them a little chance to stretch themselves. So I told Kentuck, and he said he would go; but Pan-handle was listening to that gal singing, and knowed it was no use to ax him. Well, we went out, and the pups seemed to enjoy it mightily. We walked up towards the town; and jist at the edge of it, we spied a little flag flying, with only 16 stars. Soon as Old Kentuck spied it, I seed his neck-veins swell. Says he, "Mr. Looney, that is what I call a bad sight." "What does it mean?" says I. "It means," says he, "*disunion*: free States against slave States."

Right then, up steps a good-sized, square-built fellow, that seemed to have about three drinks aboard. "Smart-looking dogs, them of your's, stranger," said he. "Clever pups," said I. "What do you call 'em?" said he. "Fillmore and Donelson," said I. "What might your name be, stranger," said he. "Dan Looney," said I. Says he, "I know the Looneys in Ireland, in the county of Cork; and, saving your presence, stranger, they were no great shakes." "No apologies necessary," says I, "for I was born in the State of Tennessee, three miles from the head-waters of the Calf-Killer. My father and two uncles fout in Jackson's war, and I am an out-and-out American." "Where do you live?" said he, and he begin to talk sassy. "On the Devil's Fork of Little Red River, in the State of Arkansaw," said I. "Why, you are one of them nigger-drivers," said he. "I reckon not," said I, "for niggers is rather scase on the Devil's Fork; but stranger, if you have anything to say agin the South, spit it out." Said he, "Look at that flag." "I have looked," said I. "Well, we are going to split this Union wide open." "Stop," said I; "when I left home, stranger, to go to the State of Ohio, my wife Sally said to me, said she, 'Dan, you are going among strangers, and you can't be too careful. Don't get in a fight on any account.' Said I, 'Sally, my

darling, I am a great man to hold in on big occasions, and unless one
of them abolitioners talks too sassy, I'll be meek as a lamb; but if
they talk about dividin' these United States, I'm bound to fight.'
'In such a case,' said she, 'fight'; and I said I would; and stranger, I
never did tell Sally a lie." So I told Kentuck to hurry the pups on
board the boat, and come back. I began to examine the chap. He
was about five feet ten inches, and put up like a jack-screw. Said I,
"My good fellow, you may as well shed your rags, for I'm gwine
to whip you, or try hard." At that he broke out in the biggest kind
of laugh. "Why, spooney, I can tan yer dog skin, and never draw
my coat." By this time old Kentuck had got back, and with him
Pan-handle. The latter's face was lighted up, and he didn't look
like the same man. I handed my coat to Kentuck, and stepping up to
the stranger, who had buttoned his, and was standing with his arms
sorter crossed. Said I, "Are you ready?" Said he, "Nobody's afraid,
if you ain't." At that I aimed to hit him about the bur of the ear;
when Whetstone, just as true as you are sitting there, he fended it off
with his left hand, as easy as ever you seed on. Oh! he ripped out
a young dog, and with his left he hit me a jo-reefer right under the
left eye. I tell you, I thought a bumblebee's nest had bursted in my
head; but I pitched in, and we clinched. We divided the under holts,
but I tell you, he was some at rastling. It wasn't long before he got
the back-lock on me, and it was no use — he flung me. Just then
Pan-handle sung out, "Hurrah for Looney!" Well, I riz with him,
and we had it round and round. I tried to come the hip-lock on him,
but he was too quick, and he come the back-lock on me, and flung
me again. "Stand up to him, Looney!" hollered Kentuck and Pan-
handle, and I riz again with him. By this time there was a big crowd
round us. "V y," says one, "that feller from Arkansaw is wasting
his time; he won't know he is fighting Dick McCormick, that whipped
the one-thumb bully from Kentucky." I heard it all, but kept in good
heart, for little Ager-Coke encouraged me all the time. This time we
had it around and about for a good while. I got so that I could keep
clear of his back-lock, but never was able to get the Piney-woods
hip-lock on him. At last he shifted his game, and tried me on the
in-turn. I found out what he was after, but he sorter got it, and
we came down a perfect dog fall — side and side — and we riz again.
I tell you, Ager-Coke and old Kentuck shouted, while one feller,
that was on McCormick's side, said, "I tell you, Arkansaw is some
punkins in a fight." "You'd better believe it," said Pan-handle; "why
Looney is just coming to himself!" Well, we had it round and about
again — he made lots of passes at me, but I had learned his locks, so
he tried the in-turn, but I was quick, and come Piney-woods onter

him. I flung him an oncommon hard fall, but he riz again. I knew now I had him — felt as sure he was my meat as Sam Adkins did of the widow Poolet, when he touched her on the naked neck with the thigh bone of a tree frog. We had it round and about, but it didn't last long. I had out-winded him — too much whisky, I reckon — and this time I flung him an old fashioned Sam Hinton fall, and he did not rise; but I played my thumbs into his eyes, and he sung out; but before they got me off, I reckon my right thumb got mighty near to the fust jint. You ought to have seen old Kentuck and Pan-handle. The way they did shout! Said Dick McCormick, after he got up and washed his face, "Well, gentlemen, I have been fighting all my life, and this is the first time I ever got whipped." "Why," said I, "that is what Davy Gibbs said when Sam Beard whipped him, and Sam said, in reply, that he had fout, man and boy, through thirteen of the old States and some of the new ones, and that Davy Gibbs was the first man he had ever found he could whip." Just then the whistle blew, and Kentucky and Pan-handle and me went board. I let on I wasn't hurt, but I tell you I was sore enough. It was an accident I whipped him. I got out at Madison. Kentuck all but shed a tear at parting, and offered me the best mule he had to go all the way to Orleans. Pan-handle said if he could he would come up and see me. I told him with bear meat and sulphur water I could knock that ager-coke all to pieces.

But I am getting tired, and must close Dan's fight and trip.

Ever yours,
PETE WHETSTONE.

William Tappan Thompson

(1812-1882)

🥀 A Northerner by birth, William Tappan Thompson was a Southerner by conviction. Thompson spent his boyhood in Ravenna, Ohio, and in Philadelphia. After studying law with James Diament Wescott, secretary of the territory of Florida, he worked with his close friend Augustus B. Longstreet on the Augusta, Georgia, *State Rights Sentinel*. In June 1842, while editor of the *Family Companion and Ladies' Mirror,* he published the first of his Major Jones letters. The periodical failed shortly thereafter, but the letters from the country major proved immediately successful. Others followed in the Madison, Georgia, *Southern Miscellany,* and in 1843 they were published as *Major Jones's Courtship.* A popular volume, it was followed by two other collections of humor, *Chronicles of Pineville* in 1845 and *Major Jones's Sketches of Travel* in 1848. In 1872 a revised and enlarged edition of the *Courtship* was published.

Thompson's best-known work, *Major Jones's Courtship,* is an epistolary novel consisting of twenty-eight letters covering a period of two years. It deals with young Joseph Jones, a major in the Pineville, Georgia, militia. Freely philosophizing on topical subjects, especially politics, the Major tells of the joys and the trials of his courtship, his marriage, and his life with Mary and their young son, Henry Clay. Here and in the later *Sketches of Travel,* the humor is derived largely from misspellings, ludicrous grammar, and incongruous situations, especially those resulting from the country major's travels to the sophisticated city. Perhaps in no other writer of the Old Southwest is the influence of Down East humor so pronounced. Thompson's creation of Major Jones was strongly influenced by the Jonathan of Royall Tyler and the Major Jack Downing letters of Seba Smith.

Unlike Thorpe's Jim Doggett and McNutt's Jim and Chunkey, Thompson's Major Jones is not a ring-tailed roarer. Unlike Harris's Sut Lovingood, Hooper's Simon Suggs, and Warren's Billy Fishback, he is not a trickster or con man. Nor is he a poor white like those who populate many Southwestern sketches. Major Jones belongs to the upper middle class. With a small plantation and a few slaves (all faithful and fun-loving), he is a respectable, small-town lad who is always intelligent if sometimes naive. He is completely honest in all things. He is a teetotaler, a devoted family man, and a loyal Whig. His impeccable morals, political certainty, and high sense of responsibility achieved for him an audience of genteel readers who frowned at more risqué humor. In fact he is almost too good; his respectability makes him much less interesting than many other figures from South-western humor. Thompson's great talent was not in creating character but in devising humorous situations: Major Jones spending the night in a sack, waiting to propose; two drunks on a coon hunt wandering in a circle all night trying to find their way home (cf. Sol Smith's "Slow Traveling by Steam"); and the country bumpkin attending a performance of Balfe's opera *The Bohemian Girl* in Philadelphia.

TEXT: Letters 12, 15, and 25 from *Major Jones's Courtship* (Madison, Ga., 1843); "A Coon-Hunt; or, A Fency Country" from *Polly Peablossom's Wedding,* ed. T. A. Burke (Philadelphia, 1851); and Letter 12 of *Major Jones's Sketches of Travel* (Philadelphia, 1848).

Major Jones Pops the Question

Pineville, December 27th, 1842.

To Mr. THOMPSON: — *Dear Sir* — Crismus is over, and the thing's ded. You know I told you in my last letter I was gwine to bring Miss Mary up to the chalk a Crismus. Well, I done it, slick as a whistle, though it come mighty nigh bein a serious undertakin. But I'll tell you all about the whole circumstance.

The fact is, I's made my mind up more'n twenty times to jest go and come rite out with the whole bisness, but whenever I got whar she was, and whenever she looked at me with her witchin eyes, and kind o' blushed at me, I always felt sort o' skeered and fainty, and all what I made up to tell her was forgot, so I couldn't think of it to save me. But you's a married man, Mr. Thompson, so I couldn't tell you nothin bout poppin the question, as they call it. Its a mighty grate favor to ax of a rite pretty gall, and to people as aint used to it, it goes monstrous hard, don't it? They say widders don't mind it no more'n nothin. But I'm making a transgression as the preacher ses.

Crismus eve I put on my new suit and shaved my face as slick as a smoothin iron and went over to old Miss Stallionses. As soon as I went into the parler whar they was all setin round the fire, Miss Carline and Miss Kesiah both laughed rite out —

"There, there," ses they, "I told you so, I knew it would be Joseph."

"What's I done, Miss Carline," ses I.

"You come under little sister's chicken bone, and I do blieve she knew you was comin when she put it over the dore."

"No I didn't — I didn't no such thing, now," ses Miss Mary, and her face blushed red all over.

"Oh, you needn't deny it," ses Miss Kesiah, "you 'long to Joseph now, jest as sure as ther's any charm in chicken bones."

I knowd that was a first rate chance to say something, but the dear little creater looked so sorry and kep blushin so, I couldn't say nothin zactly to the pint, so I tuck a chair and reached up and tuck down the bone and put it in my pocket.

"What are you gwine to do with that old bone now, Majer?" ses Miss Mary.

"I'm gwine to keep it as long as I live," ses I, "as a Crismus present from the handsomest gall in Georgia."

When I sed that, she blushed worse and worse.

"Aint you shamed, Majer?" ses she.

"Now you ought to give *her* a Crismus gift, Joseph, to keep all *her* life," ses Miss Carline.

"Ah," ses old Miss Stallions, "when I was a gall we used to hang up our stockins —"

"Why, mother!" ses all of 'em, "to say stockins rite afore —"

Then I felt a little streaked too, cause they was all blushin as hard as they could.

"Highty-tity!" ses the old lady — "what finement. I'd like to know what harm ther is in stockins. People now-a-days is gittin so mealy-mouthed they can't call nothin by its name, and I don't see as they's any better than the old time people was. When I was a gall like you, child, I use to hang up my stockins and git 'em full of presents."

The gals kep laughin.

"Never mind," ses Miss Mary, "Majer's got to give me a Crismus gift — won't you Majer?"

"Oh, yes," ses I, "you know I promised you one."

"But I didn't mean *that,*" ses she.

"I've got one for you, what I want you to keep all your life, but it would take a two bushel bag to hold it," ses I.

"Oh, that's the kind," ses she.

"But will you keep it as long as you live?" ses I.

"Certainly I will, Majer."

"Monstrous finement now-a-days — old people don't know nothin bout perliteness," said old Miss Stallions, jest gwine to sleep.

"Now you hear that, Miss Carline," ses I. "She ses she'll keep it all her life."

"Yes, I will," ses Miss Mary — "but what is it?"

"Never mind," ses I, "you hang up a bag big enuff to hold it and you'll find out what it is, when you see it in the mornin."

Miss Carline winked at Miss Kesiah, and then whispered to her —
then they both laughed and looked at me as mischievous as they could.
They spected somethin.

"You'll be sure to give it to me now, if I hang up a bag," ses Miss
Mary.

"And promise to keep it," ses I.

"Well, I will, cause I know you wouldn't give me nothin that wasn't
worth keepin."

They all agreed they would hang up a bag for me to put Miss
Mary's Crismas present in, on the back porch, and bout nine o'clock
I told 'em good evenin and went home.

I sot up till mid-night, and when they was all gone to bed I went
softly into the back gate, and went up to the porch and thar, shore
enuff, was a grate big meal bag hangin to the jice. It was monstrous
unhandy to git into it, but I was tarmined not to back out. So I sot
some chairs on top of a bench and got hold of the rope and let myself down into the bag; but jest as I was gittin in, the bag swung agin
the chairs, and down they went with a terrible racket. But no body
didn't wake up but old Miss Stallionses grate big cur dog, and here
he cum rippin and tarin through the yard like rath, and round and
round he went trying to find what was the matter. I sot down in the
bag and didn't breathe louder nor a kitten, for fear he'd find me out,
and after a while he quit barkin. The wind begun to blow bominable
cold, and the old bag kep turnin round and swinging so it made me
sea-sick as the mischief. I was afraid to move for fear the rope would
brake and let me fall, and thar I sot with my teeth ratlin like I had a
ager. It seemed like it would never come daylight, and I do blieve
if I didn't love Miss Mary so powerful I would froze to deth; for
my hart was the only spot that felt warm, and it didn't beat more'n
two licks a minit, only when I thought how she would be sprised in
the mornin, and then it went in a canter. Bimeby the cussed old dog
come up on the porch and begun to smell bout the bag, and then
he barked like he thought he'd treed something. "Bow! wow! wow!"
ses he. — Then he'd smell agin, and try to git up to the bag. "Git
out!" ses I, very low, for fear they would hear me. "Bow! wow!
wow!" ses he. "Be gone! you bominable fool," ses I, and I felt all over
in spots, for I spected every minit he'd nip me, and what made it
worse, I didn't know whar bouts he'd take hold. "Bow! wow! wow!" —
Then I tried coaxin — "come here, good feller," ses I, and whistled
a little to him, but it wan't no use. Thar he stood and kep up his
eternal whinin and barkin, all night. I couldn't tell when daylight was
breakin, only by the chickens crowin, and I was monstrous glad to

hear 'em, for if I'd had to stay thar one hour more, I don't blieve I'd ever got out o' that bag alive.

Old Miss Stallions come out fust, and as soon as she saw the bag, ses she,

"What upon yeath has Joseph put in that bag for Mary? I'll lay its a yearlin or some live animal, or Bruin wouldn't bark at it so."

She went in to call the galls, and I sot thar, shiverin all over so I couldn't hardly speak if I tried to — but I didn't say nothin. Bimeby they all come runnin out.

"My lord, what is it?" ses Miss Mary.

"Oh, it's alive!" ses Miss Kesiah, "I seed it move."

"Call Cato, and make him cut the rope," ses Miss Carline, "and less see what it is. Come here Cato and git this bag down."

"Don't hurt it for the world," ses Miss Mary.

Cato untied the rope that was round the jice, and let the bag down easy on the floor, and I tumbled out all covered with corn meal, from hed to foot.

"Goodness gracious!" ses Miss Mary, "if it aint the Majer himself!"

"Yes," ses I, "and you know you promised to keep my Crismas present as long as you lived."

The galls laughed themselves almost to deth and went to brushin off the meal as fast as they could, sayin they was gwine to hang that bag up every Crismas till they got husbands too. Miss Mary — bless her bright eyes — she blushed as butiful as a morninglory, and sed she'd stick to her word. She was rite out o' bed, and her hair wasn't comed, and her dress wasn't fixt at all, but the way she looked pretty was rale distractin. I do blieve if I was froze stif, one look at her charmin face, as she stood lookin down to the floor with her rogish eyes, and her bright curls fallin all over her snowy neck, would fotch'd me too. I tell you what, it was worth hangin' in a meal bag from one Crismas to another to feel as happy as I have ever since.

I went home after we had the laugh out, and set by the fire till I got thawed. In the forenoon all the Stallionses come over to our house and we had one of the gratest Crismus Dinners that ever was seed in Georgia, and I don't blieve a happier company ever sot down to the same table. Old Miss Stallions and mother settled the match, and talked over everything that ever happened in ther families, and laughed at me and Mary, and cried bout ther ded husbands, cause they wasn't alive to see ther children married.

Its all settled now, cept we haint sot the weddin day. I'd like to have it all over at once, but young galls always like to be engaged awhile, you know, so I spose I must wait a month or so. Mary (she ses I mustn't call her Miss Mary now) has been a good deal of trouble and botheration to me, but if you could see her, you wouldn't think I ought to grudge a little sufferin to git sich a sweet little wife.

You must come to the weddin if you possibly kin. I'll let you know when. No more from

Your frend til deth,

JOS. JONES.

N.B. I've ben thinkin bout your proposal for me to edit that little paper what you want to start. I should like to blige you if it won't be no more trouble than you say, but Mary ses she thinks I better not, cause editers dont never make nothin, and are always poor as Jobe's turky. I would like the bisness mighty well, if it would pay, but if I do go into it I wont have a single scriber what dont pay rite up when he takes the paper. When my weddin's over, I'll have considerable time to rite, and if I was certain that a rite spunky little paper, full of fun and good pieces, could git scribers enuf at sich a low price, to pay for the cost and trouble, I'd go into it like a two-year-old in a cane break.

I like to forgot to tell you bout cousin Pete. He got snapt on egnog when he heard of my gagement, and he's ben as meller as hos-apple ever sense.

The Major Avenged

Pineville, February 2nd, 1843.

To Mr. Thompson — *Dear Sir* — Ever sense I writ my last letter to you, things is gone on jest as strate as a shingle, and the only thing what troubles me is, I'm fraid it's all too good to last. It's always ben the way with me ever sense I can remember, whenever I'm the happyest sum cussed thing seems to turn up jest to upset all my calculations, and now, though the day is sot for the weddin, and the Stallionses is gittin every thing reddy as fast as they can, I wouldn't be sprised much if some bominable thing was to happen, some yeathquake or something, jest to bust it all up agin, though I should hate it monstrous.

Old Miss Stallions red that piece in the Miscellany bout the mistake in parson Miller's figers, and I do blieve she's as glad bout it as if she was shore she would live a whole thousand years more herself. She ses she hain't got no objection to the weddin' now, for me and Mary'll have plenty of time to make a fortin for our children and rais 'em up as they ought to be. She ses she always wondered how Mr. Miller could cifer the thing out so strait, to the very day, without a single mistake, but now he's made sich a terrible blunder of a whole thousand years, she ses she knows he aint no smarter nor other people, if he was raised at the north.

It's really surprisin how mazin poplar it does make a body to be engaged to be married to a butiful young lady. Sense the thing's leaked out, every body's my tickeler frend, and I can't meet nobody wherever I go, but what wants to gratilate me on my good fortin, cept cousin Pete and two or three other fellers, who look sort o' like they wanted to laugh and couldn't. Almost every night Mary and me is invited to a party. Tother night we went to one to old Squire Rogerses, whar I got my dander up a little the worst I've had it for some time. I don't blieve you have ever hearn of jest sich a fool trick as they played on me. Ther was a good many thar, and as the Squire don't 'low dancin, they all played games and tricks, and sich foolishness to pass away the time, which to my notion's a bominable site worse than dancin.

Cousin Pete was thar splurgin bout in his biggest, and with his dandy cut trowsers and big whiskers, and tried to take the shine off everybody else, jest as he always does. Well, bimeby he ses,

"Spose we play brother Bob — let's play brother Bob."

"Yes, lets play that," ses all of 'em, "won't you be brother Bob, Majer?"

"Who's brother Bob?" ses I, for I didn't know nothing 'bout it, and that's the way I cum to be so bominably tuck in.

"I tell you," ses he, "you and some body else must set down in the chairs and be blindfolded, and the rest must all walk round and round you, and keep tappin you on the head with sumthing til you gess who bob'd you."

"But how bob me?" ses I.

"Why," ses he, "when any one taps you, you must say, brother, I'm bob'd! and then they'll ax, who bob'd you? and if you gess the rite one, then they must take your place and be bob'd til they gess who bob'd 'em. If you'll be blindfolded I will," ses he, "jest for fun."

"Well," ses I, "anything for fun," and cousin Pete sot out two chairs into the middle of the room, and we sot down, and they tied a handkercher round my eyes tite as the mischief, so I couldn't see to gess no more'n if I had no eyes at all.

I hadn't sot no time fore cawhalux! some one tuck me rite side o' the hed with a dratted big book. The fire flew out o' my eyes in big live coals and I like to keeled over out of the chair. I felt my blood risin like a mill-tail but they all laughed mightily at the fun, and after a while ses I, "brother I'm bob'd." "Who bob'd you?" ses they.

I guessed the biggest-fisted feller in the room, but it wasn't him. The next minit spang went the book agin cousin Pete's head. "Whew!" ses he, "brother I'm bob'd." "Who bob'd you?" ses they. But cousin Pete didn't gess rite nother, and the fust thing I knowed, whang they tuck me agin. I was dredful anxious to gess rite, but it was no use, I missed it every time, and so did cousin Pete, and the harder they hit the harder they laughed. One time they hit me a great deal softlier than the rest. "Brother, I'm bob'd!" ses I. "Who bob'd you?" ses they. "Miss Mary Stallions," ses I. "No I never," ses she, and they all roared out worse than ever.

I begin to git monstrous tired of sich fun, which seemed so much like the frogs in the spellin book — for it was fun to them but it was deth to me — and I don't know what I would done if Mary hadn't come up and ontied the hankercher.

"Lets play something else," ses she, and her face was as red as fire, and she looked sort o' mad out of her eyes.

I seed ther was something wrong in a minit.

Well, they all went on playin "pawns" and " 'pon honor," and "Here we go round the gooseberry bush," and "Oh sister Feby, how merry we be," and sich nonsense til they played all they knowed, and while they was playin Mary told me all how cousin Pete bob'd me himself.

It was the most oudacious take in I ever hearn of. Do you think the cus didn't set rite down beside me and never blindfolded himself at all, and hit me every lick himself, now and then hittin his knee with the book, to make me blieve he was bob'd too! My hed was a singin with the licks when she told me how he done me, and I do blieve if it hadn't ben for her I'd gin cousin Pete sich a lickin rite thar in that room as he never had afore in his born days. Blazes! but I was mad at fust. But Mary begged me not to raise no fus bout it, now it was all over, and she would fix him for his smartness. I hadn't no sort of a ide how she was gwine to do it, but I knowd she was enuff for cousin Pete any time, so I jest let her go ahed. Well, she tuck the bominable fool off to one side and whispered to him like she was gwine to let him into the secret. She told him bout a new play what she learned down to Macon when she was at the college, called "Interduction to the King and Queen," what she sed was a grate deal funnyer than "Brother Bob," and swaded him to help to git 'em all to play.

After she and him made it all up, cousin Pete put out three chairs close together in a roe for a throne, and Mary she put a sheet over 'em to make 'em look a little grand. Bill Byers was to be King and Mary was to be Queen.

"Now you must all come in tother room," ses cousin Pete, "only them what belongs to the court, and then you must come in and be interduced, one at a time."

"I aint gwine," ses Tom Stallions, "for ther's some trick in it."

"No ther aint," ses cousin Pete, "I'll give you my word ther aint no trick, only a little fun."

"Well," ses I, "I's had fun enough for one nite."

Mary looked at me and kind o' winked, and ses she "you're one of the court you know, Majer, but jest go out till the court is sumonsed before the throne."

Well we all went out, and bimeby Bill Biers called out the names of all the lords and ladys what belonged to the court, and we all went in and tuck chairs on both sides of the throne.

Cousin Pete was to be the first one interduced, and Samuwell Rogers was to be the feller what interduced the company. Well bimeby the dore opened and in come cousin Pete, bowin and scrapin, and twistin and rigglein and putin on more ares nor a French dancin master — he beat Crotchett all to smash. The King sot on one side of the throne and the Queen on tother, leavin room in the middle for some one else. Sam was so full of laugh at cousin Pete's anticks that he couldn't hardly speak.

"Doctor Peter Jones," ses he, "I interduce you to ther Majestys the King and Queen."

Cousin Pete scraped about a while and then drapt on one knee, rite afore 'em.

"Rise gallant knight," ses Bill Byers, "rise, we dub you knight of the royal bath."

Cousin Pete got up and bowed and scraped a few more times, and went to set down between 'em, but they ris up jest as he went to set down, and the fust thing he knowd, kerslosh he went, rite into a big tub full of cold water, with nothing but his hed and heels stickin out.

He tried to kiss Mary as he was takin his seat, and if you could jest seed him as he went into that tub with his arms reached out to her, and his mouth sot for a kiss, I do blieve you'd laughed more'n you ever did afore in your life. The fellers was all so spicious that some trick was gwine to be played, that they left the dore open and when the thing tuck place they all run in shoutin and laughin like they would bust ther sides.

Pete got out as quick as he could, and I never seed a feller so wilted down in all my life. He got as mad as a hornet, and sed it was a d—d mean trick to sarve enny body so, specially in cold wether. And he went rite off home by himself to dry.

Mary made the niggers take out the middle chair and put the tub of water thar when we was all in tother room. Pete didn't spicion the trick was gwine to turn out that way — he thought the queen was gwine to sentence every feller what didn't kiss her as he sot down, to do something that would make fun for the rest, and he was jest gwine to open the game. I felt perfectly satisfied after that, and I don't think cousin Pete will be quite so fond of funny tricks the next time.

But I like to forget to tell you, my weddin is to take place — pervidin ther aint no more yeath quakes nor unaccountabel things to prevent — on the 22 of this month, which you know is a famous day what ought to be celebrated by every genewine patriot in the world. I shall look for you to come, and I hope you will be sure to be thar, for I know you wouldn't grudge the ride jest to see Miss Mary Jones what is to be. We's gwine to have a considerable getherin, jest to please the old folks, and old Miss Stallions ses she's gwine to give us a real Georgia weddin of the old time fashion. No more from

Your frend til deth,

JOS. JONES.

P.S. — I went over tother nite to see 'em all, and they was as bisy as bees in a tar barrel sowin and makin up finery. Mary was sowin something mighty fine and white with ruffles and jigamarees all round it. "What kind of a thing is that?" ses I. The gals looked at one another and laughed like they would die, and my poor little Mary (bless her soul) kep getherin it up in a heap and blushin dredful. — "Tell him, sis," ses Miss Carline, but Mary looked rite down and didn't say nothin. "I'll tell him," ses Miss Kesiah — "It's a —" "No you shant now — stop, stop," ses Mary, and she put her pretty little hand rite on Miss Kesiah's mouth, and looked like she'd cry for a little. I felt so sorry for her, I told 'em I didn't want to know, and they put the things away, and bimeby I went home, but I kep thinkin all the way what upon yeath it could be. I spose I'll find out some day.

Cousin Pete Goes Courting

Pineville, December 29th, 1843.

To Mr. Thompson: — *Dear Sir* — Well, Crismus and New Years is gone, and a heap of fun has gone with 'em. Down here in Pineville we had real times, you may be sure. Every body tuck Crismus, specially the niggers, and sich other carryins on — sich dancin and singin, and shootin poppers and skyrackets — you never did see. But the best joke was the way cousin Pete got tuck in 'bout gettin in sister Keziah's Crismus bag. Pete had a kind of sneakin notion of her for some time, but the dratted fool don't know no more about courtin nor a hown pup does bout 'stronomy.

He was over to our hous Crismus eve, gwine on with his nonsense, and botherin sister Kiz til she got rite tired of him — tellin her how he wanted to git marryed so bad he didn't know what would come of him, and how he wished somebody would hang up a bag for him, like Mary did for me.

"Oh, yes," ses she, "you want to fool somebody now, don't you — but you'r mighty mistaken."

"No, Miss Keziah," ses he, "if I ain't in good yearnest, I never was in my life."

"But, now, Doctor, would you give yourself away to any young lady for a Crismus gift like brother Joseph did?"

"That I would," ses he, "and glad of the chance."

"Ah," ses she, "I'm fraid you want to play some trick — you young doctors is so monstrous hard to please." And then she looked round at me and kind o' winked her pretty black eyes and smiled.

Pete looked in the glass, and sort o' slicked down his whiskers, and then ses he, "All the galls ses that; but the fact is, Miss Keziah, we's sceptible to female charms jest like common men, I can asshore you. And the fact is, I'm termined to marry the first gal that will have me for a Crismus present."

"Now, you all hear that," ses Keziah.

"Yes," we all said.

"Now mind," ses she to cousin Pete, "you ain't foolin."

I never seed Pete look so quare — he looked sort o' skeered and sort o' pleased, and he trembled all over and his voice was so husky he couldn't hardly speak.

"No, I is down right yearnest — you see if I aint."

"Well," ses she, "we'll see."

Pete seemed monstrous fidgety, and bimeby he 'lowed it was time to go, and after bidin us all good night, ses he, "Now remember, Miss Keziah," and away he went with a hart as light as a handfull of chicken feathers.

He hadn't been gone more'n no time afore Sister Keziah, bust rite out a laughin.

"Now," ses she, "if I don't fix Dr. Pomposity good, then I aint Keziah Stallins, that's all. He's always been cavortin about and makin so much of himself, as who but he! and now I'll take him down a peg."

"Why, aint you gwine to hang up no bag?" ses sister Carline.

"That I aint," ses she.

"Oh, now, sis, that's too bad to disappint him so."

"But the doctor shant be disappinted, for I'll make aunt Prissy hang up one for him to take an airin in till murnin if he's a mind to, and then we'll see if he'll be as good as his word."

And shore enuff, she called aunt Prissy and made her go up in the loft and empty the feather-bag, and fix a rope in it, and go and hang it on the porch for cousin Pete. Then she told Priss all how she must do in the mornin, and we all went to bed.

I couldn't sleep for thinkin what a bominable fool they was gwine to make out of poor Pete. Mary sed it was a great shame to serve anybody so, but she didn't blieve Keziah would quit being wild and mischievous.

It wasn't no great time fore I heard the gate squeak, and the next minit there was a monstrous racket among the dogs, and I know'd Pete was come. I could here the gals titterin and laughin in ther room, and the next thing bang went something agin the fence, and then one of the dogs set up a ki-ey! like something had hurt him, and all was still for a few minits. Then I heard Pete steppin about very cautious on the porch, and movin the table and chairs, and then the jice shuck with his weight, as he drapped into the bag. All was still agin for a little while, cept the galls snickerin in ther room, and then I heard Pete sneeze, and the dogs barked, and I thought the galls would laugh so loud he'd hear 'em, but he kep a sneezin in spite of all he could do.

"Now," ses Mary, "aint that too bad, to fool anybody that way — jest think how you would feel in that old bag what's been full of stinkin old chicken feathers for so long."

"That's a fact," ses I, but I couldn't help laughin all the time.

Pete cleared his throte a time or two, and every now and then he fetched a kind of a smothered up sneeze, and then the dogs would bark. You better keep your mouth shut, old feller, thinks I, if you don't want to git your windpipe lined with chicken feathers. Every now and then the jice would shake as Pete kep turnin and twistin round, tryin to git fixed comfortable, but I knew ther was no comfort in that bag, even if it had no fethers in it; and then when I thought what a terrible disappintment was waitin for him in the mornin, I couldn't help pityin him from the bottom of my hart.

It was a long time before we could go to sleep, but I drapt off after a while, and didn't wake til mornin. I was mighty anxious to see how the thing was gwine to turn out, and got reddy long before aunt Prissy come to see what was in her bag — the galls was up by daylight too, to see the fun. Nobody went out till all the niggers from the kitchen had got round the bag.

"Whoop-e-e-e!" ses little nigger Ned, "Mammy! see what's dat hangin on de porch."

"Kih!" ses old ant Hetty, "dat mus be ole Santa-claus heself, fell in dar when he was putting lasses candy for Pris, and can't git out."

Pete never said nothin, waitin for the galls to come.

"Oh! Miss Calline and Miss Keziah, come see what I got in my bag," ses Pris. "I spec its something what uncle Friday fotch from Gusta; he sed he was gwine to give me a Crismus."

By this time the galls was on the porch, and the niggers unswung the bag, and out tumbled Pete, all kivered with feathers from head to foot, so you couldn't see his eyes, mouth, whiskers, nor nothin else.

"Whew!" ses he, as soon as he got his hed out, and the fethers flew all over the floor, which skeered the little niggers so they split to the kitchen squallin like the very old devil was after 'em.

"God Lord, massa Pete!" ses ant Prissy, "dat you in my bag? I thought 'em was something good."

"Your bag!" ses Pete, "drat your infernal picter, who told you to hang up a bag, for white folks to go and git into? Never mind, Miss Keziah, I was only in fun, anyway," ses he, while they was all laughin fit to die, and he was trying to brush off the feathers. "Never mind, I was only jokin with you, but I had a better opinion of you than to think you would serve a body so, and ding my feathers if I aint glad I've found you out. Never mind, Miss," ses he, and he gin her a look like he could bit her hed off, and then he blowed his nose a time or two and put out.

"But aint you gwine to be as good as your word, doctor?" ses she.

"You jest go to grass," ses he; and that's the last we've seed of cousin Pete sense Crismus morning.

Mary gave the galls a rite good settin down for servin him so. But for my part I think it aint no great matter, for he is such a bominable fool, that a few pretty hard lessons won't do him no harm.

I sed ther wasn't nothin new down here — well ther haint been much — but ther was one of the curiousest live things here tother day from Augusta that ever was seen in these parts. It was sort o' tween a dandy and a gote, but on a slight examination it would have passed very well for a old monkey with its tail cut off or tucked up under its cote. The most distinguished feature about it was a little impertinent lookin gote-knot that stuck rite strate out from its chin, jest like them little gotes what they have in the mountains with tails drawed up so tight that ther hind feet don't hardly touch the ground. It had a cap on its head and a outlandish lookin bag cote. It went round town without anybody with it, and I never was so glad Mary was to home at the plantation. At first my pinter dog tried his best to set it, but soon as it turned round so he could see its face he just snuffed a little and drapped his tail and walked off. The fact was, he couldn't make out what sort of a varmint it was. Bimeby it spoke to somebody, and then Spike know'd it was some kind of a human, but he kep his eye on him all the time. I never did 'blieve in Metemsichosisism as they call it, before lately, but now I can't help but 'blieve ther's something in it. Whether people really do turn into animals or not after they're dead, I won't pretend to say; but one thing I'm certain of, and that is, that some people git to be monstrous nigh monkeys and gotes before they do die. All that little feller what was down here tother day wanted to make a complete billy gote out of him, was to have his cote-tail cut to a pint and turned up behind. If they can help it, I don't see what our young dandies make sich gotes of themselves for. If it's to be conspicuous, they don't gain nothing by it — for people is sure to ask questions about 'em, and then ther're sure to find out, that they aint much — generally some nincomnoddle, that's sprung from nothing and don't know how to live in decent people's circumstances. No more from

Your friend, til deth   Jos. JONES.

P.S. Mary's in rite good spirits, considerin. I expect to rite you a letter one of these days, old feller, that'll make your hair stand on eend with joy and gratification. But as the old sayin is, we mustn't count our chickens fore they're hatcht.

A Coon-Hunt; or, A Fency Country

'Tis really astonishin what a monstrous sight of mischief there is in a pint of rum. If one of 'em was to be submitted to an analization, as the doctors call it, it would be found to contain all manner of devilment that ever entered the hed of man, from cussin and stealin up to murder and whippin his own mother, and nonsense enuff to turn all the men in the world out of their senses. If a man's got any badness in him, it'll bring it out jest as sassafras tea does the measles, and if he's a good for nothin sort of feller, without no bad traits in pertikeler, it'll bring out all his greenness. It affects different people in different ways — it makes some men monstrous brave and full of fight, and some it makes cowards — some it makes rich and happy, and some poor and miserable; and it has a different effect on different people's eyes — some it makes see double, and some it makes so blind that they can't tell themselves from a side of bacon. One of the worst cases of rum-foolery that I've heard of for a long time, tuk place in Pineville last fall.

Bill Sweeney and Tom Culpepper is the two greatest old coveys in our settlement for coon-huntin. The fact is, they don't do much of anything else, and when *they* can't ketch nothin you may depend coons is scarce. Well, one night they had everything reddy for a regular hunt, but owin to some extra good fortin, Tom had got a pocket-pistol, as he called it, of reglar old Jimmakey, to keep off the rumatics. After takin a good startin horn, they went out on their hunt, with their lite-wood torch a blazin, and the dogs a barkin and yelpin like forty thousand. Evry now and then stoppin to wait for the dogs, they would drink one another's helth, till they begun to feel very comfortable, and chatted away bout one thing and another, without mindin much which way they was gwine. Bimeby they cum to a fence. Well, over they got, 'thout much difficulty.

"Who's fence is this?" ses Bill.

" 'Taint no matter," ses Tom, "let's take suthin to drink."

After takin a drink they went on, wonderin what on yearth had cum of the dogs. Next thing they cum to was a terrible muddy branch. After pullin through the briers and gettin on tother side, they tuck another drink, and after gwine a little ways they cum to another branch, and a little further they cum to another fence — a monstrous high one this time.

"Whar upon yearth is we got to, Culpepper?" ses Bill, "I never seed sich a heap of branches and fences in these parts."

"Why," ses Tom, "it's all old Sturlin's doins — you know he's always bildin fences and making infernal improvements, as he calls 'em. But never mind — we's through them now."

"Guess we is," ses Bill; "here's the all-firedest tall fence yet."

Shure enuff, thar they was right agin another fence. By this time, they begun to be considerable tired and limber in the gints, and it was sich a terrible high fence — Tom drapped the last piece of the torch, and thar they was in the dark.

"Now you is done it," ses Bill.

Tom know'd he had, but he thought it was no use to grieve over spilled milk, so ses he, "Never mind, old hoss — cum ahead, and I'll take you out," and the next minit kerslash he went into the water.

Bill hung on to the fence with both hands like he thought it was slewin round to throw him off.

"Hellow, Tom," ses he, "whar in the world is you got to?"

"Here I is," ses Tom, spoutin the water out of his mouth, and coffin like he'd swallowed something. "Look out, thar's another branch here."

"Name o 'sense, whar is we?" ses Bill. "If this isn't a fency country, dad fetch my buttons."

"Yes, and a branchy one, too," ses Tom; "and the highest, and deepest, and thickest that I ever seed in my born days."

"Which way is you?" ses Bill.

"Here, rite over the branch."

The next minit in Bill went, up to his middle in the branch.

"Cum ahead," ses Tom, "let's go home."

"Cum thunder! in such a place as this, whar a man haint more'n got his cote tail unhitched from a fence, fore he's over his head and ears in the water."

After gettin out and feelin about in the dark a little, they got together agin. After takin another drink, they sot out for home, denouncin the fences and the branches, and helpin one another up now and then; but they hadn't got more'n twenty yards fore they brung up all standin in the middle of another branch. After gettin thro' the branch and gwine about ten steps, they was brung to a halt by another fence.

"Dad blame my pictur," ses Bill, "if I don't think we is bewitched. Who upon yearth would bild fences all over creation this way?"

It was but a ower's job to get over this one, but after they got on the top they found the ground on tother side 'thout much trouble. This time the bottle was broke, and they come monstrous near having a fight about the catastrofy. But it was a very good thing, it was, for after crossin two or three more branches, and climbin as many more fences, it got to be daylight, and they found out that *they had been climbin the same fence all night*, not more'n a hundred yards from whar they first cum to it.

Bill Sweeney ses he can't account for it no other way but that the licker sort o' turned their heads, and he says he does really believe if it hadn't gin out they'd been climbin the same fence, and wadin that same branch till yet. Bill promised his wife to jine the Temperance Society if she won't never say no more bout that Coon-Hunt.

Major Jones at the Opera

Filladelfy, May 25, 1845.

To Mr. Thompson: — *Dear Sir* — I told you in my last letter that I was gwine to the opery, and that I'd tell you what I thought of 'em. Well, to tell you the truth, I like the opery well enuff, all but the singin. The scenery is very handsum, the actin is good, and the fiddlin is fust rate; but so much singin spiles evry thing. The opery what I went to see at the Chesnut street theatre, was the Bohemian Gall, and the acters was the celebrated Segwin Troop, as they call 'em, and I spose they done it up as well as anybody else could do it; but accordin to my notion, there's monstrous little sense in any such carryins on. If operys didn't cum from Paris, whar all the fashionable bonnets and evry thing else comes from, and it wasn't considered unfashionable not to admire 'em, I don't blieve ther's many peeple in this country what would be willin to pay a half a dollar a night to hear sich a everlastin caterwaulin as they do make.

As soon as I got my tea, I went to the theatre, what ain't a grate ways from my hotel, and after buyin a ticket of a man in a little hole outside of the green dores, I went in and tuck a seat on one of the cushioned benches what they call boxes. Ther was a good many peeple in the theatre and ever so many wimmin, all dressed out as fine as they could be, and sum of 'em lookin monstrous handsum.

Bimeby one of the fiddlers down in the place they call the orkestry, tuck up his fiddle-stick, and rapped on his desk, at which evry musicianer grabbed his instrument. Then the man with the fiddle-stick, after wavin it up and down three or four times, gin his fiddle a scrape or two what seemed to set the whole of 'em agwine; and sich another hurra's nest I never did hear before. Sumtimes all of 'em stopped but one or two; then they all struck up agin as hard as they could rip it. Sumtimes the musick was low and soft as the voice of a sick kitten, and then it was loud and terrible, as if all the lions, bulls, jackasses, and hiennys in creashun had got together, and was tryin to see which could make the biggest racket. They seemed to have evry thing in the world that would make a noise, from a base drum to a jewsharp; and evry feller tried to do his best. One old feller had a grate big fiddle of about one hundred hoss power, and the way he did rear and pitch and pull and jerk at it, was really distressin. The old feller seemed to have the highstericks for fear he couldn't make as much noise as the rest of 'em, and he rolled his eyes and twisted his mouth about enuff to frighten all the ladys out of ther senses. Bimeby they all blowed out, and at the ring of the bell up went the curtain.

Then the opery commenced, but for the soul of me I couldn't hardly make out hed nor tail to it, though I listened at 'em with all my ears, eyes, mouth, and nose. The fust thing was a grand singin match by a whole heap of Bohemian sogers and wimmin, 'bout nobody could tell what. Then thar was a big fat feller named Thadeus, what the bill sed was a Polish exile, what had run away from his country, cum on and sung a song 'bout his troubles, but he put so many dimmy-simmy quivers in it that nobody couldn't understand what hurt him. 'Bout this time ther was a gang of Murrelite lookin peeple, what they called Gipseys, made ther appearance. The hed man among them was a old feller named Devil's-hooff, what had the whitest teeth I ever seed in a white man's hed. This old cus sot to robbin the fat Polander the fust thing, but his wife, who seemed to wear the trowsers, wouldn't let him; and after a little singin the Gipseys agreed to take the fat exile into ther gang, and hide him from his pursuers. Then the Gipseys went to whar the Governor of Bohemia and his peeple was, and while they was all singin and carryin on, sumbody cum in and told them that a wild hog or sum other varmint was 'bout to eat up the Governor's baby. Then ther was a rumpus — his excellency and all his sogers run about the stage and looked at one another as much as to say, "Grate Heavens! what's to be done;" til the fat Polander tuck up a gun what was leanin agin the house, and run out and shot the varmint, whatever it was, and brung in the baby safe and sound to its mammy. Then they had another singin match. The Governor was very much obleeged to the fat man for savin his baby, and sung to him if he wouldn't take sumthing to drink. Mr. Thadeus 'lowed he didn't care if he did, and the licker was sot out; but the Governor didn't have no better sense than to propose sum political sentiment what didn't set well on the stummick of the fat Polander, who throwd down his glass and spilled the licker all over the floor. Then ther was a terrible rumpus agin. The Governor made his sogers grab the man what spilled the licker — with that, old Devil's-hooff fell to singin and rearin and shinin, tryin to git his friend out of the hands of the sogers — but they sung as loud as he did, and tuck him, too, and put him in jail with Mr. Thadeus. But while the Governor and his friends was singin about it, old Devil's-hooff got out of the jail and stole the baby what the fat Polander had saved, and run off with it. They saw him with the baby in his arms, but the sogers was afraid to shoot at him for fear of killin it; and when the old rascal got across the bridge he took out his jack-knife or sumthing else and cut it down, so they couldn't foller him. Then all fell to singin agin as hard as they could, like a barn-yard full of chickens when a hawk has jest carried off one of ther little ones. When they was about out of breth they let the curtain down for 'em to rest.

Well, thinks I, if that's what you call a opery, I'd a monstrous sight rather see a genuine old Georgia cornshuckin frollick, what ther's sum sense in.

Rite close beside me was a feller with three or four galls, what kep all the time lookin round the house at the peeple, with a kind of double-barreled spy-glass, and gabblein and chatterin like a parsel of geese. They was all dressed within a inch of ther lives, and the chap had a red and blue morocco cap on, what sot rite tite down to his hed like a ball-cover. He had a monstrous small hed, and when he had the spy-glasses up to his eyes he looked jest like a double-barreled percussion pistol, and I had half a mind jest to tap him on the hed with my cane to see if he wouldn't go off.

"Now, ladies," ses he, "we've got to wait til that baby grows to be a woman before we see any more of the opery."

"Dear me," ses one of the galls, "I hope they won't keep us waitin so long 'tween the acts as they always do; for I'm so much delighted with the opery."

"And me, too," ses another one. "It's so refreshin to hear sich delightful melody; I shall be very impatient."

"It's exceedingly foin," ses the feller with the percussion cap, lookin round the theatre with his spy glasses. "I nevaw heard Segwin in better tune. Fwazau is pwefectly delightful. But I must beg the ladies to be patient."

Thinks I, I'll be monstrous apt to be in old Georgia agin before that baby grows to be a gall; but I can set up as long as any of you, and, as I've paid my money, I'm 'termined to see it out."

But I hadn't begun to git sleepy before up went the curtain agin, and the racket commenced. Shore enuff, thar was the baby grow'd to be a grate big gall, and Mr. Thadeus, as fat as ever, was thar singin love to her.

They've both been with the gipseys ever sense, and she's fell in love with the fat Polander. The queen of the gipseys agrees to the match and the raggymuffins has a grand frollick and dance on the occasion. 'Bout this time a Miss Nancy sort of a feller, what's sum relation to the Governor, comes projectin about among the gipseys, falls in love with the Bohemian gall, and wants her to have him. The gipsey queen, who seems to have sum spite agin the pore gall, steals a medal from the booby lover, and puts it on her neck; when the feller, findin he can't git her to have nothin to say to him, has her tuck up for stealin, and carried before the governor. The governor, who's had the blues like the mischief ever sense he lost his baby, is 'bout gwine to punish her, when he finds out by some mark that she is his own daughter. Then he sings to her a heap, and she sings to him, and he takes her home to his palace, and wants her to marry his booby relation. But she's got better sense; besides, she's hard and fast in love with Mr. Thadeus, and won't have nobody else. Her father won't consent for her to marry a wanderin gipsey, and thar's the mischief to pay, with singin enuff for a dozen camp-meetins, all mixed up so nobody can't tell hed nor tail to it. 'Bout this time, Mr. Thadeus shows the governor his last tailor's bill, or sumthing else, that proves to his excellency that he was a gentleman once, and he gives his consent to the match. Mr. Thadeus and the Bohemian gall is monstrous happy, and old Devil's-hooff and the governor and all of 'em is takin another sing, when the queen of the gipseys puts up one of her vagabones to shoot Mrs. Thadeus that is to be; but the feller being a monstrous bad shot misses her and kills the queen, which puts a stop to her singin, though the rest of 'em sing away til the curtain draps.

"And that's the eend of the opery of the Bohemian Gall. I hain't got the squeelin and howlin and screechin of them 'bominable gipseys out of my hed yet, and I blieve if I was to live to be a hundred years old I wouldn't go to another opery, unless it was one that didn't have no singin in it. I like a good song as well as anybody, and have got jest as good a ear for musick as the next man, but I hain't got no notion of hearin twenty or thirty men and wimmin all singin together, in a perfect harrycane of noisy discord, so a body can't tell whether they're singin "Hail Columbia" or "Old Hundred." Ther is sich a thing as overdoin any thing; and if you want to spile the best thing in the world, that's the surest way to do it. Well, for peeple what ain't good for much else but music, like the French, Germans, and Italians, a opery full of solos and duetts and quartetts and choruses, as they call 'em, would do very well, if they would only talk a little now and then, so a body could know what they was singin about. But to sing evry thing, so that a character can't say, "Come to supper, your excellency!" without bawlin out — "Co-ho-ho-me to-oo-oo sup-up-up-e-e-er, your-r-r ex-cel-len-cy," with about five hundred dimmy-simmy quivers, so nobody can't tell whether he was called to supper, or whether he was told that his daddy was ded, is all nonsense. Let 'em sing whar ther is any sentiment — any thing to sing about — but when ther is only a word or two that is necessary to the understandin of what comes after or goes before; and whar ther ain't words enuff to make a stave of musick, what's the use of disgusin 'em so that ther ain't neither sense nor musick in 'em.

A body what never seed a opery before would swar they was evry one either drunk or crazy as loons, if they was to see 'em in one of ther grand lung-tearin, ear-bustin blowouts. Fust one begins singin and makin all sorts of motions at another, then the other one sets in and tries to drown the noise of the fust, then two or three more takes sides with the fust one, and then sum more jines in with number two, til bimeby the whole crowd gits at it, each one trying to out-squall the other, and to make more motions than the rest. That sets the fiddlers a-goin harder and harder — the singers straiten out ther necks and open ther mouths like so many carpet-bags — the fiddlers scrape away as if they was gwine to saw their fiddles in two, wakin up the ghosts of all the cats that ever was made into fiddle-strings, and makin the awfulest faces, as if it was ther own entrels they was sawin on — the clarineters and trumpeters swell and blow like bellowses, til their eyes stick out of ther heds like brass buttons on a lether trunk, and the drummer nocks away as if his salvation depended on nockin in the hed of his drum. By this time the roarin tempest of wind and sound surges and sweeps through the house like a equinoctial harrycane, risin higher and higher and gittin louder and stronger, til it almost blows the roof off the bildin, and you feel like dodgin the fallin rafters. For my part I shall have to go to singin-school a long time, and larn the keys from the pianissimo of the musketer's trumpet, up to the crashin fortissimo of a clap of thunder, before I shall have any taste for a grand opery. . . .

John S. Robb

(c. 1813-1856)

Like the hero of his narrative "The Western Wanderings of a Typo," John S. Robb found it difficult to settle down. Printer, roving reporter, editor, and wanderer, Robb traveled the country from ocean to ocean. Born in Philadelphia, he was trained as a printer and found jobs in newspaper offices wherever he went, from Detroit to New Orleans and from Philadelphia to Sacramento. For a few years he worked for the St. Louis *Reveille* under Joseph M. Field. First printer and then foreman of the composition department, he moved up in 1846 to the editorial office. Through the writings of Robb, Field, and Sol Smith, the *Reveille* in the 1840's became one of the country's leading journals of humor.

Robb left St. Louis in 1849 for California to cover the gold rush, traveling overland with the New Orleans *Picayune* correspondent, John E. Durivage. In Stockton he and Washington Bartlett, later governor of the state, established the Stockton *Journal*, its first number appearing in June 1850. In a letter of 1851 a citizen of Stockton listed Robb as one of several men in the town involved in Whig Party politics; but with the collapse of the Whigs, Robb turned to the Know-Nothing Party and actively campaigned for its cause as editor of the Sacramento *Age* in 1856.

Robb, using the pseudonym "Solitaire," began his humorous writings with two contributions to the *Reveille* in 1844. One of these was the widely reprinted sketch "Swallowing an Oyster Alive." Less original and imaginative than Longstreet or Harris, he capitalized on the perennial humor of innocence. In 1847 he collected several pieces from the *Reveille*, added a few new ones, and published his *Streaks of Squatter Life, and Far-West Scenes*. An uneven collection, it varies from the dull opening narrative of the typo to lively accounts of frontier drinking, courting, hunting, and politicking.

TEXT: "Swallowing an Oyster Alive" from *The Big Bear of Arkansas*, ed. W. T. Porter (Philadelphia, 1845); "Nettle Bottom Ball" and "Fun with a 'Bar'" from *Streaks of Squatter Life, and Far-West Scenes* (Philadelphia, 1847); "Smoking a Grizzly" from *Polly Peablossom's Wedding*, ed. T. A. Burke (Philadelphia, 1851).

Swallowing an Oyster Alive

At a late hour, the other night, the door of an oyster house in our city was thrust open, and in stalked a hero from the Sucker state. He was quite six feet high, spare, somewhat stooped, with a hungry, anxious countenance, and his hands pushed clear down to the bottom of his breeches pockets. His outer covering was hard to define, but after surveying it minutely, we came to the conclusion that his suit had been made in his boyhood, of a dingy yellow linsey-wolsey, and that, having sprouted up with astonishing rapidity, he had been forced to piece it out with all colours, in order to keep pace with his body. In spite of his exertions, however, he had fallen in arrears about a foot of the necessary length, and, consequently, stuck that far through his inexpressibles. His crop of hair was surmounted by the funniest little seal-skin cap imaginable. After taking a position, he indulged in a long stare at the man opening the *bivalves,* and slowly ejaculated — "isters?"

"Yes, sir," responded the attentive operator, — "and fine ones they are, too."

"Well, I've heard of isters afore," says he, "but that is the fust time I've seed 'm, and *pre-haps* I'll know what *thar* made of afore I git out of town."

Having expressed this desperate intention, he cautiously approached the plate and scrutinized the uncased shell-fish with a gravity and interest which would have done honour to the most illustrious searcher into the hidden mysteries of nature. At length he began to soliloquize on the difficulty of getting them out, and how queer they looked when out.

"I never seed any thin' hold on so — takes an amazin' site of screwin, hoss, to get 'em out, and aint they slick and slip'ry when they does come? Smooth as an eel! I've a good mind to give that feller lodgin', jist to realize the effects, as uncle Jess used to say about speckalation."

"Well, sir," was the reply, "down with two bits, and you can have a dozen."

"Two bits!" exclaimed the Sucker, "now come, that's stickin it on rite strong, hoss, for *isters.* A dozen on 'em aint nothin' to a chicken, and there's no gettin' more'n a picayune a piece for *them.* I've only realized forty-five picayunes on my first ventur' to St. Louis. I'll tell you what, I'll gin you two chickens for a dozen, if you'll conclude to deal."

A wag, who was standing by indulging in a dozen, winked to the attendant to shell out, and the offer was accepted.

"Now mind," repeated the Sucker, "all fair — two chickens for a dozen — you're a witness, mister," turning at the same time to the wag; "none of your tricks, for I've heard that your city fellers are mity slip'ry coons."

The bargain being fairly understood, our Sucker squared himself for the onset; deliberately put off his seal-skin, tucked up his sleeves, and, fork in hand, awaited the appearance of No. 1. It came — he saw — and quickly it was bolted! A moment's dreadful pause ensued. The wag dropped his knife and fork with a look of mingled amazement and horror — something akin to Shakespeare's Hamlet on seeing his daddy's ghost — while he burst into the exclamation —

"Swallowed alive, as I'm a Christian!"

Our Sucker hero had opened his mouth with pleasure a moment before, but now it *stood* open. Fear — a horrid dread of he didn't know what — a consciousness that all wasn't right, and ignorant of the extent of the wrong — the uncertainty of the moment was terrible. Urged to desperation, he faultered out —

"What on earth's the row?"

"Did you swallow it alive?" inquired the wag.

"I swallowed it jest as he gin it to me!" shouted the Sucker.

"You're a dead man!" exclaimed his anxious friend, "the creature is alive, and will eat right through you," added he, in a most hopeless tone.

"Get a pizen pump and pump it out!" screamed the Sucker, in a frenzy, his eyes fairly starting from their sockets. "O gracious! — what'ill I do? — It's got holds of my innards already, and I'm dead as a chicken! — do somethin' for me, do — don't let the infernal sea-toad eat me afore your eyes."

"Why don't you put some of this on it?" inquired the wag, pointing to a bottle of strong pepper-sauce.

The hint was enough — the Sucker, upon the instant, seized the bottle, and desperately wrenching out the cork, swallowed half the contents at a draught. He fairly squealed from its effects, and gasped and blowed, and pitched, and twisted, as if it were coursing through him with electric effect, while at the same time his eyes ran a stream of tears. At length becoming a little composed, his waggish adviser approached, almost bursting with suppressed laughter, and inquired,—

"How are you now old fellow — did you kill it?"

"Well, I did, hoss' — ugh, ugh o-o-o my innards. If that *ister* critter's dyin' agonies didn't stir a 'ruption in me equal to a small arthquake, then 'taint no use sayin' it — it squirmed like a sarpent, when

that killin' stuff touched it; hu' " — and here with a countenance made
up of suppressed agony and present determination, he paused to give
force to his words, and slowly and deliberately remarked, "If you
git two chickens from me for that live animal, I'm d—d!" and seizing
his seal-skin he vanished.

The shout of laughter, and the contortions of the company at
this finale, would have made a spectator believe that they had all
been *swallowing oysters alive.*

Nettle Bottom Ball

"Well, it *are* a fact, boys," said Jim Sikes, "that I promised to tell
you how I cum to git out in these Platte diggins, and I speculate you
mout as well have it at onst, kase its bin troublin' my conscience
amazin' to keep it kiver'd up. The afarr raised jessy in Nettle Bottom, and old Tom Jones' *yell,* when he swar he'd 'chaw me up,'
gives my meat a slight sprinklin' of ager whenever I think on it.

"You see, thar wur a small town called Equality, in Illin*ise,* that
some speckelators started near Nettle Bottom, cos thar wur a spon-
taneos salt lick in the diggins, and no sooner did they git it ago*in'*
and build some stores and groceries thar, than they wagon'd from
Cincinnat*e* and other up-stream villages, a p*a*cel of fellers to attend
the shops, that looked as nice, all'ays, as if they wur goin' to meetin'
or on a courtin' frolic; and 'salt their picters,' they wur etarnally pokin'
up their noses at us boys of the Bottom. Well, they got up a ball in
the village, jest to interduce themselves to the gals round the
neighborhood, and invited a few of us to make a contrary picter to
themselves, and so shine us out of site by comparison. Arter that
ball thur wan't any thin' talked on among the gals but what nice
fellers the clerks in Equality wur, and how nice and slick they wore
their *har,* and their shiny boots, and the way they stirrupp'd down
their trowsers. You couldn't go to see one on 'em, that she wouldn't
stick one of these fellers at you, and keep a talkin' how slick they
looked. It got to be parfect pizen to hear of, or see the critters, and
the boys got together at last to see what was to be done — the thing
had grown parfectly alarmin'. At last a meetin' was agreed on, down
to old Jake Bents'.

"On next Sunday night, instead of takin' the gals to meetin', whar
they could see these fellers, we left 'em at home, and met at Jake's
and I am of the opinion thur was some congregated wrath thar —
whew wan't they?

" 'Oil and scissors!' says Mike Jelt, 'let's go down and lick the town, *rite strait!*'

" 'No!' hollered Dick Butts, 'let's kitch these slick badgers comin' out of meetin', and tare the hide and feathers off on em!'

" 'Why, darn 'em, what d'ye think, boys,' busted in old Jake, 'I swar if they ain't larnt our gals to wear *starn cushins;* only this mornin' I caught my darter Sally puttin' one on and tyin' it round her. She tho't I was asleep, but I seed her, and I made the jade *re*pudiate it, and *no* mistake — *quicker!*'

"The boys took a drink on the occasion, and Equality town was slumberin', for a short spell, over a *con*-tiguous yearthquake. At last one of the boys proposed, before we attacked the town, that we should git up a ball in the Bottom, and jest out-shine the town chaps, all to death, afore we swallowed 'em. It was hard to gin in to this proposition, but the boys cum to it at last, and every feller started to put the afarr agoin'.

"I had been a long spell hankerin' arter old Tom Jones' darter, on the branch below the Bottom, and she *was* a critter good for weak eyes — maybe she hadn't a pair of her own — well, if they warn't a brace of movin' light-houses, I wouldn't say it — there was no calculatin' the extent or handsomeness of the family that gal could bring up around her, with a feller like me to look arter 'em. Talk about gracefulness, did you ever see a maple saplin' movin' with a south wind? — It warn't a crooked stick to compar' to her, but her old dad was *awful.* He could jest lick anythin' that said *boo,* in them diggins, out swar Satan, and was cross as a she *bar,* with cubs. He had a little hankerin' in favor of the fellers in town, too, fur they gin him presents of powder to hunt with, and he was precious fond of usin' his shootin' iron. I detarmin'd, anyhow, to ask his darter Betsy to be my partner at the Nettle Bottom Ball.

"Well, my sister Marth made me a bran new pair of buckskin trowsers to go in, and rile my pictur, ef she didn't put stirrups to 'em to keep 'em down. She said *straps* wur the fashion, and I should ware 'em. I jest felt with 'em on, as ef I had somethin' pressin' on me down — all my joints wur sot tight together, but Marth insisted, and I knew I could soon dance 'em off, so I gin in, and started off to the branch for Betsy Jones.

"When I arriv, the old fellar wur sittin' smokin' arter his supper, and the younger Jones' wur sittin' round the table, takin' theirs. A whappin' big pan of *mush* stood rite in the centre, and a large pan of milk beside it, with lots of corn bread and butter, and Betsy was helpin' the youngsters, while old Mrs. Jones sot by, admirin' the family collection. Old Tom took a hard star' at me, and I kind a shook, but the *straps* stood it, and I recovered myself, and gin him as good as he sent, but I wur near the door, and ready to break if he show'd fight.

" 'What the h—ll are you doin' in *disgise,*' says the old man — he swore dreadfully — 'are you comin' down here to steal?'

"I riled up at that. Says I, 'ef I wur comin' fur sich purpose, you'd be the last I'd hunt up to steal off on.'

" 'You're right,' says he, 'I'd make a hole to light your innards, ef you did.' And the old savage chuckled. *I* meant because he had nothin' worth stealin', but his darter, but he tho't 'twas cos I was afear'd on him.

"Well, purty soon I gether'd up and told him what I cum down fur, and invited him to come up and take a drink, and see that all went on rite. Betsy was in an awful way fur fear he wouldn't consent. The old 'oman here spoke in favour of the move, and old Tom thought of the licker, and gin in to the measure. Off bounced Betsy up a ladder into the second story, and one of the small gals with her, to help put on the fix-ups. I sot down in a cheer, and fell a talkin' at the old 'oman. While we wur chattin' away as nice as relations, I could hear Betsy makin' things stand round above. The floor was only loose boards kivered over wide joice, and every step made 'em shake and rattle like a small hurricane. Old Tom smoked away and the young ones at the table would hold a spoonful of mush to thur mouths and look at my straps, and then look at each other and snigger, till at last the old man seed 'em.

" 'Well, by gun flints,' says he, 'ef you ain't makin' a josey ——'

"Jest at that moment, somethin' gin way above, and may I die, ef Betsy, without any thin' on yearth on her but one of these *starn cushins,* didn't drop rite through the floor, and sot herself, *flat into the pan of mush!* I jest tho't fur a second, that heaven and yearth had kissed each other, and squeezed me between 'em. Betsy squealed like a 'scape pipe, — a spot of the mush had spattered on the old man's face, and burnt him, and he swore dreadful. I snatched up the pan of milk, and dashed it over Betsy to cool her off, — the old 'oman knocked me sprawlin' fur doing it, and away went my *straps.* The young ones let out a scream, as if the infarnal pit had broke loose, and I'd jest gin half of my hide to have bin out of the old man's reach. He did *reach* fur me, but I lent him one with my half-lows, on the smeller, that spread him, and maybe I didn't leave *sudden!* I didn't see the branch, but as I soused through it, I heerd Tom Jones swar he'd *'chaw me up,* ef an inch big of me was found in them diggins in the mornin'.'

"I didn't know fur a spell whar I was runnin', but hearing nuthin' behind me, I slacked up, and jest considered whether it was best

to go home and git my traps strait, and leave, or go see the ball.
Bein' as I was a manager, I tho't I'd go have a peep through the
winder, to see ef it cum up to my expectations. While I was lookin'
at the boys goin' it, one on 'em spied me, and they hauled me in,
stood me afore the fire, to dry, and all hands got round, insistin' on
knowin' what was the matter. I ups and tells all about it. I never
heerd such laffin', hollerin', and screamin', in all my days.

"Jest then, my trowsers gin to feel the fire, and shrink up about
an inch a minit, and the boys and gals kept it up so strong, laffin
at my scrape, and the pickle I wur in, that I gin to git riley, when all
at onst I seed one of these slick critters, from town, rite in among
'em, hollerin' wuss than the loudest.

"'Old Jones said he'd chaw you up, did he?' says the town feller,
'well, he all'ays keeps his word.'

"That minit I biled over. I grabbed his slick *har*, and may be I
didn't gin him *scissors!* Jest as I was makin' him a *chawed specimen,*
some feller holler'd out, —'don't let *old Jones* in with that ar *rifle!*'
I didn't hear any more in that Bottom, — lightnin' couldn't a got
near enough to singe my coat tail. I jumped through that winder as
easy as a bar 'ud go through a cane brake; and cuss me if I
couldn't hear the grit of old Jones' teeth, and smell his glazed powder,
until I crossed old Mississippi."

Fun with a "Bar"

At the head of a ravine on the border of the river Platte, one
bright night in June, was gathered a party of Missouri hunters, who
were encamped after a day's chase for buffalo. The evening's repast
was over, and as they stretched themselves in easy attitudes around
their stack of rifles, each looked at the other with a kind of question-
ing expression, of whether it should be *sleep* or a *yarn?* The bright
moon, with full round face, streamed down into their midst, and
sprinkled her silvery sheen over shrub and flower, investing night
in those vast solitudes with a strange charm which forbid sleep, and
with common consent they raised themselves into a sitting posture
and proposed a "talk," as the red skins say. Dan Elkhorn was the
leader of the party, and all knew his store of adventure inexhaustible,
so a unanimous call was made upon Dan for a story. "Come, Dan,"
cried a crony, "give us something to laugh at, and let us break this
silence, which seems to breed a spirit of melancholy — stir us up,
old fellow, do!"

Dan pulled his long knife out of his belt, and laying it before him, smoothed back his long grey hair. He was a genuine specimen of the hardy American mountaineer, — like the Indian, he dressed in deer skins and wore the moccason, while every seam in his iron countenance told of 'scapes and peril. Seeing that all were attention he commenced —

"Well, draw up closer, boys, so I shan't have to holler, 'cause breth is gittin' kind a short with me now, and I want to pacel it out to last pretty strong till the wind-up hunt. You, Mike, keep your eye skinned for Ingins, 'cause ef we git deep in a yarn here, without a top eye open, the cussed varmints'll pop on us unawars, and be stickin' some of thur quills in us — nothin' like havin' your eye open and insterments ready. I've a big idea to gin you an account of some fun I had with an old *bar*, on the Missouri, when I was a younker, and considerably more spry than I am jest now. I want to tell you fust, boys, that bars are knowin' animals, and they kin jest tell a younker of the human kind as easily as they kin a small pig from the old sow; — they don't fool with me now, for they've got to *know me!*

"Well, old Alic Dennison, a neighbour of mine on the Missouri, had bin about two years up in the mountains, and when he came home he gin a treat to all the fellars within thirty miles of him — that was jest seven families — and among 'em, in course, I got an invite. Alic and I had sot our cabins on opposite sides of the drink, near enough to see each other, and a red skin, ef he'd come on a scalp visit, would a bin diskivered by either. When Alic's frolic was to cum off, I was on hand, sartain. About evenin' I got my small dug-out, and fixin' my rifle carefully in the fore eend, and stickin' my knife in the edge whar it would be handy, I jest paddled over the drink.

A little above our location thar wur a bend in the stream which a kind a turned the drift tother eend up, and planted them about the spot between our cabins — snags and sawyers, jest thar, wur dreadful plenty, and it took mity nice padlin' to git across without tiltin'; howsever, I slid atween 'em, sarpentine fashion, and got over clar as a pet coon. Thar wur considerable folks at Alic's, fur some of the families in them diggins had about twenty in number, and the gals among 'em warn't any on your pigeon creaturs, that a fellar dassent tech fur fear of spilin' 'em, but raal scrougers — any on 'em over fourteen could lick a *bar*, easy. My decided opinion jest now is, that thur never was a grittyer crowd congregated before on that stream, and sich other dancin' and drinkin' and eatin' *bar* steaks, and corn dodger, and huggin' the gals, don't happen but once in a fellar's lifetime, and scarcely that often. Old Alic had a darter Molly, that

war the most enticin', gizzard-ticklin', heart-distressin' *feline* creatur
that ever made a fellar git owdacious, and I seed Tom Sellers cavortin'
round her like a young buffalo — he was puttin' in the biggest kind
a licks in the way of courtin', and between her eyes and the sweetened
whiskey he'd drank, you'd a thought the fellar would a bursted. Jest
to make matters lively, I headed up alongside of Molly, and shyed a
few soft things at her, sech as askin' how she liked bar steaks cooked,
and if Jim Tarrant warn't equal in the elbow to a mad *panter's* tail,
when he war fiddlin' that last reel, and sech amusin' light conversation. Well, boys, Tom started swellin' *instanter*. He tried to draw her
attention from me; but I got talkin' about some new improvements
I war contemplatin' about my cabin, and the cow I expected up from
St. Louis, 'sides lonely feelins I'd bin havin' lately, and Tom couldn't
git in a show of talk, edgeways. Didn't he git mad? — wur you ever
near enough to a panter when his *har* riz with wrath? Well, ef you
have, you can create some idea of Tom's state of mind, and how
electricity, from liquor and love, run out to the eends of his head
kiverin'. It wur easy to see he wur a gittin' dangerous, so I slid off
and left him alone with the gal. Arter I got a talkin' to another one
of the settlers' young women, Molly kept lookin' at me, and every
now and then sayin' somethin' pleasin' across to me, while she warn't
payin' any attention to Tom at all. He spread himself into a stiff bow
and left her; then movin' across the floor like a wounded deer, he
steadied himself on the back of my seat, and lookin' me in the
face, says:

"'*Mister* Elkhorn, I shud be strenuously obleeged to you ef you'll
step down thar with me by the old persimmen tree.'

"I nodded my head, and told him to trot outside and wait till I got
the docyments, and as soon as he moved I sent his old *daddy* to
accompany him. I jest informed the old fellar that Tom wanted a
fight, and as he was too full of corn juice to cut carefully, I didn't
want to take advantage of him. The old man said he was obleeged
to me, and moved out. Tom, thinkin' it wur me, staggered ahead of
the old man, and I concluded, as it war near mornin', to leave; 'cause I
knew when Tom found out his daddy was along with him instead of
me, he'd have a fight any how. I acknowledge the corn, boys, that
when I started my track warn't anythin' like a *bee-line;* — the
sweeten'd whiskey had made me powerful thick-legged; but arter a
fashion I got to my dug-out, with nothin' of weapon along in the
world but the paddle. Thar war jest enough light to tell that snags
wur plenty, and jest enough corn juice inside to make a fellar not
care a cuss fur 'em. I felt strong as a hoss, too, and the dug-out hadn't
more'n leaped six lengths from the bank afore — zip — chug — co-

souse I went — the front eend jest lifted itself agin a sawyer and emptied me into the ele*ment!* In about a second I came up bang agin a snag, and I guess I grabbed it sudden, while old Missouri curl'd and purl'd around me as ef she was in a hurry to git to the mouth, so she might muddy the Mississippi. I warn't much skeer'd, but still I didn't jest like to hang on thar till daylight, and I didn't want to make a fuss fur fear they'd say I war skary. I had sot myself on the eend of the snag, and was jest tryin' to cypher out some way of gittin' to shore, when I thought I diskiver'd a fellar sittin' on the bank. At fust, he looked so black in the coat I thought it war Tom Sellers, who'd sot himself down to wait fur a fight: — Tom had on at the frolic a black blanket coat with a velvet collar, and he thought it particularly nice. Arter lookin' at him move about and sit down on his hunkers once or twice, I thought I'd holler to him; but he appeared so dreadful drunk that I didn't expect much help from him.

" 'Tom,' shouted I, 'come out here with a dug-out, and help a fellar off, will you?'

"He sot still, without sayin' a word. 'Well,' says I to him, 'you're meaner than an Ingin! and would bait a trap with your daddy's leggins.' He didn't move fur a spell; at last into the drink he popped, and now, thought I, he *is* mad and *no* dispute. I could see him paddlin' right fur me, and I holler'd to him that I had no insterments, but he didn't say a whisper, ony shoved along the faster. At last up he come agin my snag, and the next minit he reached fur me, and then he tried to fix his teeth into my moccason; so guessin' it war time to do somethin', I jest grabbed fur his muzzle, and I'm blessed, boys, ef it warn't a great *he bar!* The cussed varmint had watched me from the house and seed I had no weapons, and when I upsot he just counted me his'n, and as quietly calculatin' on the bank how he'd best git me out of th. water. I had nothin' in the yearth but a small fancy pen knife, but I stuck that in him so quick that he let me go, and while he swam for one snag I reached for another. I never heerd a bar laugh out loud afore, but I'm a sucker ef he didn't snigger twice at the way he rolled me off my log.

"We sot lookin' at one another fur a spell, when I seed the varmint gittin' ready to call on me agin, and in about a second more off he dropped, and strait he took a shute for my location. As he came up close to me I slit his ear with the small blade, and he got mad; but jest as he was circling round me to git a good hold, I dropped on to his hinder eend and grabbed his har, and I guess I made him move fur shore a leetle faster than a steam boat — my little blade kept him dreadful *itchy.* Well, the fun of the thing wur, boys, as soon as the varmint teched shore, he turned right round on me, and I'm cussed if I hadn't to turn round, too, and scratch for the snag agin! with that consarned *bar* feelin' my legs with his paw every stroke I war makin' to git away from him! I got a little skary, now, and a good deal mad, fur thar the varmint war a waitin' for me, and whinin' as ef he had been ill-treated, and thar I wur perched up on a sawyer, bobbin' up and down in the water. At last I sot a hollerin' and kept on at it, and hollered louder, until I seed some one cum from the house, and singin' out agin they answered me. I asked who it war, and found that it war Molly, old Alic's darter; so I gin her a description of my siteaytion, and she war into a dug-out in a minit, and paddlin' towards me. I believe I said wonce, boys, that bars wur knowin' critters, but ef thar's anythin' true on this yearth, it's the fact, that this consarned animal had made up his mind to upsot that gal, and I'm blessed ef he didn't jest as cute as ef he'd bin human! Startin' from his snag he swam to the dug-out, put up both paws, and over it went — over went Molly into the stream, and off slid Mister *bar,* laffin' out *loud!* as I'm a white man.

"I seized Molly as she came floatin' towards me, and stuck her upon my sawyer, while I started for an adjinin' snag. I could hear Molly grittin' her teeth, she war so bilin' mad, and jest as soon as she could git breath, she hollered to me to be sure I never rested till I killed that varmint. I swore on that snag that I'd grow thin chasin' the critter, and she seemed to git pacified. Well, thar we wur, in the stream, and it a leetle too rough to swim in easy, so we had to sing out for help, and I yelled till I war nigh onto hoarse, afore anythin' livin' stirred about the house; at last, nigger Jake came down to the edge of the river, jest as day was breakin', and puttin' his hand over his eyes, he hollers —

" 'Why, Massa Dan, is dat you wot's been hollowin' eber so long for somebody!'

" 'You've jest took the notion to cum see, have you, you lazy nigger — now git a dug-out and come out here and git your missus and me off these snags, and do it quick, too, or I'll make *you* holler!'

" 'What, Missus dar, *too!'* shouted the nigger, 'well, dat's funny — de Lor!' and off the cussed blueskin started fur the house, and in a few minits all that could gethered out to see us and laugh at our water locations.

"I had bin gittin' riled by degrees, and now was at a dangerous pint — the steam began to rise off on me till thar wur a small fog above my head, and as the half drunken varmints roared a laffin, and cracked their jokes about our courtin' in the middle of the drink, I got awful excited. 'I'll make ribbons of every man among you,' says I, 'when I git whar thar's a chance to fight.' And then the cussed crew roared the louder. Tom Sellers yelled out that we'd bin tryin' to *elope,* and this made Molly mad, — her daddy got a little mad, too, and I bein' already mad, thar wur a wrathy trio on us, and the old fellow said, ef he thought I'd been playin' a two-faced game, and bitin' his friendship like a pizen varmint, he'd drop me off the log I wur on with a ball from his rifle. I jest told him to fire away and be d—d, for I wur wore out a patience. Some of the boys held him, while others got the dug-out and came to our assistance. I jest got them to drop me on my side of the river, and to send over my rifle, and as soon as it war on hand I onloosed my dog Yelp, and started to wipe out my disgrace.

"That infernal bar, as soon as he'd tossed Molly in the stream, started for the woods; but, as ef he had reasoned on the chances, the varmint came to the conclusion that he couldn't git away, and so got up into a crotch of a low tree, about a quarter of a mile from my cabin. Old Yelp smelled him, and as soon as I clapped peeper on him I let sliver, when the varmint dropped like a log, — I went to him and found he'd bin dead for an hour. My little blade couldn't a killed him, so it's my opinion, clearly entertained, that the owdacious varmint, knowin' I'd kill him for his trick, jest climbed up thar whar I could easy find him, and died to spite me!

"His hide, and hard swearin', got me and Molly out of our elopin' scrape, and the lickin' I gin Tom Sellers that spring has made us good friends ever sence. He don't wonce ventur' to say anythin' about that *bar scrape,* without my permission!"

Smoking a Grizzly

"What, you hev never seen a *live* Grizzly?" exclaimed an old Oregon gold-digger, with whom we were engaged in a *"bar"* conversation one evening on Jamestown bar.

"Never," said I, in all seriousness, "it has never been my good fortune to encounter one of the beautiful varments."

"Well, hoss, when you *do,* perhaps it won't be the pleasantest minit you've ever hed, for thar aint no varmint in these hills, nor any whar else I've ben, that kin kick wuss, either round or sideways, than a full grown Grizzly."

"But you can easily get out of the way of a clumsy animal like that," said I, provoking the old digger into a yarn of his experience in regard to Grizzlys.

"Well, when you kin get out of thur way, little feller, I gives you my advice, to get out quicker; for tho' they aint built raal beautiful for runnin, they *lope* awful smart when thur arter a humin' critter. I was desperate glad to get away from one myself once."

I had provoked him to the edge of a bar story, and knowing from his manner, that his relation of such an occurrence as getting away from a Grizzly would be interesting, I tempted him on.

"Where did you say you fell in with him?" inquired I.

"I didn't say I fell in with him anywhar," answered he; "cuss the varmint, he fell in with me, and I'd a leetle ruther hev fell in with the Old Nick jest at that minit. I was over thar, two miles 'tother side of the high ridge beyond Sullivan's, lookin' arter that gray mule of mine — and talkin' about wicked things, jest puts me thinkin' what a detarminedly vicious sarpint that gray mule was! Well, I was huntin' her, and arter runnin' over the hill, and shootin' down half a dozen gulches, I began to get out of wind; and set down to bless that gray critter for the many tramps she had given me. I'll swar no lariat 'ud hold her, not ef it was made of bull-hide an inch thick. I hadn't sot more'n a minit, when I heerd a snort, and a roar, and a growl, and a right smart sprinklin' of fast travelin', all mixed up together. Lookin' up a perpendikelar hill, right behind me, thar I saw comin' my gray mule, puttin' in her best licks, and a few yards behind her was a grizzly, not much bigger than a *yearling.* Many an infernal scrape that mule has taken me into afore, but this was rather the tightest place she ever did get me into. I hadn't a weepun about me, 'cept one of those mean, one-barreled auction pistols; and that hadn't a consarned mite of a load in, and I hadn't nothing to load it with, and no time to put it in, ef I had; and ef it had been loaded, it wouldn't hev been worth a cuss!

"You had better believe boys, that my skin got moist suddint — thar waren't no dry diggins under my red shirt, long afore that grizzly got down the hill. The infarnal mule no sooner seed me than she jest wheeled round and put me atween her and the bar, and stood off to see ef I wouldn't lick him about as easy as I used to whale her when she got stubborn. Old grizzly drawed up when he seed me, and 'gin to roll his old barrel head about, and grunt, as ef I was mor'n he bargained for; and I'd jest given him that mule, easy, to hev got off square. As the fellers say at monte, he was a lay out I didn't want to bet on.

"I commenced backin' out, and wanted to make it a draw game; but he kept shufflin' up to me, and any feller who had been close to his head, would hev giv his whole pile just to get a chance to *cut.* I considered my effects — that pan, rocker and a crow-bar — jest as good as ministered upon; and almost felt the coroner sittin' on my body. I stuck my hands into my pockets to see if there warn't a knife about me, and I pulled out half a dozen boxes of *Lucifer Matches,* that had just been bought that afternoon. I don't know what put it in my head, but I sot a box blazin', an' held it out towards old grizzly, and I reckin you havn't often seen two eyes stick out wusser than his did then. He drew back at least ten yards, and settin' the box down on the airth, I jest moved off about twenty yards in t'other direction. The bar crept up to the lucifers and took a smell, and if the muscles of my jaws hadn't been so tight with fear, I'd hev bursted into a reg'lar snort of laughin', at seein' how he turned up his nose and sniffled. The next minit he retreated at least fifty yards; and then I sot another box of the lucifers, and — boys, dar you b'lieve it — he gin to *back out!* As soon as I felt I had him skeert, I didn't keer a cuss for a whole drove of grizzlys. I jerked out another box of lucifers, teeched it off, and let out the most onairthly yell that ever woke those diggins, and the way that bar broke into a canter 'ud hev distanced any quarter nag in Christendom! He jest seemed to think that anythin' that could fire up as easy, and smell as bad as me, war rather a delicate subject to kick up a row with. As he was gettin' over the hill, I fairly squeeled out laughin', and I'll swar ef that impudent mule — which was standin' behind me — didn't snicker out too! I looked for a rock to hit her — instead of ketchin' her to ride to camp — and the ungrateful critter sot right off in a trot, and left me to walk! I made short time atween that ravine and my tent; for I was awful feer'd that my grizzly was waitin' some place to take a second look at me, and might bring a few older varmints along to get thur opinion what kind of crittur I wur.

"Ah, boys! (said he, in conclusion) Providence has helped me out of many a scrape; but it warn't him saved me from the grizzly! Ef it hadn't ben old Satan, or some Dutchman, invented brimstone and lucifer matches, thar would hev been an' end to this critter, and the verdict would hev been — *Died of a Grizzly.*"

George Washington Harris

(1814-1869)

Born near Pittsburgh, George Washington Harris grew up in Knoxville, Tennessee, between the Cumberland and Great Smoky Mountains. The thinly populated country retained its frontier character until well into the present century, and it furnished inspiration to writers of local color as well as lusty realism. Harris absorbed the idiom, folkways, and attitudes of the East Tennessee mountain people, the satisfaction they found in the fulfillment of their natural appetites, and the results — ludicrous, pathetic, and grim — of their frustrations. He infused his yarns with elements of satire and hints of humanity's predilection for devilment. The result is a density of texture beyond that of the majority of Southwestern humorists whose writings have less ulterior purpose.

Largely self-educated but certainly not unsophisticated, Harris was a careful observer and a good listener. He was also versatile, working at various times as steamboat captain, railroad conductor, farmer, metalsmith, manager of a sawmill and a copper mine, and owning land and slaves. He contributed sporting stories to the *Spirit of the Times* in 1843 and two years later a description of "a Tennessee Frolic." In 1854 Sut Lovingood, his most famous creation, made his first and only appearance in the *Spirit of the Times* in the sketch "Sut Lovingood's Daddy, Acting Horse." The Sut tales, some of them Democratic Party political propaganda, were printed frequently in Tennessee newspapers of the 1850's, and a collection, *Sut Lovingood: Yarns Spun by a "Nat'ral Born Durn'd Fool,"* was reviewed by Mark Twain.

Sut's vision is frighteningly clear and his philosophy existential. In one sketch, "Sut Lovingood's Sermon," he lists his "five pow'ful strong pints ove karactar":

> *Fustly,* that I haint got nara a soul, nuffin but a whisky proof gizzard, sorter like the wust half ove a ole par ove saddil bags. *Seconly,* that I'se too durn'd a fool tu cum even onder millertary lor. *Thudly,* that I hes the longes' par ove laigs ever hung tu eny cackus, 'sceptin only ove a grandaddy spider, an' kin beat *him* a usen ove em jis' es bad es a skeer'd dorg kin beat a crippled mud turkil. *Foufly,* that I kin chamber more cockscrew, kill-devil whisky, an' stay on aind, than enything 'sceptin only a broad bottum'd chun. *Fivety,* an' las'ly, kin git intu more durn'd misfortnit skeery scrapes, than enybody, an' then run outen them faster, by golly, nor enybody.

He emphasizes his impiety, cowardice, and capacity for whiskey and mischief and insists upon his innate character as "a nat'ral born durn'd fool." Fool he may well be, but he sees himself for what he is and he holds no illusions regarding family, church, or state. Though he has his moments of revulsion, he has decided to make out as best he can — a best which includes good food and drink, hearty wenches like Sicily Burns, belly laughs, and the occasional chance to tip the scales of justice.

For Sut is not merely a trickster, a Till Eulenspiegel or Pedro Urdemales. Himself the victim of a bad cosmic joke, he carefully selects his victims from a roster of prime drunkards, adulterers, lechers, sadists, bigots, and hypocrites. In the end his social role becomes clear. He has a triple function: advocate of healthy animal spirits, satirist, and scourge.

The world being what it is, Sut sees more of bestiality than of healthy animal spirits. In "Sut Lovingood's Daddy, Acting Horse," Sut's father, in removing his filthy rags, divests himself of the last shreds of decency and humanity, and lays bare his bestial nature. In "Parson John Bullen's Lizards," a lecherous preacher is tricked into exposing his nakedness and hypocrisy. The metaphor is classic; one recalls that the mad King Lear talks much of nakedness and tears off his clothes.

TEXT: "Sut Lovingood's Daddy, Acting Horse," "Parson John Bullen's Lizards," "Blown Up with Soda," "Sicily Burns's Wedding," "Mrs. Yardley's Quilting," "Rare Ripe Garden-Seed," and "Contempt of Court — Almost" from *Sut Lovingood: Yarns Spun by a "Nat'ral Born Durn'd Fool"* (New York, 1867).

Sut Lovingood's Daddy, Acting Horse

"Hole that ar hoss down tu the yeath." "He's a fixin fur the heavings." "He's a spreadin his tail feathers tu fly. Look out, Laigs, if you ain't ready tu go up'ards." "Wo, Shavetail." "Git a fiddil; he's tryin a jig." "Say, Long Laigs, rais'd a power ove co'n didn't yu?" "Taint co'n, hits redpepper."

These and like expressions were addressed to a queer looking, long legged, short bodied, small headed, white haired, hog eyed, funny sort of a genius, fresh from some bench-legged Jew's clothing store, mounted on "Tearpoke," a nick tailed, bow necked, long, poor, pale sorrel horse, half dandy, half devil, and enveloped in a perfect network of bridle, reins, crupper, martingales, straps, surcingles, and red ferreting, who reined up in front of Pat Nash's grocery, among a crowd of mountaineers full of fun, foolery, and mean whisky. This was SUT LOVINGOOD.

"I say, you durn'd ash cats, jis' keep yer shuts on, will ye? You never seed a rale hoss till I rid up; you's p'raps stole ur owned shod rabbits ur sheep wif borrerd saddils on, but when you tuck the fus' begrudgin look jis' now at this critter, name Tarpoke, yu wer injoyin a sight ove nex' tu the bes' hoss what ever shell'd nubbins ur toted jugs, an' he's es ded es a still wum, poor ole Tickytail!

"Wo! wo! Tarpoke, yu cussed infunnel fidety hide full ove hell fire, can't yu stan' still an listen while I'se a polishin yer karacter off es a mortul hoss tu these yere durned fools?"

Sut's tongue or his spurs brought Tearpoke into something like passable quietude while he continued:

"Say yu, sum ove yu growin hogs made a re-mark jis' now 'bout redpepper. I jis' wish tu say in a gineral way that eny wurds cupplin redpepper an Tarpoke tugether am durn'd infurnal lies."

"What killed Tickeytail, Sut?" asked an anxious inquirer after truth.

"Why nuffin, you cussed fool; he jis' died so, standin up et that. Warn't that rale casteel hoss pluck? Yu see, he froze stiff; no, not that adzactly, but starv'd fust, an' froze arterards, so stiff that when dad an' me went tu lay him out an' we push'd him over, he stuck out jis' so, (spreading his arms and legs), like ontu a carpenter's bainch, an' we hed tu wait ni ontu seventeen days fur 'im tu thaw afore we cud skin 'im."

"Skin 'im?" interrupted a fat-faced youth, whittling on a corn stalk, "I thot yu wanted tu lay the hoss out."

"The hell yu did! Ain't skinin the natral way ove layin out a hoss, I'd like tu no? See a yere, soney, yu tell yer mam tu hev yu sot back jis' bout two years, fur et the rate yu'se a climbin yu stan's a pow'ful chance tu die wif yer shoes on, an' git laid hoss way, yu dus."

The rat-faced youth shut up his knife and subsided.

"Well, thar we wer — dad, an' me, (counting on his fingers), an' Sall, an' Jake, (fool Jake we calls 'im fur short), an' Jim, an' Phineass, an' Callimy Jane, an' Sharlottyann, an' me, an' Zodiack, an' Cashus Clay, an' Noah Dan Webster, an' the twin gals, (Castur and Pollox), an' me, an' Catherin Second, an' Cleopatry Antony, an' Jane Barnum Lind, an' me, an' Benton Bullion, an' the baby what haint nam'd yet, an' me, an' the Prospect, an' mam herself, all lef in the woods alone, wifout ara hoss tu crup wif."

"Yu'se counted yersef five times, Mister Lovingood," said a tomato-nosed man in ragged overcoat.

"Yas, ole Still-tub, that's jis the perporshun I bears in the famerly fur dam fool, leavin out Dad in course. Yu jis let me alone, an' be a thinkin ove gittin more hoops ontu yu. Yus leakin now; see thar." Ha! ha! from the crowd, and "Still-tub" went into the doggery.

"Warn't that a devil's own mess ove broth fur a 'spectabil white famerly tu be sloshin about in? I be durned ef I didn't feel sorter like stealin a hoss sumtimes, an' I speck I'd a dun hit, but the stealin streak in the Lovingoods, all run tu durned fool, an' the onvartus streak all run tu laigs. Jis look down the side ove this yere hoss mos' tu the groun'. Dus yu see em?

"Well we waited, an' wished, an' rested, an' plan'd, an' wished, an' waited agin, ontil ni ontu strawberry time, hopin sum stray hoss mout cum along; but dorg my cats, ef eny sich good luck ever cums wifin reach ove whar dad is, he's so dod-dratted mean, an' lazy, an' ugly, an' savidge, an' durn fool tu kill.

"Well, one nite he lay awake till cock-crowin a-snortin, an' rollin, an' blowin, an' shufflin, an' scratchin hissef, an' a whisperin at mam a heap, an' at breckfus' I foun' out what hit ment. Says he, 'Sut, I'll tell yu what we'll du: I'll be hoss *mysef*, an' pull the plow whilst yu drives me, an' then the "Ole Quilt" (he ment that fur mam), an' the brats kin plant, an' tend, ur jis let hit alone, es they darn pleze; I ain't a carein.'

"So out we went tu the pawpaw thicket, an' peel'd a rite smart chance ove bark, an' mam an' me made geers fur dad, while he sot on the fence a-lookin at us, an' a studyin pow'rful. I arterards foun' out, he were a-studyin how tu play the kar-acter ove a hoss puffectly.

"Well, the geers becum him mitily, an' nuffin wud du 'im but he mus hev a bridil, so I gits a umereller brace — hit's a litil forked piece ove squar wire bout a foot long, like a yung pitch-fork, yu no — an' twisted hit sorter intu a bridil bit snaffil shape. Dad wanted hit made kurb, es he hedn't work'd fur a good while, an' said he mout sorter feel his keepin, an' go tu ravin an' cavortin.

"When we got the bridil fix'd ontu dad, don't yu bleve he sot in tu chompin hit jis like a rale hoss, an' tried tu bite me on the arm, (he allers were a mos' complikated durned ole fool, an' mam sed so when he warnt about). I put on the geers, an' while mam wer a-tyin the belly ban', a-strainin hit pow'rful tite, he drapt ontu his hans, sed 'Whay-a-a' like a mad hoss wud, an' slung his hine laigs at mam's hed. She step'd back a littil an' wer standin wif her arms cross'd a-restin em on her stumick, an' his heel taps cum wifin a inch ove her nose. Sez she, 'Yu plays hoss better nur yu dus husban.' He jis' run backards on all fours, an' kick'd at her agin, an' —— an' pawd the groun wif his fis.

" 'Lead him off tu the field, Sut, afore he kicks ur bites sumbody,'
sez mam. I shoulder'd the gopher plow, an' tuck hole ove the bridil.
Dad leaned back sulky, till I sed cluck cluck wif my tongue, then he
started. When we cum tu the fence I let down the gap, an' hit made
dad mad; he wanted tu jump hit on all fours hoss way. Oh' geminy!
what a durn'd ole fool kin cum tu ef he gins up tu the complaint.

"I hitch'd 'im tu the gopher, a-watchin him pow'ful clost, fur I'd
see how quick he cud drap ontu his hans, an' kick, an' away we went,
dad leanin forard tu his pullin, an we made rite peart plowin, fur tu
hev a green hoss, an' bark gears; he went over the sprowts an' bushes
same as a rale hoss, only he traveled on two laigs. I wer mitily
hope up bout co'n; I cud a'mos' see hit a cumin up; but thar's a
heap ove whisky spilt twixt the counter an' the mouf, ef hit ain't got
but two foot tu travil. 'Bout the time he wer beginin tu break sweat,
we cum tu a sassafrack bush, an tu keep up his kar-acter es a hoss,
he buljed squar intu an' thru hit, tarin down a ball ho'nets nes' ni
ontu es big es a hoss's hed, an' the hole tribe kiver'd 'im es quick
es yu cud kiver a sick pup wif a saddil blanket. He lit ontu his
hans agin, an kick'd strait up onst, then he rar'd, an' fotch a squeal
wus nur ara stud hoss in the State, an' sot in tu strait runnin away
jis es natral es yu ever seed any uther skeer'd hoss du. I let go the
line an' holler'd, Wo! dad, wo! but yu mout jis' es well say Woa! tu
a locomotum, ur Suke cow tu a gal.

"Gewhillitins! how he run: when he cum tu bushes, he'd clar the
top ove em wif a squeal, gopher an' all. P'raps he tho't thar mout
be anuther settlment ove ball ho'nets thar, an' hit wer safer tu go
over than thru, an' quicker dun eny how. Every now an' then he'd
fan the side ove his hed, fust wif wun fore laig an' then tuther, then
he'd gin hissef a roun-handed slap what soundid like a waggin
whip ontu the place whar the breechbands tetches a hoss, a-runnin
all the time an' a-kerrin that ar gopher jis 'bout as fas' an' es hi frum
the yeath es ever eny gopher were kerried I'll swar. When he cum
tu the fence, he jis tore thru hit, bustin an' scatterin ni ontu seven
panils wif lots ove broken rails. Rite yere he lef the gopher, geers,
close, clevis, an' swingltress, all mix'd up, an' not wuf a durn. Mos'
ove his shut staid ontu the aind ove a rail, an' ni ontu a pint ove
ho'nets stop'd thar a stingin all over; hits smell fool'd em. The
balance on em, ni ontu a gallun, kep' on wif dad. He seem'd tu run
jis adzactly es fas' es a ho'net cud fly; hit wer the titest race I ever
seed, fur wun hoss tu git all the whipin. Down thru a. saige field they
all went, the ho'nets making hit look like thar wer smoke roun'
dad's bald hed, an' he wif nuffin on the green yeath in the way ove
close about im, but the bridil, an' ni ontu a yard ove plow line sailin

behine, wif a tir'd out ho'net riding on the pint ove hit. I seed that he wer aimin fur the swimin hole in the krick, whar the bluff am over twenty five foot pupendiculer tu the warter, an' hits ni ontu ten foot deep.

"Well, tu keep up his karacter es a hoss, plum thru, when he got tu the bluff he loped off, ur rather jis' kep on a runnin. Kerslunge intu the krick he went. I seed the warter fly plum abuv the bluff from whar I wer.

"Now rite thar, boys, he over-did the thing, ef actin hoss tu the scribe wer what he wer arter; fur thars nara hoss ever foaldid durned fool enuf tu lope over eny sich place; a cussed muel mout a dun hit, but dad warn't actin muel, tho' he orter tuck that karacter; hits adzactly sooted tu his dispersition, all but not breedin. I crept up tu the aidge, an' peep'd over. Thar wer dad's bald hed fur all the yeath like a peeled inyin, a bobbin up an' down an' aroun, an' the ho'nets sailing roun tuckey buzzard fashun, an' every onst in a while one, an' sum times ten, wud take a dip at dad's bald head. He kep' up a rite peart dodgin onder, sumtimes afore they hit im, an' sumtimes arterard, an' the warter wer kivered wif drownded ball ho'nets. Tu look at hit frum the top ove the bluff, hit wer pow'ful inturestin, an' sorter funny; I wer on the bluff myse'f, mine yu.

"Dad cudent see the funny part frum whar he wer, but hit seem'd tu be inturestin tu him frum the 'tenshun he wer payin tu the bisness ove divin an' cussin.

"Sez I, 'Dad, ef yu's dun washin yersef, an hes drunk enuff, less go back tu our plowin, hit will soon be powful hot.' 'Hot — hell!' sez dad; 'hit am hot rite now. Don't (an onder went his hed) yer see (dip) these cussed (dip) infun — (dip) varmints arter me?' (dip). 'What,' sez I, 'them ar hoss flies thar, that's nat'ral, dad; you ain't raley fear'd ove them is yu?' 'Hoss flies! h—l an' (dip) durnation!' sez dad, 'they'se rale ginui — (dip) ball ho'nets, (dip) yu infunel ignurant cuss!' (dip). 'Kick em — bite em — paw em — switch em wif yure tail, dad,' sez I. 'Oh! soney, soney, (dip) how I'll sweeten yure — (dip) when these (dip) ho'nets leave yere.' 'Yu'd better du the levin yursef dad,' sez I. 'Leave yere! Sturn yu d—n fool! How (dip) kin I, (dip) when they won't (dip) let me stay (dip) atop (dip) the warter even.' 'Well, dad, yu'l hev tu stay thar till nite, an' arter they goes tu roos' yu cum home. I'll hev yer feed in the troft redy; yu won't need eny curyin tu-nite will yu?' 'I wish (dip) I may never (dip) see to-morrer, ef I (dip) don't make (dip) hame strings (dip) outer yure hide (dip) when I dus (dip) git outen yere,' sez dad. 'Better say yu wish yu may never see anuther ball ho'net, ef yu ever play hoss agin,' sez I.

"Them words toch dad tu the hart, an' I felt they mus' be my las, knowin dad's onmollified nater. I broke frum them parts, an' sorter cum over yere tu the copper mines. When I got tu the hous', 'Whar's yer dad?' sez mam. 'Oh, he turn'd durn fool, an' run away, busted every thing all tu cussed smash; an's in the swimin hole a divin arter minners. Look out mam, he'll cum home wif a angel's temper; better sen' fur sum strong man body tu keep him frum huggin yu tu deth. 'Law sakes!' sez mam; 'I know'd he cudent act hoss fur ten minutes wifout actin infunel fool, tu save his life.'

"I staid hid out ontil nex' arternoon, an' I seed a feller a-travelin'. Sez I, "How de do, mister? What wer agwine on at the cabin, this side the crick, when yu pass'd thar?' 'Oh, nuthin much, only a pow'ful fat man wer a lyin in the yard ontu his belly, wif no shut on, an' a 'oman wer a greasin ove his shoulders an' arms outen a gourd. A pow'ful curious, vishus, skeery lookin cuss he is tu b'shure. His head am as big es a wash pot, an' he hasent the fust durned sign ove an eye — jist two black slits. Is thar much small pox roun yere?' 'Small hell!' sez I, 'no sir.' 'Been much fightin in this neighborhood lately?' 'Nun wuf speakin ove,' sez I. He scratched his head — 'Nur French measils?' 'Not jis clost,' sez I. 'Well, do yu know what ails that man back thar?' 'Jist gittin over a vilent attack ove dam fool,' sez I. 'Well, who is he eny how?' I riz tu my feet, an' straiched out my arm, an' sez I, 'Strainger, that man is my dad.' He looked at my laigs an' pussonel feeters a moment, an' sez he, 'Yas, dam ef he ain't.'

"Now boys, I haint seed dad since, an' I dusent hev much appertite tu see im fur sum time tu cum. Less all drink! Yere's luck tu the durned old fool, an' the ho'nets too."

Parson John Bullen's Lizards

AIT ($8) DULLARS REW-ARD.
TENSHUN BELEVERS AND KONSTABLES! KETCH 'IM! KETCH 'IM!

This kash wil be pade in korn, ur uther projuce, tu be kolected at ur about nex camp-meetin, *ur thararter,* by eny wun what ketches him, fur the karkus ove a sartin wun SUT LOVINGOOD, dead ur alive, ur ailin, an' safely giv over tu the purtectin care ove Parson John Bullin, ur lef' well tied, at Squire Mackjunkins, fur the raisin ove the devil pussonely, an' permiskusly discumfurtin the wimen very powerful, an' skeerin ove folks generly a heap, an' bustin up a promisin, big warm meetin, an' a makin the wickid larf, an' wus, an' wus, insultin ove the passun orful.

Test,   JEHU WETHERO.
Sined by me,
JOHN BULLEN, the passun.

I found written copies of the above highly intelligible and vindictive proclamation, stuck up on every blacksmith shop, doggery, and store door, in the Frog Mountain Range. Its blood-thirsty spirit, its style, and above all, its chirography, interested me to the extent of taking one down from a tree for preservation.

In a few days I found Sut in a good crowd in front of Capehart's Doggery, and as he seemed to be about in good tune, I read it to him.

"Yas, George, that ar dockymint am in dead yearnist sartin. Them hard shells over thar dus want me the wus kine, powerful bad. *But,* I spect ait dullers won't fetch me, nither wud ait hundred, bekase thar's nun ove 'em fas' enuf tu ketch me, nither is thar hosses by the livin jingo! Say, George, much talk 'bout this fuss up whar yu've been?" For the sake of a joke I said yes, a great deal.

"Jes' es I 'spected, durn 'em, all git drunk, an' skeer thar fool sefs ni ontu deth, an' then lay hit ontu me, a poor innersent youf, an' es soun' a belever es they is. Lite, lite, ole feller an' let that roan ove yourn blow a litil, an' I'll 'splain this cussed misfortnit affar: hit hes ruinated my karacter es a pius pusson in the s'ciety roun' yere, an' is a spreadin faster nur meazils. When ever yu hear eny on 'em a spreadin hit, gin hit the dam lie squar, will yu? I haint dun nuffin tu one ove 'em. Hits true, I did sorter frustrate a few lizzards a littil, but they haint members, es I knows on.

"You see, las' year I went tu the big meetin at Rattlesnake Springs, an' wer a sittin in a nice shady place convarsin wif a frien' ove mine, intu the huckil berry thickit, jis' duin nuffin tu nobody an' makin no fuss, when, the fust thing I remembers, I woke up frum a trance what I hed been knocked into by a four-year old hickory-stick, hilt in the paw ove ole Passun Bullin, durn his alligater hide; an' he wer standin a striddil ove me, a foamin at the mouf, a-chompin his teeth — gesterin wif the hickory club — an' a-preachin tu me so you cud a'hearn him a mile, about a sartin sins gineraly, an' my wickedness pussonely an' mensunin the name ove my frien' loud enuf tu be hearn tu the meetin 'ous. My poor innersent frien' wer dun gone an I were glad ove hit, fur I tho't he ment tu kill me rite whar I lay, an' I didn't want her tu see me die."

"Who was she, the friend you speak of Sut?" Sut opened his eyes wide.

"Hu the devil, an' durnashun tole *yu* that hit wer a she?"

"Why, you did, Sut" ——

"I *didn't,* durn ef I did. Ole Bullin dun hit, an' I'll hev tu kill him yet, the cussed, infernel ole talebarer!" ——

"Well, well, Sut, who was she?"

"Nun ove y-u-r-e b-i-s-n-i-s-s, durn yure littil ankshus picter! I *sees yu* a lickin ove yure lips. I *will* tell you one thing, George; that night, a neighbor gal got a all-fired, overhandid stroppin frum her mam, wif a stirrup leather, an' ole Passun Bullin, hed et supper thar, an what's wus nur all, that poor innersent, skeer'd gal hed dun her levil bes' a cookin hit fur 'im. She begged him, a trimblin, an' a-cryin not tu tell on her. He et her cookin, he promised her he'd keep dark — an' then went strait an' tole her mam. Warnt that rale low down, wolf mean? The durnd infunel, hiperkritikal, pot-bellied, scaley-hided, whisky-wastin, stinkin ole groun'-hog. He'd a heap better a stole sum *man's* hoss; I'd a tho't more ove 'im. But I paid him plum up fur hit, an' I means tu keep a payin him, ontil one ur tuther, ove our toes pints up tu the roots ove the grass.

"Well, yere's the way I lifted that note ove han'. At the nex big meetin at Rattilsnaik — las' week hit wer — I wer on han' es solemn es a ole hat kivver on collection day. I hed my face draw'd out intu the shape an' perporshun ove a taylwer's sleeve-board, pint down. I hed put on the convicted sinner so pufeckly that an' ole obsarvin she pillar ove the church sed tu a ole he pillar, es I walked up tu my bainch:

" 'Law sakes alive, ef thar ain't that *orful* sinner, Sut Lovingood, pearced plum thru; hu's nex?'

"Yu see, by golly, George, I *hed* tu promis the ole tub ove soap-greas tu cum an' hev myself converted, jis' tu keep him frum killin me. An' es I know'd hit wudn't interfare wif the relashun I bore tu the still housis roun' thar, I didn't keer a durn. I jis' wanted tu git *ni* ole Bullin, onst onsuspected, an' this wer the bes' way tu du hit. I tuk a seat on the side steps ove the pulpit, an' kivvered es much ove my straitch'd face es I could wif my han's, tu prove I wer in yearnis. Hit tuck powerful — fur I hearn a sorter thankful kine ove buzzin all over the congregashun. Ole Bullin hissef looked down at me, over his ole copper specks, an' hit sed jis' es plain es a look cud say hit: 'Yu am thar, ar you — durn yu, hits well fur yu that yu cum.' I tho't sorter diffrent frum that. I tho't hit wud a been well fur *yu,* ef I hadent a-cum, but I didn't say hit jis then. Thar wer a monstrus crowd in that grove, fur the weather wer fine, an' b'levers were plenty roun' about Rattilsnaik Springs. Ole Bullin gin out, an' they sung that hyme, yu know:

> "Thar will be mournin, mournin yere, an' mournin thar,
> On that dredful day tu cum."

"Thinks I, ole hoss, kin hit be possibil enybody hes told yu what's a gwine tu happin; an' then I tho't that nobody know'd hit but me, and I wer cumforted. He nex tuck hisself a tex pow'fly mixed wif brimstone, an' trim'd wif blue flames, an' then he open'd. He cummenced ontu the sinners; he threaten'd 'em orful, tried tu skeer 'em wif all the wust varmints he cud think ove, an' arter a while he got ontu the idear ove Hell-sarpints, and he dwelt on it sum. He tole 'em how the ole Hell-sarpints wud sarve em if they didn't repent; how cold they'd crawl over thar nakid bodys, an' how like ontu pitch they'd stick tu 'em es they crawled; how they'd rap thar tails roun' thar naiks chokin clost, poke thar tungs up thar noses, an' hiss intu thar years. This wer the way they wer tu sarve men folks. Then he turned ontu the wimmen: tole 'em how they'd quile intu thar buzzims, an' how they *wud* crawl down onder thar frock-strings, no odds how tite they tied 'em, an' how sum ove the oldes' an' wus ones wud crawl up thar laigs, an' travil *onder* thar garters, no odds how tight they tied *them,* an' when the two armys ove Hell-sarpents met, then — That las' remark *fotch 'em.* Ove all the screamin' an' hollerin, an' loud cryin, I ever hearn, begun all at onst, all over the hole groun' jis' es he hollered out that word 'then.' He kep on a bellerin, but I got so buisy jis' then, that I didn't listen tu him much, fur I saw that my time fur ackshun hed cum. Now yu see, George, I'd cotch seven ur eight big pot-bellied lizzards, an' hed 'em in a littil narrer bag, what I had made a-purpus. Thar tails all at the bottim, an' so crowdid fur room that they cudent turn roun'. So when he wer a-ravin ontu his tip-toes, an' a-poundin the pulpit wif his fis' — onbenowenst tu eny-body, I ontied my bag ove reptiles, put the mouf ove hit onder the bottim ove his britches-laig, an' sot intu pinchin thar tails. Quick es gunpowder they all tuck up his bar laig, making a nise like squirrils a-climbin a shell-bark hickory. He stop't preachin rite in the middil ove the word 'damnation,' an' looked fur a moment like he wer a listenin fur sumthin — sorter like a ole sow dus, when she hears yu a-whistlin fur the dorgs. The tarifick shape ove his feeters stopp't the shoutin an' screamin; instuntly yu cud hearn a cricket chirp. I gin a long groan, an' hilt my head a-twixt my knees. He gin hisself sum orful open-handed slaps wif fust one han' an' then tuther, about the place whar yu cut the bes' steak outen a beef. Then he'd fetch a vigrus ruff rub whar a hosses tail sprouts; then he'd stomp one foot, then tuther, then bof at onst. Then he run his han' atween his waisbun an' his shut an' reach'd way down, an' roun' wif hit; then he spread his big laigs, an' gin his back a good rattlin rub agin the pulpit, like a hog scratches hisself agin a stump, leanin tu hit pow'ful, an' twitchin, an' squirmin all over, es ef he'd slept in a dorg bed, ur ontu a pisant hill. About this time, one ove my lizzards scared an' hurt by all this poundin' an' feelin, an' scratchin, popp'd out his head frum the passun's shut collar, an' his ole brown naik, an' were a-sur-veyin the crowd, when old Bullin struck at 'im, jis' too late, fur he'd dodged back agin. The hell desarvin ole raskil's speech now cum tu 'im, a'n sez he, 'Pray fur me brethren an' sisteren, fur I is a-rastilin wif the great inimy rite now!' an' his voice wer the mos' pitiful, trimblin thing I ever hearn. Sum ove the wimmen fotch a painter yell, an' a young docter, wif ramrod laigs, lean'd toward me monstrus knowin like, an' sez he, 'Clar case ove Delishus Tremenjus.' I nodded my head, an' sez I, 'Yas, spechuly the tremenjus part, an' Ise feard hit hain't at hits worst.' Ole Bullin's eyes wer a-stickin out like ontu two buckeyes flung agin a mud wall, an' he wer a-cuttin up more shines nor a cockroach in a hot skillet. Off went the clamhammer coat, an' he flung hit ahine 'im like he wer a-gwine intu a fight; he hed no jackid tu take off, so he unbuttond his galluses, an' vigrusly flung the ainds back over his head. He fotch his shut over-handed a durnd site faster nor I got outen my pasted one, an' then flung hit strait up in the air, like he jis' wanted hit tu keep on up furever; but hit lodged ontu a black-jack, an' I sed one ove my lizzards wif his tail up, a-racin about all over the ole dirty shut, skared too bad tu jump. Then he gin a shorter shake, an' a stompin kine ove twis', an' he cum outer his britches. He tuck 'em by the bottim ove the laigs, an' swung 'em roun' his head a time ur two, an' then fotch 'em down cherall-up over the frunt ove the pulpit. You cud a hearn the smash a quarter ove a mile! Ni ontu fifteen shorten'd biskits, a boiled chicken, wif hits laigs crossed, a big dubbil-bladed knife, a hunk ove ter-backer, a cob-pipe, sum copper ore, lots ove broken glass, a cork, a sprinkil ove whisky, a squirt, an' three lizzards flew permiskusly all over that meetin-groun', outen the upper aind ove them big flax britches. One ove the smartes' ove my lizzards lit head-fust intu the buzzim ove a fat 'oman, es big es a skin'd hoss, an' ni ontu es ugly, who sot thuty yards off, a fannin herself wif a tucky-tail. Smart tu the las', by golly, he imejuntly commenced runnin down the centre ove her breas'-bone, an' kep on, I speck. She wer jis' boun' tu faint; an' she did hit fust rate — flung the tucky-tail up in the air, grabbed the lap ove her gown, gin hit a big histin an' fallin shake, rolled down the hill, tangled her laigs an' garters in the top ove a huckilberry bush, wif her head in the branch an' jis' lay still. She wer interestin, she wer, ontil a serious-lookin, pale-faced 'oman hung a nankeen ridin skirt over the huckilberry bush. That wer all that wer dun to'ards bringin her too, that I seed. Now ole Bullin hed nuffin left ontu 'im but a par ove heavy, low quarter'd shoes, short woolen socks, an' eel-skin garters tu keep off the cramp. His skeer hed druv him plum crazy, fur he felt roun' in the air, abuv his head, like he wer huntin sumthin in the dark, an' he beller'd out, 'Brethren, brethren, take keer ove yerselves, the Hell-sarpints *hes got me!*' When this cum out yu cud a'hearn the screams tu Halifax. He jis' spit in his han's, an' loped over the frunt ove the pulpid *kerdiff!* He lit on top ove, an' rite amung the mos' pius part ove the congregashun. Ole Misses Chaneyberry sot wif her back tu the pulpit, sorter stoopin forrid.

He lit a-stradil ove her long naik, a shuttin her up wif a snap, her head atwix her knees, like shuttin up a jack-knife, an' he sot intu gittin away his levil durndest; he went in a heavy lumberin gallop, like a ole fat waggon hoss, skared at a locomotive. When he jumpt a bainch he shook the yeath. The bonnets, an' fans clar'd the way an' jerked most ove the children wif em, an' the rest he scrunched. He open'd a purfeckly clar track tu the woods, ove every livin thing. He weighed ni ontu three hundred, hed a black stripe down his back, like ontu a ole bridil rein, an' his belly wer 'bout the size an' color ove a beef paunch, an' hit a-swingin out frum side tu side; he leand back frum hit, like a littil feller a-totin a big drum, at a muster, an' I hearn hit plum tu whar I wer. Thar wer cramp-knots on his laigs es big es walnuts, an' mottled splotches on his shins; an' takin him all over, he minded ove a durnd crazy ole elephant, pussessed ove the devil, rared up on hits hind aind, an' jis' *gittin* frum sum imijut danger ur tribulashun. He did the loudest, an' skariest, an' fussiest runnin I ever seed, tu be no faster nur hit wer, since dad tried tu outrun the ho'nets.

"Well, he disapear'd in the thicket jis' bustin — an' ove all the noises yu ever hearn, wer made thar on that camp groun': sum wimen screamin — they wer the skeery ones; sum larfin — they wer the wicked ones; sum cryin — they wer the fool ones, (sorter my stripe yu know); sum trying tu git away wif thar faces red — they wer the modest ones; sum lookin arter ole Bullin — they wer the curious ones; sum hangin clost tu thar sweethearts — they wer the sweet ones; sum on thar knees wif thar eyes shot, but facin the way the old mud turtil wer a-runnin — they wer the 'saitful ones; sum duin nuthin — they wer the waitin ones; an' the mos' dangerus ove all ove em by a durnd long site.

"I tuck a big skeer mysef arter a few rocks, an' sich like fruit, spattered ontu the pulpit ni ontu my head; an' es the Lovingoods, durn em! knows nuffin but tu run, when they gits skeerd, I jis' put out fur the swamp on the krick. As I started, a black bottil ove baldface smashed agin a tree furninst me, arter missin the top ove my head 'bout a inch. Sum durn'd fool professor dun this, who hed more zeal or sence; fur I say that eny man who wud waste a quart ore even mean sperrits, fur the chance ove knockin a poor ornary devil like me down wif the bottil, is a bigger fool nor ole Squire Mackmullen, an' he tried tu shoot hissef wif a onloaded hoe-handle."

"Did they catch you Sut?"

"Ketch thunder!" *No sir!* jis' look at these yere laigs! Skeer me, hoss, jis' skeer me, an' then watch me while I stay in site, an' yu'll never ax that fool question agin. Why, durn it, man, that's what the ait dullers am fur.

"Ole Barbelly Bullin es they calls 'im now, never preached ontil yesterday, an' he hadn't the fust durn'd 'oman tu hear 'im, *they hev seed too much ove im.* Passuns ginerly hev a pow'ful strong holt on wimen; but, hoss, I tell yu thar ain't meny ove em kin run start nakid over an' thru a crowd ove three hundred wimen an' not injure thar karacters *sum.* Enyhow, hits a kind ove show they'd ruther see one at a time, an' pick the passun at that. His tex' wer, 'Nakid I cum intu the world, an' nakid I'm a gwine outen hit, ef I'm spard ontil then.' He sed nakidness warnt much ove a sin, purtickerly ove dark nights. That he wer a weak, frail wum ove the dus', an' a heap more sich truck. Then he totch ontu me; sed I wer a living proof ove the hell-desarvin nater ove man, an' that thar warnt grace enuf in the whole 'sociation tu saften my outside rind; that I wer 'a lost ball' forty years afore I wer born'd, an' the bes' thing they cud du fur the church, wer tu turn out, an' still hunt fur me ontil I wer shot. An' he never said Hell-sarpints onst in the hole preach. I b'leve, George, the durnd fools am at hit.

"Now, I wants yu tu tell ole Barbelly this fur me, ef he'll let me an' Sall alone, I'll let him alone — a-while; an' ef he don't, ef I don't lizzard him agin, I jis' wish I may be dod durnd! *Skeer him if yu ken.*

"Let's go tu the spring an' take a ho'n.

"Say George, didn't that ar Hell-sarpint sermon ove his'n, hev sumthin like a Hell-sarpint aplicashun? Hit looks sorter so tu me."

Blown Up with Soda

Sut's hide is healed — the wounds received in his sudden separation from his new shirt have ceased to pain, and, true to his instincts, or rather "a famerly dispersition," as he calls it, he "pitches in," and gets awfully blown up by a wild mountain girl. Hear him, poor fellow!

"George, did yu ever see Sicily Burns? Her dad lives at the Rattilsnake Spring, clost ontu the Georgia line."

"Yes, a very handsome girl."

"Handsome! that ar word don't kiver the case; hit souns sorter like callin good whiskey strong water, when yu ar ten mile frum a still-hous, hit a rainin, an' yer flask only haf full. She shows amung wimen like a sunflower among dorg fennil, ur a hollyhawk in a patch ove smartweed. Sich a buzzim! Jis' think ove two snow balls wif a strawberry stuck but-ainded intu bof on em. She takes adzactly fifteen inches ove garter clar ove the knot, stans sixteen an' a 'alf hans hi, an weighs one hundred an' twenty-six in her petticoatail afore brekfus'. She cudent crawl thru a whisky barrel wif bof heads stove out, nur sit in a common arm-cheer, while yu cud lock the top hoop ove a chun, ur a big dorg collar, roun the huggin place."

"The *what*, Sut?"

"The *wais'* yu durn oninishiated gourd, yu! Her har's es black es a crow's wing et midnite, ur a nigger hanlin charcoal when he's hed no brekfus'; hit am es slick es this yere bottil, an' es long es a hoss's tail. I've seed her jump over a split-bottim cheer wifout showin her ankils, ur ketchin her dress ontu the knobs. She cud cry an' larf et the same time, an' either lov'd ur hated yu all over. Ef her hate fell ontu yu, yu'd feel like yu'd been whipp'd wif a pizen vine, ur a broom made outen nettils when yer breeches an' shut wer bof in the wash-tub. She kerried enuf devil about her tu run crazy a big settilment ove Job's children; her skin wer es white es the inside ove a frogstool, an' her cheeks an' lips es rosey es a pearch's gills in dorgwood blossom time — an' sich a smile! why, when hit struck yu far an' squar hit felt jis' like a big ho'n ove onrectified ole Munongahaley, arter yu'd been sober fur a month, a tendin ove a ten hoss prayer-meetin twist a day, an' mos' ove the nites.

"Three ove her smiles when she wer a tryin ove hersef, taken keerfully ten minutes apart, wud make the gran' captin ove a temprunce s'iety so durn'd drunk, he wudn't no his britches frum a par ove bellowses ur a pledge frum a — a — warter-pot. Oh! I be durned ef hits eny use talkin, that ar gal cud make me murder ole Bishop Soul, hissef, ur kill mam, not tu speak ove dad, ef she jis' hinted she wanted sich a thing dun. Sich an 'oman cud du more devilmint nur a loose stud hoss et a muster groun', ef she only know'd what tools she totes, an' I'se sorter beginin tu think she no's the use ove the las' durnd wun, tu a dot. Her ankils wer es roun', an' not much bigger nur the wrist ove a rifle-gun, an' when she were a-dancin, ur makin up a bed, ur gittin over a fence —— Oh durn sich wimen! Why ain't they all made on the hempbreak plan, like mam, ur Betts Carr, ur Suke Miller, so they wudn't bother a feller's thinker et all.

"George, this worl am all 'rong enyhow, more temtashun than perventitive; ef hit wer ekal, I'd stand hit. What kin the old prechurs an' the ugly wimen 'spect ove us, 'sposed es we ar tu sich invenshuns es she am? Oh, hits jis' no use in thar talkin, an' groanin, an' sweatin tharsefs about hit; they mus jis' upset nater ontu her head, an' keep her thar, ur shet up. Less taste this yere whisky."

Sut continued, wiping his mouth on his shirt-sleeve:

"I'se hearn in the mountins a fust rate fourth proof smash ove thunder cum onexpected, an' shake the yeath, bringin along a string ove litenin es long es a quarter track, an' es bright es a weldin heat, a-racin down a big pine tree, tarin hit intu broom-splits, an' toof pickers, an' raisin a cloud ove dus', an' bark, an' a army ove lim's wif a smell sorter like the devil wer about, an' the long darnin needil leaves fallin roun wif a tif — tif — quiet sorter soun, an' then a quiverin on the yeath es littil snakes die; an' I felt quar in my in'ards, sorter ha'f cumfurt, wif a littil glad an' rite smart ove sorry mix'd wif hit.

"I'se seed the rattil-snake squar hissef tu cum at me, a sayin z-e-e-e-e, wif that nisey tail ove his'n, an' I felt quar agin — mons'rous quar. I've seed the Oconee River jumpin mad frum rock tu rock wif hits clear, cool warter, white foam, an' music" ——

"What, Sut?"

"Music; the rushin warter dus make music; so dus the wind, an' the fire in the mountin, an' hit gin me an oneasy queerness agin; but every time I look'd at that gal Sicily Burns, I hed all the feelins mix'd up, ove the litenin, the river, an' the snake, wif a totch ove the quicksilver sensashun a huntin thru all my veins fur my ticklish place.

"Tu gether hit all in a bunch, an' tie hit, she wer gal all over, frum the pint ove her toe-nails tu the aind ove the longes' har on the highis knob on her head — gal all the time, everywhar, an' wun ove the exhitenis kine. Ove corse I lean'd up tu her, es clost es I dar tu, an' in spite ove these yere laigs, an' my appertite fur whisky, that ar shut-skinin bisness, an' dad's actin hoss, she sorter lean'd tu me, jis' a scrimpshun, sorter like a keerful man salts uther pepil's cattil in the mountin, barly enuf tu bring em back tu the lick-log sum day — that's the way she salted me, an' I 'tended the lick-log es reg'lar es the old bell cow; *an'* I wer jis' beginin tu think I wer ontu the rite trail tu es much cumfurt, an' stayin awake a-purpus, es old Brigham Young wif all his saddil-culler'd wimen, an' the papers tu fetch more, ef he wants em.

"Well, wun day a cussed, palaverin, inyun-eatin Yankee pedlar, all jack-nife, an' jaw, cum tu ole man Burns wif a carryall full ove appil-parin-mersheens, jewsharps, calliker, ribbons, sody-powder, an' uther durn'd truck.

"Now mine, I'd never hearn tell ove sody-powder in *my* born'd days; I didn't know hit from Beltashazur's off ox; but I no's now that hit am wus nur gunpowder fur hurtin, an' durn'd ni es smart tu go off.

"Thar ar Yankee pedlar hes my piusest prayer, an' I jis wish I hed a kaig ove the truck intu his cussed paunch, wif a slow match cumin out at his mouf, an' I hed a chunk ove fire. The feller what foun a mossel ove 'im big enuf tu feed a cockroach, orter be turn'd loose tu pastur amung seventy-five purty wimen, an' foun in whisky fur life, becase ove his good eyes in huntin los' things. George, a Yankee pedlar's soul wud hev more room in a turnip-seed tu fly roun in than a leather-wing bat hes in a meetin-hous; that's jis' so.

"Sicily hed bot a tin box ove the cold bilin truck an' hid hit till I cum tu the lick-log agin, yu know. Well, I jis' happen'd tu pas nex' day, an' ove corse stopp'd tu injoy a look at the temtashun, an' she wer mity luvin tu me. I never felt the like — put wun arm roun my naik, an' tuther whar the susingil goes roun a hoss, tuck the inturn ontu me wif her lef' foot, an' gin me a kiss. Sez she —

"Sutty, luv, I'se got sumthin fur yu, *a new sensashun*" —

"An' I b'leve in hit strong, fur I begun tu feel hit pow'ful. My toes felt like I wer in a warm krick wif minners a-nibblin at em; a cole streak wer a racin up an' down my back like a lizzard wif a tucky hen arter 'im; my hans tuck the ager, an' my hart felt hot an onsatisfied like. Then hit wer that I'd a-cut ole Soul's froat wif a hansaw, an' never batted my eye, ef she'd a-hinted the needsesity.

"Then she pour'd 'bout ten blue papers ove the fizilin powder intu a great big tumbler, an' es meny white papers intu anuther, an' put ni ontu a pint ove warter intu bof on em, stir'd em up wif a case-nife, an' gritted a morsel ove nutmaig on top, the 'saitful she torment lookin es solemn es a jasack in a snow storm, when the fodder gin out. She hilt wun, an' tole me tu drink tuther. I swaller'd hit at wun run; tasted sorter salty like, but I tho't hit were part ove the sensashun. But I wer slitely mistaken'd; hit wer yet tu cum, an' warn't long 'bout hit, hoss, better b'leve. Ternally durn all sensashuns ove every spot an' stripe! I say. Then she gin me tuther, an' I sent hit a chasin the fus' instalmint tu the sag ove my paunch, race-hoss way. Yu see I'd got the idear onder my har that hit wer *luv-powders*, an' I'd swaller'd the devil red hot frum home, a-thinkin that. Luv-powders *frum her!* jis' think ove hit yerse'f solemnly a minit, an' sit still ef yu kin.

"Jis' 'bout the time I were ketchin my breff, I tho't I'd swaller'd a thrashin-meersheen in full blast, wif a cuppil ove bull-dorgs, an' they hed sot intu fitin; an' I felt sumthin cumin up my swaller, monstrus like a hi pressur steamboat. I cud hear hit a-snortin, and scizzin. *Kotch agin, by the great golly!* tho't I; same famerly dispersishun to make a durn'd fool ove myse'f jis' es ofen es the sun sets, an' fifteen times ofener ef thar's a half a chance. Durn dad evermore, amen! I say.

"I happen'd tu think ove my hoss, an' I broke fur him. I stole a hang-dorg look back, an' thar lay Sicily, flat ove her back in the porch, clapin her hans, screamin wif laughin, her feet up in the air, a-kickin em a-pas' each uther like she wer tryin tu kick her slippers off. I'se pow'ful sorry I wer too bizzy tu look at em. Thar wer a road ove foam frum the hous' tu the hoss two foot wide, an' shoe mouf deep — looked like hit hed been snowin — a poppin, an' a-hissin, an' a-bilin like a tub ove soap-suds wif a red hot mole-board in hit. I gethered a cherry tree lim' es I run, an' I lit a-straddil ove ole Blackey, a-thrashin his hide like the devil beatin tan-bark, an' a-hissin wur nur four thousin mad ganders outen my mouf, eyes, noes, an' years. All this waked the ole hoss, an' he fotch one rar, one kiek, an' then he went — he jis' mizzel'd, skar'd. Oh lordy! how the foam rolled, an' the hoss flew! Es we turned the corner ove the gardin lot, I hearn Sicily call, es clar es a bugle:

" 'Hole hit down, Mister Lovingood! hole hit down! hits a cure fur puppy luv; hole hit *down!*'

"Hole hit down! Hu ever hearn sich a onpossibil — Why, *rite then* I wer a-feelin the bottim ove my paunch cumin up arter hit, inside out, jis' like the bottim ove a green champain bottil. I wer spectin tu see hit every blast. That, wif what Sicily sed, wer a-hurtin my thinker pow'ful bad, an' then the ise-warter idear, that hit warn't a luv-powder arter all that hurtin — takin all tugether, I wer sorter wishin hit mout keep on til I wer all biled tu foam, plum tu my heel-strings.

"I wer aimin fur Dr. Goodman's, at the Hiwasee Copper Mine, tu git sumthin tu simmer hit down wif, when I met ole Clapshaw, the suckit-rider, a-travelin to'ards sumbody's hot biskit an' fried chicken. As I cum tarin along, he hilt up his hans like he wanted tu pray fur me; but es I wanted sumthin tu reach furder, an' take a ranker holt nur his prars cud, I jis' rambled ahead. I wer hot arter a ten-hoss dubbil-actin steam paunch-pump, wif wun aind sock'd deep intu my soda lake, an' a strong manbody doctur at tuther; hit wer my *big want* jis' then. *He* tuck a skeer, es I wer cumin strait fur him; his faith gin out, an' he dodged, flat hat, hoss, an' saddil-bags, intu the thicket. I seed his hoss's tail fly up over his back, es he disappear'd intu the bushes; thar mus' a-been spurrin gwine on 'bout thar. I liked his moshuns onder a skeer rite well; he made that dodge jis' like a mud-turkil draps ofen a log when a big steamboat cums tarin a-pas'. Es he pass'd ole man Burns's, Sicily hailed 'im tu ax ef he met enybody gwine up the road in a sorter hurry. The poor devil tho't that p'raps he mout; warnt sure, but he hed seed a dreadful forewarnin, ur a ghos', ur ole Belzebub, ur the Tariff. Takin all things tugether, however, in the litil time spar'd tu 'im fur 'flection, hit mus' a-been a crazy, long-laiged shakin Quaker, fleein frum the rath tu cum, on a black an' white spotted hoss, a-whipin 'im wif a big brush; an' he hed a white beard what cum frum jis onder his eyes down tu the pumil ove the saddil, an' then forked an' went tu his knees, an' frum thar drapp'd in bunches es big es a crow's nes', tu the groun; an' he hearn a soun like ontu the rushin ove mitey warters, an' he wer pow'fully exersized 'bout hit enyhow. Well, I guess he wer, an' so wer his fat hoss, an' so wer old Blackey, an' more so by a durn'd site wer me mysef. Arter he cumpos'd hissef he rit out his fool noshuns fur Sicily, that hit wer a new steam invenshun, tu spread the Catholic doctrin, an' tote the Pope's bulls tu pastur in distunt lans, made outen sheet iron, ingin rubber, tann'd leather, ise cream, an' fat pine, an' that the hoss's tail wer made outen iron wire, red hot at the pint, an' a stream ove sparks es long es the steerin-oar ove a flatboat foller'd thararter; an' takin hit all tugether hit warnt a safe thing tu meet in a lane ove a dark nite; an' he tho't he hed a call over the mountin tu anuther sarkit; that chickens warnt es plenty over thar, but then he wer a self-denyin man.

"Now, George, all this beard, an' spotted hoss, an' steam, an' fire, an' snow, an' wire tails, wer durn'd skeer'd suckit rider's humbug; hit all cum outen my paunch, wifout eny vomitin ur coaxin, an' ef hit hedn't, I'd a dun been busted intu more scraps nur thar's aigs in a big catfish.

" 'Hole hit down, Mister Lovingood! hole hit down!' Now warnt that jis' the durndes' onreasonabil reques' ever an 'oman made ove man? She mout jis es well ax'd me tu swaller my hoss, an' then skin the cat on a cob-web. She's pow'ful on docterin tho', I'll swar tu that."

"Why, Sut?"

"Kase she cur'd my puppy-luv wif wun dost, durn her! George, am sody *pizen?*"

"No; why?"

"I sorter 'spected hit wer, an' I sot in, an' et yarbs, an' grass, an' roots, till I'se pounch'd out like ontu a ole cow; my hole swaller an' paunch am tann'd hard es sole leather. I axes rot-gut no odds now. Yere's a drink tu the durndes' fool in the worl' — jis' me!"

And the bottom of Sut's flask flashed in the sunlight.

Sicily Burns's Wedding

"Hey Ge-orge!" rang among the mountain slopes; and looking up
to my left, I saw "Sut," tearing along down a steep point, heading me
off, in a long kangaroo lope, holding his flask high above his head,
and hat in hand. He brought up near me, banteringly shaking the
half-full "tickler," within an inch of my face.

"Whar am yu gwine? take a suck, hoss? This yere truck's *ole*.
I kotch hit myse'f, hot this mornin frum the still wum. Nara durn'd
bit ove strike-nine in hit — I put that ar piece ove burnt dried peach
in myse'f tu gin hit color — better nur ole Bullen's plan: he puts in
tan ooze, in what he sells, an' when that haint handy, he uses the
red warter outen a pon' jis' below his barn; — makes a pow'ful natral
color, but don't help the taste much. Then he correcks that wif red
pepper; hits an orful mixtry, that whisky ole Bullen makes; no
wonder he seed 'Hell-sarpints.' He's pisent ni ontu three quarters ove
the b'levin parts ove his congregashun wif hit, an' tuther quarter he's
sot intu ruff stealin an' cussin. Ef his still-ous don't burn down, ur
he peg out hisse'f, the neighborhood am ruinated a-pas' salvashun.
Haint he the durndes sampil ove a passun yu ever seed enyhow?

"Say George, du yu see these yere well-poles what I uses fur laigs?
Yu sez yu sees em, dus yu?"

"Yes."

"Very well; I passed 'em a-pas' each uther tuther day, right peart.
I put one out a-head jis' so, an' then tuther 'bout nine feet a-head ove
hit agin jis' so, an' then kep on a-duin hit. I'll jis' gin yu leave tu
go tu the devil ha'f hamon, ef I didn't make fewer tracks tu the mile,
an' more tu the minit, than wer ever made by eny human man body,
since Bark Wilson beat the saw-log frum the top ove the Frog Mountin
intu the Oconee River, an' dove, an' dodged hit at las'. I hes allers
look'd ontu that performince ove Bark's as onekel'd in histery, allers
givin way tu dad's ho'net race, however.

"George, every livin thing hes hits pint, a pint ove sum sort. Ole
Bullen's pint is a durn'ed fust rate, three bladed, dubbil barril'd,
warter-proof, hypockracy, an' a never-tirein appertite fur bal'-face.
Sicily Burns's pint am tu drive men folks plum crazy, an' then bring
em too agin. Gin em a rale Orleans fever in five minits, an' then
in five minits more, gin them a Floridy ager. Durn her, she's down on
her heels flat-footed now. Dad's pint is tu be king ove all durn'd
fools, ever since the day ove that feller what cribb'd up so much co'n

down in Yegipt, long time ago, (he ran outen his coat yu minds). The Bibil tell us hu wer the stronges' man — hu wer the bes' man — hu wer the meekis' man, an' hu the wises' man, but leaves yu tu guess hu wer the bigges' fool.

"Well, eny man what cudent guess arter readin that ar scrimmage wif an 'oman 'bout the coat, haint sense enuf tu run intu the hous', ef hit wer rainin ded cats, that's all. Mam's pint am in kitchen insex, bakin hoe-cake, biling greens, an' runnin bar laiged. My pint am in taking aboard big skeers, an' then beatin enybody's hoss, ur skared dorg, a-runnin frum onder em agin. I used tu think my pint an' dad's wer jis' the same, sulky, unmix'd king durn'd fool; but when he acted hoss, an' mistook hossflies fur ho'nets, I los' heart. Never mine, when I gits his 'sperence, I may be king fool, but yet great golly, he gets frum bad tu wus, monstrus fas'.

"Now ef a feller happens tu know what his pint am, he kin allers git along, sumhow, purvided he don't swar away his liberty tu a temprins s'ciety, live tu fur frum a still-hous, and too ni a chu'ch ur a jail. Them's my sentimints on 'pints,' — an' yere's my sentimints ontu folks: Men wer made a-purpus jis' tu eat, drink, an' fur stayin awake in the yearly part ove the nites: an' wimen wer made tu cook the vittils, mix the sperits, an' help the men du the stayin awake. That's all, an' nuthin more, onless hits fur the wimen tu raise the devil atwix meals, an' knit socks atwix drams, an' the men tu play short kerds, swap hosses wif fools, an' fite fur exersise at odd spells.

"George, yu don't onderstan life yet scarcely at all, got a heap tu larn, a heap. But 'bout my swappin my laigs so fas' — these yere very par ove laigs. I hed got about a fox squirril skin full ove biled co'n juice packed onder my shut, an' onder my hide too, I mout es well add, an' wer aimin fur Bill Carr's on foot. When I got in sight ove ole man Burns's, I seed ni ontu fifty hosses an' muels hitch'd tu the fence. Durnashun! I jis' then tho't ove hit, 'twer Sicily's wedding day. She married ole Clapshaw, the suckit rider. The very feller hu's faith gin out when he met me sendin sody all over creashun. Suckit-riders am surjestif things tu me. They preaches agin me, an' I hes no chance tu preach back at them. Ef I cud I'd make the institushun behave hitsef better nur hit dus. They hes sum wunderful pints, George. Thar am two things nobody never seed: wun am a dead muel, an' tuther is a suckit-rider's grave. Kaze why, the he muels all turn intu old field school-masters, an' the she ones intu strong minded wimen, an' then when thar times cums, they dies sorter like uther folks. An' the suckit-riders ride ontil they marry; ef they marrys money, they turns intu store-keepers, swaps hosses, an' stays away ove colleckshun Sundays. Them what marrys, an' by sum orful mistake *misses the money,* jis' turns intu polertishuns, sells 'ile well stock,' and dies sorter in the human way too.

"But 'bout the wedding. Ole Burns hed a big black an' white bull, wif a ring in his snout, an' the rope tied up roun his ho'ns. They rid 'im tu mill, an' sich like wif a saddil made outen two dorgwood forks, an' two clapboards, kivered wif a ole piece ove carpet, rope girth, an' rope stirrups wif a loop in hit fur the foot. Ole 'Sock,' es they call'd the bull, hed jis' got back frum mill, an' wer turn'd intu the yard, saddil an' all, tu solace hissef a-pickin grass. I wer slungin roun the outside ove the hous', fur they hedn't hed the manners tu ax me in, when they sot down tu dinner. I wer pow'fully hurt 'bout hit, an' happen'd tu think — SODY. So I sot in a-watchin fur a chance tu du sumthin. I fus' tho't I'd shave ole Clapshaw's hoss's tail, go tu the stabil an' shave Sicily's mare's tail, an' ketch ole Burns out, an' shave his tail too. While I wer a-studyin 'bout this, ole Sock wer a-nosin 'roun, an' cum up ontu a big baskit what hilt a littil shattered co'n; he dipp'd in his head tu git hit, an' I slipp'd up an' jerked the handil over his ho'ns.

"Now, George, ef yu knows the nater ove a cow brute, they is the durndes' fools amung all the beastes, ('scept the Lovingoods); when they gits intu tribulashun, they knows nuffin but tu shot thar eyes, beller, an' back, an' keep a-backin. Well, when ole Sock raised his head an' foun hissef in darkness, he jis' twisted up his tail, snorted the shatter'd co'n outen the baskit, an' made a tremenjus lunge agin the hous'. I hearn the picters a-hangin agin the wall on the inside a-fallin. He fotch a deep loud rusty beller, mout been hearn a mile, an' then sot intu a onendin sistem ove backin. A big craw-fish wif a hungry coon a-reachin fur him, wer jis' nowhar. Fust agin one thing, then over anuther, an' at las' agin the bee-bainch, knockin hit an' a dozen stan ove bees heads over heels, an' then stompin back'ards thru the mess. Hit haint much wuf while tu tell what the bees did, ur how soon they sot intu duin hit. They am pow'ful quick-tempered littil critters, enyhow. The air wer dark wif 'em, an' Sock wer kivered all over, frum snout tu tail, so clost yu cudent a-sot down a grain ove wheat fur bees, an' they wer a-fitin one anuther in the air, fur a place on the bull. The hous' stood on sidelin groun, an' the back door wer even wif hit. So Sock happen tu hit hit plum, jis' backed intu the hous' onder 'bout two hundred an' fifty pouns ove steam, bawlin orful, an' every snort he fotch he snorted away a quart ove bees ofen his sweaty snout. He wer the leader ove the bigges' an' the madest army ove bees in the worild. Thar wer at leas' five solid bushels ove 'em. They hed filled the baskit, an' hed lodged ontu his tail, ten deep, ontil hit wer es thick es a waggin tung. He hed hit stuck strait up in the air, an' hit looked adzackly like a dead pine kivered wif ivey. I think he wer the hottes' and wus hurtin bull then livin; his temper, too, seemed tu be pow'fully flustrated. Ove *all* the durn'd times an' kerryins on yu *ever* hearn tell on wer thar an' thar abouts. He cum tail fust agin the old two story Dutch clock, an' fotch hit, bustin hits runnin geer outen hit, the littil wheels a-trundlin over the floor, an' the bees even chasin them. Nex pass, he fotch up agin the foot ove a big dubbil injine bedstead, rarin hit on aind, an' punchin one ove the posts thru a glass winder. The nex tail fus' experdishun wer made aginst the caticorner'd cupboard, outen which he made a perfeck momox. Fus' he upsot hit, smashin in the glass doors, an' then jis' sot in an' stomp'd everything on the shelves intu giblits, a-tryin tu back furder in that direckshun, an' tu git the bees ofen his laigs.

"Pickil crocks, perserves jars, vinegar jugs, seed bags, yarb bunches, paragorick bottils, aig baskits, an' delf war — all mix'd dam permiskusly, an' not worth the sortin, by a duller an' a 'alf. Nex he got a far back acrost the room agin the board pertishun; he went thru hit like hit hed been paper, takin wif him 'bout six foot squar ove hit in splinters, an' broken boards, intu the nex room, whar they wer eatin dinner, an' rite yere the fitin becum gineral, an' the dancin, squawkin, cussin, an' dodgin begun.

"Clapshaw's ole mam wer es deaf es a dogiron, an sot at the aind ove the tabil, nex tu whar ole Sock busted thru the wall; tail fus' he cum agin her cheer, a-histin her an' hit ontu the tabil. Now, the smashin ove delf, an' the mixin ove vittils begun. They hed sot severil tabils tugether tu make hit long enuf. So he jis' rolled 'em up a-top ove one anuther, an' thar sot ole Missis Clapshaw, a-straddil ove the top ove the pile, a-fitin bees like a mad wind-mill, wif her calliker cap in one han, fur a wepun, an' a cract frame in tuther, an' a-kickin, an' a-spurrin like she wer ridin a lazy hoss arter the doctor, an' a-screamin rape, fire, an' murder, es fas' es she cud name 'em over.

"Taters, cabbige, meat, soup, beans, sop, dumplins, an' the truck what yu wallers 'em in; milk, plates, pies, puddins, an' every durn fixin yu cud think ove in a week, wer thar, mix'd an' mashed, like hit had been thru a thrashin-meesheen. Ole Sock still kep a-backin, an' backed the hole pile, ole 'oman an' all, also sum cheers, outen the frunt door, an' down seven steps intu the lane, an' then by golly, turn'd a fifteen hundred poun summerset hissef arter em, lit a-top ove the mix'd up mess, flat ove his back, an' then kicked hissef ontu his feet agin. About the time he ris, ole man Burns —yu know how fat, an' stumpy, an' cross-grained he is, enyhow — made a vigrus mad snatch at the baskit, an' got a savin holt ontu hit, but cudent *let go quick enuf;* fur ole Sock jis' snorted, bawled, an' histed the ole cuss heels fust up intu the air, an' he lit on the bull's back, an' hed the baskit in his han.

"Jis' es soon es old Blackey got the use ove his eyes, he tore off down the lane tu out-run the bees, so durn'd fas' that ole Burns wer feard tu try tu git off. So he jis' socked his feet intu the rope loops, an' then cummenc'd the durndes' bull-ride ever mortal man ondertuck. Sock run atwix the hitched critters an' the railfence, ole Burns fust fiting him over the head wif the baskit tu stop him, an' then fitin the bees wif hit. I'll jis' be durn'd ef I didn't think he hed four ur five baskits, hit wer in so meny places at onst. Well, Burns, baskit, an' bull, an' bees, skared every durn'd hoss an' muel loose frum that fence — bees ontu all ove 'em, bees, by golly, everywhar. Mos' on 'em, too, tuck a fence rail along, fas' tu the bridil reins. Now I'll jis' gin yu leave tu kiss my sister Sall till she squalls, ef ever sich a sight wer seed ur sich nises hearn, es filled up that long lane. A heavy cloud ove dus', like a harycane hed been blowin, hid all the hosses, an' away abuv hit yu cud see tails, an' ainds ove fence-rails a-flyin about; now an' then a par ove bright hine shoes wud flash in the sun like two sparks, an' away ahead wer the basket a-sirklin roun an' about at ran-dum. Brayin, nickerin, the bellerin ove the bull, clatterin ove runnin hoofs, an' a mons'ous rushin soun, made up the noise. Lively times in that lane jis' then, warnt thar?

"I swar ole Burns kin beat eny man on top ove the yeath a-fitin bees wif a baskit. Jis' set 'im a-straddil ove a mad bull, an' let thar be bees enuf tu exhite the ole man, an' the man what beats him kin break me. Hosses an' muels wer tuck up all over the county, an' sum wer forever los'. Yu cudent go eny course, in a cirkil ove a mile, an' not find buckils, stirrups, straps, saddil blankits, ur sum-thin belongin tu a saddil hoss. Now don't forgit that about that hous' thar wer a good time bein had ginerally. Fellers an' gals loped outen windows, they rolled outen the doors in bunches, they clomb the chimleys, they darted onder the house jis' tu dart out agin, they tuck tu the thicket, they rolled in the wheat field, lay down in the krick, did everything but stan still. Sum made a strait run *fur* home, an' sum es strait a run *frum* home; livelyest folks I ever did see. Clapshaw crawled onder a straw pile in the barn, an' sot intu prayin — yu cud a-hearn him a mile — sumthin 'bout the plagues ove Yegipt, an' the pains ove the secon death. I tell yu now he lumbered.

"Sicily, she squatted in the cold spring, up tu her years, an turn'd a milk crock over her head, while she wer a drownin a mess ove bees onder her coats. I went tu her, an' sez I, 'Yu hes got anuther new sensashun haint yu?' Sez she —

" 'Shet yer mout, yu cussed fool!'

"Sez I, 'Power'ful sarchin' feelin bees gins a body, don't they?'

" 'Oh, lordy, lordy, Sut, these yere 'bominabil insex is jis' burnin me up!'

" 'Gin 'em a mess ove SODY,' sez I, 'that'll cool 'em off, an' skeer the las' durn'd one ofen the place.'

"She lifted the crock, so she cud flash her eyes at me, an' sed, 'Yu go tu hell!' *jis es plain.* I thought, takin all things tugether, that p'raps I mout es well put the mountin atwix me an' that plantashun; an' I did hit.

"Thar warnt an' 'oman, ur a gal at that weddin, but what thar frocks, an' stockins wer too tite fur a week. Bees am wus on wimen than men, enyhow. They hev a farer chance at 'em. Nex day I passed ole Hawley's, an' his gal Betts wer sittin in the porch, wif a white hankerchef tied roun her jaws; her face wer es red es a beet, an' her eyebrows hung 'way over heavy. Sez I, 'Hed a fine time at the weddin, didn't yu?' 'Yu mus' be a durn'd fool,' wer every word she sed. I hadent gone a hundred yards, ontil I met Missis Brady, her hans fat, an' her ankils swelled ontil they shined. Sez she, —

" 'Whar yu gwine, Sut?'

" 'Bee huntin,' sez I.

" 'Yu jis' say bees agin, yu infunel gallinipper, an' I'll scab yer head wif a rock.'

"Now haint hit strange how tetchus they am, on the subjick ove bees?

"Ove all the durn'd misfortinit weddins ever since ole Adam married that heifer, what wer so fon' ove talkin tu snaix, an' eatin appils, down ontil now, that one ove Sicily's an' Clapshaw's wer the worst one fur noise, disappintment, skeer, breakin things, hurtin, trubbil, vexashun ove spirrit, an' gineral swellin. Why, George, her an' him cudent sleep tugether fur ni ontu a week, on account ove the doins ove them ar hot-footed, 'vengeful 'bominabil littil insex. They never will gee tugether, got tu bad a start, mine what I tell yu. Yu haint time now tu hear how ole Burns finished his bull-ride, an' how I cum tu du that lofty, topliftical speciment ove fas' runnin. I'll tell yu all that sum uther time. Ef eny ove 'em axes after me, tell 'em that I'm over in Fannin, on my way tu Dahlonega. They is huntin me tu kill me, I is fear'd.

"Hit am an orful thing, George, tu be a natral born durn'd fool. Yu'se never 'sperienced hit pussonally, hev yu? Hits made pow'fully agin our famerly, an all owin tu dad. I orter bust my head open agin a bluff ove rocks, an' jis' wud du hit, ef I warnt a cussed coward. All my yeathly 'pendence is in these yere laigs — d'ye see 'em? Ef they don't fail, I may turn human sum day, that is sorter human, enuf tu be a Squire, ur school cummisiner. Ef I wer jis' es smart es I am mean, an' ornary, I'd be President ove a Wild Cat Bank in less nor a week. Is sperrits plenty over wif yu?"

Mrs. Yardley's Quilting

"Thar's one durn'd nasty muddy job, an' I is jis' glad enuf tu take a ho'n ur two, on the straingth ove hit."

"What have you been doing, Sut?"

"Helpin tu salt ole Missis Yardley down."

"What do you mean by that?"

"Fixin her fur rotten cumfurtably, kiverin her up wif sile, tu keep the buzzards from cheatin the wurms."

"Oh, you have been helping to bury a woman."

"That's hit, by golly! Now why the devil can't I 'splain myself like yu? I ladles out my words at random, like a calf kickin at yaller-jackids; yu jis' rolls em out tu the pint, like a feller a-layin bricks — every one fits. How is it that bricks fits so clost enyhow? Rocks won't ni du hit."

"Becaze they'se all ove a size," ventured a man with a wen over his eye.

"The devil yu say, hon'ey-head! haint reapin-mersheens ove a size? I'd like tu see two ove em fit clost. Yu wait ontil yu sprouts tuther ho'n, afore yu venters tu 'splain mix'd questions. George, did yu know ole Missis Yardley?"

"No."

"Well, she wer a curious 'oman in her way, an' she wore shiney specks. Now jis' listen: Whenever yu see a ole 'oman ahine a par ove *shiney* specks, yu keep yer eye skinn'd; they am dang'rus in the extreme. Thar is jis' no knowin' what they ken du. I hed one a-stradil ove me onst, fur kissin her gal. She went fur my har, an' she went fur my skin, ontil I tho't she ment tu kill me, an' wud a-dun hit, ef my hollerin hadent fotch ole Dave Jordan, a *bacheler*, tu my aid. He, like a durn'd fool, cotch her by the laig, an' drug her back'ards ofen me. She jis' kivered him, an' I run, by golly! The nex time I seed him he wer bald headed, an' his face looked like he'd been a-fitin wildcats.

"Ole Missis Yardley wer a great noticer ove littil things, that nobody else ever seed. She'd say right in the middil ove sumbody's serious talk: 'Law sakes! thar goes that yaller slut ove a hen, a-flingin straws over her shoulder; she's arter settin now, an' haint laid but seven aigs. I'll disapint *her,* see ef I don't; I'll put a punkin in her ne's, an' a feather in her nose. An' bless my soul! jis' look at that cow wif the wilted ho'n, a-flingin up dirt an' a-smellin the place whar hit cum frum, wif the rale ginuine still-wurim twis' in her tail, too; what upon the face ove the yeath kin she be arter now, the ole fool? watch her, Sally. An' sakes alive jis' look at that ole sow; she's a-gwine in a fas' trot, wif her empty bag a-floppin agin her sides. Thar, she hes stop't, an's a-listenin! massy on us! what a long yearnis grunt she gin; hit cum frum way back ove her kidneys. Thar she goes agin; she's arter no good, sich kerryin on means no good.'

"An' so she wud gabble, no odds who wer a-listenin. She looked like she mout been made at fust 'bout four foot long, an' the common thickness ove wimen when they's at tharsefs, an' then had her har tied tu a stump, a par ove steers hitched to her heels, an' then straiched out a-mos' two foot more — mos' ove the straichin cumin outen her laigs an' naik. Her stockins, a-hangin on the clothes-line tu dry, looked like a par ove sabre scabbards, an' her naik looked like a dry beef shank smoked, an' mout been ni ontu es tough. I never felt hit mysef, I didn't, I jis' jedges by looks. Her darter Sal wer bilt at fust 'bout the laingth ove her mam, but wer never straiched eny by a par ove steers an' she wer fat enuf tu kill; she wer taller lyin down than she wer a-standin up. Hit wer her who gin me the 'hump shoulder.' Jis' look at me; haint I'se got a tech ove the dromedary back thar bad? haint I humpy? Well, a-stoopin tu kiss that squatty lard-stan ove a gal is what dun hit tu me. She wer the fairest-lookin gal I ever seed. She allers wore thick woolin stockins 'bout six inches too long fur her laig; they rolled down over her garters, lookin like a par ove life-preservers up thar. I tell yu she wer a tarin gal enyhow. Luved kissin, wrastlin, an' biled cabbige, an' hated tite clothes, hot weather, an suckit-riders. B'leved strong in married folk's ways, cradles, an' the remishun ove sins, an' didn't b'leve in corsets, fleas, peaners, nur the fashun plates."

"What caused the death of Mrs. Yardley, Sut?"

"Nuffin, only her heart stop't beatin 'bout losin a nine dimunt quilt. True, she got a skeer'd hoss tu run over her, but she'd a-got over that ef a quilt hadn't been mix'd up in the catastrophy. Yu see quilts wer wun ove her speshul gifts; she run strong on the bed-kiver question. Irish chain, star ove Texas, sun-flower, nine dimunt, saw teeth, checker board, an' shell quilts; blue, an' white, an' yaller an' black coverlids, an' callickercumfurts reigned triumphan' 'bout her hous'.

They wer packed in drawers, layin in shelfs full, wer hung four dubbil on lines in the lof, packed in chists, piled on cheers, an' wer everywhar, even ontu the beds, an' wer changed every bed-makin. She told everybody she cud git tu listen tu hit that she ment tu give every durn'd one ove them tu Sal when she got married. Oh, lordy! what es fat a gal es Sal Yardley cud ever du wif half ove em, an' sleepin wif a husbun at that, is more nor I ever cud see through. Jis' think ove her onder twenty layer ove quilts in July, an' yu in thar too. Gewhillikins! George, look how I is sweatin' now, an' this is December. I'd 'bout es lief be shet up in a steam biler wif a three hundred pound bag ove lard, es tu make a bisiness ove sleepin wif that gal — 'twould kill a glass-blower.

"Well, tu cum tu the serious part ove this conversashun, that is how the old quilt-mersheen an' coverlid-loom cum tu stop operashuns on this yeath. She hed narrated hit thru the neighborhood that nex Saterday she'd gin a quiltin — three quilts an' one cumfurt tu tie. 'Goblers, fiddils, gals, an' whisky,' wer the words she sent tu the men-folk, an' more tetchin ur wakenin words never drap't ofen an 'oman's tongue. She sed tu the gals, 'Sweet toddy, huggin, dancin, an' huggers in 'bundunce.' Them words struck the gals rite in the pit ove the stumick, an' spread a ticklin sensashun bof ways, ontil they scratched thar heads wif one han, an' thar heels wif tuther.

"Everybody, he an' she, what wer baptized b'levers in the righteousnes ove quiltins wer thar, an' hit jis' so happen'd that everybody in them parts, frum fifteen summers tu fifty winters, were unannamus b'levers. Strange, warn't hit? Hit wer the bigges' quiltin ever Missis Yardley hilt, an' she hed hilt hundreds; everybody wer thar, 'scept the constibil an' suckit-rider, two dam easily-spared pussons; the numbers ni ontu even too; jis' a few more boys nur gals; that made hit more exhitin, fur hit gin the gals a chance tu kick an' squeal a littil, wifout runnin eny risk ove not gittin kissed at all, an' hit gin reasonabil grouns fur a few scrimmages amung the he's. Now es kissin an' fitin am the pepper an' salt ove all soshul getherins, so hit were more espishully wif this ove ours. Es I swung my eyes over the crowd, George, I thought quiltins, managed in a morril an' sensibil way, truly am good things — good fur free drinkin, good fur free eatin, good fur free huggin, good fur free dancin, good fur free fitin, an' goodest ove all fur poperlatin a country fas'.

"Thar am a fur-seein wisdom in quiltins, ef they hes proper trimmins: 'vittils, fiddils, an' sperrits in 'bundunce.' One holesum quiltin am wuf three old pray'r meetins on the poperlashun pint, purtickerly ef hits hilt in the dark ove the moon, an' runs intu the night a few hours, an' April ur May am the time chosen. The moon don't suit quiltins whar everybody is well acquainted an' already fur along in courtin. She dus help pow'ful tu begin a courtin match onder, but when hit draws ni ontu a head, nobody wants a moon but the ole mammys.

"The mornin cum, still, saft, sunshiney; cocks crowin, hens singin, birds chirpin, tuckeys gobblin — jis' the day tu sun quilts, kick, kiss, squeal, an' make love.

"All the plow-lines an' clothes-lines wer straiched tu every post an' tree. Quilts purvailed. Durn my gizzard ef two acres round that ar house warn't jis' one solid quilt, all out a-sunnin, an' tu be seed. They dazzled the eyes, skeered the hosses, gin wimen the heart-burn, an' perdominated.

"To'ards sundown the he's begun tu drap in. Yearnis' needil-drivin cummenced tu lose groun; threads broke ofen, thimbils got los', an' quilts needed anuther roll. Gigglin, winkin, whisperin, smoofin ove har, an' gals a-ticklin one anuther, wer a-gainin every inch ove groun what the needils los'. Did yu ever notis, George, at all soshul gether-ins, when the he's begin tu gather, that the young she's begin tu tickil one anuther an' the ole maids swell thar tails, roach up thar backs, an' sharpen thar nails ontu the bed-posts an' door jams, an' spit an' groan sorter like cats a-courtin? Dus hit mean *rale* rath, ur is hit a dare tu the he's, sorter kivered up wif the outside signs ove danger? I honestly b'leve that the young shes' ticklin means, 'Cum an' take this job ofen our hans.' But that swellin I jis' don't onderstan; dus yu? Hit looks skeery, an' I never tetch one ove em when they am in the swellin way. I may be mistaken'd 'bout the ticklin bisiness too; hit may be dun like a feller chaws poplar bark when he haint got eny terbacker, a-sorter better nur nun make-shif. I dus know one thing tu a certainty: is, when the he's take hold the ticklin quits, an' ef yu gits one ᵕᵕᵉ the ole maids out tu hersef, then she subsides an' is the smoofes, sleekes, saft thing yu ever seed, an' dam ef yu can't hear her purr, jis' es plain!

"But then, George, gals an' ole maids haint the things tu fool time away on. Hits widders, by golly, what am the rale sensibil, steady-goin, never-skeerin, never-kickin, willin, sperrited, smoof pacers. They cum clost up tu the hoss-block, standin still wif thar purty silky years playin, an' the naik-veins a-throbbin, an' waits fur the word, which ove course yu gives, arter yu finds yer feet well in the stirrup, an' away they moves like a cradil on cushioned rockers, ur a spring buggy runnin in damp san'. A tetch ove the bridil, an' they knows yu wants em tu turn, an' they dus hit es willin es ef the idear wer thar own. I be dod rabbited ef a man can't 'propriate happiness by the skinful ef he is in contack wif sumbody's widder, an' is smart.

Gin me a willin widder, the yeath over: what they don't know, haint worth larnin. They hes all been tu Jamakey an' larnt how sugar's made, an' knows how tu sweeten wif hit; an' by golly, they is always ready tu use hit. All yu hes tu du is tu find the spoon, an' then drink cumfort till yer blind. Nex tu good sperrits an' my laigs, I likes a twenty-five year ole widder, wif roun ankils, an' bright eyes, honestly an' squarly lookin intu yurn, an' sayin es plainly es a partrige sez 'Bob White,' 'Don't be afraid ove me; I hes been thar; yu know hit ef yu hes eny sense, an' thar's no use in eny humbug, old feller — cum ahead!'

"Ef yu onderstans widder nater, they ken save yu a power ove troubil, onsartinty, an' time, an ef you is interprisin yu gits mons'rous well paid fur hit. The very soun ove thar littil shoe-heels speak full trainin, an' hes a knowin click as they tap the floor; an' the rustil ove thar dress sez, 'I dar yu tu ax me.'

"When yu hes made up yer mind tu court one, jis' go at hit like hit wer a job ove rail-maulin. Ware yer workin close, use yer common, every-day moshuns an' words, an' abuv all, fling away yer cinamint ile vial an' burn all yer love songs. No use in tryin tu fool em, fur they sees plum thru yu, a durn'd sight plainer than they dus thru thar veils. No use in a pasted shut; she's been thar. No use in borrowin a cavortin fat hoss; she's been thar. No use in har-dye; she's been thar. No use in cloves, tu kill whisky breff; she's been thar. No use in buyin clost curtains fur yer bed, fur she has been thar. Widders am a speshul means, George, fur ripenin green men, killin off weak ones, an makin 'ternally happy the soun ones.

"Well, es I sed afore, I flew the track an' got ontu the widders. The fellers begun tu ride up an' walk up, sorter slow, like they warn't in a hurry, the durn'd 'saitful raskils, hitchin thar critters tu enything they cud find. One red-comb'd, long-spurr'd, dominecker feller, frum town, in a red an' white grid-iron jackid an' patent leather gaiters, hitched his hoss, a wild, skeery, wall-eyed devil, inside the yard palins, tu a cherry tree lim'. Thinks I, that hoss hes a skeer intu him big enuf tu run intu town, an' perhaps beyant hit, ef I kin only tetch hit off; so I sot intu thinkin.

"One aind ove a long clothes-line, wif nine dimunt quilts ontu hit, wer tied tu the same cherry tree that the hoss wer. I tuck my knife and socked hit thru every quilt, 'bout the middil, an' jis' below the rope, an' tied them thar wif bark, so they cudent slip. Then I went tu the back aind, an' ontied hit frum the pos', knottin in a hoe-handil, by the middil, tu keep the quilts frum slippin off ef my bark strings failed, an' laid hit on the groun. Then I went tu the tuther aind: thar wer 'bout ten foot tu spar, a-lyin on the groun arter tyin tu the tree. I tuck hit atwix Wall-eye's hine laigs, an' tied hit fas' tu bof stirrups, an' then cut the cherry tree lim' betwix his bridil an' the tree, almos' off. Now, mine yu thar wer two ur three uther ropes full ove quilts atween me an' the hous', so I wer purty well hid frum thar. I jis' tore off a palin frum the fence, an' tuck hit in bof hans, an' arter raisin hit 'way up yander, I fotch hit down, es hard es I cud, flatsided to'ards the groun, an' hit acksidentally happen'd tu hit Wall-eye, 'bout nine inches ahead ove the root ove his tail. Hit landed so hard that hit made my hans tingle, an' then busted intu splinters. The first thing I did, wer tu feel ove mysef, on the same spot whar hit hed hit the hoss. I cudent help duin hit tu save my life, an' I swar I felt sum ove Wall-eye's sensashun, jis' es plain. The fust thing he did, wer tu tare down the lim' wif a twenty foot jump, his head to'ards the hous. Thinks I, now yu hev dun hit, yu durn'd wall-eyed fool! tarin down that lim' wer the beginin ove all the troubil, an' the hoss did hit hissef; my conshuns felt clar es a mountin spring, an' I wer in a frame ove mine tu obsarve things es they happen'd, an' they soon begun tu happen purty clost arter one anuther rite then, an' thar, an' tharabouts, clean ontu town, thru hit, an' still wer a-happenin, in the woods beyant thar ni ontu eleven mile frum ole man Yardley's gate, an' four beyant town.

"The fust line ove quilts he tried tu jump, but broke hit down; the nex one he ran onder; the rope cotch ontu the ho'n ove the saddil, broke at bof ainds, an' went along wif the hoss, the cherry tree lim' an' the fust line ove quilts, what I hed proverdensally tied fas' tu the rope. That's what I calls foresight, George. Right furnint the frunt door he cum in contack wif ole Missis Yardley hersef, an' anuther ole 'oman; they wer a-holdin a nine dimunt quilt spread out, a-'zaminin hit an' a-praisin hits perfeckshuns. The durn'd onmanerly, wall-eyed fool run plum over Missis Yardley frum ahine, stompt one hine foot through the quilt takin hit along, a-kickin ontil he made hits corners snap like a whip. The gals screamed, the men hollered wo! an' the ole 'oman wer toted intu the hous' limber es a wet string, an' every word she sed wer, 'Oh, my preshus nine dimunt quilt!'

"Wall-eye busted thru the palins, an' Dominicker sed 'im, made a mortal rush fur his bitts, wer too late fur them, but in good time fur the strings ove flyin quilts, got tangled amung em, an' the gridiron jackid patren wer los' tu my sight amung star an' Irish chain quilts; he went frum that quiltin at the rate ove thuty miles tu the hour. Nuffin lef on the lot ove the hole consarn, but a nine biler hat, a par ove gloves, an' the jack ove hearts.

"What a onmanerly, suddin way ove leavin places sum folks hev got, enyhow.

"Thinks I, well, that fool hoss, tarin down that cherry tree lim', hes dun sum good, enyhow; hit hes put the ole 'oman outen the way fur the balance ove the quiltin, an' tuck Dominicker outen the way an' outen danger, fur that gridiron jackid wud a-bred a scab on his nose afore midnite; hit wer morrily boun tu du hit.

"Two months arterwards, I tracked the route that hoss tuck in his kalamatus skeer, by quilt rags, tufts ove cotton, bunches ove har, (human an' hoss), an' scraps ove a gridiron jackid stickin ontu the bushes, an' plum at the aind ove hit, whar all signs gin out, I foun a piece ove watch chain an' a hosses head. The places what know'd Dominicker, know'd 'im no more.

"Well, arter they'd tuck the ole 'oman up stairs an' camfired her tu sleep, things begun tu work agin. The widders broke the ice, an' arter a littil gigilin, goblin, an' gabblin, the kissin begun. *Smack!* — 'Thar, now,' a widder sed that. *Pop!* — 'Oh, don't!' *Pfip!* — 'Oh, yu quit!' *Plosh!* — 'Go *way* yu awkerd critter, yu kissed me in the eye!' anuther widder sed that. *Bop!* 'Now yu ar satisfied, I recon, big mouf!' *Vip!* — 'That haint fair!' *Spat!* — 'Oh, lordy! May, cum pull Bill away; he's a-tanglin my har.' *Thut!* — 'I jis' d-a-r-e yu tu du that agin!" a widder sed that, too. Hit sounded all 'roun that room like poppin co'n in a hot skillet, an' wer pow'ful sujestif.

"Hit kep on ontil I be durn'd ef *my* bristils didn't begin tu rise, an' sumthin like a cold buckshot wud run down the marrow in my back-bone 'bout every ten secons, an' then run up agin, tolerabil hot. I kep a swallerin wif nuthin tu swaller, an' my face felt swell'd: an' yet I wer fear'd tu make a bulge. Thinks I, I'll ketch one out tu hersef torreckly, an' then I guess we'll rastil. Purty soon Sal Yardley started fur the smoke 'ous, so I jis' gin my head a few short shakes, let down one ove my wings a-trailin, an' sirkiled roun her wif a side twis' in my naik, steppin sidewise, an' a-fetchin up my hinmos' foot wif a sorter jerkin slide at every step. Sez I, 'Too coo-took a-too.' She onderstood hit, an' stopt, sorter spreadin her shoulders. An' jis' es I hed pouch'd out my mouf, an' wer a-reachin forrid wif hit, fur the article hitself, sunthin interfared wif me, hit did. George, wer yu ever ontu yer hans an' knees, an' let a hell-tarin big, mad ram, wif a ten-yard run, but yu yearnis'ly, jis' onst, right squar ontu the pint ove yer back-bone?"

"No, you fool, why do you ask?"

"Kaze I wanted tu know ef yu cud hev a realizin' noshun ove my shock. Hits scarcely worth while tu try tu make yu onderstan the case by words only, onless yu hev been tetched in that way. Gr-eat golly! the fust thing I felt, I tuck hit tu be a back-ackshun yeathquake; an' the fust thing I seed wer my chaw'r terbacker a-flyin' over Sal's head like a skeer'd bat. My mouf wer pouch'd out, ready fur the article hitsef, yu know, an' hit went outen the roun hole like the wad outen a pop-gun — thug! an' the fust thing I know'd, I wer a flyin over Sal's head too, an' a-gainin on the chaw'r terbacker fast. I wer straitened out strait, toes hinemos', middil finger-nails foremos', an' the fust thing I hearn wer, 'Yu dam Shanghi!' Great Jerus-a-lam! I lit ontu my all fours jis' in time tu but the yard gate ofen hits hinges, an' skeer loose sum more hosses — kep on in a four-footed gallop, clean acrost the lane afore I cud straiten up, an' yere I cotch up wif my chaw'r terbacker, stickin flat agin a fence-rail. I hed got so good a start that I thot hit a pity tu spile hit, so I jis' jump'd the fence an' tuck thru the orchurd. I tell yu I dusted these yere close, fur I tho't hit wer arter me.

"Arter runnin a spell, I ventered tu feel roun back thar, fur sum signs ove what hed happened tu me. George, arter two pow'ful hard tugs, I pull'd out the vamp an' sole ove one ove ole man Yardley's big brogans, what he hed los' amung my coat-tails. Dre'ful! dre'ful! Arter I got hit away frum thar, my flesh went fas' asleep, frum abuv my kidneys tu my knees; about now, fur the fust time, the idear struck me, what hit wer that hed interfar'd wif me, an' los' me the kiss. Hit wer ole Yardley hed kicked me. I walked fur a month like I wer straddlin a thorn hedge. Sich a shock, at sich a time, an' on sich a place — jis' think ove hit! hit am tremenjus, haint hit? The place feels num, right now."

"Well, Sut, how did the quilting come out?"

"How the hell du yu 'speck me tu know? I warn't thar eny more."

Rare Ripe Garden-Seed

"I tell yu now, I minds my fust big skeer jis' es well as rich boys minds thar fust boots, ur seein the fust spotted hoss sirkis. The red top ove them boots am still a rich red stripe in thar minds, an' the burnin red ove my fust skeer hes lef es deep a scar ontu my thinkin works. Mam hed me a standin atwixt her knees. I kin feel the knobs ove her jints a-rattlin a-pas' my ribs yet. She didn't hev much petticoats tu speak ove, an' I hed but one, an' hit wer calliker slit frum the nap ove my naik tu the tail, hilt together at the top wif a draw-string, an' at the bottom by the hem; hit wer the handiest close I ever seed, an' wud be pow'ful cumfurtin in summer if hit warn't fur the flies. Ef they was good tu run in, I'd war one yet. They beats pasted shuts, an' britches, es bad es a feather bed beats a bag ove warnut shells fur sleepin on.

"Say, George, wudn't yu like tu see me intu one 'bout haf fadid, slit, an' a-walkin jis' so, up the middil street ove yure city chuch, a-aimin fur yure pew pen, an' hit chock full ove yure fine city gal friends, jis' arter the peopil hed sot down frum the fust prayer, an' the orgin beginin tu groan; what wud yu du in sich a margincy? say hoss?"

"Why, I'd shoot you dead, Monday morning before eight o'clock," was my reply.

"Well, I speck yu wud; but yu'd take a rale ole maid faint fus, rite amung them ar gals. Lordy! wudn't yu be shamed ove me! Yit why not ten chuch in sich a suit, when yu hesn't got no store clothes?

"Well, es I wer sayin mam wer feedin us brats ontu mush an' milk, wifout the milk, an' es I were the baby then, she hilt me so es tu see that I got my sheer. Whar thar ain't enuf feed, big childer roots littil childer outen the troff, an' gobbils up thar part. Jis' so the yeath over: bishops eats elders, elders eats common peopil; they eats sich cattil es me, I eats possums, possums eats chickins, chickins swallers wums, an' wums am content tu eat dus, an' the dus am the aind ove hit all. Hit am all es regilur es the souns frum the tribil down tu the bull base ove a fiddil in good tchune, an' I speck hit am right, ur hit wudn't be 'lowed.

"'*The sheriff!*' his'd mam in a keen trimblin whisper; hit sounded tu me like the skreech ove a hen when she sez 'hawk,' tu her little roun-sturn'd, fuzzy, bead-eyed, stripid-backs.

"I actid jis' adzacly as they dus; I darted on all fours onder mam's petticoatails, an' thar I met, face tu face, the wooden bowl, an' the mush, an' the spoon what she slid onder frum tuther side. I'se mad at mysef yet, fur rite thar I show'd the fust flash ove the nat'ral born durn fool what I now is. I orter et hit all up, in jestis tu my stumick an' my growin, while the sheriff wer levyin ontu the bed an' the cheers. Tu this day, ef enybody sez 'sheriff,' I feels skeer, an' ef I hears constabil menshun'd, my laigs goes thru runnin moshuns, even ef I is asleep. Did yu ever watch a dorg dreamin ove rabbit huntin? Thems the moshuns, an' the feelin am the rabbit's.

"Sherifs am orful 'spectabil peopil; everybody looks up tu em. I never adzacly seed the 'spectabil part mysef. I'se too fear'd ove em, I reckon, tu 'zamin fur hit much. One thing I knows, no country atwix yere an' Tophit kin ever 'lect me tu sell out widders' plunder, ur poor men's co'n, an' the tho'ts ove hit gins me a good feelin; hit sorter flashes thru my heart when I thinks ove hit. I axed a passun onst, whan hit cud be, an' he pernounced hit tu be *onregenerit pride,* what

I orter squelch in prayer, an' in tendin chuch on colleckshun days. I wer in hopes hit mout be 'ligion, ur sense, a-soakin intu me; hit feels good, enyhow, an' I don't keer ef every suckit rider outen jail knows hit. Sheriffs' shuts allers hes nettil dus ur fleas inside ove em when they lies down tu sleep, an' I'se glad ove hit, fur they'se allers discumfortin me, durn em. I scarcely ever git tu drink a ho'n, ur eat a mess in peace. I'll hurt one sum day, see ef I don't. Show me a sheriff a-steppin softly roun, an' a-sorter sightin at me, an' I'll show yu a far sampil ove the speed ove a express ingine, fired up wif rich, dry, rosiny skeers. They don't ketch me *much,* usin only human laigs es wepuns.

"Ole John Doltin wer a 'spectabil sheriff, monsusly so, an' hed the bes' scent fur poor fugatif devils, an' wimen, I ever seed; he wer sure fire. Well, he toted a warrun fur this yere skinful ove durn'd fool, 'bout that ar misfortnit nigger meetin bisness, ontil he wore hit intu six seperit squar bits, an' hed wore out much shoe leather a-chasin ove me. I'd foun a doggery in full milk, an' hated pow'ful bad tu leave that settilment while hit suck'd free; so I sot intu sorter try an' wean him off frum botherin me so much. I suckseedid so well that he not only quit racin ove me, an' wimen, but he wer tetotaly spiled es as a sheriff, an' los' the 'spectabil seckshun ove his karacter. Tu make yu fool fellers onderstan how hit wer done, I mus' interjuice yure minds tu one Wat Mastin, a bullit-headed yung blacksmith.

"Well, las' year — no hit wer the year afore las' — in struttin an' gobblin time, Wat felt his keepin right warm, so he sot intu bellerin an' pawin up dus in the neighborhood roun the ole widder McKildrin's. The more dus he flung up, the wus he got, ontil at las' he jis cudn't stan the ticklin sensashuns anuther minnit; so he put fur the county clark's offis, wif his hans sock'd down deep intu his britchis pockets, like he wer fear'd ove pick-pockets, his back roach'd roun, an' a-chompin his teef ontil he splotch'd his whiskers wif foam. Oh! he wer yearnis' hot, an' es restless es a cockroach in a hot skillit."

"What was the matter with this Mr. Mastin? I cannot understand you, Mr. Lovingood; had he hydrophobia?" remarked a man in a square-tail coat, and cloth gaiters, who was obtaining subscribers for some forthcoming Encyclopedia of Useful Knowledge, who had quartered at our camp, uninvited, and really unwanted.

"What du yu mean by high-dry-foby?" and Sut looked puzzled.

"A madness produced by being bit by some rabid animal," explained Square-tail, in a pompous manner.

"Yas, hoss, he hed high-dry-foby *orful,* an' Mary McKildrin, the widder McKildrin's only darter, hed gin him the complaint; I don't know whether she bit 'im ur not; he mout a-cotch hit frum her bref, an' he wer now in the roach back, chompin stage ove the sickness, so he wer arter the clark fur a tickit tu the hospital. Well, the clark sole 'im a piece ove paper, part printin an' part ritin, wif a picter ove two pigs' hearts, what sum boy hed shot a arrer thru, an' lef hit stickin, printed at the top. That paper wer a splicin pass — sum calls hit a par ove licins — an' that very nite he tuck Mary, fur better, fur wus, tu hev an' tu hole tu him his heirs, an' —"

"Allow me to interrupt you," said our guest; "you do not quote the marriage ceremony correctly."

"Yu go tu *hell*, mistofer; yu bothers me."

This outrageous rebuff took the stranger all aback, and he sat down.

"Whar wer I? Oh yas, he married Mary tight an' fas', an' nex day he wer abil tu be about. His coat tho', an' his trousis look'd jis' a skrimshun too big, loose like, an' heavy tu tote. I axed him ef he felt soun. He sed yas, but he'd welded a steamboat shaftez the day afore, an' wer sorter tired like. Thar he tole a durn lie, fur he'd been a-ho'nin up dirt mos' ove the day, roun the widder's garden, an' bellerin in the orchard. Mary an' him sot squar intu hous'-keepin, an' 'mung uther things he bot a lot ove *rar ripe garden-seed,* frum a Yankee peddler. Rar ripe co'n, rar ripe peas, rar ripe taters, rar ripe everything, an' the two yung durn'd fools wer dreadfully exercis'd 'bout hit. Wat sed he ment tu git him a rar ripe hammer an' anvil, an' Mary vow'd tu grashus, that she'd hev a rar ripe wheel an' loom, ef money wud git em. Purty soon arter he hed made the garden, he tuck a noshun tu work a spell down tu Ataylanty, in the railroad shop, es he sed he hed a sorter ailin in his back, an' he tho't weldin rail car-tire an' ingine axiltrees, wer lighter work nur sharpinin plows, an' puttin lap-links in trace-chains. So down he went, an' foun hit agreed wif him, fur he didn't cum back ontil the middil ove August. The fust thing he seed when he landid intu his cabin-door, wer a shoebox wif rockers onder hit, an' the nex thing he seed, wer Mary hersef, propped up in bed, an' the nex thing he seed arter that, wer a par ove littil rat-eyes a-shinin abuv the aind ove the quilt, ontu Mary's arm, an' the next an' las thing he seed wer the two littil rat-eyes aforesed, a-turnin into two hundred thousand big green stars, an' a-swingin roun an' roun the room, faster an' faster, ontil they mix'd intu one orful green flash. He drap't intu a limber pile on the floor. The durn'd fool what hed weldid the steamboat shaftez hed fainted safe an' soun es a gal skeered at a mad bull. Mary fotch a weak cat-scream, an' kivered her hed, an' sot intu work ontu a whifflin dry cry, while littil Rat-eyes gin hitssef up tu suckin. Cryin an' suckin bof at onst ain't far; mus' cum pow'ful strainin on the wet seckshun ove an' 'oman's constitushun; yet hit am ofen dun, an' more too. Ole

Missis McKildrin, what wer a-nussin Mary, jis' got up frum knittin, an' flung a big gourd ove warter squar intu Wat's face, then she fotch a glass bottil ove swell-skull whisky outen the three-cornered cupboard, an' stood furnint Wat, a-holdin hit in wun han, an' the tincup in tuther, waitin fur Wat tu cum to. She wer the piusses lookin ole 'oman jis' then, yu ever seed outside ove a prayer-meetin. Arter a spell, Wat begun tu move, twitchin his fingers, an' battin his eyes, sorter 'stonished like. That pius lookin statue sed tu him: " 'My son, jis' take a drap ove sperrits, honey. Yu'se very sick, dumplin, don't take on darlin, ef yu kin help hit, ducky, fur poor Margarit Jane am mons'ous ailin, an' the leas' nise ur takin on will kill the poor sufferin dear, an' yu'll loose yure tuckil ducky duv ove a sweet wifey, arter all she's dun gone thru fur yu. My dear son Watty, yu mus' consider her feelins a littil.' Sez Wat, a-turnin up his eyes at that vartus ole relick, sorter sick like —
" 'I is a-considerin em a heap, rite now.'
" 'Oh that's right, my good kine child.'

"Oh dam ef ole muther-in-lors can't plaster humbug over a feller, jis' es saft an' easy es they spreads a camrick hanketcher over a three hour ole baby's face; yu don't feel hit at all, but hit am thar, a plum inch thick, an' stickin fas es court-plaster. She raised Wat's head, an' sot the aidge ove the tin cup agin his lower teef, an' turned up the bottim slow an' keerful, a-winkin at Mary, hu wer a-peepin over the aidge ove the coverlid, tu see ef Wat *tuck the perskripshun,* fur a heap ove famerly cumfort 'pended on that ar ho'n ove sperrits. *Wun* ho'n allers saftens a man, the yeath over. Wat keep a-battin his eyes, wus nur a owl in daylight; at las' he raised hissef ontu wun elbow, an' rested his head in that han, sorter weak like. Sez he, mons'ous trimblin an' slow: 'Aprile — May — June — July — an' mos' — haf — ove — August,' a-countin the munths ontu the fingers ove tuther han, wif the thumb, a-shakin ove his head, an' lookin at his spread fingers like they warn't his'n, ur they wer nastied wif sumfin. Then he counted em agin, slower, Aprile — May — June — July — an', mos' haf ove August, an' he run his thumb atwixt his fingers, es meanin mos' haf ove August, an' look'd at the pint ove hit, like hit mout be a snake's head. He raised his eyes tu the widder's face, who wer standin jis' es steady es a hitchin pos', an' still a-warin that pius 'spression ontu her pussonal feturs, an' a flood ove saft luv fur Wat, a-shining strait frum her eyes intu his'n. Sez he, 'That jis' makes four munths, an' mos' a half, don't hit, Missis McKildrin?' She never sed one word. Wat reached fur the hath, an' got a dead fire-coal; then he made a mark clean acrost a floor-plank. Sez he, 'Aprile,' a-holdin down the coal ontu the aind ove the mark, like he wer fear'd hit mout blow away afore he got hit christened Aprile. Sez he, 'May' — an' he marked across the board agin; then he counted the marks, one, two, a-dottin at em wif the coal. 'June,' an' he marked agin, one, two, three; counted wif the pint ove the coal. He scratched his head wif the littil finger ove the han holdin the charcoal, an' he drawed hit slowly acrost the board agin, peepin onder his wrist tu see when hit reached the crack, an' sez he 'July,' es he lifted the coal; 'one, two three, four,' countin frum lef tu right, an' then frum right tu lef. 'That haint but four, no way I kin fix hit. Ole Pike hissef cudn't make hit five, ef he wer tu sifer ontu hit ontil his laigs turned intu figger eights.' Then he made a mark, haf acrost a plank, spit on his finger, an' rubbed off a haf inch ove the aind, an' sez he, 'Mos' haf ove August.' He looked up at the widder, an' thar she wer, same es ever, still a-holdin the flask agin her bussum, an' sez he 'Four months, an' mos' a haf. *Haint enuf, is hit mammy?* hits jis' 'bout (lackin a littil) *haf enuf,* haint hit, mammy?'

"Missis McKildrin shuck her head sorter onsartin like, an' sez she, 'Take a drap more sperrits, Watty, my dear pet; dus yu mine buyin that ar rar ripe seed, frum the peddler?' Wat nodded his head, an' looked 'what ove hit,' but didn't say hit.

" 'This is what cums ove hit, an' four months an' a half am rar ripe time fur babys, adzackly. Tu be sure, hit lacks a day ur two, but Margarit Jane wer allers a pow'ful interprizin gal, an' a yearly rizer.' Sez Wat,

" 'How about the 'taters?'

" 'Oh, *we* et 'taters es big es goose aigs, afore ole Missis Collinze's blossomed.'

" 'How 'bout co'n?'

" 'Oh, we shaved down roasin years afore hern tassel'd ——'

" 'An' peas?'

" 'Yes son, we hed gobs an' lots in three weeks. Everything cums in adzackly half the time that hit takes the ole sort, an' yu *knows,* my darlin son, yu planted hit waseful. I tho't then yu'd rar ripe everything on the place. Yu planted *often,* too, didn't yu luv? fur fear hit wudn't cum up.'

" 'Ye-ye-s-s he — he did,' sed Mary a-cryin. Wat studied pow'ful deep a spell, an' the widder jis' waited. Widders allers wait, an' allers win. At las, sez he, 'Mammy.' She looked at Mary, an' winked these yere words at her, es plain es she cud a-talked em. 'Yu hearn him call me *mammy twiste.* I'se *got him* now. His back-bone's a-limberin fas', he'll own the baby yet, see ef he don't. Jis' hole still my darter, an' let yer mammy knead this dough, then yu may bake hit es brown es yu please.'

" 'Mammy, when I married on the fust day of Aprile" —— The wid-der look'd oneasy; she tho't he mout be a-cupplin that day, his weddin, an' the idear, dam fool, tugether. But he warn't, fur he sed 'That day I gin ole man Collins my note ove han fur a hundred dul-lars, jew in one year arter date, the balluns on this lan. Dus yu think that ar seed will change the *time* eny, ur will hit alter the *amount?*' An' Wat looked at her powerful ankshus. She raised the whisky bottil way abuv her head, wif her thumb on the mouf, an' fotch the bottim down ontu her han, spat. Sez she, 'Watty, my dear b'lovid son, pripar tu pay *two* hundred dullars 'bout the fust ove October, fur hit'll be jew jis' then, *es* sure es that littil black-eyed angel in the bed thar, am yer darter.'

"Wat drap't his head, an' sed, *'Then hits a dam sure thing.'* Rite yere, the baby fotch a rattlin loud squall, (I speck Mary wer sorter figetty jis' then, an' hurt hit). 'Yas,' sez Wat, a-wallin a red eye to'ards the bed; 'my littil she — what wer hit yu called her name, mammy?' 'I called her a sweet littil angel, an' she is wun, es sure es yu're her daddy, my b'loved son.' 'Well,' sez Wat, 'my littil sweet, patent rar ripe she angel, ef yu lives tu marryin time, yu'll 'stonish sum man body outen his shut, ef yu don't rar ripe lose hits vartu arter the fust plantin, that's all.' He rared up on aind, wif his mouf pouch'd out. He had a pow'ful forrid, fur-reachin, bread funnel, enyhow — cud a-bit the aigs outen a catfish, in two-foot warter, wifout wettin his eyebrows. 'Dod durn rar ripe seed, an' rar ripe pedlers, an' rar ripe notes tu the hottes' corner ove ——'

" 'Stop Watty, *darlin,* don't swar; 'member yu belongs tu meetin.'

" 'My blacksmith's fire,' ainded Wat, an' he studied a long spell; sez he,

" 'Did you save eny ove that infunnel doubil-trigger seed?' 'Yas,' sez the widder, 'thar in that bag by the cupboard.' Wat got up ofen the floor, tuck a countin sorter look at the charcoal marks, an' reached down the bag; he went tu the door an' called 'Suke, muley! Suke, Suke, cow, chick, chick, chicky chick.' 'What's yu gwine tu du now, my dear son?' sed Missis McKildrin. 'I'se jis' gwine tu feed this actif *smart* truck tu the cow, an' the hens, that's what I'se gwine tu du. Ole muley haint hed a calf in two years, an' I'll eat sum rar ripe aigs.' Mary now venter'd tu speak: 'Husban, I ain't sure hit'll work on hens; cum an' kiss me my luv.' 'I haint sure hit'll work on hens, either,' sed Wat. 'They's powerful onsartin in thar ways, well es wimen,' an' he flung out a hanful spiteful like. 'Takin the rar ripe invenshun all tugether, frum 'taters an' peas tu notes ove han, an' childer, I can't say I likes hit much,' an' he flung out anuther hanful. 'Yer mam hed thuteen the ole way, an' ef this truck stays 'bout the

hous', yu'se good fur twenty-six, maybe thuty, fur yu'se a pow'ful
interprizin gal, yer mam sez,' an' he flung out anuther hanful, overhandid, es hard es ef he wer flingin rocks at a stealin sow. 'Make yere
mine easy,' sed the widder; 'hit never works on married folks only
the fust time.' 'Say them words agin,' sed Wat, 'I'se glad tu hear em.
Is hit the same way wif notes ove han?' 'I speck hit am,' answer'd
the widder, wif jis' a taste ove strong vinegar in the words, es she
sot the flask in the cupboard wif a push.

"Jis' then ole Doltin, the sheriff, rid up, an' started 'stonished when
he seed Wat, but he, quick es an 'oman kin hide a strange hat, drawed
the puckerin-string ove that legil face ove his'n, an' fotch hit up tu
the 'know'd yu wer at home,' sorter look, an' wishin Wat much joy,
sed he'd fotch the baby a present, a par ove red shoes, an' a calliker
dress, fur the luv he bore hits granmam. Missis McKildrin tole him
what the rar ripe hed dun, an' he swore hit allers worked jis' that
way, an' wer 'stonished at Wat's not knowin hit; an' they talked
so fas', an' so much, that the more Wat listened the less he know'd.

"Arter the sheriff lef, they onrolled the bundil, an' Wat straitched
out the calliker in the yard. He step't hit off keerfully, ten yards, an
a littil the rise. He puss'd up his mouf, an' blow'd out a whistil seven
foot long, lookin up an' down the middil stripe ove the drygoods,
frum aind tu aind. Sez he, 'Missis McKildrin, that'll make Rar Ripe
a good *full* frock, won't hit?' 'Y-a-s,' sed she, wif her hans laid up
along her jaw, like she wer studyin the thing keerfully. 'My son, I
thinks hit will, an' I wer jis' a-thinkin ef hit wer cut tu 'vantage, thar
mout be nuff lef, squeezed out tu make yu a Sunday shutin shut,
makin the ruffils an' ban outen sumthin else.' 'Put hit in the bag
what the rar ripe wer in, an' by mornin thar'll be nuff fur the ruffils
an' bans, an' yu mout make the tail tu drag the yeath, wifout squeezin
ur pecin', sez Wat, an' he put a few small wrinkils in the pint ove his
nose, what seemed tu bother the widder tu make out the meanin ove;
they look'd mons'ous like the outward signs ove an onb'lever. Jis' then
his eyes sot fas' ontu sumthin a-lyin on the groun whar he'd onrolled
the bundil; he walk'd up tu hit slow, sorter like a feller goes up tu a
log, arter he thinks he seed a snake run onder. He walk'd clean roun
hit twiste, never takin his eyes ofen hit. At las' he lifted hit on his
instep, an' hilt out his laig strait at that widdered muther-in-lor ove
his'n. Sez he, 'What mout yu call that? Red baby's shoes don't gin-
er'lly hev teeth, dus they?' 'Don't yu *know* hits a tuckin comb, Watty?
The store-keeper's made a sorter blunder, I speck,' sed that vartus
petticoatful ove widderhood. 'Maybe he hes; I'se durn sure I hes,' sed
Wat, an' he wrinkil'd his nose agin, mons'ous botherinly tu that watch-
ful widder. He scratched his head a spell; sez he, 'Ten yards an'

the rise fur a baby's frock, *an' hit rar ripe at that, gits me;* an' that ar tuckin comb gits me wus.' 'Oh, fiddlesticks an' flusterashun,' sez she. 'Save the comb; baby'll soon want hit.' 'That's so, mammy, I'm dam ef hit don't,' an' he slip't his foot frum onder hit, an' hit scarcely totch the yeath afore he stomp't hit, an' the teeth flew all over the widder. He look'd like he'd been stompin a blowin adder, an' went apas' the 'oman intu the cabin, in a rale Aprile tucky gobbler strut. When he tore the rapper off the sheriff's present, I seed a littil bit ove white paper fall out. Onbenowenst tu enybody, I sot my foot ontu hit, an' when they went in I socked hit deep intu my pocket, an' went over tu the still-'ous. I tuck Jim Dunkin out, an' arter swarin 'im wif a uplifted han', tu keep dark, got him tu read hit tu me, ontil hit wer printed on the mindin seckshun ove my brain. Hit run jis' so:

"MY SWEET MARY:

I mayn't git the chance tu talk eny tu yu, so when Wat gits home, an' axes enything 'bout the *comb* an' *calliker,* yu tell him yer mam foun the bundil in the road. She'll back yu up in that ar statemint, ontil thar's enuf white fros' in hell tu kill snap-beans.

Notey Beney. — I hope Wat'll stay in Atlanty ontil the merlenium, don't yu, my dear duv?

Yures till deth,

DOLTIN.

An' tu that ar las' remark he'd sot a big D. I reckon he ment that fur dam Wat.

"Now, I jis' know'd es long es I hed that paper, I hilt four aces ontu the sheriff, an' I ment tu bet on the han, an' *go halves wif Wat,* fur I wer sorry fur him, he wer so infunely 'posed upon. I went tu school tu Sicily Burns, tu larn 'oman tricks, an' I tuck a dirplomer, I did, an' now I'd jes' like tu see the pussonal feeters ove the she 'oman what cud stock rar ripe kerds on me, durn'd fool es I is. I hed a talk wif Wat, an' soon foun out that his mine hed simmer'd down intu a strong belief that the sheriff an' Mary wer doin thar weavin in the same loom.

"Then I show'd him my four aces, an' that chip made the pot bile over, an' he jis' 'greed tu be led by me, spontanashusly.

"Jis' think on that fac' a minnit boys; a man what hed sense enuf tu turn a hoss shoe, an' then nail hit on toe aind foremos' bein led by me, looks sorter like a plum tree barin tumil bug-balls, but hit wer jis' so, an' durn my pictur, ef I didn't lead him tu victory, strait along.

"Wat narrated hit, that he b'leved strong in rar ripe, frum beans, thru notes ove han, plum tu babys, an' that his cabin shud never be wifout hit. The widder wer cheerful, Mary wer luvin, an' the sheriff wer told on the sly, by ole Mister McKildrin's remainin, an' mos' pius she half, that Wat wer es plum blind es ef his eyes wer two tuckil aigs. So the wool grow'd over *his* eyes, ontil hit wer fit tu shear, an' *dam ef I warn't at the shearin.*

"Things, tharfore, went smoof, an' es quiet es a greased waggin, runnin in san. Hits allers so, jis' afore a tarin big storm.

"By the time littil Rar Ripe wer ten weeks ole, Doltin begun tu be pow'ful plenty in the neighborhood. Even the brats know'd his hoss's tracks, an' go whar he wud, the road led ni ontu Wat's, ur the widder's, tu git thar. My time tu play my four aces hed 'bout cum."

"And so has orderly bed time. I wish to repose," remarked the man of Useful Knowledge, in the square-tail coat, and cloth gaiters.

Sut opened his eyes in wonder.

"Yu wish tu du what?"

"I wish to go to sleep."

"Then why the h—l didn't yu say so? Yu mus' talk Inglish tu me, ur not git yersef onderstood. I warn't edikated at no Injun ur nigger school. Say, bunty, warn't yu standid deep in sum creek, when the taylure man put the string to yu, fur that ar cross atwix a rounabout an' a flour barril, what yu'se got on in place of a coat?"

My self-made guest looked appealingly at me, as he untied his gaiters, evidently deeply insulted. I shook my head at Sut, who was lying on his breast, with his arms crossed for a pillow, but with head elevated like a lizard's, watching the traveler's motions with great interest.

"Say, George, what dus repose mean? That wurd wer used at me jis' now."

"Repose means rest."

"Oh, the devil hit dus! I'se glad tu hear hit, I tho't hit wer pussonal. I kin repose now, mysef. Say, ole Onsightly Peter, repose sum tu, ef yu kin in that flour barril. I ain't gwine tu hunt fur yure har ontil mor ——" and Sut slept. When morning broke, the Encyclopedia, or Onsightly Peter as Sut pronounced it, had

"Folded his tent like the Arab,
And as silently stole away."

Contempt of Court — Almost

"Ole Onsightly Peter tuck his squar-tail cackus kiver away frum this yere horspitable camp, wifout axin fur his bill, ur even sayin 'mornin,' tu us. Le's look roun a littil; I bet he'se stole sumfin. Fellers ove his stripe allers dus. They never thinks a night's lodgin cumplete, onless they hooks a bed-quilt, ur a candilstick, ur sum sichlike. I hates ole Onsightly Peter, jis' caze he didn't seem tu like tu hear me narrate las' night; that's human nater the yeath over, an' yere's more universal onregenerit human nater: ef ever yu dus enything tu enybody wifout cause, yu hates em allers arterwards, an' sorter wants tu hurt em agin. An' yere's anuther human nater: ef enything happens sum feller, I don't keer ef he's yure bes frien, an' I don' keer how sorry yu is fur him, thar's a streak ove satisfackshun 'bout like a sowin thread a-runnin all thru yer sorrer. Yu may be shamed ove hit, but durn me ef hit ain't thar. Hit will show like the white cottin chain in mean cassinett; brushin hit onder only hides hit. An' yere's a littil more; no odds how good yu is tu yung things, ur how kine yu is in treatin em, when yu sees a littil long laiged lamb a-shakin hits tail, an' a-dancin staggerinly onder hits mam a-huntin fur the tit, ontu hits knees, yer fingers *will* itch tu seize that ar tail, an' fling the littil ankshus son ove a mutton over the fence amung the blackberry briars, not tu hurt hit, but jis' tu disapint hit. Ur say, a littil calf, a-buttin fas' under the cow's fore-laigs, an' then the hine, wif the pint ove hits tung stuck out, makin suckin moshuns, not yet old enuf tu know the bag aind ove hits mam frum the hookin aind, don't yu want tu kick hit on the snout, hard enough tu send hit backwards, say fifteen foot, jis' tu show hit that buttin won't allers fetch milk? Ur a baby even, rubbin hits heels apas' each uther, a-rootin an' a-snifflin arter the breas', an' the mam duin her bes' tu git hit out, over the hem ove her clothes, don't yu feel hungry tu gin hit jis' one 'cussion cap slap, rite ontu the place what sum day'll fit a saddil, ur a sowin cheer, tu show hit what's atwixt hit an' the grave; that hit stans a pow'ful chance not tu be fed every time hits hungry, ur in a hurry? An' agin: ain't thar sum grown up babys what yu meets, that the moment yer eyes takes em in, yer toes itch tu tetch thar starns, jis' 'bout es saftly es a muel kicks in playin; a histin kine ove a tetch, fur the way they wares thar har, hat, ur watch-chain, the shape ove thar nose, the cut ove thar eye, ur sumthin ove a like littil natur. Jis' tu show the idear, a strange fellow onst cum intu a doggery whar I wer buzzy a-raisin steam, an' had got hit a few poun abuv a bladder bustin pint.

"He tuck off his gloves, slow an' keerful, a-lookin at me like I mout smell bad. Then he flattened em ontu the counter, an' laid em in the crown ove his hat, like he wer packin shuts in a trunk. Then sez he —

" 'Baw-keepaw, ole Champaigne Brandy, vintage ove thuty-eight, ef yu please, aw.'

"He smelt hit slow, a-lookin at hissef in the big lookin-glass ahine the counter, shook his head, an' turned up his mustachus, sorter like a goat hists hits tail.

"Mustachus am pow'ful holesum things I speck, tu them what hes the stumick tu wear em. Bes' buttermilk strainers on yeath. All the scrimpshuns ove butter lodges in the har, an' rubbed in makes it grow, like chicken dung dus inyuns. Strains whisky powerful good, what hes dead flies in hit, an' then yu kin comb em off ur let em stay, 'cordin tu yer taste. They changes the taste ove a kiss clear over; makes hit tas' an' smell like a mildew'd saddil-blankit, arter hit hed been rid on a sore-back hoss three hundred miles in August, an' increases yer apper-tite fur sich things 'cordinly. I seed a blue-bird devil a feller onst, all one spring, a-tryin tu git intu his mouf tu bild a nestes, an' the durn'd fool wer proud ove the bird's preferens, but wudn't let hit git in.

"Rite then, I thought, well, durn yure artifishul no-count soul, an' my toes begun tu tingle. He tuck four trials, a-pourin back an' forrid, afore he got his dram the right depth, a-lookin thru the tumbler like he spected tu see a minner, ur a warter-mockasin in hit. Then he drunk hit, like hit wer caster ile, the infunel fool. Lordy crimminy! how bad my toes wer itchin now. He lit a seegar, cocked hit up to'ards one eye, an' looked at me agin thru the smoke, while he shook his hat over ontu one ove his years. Sez I, 'Mornin mister.'

"He never sed a word, but turned an' started fur the door. When he got six foot nine inches distunt, (that's my bes' kickin range), the durned agravatin toe itch overcum me, an' I let one ove these yere hoss-hide boots *go arter 'im;* hit imejuntly cotch up wif the fork ove his coatail, an' went outen my sight, mos' up tu the straps. He went flyin outen the doggery door, over the hoss-rack. While he wer in the air, he turned plum roun an' lit facin me wif a cock't Derringer, a-starin me squar in the face. I tho't I seed the bullit in hit lookin es big es a hen's aig. Es I dodged, hit plowed a track acrost the door-jam, jis' es high es my eye-brows. I wer one hundred an' nineteen yards deep in the wheat-field when I hearn hits mate bark, an' he wer a pow'rful quick moshun'd man wif shootin irons.

"I wer sorter fooled in the nater ove that feller, that's a fac'. The idear ove Derringers, an' the melt tu use em, bein mix't up wif es much durned finekey fool es he show'd, never struck me at all, but I made my pint on 'im, I cured my toe itch.

"Well, I allers tuck the cumplaint every time I seed ole Jedge Smarty, but I dusn't try tu cure hit on him, an' so hit jis' hed tu run hits course, onless I met sumthin I cud kick.

"Wirt Staples got him onst, bad; 'stonished the ole bag ove lor amos' outen his dignity, dam ef he didn't, an' es Wirt tuck a skeer in what's tu cum ove my narashun about th consekinses ove foolin wif uther men's wives, I'll tell you how he 'stonished old Smarty, an' then yu'll better onderstand me when I cums tu tell yu how he help't tu 'stonish ole Doltin.

"Wirt hed changed his grocery range, an' the sperrits at the new lick-log hed more scrimmage seed an' raise-devil intu hit than the old biled drink he wer used tu, an' three ho'ns histed his tail, an' sot his bristils 'bout es stiff es eight ove the uther doggery juice wud. So when cort sot at nine o'clock, Wirt wer 'bout es fur ahead as cleaving, ur half pas' that.

"The hollerin stage ove the disease now struck him, so he roar'd one good year-quiverin roar, an' riz three foot inside the doggery door, an' lit nine more out in the mud, sploshin hit all over the winders, tuther side the street. He hed a dried venerson ham in one han, an' a ten-year old he nigger by hits gallus-crossin in tuther. He waved fus' the nigger an' then the venerson over his head, steppin short an' high, like ontu a bline hoss, an lookin squar atwixt his shoe-heels, wif his shoulders hump'd hi up. Sez he,

" 'Hu — wee,' clear an' loud es a tin ho'n, 'run onder the hen, yere's the blue-tail hawk, an' he's a-flyin low. The Devil's grist mill-dam's broke; take tu yer canoes.' Then he roared a time ur two, an' look'd up an' down the street, like a bull looks fur tuther one, when he thinks he hearn a beller. He riz ontu his tip-toes, an' finished a good loud 'Hu-wee.' Es he drap't ontu his heels agin, he yelled so hard his head shook an' his long black har quivered agin; he then shook hit outen his eyes, wipin the big draps ove sweat ofen his snout wif his shut-sleeve, still hangin tu the venerson an' the nigger. Sez he,

" 'Look out fur the ingine when yu hears hit whistil; hits a-whistlin rite now. *Nine*teen hundred an' eighty pouns tu the squar scrimpshun by golly, an' *eighty*-nine miles in the shake ove a lamb's tail. Pur-feckly clear me jis' ten acres tu du my gesterin on, yu durned Jews, tape-sellers, gentiles, an' jackasses, I'se jis' a mossel ove the bes' man what ever laid a shadder ontu this dirt. Hit wilts grass, my breff pizins skeeters, my yell breaks winders, an' my tromp gits yeath-quakes. I kin bust the bottom outen a still by blowin in at the wum,

I kin addil a room full ove goose aigs by peepin in at the key-hole, an' *I kin spit a blister ontu a washpot, ontil the flies blow hit.* Listen tu me, oh yu dam puney, panady eating siterzens, an' sojourners in this half-stock't town, I'se in yearnis' now.' Then he reared a few times agin, an' cut the pidgeon-wing three foot high, finished off wif 'bout haf ove a ho'n-pipe, keepin time abuv his head wif the venerson an' the littil son ove midnite. He hilt em straight out at arm's laingth, leaned way back, an' lookin straight up at the sky, sung 'bout es loud es a cow bellers, one vearse ove the sixteen hundred an' ninety-ninth hyme —

> The martins bilds in boxis,
> The foxis dens in holes,
> The sarpints crawls in rocksis,
> The yeath's the home ove moles.
> Cock a-doodil-do, hits movin,
> An' dram time's cum agin.

'*Yere's* what kin jis' sircumstansully flax out that ar court-hous' full tu the chimbly tops, ove bull-dorgs, Bengal tigers, an' pizen bitin things, wif that ar pusley-gutted, leather whisky jug ove a jedge, tu laig fur em. Cum out yere, yu ole false apostil ove lor, yu cussed, termatis-nosed desipil ove supeners, an' let me gin *yu* a charge. I'll bet high hit busts yu plum open, frum fork tu forrid, yu hary, sulky, choliky durn'd son ove a slush-tub. Cum out yere, oh yu coward's skeer, yu widder's night-mar, yu poor man's heart ache, yu constabil's god, yu lawyer's king, yu treasury's tape-wum, yer wife's dam barril ove soap-grease, saften'd wif unbought whisky.'

"Thinks I, *that's hit;* now Wirt yu'se draw'd an ace kerd at las', fur the winders wer histed an' the cort hearn every word.

"Wirt wer bilin hot; nobody tu gainsay him, hed made him piedied all over: he wer plum pizen. So arter finishin his las' narashun, aim'd at Jedge Smarty, he tuck a vigrus look at the yung nigger, what he still hilt squirmin an' twistin his face, what warn't eyes, glazed all over wif tears, an' starch outen his nose, an' sez he, 'Go.' He flung hit up'ards, an' es hit cum down, hit met one ove Wirt's boots. Away hit flew, spread like ontu a flyin squirrel, smash thru a watch-tinker's winder, totin in broken sash, an' glass, an' bull's-eye watches, an' sasser watches, an' spoons, an' doll heads, an' clay pipes, an' fishin reels, an' sum noise. A ole ball-headed cuss wer a-sittin a-peepin intu a ole watch, arter spiders, wif a thing like a big black wart kiverin one eye, when the smashery cum, an' the fus' thing he knowed, he wer flat ove his back, wif a small, pow'fully skeer'd, ash-culler'd nigger, a-straddil his naik, littil brass wheels spinnin on the floor, an' watches singin like rattil-snakes all roun. I wer a-peepin outen the ole doggery door, an' thinks I, thar, by jingo, Wirt, yu'se draw'd *anuther ace,* an' ef yu hilt enything ove a han afore, yu hes got a sure thing now; so better bet fas', ole feller, fur I rather think the jedge'll 'call yu' purty soon. Wirt seed me, an' ove course tho't ove whisky that moment; so he cum over tu lay on a littil more kindlin wood. I'll swar, tu look at him, yu cudn't think fur the life ove yu, that he hed over-bragged a single word. His britches wer buttoned tite roun his loins, an' stuffed 'bout half intu his boots, his shut bagg'd out abuv, an' wer es white es milk, his sleeves wer rolled up tu his arm-pits, an' his collar wer es wide open es a gate, the mussils on his arms moved about like rabbits onder the skin, an ontu his hips an' thighs they play'd like the swell on the river, his skin wer clear red an' white, an' his eyes a deep, sparklin, wickid blue, while a smile fluttered like a hummin bird roun his mouf all the while. When the State-fair offers a premin fur *men* like they now dus fur jackasses, I means tu enter Wirt Staples, an' I'll git hit, ef thar's five thousand entrys. I seed ole Doltin cumin waddlin outen the court-hous', wif a paper in his han, an' a big stick onder his arm, lookin to'ards the doggery wif his mouf puss'd up, an' his brows draw'd down. Sez I, "Wirt, look thar, thar's a 'herearter,' a-huntin yu; du yu see hit? whar's yer hoss?' He tuck one wickid, blazin look, an' slip't intu the stret wif his arms folded acrost his venerson laig.

"Now Wirt wer Wat Mastin's cuzzin, *an' know'd all about the rar ripe bisness,* an' tuck sides wif Wat strong. I'd show'd him the sheriff's note tu Mary, an' he hed hit by heart. The crowd wer now follerin Doltin tu see the fun. When he got in about ten steps, sez Wirt:

" 'Stop rite thar; ef yu don't, thar's *no calliker ur combs in Herrin's store,* ef I don't make yu fear'd ove lightnin. I'll stay wif yu till *thar's enuf fros' in hell tu kill snap-beans.'*

"When Wirt menshun'd snap-beans, I seed the sheriff sorter start, an git pale ahine the years.

" 'Git intu that ar hog-pen, quick, (a-pintin at the court-hous' wif the venerson laig), ur I'll split yer head plum tu the swaller wif this yere buck's laig, yu durn'd ole skaley-heel'd, bob-tail old muley bull; I'll spile yer appertite fur the grass in uther men's pasturs.'

" 'Don't talk so loud, Mister Staples; hit discomboberates the court. I hes no papers agin yu. Jis' keep quiet,' sez Doltin, aidgin up slow, an' two ur three depertys sorter flankin.

"Wirt seed the signs. He jis' roared 'the lion's loose! Shet yer doors.' I seed his har a-flyin es he sprung, an' I hearn a soun like smashin a dry gourd. Thar wer a rushin tugether ove depertys an' humans, an' hit look'd like bees a-swarmin. Yere cum Wirt, mowin his way outen the crowd, wif his venerson, an' sprung ontu his hoss. Thar lay Doltin, flat ove his back, his belly pintin up like a big tater-hill, an' eight ur nine more in es many shapes, lying all about, every durned wun a-holdin his head, 'sceptin Doltin, an' he wer plum limber. Wirt hed a pow'ful fine hoss, an' he rid 'im roun that crowd like a Cumanche Injun, ur a suckis, es fas' es quarter racin, jis' bustin his froat a-hollerin. Then he went fur the court-hous', rid in at one door, an' out at tuther. Es he went, he flung that mortul buck's hine laig at the jedge's head sayin:

" 'Thar's a dried supeaner fur yu, yu dam ole cow's paunch.'

"Es hit cum hit hit the tabil afore him, an' sent a head ove hit, the broken glass ove a big inkstand, an' a half pint ove ink, intu the face ove the court, then glancin up, hit tuck a par ove specks what hed been rared back ontu his head, outen the winder wif hit. Ole Smarty hes a mity nice idear ove when tu duck his head, even ef a rain-storm ove ink am cumin upwards intu his face. Warn't that mons'ous nigh bein a case ove contempt ove court?"

Johnson Jones Hooper

(1815-1862)

✣ Johnson Jones Hooper, the creator of that comic opportunist Simon Suggs, was born in the coastal town of Wilmington, North Carolina. The modest means of his rather distinguished family made it impossible for him to attend college; so he soon pushed westward toward the frontier. When he was twenty he began a half-hearted study of law in the office of his elder brother in La Fayette, Alabama, but law never interested him as much as the raw life of the folk about him. In 1840 he helped take the census in Tallapoosa County, a hazardous intrusion into the private lives of the backwoodsmen. The editorship of country newspapers proved more to Hooper's liking than a legal career. In 1842 he became the editor of the La Fayette *East Alabamian* and published in it his first humorous sketch, "Taking the Census in Alabama." William T. Porter, editor of the New York *Spirit of the Times*, reprinted the sketch and encouraged Hooper to write more like it. Many humorous sketches did follow, including those collected in two books, *Some Adventures of Captain Simon Suggs, Late of the Tallapoosa Volunteers; Together with "Taking the Census" and Other Alabama Sketches* in 1845 and *The Widow Rugby's Husband* in 1851; but Hooper thought of himself principally as a newspaper editor and as an active participant in politics. He held minor political offices in Alabama and at his death in 1862 was Secretary to the Provisional Confederate Congress.

Some Adventures of Simon Suggs is a "campaign biography" of one of the most notorious rogues in Southern literature. Mark Twain knew the book well and more than likely had Suggs's activities at the camp meeting in mind when he wrote "The King Turns Parson" for *Huckleberry Finn*. A picaresque novel, the work presents episodes in the life of Suggs from his early youth, when he swindled his father in cards, to middle age, when he is thinking of running for public office. His credo is "It is good to be shifty in a new country." Like the King in Twain's novel, Suggs is neither a lovable rogue nor a hateful villain. In his shady dealings he is so ridiculously funny that the reader finds it hard to despise him, but he is too heartless to be mistaken for a backwoods Robin Hood. One follows the adventures of Simon Suggs with a fascinated disinterest; the world Hooper has created is one in which the comic but conscienceless thief succeeds chiefly because he knows human nature so well and profits by the selfishness, affectation, and avarice of his fellows.

TEXT: Chapters 1, 2, 5, 7, 10, and "Daddy Biggs' Scrape at Cockerell's Bend" from *Some Adventures of Captain Simon Suggs* (Philadelphia, 1846); "Shifting the Responsibility" from *Polly Peablossom's Wedding,* ed. T. A. Burke (Philadelphia, 1851).

Simon Plays the "Snatch" Game

It is not often that the living worthy furnishes a theme for the biographer's pen. The pious task of commemorating the acts, and depicting the character of the great or good, is generally and properly deferred until they are past blushing, or swearing — constrained to a decorous behaviour by the folds of their cerements. Were it otherwise, who could estimate the pangs of wounded modesty which would result! Who could say how keen would be the mortification, or how crimson the cheek of Grocer Tibbetts, for instance, should we present him to the world in all the resplendent glory of his public and his private virtues! — dragging him, as it were, from the bosom of retirement and Mrs. Tibbetts, to hold him up before the full gaze of "the community," with all his qualities, characteristics, and peculiarities written on a large label and pasted to his forehead! Wouldn't Mr. Tibbetts almost die of bashfulness? And wouldn't Mrs. Tibbetts tell all her neighbours, that she would just as soon they put Mr. Tibbetts in the stocks, if it were not for the concomitant little boys and rotten eggs? Certainly: and Mrs. Tabitha Tibbetts in making such a remark, would be impelled by a principle which exists in a majority of human minds — a principle which makes the idea revolting, that everybody should know all about us in our life-times, notwithstanding our characters may present something better even than a fair average of virtue and talent.

But "there is no rule without an exception," and notwithstanding that it is both unusual and improper, generally, to publish biographies of remarkable personages during their lives, for the reason already explained, as well as because such histories must, of necessity, be incomplete and require *post mortem* additions — notwithstanding all this, we say, there are cases and persons, in which and to whom, the general rule cannot be considered to apply. Take, by way of illustration, the case of a candidate for office — for the Presidency we'll say. His life, up to the time when his reluctant acquiescence in the wishes of his friends was wrung from him, by the stern demands of a self-immolating patriotism, MUST be written. It is an absolute, political necessity. His enemies *will* know enough to attack; his friends *must* know enough to defend. — Thus Jackson, Van Buren, Clay, and Polk have each a biography published while they live. Nay, the thing has been carried further; and in the first of each "Life" there is found what is termed a "counterfeit presentment" of the subject of the pages which follow. And so, not only are the moral and intellectual endowments of the candidate heralded to the world of voters; but an attempt is made to create an idea of his *physique.* By this means, all the country has in its mind's eye, an image of a little gentleman with a round, oily face — sleek, bald pate, delicate whiskers, and foxy smile, which they call Martin Van Buren; and future generations of naughty children who will persist in sitting up when they should be a-bed, will be frightened to their cribs by the lithograph of "Major General Andrew Jackson," which their mammas will declare to be a faithful representation of the Evil One — an atrocious slander, by the bye, on the potent, and comparatively well-favoured, prince of the infernal world.

What we have said in the preceding paragraphs was intended to prepare the minds of our readers for the reception of the fact, that we have not undertaken to furnish for their amusement and instruction, in this and the chapters which shall come after, a few incidents — for we are by far too modest to attempt a connected memoir — in the life of CAPTAIN SIMON SUGGS, OF TALLAPOOSA, without the profoundest meditation on the propriety of doing so ere the captain has been "gathered to his fathers." No! no! we have chewed the cud of this matter, until we flatter ourself all its juices have been expressed; and the result is, that as Captain Simon Suggs thinks it "more than probable" he shall "come before the people of Tallapoosa" in the course of a year or two, he is, in our opinion, clearly "within the line of safe precedents," and bound in *honor* to furnish the Suggs party with such information respecting himself, as will enable them to vindicate his character whenever and wherever it may be attacked by the ruthless and polluted tongues of Captain Simon Suggs' enemies. And in order that our hero should not appear before his fellow citizens under circumstances less advantageous than those which mark the introduction to the public of other distinguished individuals, we have, at the outlay of much trouble and expense, obtained the services of an artist competent to delineate his countenance, so that all who have never yet seen the Captain may be able to recognize him immediately whenever it shall be their good fortune to be inducted into his presence. His autograph, — which was only produced unblotted and in orthographical correctness, after three several efforts, "from a rest," on the counter of Bill Griffin's confectionary — we have presented with a view to humor the whim of those who fancy they can read character in a signature. All such, we suspect, would pronounce the Captain *rugged, stubborn, and austere* in his disposition; whereas in fact, he is *smooth, even-tempered, and facile!*

In aid of the portrait, however, it is necessary we should add a verbal description, in order to perfect the reader's conceptions of the Captain.

Beginning then, at our friend Simon's intellectual extremity: — His head is somewhat large, and thinly covered with coarse, silver-white hair, a single lock of which lies close and smooth down the middle of a forehead which is thus divided into a couple of very acute triangles, the base of each of which is an eye-brow, lightly defined, and seeming to owe its scantiness to the depilatory assistance of a pair of tweezers. Beneath these almost shrubless cliffs, a pair of eyes with light-grey pupils and variegated whites, dance and twinkle in an aqueous humor which is constantly distilling from the corners. Lids without lashes complete the optical apparatus of Captain Suggs; and the edges of these, always of a sanguineous hue, glow with a reduplicated brilliancy whenever the Captain has remained a week or so in town, or elsewhere in the immediate vicinity of any of those citizens whom the county court has vested with the important privilege of vending "spirituous liquors in less quantities than one quart." The nose we find in the neighbourhood of these eyes, is long and low, with an extremity of singular acuteness, overhanging the subjacent mouth. Across the middle, which is slightly raised, the skin is drawn with exceeding tightness, as if to contrast with the loose and wrinkled abundance supplied to the throat and chin. But the mouth of Captain Simon Suggs is his great feature, and measures about four inches horizontally. An ever-present sneer — not all malice, however — draws down the corners, from which radiate many small wrinkles that always testify to the Captain's love of the "filthy weed." A sharp chin monopolizes our friend's bristly, iron-gray beard. All these facial beauties are supported by a long and skinny, but muscular neck, which is inserted after the ordinary fashion in the upper part of a frame, lithe, long, and sinewy, and clad in Kentucky jeanes, a trifle worn. Add to all this, that our friend is about fifty years old, and seems to indurate as he advances in years, and our readers will have as accurate an idea of the personal appearance of Captain Simon Suggs, late of the Tallapoosa Volunteers, as we are able to give them.

The moral and intellectual qualities which, with the physical proportions we have endeavoured to portray, make up the entire entity of Captain Suggs, may be readily described. His whole ethical system lies snugly in his favourite aphorism — "It is good to be shifty in a new country" — which means that it is right and proper that one should live as merrily and as comfortably as possible at the expense of others; and of the practicability of this in particular instances, the Captain's whole life has been a long series of the most convincing illustrations. But notwithstanding this fundamental principle of Captain Suggs' philosophy, it were uncandid not to say that his actions often indicate the most benevolent emotions; and there are well-authenticated instances within our knowledge, wherein he has divided with a needy friend, the five or ten dollar bill which his consummate address had enabled him to obtain from some luckless individual, without the rendition of any sort of equivalent, excepting only solemnly reiterated promises to repay within two hours at farthest. To this amiable trait, and his riotous good-fellowship, the Captain is indebted for his great popularity among a certain class of his fellow citizens — that is, the class composed of the individuals with whom he divides the bank bills, and holds his wild nocturnal revelries.

The shifty Captain Suggs is a miracle of shrewdness. He possesses, in an eminent degree, that tact which enables man to detect the *soft spots* in his fellow, and to assimilate himself to whatever company he may fall in with. Besides, he has a quick, ready wit, which has extricated him from many an unpleasant predicament, and which makes him whenever he chooses to be so — and that is always — very companionable. In short, nature gave the Captain the precise intellectual outfit most to be desired by a man of his propensities. She sent him into the world a sort of he-Pallas, ready to cope with his kind, from his infancy, in all the arts by which men *"get along"* in the world; if she made him, in respect to his moral conformation, a beast of prey, she did not refine the cruelty by denying him the fangs and the claws.

But it is high time we were beginning to record some of those specimens of the worthy Captain's ingenuity, which entitle him to the epithet *"Shifty."* We shall therefore relate the earliest characteristic anecdote which we have been able to obtain; and we present it to our readers with assurances that it has come to our knowledge in such a way as to leave upon our mind not "a shadow of doubt" of its perfect genuineness. It will serve, if no other purpose, at least to illustrate the precocious development of Captain Suggs' peculiar talent.

Until Simon entered his seventeenth year, he lived with his father, an old "hard shell" Baptist preacher; who, though very pious and remarkably austere, was very avaricious. The old man reared his boys —or endeavoured to do so — according to the strictest requisitions of the moral law. But he lived, at the time to which we refer, in Middle

Georgia, which was then newly settled; and Simon, whose wits from the time he was a "shirt-tail boy," were always too sharp for his father's, contrived to contract all the coarse vices incident to such a region. He stole his mother's roosters to fight them at Bob Smith's grocery, and his father's plough-horses to enter them in "quarter" matches at the same place. He pitched dollars with Bob Smith himself, and could "beat him into doll rags" whenever it came to a measurement. To crown his accomplishments, Simon was tip-top at the game of "old sledge," which was the fashionable game of that era; and was early initiated in the mysteries of "stocking the papers." The vicious habits of Simon were, of course, a sore trouble to his father, Elder Jedediah. He reasoned, he counselled, he remonstrated, and he lashed — but Simon was an incorrigible, irreclaimable devil. One day the simple-minded old man returned rather unexpectedly to the field where he had left Simon and Ben and a negro boy named Bill, at work. Ben was still following his plough, but Simon and Bill were in a fence corner very earnestly engaged at "seven up." Of course the game was instantly suspended, as soon as they spied the old man sixty or seventy yards off, striding towards them.

It was evidently a "gone case" with Simon and Bill; but our hero determined to make the best of it. Putting the cards into one pocket, he coolly picked up the small coins which constituted the stake, and fobbed them in the other, remarking, "Well, Bill, this game's blocked; we'd as well quit."

"But, mass Simon," remarked the boy, "half dat money's mine. An't you gwine to lemme hab 'em?"

"Oh, never mind the money, Bill; the old man's going to take the bark off both of us — and besides, with the hand I helt when we quit, I should 'a beat you and won it all any way."

"Well, but mass Simon, we nebber finish de game, and de rule ——"

"Go to an orful h—l with your rule," said the impatient Simon — "don't you see daddy's right down upon us, with an armful of hickories? I tell you I helt nothin' but trumps, and could 'a beat the horns off of a billygoat. Don't that satisfy you? Somehow or another you're d—d hard to please!" About this time a thought struck Simon, and in a low tone — for by this time the Reverend Jedediah was close at hand — he continued, "But maybe daddy don't know, *right down sure*, what we've been doin'. Let's try him with a lie — twon't hurt, no way — let's tell him we've been playin' mumble-peg."

Bill was perforce compelled to submit to this inequitable adjustment of his claim to a share of the stakes; and of course agreed to swear to the game of mumble-peg. All this was settled and a peg driven into the ground, slyly and hurriedly, between Simon's legs as he sat on the ground, just as the old man reached the spot. He carried under his left arm, several neatly-trimmed sprouts of formidable length, while in his left hand he held one which he was intently engaged in divesting of its superfluous twigs.

"Soho! youngsters! — *you* in the fence corner, and the *crap* in the grass; what saith the Scriptur', Simon? 'Go to the ant, thou sluggard,' and so forth, and so on. What in the round creation of the yeath have you and that nigger been a-doin'?"

Bill shook with fear, but Simon was cool as a cucumber, and answered his father to the effect that they had been wasting a little time in the game of mumble-peg.

"Mumble-peg! mumble-peg!" repeated old Mr. Suggs, "what's that?"

Simon explained the process of *rooting* for the peg; how the operator got upon his knees, keeping his arms stiff by his sides, leaned forward and extracted the peg with his teeth.

"So you git *upon your knees,* do you, to pull up that nasty little stick! you'd better git upon 'em to ask mercy for your sinful souls and for a dyin' world. But let's see one o' you git the peg up now."

The first impulse of our hero was to volunteer to gratify the curiosity of his worthy sire, but a glance at the old man's countenance changed his "notion," and he remarked that "Bill was a long ways the best hand." Bill who did not deem Simon's modesty an omen very favourable to himself, was inclined to reciprocate compliments with his young master; but a gesture of impatience from the old man set him instantly upon his knees; and, bending forward, he essayed to lay hold with his teeth of the peg, which Simon, just at that moment, very wickedly pushed a half inch further down. Just as the breeches and hide of the boy were stretched to the uttermost, old Mr. Suggs brought down his longest hickory, with both hands, upon the precise spot where the tension was greatest. With a loud yell, Bill plunged forward, upsetting Simon, and rolled in the grass; rubbing the castigated part with fearful energy. Simon, though overthrown, was unhurt; and he was mentally complimenting himself upon the sagacity which had prevented his illustrating the game of mumble-peg for the paternal amusement, when his attention was arrested by the old man's stooping to pick up something — what is it? — a card upon which Simon had been sitting, and which, therefore, had not gone with the rest of the pack into his pocket. The simple Mr. Suggs had only a vague idea of the pasteboard abomination called *cards;* and though he decidedly inclined to the opinion that this was one, he was by no means certain of the fact. Had Simon known this he would certainly have escaped; but he did not. His father assuming the look of extreme sapiency which is always worn by the interrogator who does not desire or expect to increase his knowledge by his questions, asked —

"What's this, Simon?"

"The Jack-a-dimunts," promptly responded Simon, who gave up all as lost after this *faux pas.*

"What was it doin' down thar Simon, my sonny?" continued Mr. Suggs, in an ironically affectionate tone of voice.

"I had it under my leg, thar, to make it on Bill, the first time it come trumps," was the ready reply.

"What's trumps?" asked Mr. Suggs, with a view of arriving at the import of the word.

"Nothin' a'n't trumps *now*," said Simon, who misapprehended his father's meaning — "but *clubs* was, when you come along and busted up the game."

A part of this answer was Greek to the Reverend Mr. Suggs, but a portion of it was full of meaning. They had then, most unquestionably, been "throwing" cards, the scoundrels! the "oudacious" little hellions!

"To the 'mulberry' with both on ye, in a hurry," said the old man sternly. But the lads were not disposed to be in a "hurry," for "the mulberry" was the scene of all formal punishment administered during work hours in the field. Simon followed his father, however, but made, as he went along, all manner of "faces" at the old man's back; gesticulated as if he were going to strike him between the shoulders with his fists, and kicking at him so as almost to touch his coat tail with his shoe. In this style they walked on to the mulberry tree, in whose shade Simon's brother Ben was resting. Of what transpired there, we shall speak in the next chapter.

Simon Gets a "Soft Snap" out of His Daddy

It must not be supposed that, during the walk to the place of punishment, Simon's mind was either inactive, or engaged in suggesting the grimaces and contortions wherewith he was pantomimically expressing his irreverent sentiments toward his father. Far from it. The movements of his limbs and features were the mere workings of habit — the self-grinding of the corporeal machine — for which his reasoning half was only remotely responsible. For while Simon's person was thus, on its own account, "making game" of old Jed'diah, his wits, in view of the anticipated flogging, were dashing, springing, bounding, darting about, in hot chase of some expedient suitable to the necessities of the case; much after the manner in which puss — when Betty, armed with the broom, and hotly seeking vengeance for pantry robbed or bed defiled, has closed upon her the garret doors and windows — attempts all sorts of impossible exits, to come down at last in the corner, with panting side and glaring eye, exhausted and defenceless. Our unfortunate hero could devise nothing by which he could reasonably expect to escape the heavy blows of his father. Having arrived at this conclusion and the "mulberry" about the same time, he stood with a dogged look awaiting the issue.

The old man Suggs made no remark to any one while he was seizing up Bill—a process which, though by no means novel to Simon, seemed to excite in him a sort of painful interest. He watched it closely, as if endeavouring to learn the precise fashion of his father's knot; and when at last Bill was swung up a-tiptoe to a limb, and the whipping commenced, Simon's eye followed every movement of his father's arm; and as each blow descended upon the bare shoulders of his sable friend, his own body writhed and "wriggled" in involuntary sympathy.

"It's the devil — it's hell," said Simon to himself, "to take such a wallopin' as that. Why the old man looks like he wants to git to the holler, if he could — rot his old picter! It's wuth, at the least, fifty cents — je-e-miny how that hurt! — yes, it's wuth three-quarters of a dollar to take that 'ere lickin'! Wonder if I'm 'predestinated,' as old Jed'diah says, to git the feller to it? Lord, how daddy blows! I do wish to God he'd bust wide open, the durned old deer-face! If 'twa'n't for Ben helpin' him, I b'lieve I'd give the old dog a tussel when it come to my turn. It couldn't make the thing no wuss, if it didn't make it no better. 'D rot it! what do boys have daddies for, any how? 'Taint for nuthin' but jist to beat 'em and work 'em. — There's some use in mammies — I kin poke my finger right in the old 'oman's eye, and keep it thar, and if I say it aint thar, she'll say so too. I wish she was here to hold daddy off. If 'twa'n't so fur, I'd holler for her, any how. How she would cling to the old feller's coat tail!"

Mr. Jedediah Suggs let down Bill and untied him. Approaching Simon, whose coat was off, "Come, Simon, son," said he, "cross them hands; I'm gwine to correct you."

"It aint no use, daddy," said Simon.

"Why so, Simon?"

"Jist bekase it aint. I'm gwine to play cards as long as I live. When I go off to myself, I'm gwine to make my livin' by it. So what's the use of beatin' me about it?"

Old Mr. Suggs groaned, as he was wont to do in the pulpit, at this display of Simon's viciousness.

"Simon," said he, "you're a poor ignunt creetur. You don't know nuthin', and you've never bin no whars. If I was to turn you off, you'd starve in a week —"

"I wish you'd try me," said Simon, "and jist see. I'd win more money in a week than you can make in a year. There ain't nobody round here kin make seed corn off o' me at cards. I'm rale smart," he added with great emphasis.

"Simon! Simon! you poor unlettered fool. Don't you know that all card-players, and chicken-fighters, and horse-racers go to hell? You crack-brained creetur you. And don't you know that them that plays cards always loses their money, and —"

"Who win's it all then, daddy?" asked Simon.

"Shet your mouth, you imperdent, slack-jawed dog. Your daddy's a-tryin' to give you some good advice, and you a-pickin' up his words that way. I knowed a young man once, when I lived in Ogletharp, as went down to Augusty and sold a hundred dollars worth of cotton for his daddy, and some o' them gambollers got him to drinkin', and the *very first* night he was with 'em they got every cent of his money."

"They couldn't get my money in a *week*," said Simon. "Any body can git these here green feller's money; them's the sort I'm a-gwine to watch for myself. Here's what kin fix the papers jist about as nice as any body."

"Well, it's no use to argify about the matter," said old Jed'diah; "What saith the Scriptur'? 'He that begetteth a fool, doeth it to his sorrow.' Hence, Simon, you're a poor, misubble fool — so cross your hands!"

"You'd jist as well not, daddy; I tell you I'm gwine to follow playin' cards for a livin', and what's the use o' bangin' a feller about it? I'm as smart as any of 'em, and Bob Smith says them Augusty fellers can't make rent off o' me."

The Reverend Mr. Suggs had once in his life gone to Augusta; an extent of travel which in those days was a little unusual. His consideration among his neighbours was considerably increased by the circumstance, as he had all the benefit of the popular inference, that no man could visit the city of Augusta without acquiring a vast superiority over all his untravelled neighbors, in every department of human knowledge. Mr. Suggs then, very naturally, felt ineffably indignant that an individual who had never seen any collection of human habitations larger than a log-house village — an individual, in short, no other or better than Bob Smith, should venture to express an opinion concerning the manners, customs, or any thing else apper- taining to, or in any wise connected with, the *ultima Thule* of back- woods Georgians. There were two propositions which witnessed their own truth to the mind of Mr. Suggs — the one was, that a man who had never been at Augusta, could not know any thing about that city, or any place, or any thing else; the other, that one who *had* been there must, of necessity, be not only well informed as to all things connected with the city itself, but perfectly *au fait* upon all subjects whatsoever. It was, therefore, in a tone of mingled indignation and contempt that he replied to the last remark of Simon.

"*Bob Smith* says, does he? And who's *Bob Smith? Much does Bob Smith* know about Augusty! he's *been thar,* I reckon! Slipped off yerly some mornin', when nobody warn't noticin', and got back afore night! It's *only* a hundred and fifty mile. Oh, yes, *Bob Smith* knows *all* about it! *I* don't know nothin' about it! *I* a'n't never been to Augusty — *I* couldn't find the road thar, I reckon — ha! ha! *Bob — Smi-th!* The eternal stink! if he was only to see one o' them fine gentlemen in Augusty, with his fine broad-cloth, and bell-crown hat, and shoe- boots a-shinin' like silver, he'd take to the woods and kill himself a-runnin'. Bob Smith! that's whar all your devilment comes from, Simon."

"Bob Smith's as good as any body else, I judge; and a heap smarter than some. He showed me how to cut Jack," continued Simon, "and that's more nor some people can do, if they *have* been to Au- gusty."

"If Bob Smith kin do it," said the old man, "I kin too. I don't know it by that name; but if it's book knowledge or plain sense, and Bob kin do it, it's reasonable to s'pose that old Jed'diah Suggs won't be bothered *bad.* Is it any ways similyar to the rule of three, Simon?"

"Pretty much, daddy, but not adzactly," said Simon, drawing a pack from his pocket, to explain. "Now daddy," he proceeded, "you see these here four cards is what we calls the Jacks. Well, now the idee is, if you'll take the pack and mix 'em all up together, I'll take off a passel from top, and the bottom one of them I take off will be one of the Jacks."

"Me to mix 'em fust?" said old Jed'diah.

"Yes."

"And you not to see but the back of the top one, when you go to 'cut,' as you call it?"

"Jist so, daddy."

"And the backs all jist as like as kin be?" said the senior Suggs, examining the cards.

"More alike nor cow-peas," said Simon.

"It can't be done, Simon," observed the old man, with great solemnity.

"Bob Smith kin do it, and so kin I."

"It's agin nater, Simon; thar a'n't a man in Augusty, nor on top of the yeath that kin do it!"

"Daddy," said our hero, "ef you'll bet me ——"

"What!" thundered old Mr. Suggs. *"Bet,* did you say?" and he came down with a *scorer* across Simon's shoulders — "me, Jed'diah Suggs, that's been in the Lord's sarvice these twenty years — *me* bet, you nasty, sassy, triflin' ugly —"

"I didn't go to say *that* daddy; that warn't what I meant, adzackly. I went to say that ef you'd let me off from this here maulin' you owe me, and *give me* 'Bunch,' ef I cut Jack; I'd *give you* all this here silver, ef I didn't — that's all. To be sure, I allers knowed *you* wouldn't *bet.*"

Old Mr. Suggs ascertained the exact amount of the silver which his son handed him, in an old leathern pouch, for inspection. He also, mentally, compared that sum with an imaginary one, the supposed value of a certain Indian poney, called "Bunch," which he had bought for his "old woman's" Sunday riding, and which had sent the old lady into a fence corner, the first and only time she ever mounted him. As he weighed the pouch of silver in his hand, Mr. Suggs also endeavoured to analyze the character of the transaction proposed by Simon. "It sartinly *can't* be nothin' but *givin',* no way it kin be twisted," he murmured to himself. "I *know* he can't do it, so there's no resk. What makes bettin'? The resk. It's a one-sided business, and I'll jist let him give me all his money, and that'll put all his wild sportin' notions out of his head."

"Will you stand it, daddy?" asked Simon, by way of waking the old man up. "You mought as well, for the whippin' won't do you no good, and as for Bunch, nobody about the plantation won't ride him but me."

"Simon," replied the old man, "I agree to it. Your old daddy is in a close place about payin' for his land; and this here money — it's jist eleven dollars, lacking of twenty-five cents — will help out mightily. But mind, Simon, ef any thing's said about this, herearter, remember, you *give* me the money."

"Very well, daddy; and ef the thing works up instid o' down, I s'pose we'll say you give *me* Bunch — eh?"

"You won't never be troubled to tell how you come by Bunch; the thing's agin nater, and can't be done. What old Jed'diah Suggs knows, he knows as good as any body. Give me them fixments, Simon."

Our hero handed the cards to his father, who, dropping the plough-line with which he had intended to tie Simon's hands, turned his back to that individual, in order to prevent his witnessing the operation of *mixing*. He then sat down, and very leisurely commenced shuffling the cards, making, however, an exceedingly awkward job of it. Restive *kings* and *queens* jumped from his hands, or obstinately refused to slide into the company of the rest of the pack. Occasionally a sprightly *knave* would insist on *facing* his neighbour; or, press-ing his edge against another's, half double himself up, and then skip away. But Elder Jed'diah perseveringly continued his attempts to subdue the refractory, while heavy drops burst from his fore-head, and ran down his cheeks. All of a sudden an idea, quick and penetrating as a rifleball, seemed to have entered the cranium of the old man. He chuckled audibly. The devil had suggested to Mr. Suggs an *impromptu* "stock," which would place the chances of Simon, already sufficiently slim, in the old man's opinion, without the range of possibility. Mr. Suggs forthwith proceeded to cull out all the *picter ones*, so as to be certain to include the *Jacks*, and place them at the bottom; with the evident intention of keeping Simon's fingers above these when he should cut. Our hero, who was quietly looking over his father's shoulders all the time, did not seem alarmed by this disposition of the cards; on the contrary, he smiled as if he felt perfectly confident of success, in spite of it.

"Now, daddy," said Simon, when his father had announced him-self ready, "narry one of us aint got to look at the cards, while I'm a cuttin'; if we do, it'll spile the conjuration."

"Very well."

"And another thing — you've got to look me right dead in the eye, daddy — will ᴠu?"

"To be sure — to be sure;" said Mr. Suggs; "fire away."

Simon walked up close to his father, and placed his hand on the pack. Old Mr. Suggs looked in Simon's eye, and Simon returned the look for about three seconds, during which a close observer might have detected a suspicious working of the wrist of the hand on the cards, but the elder Suggs did not remark it.

"Wake snakes! day's a-breakin'! Rise Jack!" said Simon, cutting half a dozen cards from the top of the pack, and presenting the face of the bottom one for the inspection of his father.

It was the Jack of hearts!

Old Mr. Suggs staggered back several steps with uplifted eyes and hands!

"Marciful master!" he exclaimed, "ef the boy haint! well, how in the round creation of the ———! Ben, did you ever? to be sure and sartin,

Satan has power on this yeath!" and Mr. Suggs groaned in very bitterness.

"You never seed nothin' like that in *Augusty*, did ye, daddy?" asked Simon, with a malicious wink at Ben.

"Simon, how *did* you do it?" queried the old man, without noticing his son's question.

"Do it daddy? Do it? 'Taint nothin'. I done it jist as easy as — shootin'."

Whether this explanation was entirely, or in any degree, satisfactory to the perplexed mind of Elder Jed'diah Suggs, cannot, after the lapse of time which has intervened, be sufficiently ascertained. It is certain, however, that he pressed the investigation no farther, but merely requested his son Benjamin to witness the fact, that in consideration of his love and affection for his son Simon, and in order to furnish the donee with the means of leaving that portion of the state of Georgia, he bestowed upon him the impracticable poney, "Bunch."

"Jist so, daddy; jist so; I'll witness that. But it 'minds me mightily of the way mammy *give* Old Trailler the side of bacon, last week. She a-sweepin' up the hath; the meat on the table — old Trailler jumps up, gethers the bacon and darts! mammy arter him with the broomstick, as fur as the door — but seein' the dog has got the start, she shakes the stick at him and hollers, 'You sassy, aig-sukkin', roguish, gnatty, flop-eared varmint! take it along! take it along! I only wish 'twas full of a'snic, and ox-vomit, and blue vitrul, so as 'twould cut your interls into chitlins!' That's about the way you give Bunch to Simon."

"Oh, shuh! Ben," remarked Simon, "I wouldn't run on that way; daddy couldn't help it, it was *predestinated* — 'whom he hath, he will,' you know;" and the rascal pulled down the under lid of his left eye at his brother. Then addressing his father, he asked, "Warn't it, daddy?"

"To be sure — to be sure — all fixed aforehand," was old Mr. Suggs' reply.

"Didn't I tell you so, Ben?" said Simon — "*I* knowed it was all fixed aforehand;" and he laughed until he was purple in the face.

"What's in ye? What are ye laughin' about?" asked the old man wrothily.

"Oh, it's so funny that it could all a' been *fixed aforehand!*" said Simon, and laughed louder than before.

The obtusity of the Reverend Mr. Suggs, however, prevented his making any discoveries. He fell into a brown study, and no further allusion was made to the matter.

It was evident to our hero that his father intended he should remain but one more night beneath the paternal roof. What mattered it to Simon?

He went home at night, curried and fed Bunch; whispered confidentially in his ear that he was the "fastest piece of hoss-flesh, accordin' to size, that ever shaded the yeath;" and then busied himself in preparing for an early start on the morrow.

Simon Fights "The Tiger" and Gets Whipped

As a matter of course, the first thing that engaged the attention of Captain Suggs upon his arrival in Tuskaloosa, was his proposed attack upon his enemy. Indeed, he scarcely allowed himself time to bolt, without mastication, the excellent supper served to him at Duffie's, ere he outsallied to engage the adversary. In the street, he suffered not himself to be beguiled into a moment's loitering, even by the strange sights which under other circumstances would certainly have enchained his attention. The windows of the great drug store cast forth their blaze of varied light in vain; the music of a fine amateur band preparing for a serenade, was no music for him; he paused not in front of the bookseller's, to inspect the prints, or the huge-lettered advertising cards. In short, so eager was he to give battle to the "Tiger," that the voice of the ring-master, as it came distinctly into the street from the circus — the sharp joke of the clown, and the perfectly-shadowed figures of "Dandy Jack" and the other performers, whisking rapidly round upon the canvas — failed to shake, in the slightest degree, the resolute determination of the courageous and indomitable Captain.

As he hurried along, however, with the long stride of the backwoods, hardly turning his head, and to all appearance, oblivious altogether of things external, he held occasional "confabs" with himself in regard to the unusual objects which surrounded him — for Suggs is an observant man, and notes with much accuracy whatever comes before him, all the while a body would suppose him to be asleep, or in a "turkey dream" at least. On the present occasion his communings with himself commenced opposite the window of the drug-store, — "Well, thar's the most deffrunt sperrets in *that grocery* ever *I* seed! Thar's koniac, and old peach, and rectified, and lots I can't tell thar names! That light-yaller bottle tho', in the corner thar, that's Tenne*see!* I'd know that *any whar!* And that tother bottle's rot-gut, ef I know myself — bit a drink, I reckon, as well's the rest! What a power o' likker they do keep in this here town; ef I warn't goin' to run agin the bank, I'd sample some of it, too, I reether expect. But it don't do for a man to sperrets much when he's pursuin' the beast —"

"H—ll and scissors! who ever seed the like of the books! Aint thar a pile! Do wonder what sort of a office them fellers in thar keeps, makes 'em want so many! They don't read 'em *all*, I judge! Well, mother-wit kin beat book-larnin, at *any* game! Thar's 'squire Haden-skelt up home, he's got two cart-loads of law books — tho' that's no tech to this feller's — and here's what knocked a fifty outen him once, at short cards, afore a right smart, active sheep could flop his tail *ary* time; and kin do it agin, whenever he gits over his shyness! Human natur' and the human family is *my* books, and I've never seed many but what I could hold my own with. Let me git one o' these book-larnt fellers over a bottle of "old corn," and a handful of the dokky-ments, and I'm d—d apt to git what he knows, and in a ginral way give *him* a wrinkle into the bargain! Books aint fitten for nothin' but jist to give to childen goin' to school, to keep 'em outen mischief. As old Jed'diah used to say, book-larnin spiles a man ef he's got mother-wit, and ef he aint got that, it don't do him no good —"

"Hello agin! Here's a sirkis, and ef I warnt in a hurry, right here I'd drop a quarter, providin' I couldn't fix it to slip in for nothin', which is always the cheapest in a ginral way!"

Thus ruminating, Simon at length reached CLARE'S. Passing into the bar-room, he stood a moment, looking around to ascertain the direc-tion in which he should proceed to find the faro banks, which he had heard were nightly exhibited there. In a corner of the room he discovered a stair-way, above which was burning a lurid-red lamp. Waiting for no other indication, he strode up the stairs. At the landing-place above he found a door which was closed and locked, but light came through the key-hole, and the sharp rattling of dice and jingling of coin, spoke conclusively of the employment of the occu-pants of the room.

Simon knocked.

"Hello!" said somebody within.

"Hello yourself!" said the Captain.

"What do you want?" said the voice from the room.

"A game," was the Captain's laconic answer.

"What's the name?" again inquired the person within.

"Cash," said Simon.

"He'll do," said another person in the room; "let 'Cash' in."

The door was opened and Simon entered, half-blinded by the sudden burst of light which streamed from the chandeliers and lamps, and was reflected in every direction by the mirrors which almost walled the room. In the centre of the room was a small but unique "bar," the counter of which, except a small space occupied by a sliding door at which customers were served, was enclosed with burnished brass rods. Within this "magic circle" stood a pock-marked clerk, who vended to the company wines and liquors too costly to be imbibed by any but men of fortune or gamesters, who, alternately rich and penniless, indulge every appetite without stint while they have the means; eating viands and drinking wines one day, which a prince might not disdain, to fast entirely the next, or make a disgusting meal from the dirty counter of a miserable eating-house. Disposed at regular intervals around the room, were tables for the various games usually played; all of them thronged with eager "customers," and covered with heavy piles of doubloons, and dollars, and bank notes. Of these tables the "tiger" claimed three — for faro was predominant in those days, when a cell in the penitentiary was not the penalty for exhibiting it. Most of the persons in the room were well-dressed, and a large proportion members of the legislature. There was very little noise, no loud swearing, but very deep playing.

As Simon entered, he made his rustic bow, and in an easy, familiar way, saluted the company with

"Good evenin' gentle*men!*"

No one seemed inclined to acknowledge, on behalf of the company, their pleasure at seeing Captain Suggs. Indeed, nobody appeared to notice him at all after the first half second. The Captain, therefore, repeated his salutation:

"*I say,* GOOD EVENIN', gentle*men!*"

Notwithstanding the emphasis with which the words were re-spoken, there was only a slight laugh from some of the company, and the Captain began to feel a little awkward standing up before so many strangers. While he was hesitating whether to begin business at once by walking up to one of the faro tables and commencing the "fight," he overheard a young man standing a few feet from him, say to another,

"Jim, isn't that your uncle, General Witherspoon, who has been expected here for several days with a large drove of hogs?"

"By Jupiter," said the person addressed, "I believe it is; though I'm not certain, as I haven't seen him since I was a little fellow. But what makes *you* think it's him: you never saw him?"

"No, but he suits the description given of your uncle, very well — white hair, red eyes, wide mouth, and so forth. Does your uncle gamble?"

"They say he does; but my mother, who is his sister, knows hardly any more about him than the rest of the world. We've only seen him once in fifteen years. I'll be d—d," he added, looking steadfastly at

Simon, "if that isn't he! He's as rich as mud, and a jovial old cock of a bachelor, so I must claim kin with him."

Simon could, of course, have no reasonable objection to being believed to be General Thomas Witherspoon, the rich hog drover from Kentucky. Not he! The idea pleased him excessively, and he determined if he was not respected as General Witherspoon for the remainder of that evening, it should be "somebody else's fault," not his! In a few minutes, indeed, it was whispered through the company, that the red-eyed man with white hair, was the wealthy field-officer who drove swine to increase his fortune; and in consequence of this, Simon thought he discovered a very considerable improvement in the way of politeness, on the part of all present. The bare suspicion that he was rich, was sufficient to induce deference and attention.

Sauntering up to a faro bank with the intention of betting, while his money should hold out, with the spirit and liberality which General Witherspoon would have displayed had he been personally present, he called for

"Twenty, five-dollar checks, and that pretty toloble d—d quick!"

The dealer handed him the red checks, and he piled them upon the "ten."

"Grind on!" said Simon.

A card or two was dealt, and the keeper, with a profound bow, handed Simon twenty more red checks.

"Deal away," said Simon, heaping the additional checks on the same card.

Again the cards flew from the little box, and again Simon won.

Several persons were now over-looking the game; and among the rest, the young man who was so happy as to be the nephew of General Witherspoon.

"The old codger has nerve; I'll be d—d if he hasn't," said one.

"And money too," said another, "from the way he bets."

"To be sure he has," said a third; "that's the rich hog drover from Kentucky."

By this time Simon had won seven hundred dollars. But the Captain was not at all disposed to discontinue. "Now!" he thought was the "golden moment" in which to press his luck; "now!" the hour of the "tiger's" doom, when he should be completely flayed.

"That brings the fat in great fleeks as big as my arm!" observed the Captain, as he won the fifth consecutive bet: "it's hooray, brother John, every fire a turkey! as the boy said. Here goes again!" and he staked his winnings and the original stake on the Jack.

"Gracious heavens! General, I wouldn't stake so much on a single card," said a young man who was inclined to boot-lick anybody suspected of having money.

"*You* wouldn't, young man," said the Captain, turning round and facing him, "bekase *you* never tote a pile of that size."

The obtrusive individual shrunk back under this rebuke, and the crowd voted Simon not only a man of spunk, but a man of wit.

At this moment the Jack won, and the Captain was better off, by fifteen hundred dollars, than when he entered the saloon.

"That's better — jist the least grain in the world better — than drivin' hogs from Kaintucky and sellin' 'em at four cents a pound!" triumphantly remarked Suggs.

The nephew of General Witherspoon was now confident that Captain Suggs was his uncle. He accordingly pushed up to him with —

"Don't you know me, uncle?" at the same time extending his hand.

Captain Suggs drew himself up with as much dignity as he supposed the individual whom he personated would have assumed, and remarked that he did *not* know the young man then in his immediate presence.

"Don't know me, uncle? Why, I'm James Peyton, your sister's son. She has been expecting you for several days;" said the much-humbled nephew of the hog drover.

"All very well, Mr. Jeemes Peyton, but as this little world of ourn is tolloble d—d full of rascally impostors; and gentle*men* of my — that is to say — you see — persons that have got somethin', is apt to be tuk in, it stands a man in hand to be a leetle perticler. So jist answer me a strait forrard question or two," said the Captain, subjecting Mr. Peyton to a test, which if applied to himself, would have blown him sky-high. But Simon was determined to place his own identity as General Witherspoon above suspicion, by seeming to suspect something wrong about Mr. James Peyton.

"Oh," said several of the crowd, "everybody knows he's the widow Peyton's son, and your nephew, of course."

"Wait for the wagin, gentle*men*," said Simon; "*everybody* has give me several sons, which, as I aint married, I don't want, and" added he with a very facetious wink and smile, "I don't care about takin' a nephy on the same terms without he's giniwine."

"Oh, he's genuine," said several at once.

"Hold on, gentle*men;* this young man might want to borrow money of me —"

Mr. Peyton protested against any such supposition.

"Oh, well!" said the Captain, "*I* might want to borrow of *you,* and —"

Mr. Peyton signified his willingness to lend his uncle the last dollar in his pocket book.

"Very good! very good! but *I* happen to be a little *notiony* about sich matters. It aint every man I'd borrer from. Before I handle a man's money in the way of borrerin, in the fust place I must know him to be a gentleman; in the second place, he must be my friend; and in the third place, I must think he's both able and willin' to afford the accommodation" — and the Captain paused and looked around to receive the applause which he knew must be elicited by the magnanimity of the sentiment.

The applause *did* come; and the crowd thought while they gave it, how difficult and desirable a thing it would be, to lend money to General Thomas Witherspoon, the rich hog drover.

The Captain now resumed his examination of Mr. Peyton.

"What's your mother's fust name?" he asked.

"Sarah," said Mr. Peyton meekly.

"Right! so fur," said the Captain, with a smile of approval: "how many children has she?"

"Two: myself and brother Tom."

"Right again!" observed the Captain. "Tom, gentle*men*," added he, turning to the crowd, and venturing a shrewd guess; "Tom, gentle*men*, was named arter *me*. Warn't he, sir?" said he to Mr. Peyton, sternly.

"He was, sir — his name is Thomas Witherspoon."

Captain Suggs bobbed his head at the company, as much as to say, "*I* knew it;" and the crowd in their own minds, decided that the *ci-devant* General Witherspoon was "a devilish sharp old cock" — and the crowd wasn't far out of the way.

Simon was not acting in this matter without an object. He intended to make a bold attempt to win a small fortune, and he thought it quite possible he should lose the money he had won; in which case it would be convenient to have the credit of General Witherspoon to operate upon.

"Gentle*men*," said he to the company, with whom he had become vastly popular; "your attention, *one* moment, ef you please!"

The company accorded him its most obsequious attention.

"Come here, Jeemes!"

Mr. James Peyton approached to within eighteen inches of his supposititious uncle, who raised his hands above the young man's head, in the most impressive manner.

"One and all, gentle*men*," said he, "I call on you to witness that I reckognize this here young man as my proper, giniwine nephy — my sister Sally's son; and wish him respected as sich. Jeemes, hug your old uncle!"

Young Mr. James Peyton and Captain Simon Suggs then embraced. Several of the bystanders laughed, but a large majority sympathized with the Captain. A few wept at the affecting sight, and one person expressed the opinion that nothing so soul-moving had ever before taken place in the city of Tuskaloosa. As for Simon, the tears rolled down his face, as naturally as if they had been called forth by real emotion, instead of being pumped up mechanically to give effect to the scene.

Captain Suggs now renewed the engagement with the tiger, which had been temporarily suspended that he might satisfy himself of the identity of James Peyton. But the "fickle goddess," jealous of his attention to the nephew of General Witherspoon, had deserted him as a pet.

"Thar goes a dozen d—d fine, fat hogs!" said the Captain, as the bank won a bet of two hundred dollars.

Suggs shifted about from card to card, but the bank won always! At last he thought it best to return to the "ten," upon which he bet five hundred dollars.

"Now, I'll wool you," said he.

"Next time!" said the dealer, as he threw the winning card upon his own pile.

"That makes my hogs squeal," said the Captain; and everybody admired the fine wit and nerve of the hog drover.

In half an hour Suggs was "as flat as a flounder." Not ᵔ dollar remained of his winnings or his original stake. It was, therefore, time to "run his face," or rather, the "face" of General Witherspoon.

"Could a body bet a few mighty fine bacon hogs, agin money at this table?" he inquired.

The dealer would be happy to accommodate the General, upon his word of honor.

It was not long before Suggs had bet off a very considerable number of the very fine hogs in General Witherspoon's uncommonly fine drove. He began to feel, too, as if a meeting with the veritable drover might be very disagreeable. He began, therefore, to entertain serious notions of borrowing some money and leaving in the stage, that night, for Greensboro'. Honor demanded, however, that he should "settle" to the satisfaction of the dealer. He accordingly called

"Jeemes!"

Mr. Peyton responded very promptly to the call.

"Now," said Simon, "Jeemes, I'm a little behind to this gentleman here, and I'm obleeged to go to Greensboro' in to-night's stage, on account of seein' ef I can engage pork thar. Now ef *I* shouldn't be *here*, when my hogs *come in*, do *you*, Jeemes, take this gentleman to wherever the boys puts 'em up, and let him pick thirty of the finest in the drove. D'ye *hear*, Jeemes?"

James promised to attend to the delivery of the hogs.

"Is that satisfactory?" asked Simon.

"Perfectly," said the dealer; "let's take a drink."

Before the Captain went up to the bar to drink, he patted "Jeemes" upon the shoulder, and intimated that he desired to speak to him privately. Mr. Peyton was highly delighted at this mark of his rich uncle's confidence, and turned his head to see whether the company noted it. Having ascertained that they did, he accompanied his uncle to an unoccupied part of the saloon.

"Jeemes," said the Captain thoughtfully, "has your — mother bought — her — her — pork yet?"

James said that she had not.

"Well, Jeemes, when my drove comes in, do you go down and pick her out ten of the best. Tell the boys to show you them new breed — the Berkshears."

Mr. Peyton made his grateful acknowledgements for his uncle's generosity, and they started back towards the crowd. Before they had advanced more than a couple of steps, however —

"Stop!" said Simon, "I'd like to a'forgot. Have you as much as a couple of hunderd by you, Jeemes, that I could use twell I git back from Greensboro'?"

Mr. Peyton was very sorry he hadn't more than fifty dollars about him. His uncle could take that, however — as he did forthwith — and he would "jump about" and get the balance in ten minutes.

"Don't do it, ef it's any trouble at all, Jeemes," said the Captain cunningly.

But Mr. James Peyton was determined that he would "raise the wind" for his uncle, let the "trouble" be what it might; and so energetic were his endeavours, that in a few moments he returned to the Captain and handed him the desired amount.

"Much obleeged to you, Jeemes; I'll remember you for this;" and no doubt the Captain has kept his word; for whenever he makes a promise which it costs nothing to perform, Captain Simon Suggs is the most punctual of men.

After Suggs had taken a glass of "sperrets" with his friend the dealer — whom he assured he considered the "smartest and cleverest" fellow out of Kentucky — he wished to retire. But just as he was leaving, it was suggested in his hearing, that an oyster supper would be no inappropriate way of testifying his joy at meeting his clever nephew and so many true-hearted friends.

"Ah, gentlemen, the old hog drover's broke now, or he'd be proud to treat to something of the sort. They've knocked the leaf fat outen him to-night, in wads as big as mattock handles," observed Suggs, looking at the bar-keeper out of the corner of his left eye.

"Anything this house affords is at the disposal of General Witherspoon," said the bar-keeper.

"Well! well!" said Simon, "you're all so clever, I must stand it I suppose, tho' I oughtn't to be so extravagant."

"Take the crowd, sir?"

"Certainly," said Simon.

"How much champagne, General?"

"I reckon we can make out with a couple of baskets," said the Captain, who was determined to sustain any reputation for liberality which General Witherspoon might, perchance, possess.

There was a considerable ringing of bells for a brief space, and then a door which Simon hadn't before seen, was thrown open, and the company ushered into a handsome supping apartment. Seated at the convivial board, the Captain outshone himself; and to this day, some of the *bon mots* which escaped him on that occasion, are remembered and repeated.

At length, after the proper quantity of champagne and oysters had been swallowed, the young man whom Simon had so signally rebuked early in the evening, rose and remarked that he had a sentiment to propose:_"I give you, gentlemen," said he, "the health of General Witherspoon. Long may he live, and often may he visit our city and partake of its hospitalities!"

Thunders of applause followed this toast, and Suggs, as in duty bound, got up in his chair to respond.

"Gentle*men,*" said he, "I'm devilish glad to see you all, and much obleeged to you, besides. You are the finest people I ever was amongst, and treat me a d—d sight better than they do at home" — which was a fact! "Hows'ever, I'm a poor hand to speak, but here's wishing of luck to you all" — and then wickedly seeming to blunder in his little speech — "and if I forgit you, I'll be d—d if you'll ever forgit me!"

Again there was a mixed noise of human voices, plates, knives, and forks, glasses and wine bottles, and then the company agreed to disperse. "What a noble-hearted fellow!" exclaimed a dozen in a breath, as they were leaving.

As Simon and Peyton passed out, the bar-keeper handed the former a slip of paper, containing such items as — "twenty-seven dozen of oysters, twenty-seven dollars; two baskets of champagne, thirty-six dollars," — making a grand total of sixty-three dollars.

The Captain, who "felt his wine," only hiccoughed, nodded at Peyton, and observed,

"Jeemes, you'll attend to this?"

"Jeemes" said he would, and the pair walked out and bent their way to the stage-office, where the Greensboro' coach was already drawn up. Simon wouldn't wake the hotel keeper to get his saddle-bags, because, as he said, he would probably return in a day or two.

"Jeemes," said he, as he held that individual's hand; "Jeemes, has your mother bought her pork yet?"

"No, sir," said Peyton, "you know you told me to take ten of your hogs for her — don't you recollect?"

"Don't do that," said Simon, sternly.

Peyton stood aghast! "Why sir?" he asked.

"Take TWENTY!" said the Captain, and wringing the hand he held, he bounced into the coach, which whirled away, leaving Mr. James Peyton on the pavement, in profound contemplation of the boundless generosity of his uncle, General Thomas Witherspoon of Kentucky!

Simon Becomes Captain

By reference to memoranda, contemporaneously taken, of incidents to be recorded in the memoirs of Captain Suggs, we find that we have reached the most important period in the history of our hero — his assumption of a military command. And we beg the reader to believe, that we approach this portion of our subject with a profound regret at our own incapacity for its proper illumination. Would that thy pen, O! Kendall, were ours! Then would thy hero and ours — the nation's Jackson and the country's Suggs — go down to far posterity, equal in fame and honors, as in deeds! But so the immortal gods have not decreed! Not to Suggs was Amos given! Aye, jealous of his mighty feats, the thundering Jove denied an historian worthy of his puissance! Would that, like Caesar, he could write himself! Then, indeed, should Harvard yield him honors, and his country — justice!

Early in May of the year of grace — and excessive bank issues — 1836, the Creek war was discovered to have broken out. During that month several persons, residing in the county of Tallapoosa, were cruelly murdered by the "inhuman savages;" and an exceedingly large number of the peaceful citizens of the state — men, women and children — excessively frightened. Consternation seized all! "Shrieks inhuman" rent the air! The more remote from the scenes of blood, the greater the noise. The yeomanry of the country — those to whom, as we are annually told, the nation looks with confidence in all her perils — packed up their carts and wagons, and "incontinently" departed for more peaceful regions! We think we see them now, "strung along the road," a day or two after the intelligence of the massacres below had reached the "settlement" of Captain Suggs! There goes old man Simmons, with his wife and three daughters, together with two feather beds, a few chairs, and a small assortment of pots and ovens, in a cart drawn by a bob-tail, gray pony. On the top-most bed, and forming the apex of this pile of animate and inanimate "luggage," sits the old tom-cat, whom the youngest daughter would not suffer to remain lest he might come to harm. "Who knows," she exclaims, *"what* they might do to the poor old fellow?" On they toil! the old man's head, ever and anon, turned back to see if they are pursued by the remorseless foe; while the wife and daughters scream direfully, every ten minutes, as they discover in the distance a cow or a hog — "Oh, they'll kill us! they'll skelp us! they'll tar us all *to* pieces! Oh, Lord! daddy! oh, Lord!" But the old tom-cat sits there, gravely and quietly, the very incarnation of tom philosophy!

It was on Sunday that the alarm was sounded in the "Suggs settle-ment," and most of the neighbours were in attendance upon the "preaching of the word" by brother Snufflenosey, at Poplar Spring meeting-house, when the "runner" who brought the woful tidings, disclosed them at old Tom Rollins', by yelling, as he sat on his horse before the door, — "the Injuns is a-killin everybody below! I aint got time to stop! tell the neighbours!" Now, old Mr. Rollins and the "gals" were already at meeting, but the old lady, having stayed behind "to fix up a leetle," was, at the identical moment of the mes-senger's arrival, *en chemise* before a very small glass set in a frame of red paper, preparing to adorn her person with divers new articles of apparel, inclusive of a new blue-and-red-calico gown. But no sooner did her mind comprehend the purport of the words from without, than she sprang out of the house, "accoutred as she was," shrieking at every bound, "the Injuns! the Injuns!" — nor stopped until with face, neck, and bosom crimson as a strutting gobbler's snout, she burst into the meeting-house, and having once more screamed "the Injuns!" fell exhausted, at full length, upon the floor. "Will any of the breethring lend me a horse?" asked the Reverend Mr. Snufflenosey, wildly, as he bounded out of the pulpit, in very creditable style — "Wont *none* of you lend me one?" he repeated emphatically; and obtaining no answer, dashed off precipitately afoot! Then went up to Heaven the screams of fifty frightened women, in one vast discord, more dreadful than the war-squalls of an hundred cats in fiercest battle. Men, too, looked pale and trembled; while, strange to relate, all of the dozen young babies in attendance silently dilated their astonished eyes — struck utterly dumb at being so signally beaten at their own peculiar game!

At length an understanding was somehow effected, that Taylor's store, five miles thence, should be the place of rendezvous, for that night at least; and then Mr. Snufflenosey's congregation tumbled itself forth as expeditiously as was possible.

Simon was "duly" at the store with his family, when the wagon, cart, and pony loads of "badly-scared" mortality began to arrive in the afternoon. He was there of course, and he was in his element. Not that Suggs is particularly fond of danger — albeit, he is a hero — but because he delighted in the noise and confusion, the fun and the free drinking, incident to such occasions. And he enjoyed these to the uttermost now, because he was well informed as to the state of feeling of the Indians, in all the country for ten miles around, and knew there was no danger. But Simon did not disclose this to the terrified throng at the store. Not he! Suggs was never the man to destroy his own importance in that sort of way. On the contrary, he magnified the danger, and endeavoured to impress upon the minds of the miscellaneous crowd "then and there" assembled, that he, Simon Suggs, was the only man at whose hands they could expect a deliverance from the imminent peril which impended.

"Gentle*men*," said he impressively, "this here is a critercle time; the wild savage of the forest are beginnin' of a bloody, hostile war, which they're not a-goin' to spar nither age nor sek — not even to the women and children!"

"Gracious Lord above! what *is* a body to do!" exclaimed the portly widow Haycock, who was accounted wealthy, in consideration of the fact that she had a hundred dollars in money, and was the undisputed owner of one entire negro — "we shall all be skelped, and our truck all burnt up and destr'yed! What shall we do!"

"That's the question," remarked Simon, as he stooped to draw a glass of whiskey from a barrel of that article — the only thing on sale in the "store" — "that's the question. Now, as for you women-folks" — here Suggs dropped a lump of brown sugar in his whiskey, and began to stir it with his finger, looking intently in the tumbler, the while — "as for you women-folks, it's plain enough what *you*'ve got to do" — here Simon tasted the liquor and added a little more sugar — "plain *enough!* You've only got to look to the Lord and hold your jaws; for that's all you *kin* do! But what's the 'sponsible *men*" — taking his finger out of the tumbler, and drawing it through his mouth — "of this crowd to do? The inemy will be down upon us right away, and before mornin'" — Simon drank half the whiskey — "blood will flow like — like" — the Captain was bothered for a simile, and looked around the room for one, but finding none, continued — "like all the world! Yes, like all the world" — an idea suggested itself — "and the Tallapussey river! It'll pour out," he continued, as his fancy got rightly to work, "like a great gulpin ocean! — d—d if it don't!" And then Simon swallowed the rest of the whiskey, threw the tumbler down, and looked around to observe the effect of this brilliant exordium.

The effect was tremendous!

Mrs. Haycock clasped her hands convulsively, and rolled up her eyes until the "whites" only could be seen. Old Mrs. Rollins — who by this time was fully clothed — and her two daughters had what Simon termed the "high-strikes" in one corner of the room, and kicked up their heels at a prodigious rate; while in another, a group of young women hugged one another most affectionately, sobbing hysterically all the time. Old granny Gilbreth sat in the middle of the floor, rocking her body back and forth, striking the palms of her hands on the planks as she bent forward, and clapping them together as she re-attained the perpendicular.

"My apinion," continued Simon, as he stooped to draw another tumbler of whiskey; "my apinion, folks, is this here. We ought to form a company right away, and make some man capting that aint afeard to fight — mind what I say, now — *that-aint-afeard-to-fight!* — some sober, stiddy feller" — here he sipped a little from the tumbler — "that's a good hand to manage women and keep 'em from hollerin — which they're a-needin' somethin' of the sort most damdibly, and I eech to git holt o' that one a-making that devilish racket in the corner, thar" — the noise in the corner was suddenly suspended — "and more'n all, a man that's acquainted with the country and the ways of the Injuns!" Having thus spoken, Suggs drank off the rest of the whiskey, threw himself into a military attitude, and awaited a reply.

"Suggs is the man," shouted twenty voices.

"Keep close to *him,* and you'll never git hurt," said a diminutive, yellow-faced, spindle-legged young man.

"D'ye think so now?" exclaimed Simon furiously, as he "planted" a tremendous kick on that part of the joker's person at which the boot's point is most naturally directed. "D'ye think so, now? Take *that* along, and next time keep your jaw, you slink, or I'll kick more clay outen you in a minute, than you can eat again in a month, you durned, little, dirt-eatin' deer-face!"

"Keep the children outen the way," said the little fellow, as he lay sprawling in the farthest corner of the room; "ef you don't, *Cap'en* Suggs will whip 'em all. He's a sight on children and people what's got the *yaller janders!*"

Simon heeded not the sarcasm, but turning to the men he asked —

"Now gentle*men*, who'll you have for capting?"

"Suggs! Suggs! Suggs!" shouted a score and a half of masculine voices.

The women said nothing — only frowned.

"Gentle*men*," said Simon, a smile of gratified, but subdued pride playing about his mouth; "Gentle*men*, my respects — ladies, the same to you!" — and the Captain bowed — "I'm more'n proud to sarve my country at the head of sich an independent and patriotic cumpany! Let who will run, gentle*men*, Simon Suggs will allers be found sticking thar, like a tick onder a cow's belly —"

"Whar do you aim to bury your dead Injuns, Cap'en?" sarcastically inquired the little dirt-eater.

"I'll bury *you*, you little whifflin fice," said Captain Suggs in a rage; and he dashed at yellow-legs furiously.

"Not afore a body's dead, I reckon," replied the dirt-eater, running round the room, upsetting the women and trampling the children, in his efforts to escape. At last he gained the door, out of which he bounced and ran off.

"Durn the little cuss," said the Captain, when he saw that pursuit would be useless; "I oughtent to git aggrawated at him, no how. He's a poor signifiken runt, that's got the mark of the huckle-berry ponds on his legs yit, whar the water come to when he was a-getherin 'em, in his raisin' in Northkurliny. But I must put a stop to sich, and that right away;" and striding to the door, out of which he thrust his head, he made proclamation: "Oh yes! gentle*men*! Oh yes! This here store-house and two acres all round is now onder *martial law!* If any man or woman don't mind my orders, I'll have 'em shot right away; and children to be whipped accordin' to size. By order of me, Simon Suggs, Capting of the" — the Captain paused.

"Tallapoosy Vollantares," suggested Dick Cannifax.

"The Tallapoosy Vollantares," added Suggs, adopting the suggestion; "so let everybody look out, and walk the chalk!"

Thus was formed the nucleus of that renowned band of patriot soldiers, afterwards known as the "Forty Thieves" — a name in the highest degree inappropriate, inasmuch as the company, from the very best evidence we have been able to procure, never had upon its roll, at any time, a greater number of names than *thirty-nine!*

As became a prudent commander, Captain Suggs, immediately after the proclamation of martial law, set about rendering his position as strong as possible. A rude rail fence near by was removed and made to enclose the log store, and another building of the same sort, which was used as a stable. The company was then paraded, and a big drink dealt out to each man, and five men were detailed to serve as sentinels, one at each corner of the enclosure, and one at the fence in front of the store door. The Captain then announced that he had appointed Andy Snipes, "fust lewtenant," Bird Stinson "sekkunt ditto," and Dave Lyon "sarjunt."

The guard was set, the women summarily quieted, the mass of the company stowed away in the stable for the night; and the Captain and "Lewtenant Snipes" sat down, with a bottle of bald-face between them, to a social game of "six cards, seven up," by a fire in the middle of the enclosure. About this time, the widow Haycock desired to possess herself of a certain "plug" of tobacco, wherewithal to supply her pipe during the watches of the night. The tobacco was in her cart, which, with a dozen others, stood in the road twenty steps or so from the front door. Now, as the widow Haycock was arrayed rather grotesquely — in a red-flannel wrapper, with a cotton handkerchief about her head — she did not wish to be seen as she passed out. She therefore noiselessly slipped out, and, the sentinel having deserted his post for a few moments to witness the playing between his officers, succeeded in reaching the cart unobserved. As she returned, however, with the weed of comfort in her hand, she was challenged by the sentinel, who, hearing a slight noise, had come back to his post.

"Stand!" said he, as the old lady was climbing the fence.

"Blessed Master!" exclaimed Mrs. Haycock; but the soldier was too much frightened to observe that she spoke English, or to recognize her voice.

"Give the counter-sign or I'll shoot," said he, bringing his gun to a "present," but receding towards the fire as he spoke.

Instead of the counter-sign, Mrs. Haycock gave a scream, which the sentinel, in his fright, mistook for the war-whoop, and instantly fired. The widow dropped from the fence to the ground, on the outside, and the sentinel ran to the Captain's fire.

In a moment was heard the thundering voice of Captain Suggs:

"Turn out, men! Kumpny fo-r-m!"

The women in the store screamed, and the company formed immediately in front of the door. The Captain was convinced that the alarm was a humbug of some sort; but keeping up the farce, kept up his own importance.

"Bring your guns to a level with your breasts, and fire through the cracks of the fence!" he ordered.

An irregular volley was fired, which brought down a poney and a yoke of steers, haltered to their owner's carts in the road; and frightened "yellow-legs," (who had slyly taken lodgings in a little wagon), nearly to death.

"Over the fence now! Hooraw! my galyunt voluntares!" shouted the Captain, made enthusiastic by the discharge of the guns.

The company scaled the fence.

"Now charge baggonets! Hooraw! Let 'em have the cold steel, my brave boys!"

This manoeuvre was executed admirably, considering the fact, that the company was entirely without bayonets or a foe. The men brought their pieces to the proper position, ran ten steps, and finding nothing else to pierce, drove the long, projecting ram-rods of their rifles deep in the mellow earth!

"Pickle all them skelps, Cap'en Suggs, or they'll *spile!*" said a derisive voice, which was recognized as belonging to Yellow-legs, and a light form flitted from among the wagons and carts, and was lost in the darkness.

"Somebody kill that critter!" said Suggs, much excited. But the "critter" had "evaporated."

A careful examination of the field of battle was now made, and the prostrate bodies of the pony, the oxen, and the widow Haycock discovered, lying as they had fallen. From the last a slight moaning proceeded. A light was soon brought.

"What's the matter, widder — hurt?" inquired Suggs, raising up one of Mrs. Haycock's huge legs upon his foot, by way of ascertaining how much life was left.

"Only dead — that's all," said the widow as her limb fell heavily upon the ground, with commendable resignation.

"Pshaw!" said Suggs, "you aint bad hurt. Whar-abouts did the bullet hit?"

"All over! *only* shot all to pieces! It makes *no* odds tho' — kleen through and through — I'm a-goin' mighty fast!" replied the widow, as four stout men raised her from the ground and carried her into the house, where her wounds were demonstrated to consist of a contusion on the bump of philo-progenitiveness, and the loss of a half square inch of the corrugated integument of her left knee.

Captain Suggs and Lieutenant Snipes now resumed their game.

"Lewtenant," — said Suggs, as he dealt the cards — "we must — there's the tray for low — we must *court-martial* that old 'oman in the mornin'."

" 'Twon't do, Capting — the tray I mean — to be sure we must! She's vierlated the rules of war!"

"And Yaller-legs, *too!*" said Suggs.

"Yes, yes; and Yaller-legs too, ef we kin ketch him," replied Lewtenant Snipes.

"Yes, d—d ef I don't! — court-martial 'em both, as sure as the sun rises —*drum-head* court-martial at that!"

The Captain Attends a Camp-Meeting

Captain Suggs found himself as poor at the conclusion of the Creek war, as he had been at its commencement. Although no "arbitrary," "despotic," "corrupt," and "unprincipled" judge had fined him a thousand dollars for his proclamation of martial law at Fort Suggs, or the enforcement of its rules in the case of Mrs. Haycock; yet somehow — the thing is alike inexplicable to him and to us — the money which he had contrived, by various shifts to obtain, melted away and was gone forever. To a man like the Captain, of intense domestic affections, this state of destitution was most distressing. "He could stand it himself — didn't care a d——n for it, no way," he observed, "but the old woman and the children; *that* bothered him!"

As he sat one day, ruminating upon the unpleasant condition of his "financial concerns," Mrs. Suggs informed him that "the sugar and coffee was nigh about out," and that there were not "a dozen j'ints and middlins, *all put together,* in the smoke-house." Suggs bounced up on the instant, exclaiming, "D——n it! *somebody* must suffer!" But whether this remark was intended to convey the idea that he and his family were about to experience the want of the necessaries of life; or that some other, and as yet unknown individual should "suffer" to prevent that prospective exigency, must be left to the commentators, if perchance any of that ingenious class of persons should hereafter see proper to write notes for this history. It is enough for us that we give all the facts in this connection, so that ignorance of the subsequent conduct of Captain Suggs may not lead to an erroneous judgment in respect to his words.

Having uttered the exclamation we have repeated — and perhaps, hurriedly walked once or twice across the room — Captain Suggs drew on his famous old green-blanket overcoat, and ordered his horse, and within five minutes was on his way to a camp-meeting, then in full blast on Sandy creek, twenty miles distant, where he hoped to find amusement, at least. When he arrived there, he found the hollow square of the encampment filled with people, listening to the mid-day sermon and its dozen accompanying "exhortations." A half-dozen preachers were dispensing the word; the one in the pulpit, a meek-faced old man, of great simplicity and benevolence. His voice was weak and cracked, notwithstanding which, however, he contrived to make himself heard occasionally, above the din of the exhorting, the singing, and the shouting which were going on around him. The rest were walking to and fro, (engaged in the other exercises we have indicated), among the "mourners" — a host of whom occupied the seat set apart for their especial use — or made personal appeals to the mere spectators. The excitement was intense. Men and women rolled about on the ground, or lay sobbing or shouting in promiscuous heaps. More than all, the negroes sang and screamed and prayed. Several, under the influence of what is technically called "the jerks," were plunging and pitching about with convulsive energy. The great object of all seemed to be, to see who could make the greatest noise —

> "And each — for madness ruled the hour —
> Would try his own expressive power."

"Bless my poor old soul!" screamed the preacher in the pulpit; "ef yonder aint a squad in that corner that we aint got one outen yet! It'll never do" — raising his voice — "you must come outen that! Brother Fant, fetch up that youngster in the blue coat! I see the Lord's a-workin' upon him! Fetch him along — glory — yes! — hold to him!"

"Keep the thing warm!" roared a sensual seeming man, of stout mould and florid countenance, who was exhorting among a bevy of young women, upon whom he was lavishing caresses. "Keep the thing warm, breethring! — come to the Lord, honey!" he added, as he vigorously hugged one of the damsels he sought to save.

"Oh, I've got him!" said another in exulting tones, as he led up a gawky youth among the mourners — "I've got him — he tried to git off, but — ha! Lord!" — shaking his head as much as to say, it took a smart fellow to escape him — "ha! Lord!" — and he wiped the perspiration from his face with one hand, and with the other, patted his neophyte on the shoulder — "he couldn't do it! No! Then he tried to argy wi' me — but bless the Lord! — he couldn't do that nother! Ha! Lord! I tuk him, fust in the Old Testament — bless the Lord! — and I argyed him all thro' Kings — then I throwed him into Proverbs! — and from that, here we had it up and down, kleer down to the New Testament, and then I begun to see it work him! — then we got into Matthy, and from Matthy right straight along to Acts; and *thar* I throwed him! Y-e-s L-o-r-d!" — assuming the nasal twang and high pitch which are, in some parts, considered the perfection of rhetorical art — "Y-e-s L-o-r-d! and h-e-r-e he is! Now g-i-t down thar," addressing the subject, "and s-e-e ef the L-o-r-d won't do somethin' f-o-r you!" Having thus deposited his charge among the mourners, he started out, summarily to convert another soul!

"Gl-o-*ree!*" yelled a huge, greasy negro woman, as in a fit of the jerks, she threw herself convulsively from her feet, and fell "like a thousand of brick," across a diminutive old man in a little round hat, who was squeaking consolation to one of the mourners.

"Good Lord, have mercy!" ejaculated the little man earnestly and unaffectedly, as he strove to crawl from under the sable mass which was crushing him.

In another part of the square a dozen old women were singing. They were in a state of absolute ecstasy, as their shrill pipes gave forth,

> "I rode on the sky,
> Quite ondestified I,
> And the moon it was under my feet!"

Near these last, stood a delicate woman in that hysterical condition in which the nerves are incontrollable, and which is vulgarly — and almost blasphemously — termed the "holy laugh." A hideous grin distorted her mouth, and was accompanied with a maniac's chuckle; while every muscle and nerve of her face twitched and jerked in horrible spasms.*

Amid all this confusion and excitement Suggs stood unmoved. He viewed the whole affair as a grand deception — a sort of "opposition line" running against his own, and looked on with a sort of professional jealousy. Sometimes he would mutter running comments upon what passed before him.

"Well now," said he, as he observed the full-faced brother who was "officiating" among the women, "that ere feller takes *my* eye! — thar he's been this half-hour, a-figurin amongst them galls, and's never said the fust word to nobody else. Wonder what's the reason these here preachers never hugs up the old, ugly women? Never seed one do it in my life — the sperrit never moves 'em that way! It's nater tho'; and the women, *they* never flocks round one o' the old dried-up breethring — bet two to one old splinter-legs thar," — nodding at one of the ministers — "won't git a chance to say turkey to a good-looking gall

---

* The reader is requested to bear in mind, that the scenes described in this chapter are not *now* to be witnessed. Eight or ten years ago, all classes of population of the Creek country were very different from what they now are. Of course, no disrespect is intended to any denomination of Christians. We believe that camp-meetings are not peculiar to any church, though most usual in the Methodist — a denomination whose respectability in Alabama is attested by the fact, that *very many* of its worthy clergymen and lay members, hold honourable and profitable offices in the gift of the state legislature; of which, indeed, almost a controlling portion are themselves Methodists. [Author's note]

to-day! Well! who blames 'em? Nater will be nater, all the world over; and I judge ef I was a preacher, I should save the purtiest souls fust, myself!"

While the Captain was in the middle of this conversation with himself, he caught the attention of the preacher in the pulpit, who inferring from an indescribable something about his appearance that he was a person of some consequence, immediately determined to add him at once to the church if it could be done; and to that end began a vigorous, direct personal attack.

"Breethring," he exclaimed, "I see yonder a man that's a sinner; I *know* he's a sinner! Thar he stands," pointing at Simon, "a missubble old crittur, with his head a-blossomin for the grave! A few more short years, and d-o-w-n he'll go to perdition, lessen the Lord have mer-cy on him! Come up here, you old hoary-headed sinner, a-n-d git down upon your knees, a-n-d put up your cry for the Lord to snatch you from the bottomless pit! You're ripe for the devil — you're b-o-u-n-d for hell, and the Lord only knows what'll become of you!"

"D—n it," thought Suggs, *"ef* I only had you down in the krick swamp for a minit or so, *I'd* show you who's *old! I'd* alter your tune *mighty* sudden, you sassy, 'saitful old rascal!" But he judiciously held his tongue and gave no utterance to the thought.

The attention of many having been directed to the Captain by the preacher's remarks, he was soon surrounded by numerous well-meaning, and doubtless very pious persons, each one of whom seemed bent on the application of his own particular recipe for the salvation of souls. For a long time the Captain stood silent, or answered the incessant stream of exhortation only with a sneer; but at length, his countenance began to give token of inward emotion. First his eye-lids twitched — then his upper lip quivered — next a transparent drop formed on one of his eye-lashes, and a similar one on the tip of his nose — and, at last, a sudden bursting of air from nose and mouth, told that Captain Suggs was overpowered by his emotions. At the moment of the explosion, he made a feint as if to rush from the crowd, but he was in experienced hands, who well knew that the battle was more than half won.

"Hold to him!" said one — "it's a-workin in him as strong as a Dick horse!"

"Pour it into him," said another, "it'll all come right directly!"

"That's the way I love to see 'em do," observed a third; "when you begin to draw the water from their eyes, taint gwine to be long afore you'll have 'em on their knees!"

And so they clung to the Captain manfully, and half dragged, half led him to the mourner's bench; by which he threw himself down, altogether unmanned, and bathed in tears. Great was the rejoicing of the brethren, as they sang, shouted, and prayed around him — for by this time it had come to be generally known that the "convicted" old man was Captain Simon Suggs, the very "chief of sinners" in all that region.

The Captain remained grovelling in the dust during the usual time, and gave vent to even more than the requisite number of sobs, and groans, and heart-piercing cries. At length, when the proper time had arrived, he bounced up, and with a face radiant with joy, commenced a series of vaultings and tumblings, which "laid in the shade" all previous performances of the sort at that camp-meeting. The brethren were in ecstasies at this demonstrative evidence of completion of the work; and whenever Suggs shouted "Gloree!" at the top of his lungs, every one of them shouted it back, until the woods rang with echoes.

The effervescence having partially subsided, Suggs was put upon his pins to relate his experience, which he did somewhat in this style — first brushing the tear-drops from his eyes, and giving the end of his nose a preparatory wring with his fingers, to free it of the superabundant moisture:

"Friends," he said, "it don't take long to curry a short horse, accordin' to the old sayin', and I'll give you the perticklers of the way I was 'brought to a knowledge' " — here the Captain wiped his eyes, brushed the tip of his nose and snuffled a little — "in less'n no time."

"Praise the Lord!" ejaculated a bystander.

"You see I come here full o' romancin' and devilment, and jist to make game of all the purceedins. Well, sure enough, I done so for some time, and was a-thinkin how I should play some trick —"

"Dear soul alive! *don't* he talk sweet!" cried an old lady in black silk — "Whar's John Dobbs? You Sukey!" screaming at a negro woman on the other side of the square — "ef you don't hunt up your mass John in a minute, and have him here to listen to this 'sperience. I'll tuck you up when I git home and give you a hundred and fifty lashes, madam! — see ef I don't! Blessed Lord!" — referring again to the Captain's relation — "aint it a *precious* 'scource!"

"I was jist a-thinkin' how I should play some trick to turn it all into redecule, when they began to come round me and talk. Long at fust I didn't mind it, but arter a little that brother" — pointing to the reverend gentlemen who had so successfully carried the unbeliever through the Old and New Testaments, and who Simon was convinced was the "big dog of the tanyard" — "that brother spoke a word that struck me kleen to the heart, and run all over me, like fire in dry grass —"

"*I – I – I* can bring 'em!" cried the preacher alluded to, in a tone of exultation — "Lord thou knows ef thy servant can't stir 'em up, nobody else needn't try — but the glory aint mine! I'm a poor worrum of the dust," he added, with ill-managed affectation.

"And so from that I felt somethin' a-pullin' me inside —"

"Grace! grace! nothin' but grace!" exclaimed one; meaning that "grace" had been operating in the Captain's gastric region.

"And then," continued Suggs, "I wanted to git off, but they hilt me, and bimeby I felt so missuble, I had to go yonder" — pointing to the mourners' seat — "and when I lay down thar it got wuss and wuss, and 'peared like somethin' was a-mashin' down on my back —"

"That was his load o' sin," said one of the brethren — "never mind, it'll tumble off presently; see ef it don't!" and he shook his head professionally and knowingly.

"And it kept a-gittin heavier and heavier, ontwell it looked like it might be a four year old steer, or a big pine log, or somethin' of that sort —"

"Glory to my soul," shouted Mrs. Dobbs, "it's the sweetest talk I *ever* hearn! You Sukey! aint you got John yit? never mind, my lady, *I'll* settle wi' you!" Sukey quailed before the finger which her mistress shook at her.

"And arter awhile," Suggs went on, " 'peared like I fell into a trance, like, and I seed —"

"Now we'll git the good on it!" cried one of the sanctified.

"And I seed the biggest, longest, rip-roarenest, blackest, scaliest —" Captain Suggs paused, wiped his brow, and ejaculated "Ah, L-o-r-d!" so as to give full time for curiosity to become impatience to know what he saw.

"*Sarpent!* warn't it?" asked one of the preachers.

"No, not a sarpent," replied Suggs, blowing his nose.

"Do tell us *what* it war, soul alive! — whar *is* John?" said Mrs. Dobbs.

"Allegator!" said the Captain.

"Alligator!" replied every woman present, and screamed for very life.

Mrs. Dobbs' nerves were so shaken by the announcement, that after repeating the horrible word, she screamed to Sukey, "you Sukey, I say, you Su-u-ke-e-y! ef you let John come a-nigh this way, whar the dreadful alliga — shaw! what am I thinkin' 'bout? 'Twarn't nothin' but a vishin!"

"Well," said the Captain in continuation, "the allegator kept a-comin' and a-comin' to'ards me, with his great long jaws a-gapin' open like a ten-foot pair o' tailors' shears —"

"Oh! oh! oh! Lord! gracious above!" cried the women.

"SATAN!" was the laconic ejaculation of the oldest preacher present, who thus informed the congregation that it was the devil which had attacked Suggs in the shape of an alligator.

"And then I concluded the jig was up, 'thout I could block his game some way; for I seed his idee was to snap off my head —"

The women screamed again.

"So I fixed myself jist like I was purfectly willin' for him to take my head, and rather he'd do it as not" — here the women shuddered perceptibly — "and so I hilt my head straight out" — the Captain illustrated by elongating his neck — "and when he come up and was a gwine to *shet down* on it, I jist pitched in a big rock which choked him to death, and that minit I felt the weight slide off, and I had the best feelins — sorter like you'll have from *good* sperrits — any body ever had!"

"Didn't I *tell* you so? Didn't I *tell* you so?" asked the brother who had predicted the off-tumbling of the load of sin. "Ha, Lord! fool *who!* I've been *all* along thar! — yes, *all along thar!* and I know every inch of the way jist as good as I do the road home!" — and then he turned round and round, and looked at all, to receive a silent tribute to his superior penetration.

Captain Suggs was now the "lion of the day." Nobody could pray so well, or exhort so movingly, as "brother Suggs." Nor did his natural modesty prevent the proper performance of appropriate exercises. With the reverend Bela Bugg (him to whom, under providence, he ascribed his conversion), he was a most especial favourite. They walked, sang, and prayed together for hours.

"Come, come up; thar's room for all!" cried brother Bugg, in his evening exhortation. "Come to the 'seat,' and ef you won't pray yourselves, let *me* pray for you!"

"Yes!" said Simon, by way of assisting his friend; "it's a game that all can win at! Ante up! ante up, boys — friends I mean — don't back out!"

"Thar aint a sinner here," said Bugg, "no matter ef his soul's black as a nigger, but what thar's room for him!"

"No matter what sort of a hand you've got," added Simon in the fulness of his benevolence; "take stock! Here am *I*, the wickedest and blindest of sinners — has spent my whole life in the sarvice of the devil — has now come in on *narry pair* and won a *pile!*" and the Captain's face beamed with holy pleasure.

"D-o-n-'t be afeard!" cried the preacher; "come along! the meanest won't be turned away! humble yourselves and come!"

"No!" said Simon, still indulging in his favourite style of metaphor; "the bluff game aint played here! No runnin' of a body off! Every body holds four aces, and when you bet, you win!"

And thus the Captain continued, until the services were concluded, to assist in adding to the number at the mourners' seat; and up to the hour of retiring, he exhibited such enthusiasm in the cause, that he was unanimously voted to be the most efficient addition the church had made during that meeting.

The next morning, when the preacher of the day first entered the pulpit, he announced that "brother Simon Suggs," mourning over his past iniquities, and desirous of going to work in the cause as speedily as possible, would take up a collection to found a church in his own neighbourhood, at which he hoped to make himself useful as soon as he could prepare himself for the ministry, which the preacher didn't doubt, would be in a very few weeks, as brother Suggs was "a man of mighty good judge*ment,* and of *a great discorse.*" The funds were to be collected by "brother Suggs," and held in trust by brother Bela Bugg, who was the financial officer of the circuit, until some arrangement could be made to build a suitable house.

"Yes, breethring," said the Captain, rising to his feet; "I want to start a little 'sociation close to me, and I want you all to help. I'm mighty poor myself, as poor as any of you — don't leave breethring" — observing that several of the well-to-do were about to go off — "don't leave; ef you aint able to afford any thing, jist give us your blessin' and it'll be all the same!"

This insinuation did the business, and the sensitive individuals re-seated themselves.

"It's mighty little of this world's goods I've got," resumed Suggs, pulling off his hat and holding it before him; "but I'll bury *that* in the cause any how," and he deposited his last five-dollar bill in the hat."

There was a murmur of approbation at the Captain's liberality throughout the assembly.

Suggs now commenced collecting, and very prudently attacked first the gentlemen who had shown a disposition to escape. These, to exculpate themselves from anything like poverty, contributed handsomely.

"Look here, breethring," said the Captain, displaying the bank-notes thus received, "brother Snooks has drapt a five wi' me, and Brother Snodgrass a ten! In course 'taint expected that you *that aint as well off as them,* will give *as much;* let every one give *accordin'* to ther means."

This was another chain-shot that raked as it went!

"Who so low" as not to be able to contribute as much as Snooks and Snodgrass?

"Here's all the *small* money I've got about me," said a burly old fellow, ostentatiously handing to Suggs, over the heads of a half dozen, a ten dollar bill.

"That's what I call maganimus!" exclaimed the Captain; "that's the way *every* rich man ought to do!"

These examples were followed, more or less closely, by almost all present, for Simon had excited the pride of purse of the congregation, and a very handsome sum was collected in a very short time.

The reverend Mr. Bugg, as soon as he observed that our hero had obtained all that was to be had at that time, went to him and inquired what amount had been collected. The Captain replied that it was still uncounted, but that it couldn't be much under a hundred.

"Well, brother Suggs, you'd better count it and turn it over to me now. I'm goin' to leave presently."

"No!" said Suggs — "can't do it!"

"Why? — what's the matter?" inquired Bugg.

"It's got to be *prayed over,* fust!" said Simon, a heavenly smile illuminating his whole face.

"Well," replied Bugg, "less go one side and do it!"

"No!" said Simon, solemnly.

Mr. Bugg gave a look of inquiry.

"You see that krick swamp?" asked Suggs — "I'm gwine down in *thar,* and I'm gwine to lay this money down *so*" — showing how he would place it on the ground — "and I'm gwine to git on these here knees" — slapping the right one — "and I'm *n-e-v-e-r* gwine to quit the grit ontwell I feel it's got the blessin'! And nobody aint got to be thar but me!"

Mr. Bugg greatly admired the Captain's fervent piety, and bidding him God-speed, turned off.

Captain Suggs "struck for" the swamp sure enough, where his horse was already hitched. "Ef them fellers aint done to a cracklin," he muttered to himself as he mounted, *"I'll* never bet on two pair agin! They're peart at the snap game, theyselves; but they're badly lewed this hitch! Well! Live and let live is a good old motter, and it's my sentiments adzactly!" And giving the spur to his horse, off he cantered.

Daddy Biggs' Scrape at Cockerell's Bend

Cockerell's Bend is a well-known rendezvous for the hunter and fisher of the Tallapoosa; and a beautiful place it is. The upper end of the curve is lake-like in its stillness, and is very deep; while a half mile below the river spreads itself to double its usual width, and brawls among rocks and islets fringed with the tall river grass. The part above is resorted to by those who fish with the rod; and that below, by seiners. Opposite the deep water, the hills come towering down to within twenty yards of the river, the narrow intervening strip being low land, covered with a tremendous growth of gum, poplar, and white-oak. Late in the afternoon of a warm May day, this part of the Bend is a most delightful spot. The little mountains on the south and west exclude the sun-glare completely, and the mere comfort-seeker may lay himself flat in the bottom of the old Indian canoe he finds moored there by a grape vine, and float and look at the clouds, and dream — as I have often done — with no living thing in sight to disturb his meditations, except the muskrat on the end of the old projecting log, and the matronly summer duck with her brood of tiny ducklings, swimming, close huddled, in the shadow of the huge wateroak, whose overhanging limbs are covered with a close net-work of muscadine vines — whereof, (of the vines I mean), I have a story of my friend Captain Suggs, which will be related at the proper time. Take care! ye little downy rascals! — especially you, little fellow, with half an egg-shell stuck to your back! — true, there are not many or large trout in the Tallapoosa: but there are *some;* and occasionally one is found of mouth sufficient to engorge a young duck! — and almost always in a cool quiet shade just like — hist! snap! — there you go, precisely as I told you! Now, old lady, quit that fussing and fluttering, and take the "young 'uns" out of the way of that *other one* that isn't far off! Trituration in a trout's maw *must* be unpleasant one would think!

The "Bend" took its name from one Bob Cockerell, who, some years ago, inhabited a log hut on the north side, within halloo of the river. Bob, by the bye, was an equivocal sort of fellow — *people* said he subsisted on stolen beef! — he challenged them, always, to "perduce the years;" and swore that he lived honestly, by fishing. Be this as it may, it is certain that his daughters, Betsy and Margaret, were the naiads of the Bend; and all the "old settlers" thereabouts have, at one time or another, been indebted to them for a passage across. They were not, we may well suppose, as graceful or romantic as the Lady of the Lake; but "Mag," with her blue eyes, flowing hair, and "cutty sark" — arranged with special reference to the average depth of water in the bottom of the canoe — was, at least, as pretty. And "the best day" the Scotch woman "ever saw," I'd venture the little Tallapoosian could have beaten her, easily, in a "single dash of a mile," with the paddles! They are gone now! but wherever they are, bless them! — they never kept one waiting as some male ferry-keepers do, but were aye at the "landing," and in the boat, before the echo of your shout had crossed the river!

It chanced once, that the writer encamped for a day or two on the narrow strip spoken of, with a company of the unsophisticated dwellers of the rough lands in that region, of whom the principal personage was "DADDY ELIAS BIGGS," sometimes called "DADDY 'LIAS," but more commonly, *"Daddy Biggs."* We were on a fishing expedition, and at night hung a short line or two from the branches of the trees which oversweep the water there, for "cat." One night, as we had just done this, and were gathered around the fire, a gallon jug passing from hand to hand, "Daddy Biggs" — who was a short, squat man, rosy-cheeked, bald, and "inclining to three-score" — remarked, as he extended his hand towards a long, gaunt fellow, with a very long nose, and a very black beard —

"Boys, aint you never hearn what a h—ll of a scrape I had here, at this very spot, last year? Billy Teal, let me have a suck at that yeathen-war, and I'll tell you all about it."

The old man tuk "a suck," smacked his lips, and began his relation: "You all 'member the time, boys, when them Chatohospa fellows come here a fishin'? D—n 'em, I wish they could fish about home, without goin' twenty mile to interrupt other people's range! Well, they 'camped right here, and *right here* THEY SEED THE DEVIL!"

"Seed the Devil!" exclaimed Billy Teal.

"Did they, in right down airnest, now?" asked Jim Waters, looking around at the dark woods, and insinuating himself between Abe Ludlow and the fire, in evident fright.

"They seed the Devil," repeated Daddy Biggs, with emphasis, "and ketcht him too!" he added; "but they couldn't hold him."

"Good Gracious!" said Jim Waters, looking around again — "do you think he stays about here?" — and Jim got nearer to the fire.

"He stays about here *some,*" replied Daddy Biggs. "But Jim, son, get out from the fire! — you'll set your over-halls afire! — and get me the sperrets. I'll buss the jug agin, and tell you all about it."

Bill Teal had deposited the jug behind a log, some ten feet off; but Jim Waters was not the lad to back out, if the Devil *was* about: so he

made two desperate strides and grabbed the "yeathen-war," and then
made two more, which brought him, head first, jug and all, into the
fire. Chunks and sparks flew everywhere, as he ploughed through!

"He's got you, Jim!" shouted Abe.

"Pull the boy out!" exclaimed Bill and myself in a breath, "or he'll
burn up!"

"Some on ye save the —— *jug!*" screamed Daddy Biggs, who was
standing horror-stricken at the idea of being left without liquor in
the woods.

In a minute both boy and jug were rescued; the former with burnt
face and hands, and singed hair; the latter entirely uninjured.

"Well, well," chuckled Daddy Biggs, "we come outen *that* fust-rate
— the jug aint hurt, nor no liquor spilt. But Jim, I'm raaly 'stonished
at *you!* pitchin' in the fire that way, and you a-knowin' that was every
drop o' sperrets we had!"

"Oh, but Daddy 'Lias," interposed Dick McCoy, "you must look
over that — *he seed the Devil!*"

"Well, well, that 'minds me I was gwine to tell you all about that
h—ll of a scrape I had wi' them Chatohospa fellows, last summer;
so I'll squeeze the jug one time more, and tell you all about it."

Throwing his head into an admirable position for taking a view
of things heavenly, Daddy Biggs inserted the mouth of the jug in his
own mouth, when for a short space there was a sound which might
be spelled, "*luggle-ugle-luggle-lul-uggle;*" and then Daddy Biggs set the
jug down by him, and began his story once more.

"Well boys, they was 'camped right here, and had sot out their
hooks for cat[fish], jist as we've done to-night. Right thar, this side
o' whar Bill's line hengs, some on 'em had tied a most a devil of a
hook, from that big limb as goes strait out thar. He must a' had a
kunnoo to fasten it whar he did, else cooned it on the top o' the limb.
Well, it's allers swimmin' under that limb, but thar's a big rock, in
the shape of a sugar-loaf, comes up in six inches o' the top. Right
round *that* was whar I'd ketcht the monstousest, most oudaciousest
Appeloosas cat, the week before, that ever come outen the Tallapoosy;
and *they'd* hearn of it, and the fellow with the big hook was a fishin'
for hit's mate. D—n it boys, it makes me mad to think how them
Chatohospa fellows and the town folks do 'trude on we roover people,
and when I'm aggrawated I allers drinks, so here goes agin."

Daddy Biggs threw back his head again — again put the jug's
mouth in his own — and again produced the sound of "guggle-uggle-
lu-uggle!" and then resumed:

"This big-hook fellow I was tellin' about, his name were Jess Cole, which lives in the bottom, thar whar Chatohospa falls into the Hoota Locko; and aint got more'n half sense at that."

"That's the fellow used to strike for Vince Kirkland, in the black-smith's shop at Dodd's, afore Vince died, aint it?" asked Bill Teal.

"That's him," said Daddy Biggs, "and that's how I come to know him, for I seed him thar once, tho' I can't say he know'd me. Well, he waked up in the night, and heerd a most a h—ll of a sloshin' at the end of his line, and says he, 'Rise boys! I've got him! Durn my skin ef I hain't!' And sure enough there was somethin' a flouncin' and sloshin', and makin' a devil of a conbobberation at the eend of the line. Jess he sprung up and got a long stick with a hook at one eend, and retched out and cotcht the line and tried to pull it in; but the thing on the hook give a flirt, and the stick bein' a leetle too short, which made him stoop forard, in *he* fell! He scuffled out tho' tolloble quick, and ses he, 'boys, he's a whaler! — cuss my etarnal buttons if he aint the rise of sixty pounds! Old Biggs may go to h—ll *now* with his *forty-pound* cats, he can't shine no way!' When I heered that, boys, I——"

"When *you* heerd it?" exclaimed all.

"Yes! *me!*" said Biggs laughingly; "didn't I tell you that before? Well, I oughter done it but forgot. D—n it, we'll take a drink on that, any way!" and so he did.

"So 'twas *you* instid o' the Devil, he cotched," observed Jim Waters, apparently much relieved by the disclosure.

"Jist so; and the way it was, I seed the rascals as they were comin' here, and knowed what they were arter. So when night comes, I slips down the roover bank mighty easy and nice, twell I could see the camp-fire. But thar was a dog along, and I was afraid to ventur up that way. See, I was arter stealin' their fish they'd cotched thro' the day, which I knowd in reason they'd have a string on 'em in the water, at the kunnoo landin', to keep fresh. Well, seein' of the dog I 'cluded I'd 'tack the inimy by water, instid o' land. So with that I took the roover about thirty yards above here, and sure enough, finds the string of fish jist whar I knowed they'd be; and then I starts to swim down the roover a little ways, and git out below, and go to Jerry White's, and tell him the joke. Boys, aint you all gittin' mighty dry, *I* am."

And Daddy Biggs drank again!

"Well, boys, jist as I got whar that d—d hook was, not a thinkin' o' nuthin but the fun, the cussed thing ketcht in one thigh of my over-hauls and brought me up short. I tried the cussedest ever a feller did to get loose, *and* couldn't. I had no knife, and thar I flew round, and pulled first forard and then backards, and reared and pitched, and made the water bile. Fact boys, I was 'hitched to a swingin' limb,' and no mistake. Once or twice I got on the top of the sugar-loaf rock, and *je-e-est* about the time I'd go to untie the d—d rope of a line, the blasted rock was so slippery *off I'd slaunch!* — Fact boys! — And it aggrawated me; it aggrawated me *smartly,* so it did! Ef I'd a' had liquor then, I'd a' took some, I was so *d—d* mad! Well, in this time, that long-legged cuss, Jess Cole, wakes up as I tell'd you, and hollers out the way I norated. Boys, what do you all say to another drink. It makes me so *cussed* mad every time I think 'bout it!"

Once more Daddy Biggs gazed at the stars!

"Yes, boys, it *does* make me mad. But its *allers* been so, ever sence I left old Pedee! Fust I went over to the Forky-Deer country — well! they driv me off from *thar!* Then I struck for the mountain country high up in Jurgy, and I finds me a place by the side of a nice big krick; and thinks I, nobody never *kin* pester me *here,* certain; for ef they git down in the bottom, they'll be overflowed, and ef they ondertake to bild housen on the hill-sides, they're so durned, infernal steep, they'll have to *rope 'em to the trees!* Well, what do you think? — hadn't been *thar* but little better'n two year, afore they was as thick all round me, as cuckle-burrs in a colt's tail, a-huntin and a fishin all about me — and had bilt lanes — *lanes,* i' God! every whar! So I flings the old 'oman 'cross a poney, and comes *here* — and I've bettered the thing mightily, to be sure, with this d—d scatter-gun crowd, from town and Chatohospa, a-makin the woods and roover farly roar from one day's eend to another — aint I? But, as I was a-sayin about that scrape I had wi' 'em — Soon as Jess said that about *his* cat bein' bigger'n *mine,* I said in my mind, 'I'll whip *you,* certin!' Well, they all kept a most a h—ll of a hollerin', and every now and then, some on 'em would throw a long log o' wood as they had cut for fire, as nigh at me as they could guess, *to stunt the cat,* you see; but the branches of the tree favoured me mightily in keepin' 'em off — tho' they'd hit pretty close by me 'casionally, ca-junk! strikin' eend-foremost, you see. So *they* kept up a right smart throwin' o' logs, and *me,* a right peart dodgin', for some time; and I tell you, it took raal nice judgment to keep the infernal hook outen my meat; it grained the skin several times, as 'twas. At last, Jess he climbs into the tree and gits on the limb right over me, and ses he, 'boys, I b'lieve hit's a mud turkle, for I see somethin' like the form o' one, right under me.' Thinks I, *you'll* find it one o' the *snappin'* sort, I judge. Then another one ses, 'thar's a way to try that, Jess, ef you see him;' and he hands Jess a gig. 'Now,' ses he, '*gig him!*' "

"Gig THE DEVIL! ses I, for I *was* pestered!"

"Great G—d!" squalled Jess, "hit's the Devil!" and down *he* tumbled right a top o' me! I thought I was busted open from one eend to 'tother! Sure enough tho', I warn't, but only busted loose from the line. Both on us put for the bank quick, but on account of my gittin' holt of the gig, which ruther bothered me, Jess got ashore fust. I was *right arter him* tho', I tell you, *with the gig!* When I clum up the bank, I found the rest was all kleen gone, and thar lay Jess, which had stumped his toe agin' somethin', right flat of his face, a-moanin' dreadful!"

"Oh, I've got you *now,* Jess," ses I.

"Please Devil!" ses Jess.

"Must take you along wi' me," ses I, in the d—dest most onyeathly voice you *ever* heered.

"The hogs I took warn't *marked,*" ses Jess, a-shiverin' all over.

"They warn't *yourn,*" ses I.

"I'll never do so no more," ses Jess, shiverin' wuss and wuss, "ef you'll let me off this time."

"Can't do it, Jess; want you down in Tophet, *to strike for Vince Kirkland.* I've got *him* thar, a-blacksmithin' of it. He does all my odd jobs, like pinetin' of my tail and sich like! Can't let you off — *I've come a purpose for you!*"

"I seed the poor devil shudder when I called Vince's name, but he didn't say no more, so I jobs the gig thro' the hind part of his overhauls and starts down to the kunnoo landin' with him, in a peart trot. The way he scratched up the dirt as he travelled backards on his all-fours, was a perfect sight! But jist as I struck the roover, he got holt of a grub, and the gig tore out, *and he started 'tother way!* I never seed runnin' twell *then* — 'taint no use to try to tell you how fast he *did* run; I couldn't do it in a week. A "scared wolf," warn't nothin' to him. He run faster'n six scared wolves and a yearlin' deer. Soon as he got a start I made for a log whar I seed their guns, and behind that I finds the big powder gourd they all kept their powder in that they warn't a-usin'. Thinks I, ef you aint all *kleen* gone, I'll finish the job for you; so I pitched the gourd — it hilt fully a gallon —smack into the fire, and then jumped in the roover myself. I hadn't more'n got properly in before it blowed up. Sich a blaze I never seed before. The n'ise was some itself, but the blaze covered all creation, and retched higher than the trees. It spread out to the logs whar the guns was and fired *them* off! Pop! pop! pop! No wonder them Chatohospa fellows never come back! Satan, hisself, couldn't a done it no better, ef he had been thar, in the way of racket and n'ise!"

Daddy Biggs now took a long breath, and a longer drink.

"Boys," he then added, "I got them fellers' fish and a two-gallon jug o' sperrets, and I throwed their guns in the roover, besides givin' 'em the all-gortiest scare they ever had; and they aint been back sence, which I hope they never will, for its oudacious the way the roover folks is 'posed upon. And now, boys, that's my 'scrape;' so less take another drink, look at the hooks, and then lay down!"

Shifting the Responsibility

While attending court, recently, in the adjoining county of Randolph, a friend who is fond of jokes of all sorts, and who relates them almost as humorously as "his Honour," gave us the following, vouching for the substantial, sub-lunar existence of the parties and their present residence "in the county aforesaid:"

Brethren Crump and Noel were both members of the Primitive Baptist Church, and both clever, honest men who paid their taxes and debts as the same annually accrued, with a regularity at once Christian and commendable. If, when settling day came round, Brother Noel was "short," Brother Crump was sure to be in funds; and on the other hand, it almost seemed providential how, if Brother Crump fell "behind," Brother Noel always had a surplus. Thus, borrowing from and lending to each other, worshipping at the same church, and living only a mile apart, an intimacy gradually ripened between them; so that at last they did not hesitate to speak in the freest and most familiar manner to each other, even in regard to their respective foibles.

Now, it came to pass that Brother Crump, during the liveliest period of the cotton season, drove into Wetumpka and disposed of his "crap" of ten bales, at the very fair price of 12½ cents per pound. It was more than he expected, and as the world was easy with him, he determined to invest, and did actually invest, a portion of the proceeds of the sale of his cotton, in a barrel of Western whiskey; paying therefor at the rate of, precisely two pounds of middling cotton for one gallon of "ditto" whiskey.

Of course it was "norated in the settlement" that old man Crump had bought a whole barrel, and after a few weeks people began to observe that his nose grew redder and his eye more moist. The idea that Brother Crump was "drinking too much" diffused itself in the neighbourhood, until, as one might say, it became epidemical. People talked and talked — more especially "what few" of other denominations of Christians dwell thereabouts.

Brother Noel was "sore troubled" at the scandal which circulated about his brother and friend, and especially regretted the injury it brought to the " 'ciety at Sharon. " So one morning he stepped over to Brother Crump's and found the old man in a half doze in his little porch.

"Won't you take a dram?" asked Brother Crump, as soon as he was aware of the presence of his neighbour.

"Why, yes, I'm not agin a dram when a body wants it."

Brother Crump got his bottle, and the friends took a dram apiece.

"Don't you think, Brother Noel," said Crump, "that sperits is a blessin'?"

"Y-e-s!" responded Noel; "sperits is a blessin', but accordin' to my notion, its a blessin' that some of us abuses."

"Well now, Brother Noel, *who* do you think abuses the blessin'?"

"Well, it's hard to say — but people talk — don't you think *you* drink too much, Brother Crump?"

"It's hard to say — it's hard to say," returned Crump. "Sometimes I've thought I *was* a drinkin' too much — then again, I'd think *may be not*. What is man? A weak *wurrum* of the dust! What the Lord saith, that shall be done! So I left it to the Lord to say whether I was goin' too fur in sperits. I put the whole *'sponsibility on him;* I prayed to him, if I was drinkin' too much, to *take away my appetite for sperits.*"

Here Brother Noel groaned piously, and asked, "What then, Brother Crump?"

"And," replied Crump, "I've prayed that prayer three times, and HE HAIN'T DONE IT! So I'm clear of the 'sponsibility any way."

"The Lord's will be done!" ejaculated Noel, and after taking another dram he went home, thinking all the way, how cleverly Brother Crump had *shifted the responsibility!*

Joseph Glover Baldwin

(1815-1864)

🙥 The career of Joseph Glover Baldwin as a lawer and writer reflects the attractions which he felt for order and refinement on the one hand and raw vitality on the other. Born near Winchester in the Shenandoah Valley of Virginia, he was working as a clerk in the district court by the time he was twelve, and at seventeen was editing a newspaper and studying Blackstone's *Commentaries* under the direction of a lawyer uncle. At eighteen, impatient at the prospects for a young lawyer in so staid a situation as his own, he set out on horseback, with his belongings in his saddlebags, for the Southwest. In a frankly autobiographical sketch, "The Bench and Bar," he relates how, "Urged by hunger and the request of friends" and propelled by the "gentle momentum of a female slipper," he left for a country reputed to be "a California of Law, whose surface strife indicated the vast *placers* of legal dispute waiting in untold profusion."

Baldwin alighted in the Mississippi village of DeKalb, a "legal Utopia," and remained there because competition was not excessive and a license to practice was easy to come by. A recently signed Indian treaty had opened the territory for settlement, and conflicting land claims offered endless opportunities for litigation. Financial conditions encouraged land speculation. Law enforcement was as casual as the behavior of many of the lawyers themselves, though among the adventurers who poured into the new country were a few sedate barristers, competently trained and irreproachable in their conduct. In the early years of the "flush times," however, legal sanctions were almost impossible to impose because it was easy for the culprit to dig his way out of the log pens that served as jails and head for the even more tolerant lands to the west.

In 1839 Baldwin moved to Gainesville, Alabama, a respectable community where a few Virginia families and some educated New Englanders set the tone. Here he married the daughter of a judge, became a prominent lawyer, and in 1844 was elected as a Whig to the state legislature. In 1850 he moved to Livingston, Alabama, attracted by a lucrative partnership, and in 1853 to Mobile.

The end of the "flush times" in Alabama and Mississippi and the beginning of middle age caused Baldwin to reminisce, one suspects a bit wistfully, and to attempt to recapture the past. The form he chose was the literary essay, though flavored with the vigorous language of the courtroom and influenced by the oral tradition of the back country. In 1852 he sent his first essay, "Ovid Bolus, Esq.," not to a rural newspaper or sporting journal, but to the more pretentious *Southern Literary Messenger*. John R. Thompson, the editor, accepted it and others by Baldwin and even traveled with him to New York to arrange for their publication as a collection entitled *The Flush Times of Alabama and Mississippi*. Issued first in 1853, it was reprinted six times in six months.

The book begins with the sketch of Ovid Bolus and ends with an essay, "The Hon. Francis Strother," a tribute to Francis Strother Lyon, a distinguished lawyer and bank commissioner of Alabama. It was Lyon, according to Baldwin, who put an end to the period of wild speculation, "redeeming the State from *Flush Times.*" Yet Baldwin implies that for all the initial chaos, a society based on economic and legal stability could develop only in a new country where opportunity was relatively unrestricted. For himself, he was willing to leave stability behind and emigrate to California.

In November 1853, the *Southern Literary Messenger* printed his "California Flush Times." He found the legal situation in San Francisco chaotic and again joined in the effort to bring law to a lawless country. So successful was he that his practice flourished and he was appointed an associate justice of the state supreme court. His second book, *Party Leaders* (1855), consists of sober essays on Jefferson, Hamilton, John Randolph, Jackson, and Clay.

Baldwin's humor is sometimes earthy but never crude. His sketches do not fall apart or descend to the level of horseplay. If someone must be the butt of the joke, it is always someone who deserves to be — the village braggart, the bully, the pedant, the sharper. Justice always triumphs and no one is really hurt. This genteel quality, the tendency to assert rather than demonstrate, to generalize rather than give particulars, and to rephrase rather than let his characters speak for themselves, are limitations consistent with Baldwin's ambivalent response to "the flush times."

Abraham Lincoln, a one-time circuit-riding lawyer who could tell a good story himself, is said to have enjoyed reading aloud from his copy of *Flush Times*. The copy of another good judge, Washington Irving, may still be seen in his library at "Sunnyside."

TEXT: "Ovid Bolus, Esq., Attorney at Law and Solicitor in Chancery," "Sharp Financiering," "The Bar of the South-West," and "Jo. Heyfron" from *The Flush Times of Alabama and Mississippi* (New York, 1853).

Ovid Bolus, Esq.,
Attorney at Law and Solicitor in Chancery

A Fragment

*   *   *   *   *   *   *   *   *   *   *

And what history of that halcyon period, ranging from the year of
Grace, 1835, to 1837; that golden era, when shin-plasters were the sole
currency; when bank-bills were "as thick as Autumn leaves in Vallambrosa," and credit was a franchise — what history of those times
would be complete, that left out the name of Ovid Bolus? As well
write the biography of Prince Hal, and forbear all mention of Falstaff.
In law phrase, the thing would be a "deed without a name," and void;
a most unpardonable *casus omissus.*

I cannot trace, for reasons the sequel suggests, the early history,
much less the birth-place, pedigree, and juvenile associations of this
worthy. Whence he or his forbears got his name or how, I don't
know: but for the fact that it is to be inferred he got it in infancy, I
should have thought he borrowed it: he borrowed every thing else he
ever had, such things as he got under the credit system only excepted:
in deference, however, to the axiom, that there is *some* exception to
all general rules, I am willing to believe that he got this much
honestly, by *bona fide* gift or inheritance, and without false pretense.

I have had a hard time of it in endeavoring to assign to Bolus his
leading vice: I have given up the task in despair; but I have essayed
to designate that one which gave him, in the end, most celebrity. I
am aware that it is invidious to make comparisons, and to give pre-
eminence to one over other rival qualities and gifts, where all have
high claims to distinction: but, then, the stern justice of criticism, in
this case, requires a discrimination, which, to be intelligible and definite,
must be relative and comparative. I, therefore, take the responsibility
of saying, after due reflection, that in my opinion, Bolus's reputation
stood higher for lying than for anything else; and in thus assigning
pre-eminence to this poetic property, I do it without any desire to
derogate from other brilliant characteristics belonging to the same
general category, which have drawn the wondering notice of the world.

Some men are liars from interest; not because they have no regard
for truth, but because they have less regard for it than for gain:
some are liars from vanity, because they would rather be well thought
of by others, than have reason for thinking well of themselves: some

are liars from a sort of necessity, which overbears, by the weight of temptation, the sense of virtue: some are enticed away by the allurements of pleasure, or seduced by evil example and education. Bolus was none of these: he belonged to a higher department of the fine arts, and to a higher class of professors of this sort of Belles-Lettres. Bolus was a natural liar, just as some horses are natural pacers, and some dogs natural setters. What he did in that walk, was from the irresistible promptings of instinct, and a disinterested love of art. His genius and his performances were free from the vulgar alloy of interest or temptation. Accordingly, he did not labor a lie: he lied with a relish: he lied with a coming appetite, growing with what it fed on: he lied from the delight of invention and the charm of fictitious narrative. It is true he applied his art to the practical purposes of life; but in so far did he glory the more in it; just as an ingenious machinist rejoices that his invention, while it has honored science, has also supplied a common want.

Bolus's genius for lying was encyclopediacal: it was what German criticism calls many-sided. It embraced all subjects without distinction or partiality. It was equally good upon all, "from grave to gay, from lively to severe."

Bolus's lying came from his greatness of soul and his comprehensiveness of mind. The truth was too small for him. Fact was too dry and common-place for the fervor of his genius. Besides, great as was his memory — for he even remembered the outlines of his chief lies — his invention was still larger. He had a great contempt for history and historians. He thought them tame and timid cobblers; mere tinkers on other people's wares — simple parrots and magpies of other men's sayings or doings; borrowers of and acknowledged debtors for others' chattels, got without skill; they had no separate estate in their ideas: they were bailees of goods, which they did not pretend to hold by adverse title; buriers of talents in napkins making no usury; barren and unprofitable non-producers in the intellectual vineyard — *nati consumere fruges.*

He adopted a fact occasionally to start with, but, like a Sheffield razor and the crude ore, the workmanship, polish and value were all his own: a Thibet shawl could as well be credited to the insensate goat that grew the wool, as the author of a fact Bolus honored with his artistical skill, could claim to be the inventor of the story.

His experiments upon credulity, like charity, began at home. He had long torn down the partition wall between his imagination and his memory. He had long ceased to distinguish between the impressions made upon his mind by what came *from* it, and what came *to* it: all ideas were facts to him.

Bolus's life was not a common man's life. His world was not the hard, work-day world the groundlings live in: he moved in a sphere of poetry: he lived amidst the ideal and romantic. Not that he was not practical enough, when he chose to be: by no means. He bought goods and chattels, lands and tenements, like other men; but he got them under a state of poetic illusion, and paid for them in an imaginary way. Even the titles he gave were not of the *earthy* sort — they were sometimes *clouded.* He gave notes, too, — how well I know it! — like other men; he paid them like himself.

How well he asserted the Spiritual over the Material! How he delighted to turn an abstract idea into concrete cash — to make a few blots of ink, representing a little thought, turn out a labor-saving machine, and bring into his pocket money which many days of hard exhausting labor would not procure! What pious joy it gave him to see the days of the good Samaritan return, and the hard hand of avarice relax its grasp on land and negroes, pork and clothes, beneath the soft speeches and kind promises of future rewards — blending in the act the three cardinal virtues, Faith, Hope, and Charity; while, in the result, the chief of these three was *Charity!*

There was something sublime in the idea — this elevating the spirit of man to its true and primeval dominion over things of sense and grosser matter.

It is true, that in these practical romances, Bolus was charged with a defective taste in repeating himself. The justice of the charge must be, at least, partially acknowledged: this I know from a client, to whom Ovid sold a tract of land after having sold it twice before: I cannot say, though, that his forgetting to mention this circumstance made any difference, for Bolus originally had no title.

There was nothing narrow, sectarian, or sectional, in Bolus's lying. It was on the contrary broad and catholic. It had no respect to times or places. It was as wide, illimitable, as elastic and variable as the air he spent in giving it expression. It was a generous, gentlemanly, whole-souled faculty. It was often employed on occasions of this sort, but no more; and no more zealously on these than on others of no profit to himself. He was an Egotist, but a magnificent one; he was not a liar because an egotist, but an egotist because a liar. He usually made himself the hero of the romantic exploits and adventures he narrated; but this was not so much to exalt himself, as because it was more convenient to his art. He had nothing malignant or invidious in his nature. If he exalted himself, it was seldom or never to the disparagement of others, unless, indeed, those others were merely imaginary persons, or too far off to be hurt. He would as soon lie for you as for himself. It was all the same, so there was something doing in his line of business, except in those cases in which his necessities required to be fed at your expense.

He did not confine himself to mere lingual lying: one tongue was not enough for all the business he had on hand. He acted lies as well. Indeed, sometimes his very silence was a lie. He made nonentity fib for him, and performed wondrous feats by a "masterly inactivity."

The *personnel* of this distinguished Votary of the Muse, was happily fitted to his art. He was strikingly handsome. There was something in his air and bearing almost princely, certainly quite distinguished. His manners were winning, his address frank, cordial and flowing. He was built after the model and structure of Bolingbroke in his youth, *Americanized* and *Hoosierized* a little by a "raising in," and an adaptation to, the Backwoods. He was fluent but choice of diction, a little sonorous in the structure of his sentences to give effect to a voice like an organ. His countenance was open and engaging, usually sedate of expression, but capable of any modifications at the shortest notice. Add to this his intelligence, shrewdness, tact, humor, and that he was a ready debater and elegant declaimer, and had the gift of bringing out, to the fullest extent, his resources, and you may see that Ovid, in a new country, was a man apt to make no mean impression. He drew the loose population around him, as the magnet draws iron filings. He was the man for the "boys" — then a numerous and influential class. His generous profusion and free-handed manner impressed them as the bounty of Caesar the loafing commonalty of Rome: Bolus was no niggard. He never higgled or chaffered about small things. He was as free with his own money — if he ever had any of his own — as with yours. If he never paid borrowed money, he never asked payment of others. If you wished him to lend you any, he would give you a handful without counting it: if you handed him any, you were losing time in counting it, for you never saw anything of it again: Shallow's funded debt on Falstaff were as safe an investment: this would have been an equal commerce, but, unfortunately for Bolus's friends, the proportion between his disbursements and receipts was something scant. Such a spendthrift never made a track even in the flush times of 1836. It took as much to support him as a first class steamboat. His bills at the groceries were as long as John Q. Adams' Abolition petition, or, if pasted together, would have matched the great Chartist memorial. He would as soon treat a regiment or charter the grocery for the day, as any other way; and after the crowd had heartily drank — some of them "laying their souls in soak," — if he did not have the money convenient — as when did he? — he would fumble in his pocket, mutter something about nothing less than $100 bill, and direct the score, with a lordly familiarity, to be charged to his account.

Ovid had early possessed the faculty of ubiquity. He had been born in more places than Homer. In an hour's discourse, *he* would, with more than the speed of Ariel, travel at every point of the compass, from Portland to San Antonio, some famous adventure always occurring just as he "rounded to," or while stationary, though he did not remain longer than to see it. He was present at every important debate in the Senate at Washington, and had heard every popular speaker on the hustings, at the bar and in the pulpit, in the United States. He had been concerned in many important causes with Grymes and against Mazereau in New Orleans, and had borne no small share in the fierce forensic battles, which, with singular luck, *he* and Grymes always won in the courts of the Crescent City. And such frolics as they had when they laid aside their heavy armor, after the heat and burden of the day! Such gambling! A negro *ante* and twenty on the call, was moderate playing. What lots of "Ethiopian captives" and other plunder *he raked down* vexed Arithmetic to count and credulity to believe; and, had it not been for Bolus's generosity in giving "the boys" a chance to win back *by doubling off on the high hand,* there is no knowing what changes of owners would not have occurred in the Rapides or on the German Coast.

The Florida war and the Texas Revolution, had each furnished a brilliant theatre for Ovid's chivalrous emprise. Jack Hays and he were great chums. Jack and he had many a hearty laugh over the odd trick of Ovid, in lassoing a Camanche Chief, while galloping a stolen horse bare-backed, up the San Saba hills. But he had the rig on Jack again, when he made him charge on a brood of about twenty Camanches, who had got into a mot of timber in the prairies, and were shooting their arrows from the covert, Ovid, with a six-barrelled rifle, taking them on the wing as Jack rode in and flushed them!

It was an affecting story and feelingly told, that of his and Jim Bowie's rescuing an American girl from the Apaches, and returning her to her parents in St. Louis; and it would have been still more tender, had it not been for the unfortunate necessity Bolus was under of shooting a brace of gay lieutenants on the border, one frosty morning, before breakfast, back of the fort, for taking unbecoming liberties with the fair damosel, the spoil of his bow and spear.

But the girls Ovid courted, and the miraculous adventures he had met with in love beggared by the comparison, all the fortune of war had done for him. Old Nugent's daughter, Sallie, was his narrowest escape. Sallie was accomplished to the romantic extent of two ocean steamers, and four blocks of buildings in Boston, separated only from immediate "perception and pernancy," by the contingency of old Nugent's recovering from a confirmed dropsy, for which he had been twice ineffectually tapped. The day was set — the presents made — superb of course — the guests invited: the old Sea Captain insisted on Bolus's setting his negroes free, and taking five thousand dollars apiece for the loss. Bolus's love for the "peculiar institution" wouldn't stand it. Rather than submit to such degradation, Ovid broke off the match, and left Sallie broken-hearted; a disease from which she did not recover until about six months afterwards, when she ran off with the mate of her father's ship, the Sea Serpent, in the Rio trade.

Gossip and personal anecdote were the especial subjects of Ovid's elocution. He was intimate with all the notabilities of the political circles. He was a privileged visitor of the political green-room. He was admitted back into the laboratory where the political thunder was manufactured, and into the office where the magnetic wires were worked. He knew the origin of every party question and movement, and had a finger in every pie the party cooks of Tammany baked for the body politic.

One thing in Ovid I can never forgive. This was his coming it over poor Ben. I don't object to it on the score of the swindle. That was to have been expected. But swindling Ben was degrading the dignity of the art. True, it illustrated the universality of his science, but it lowered it to a beggarly process of mean deception. There was no skill in it. It was little better than crude larceny. A child could have done it; it had as well been done to a child. It was like catching a cow with a lariat, or setting a steel trap for a pet pig. True, Bolus had nearly practised out of custom. He had worn his art threadbare. Men, who could afford to be cheated, had all been worked up or been scared away. Besides, Frost couldn't be put off. He talked of money in a most ominous connection with blood. The thing could be settled by a bill of exchange. Ben's name was unfortunately good — the amount some $1,600. Ben *had* a fine tract of land in S—r. He has not got it now. Bolus only gave Ben one wrench — that was enough. Ben never breathed easy afterwards. All the V's and X's of ten years' hard practice, went in that penful of ink. Fie! Bolus, Monroe Edwards wouldn't have done that. He would sooner have sunk down to the level of some honest calling for a living, than have put his profession to so mean a shift. I can conceive of but one extenuation; Bolus was on the lift for Texas, and the desire was natural to qualify himself for citizenship.

The genius of Bolus, strong in its unassisted strength, yet gleamed out more brilliantly under the genial influence of "the rosy." With boon companions and "reaming suats," it was worth while to hear him of a winter evening. He could "gild the palpable and the familiar, with golden exhalations of the dawn." The most common-place objects became dignified. There was a history to the commonest articles about him: that book was given him by Mr. Van Buren — the walking stick was a present from Gen. Jackson. The thrice-watered Monongahela, just drawn from the grocery hard by, was the last of a distillation of 1825, smuggled in from Ireland, and presented to him by a friend in New Orleans, on easy terms with the collector; the cigars, not too fragrant, were of a box sent him by a schoolmate from Cuba, in 1834 — *before* he visited the Island. And talking of Cuba — he had met with an adventure there, the impression of which never could be effaced from his mind. He had gone, at the instance of Don Carlos y Cubanos, (an intimate classmate in a Kentucky Catholic College), whose life he had saved from a mob in Louisville, at the imminent risk of his own. The Don had a sister of blooming sixteen, the least of whose charms was two or three coffee plantations, some hundreds of slaves, and a suitable garnish of doubloons, accumulated during her minority, in the hands of her uncle and guardian, the Captain General. All went well with the young lovers — for such, of course, they were — until Bolus, with his usual frank indiscretion, in a conversation with the Priest, avowed himself a Protestant. Then came trouble. Every effort was made to convert him; but Bolus's faith resisted the eloquent tongue of the Priest, and the more eloquent eyes of Donna Isabella. The brother pleaded the old friendship — urged a seeming and formal conformity — the Captain General argued the case like a politician — the Señorita like a warm and devoted woman. All would not do. The Captain General forbade his longer sojourn on the Island. Bolus took leave of the fair Señorita: the parting interview held in the orange bower, was affecting: Donna Isabella, with dishevelled hair, threw herself at his feet; the tears streamed from her eyes: in liquid tones, broken by grief, she implored him to relent, — reminded him of her love, of her trust in him, and of the consequences — now not much longer to be concealed — of that love and trust; ("though I protest," Bolus would say, "I don't know what she meant exactly by *that*.") "Gentlemen," Bolus continued, "I confess to the weakness — I wavered — but then my eyes happened to fall on the breast-pin with a lock of my mother's hair — I recovered my courage: I shook her gently from me. I felt my last hold on earth was loosened — my last hope of peace destroyed. Since that hour, my life has been a burden. Yes, gentlemen, you see before you a broken man — a martyr to his Religion. But, away with these melancholy thoughts: boys, pass around the jorum." And wiping his eyes, he drowned the wasting sorrow in a long draught of the poteen; and, being much refreshed, was able to carry the burden on a little further, — *videlicet,* to the next lie.

It must not be supposed that Bolus was destitute of the tame virtue of prudence — or that this was confined to the avoidance of the improvident habit of squandering his money in paying old debts. He took reasonably good care of his person. He avoided all unnecessary exposures, chiefly from a patriotic desire, probably, of continuing his good offices to his country. His recklessness was, for the most part, lingual. To hear him talk, one might suppose he held his carcass merely for a target to try guns and knives upon; or that the business of his life was to draw men up to ten paces or less, for sheer improvement in marksmanship. Such exploits as he had gone through with, dwarfed the heroes of romance to very pigmy and sneaking proportions. Pistol at the Bridge when he bluffed at honest Fluellen, might have envied the swash-buckler airs, Ovid would sometimes put on. But I never could exactly identify the place he had laid out for his burying-ground. Indeed, I had occasion to know that he declined to understand several not very ambiguous hints, upon which he might, with as good a grace as Othello, have spoken, not to mention one or two pressing invitations which his modesty led him to refuse. I do not know that the base sense of fear had anything to do with these declinations: possibly he might have thought he had done his share of fighting, and did not wish to monopolize: or his principles forbade it — I mean those which opposed his paying a debt: knowing he could not cheat that inexorable creditor, Death, of his claim, he did the next thing to it; which was to delay and shirk payment as long as possible.

It remains to add a word of criticism on this great *Lyric* artist.

In lying, Bolus was not only a successful, but he was a very able practitioner. Like every other eminent artist, he brought all his faculties to bear upon his art. Though quick of perception and prompt of invention, he did not trust himself to the inspirations of his genius for *improvising* a lie, when he could well premeditate one. He deliberately built up the substantial masonry, relying upon the occasion and its accessories, chiefly for embellishment and collateral supports: as Burke excogitated the more solid parts of his great speeches, and left unprepared only the illustrations and fancy-work.

Bolus's manner was, like every truly great man's, his own. It was excellent. He did not come blushing up to a lie, as some otherwise very passable liars do, as if he were making a mean compromise between his guilty passion or morbid vanity, and a struggling conscience. Bolus had long since settled all disputes with *his* conscience. He and it were on very good terms — at least, if there was no affection between the couple, there was no fuss in the family; or, if there were any scenes or angry passages, they were reserved for strict privacy and never got out. My own opinion is, that he was as destitute of the article as an ostrich. Thus he came to his work bravely, cheerfully and composedly. The delights of composition, invention and narration, did not fluster his style or agitate his delivery. He knew how, in the tumult of passion, to assume the "temperance to give it smoothness." A lie never ran away with him, as it is apt to do with young performers: he could always manage and guide it; and to have seen him fairly mounted, would have given you some idea of the polished elegance of D'Orsay, and the superb *menage* of Murat. There is a tone and manner of narration different from those used in delivering ideas just conceived; just as there is a difference between the sound of the voice in reading and in speaking. Bolus knew this, and practised on it. When he was narrating, he put the facts in order, and seemed to speak them out of his memory; but not formally, or as if by rote. He would stop himself to correct a date; recollect he was wrong — he was *that* year at the White Sulphur or Saratoga, &c.: having got the date right, the names of persons present would be incorrect, &c.: and these he corrected in turn. A stranger hearing him, would have feared the marring of a good story by too fastidious a conscientiousness in the narrator.

His zeal in pursuit of a lie under difficulties, was remarkable. The society around him — if such it could be called — was hardly fitted, without some previous preparation, for an immediate introduction to Almacks' or the classic precincts of Gore House. The manners of the natives were rather plain than ornate, and candor rather than polish, predominated in their conversation. Bolus had need of some forbearance to withstand the interruptions and cross-examinations, with which his revelations were sometimes received. But he possessed this in a remarkable degree. I recollect, on one occasion, when he was giving an account of a providential escape he was signally favored with, (when boarded by a pirate off the Isle of Pines, and he pleaded masonry, and gave a sign he had got out of the Disclosures of Morgan), Tom Johnson interrupted him to say that he had heard *that* before, (which was more than Bolus had ever done.) B. immediately rejoined, that he had, he believed, given him, Tom, a *running* sketch of the incident. "Rather," said Tom, "I think, a *lying* sketch." Bolus scarcely smiled, as he replied, that Tom was a wag, and couldn't help turning the most serious things into jests; and went on with his usual brilliancy, to finish the narrative. Bolus did not overcrowd his canvas. His figures were never confused, and the subordinates and accessories did not withdraw attention from the main and substantive lie. He never squandered his lies profusely: thinking, with the poet, that "bounteous, not prodigal, is kind Nature's hand," he kept the golden mean between penuriousness and prodigality; never stingy of his lies, he was not wasteful of them, but was rather forehanded than pushed, or embarrassed, having, usually, fictitious stock to be freshly put on 'change, when he wished to "make a raise." In most of his fables, he inculcated but a single leading idea; but contrived to make the several facts of the narrative fall in very gracefully with the principal scheme.

The rock on which many promising young liars, who might otherwise have risen to merited distinction, have split, is vanity: this marplot vice betrays itself in the exultation manifested on the occasion of a decided hit, an exultation too inordinate for mere recital, and which betrays authorship; and to betray authorship, in the present barbaric, moral and intellectual condition of the world is fatal. True, there seems to be some inconsistency here. Dickens and Bulwer can do as much lying, for money too, as they choose, and no one blame them, any more than they would blame a lawyer regularly *fee'd* to do it; but let any man, gifted with the same genius, try his hand at it, not deliberately and in writing, but merely orally, and ugly names are given him, and he is proscribed! Bolus heroically suppressed exultation over the victories his lies achieved.

Alas! for the beautiful things of Earth, its flowers, its sunsets — its lovely girls — its lies — brief and fleeting are their date. Lying is a very delicate accomplishment. It must be tenderly cared for, and jealously guarded. It must not be overworked. Bolus forgot this salutary caution. The people found out his art. However dull the commons are as to other matters, they get sharp enough after awhile, to whatever concerns their bread and butter. Bolus not having confined his art to political matters, sounded, at last, the depths, and explored the limits of popular credulity. The denizens of this degenerate age, had not the disinterestedness of Prince Hal, who "cared not how many fed at his cost"; they got tired, at last, of promises to pay. The credit system, common before as pump-water, adhering, like the elective franchise to every voter, began to take the worldly wisdom of Falstaff's mercer, and ask security; and security liked something more substantial than plausible promises. In this forlorn condition of the country, returning to its savage state, and abandoning the refinements of a ripe Anglo-Saxon civilization for the sordid safety of Mexican or Chinese modes of traffic; deserting the sweet simplicity of its ancient trustfulness and the poetic illusions of Augustus Tomlinson, for the vulgar saws of poor Richard — Bolus, with a sigh like that breathed out by his great prototype after his apostrophe to London, gathered up, one bright moonlight night, his articles of value, shook the dust from his feet, and departed from a land unworthy of his longer sojourn. With that delicate consideration for the feelings of his friends, which, like the politeness of Charles II, never forsook him, he spared them the pain of a parting interview. He left no greetings of kindness; no messages of love: nor did he ask assurances of their lively remembrance. It was quite unnecessary. In every house he had left an autograph, in every ledger a souvenir. They will never forget him. Their connection with him will be ever regarded as

> —— "The *greenest* spot
> In memory's waste."

Poor Ben, whom he had honored with the last marks of his confidence, can scarcely speak of him to this day, without tears in his eyes. Far away towards the setting sun he hied him, until, at last, with a hermit's disgust at the degradation of the world, like Ignatius turned monk, he pitched his tabernacle amidst the smiling prairies that sleep in vernal beauty, in the shadow of the San Saba mountains. There let his mighty genius rest. It has earned repose. We leave Themistocles to his voluntary exile.

Sharp Financiering

In the times of 1836, there dwelt in the pleasant town of T. a smooth oily-mannered gentleman, who diversified a commonplace pursuit by some exciting episodes of finance — dealing occasionally in exchange, buying and selling uncurrent money, &c. We will suppose this gentleman's name to be Thompson. It happened that a Mr. Ripley of North Carolina, was in T., having some $1200, in North Carolina money, and desiring to return to the old North State with his funds, not wishing to encounter the risk of robbery through the Creek country, in which there were rumors of hostilities between the whites and the Indians, he bethought him of buying exchange on Raleigh, as the safest mode of transmitting his money. On inquiry he was referred to Mr. Thompson, as the only person dealing in exchange in that place. He called on Mr. T. and made known his wishes. With his characteristic politeness, Mr. Thompson agreed to accommodate him with a sight bill on his correspondent in Raleigh, charging him the moderate premium of five per cent. for it. Mr. Thompson retired into his counting-room, and in a few minutes returned with the bill and a letter, which he delivered to Mr. Ripley, at the same time receiving the money from that gentleman plus the exchange. As the interlocutors were exchanging valedictory compliments, it occurred to Mr. Thompson that it would be a favor to him if Mr. Ripley would be so kind as to convey to Mr. T.'s correspondent a package he was desirous of sending, which request Mr. Ripley assured Mr. T. it would afford him great pleasure to comply with. Mr. Thompson then handed Mr. Ripley a package, strongly enveloped and sealed, addressed to the Raleigh Banker, after which the gentlemen parted with many polite expressions of regard and civility.

Arriving without any accident or hindrance at Raleigh, Mr. Ripley's first care was to call on the Banker and present his documents. He found him at his office, presented the bill and letter to him, and requested payment of the former. That, said the Banker, will depend a good deal upon the contents of the package. Opening which, Mr. Ripley found the identical bills, minus the premium, he had paid Mr. T. for his bill: and which the Banker paid over to that gentleman, who was not a little surprised to find that the expert Mr. Thompson had charged him five per cent. for carrying his own money to Raleigh, to avoid the risk and trouble of which he had bought the exchange.

T. used to remark that that was the safest operation, all around, he ever knew. He had got his exchange — the buyer had got his bill and the money, too, — and the drawee was fully protected! There was profit without outlay or risk.

The Bar of the South-West

. . . .

In trying to arrive at the character of the South-Western bar, its opportunities and advantages for improvement are to be considered. It is not too much to say that, in the United States at least, no bar ever had such, or so many: it might be doubted if they were *ever* enjoyed to the same extent before. Consider that the South-West was the focus of an emigration greater than any portion of the country ever attracted, at least, until the golden magnet drew its thousands to the Pacific coast. But the character of emigrants was not the same. Most of the gold-seekers were mere gold-diggers — not bringing property, but coming to take it away. Most of those coming to the South-West brought property — many of them a great deal. Nearly every man was a speculator; at any rate, a trader. The treaties with the Indians had brought large portions of the States of Alabama, Mississippi and Louisiana into market; and these portions, comprising some of the

most fertile lands in the world, were settled up in a hurry. The Indians claimed lands under these treaties — the laws granting preemp-
tion rights to settlers on the public lands, were to be construed, and
the litigation growing out of them settled, the public lands afforded a
field for unlimited speculation, and combinations of purchasers, part-
nerships, land companies, agencies, and the like, gave occasion to
much difficult litigation in after times. Negroes were brought into
the country in large numbers and sold mostly upon credit, and bills
of exchange taken for the price; the negroes in many instances were
unsound — some as to which there was no title; some falsely pretended to be unsound, and various questions as to the liability of
parties on the warranties and the bills, furnished an important addition to the litigation: many land titles were defective; property was
brought from other States clogged with trusts, limitations, and uses, to
be construed according to the laws of the State from which it was
brought: claims and contracts made elsewhere to be enforced here:
universal indebtedness, which the hardness of the times succeeding
made it impossible for many men to pay, and desirable for all to
escape paying: hard and ruinous bargains, securityships, judicial sales;
a general looseness, ignorance, and carelessness in the public officers in
doing business; new statutes to be construed; official liabilities, especially those of sheriffs, to be enforced; banks, the laws governing
their contracts, proceedings against them for forfeiture of charter;
trials of right of property; an elegant assortment of frauds constructive
and actual; and the whole system of chancery law, admiralty proceedings; in short, all the flood-gates of litigation were opened and the
pent-up tide let loose upon the country. And such a criminal docket!
What country could boast more largely of its crimes? What more
splendid rôle of felonies! What more terrific murders! What more
gorgeous bank robberies! What more magnificent operations in the
land offices! Such McGregor-like levies of black mail, individual and
corporate! Such superb forays on the treasuries, State and National!
Such expert transfers of balances to undiscovered bournes! Such
august defalcations! Such flourishes of rhetoric on ledgers auspicious
of gold which had departed for ever from the vault! And in INDIAN
affairs! — the very mention is suggestive of the poetry of theft — the
romance of a wild and weird larceny! What sublime conceptions of
super-Spartan roguery! Swindling Indians by the nation! (*Spirit of
Falstaff, rap!*) Stealing their land by the township! (*Dick Turpin and
Jonathan Wild! tip the table!*) Conducting the nation to the Mississippi river, stripping them to the flap, and bidding them God speed
as they went howling into the Western wilderness to the friendly
agency of some sheltering Suggs duly empowered to receive their

coming annuities and back rations! What's Hounslow heath to this? Who Carvajal? Who Count Boulbon?

And all these merely forerunners, ushering in the Millennium of an accredited, official Repudiation; and IT but vaguely suggestive of what men could do when opportunity and capacity met — as shortly afterwards they did — under the Upas-shade of a perjury-breathing bankrupt law! — But we forbear. The contemplation of such hyperboles of mendacity stretches the imagination to a dangerous tension. There was no end to the amount and variety of lawsuits, and interests involved in every complication and of enormous value were to be adjudicated. The lawyers were compelled to work, and were forced to learn the rules that were involved in all this litigation.

Many members of the bar, of standing and character, from the other States, flocked in to put their sickles into this abundant harvest. Virginia, Kentucky, North Carolina and Tennessee contributed more of these than any other four States; but every State had its representatives.

Consider, too, that the country was not so new as the practice. Every State has its peculiar tone or physiognomy, so to speak, of jurisprudence imparted to it, more or less, by the character and temper of its bar. That had yet to be given. Many questions decided in older States, and differently decided in different States, were to be settled here; and a new state of things, peculiar in their nature, called for new rules or a modification of old ones. The members of the bar from different States had brought their various notions, impressions and knowledge of their own judicature along with them; and thus all the points, dicta, rulings, offshoots, quirks and quiddities of all the law, and lawing, and law-mooting of all the various judicatories and their satellites, were imported into the new country and tried on the new jurisprudence.

After the crash came in 1837 — (there were some *premonitory fits* before, but *then* the *great convulsion* came on) — all the assets of the country were marshalled, and the suing material of all sorts, as fast as it could be got out, put into the hands of the workmen. Some idea of the business may be got from a fact or two: in the county of Sumpter, Alabama, in one year, some four or five thousand suits, in the common-law courts alone, were brought; but in some other counties the number was larger; while in the lower or river counties of Mississippi, the number was at least double. The United States Courts were equally well patronized in proportion — indeed, rather more so. The white *suable* population of Sumpter was then some 2,400 men. It was a merry time for us craftsmen; and we brightened up mightily, and shook our quills joyously, like goslings in the midst of a shower. We look back to that good time, "now past and gone," with the pious gratitude and serene satisfaction with which the wreckers near the Florida Keys contemplate the last fine storm. . . .

Jo. Heyfron

Judge Starling, of Mississippi, had become very sensitive because the lawyers insisted on arguing points after he had decided them. So he determined to put a stop to it. But Jo. Heyfron, an excellent lawyer, who had everything of the Emerald Isle about him, but its greenness, — was the wrong one for the decisive judicial experiment to be commenced on. Jo. knew too much law, and the judge too little, for an equality of advantages. On the occasion referred to, just as the judge had pronounced a very peremptory and very ridiculous decision, Jo. got up in his deprecating way, with a book in his hand, and was about to speak, when the Judge thundered out, "Mr. Heyfron! you have been practising, sir, before *this* Court long enough to know that when *this* Court has once decided a question, the propriety of its decision can only be reviewed in the High Court of Errors & Appeals! Take your seat, sir!"

"If your honor plase!" broke out Jo., in a manner that would have passed for the most beseeching, if a sly twinkle in the off corner of his eye had not betokened the contrary, — "If your honor plase! far be it from *me* to impugn in the slightest degray, the wusdom and proprietay of your honor's decision! I marely designed to rade a few lines from the volume I hold in my hand, that your honor might persave how profoundly aignorant Sir Wulliam Blockstone was upon this subject."

The judge looked daggers, but spoke none; and Heyfron sat down, immortal. His body is dead, but he still lives, for his brilliant retort, in the anecdotal reminiscences of the South-Western bar. The anecdote has already (in a different, but incorrect form) had the run of the newspapers.

Thomas Bangs Thorpe

(1815-1875)

🌿 "The Big Bear of Arkansas" by Thomas Bangs Thorpe is the finest example of the many stories of legendary hunters who pursued fabulous bears, a genre coeval with the arrival of the white man on the Atlantic frontier. The tale itself became so popular and exemplary that it provided a designation, "the big bear school," for the Southwestern frontier writers who followed Thorpe. Though comic in tone and modest in scope, Thorpe's yarn has much in common with two other important American hunting stories, Melville's *Moby-Dick* (1851), and Faulkner's *The Bear* (1942).

The son of a Methodist minister, Thorpe was born in Westfield, Massachusetts, and grew up in New York. He sought instruction in painting from the eccentric artist John Quidor, neglected in his own time but now acclaimed for his fantastic paintings based on Washington Irving's tales. In 1834-1835 Thorpe was a student at Wesleyan University, Middletown, Connecticut, where he continued to paint. Poor health led him to seek a more salubrious climate, and at the urging of several of his Southern classmates he moved to Baton Rouge, Louisiana, in 1836. He remained in Louisiana for the next twenty years.

Thorpe became a painter of portraits and wildlife, a newspaper editor, postmaster, contributor to sporting magazines, war correspondent, author of three books on the Mexican War, and a Whig politician. His first magazine article, "Tom Owen, the Bee-Hunter," which appeared in the *Spirit of the Times* in 1839, met with great success and was followed by dozens of other sketches for the same publication, some of which were collected in *The Mysteries of the Backwoods; or Sketches of the Southwest.* His realistic and humorous sketches of the frontier were translated into German, Italian, and French, and his competent but less imaginative articles found acceptance in the Eastern literary magazines. His portrait of General Zachary Taylor was purchased by the Louisiana legislature for $1,000. But he was unable to achieve the income and status which he hoped for, and he returned to New York in 1853.

In New York Thorpe met with modest success as a professional writer. He contributed regularly to *Harper's New Monthly Magazine, The Knickerbocker Magazine, Godey's Lady's Book,* and other popular journals. He collected the best of his Southwestern sketches, revised them carefully, and published them as *The Hive of "The Bee-Hunter";* and he wrote a reform novel on the evils of slavery, *The*

Master's House: A Tale of Southern Life (1854). He also exhibited regularly at the National Academy of Design. Thorpe continued to write for the *Spirit of the Times* and in 1859 bought an interest in it which he retained until 1861. Commissioned a colonel in the Union Army, in 1862 he went back to New Orleans with the occupation forces as a city administrator. In 1864 he returned to New York where he continued to write and paint, and from 1869 until his death he held a political appointment in the Custom House.

As a popular magazinist, Thorpe successfully employed the romantic themes and genteel style that were conventional in his day. He remains of literary interest, however, for his originality, earthy comedy, realism, and the sense of the dignity which he saw in the life and people of the Southwestern frontier.

TEXT: "The Big Bear of Arkansas" from *The Hive of "The Bee-Hunter"* (New York, 1854); "A Piano in 'Arkansaw'" and "The Disgraced Scalp-Lock" from *The Mysteries of the Backwoods* (Philadelphia, 1846).

The Big Bear of Arkansas

A steamboat on the Mississippi, frequently, in making her regular trips, carries between places varying from one to two thousand miles apart; and, as these boats advertise to land passengers and freight at "all intermediate landings," the heterogeneous character of the passengers of one of these up-country boats can scarcely be imagined by one who has never seen it with his own eyes.

Starting from New Orleans in one of these boats, you will find yourself associated with men from every State in the Union, and from every portion of the globe; and a man of observation need not lack for amusement or instruction in such a crowd, if he will take the trouble to read the great book of character so favorably opened before him.

Here may be seen, jostling together, the wealthy Southern planter and the pedler of tin-ware from New England — the Northern merchant and the Southern jockey — a venerable bishop, and a desperate gambler — the land speculator, and the honest farmer — professional men of all creeds and characters — Wolvereens, Suckers, Hoosiers, Buckeyes, and Corncrackers, beside a "plentiful sprinkling" of the half-horse and half-alligator species of men, who are peculiar to "old Mississippi," and who appear to gain a livelihood by simply going up and down the river. In the pursuit of pleasure or business, I have frequently found myself in such a crowd.

On one occasion, when in New Orleans, I had occasion to take a trip of a few miles up the Mississippi, and I hurried on board the well-known "high-pressure-and-beat-every-thing" steamboat "Invincible," just as the last note of the last bell was sounding; and when the confusion and bustle that is natural to a boat's getting under way had subsided, I discovered that I was associated in as heterogeneous a crowd as was ever got together. As my trip was to be of a few hours' duration only, I made no endeavors to become acquainted with my fellow-passengers, most of whom would be together many days. Instead of this, I took out of my pocket the "latest paper," and more critically than usual examined its contents; my fellow-passengers, at the same time, disposed of themselves in little groups.

While I was thus busily employed in reading, and my companions were more busily still employed, in discussing such subjects as suited their humors best, we were most unexpectedly startled by a loud Indian whoop, uttered in the "social hall," that part of the cabin fitted off for a bar; then was to be heard a loud crowing, which would not have continued to interest us — such sounds being quite common in that *place of spirits* — had not the hero of these windy accomplishments stuck his head into the cabin, and hallooed out, "Hurra for the Big Bear of Arkansaw!"

Then might be heard a confused hum of voices, unintelligible, save in such broken sentences as "horse," "screamer," "lightning is slow," &c.

As might have been expected, this continued interruption, attracted the attention of every one in the cabin; all conversation ceased, and in the midst of this surprise, the "Big Bear" walked into the cabin, took a chair, put his feet on the stove, and looking back over his shoulder, passed the general and familiar salute — "Strangers, how are you?"

He then expressed himself as much at home as if he had been at "the Forks of Cypress," and "prehaps a little more so."

Some of the company at this familiarity looked a little angry, and some astonished; but in a moment every face was wreathed in a smile. There was something about the intruder that won the heart on sight. He appeared to be a man enjoying perfect health and contentment; his eyes were as sparkling as diamonds, and good-natured to simplicity. Then his perfect confidence in himself was irresistibly droll.

"Prehaps," said he, "gentlemen," running on without a person interrupting, "prehaps you have been to New Orleans often; I never made *the first visit before,* and I don't intend to make another in a crow's life. I am thrown away in that ar place, and useless, that ar a fact. Some of the gentlemen thar called me *green* — well, prehaps I am, said I, *but I arn't so at home;* and if I ain't off my trail much, the heads of them perlite chaps themselves wern't much the hardest; for according to my notion, they were *real know-nothings,* green as a pumpkin-vine — couldn't, in farming, I'll bet, raise a crop of turnips; and as for shooting, they'd miss a barn if the door was swinging, and that, too, with the best rifle in the country. And then they talked to me 'bout hunting, and laughed at my calling the principal game in Arkansaw poker, and high-low-jack.

" 'Prehaps,' said I, 'you prefer checkers and roulette;' at this they laughed harder than ever, and asked me if I lived in the woods, and didn't know what *game* was?

"At this, I rather think *I* laughed.

" 'Yes,' I roared, and says, I, 'Strangers, if you'd ask me *how we got our meat* in Arkansaw, I'd a told you at once, and given you a list of varmints that would make a caravan, beginning with the bar, and ending off with the cat; that's *meat* though, not game.

"Game, indeed, — that's what city folks call it; and with them it means chippen-birds and shite-pokes; may be such trash live in my diggins, but I arn't noticed them yet: a bird anyway is too trifling. I never did shoot at but one, and I'd never forgiven myself for that, had it weighed less than forty pounds. I wouldn't draw a rifle on anything less heavy than that; and when I meet with another wild turkey of the same size, I will drap him."

"A wild turkey weighing forty pounds!" exclaimed twenty voices in the cabin at once.

"Yes, strangers, and wasn't it a whopper? You see, the thing was so fat that it couldn't fly far; and when he fell out of the tree, after I shot him, on striking the ground he bust open behind, and the way the pound gobs of tallow rolled out of the opening was perfectly beautiful."

"Where did all that happen?" asked a cynical-looking Hoosier.

"Happen! happened in Arkansaw: where else could it have happened, but in the creation State, the finishing-up country — a State where the *sile* runs down to the centre of the 'arth, and government gives you a title to every inch of it? Then its airs — just breathe them, and they will make you snort like a horse. It's a State without a fault, it is."

"Excepting mosquitoes," cried the Hoosier.

"Well, stranger, except them; for it ar a fact that they are rather *enormous,* and do push themselves in somewhat troublesome. But, stranger, they never stick twice in the same place; and give them a fair chance for a few months, and you will get as much above noticing them as an alligator. They can't hurt my feelings, for they lay under the skin; and I never knew but one case of injury resulting from them, and that was to a Yankee: and they take worse to foreigners, any how, than they do to natives. But the way they used that fellow up! first they punched him until he swelled up and busted; then he sup-per-a-ted, as the doctor called it, until he was as raw as beef; then, owing to the warm weather, he tuck the ager, and finally he tuck a steamboat and left the country. He was the only man that ever tuck mosquitoes at heart that I knowd of.

"But mosquitoes is natur, and I never find fault with her. If they ar large, Arkansaw is large, her varmints ar large, her trees ar large, her rivers ar large, and a small mosquito would be of no more use in Arkansaw than preaching in a cane-brake."

This knock-down argument in favor of big mosquitoes used the Hoosier up, and the logician started on a new track, to explain how numerous bear were in his "diggins," where he represented them to be "about as plenty as blackberries, and a little plentifuller."

Upon the utterance of this assertion, a timid little man near me inquired, if the bear in Arkansaw ever attacked the settlers in numbers.

"No," said our hero, warming with the subject, "no, stranger, for you see it ain't the natur of bear to go in droves; but the way they squander about in pairs and single ones is edifying.

"And then the way I hunt them — the old black rascals know the crack of my gun as well as they know a pig's squealing. They grow thin in our parts, it frightens them so, and they do take the noise dreadfully, poor things. That gun of mine is a perfect *epidemic among bear:* if not watched closely, it will go off as quick on a warm scent as my dog Bowieknife will: and then that dog — whew! why the fellow thinks that the world is full of bear, he finds them so easy. It's lucky he don't talk as well as think; for with his natural modesty, if he should suddenly learn how much he is acknowledged to be ahead of all other dogs in the universe, he would be astonished to death in two minutes.

"Strangers, that dog knows a bear's way as well as a horse-jockey knows a woman's: he always barks at the right time, bites at the exact place, and whips without getting a scratch.

"I never could tell whether he was made expressly to hunt bear, or whether bear was made expressly for him to hunt; any way, I believe they were ordained to go together as naturally as Squire Jones says a man and woman is, when he moralizes in marrying a couple. In fact, Jones once said, said he, 'Marriage according to law is a civil contract of divine origin; it's common to all countries as well as Arkansaw, and people take to it as naturally as Jim Doggett's Bowie-knife takes to bear.' "

"What season of the year do your hunts take place?" inquired a gentlemanly foreigner, who, from some peculiarities of his baggage, I suspected to be an Englishman, on some hunting expedition, probably at the foot of the Rocky Mountains.

"The season for bear hunting, stranger," said the man of Arkansaw, "is generally all the year round, and the hunts take place about as regular. I read in history that varmints have their fat season, and their lean season. That is not the case in Arkansaw, feeding as they do upon the *spontenacious* productions of the sile, they have one continued fat season the year round; though in winter things in this way is rather more greasy than in summer, I must admit. For that reason bear with us run in warm weather, but in winter they only waddle.

"Fat, fat! its an enemy to speed; it tames every thing that has plenty of it. I have seen wild turkeys, from its influence, as gentle as chickens. Run a bear in this fat condition, and the way it improves the critter for eating is amazing; it sort of mixes the ile up with the meat, until you can't tell t'other from which. I've done this often.

"I recollect one perty morning in particular, of putting an old he fellow on the stretch, and considering the weight he carried, he run well. But the dogs soon tired him down, and when I came up with him wasn't he in a beautiful sweat — I might say fever; and then to see his tongue sticking out of his mouth a feet, and his sides sinking and opening like a bellows, and his cheeks so fat that he couldn't look cross. In this fix I blazed at him, and pitch me naked into a briar patch, if the steam didn't come out of the bullet-hole ten foot in a straight line. The fellow, I reckon, was made on the high-pressure system, and the lead sort of bust his biler."

"That column of steam was rather curious, or else the bear must have been very *warm,*" observed the foreigner, with a laugh.

"Stranger, as you observe, that bear was WARM, and the blowing off of the steam show'd it, and also how hard the varmint had been run. I have no doubt if he had kept on two miles farther his insides would have been stewed; and I expect to meet with a varmint yet of extra bottom, that will run himself into a skinfull of bear's grease: it is possible; much onlikelier things have happened."

"Whereabouts are these bears so abundant?" inquired the foreigner, with increasing interest.

"Why, stranger, they inhabit the neighborhood of my settlement, one of the prettiest places on old Mississipp — a perfeet location, and no mistake; a place that had some defects until the river made the 'cut-off' at 'Shirt-tail bend,' and that remedied the evil, as it brought my cabin on the edge of the river — a great advantage in wet weather, I assure you, as you can now roll a barrel of whiskey into my yard in high water from a boat, as easy as falling off a log. It's a great improvement, as toting it by land in a jug, as I used to do, *evaporated* it too fast, and it became expensive.

"Just stop with me, stranger, a month or two, or a year, if you like, and you will appreciate my place. I can give you plenty to eat; for beside hog and hominy, you can have bear-ham, and bear-sausages, and a mattrass of bear-skins to sleep on, and a wildcat-skin, pulled off hull, stuffed with corn-shucks, for a pillow. That bed would put you to sleep if you had the rheumatics in every joint in your body. I call that ar bed, a *quietus.*

"Then look at my 'pre-emption' — the government ain't got another like it to dispose of. Such timber, and such bottom land, — why you can't preserve anything natural you plant in it unless you pick it young, things thar will grow out of shape so quick.

"I once planted in those diggins a few potatoes and beets; they took a fine start, and after that, an ox team couldn't have kept them from growing. About that time I went off to old Kaintuck on business, and did not hear from them things in three months, when I accidentally stumbled on a fellow who had drapped in at my place, with an idea of buying me out.

" 'How did you like things?' said I.

" 'Pretty well,' said he; 'the cabin is convenient, and the timber land is good; but that bottom land ain't worth the first red cent.' "

" 'Why?' said I.

" ' 'Cause,' said he.

" ' 'Cause what?' said I.

" ' 'Cause it's full of cedar stumps and Indian mounds, and *can't be cleared.'*

" 'Lord,' said I, 'them ar "cedar stumps" is beets, and them ar "Indian mounds" tater hills.'

"As I had expected, the crop was overgrown and useless: the sile is too rich, *and planting in Arkansaw is dangerous.*

"I had a good-sized sow killed in that same bottom land. The old thief stole an ear of corn, and took it down to eat where she slept at night. Well, she left a grain or two on the ground, and lay down on them: before morning the corn shot up, and the percussion killed her dead. I don't plant any more: natur intended Arkansaw for a hunting ground, and I go according to natur."

The questioner, who had thus elicited the description of our hero's settlement, seemed to be perfectly satisfied, and said no more; but the "Big Bear of Arkansaw" rambled on from one thing to another with a volubility perfectly astonishing, occasionally disputing with those around him, particularly with a "live Sucker" from Illinois, who had the daring to say that our Arkansaw friend's stories "smelt rather tall."

The evening was nearly spent by the incidents we have detailed; and conscious that my own association with so singular a personage would probably end before morning, I asked him if he would not give me a description of some particular bear hunt; adding, that I took great interest in such things, though I was no sportsman. The desire seemed to please him, and he squared himself round towards me, saying, that he could give me an idea of a bear hunt that was never beat in this world, or in any other. His manner was so singular, that half of his story consisted in his excellent way of telling it, the great peculiarity of which was, the happy manner he had of emphasizing the prominent parts of his conversation. As near as I can recollect, I have italicized the words, and given the story in his own way.

"Stranger," said he, "in bear hunts *I am numerous,* and which particular one, as you say, I shall tell, puzzles me.

"There was the old she devil I shot at the Hurricane last fall — then there was the old hog thief I popped over at the Bloody Crossing, and then — Yes, I have it! I will give you an idea of a hunt, in which the greatest bear was killed that ever lived, *none excepted;* about an old fellow that I hunted, more or less, for two or three years; and if that ain't a *particular bear hunt,* I ain't got one to tell.

"But in the first place, stranger, let me say, I am pleased with you, because you ain't ashamed to gain information by asking and listening; and that's what I say to Countess's pups every day when I'm home; and I have got great hopes of them ar pups, because they are continually *nosing* about; and though they stick it sometimes in the wrong place, they gain experience any how, and may learn something useful to boot.

"Well, as I was saying about this big bear, you see when I and some more first settled in our region, we were drivin to hunting naturally; we soon liked it, and after that we found it an easy matter to make the thing our business. One old chap who had pioneered 'afore us, gave us to understand that we had settled in the right place. He dwelt upon its merits until it was affecting, and showed us, to prove his assertions, more scratches on the bark of the sassafras trees, than I ever saw chalk marks on a tavern door 'lection time.

" 'Who keeps that ar reckoning?' said I.

" 'The bear,' said he.

" 'What for?' said I.

" 'Can't tell,' said he; 'but so it is: the bear bite the bark and wood too, at the highest point from the ground they can reach, and you can tell, by the marks,' said he, 'the length of the bear to an inch.'

" 'Enough,' said I; 'I've learned something here a'ready, and I'll put it in practice.'

"Well, stranger, just one month from that time I killed a bear, and told its exact length before I measured it, by those very marks; and when I did that, I swelled up considerably — I've been a prouder man ever since.

"So I went on, larning something every day, until I was reckoned a buster, and allowed to be decidedly the best bear hunter in my district; and that is a reputation as much harder to earn than to be reckoned first man in Congress, as an iron ramrod is harder than a toadstool.

"Do the varmints grow over-cunning by being fooled with by greenhorn hunters, and by this means get troublesome, they send for me, as a matter of course; and thus I do my own hunting, and most of my neighbors'. I walk into the varmints though, and it has become about as much the same to me as drinking. It is told in two sentences —

"A bear is started, and he is killed.

"The thing is somewhat monotonous now — I know just how much they will run, where they will tire, how much they will growl, and what a thundering time I will have in getting their meat home. I could give you the history of the chase with all the particulars at the commencement, I know the signs so well — *Stranger, I'm certain.* Once I met with a match, though, and I will tell you about it; for a common hunt would not be worth relating.

"On a fine fall day, long time ago, I was trailing about for bear, and what should I see but fresh marks on the sassafras trees, about eight inches above any in the forests that I knew of. Says I, 'Them marks is a hoax, or it indicates the d—t bear that was ever grown.' In fact, stranger, I couldn't believe it was real, and I went on. Again I saw the same marks, at the same height, and *I knew the thing lived.* That conviction came home to my soul like an earthquake.

"Says I, 'Here is something a-purpose for me: that bear is mine, or I give up the hunting business.' The very next morning, what should I see but a number of buzzards hovering over my corn-field. 'The rascal has been there,' said I, 'for that sign is certain'; and, sure enough, on examining, I found the bones of what had been as beautiful a hog the day before, as was ever raised by a Buckeye. Then I tracked the critter out of the field to the woods, and all the marks he left behind, showed me that he was *the bear.*

"Well, stranger, the first fair chase I ever had with that big critter, I saw him no less than three distinct times at a distance; the dogs run him over eighteen miles and broke down, my horse gave out, and I was as nearly used up as a man can be, made on *my* principle, *which is patent.*

"Before this adventure, such things were unknown to me as possible; but, strange as it was, that bear got me used to it before I was done with him; for he got so at last, that he would leave me on a long chase *quite easy.* How he did it, I never could understand.

"That a bear runs at all, is puzzling; but how this one could tire down and bust up a pack of hounds and a horse, that were used to overhauling everything they started after in no time, was past my understanding. Well, stranger, that bear finally got so sassy, that he used to help himself to a hog off my premises whenever he wanted one; the buzzards followed after what he left, and so, between *bear and buzzard,* I rather think I got *out of pork.*

"Well, missing that bear so often took hold of my vitals, and I wasted away. The thing had been carried too far, and it reduced me in flesh faster than an ager. I would see that bear in every thing I did: *he hunted me,* and that, too, like a devil, which I began to think he was.

"While in this shaky fix, I made preparations to give him a last brush, and be done with it. Having completed everything to my satisfaction, I started at sunrise, and to my great joy, I discovered from the way the dogs run, that they were near him. Finding his trail was nothing, for that had become as plain to the pack as a turnpike road.

"On we went, and coming an an open country, what should I see but the bear very leisurely ascending a hill, and the dogs close at his heels, either a match for him this time in speed, or else he did not care to get out of their way — I don't know which. But wasn't he a beauty, though! I loved him like a brother.

"On he went, until he came to a tree, the limbs of which formed a crotch about six feet from the ground. Into this crotch he got and seated himself, the dogs yelling all around it; and there he sat eyeing them as quiet as a pond in low water.

"A greenhorn friend of mine, in company, reached shooting distance before me, and blazed away, hitting the critter in the centre of his forehead. The bear shook his head as the ball struck it, and then walked down from that tree, as gently as a lady would from a carriage.

" 'Twas a beautiful sight to see him do that — he was in such a rage, that he seemed to be as little afraid of the dogs as if they had been sucking pigs; and the dogs warn't slow in making a ring around him at a respectful distance, I tell you; even Bowieknife himself, stood off. Then the way his eyes flashed! — why the fire of them would have singed a cat's hair; in fact, that bear was in a *wrath all over*. Only one pup came near him, and he was brushed out so totally with the bear's left paw, that he entirely disappeared; and that made the old dogs more cautious still. In the mean time, I came up, and taking deliberate aim, as a man should do, at his side, just back of his foreleg, *if my gun did not snap,* call me a coward, and I won't take it personal.

"Yes, stranger, *it snapped,* and I could not find a cap about my person. While in this predicament, I turned round to my fool friend — 'Bill,' says I, 'you're an ass — you're a fool — you might as well have tried to kill that bear by barking the tree under his belly, as to have done it by hitting him in the head. Your shot has made a tiger of him; and blast me, if a dog gets killed or wounded when they come to blows, I will stick my knife into your liver, I will ——.' My wrath was up. I had lost my caps, my gun had snapped, the fellow with me had fired at the bear's head, and I expected every moment to see him close in with the dogs and kill a dozen of them at least. In this thing I was mistaken; for the bear leaped over the ring formed by the dogs, and giving a fierce growl, was off — the pack, of course, in full cry after him. The run this time was short, for coming to the edge of a lake, the varmint jumped in, and swam to a little island in the lake, which it reached, just a moment before the dogs.

" 'I'll have him now,' said I, for I had found my caps in the *lining of my coat* — so, rolling a log into the lake, I paddled myself across to the island, just as the dogs had cornered the bear in a thicket. I rushed up and fired — at the same time the critter leaped over the dogs and came within three feet of me, running like mad; he jumped into the lake, and tried to mount the log I had just deserted, but every time he got half his body on it, it would roll over and send him under; the dogs, too, got around him, and pulled him about, and finally Bowieknife clenched with him, and they sunk into the lake together.

"Stranger, about this time I was excited, and I stripped off my coat, drew my knife, and intended to have taken a part with Bowieknife myself, when the bear rose to the surface. But the varmint staid under — Bowieknife came up alone, more dead than alive, and with the pack came ashore.

" 'Thank God!' said I, 'the old villain has got his deserts at last.'

"Determined to have the body, I cut a grape-vine for a rope, and dove down where I could see the bear in the water, fastened my rope to his leg, and fished him, with great difficulty, ashore. Stranger, may I be chawed to death by young alligators, if the thing I looked at wasn't a *she bear, and not the old critter after all.*

"The way matters got mixed on that island was onaccountably curious, and thinking of it made me more than ever convinced that I was hunting the devil himself. I went home that night and took to my bed — the thing was killing me. The entire team of Arkansaw in bear-hunting acknowledged himself used up, and the fact sunk into my feelings as a snagged boat will in the Mississippi. I grew as cross as a bear with two cubs and a sore tail. The thing got out 'mong my neighbors, and I was asked how come on that individ-u-al that never lost a bear when once started? and if that same individ-u-al didn't wear telescopes when he turned a she-bear, of ordinary size, into an old he one, a little larger than a horse?

"'Prehaps,' said I, 'friends' — getting wrathy — 'prehaps you want to call somebody a liar?'

"'Oh, no,' said they, 'we only heard of such things being *rather common* of late, but we don't believe one word of it; oh, no,' — and then they would ride off, and laugh like so many hyenas over a dead nigger.

"It was too much, and I determined to catch that bear, go to Texas, or die, — and I made my preparations accordin'.

"I had the pack shut up and rested. I took my rifle to pieces, and iled it.

"I put caps in every pocket about my person, *for fear of the lining.*

"I then told my neighbors, that on Monday morning — naming the day — I would start THAT BEAR, and bring him home with me, or they might divide my settlement among them, the owner having disappeared.

"Well, stranger, on the morning previous to the great day of my hunting expedition, I went into the woods near my house, taking my gun and Bowieknife along, just *from habit,* and there sitting down, also from habit, what should I see, getting over my fence, but *the bear!* Yes, the old varmint was within a hundred yards of me, and the way he walked *over that fence* — stranger; he loomed up like a *black mist,* he seemed so large, and he walked right towards me.

"I raised myself, took deliberate aim, and fired. Instantly the varmint wheeled, gave a yell, and *walked through the fence,* as easy as a falling tree would through a cobweb.

"I started after, but was tripped up by my inexpressibles, which, either from habit or the excitement of the moment, were about my heels, and before I had really gathered myself up, I heard the old varmint groaning, like a thousand sinners, in a thicket near by, and, by the time I reached him, he was a corpse.

"Stranger, it took five niggers and myself to put that carcass on a mule's back, and old long-ears waddled under his load, as if he was foundered in every leg of his body; and with a common whopper of a bear, he would have trotted off, and enjoyed himself.

"'Twould astonish you to know how big he was: I made a *bedspread of his skin,* and the way it used to cover my bear mattress, and leave several feet on each side to tuck up, would have delighted you. It was, in fact, a creation bear, and if it had lived in Samson's time, and had met him in a fair fight, he would have licked him in the twinkling of a dice-box.

"But, stranger, I never liked the way I hunted him, *and missed him.* There is something curious about it, that I never could understand, — and I never was satisfied at his giving in *so easy at last.* Prehaps he had heard of my preparations to hunt him the next day, so he jist guv up, like Captain Scott's coon, to save his wind to grunt with in dying; but that ain't likely. My private opinion is, that that bear was an *unhuntable bear, and died when his time come."*

When this story was ended, our hero sat some minutes with his auditors, in a grave silence; I saw there was a mystery to him connected with the bear whose death he had just related, that had evidently made a strong impression on his mind. It was also evident that there was some superstitious awe connected with the affair, — a feeling common with all "children of the wood," when they meet with any thing out of their every-day experience.

He was the first one, however, to break the silence, and, jumping up, he asked all present to "liquor" before going to bed, — a thing which he did, with a number of companions, evidently to his heart's content.

Long before day, I was put ashore at my place of destination, and I can only follow with the reader, in imagination, our Arkansas friend, in his adventures at the "Forks of Cypress," on the Mississippi.

A Piano in "Arkansaw"

We shall never forget the excitement which seized upon the inhabitants of the little village of Hardscrabble, as the report spread through the community that a real piano had actually arrived within its precincts. Speculation was afloat as to its appearance and its use. The name was familiar with everybody; but what it precisely meant, no one could tell. That it had legs was certain; for a stray volume of some traveller was one of the most conspicuous works in the floating library of Hardscrabble; and said traveller stated he had seen a piano somewhere in New England with pantalettes on. An old foreign paper was brought forward, in which there was an advertisement headed "Soiree," which informed the "citizens generally," that Mr. Bobolink would preside at the piano.

This was presumed by several wiseacres, who had been to a menagerie, to mean that Mr. Bobolink stirred the piano up with a long pole, in the same way the showman did the lions and rhi-no-ce-rus. So public opinion was in favour of its being an animal, though a harmless one; for there had been a land speculator through the village a few weeks before, who distributed circulars of a "Female Academy," for the accomplishment of young ladies. These circulars distinctly stated "the use of the piano to be one dollar per month." One knowing old chap said, if they would tell him what so-i-ree meant, he would tell them what a piano was, and no mistake.

The owner of this strange instrument was no less than a very quiet and very respectable late merchant in a little town somewhere "north," who, having failed at home, had emigrated into the new and hospitable country of Arkansas, for the purpose of bettering his fortune, and escaping the heartless sympathy of his more lucky neighbours, who seemed to consider him an indifferent and degraded man because he had become honestly poor.

The newcomers were strangers of course. The house in which they were setting up their furniture, was too little arranged "to admit of calls"; and as the family seemed very little disposed to court society, all prospects of immediately solving the mystery that hung about the piano seemed hopeless. In the mean time public opinion was "rife." The depository of this strange thing was looked upon by the passers-by with indefinable awe; and as noises unfamiliar reached the street, it was presumed that the piano made them, and the excitement rose higher than ever. In the midst of it, one or two ladies, presuming upon their age and respectability, called upon the strangers and inquired after their health, and offered their services and friendship; meantime everything in the house was eyed with the greatest intensity, but seeing nothing strange, a hint was given about the piano. One of the new family observed carelessly, "that it had been much injured by bringing out, that the damp had affected its tones, and that one of its legs was so injured that it would not stand up, and that for the present it would not ornament the parlour."

Here was an explanation, indeed: injured in bringing out — damp affecting its tones — leg broken. "Poor thing!" ejaculated the old ladies with real sympathy, as they proceeded homeward; "travelling has evidently fatigued it; the Mass-is-sip fogs have given it a cold, poor thing!" and they wished to see it with increased curiosity. "The village" agreed that if Moses Mercer, familiarly called "Mo Mercer," was in town, they would have a description of the piano, and the uses to which it was put; and fortunately, in the midst of the excitement, "Mo" arrived, he having been temporarily absent on a hunting expedition.

Moses Mercer was the only son of "old Mercer," who was, and had been, in the state senate ever since Arkansas was admitted into the "Union." Mo, from this fact, received great glory, of course; his father's greatness alone would have stamped him with superiority; but his having been twice to the "Capitol," when the legislature was in session, stamped his claims to pre-eminence over all competitors; and Mo Mercer was the oracle of the renowned village of Hardscrabble.

"Mo" knew every thing; he had all the consequence and complacency of a man who had never seen his equal, and never expected to. "Mo" bragged extensively upon his having been to the "Capitol" twice, — of his there having been in the most "fashionable society," — of having seen the world. His return to town was received with a shout. The arrival of the piano was announced to him, and *he alone* of all the community was not astonished at the news.

His insensibility was considered wonderful. He treated the piano as a thing he was used to, and went on, among other things to say, that he had seen more pianos in the "Capitol," than he had ever seen woodchucks; and that it was not an animal, but a musical instrument, played upon by the ladies; and he wound up his description by saying that the way "the dear creeters could pull music out of it was a caution to hoarse owls."

The new turn given to the piano excitement in Hardscrabble, by Mo Mercer, was like pouring oil on fire to extinguish it, for it blazed out with more vigour than ever. That it was a musical instrument, made it a rarer thing than if it had been an animal in that wild country, and people of all sizes, colours, and degrees, were dying to see and hear it.

Jim Cash was Mo Mercer's right hand man; in the language of refined society, he was "Mo's toady," — in the language of Hardscrabble, he was "Mo's wheel-horse." Cash believed in Mo Mercer with an abandonment perfectly ridiculous. Mr. Cash was dying to see the piano, and the first opportunity he had alone with his Quixotte, he expressed the desire that was consuming his vitals.

"We'll go at once and see it," said Mercer.

"Strangers!" echoed the frightened Cash.

"Humbug! Do you think I have visited the 'Capitol' twice, and don't know how to treat fashionable society? Come along at once, Cash," said Mercer.

Off the pair started, Mercer all confidence, and Cash all fears, as to the propriety of the visit. These fears Cash frankly expressed; but Mercer repeated, for the thousandth time, his experience in the fashionable society of the "Capitol," and with pianos, which he said, "was synonymous." And he finally told Cash, to comfort him, that however abashed and ashamed he might be in the presence of the ladies, "that he needn't fear of sticking, for he would put him through."

A few minutes' walk brought the parties on the broad galleries of the house that contained the object of so much curiosity. The doors and windows were closed, and a suspicious look was on everything.

"Do they always keep a house closed up this way that has a piano in it?" asked Cash, mysteriously.

"Certainly," replied Mercer, "the damp would destroy its tones."

Repeated knocks at the doors, and finally at the windows, satisfied both Cash and Mercer that nobody was at home. In the midst of their disappointment, Cash discovered a singular machine at the end of the gallery, crossed by bars and rollers, and surmounted with an enormous crank. Cash approached it on tiptoe; he had a presentiment that he beheld the object of his curiosity, and as its intricate character unfolded itself, he gazed with distended eyes, and asked Mercer, with breathless anxiety, *"what that was?"*

Mercer turned to the thing as coolly as a north wind to an icicle, and said, "that was it."

"That IT!!" exclaimed Cash, opening his eyes still wider; and then, recovering himself, he asked to see "the tones."

Mercer pointed to the cross-bars and rollers. With trembling hands, and a resolution that would enable a man to be scalped without winking, Cash reached out his hand, and seized the handle of the crank; (Cash at heart was a brave and fearless man); he gave it a turn, the machinery grated harshly, and seemed to clamour for something to be put in its maw.

"What delicious sounds!" said Cash.

"Beautiful!" observed the complacent Mercer, at the same time seizing Cash's arm, and asking him to desist, for fear of breaking the instrument or getting it out of tone.

The simple caution was sufficient; and Cash, in the joy of the moment at what he had done and seen, looked as conceited as Mo Mercer himself. Busy indeed was Cash, from this time forward, in explaining to gaping crowds the exact appearance of the piano, how he had actually taken hold of it, and, as his friend Mo Mercer observed, "pulled music out of it."

The curiosity of the village was thus allayed, and it died comparatively away; Cash, however, having rose to almost as much importance as Mo Mercer, for having seen and handled the thing.

Our "northern family" knew little or nothing of all this excitement; they received the visits and congratulations of the hospitable villagers, and resolved to give a grand party to return some of the kindness they had received, and the piano was for the first time moved into the parlour. No invitation on this occasion was neglected; early at the post was every visitor, for it was rumoured that Miss Patience Doolittle would, in course of the evening, "perform on the piano."

The excitement was immense. The supper was passed over with a contempt that rivals that cast upon an excellent farce played preparatory to a dull tragedy, in which the *star* is to appear. The furniture was all critically examined; but nothing could be discovered answering Cash's description. An enormously *thick-leafed table,* with a "spread" upon it, attracted little attention, *timber* being so cheap in a new country, and so everybody expected soon to see the piano "brought in."

Mercer, of course, was the hero of the evening; he talked much and loud. Cash, as well as several young ladies, went into hysterics at his wit. Mercer grew exceedingly conceited even for him, as the evening wore away; he asserted the company present reminded him of his two visits to the "Capitol," and other associations equally exclusive and peculiar.

The evening wore on apace, and still no piano. The hope deferred that maketh the heart sick, was felt by some elderly ladies, and by a few younger ones; and Mercer was solicited to ask Miss Patience Doolittle to favour the company with the presence of the piano.

"Certainly," said Mercer. With the grace of a city dandy, he called upon the lady to gratify all present with a little music, prefacing his request with the remark, that if she was fatigued, "his friend Cash could give the machine a *turn.*"

Miss Patience smiled, and looked at Cash.

Cash's knees trembled.

All eyes in the room turned upon him.

Cash sweat all over.

Miss Patience said she was gratified to hear that Mr. Cash was a musician; she admired people who had a musical taste. Whereupon Cash fell into a chair, as he afterwards observed, "chawed-up."

Oh that Beau Brummel or any of his admirers could have seen Mo Mercer all this while! Calm as a summer morning, and as complacent as a newly painted sign; he smiled and patronised, and was the only unexcited person in the room.

Miss Patience rose, a sigh escaped from all present, — the piano was evidently to be brought in. She approached the thick-leafed table, and removed the covering, throwing it carelessly and gracefully aside; opened it, and presented the beautiful arrangement of dark and white keys.

Mo Mercer at this, for the first time in his life, looked confused; he was Cash's authority in his descriptions of the appearance of the piano; while Cash himself began to recover the moment he ceased to be an object of attention. Many a whisper now ran through the room as to the "tones," and more particularly the "crank"; none could see them.

Miss Patience took her seat, ran her fingers over a few octaves, and if "Moses in Egypt" was not perfectly *executed*, Moses in Hardscrabble *was*. The music ceased. "Miss," said Cash, the moment he could express himself, so entranced was he by the music, — "Miss Doolittle, what was that instrument Mo Mercer showed me in your gallery once, that went by a crank, and had rollers in it?"

It was now the time for Miss Patience to blush; so away went the blood to her cheeks, with confusion; she hesitated, stammered, and said, "if Mr. Cash must know, that it was a-a-a-*yankee washing machine.*"

The name grated on Mo Mercer's ears as if rusty nails had been thrust into them; the heretofore invulnerable Mercer's knees trembled; the sweat started to his brow as he heard the taunting whispers of "visiting the Capitol twice," and seeing pianos as plenty as woodchucks.

The fashionable vices of envy and maliciousness were that moment sown in the village of Hardscrabble; and Mo Mercer, the great and confident, the happy and self-possessed, surprising as it may seem, was the first victim sacrificed to their influence. Time wore on, and pianos became common, and Mo Mercer less popular; and he finally disappeared altogether on the evening of the day a yankee pedler of notions sold, to the highest bidder, "six patent, warranted, and improved Mo Mercer pianos."

The Disgraced Scalp-Lock

Occasionally may be seen on the Ohio and Mississippi rivers singularly hearty-looking men, that puzzle a stranger as to their history and age. Their forms always exhibit a powerful development of muscle and bone; their cheeks are prominent, and you would pronounce them men enjoying perfect health in middle life, were it not for their heads, which, if not bald, will be sparsely covered with steel-gray hair. Another peculiarity about this people is, that they have a singular knowledge of all the places on the river; every bar and bend is spoken of with precision and familiarity; every town is recollected before it was half as large as the present, or no town at all. Innumerable places are marked out where once was an Indian fight, or a rendezvous of robbers. The manner, the language, and the dress of these individuals are all characteristic of sterling common sense — the manner modest, yet full of self-reliance; the language strong and forcible, from superiority of mind rather than from education; the dress studied for comfort, rather than fashion — on the whole, you become attached to them and court their society. The good humour, the frankness, the practical sense, the reminiscences, the powerful frame — all indicate a character, at the present day anomalous; and such indeed is the case, for your acquaintance will be one of the few remaining people now spoken of as the "last of the flat-boatmen."

Thirty years ago the navigation of the western waters was confined to this class of men; the obstacles presented to the pursuit in those swift-running and wayward waters had to be overcome by physical force alone; the navigator's arm grew strong as he guided his rude craft past the "snag" and "sawyer," or kept off the no less dreaded "bar." Besides all this, the deep forests that covered the river banks concealed the wily Indian, who gloated over the shedding of blood. The qualities of the frontier warrior associated themselves with the boatmen, while he would, when at home, drop both these characters in the cultivator of the soil. It is no wonder, then, that they were brave, hardy, and open-handed men: their whole lives were a round of manly excitement; they were hyperbolical in thought and in deed, when most natural, compared with any other class of men. Their bravery and chivalrous deeds were performed without a herald to proclaim them to the world — they were the mere incidents of a border life, considered too common to outlive the time of a passing wonder. Obscurity has nearly obliterated the men, and their actions. A few of the former still exist, as if to justify their wonderful exploits, which now live almost exclusively as traditions.

Among the flat-boatmen there were none that gained the notoriety of *Mike Fink*. His name is still remembered along the whole of the Ohio as a man who excelled his fellows in everything, — particularly in his rifle-shot, which was acknowledged to be unsurpassed. Probably no man ever lived who could compete with Mike Fink in the latter accomplishment. Strong as Hercules, free from all nervous excitement, possessed of perfect health, and familiar with his weapon from childhood, he raised the rifle to his eye, and, having once taken sight, it was as firmly fixed as if buried in a rock. It was Mike's pride, and he rejoiced on all occasions where he could bring it into use, whether it was turned against the beast of prey or the more savage Indian; and in his day these last named were the common foe with whom Mike and his associates had to contend. On the occasion that we would particularly introduce Mike to the reader, he had bound himself for a while to the pursuits of trade, until a voyage from the head-waters of the Ohio, and down the Mississippi, could be completed. Heretofore he had kept himself exclusively to the Ohio, but a liberal reward, and some curiosity, prompted him to extend his business character beyond his ordinary habits and inclinations. In accomplishment of this object, he was lolling carelessly over the big "sweep" that guided the "flat" on which he officiated; the current of the river bore the boat swiftly along, and made his labour light; his eye glanced around him, and he broke forth in ecstasies at what he saw and felt. If there is a river in the world that merits the name of beautiful, it is the Ohio, when its channel is

"Without o'erflowing, full."

The scenery is everywhere soft; there are no jutting rocks, no steep banks, no high hills; but the clear and swift current laves beautiful and undulating shores, that descend gradually to the water's edge. The foliage is rich and luxuriant, and its outlines in the water are no less distinct than when it is relieved against the sky. Interspersed along its route are islands, as beautiful as ever figured in poetry as the land of the fairies; enchanted spots indeed, that seem to sit so lightly on the water that you almost expect them, as you approach, to vanish into dreams. So late as when Mike Fink disturbed the solitudes of the Ohio with his rifle, the canoe of the Indian was hidden in the little recesses along the shore; they moved about in their frail barks like spirits; and clung, in spite of the constant encroachments of civilization, to the places which tradition had designated as the happy places of a favoured people.

Wild and uncultivated as Mike appeared, he loved nature, and had a soul that sometimes felt, while admiring it, an exalted enthusiasm. The Ohio was his favourite stream. From where it runs no stronger than a gentle rivulet, to where it mixes with the muddy Mississippi, Mike was as familiar with its meanderings as a child could be with those of a flower-garden. He could not help noticing with sorrow the desecrating hand of improvement as he passed along, and half soliloquizing, and half addressing his companions, he broke forth:
— "I knew these parts afore a squatter's axe had blazed a tree; 'twasn't

then pulling a —— sweep to get a living; but pulling the trigger's the business. Those were times to see; a man might call himself lucky. What's the use of improvements? When did cutting down trees make deer more plenty? Who ever found wild buffalo or a brave Indian in a city? Where's the fun, the frolicking, the fighting? Gone! Gone! The rifle won't make a man a living now — he must turn nigger and work. If forests continue to be used up, I may yet be smothered in a settlement. Boys, this 'ere life won't do. I'll stick to the broadhorn 'cordin' to contract; but once done with it, I'm off for a frolic. If the Choctaws or Cherokees on the Massassip don't give us a brush as we pass along, I shall grow as poor as a starved wolf in a pitfall. I must, to live peaceably, point my rifle at something more dangerous than varmint. Six months and no fight would spile me worse than a dead horse on a prairie."

Mike ceased speaking. The then beautiful village of Louisville appeared in sight; the labour of landing the boat occupied his attention — the bustle and confusion that followed such an incident ensued, and Mike was his own master by law until his employers ceased trafficking, and again required his services.

At the time we write of, there were a great many renegade Indians who lived about the settlements, and which is still the case in the extreme south-west. These Indians generally are the most degraded of their tribe — outcasts, who, for crime or dissipation, are no longer allowed to associate with their people; they live by hunting or stealing, and spend their precarious gains in intoxication. Among the throng that crowded on the flat-boat on his arrival, were a number of these unfortunate beings; they were influenced by no other motive than that of loitering round in idle speculation at what was going on. Mike was attracted towards them at sight; and as he too was in the situation that is deemed most favourable to mischief, it struck him that it was a good opportunity to have a little sport at the Indians' expense. Without ceremony, he gave a terrific war-whoop; and then mixing the language of the aborigines and his own together, he went on in savage fashion and bragged of his triumphs and victories on the war-path, with all the seeming earnestness of a real "brave." Nor were taunting words spared to exasperate the poor creatures, who, perfectly helpless, listened to the tales of their own greatness, and their own shame, until wound up to the highest pitch of impotent exasperation. Mike's companions joined in; thoughtless boys caught the spirit of the affair; and the Indians were goaded until they in turn made battle with their tongues. Then commenced a system of running against them, pulling off their blankets, together with a thousand other indignities; finally they made a precipitate retreat ashore, amid the hooting and jeering of an unfeeling crowd, who considered them poor devils destitute of feeling and humanity. Among this crowd of outcasts was a Cherokee, who bore the name of Proud Joe; what his real cognomen was, no one knew, for he was taciturn, haughty — and, in spite of his poverty and his manner of life won the name we have mentioned. His face was expressive of talent, but it was furrowed by the most terrible habits of drunkenness. That he was a superior Indian was admitted; and it was also understood that he was banished from his mountain home, his tribe being then numerous and powerful, for some great crime. He was always looked up to by his companions, and managed, however intoxicated he might be, to sustain a singularly proud bearing, which did not even depart from him while prostrated on the ground. Joe was filthy in his person and habits — in this respect he was behind his fellows; but one ornament of his person was attended to with a care which would have done honour to him if surrounded by his people, and in his native woods. Joe still wore with Indian dignity his scalp-lock; he ornamented it with taste, and cherished it, as report said, that some Indian messenger of vengeance might tear it from his head, as expiatory of his numerous crimes. Mike noticed this peculiarity; and reaching out his hand, plucked from it a hawk's feather, which was attached to the scalp-lock. The Indian glared horribly on Mike as he consummated the insult, snatched the feather from his hand, then shaking his clenched fist in the air, as if calling on Heaven for revenge, retreated with his friends. Mike saw that he had roused the savage's soul, and he marvelled wonderfully that so much resentment should be exhibited; and as an earnest to Proud Joe that the wrong he had done him should not rest unrevenged, he swore he would cut the scalp-lock off close to his head the first convenient opportunity he got, and then he thought no more about it.

The morning following the arrival of the boat at Louisville was occupied in making preparations to pursue the voyage down the river. Nearly everything was completed, and Mike had taken his favourite place at the sweep, when looking up the river-bank, he beheld at some distance Joe and his companions, and perceived from their gesticulations that they were making him the subject of conversation.

Mike thought instantly of several ways in which he could show them altogether a fair fight, and then whip them with ease; he also reflected with what extreme satisfaction he would enter into the spirit of the arrangement, and other matters to him equally pleasing, when all the Indians disappeared, save Joe himself, who stood at times reviewing him in moody silence, and then staring round at passing objects. From the peculiarity of Joe's position to Mike, who was below him, his head and upper part of his body relieved boldly against the sky, and in one of his movements he brought his profile face to view. The prominent scalp-lock and its adornments seemed to be more striking than ever, and it again roused the pugnacity of Mike Fink; in an instant he raised his rifle, always loaded and at command, brought it to his eye, and, before he could be prevented, drew sight upon Proud Joe and fired. The ball whistled loud and shrill, and Joe, springing his whole length into the air, fell upon the ground. The cold-blooded murder was noticed by fifty persons at least, and there arose from the crowd an universal cry of horror and indignation at the bloody deed. Mike himself seemed to be much astonished, and in an instant reloaded his rifle, and as a number of white persons rushed towards the boat, Mike threw aside his coat, and, taking his powder horn between his teeth, leaped, rifle in hand, into the Ohio, and commenced swimming for the opposite shore. Some bold spirits determined Mike should not so easily escape, and jumping into the only skiff at command, pulled swiftly after him. Mike watched their movements until they came within a hundred yards of him, then turning in the water, he supported himself by his feet alone, and raised his deadly rifle to his eye. Its muzzle, if it spoke hostilely, was as certain to send a messenger of death through one or more of his pursuers, as if it were lightning, and they knew it; dropping their oars and turning pale, they bid Mike not to fire. Mike waved his hand towards the little village of Louisville, and again pursued his way to the opposite shore.

The time consumed by the firing of Mike's rifle, the pursuit, and the abandonment of it, required less time than we have taken to give the details; and in that time, to the astonishment of the gaping crowd around Joe, they saw him rising with a bewildered air; a moment more and he recovered his senses and stood up — *at his feet lay his scalp-lock!* The ball had cut it clear from his head; the cord around the root of it, in which were placed feathers and other ornaments, held it together; the concussion had merely stunned its owner; farther, he had escaped all bodily harm! A cry of exultation rose at the last evidence of the skill of Mike Fink — the exhibition of a shot that established his claim, indisputable, to the eminence he ever afterwards held — the unrivalled marksman of all the flat-boat-men of the western waters. Proud Joe had received many insults. He looked upon himself as a degraded, worthless being; and the ignominy heaped upon him he never, except by reply, resented; but this last insult was like seizing the lion by the mane, or a Roman senator by the beard — it roused the slumbering demon within, and made him again thirst to resent his wrongs with an intensity of emotion that can only be felt by an Indian. His eye glared upon the jeering crowd around like a fiend; his chest swelled and heaved until it seemed that he must suffocate. No one noticed this emotion. All were intent upon the exploit that had so singularly deprived Joe of his war-lock; and, smothering his wrath, he retreated to his associates with a consuming fire at his vitals. He was a different man from an hour before; and with that desperate resolution on which a man stakes his all, he swore by the Great Spirit of his forefathers that he would be revenged.

An hour after the disappearance of Joe, both he and Mike Fink were forgotten. The flat-boat, which the latter had deserted, was got under way, and dashing through the rapids in the river opposite Louisville wended on its course. As is customary when night sets in, the boat was securely fastened in some little bend or bay in the shore, where it remained until early morn.

Long before the sun had fairly risen, the boat was again pushed into the stream, and it passed through a valley presenting the greatest possible beauty and freshness of landscape the mind can conceive.

It was spring, and a thousand tints of green developed themselves in the half-formed foliage and bursting buds. The beautiful mallard skimmed across the water, ignorant of the danger of the white man's approach; the splendid spoon-bill decked the shallow places near the shore, while myriads of singing-birds filled the air with their unwritten songs. In the far reaches down the river, there occasionally might be seen a bear stepping along the ground as if dainty of its feet, and, snuffing the intruder on his wild home, he would retreat into the woods. To enliven all this, and give the picture the look of humanity, there might also be seen, struggling with the floating mists, a column of blue smoke, that came from a fire built on a projecting point of land, around which the current swept rapidly, and carried everything that floated on the river. The eye of the boatman saw the advantage of the situation which the place rendered to those on shore, to annoy and attack, and as wandering Indians, in those days, did not hesitate to rob, there was much speculation as to what reception the boat would receive from the builders of the fire.

The rifles were all loaded, to be prepared for the worst, and the loss of Mike Fink lamented, as a prospect of a fight presented itself, where he could use his terrible rifle. The boat in the mean time swept round the point; but instead of an enemy, there lay, in a profound sleep, Mike Fink, with his feet toasting at the fire, his pillow was a huge bear, that had been shot on the day previous, while at his sides, and scattered in profusion around him, were several deer and wild turkeys. Mike had not been idle. After picking out a place most eligible to notice the passing boat, he had spent his time in hunting, and he was surrounded by trophies of his prowess. The scene that he presented was worthy of the time and the man, and would have thrown Landseer into a delirium of joy, could he have witnessed it. The boat, owing to the swiftness of the current, passed Mike's resting place, although it was pulled strongly to the shore. As Mike's companions came opposite to him, they raised such a shout, half exultation of meeting him, and half to alarm him with the idea that Joe's friends were upon him. Mike, at the sound, sprang to his feet, rifle in hand, and as he looked around, he raised it to his eyes, and by the time he discovered the boat, he was ready to fire. "Down with your shooting-iron, you wild critter," shouted one of the boatmen. Mike dropped the piece, and gave a loud halloo, that echoed among the solitudes like a piece of artillery. The meeting between Mike and his fellows was characteristic. They joked, and jibed him with their rough wit, and he parried it off with a most creditable ingenuity. Mike soon learned the extent of his rifle-shot — he seemed perfectly indifferent to the fact that Proud Joe was not dead. The only sentiment he uttered, was regret that he did not fire at the vagabond's head, and if he hadn't hit it, why, he made the first bad shot in twenty years. The dead game was carried on board of the boat, the adventure was forgotten, and everything resumed the monotony of floating in a flat-boat down the Ohio.

A month or more elapsed, and Mike had progressed several hundred miles down the Mississippi; his journey had been remarkably free from incident; morning, noon, and night, presented the same banks, the same muddy water, and he sighed to see some broken land, some high hills, and he railed and swore, that he should have been such a fool as to desert his favourite Ohio for a river that produced nothing but alligators, and was never at best half finished.

Occasionally, the plentifulness of game put him in spirits, but it did not last long; he wanted more lasting excitement, and declared himself as perfectly miserable and helpless as a wild-cat without teeth or claws.

In the vicinity of Natchez rise a few abrupt hills, which tower above the surrounding lowlands of the Mississippi like monuments; they are not high, but from their loneliness and rarity they create sensations of pleasure and awe.

Under the shadow of one of these bluffs, Mike and his associates made the customary preparations to pass the night. Mike's enthusiasm knew no bounds at the sight of land again; he said it was as pleasant as "cold water to a fresh wound"; and, as his spirits rose, he went on making the region round about, according to his notions, an agreeable residence.

"The Choctaws live in these diggins," said Mike, "and a cursed time they must have of it. Now if I lived in these parts I'd declare war on 'em just to have something to keep me from growing dull; without some such business I'd be as musty as an old swamp moccasin. I could build a cabin on that ar hill yonder that could, from its location, with my rifle, repulse a whole tribe if they came after me. What a beautiful time I'd have of it! I never was particular about what's called a fair fight; I just ask half a chance, and the odds against me, and if I then don't keep clear of snags and sawyers, let me spring a leak and go to the bottom. It's natur that the big fish should eat the little ones. I've seen trout swallow a perch, and a cat would come along and swallow the trout, and perhaps, on the Mississippi, the alligators use up the cat, and so on to the end of the row. Well, I will walk tall into varmint and Indian; it's a way I've got, and it comes as natural as grinning to a hyena. I'm a regular tornado, tough as a hickory, and long-winded as a nor'-wester. I can strike a blow like a falling tree, and every lick makes a gap in the crowd that lets in an acre of sunshine. Whew, boys!" shouted Mike, twirling his rifle like a walking-stick around his head, at the ideas suggested in his mind. "Whew, boys! if the Choctaw divils in them ar woods thare would give us a brush, just as I feel now, I'd call them gentlemen. I must fight something, or I'll catch the dry rot — burnt brandy won't save me." Such were some of the expressions which Mike gave utterance to, and in which his companions heartily joined; but they never presumed to be quite equal to Mike, for his bodily prowess, as well as his rifle, were acknowledged to be unsurpassed. These displays of animal spirits generally ended in boxing and wrestling-matches, in which falls were received, and blows were struck without being noticed, that would have destroyed common men. Occasionally angry words and blows were exchanged, but, like the summer storm, the cloud that emitted the lightning purified the air; and when the commotion ceased, the combatants immediately made friends and became more attached to each other than before the cause that interrupted the good feelings occurred. Such were the conversation and amusements of the evening when the boat was moored under the bluffs we have alluded to. As night wore on, one by one of the hardy boatmen fell asleep, some in its confined interior, and others protected by a light covering in the open air. The moon arose in beautiful majesty; her silver light, behind the highlands, gave them a power and theatrical effect as it ascended; and as its silver rays grew perpendicular, they finally kissed gently the summit of the hills, and poured down their full light upon the boat, with almost noonday brilliancy. The silence with which the beautiful changes of darkness and light were produced made it mysterious. It seemed as if some creative power was at work, bringing form and life out of darkness. In the midst of the witchery of this quiet scene, there sounded forth the terrible rifle, and the more terrible war-whoop of the Indian. One of the flat-boatmen, asleep on deck, gave a stifled groan, turned upon his face, and with a quivering motion, ceased to live. Not so with his companions — they in an instant, as men accustomed to danger and sudden attacks, sprang ready-armed to their feet, but before they could discover their foes, seven sleek and horribly painted savages leaped from the hill into the boat. The firing of the rifle was useless, and each man singled out a foe and met him with the drawn knife.

The struggle was quick and fearful; and deadly blows were given amid screams and imprecations that rent the air. Yet the voice of Mike Fink could be heard in encouraging shouts above the clamour. "Give it to them, boys!" he cried, "cut their hearts out! choke the dogs! Here's hell a-fire and the river rising!" then clenching with the most powerful of the assailants, he rolled with him upon the deck of the boat. Powerful as Mike was, the Indian seemed nearly a match for him. The two twisted and writhed like serpents, — now one seeming to have the advantage, and then the other.

In all this confusion there might occasionally be seen glancing in the moonlight the blade of a knife; but at whom the thrusts were made, or who wielded it, could not be discovered.

The general fight lasted less time than we have taken to describe it. The white men gained the advantage; two of the Indians lay dead upon the boat, and the living, escaping from their antagonists leaped ashore, and before the rifle could be brought to bear they were out of its reach. While Mike was yet struggling with his antagonist, one of his companions cut the boat loose from the shore, and, with powerful exertion, managed to get its bows so far into the current, that it swung round and floated; but before this was accomplished, and before any one interfered with Mike, he was on his feet, covered with blood, and blowing like a porpoise: by the time he could get his breath, he commenced talking. "Ain't been so busy in a long time," said he, turning over his victim with his foot; "that fellow fou't beautiful; if he's a specimen of the Choctaws that live in these parts, they are screamers; the infernal sarpents! the d—d possums!" Talking in this way, he with others, took a general survey of the killed and wounded. Mike himself was a good deal cut up with the Indian's knife; but he called his wounds blackberry scratches. One of Mike's associates was severely hurt; the rest escaped comparatively harmless. The sacrifice was made at the first fire; for beside the dead Indians, there lay one of the boat's crew, cold and dead, his body perforated with four different balls. That he was the chief object of attack seemed evident, yet no one of his associates knew of his having a single fight with the Indians. The soul of Mike was affected, and, taking the hand of his deceased friend between his own, he raised his bloody knife towards the bright moon, and swore that he would desolate "the nation" that claimed the Indians who made war upon them that night, and turned to his stiffened victim, that, dead as it was, retained the expression of implacable hatred and defiance, he gave it a smile of grim satisfaction, and then joined in the general conversation which the occurrences of the night would naturally suggest. The master of the "broad horn" was a business man and had often been down the Mississippi. This was the first attack he had received, or knew to have been made from the shores inhabited by the Choctaws, except by the white man, and he, among other things, suggested the keeping the dead Indians until daylight, that they might have an opportunity to examine their dress and features, and see with certainty who were to blame for the occurrences of the night. The dead boatman was removed with care to a respectful distance; and the living, except the person at the sweep of the boat, were soon buried in profound slumber.

Not until after the rude breakfast was partaken of, and the funeral rites of the dead boatman were solemnly performed, did Mike and his companions disturb the corpses of the red men.

When both these things had been leisurely and gently got through with, there was a different spirit among the men.

Mike was astir, and went about his business with alacrity. He stripped the bloody blanket from the Indian he had killed, as if it enveloped something disgusting, and required no respect. He examined carefully the moccasins on the Indian's feet, pronouncing them at one time Chickasas, at another time, the Shawnese. He stared at the livid face, but could not recognize the style of paint that covered it.

That the Indians were not strictly national in their adornments, was certain, for they were examined by practised eyes, that could have told the nation of the dead, if such had been the case, as readily as a sailor could distinguish a ship by its flag. Mike was evidently puzzled; and as he was about giving up his task as hopeless, the dead body he was examining, from some cause, turned on its side. Mike's eyes distended, as some of his companions observed, "like a choked cat," and became riveted. He drew himself up in a half serious, and half comic expression, and pointing at the back of the dead Indian's head, there was exhibited a dead warrior in his paint, destitute of his scalp-lock, the small stump which was only left, being stiffened with *red paint*. Those who could read Indians' symbols learned a volume of deadly resolve in what they saw. The body of Proud Joe was stiff and cold before them.

The last and best shot of Mike Fink cost a brave man his life. The corpse so lately interred, was evidently taken in the moonlight by Proud Joe and his party, as that of Mike's, and they had risked their lives, one and all, that he might with certainty be sacrificed. Nearly a thousand miles of swamp had been threaded, large and swift running rivers had been crossed, hostile tribes passed through by Joe and his friends, that they might revenge the fearful insult, of destroying *without the life,* the sacred scalp-lock.

Harden E. Taliaferro

(1818-1875)

✻ As a young man Harden E. Taliaferro worked on a farm in his native Surry County, North Carolina, during the week and preached on Sundays. About 1837 he moved to Alabama where he became a Baptist minister in Talladega and Eufaula and edited a religious periodical, the *Southwestern Baptist*. According to the introduction to his *Fisher's River (North Carolina) Scenes and Characters*, a visit "in 1857 after an absence of twenty years" to his birthplace in the northwestern corner of North Carolina led him to record the customs and stories of the people he had known there a generation before.

An appreciative reviewer writing in *Harper's New Monthly Magazine* for July, 1862, asserted that while the rest of the United States was assuming a bland uniformity, the isolated mountain folk of Fisher's River, indifferent to the world beyond, clung to their individualism and went their own way. He concluded that Taliaferro's book was "deserving to rank with Judge Longstreet's 'Georgia Scenes,'" but what seems to have especially struck his fancy were the yarns about fantastic snakes and fabulous hunters whose adventures were close to those of Baron Munchausen. Taliaferro's graphic transcriptions of tales, dialects, proverbs, superstitions, and folkways of the North Carolina back country command the interest of folklorists. Such characters as Ham Rachel of Alabama, a Southern poor white whose literary (and sociological) forebears lived in William Byrd's Lubberland and whose descendants inhabit William Faulkner's Yoknapatawpha County, merit more attention than they have received. Taliaferro contributed additional sketches of the Fisher's River type to the *Southern Literary Messenger* in the early 1860's.

TEXT: "'Famus or No Famus,'" "Larkin Snow, the Miller," and "Ham Rachel, of Alabama" from *Fisher's River (North Carolina) Scenes and Characters* (New York, 1859).

"Famus or No Famus"

Fisher's River was one of the last places for the importance of militia musters, in the expressive language of that section, "to give up the ghost." I account for it from the fact that a few old Revolutionary soldiers lived in the community, and kept the "militeer sperit" always at blood heat in the rising generation.

Their musters were semi-annual, held in May and November, and the old "Revolutionaries" were ever present. The "capting," "leftenant," "sargint" — all the "ossifers" — were proud to perform "revolutions" before them. "They knowed a thing or two about militeer tacktucks, just as well as old Steuben ur Duane tharselves." And the "cap'en" never thought for once of giving the word "Right face! dismissed!" till they were gravely reviewed by the "old sogers."

There was another matter of powerful attraction to the old " 'Lutionaries" and the " 'Litia" — the "knock-'em-stiff" — that was as punctual in attendance as any of the "patriots." "Nigger Josh Easley" with his "gingy cakes," and Hamp Hudson with his "licker," were men and things as much looked for as "Capting Moore with his militeer uniform."

Hamp Hudson was the only man in that whole country who kept a "still-house" running all the year; the weaker ones would "run dry." Of course, Hamp and his still-house, and all the "appurtenances thereof," were well known to the whole country.

Hamp also had a noted dog, named "Famus," as *famous* for being in the distillery as Hamp himself, and quite as well known in that entire region as his master.

Now it came to pass in the course of human and dog events that Famus fell into a "mash-tub" and was drowned. It was "narrated" all through the country "that Famus was drownded in a mash-tub, and Hamp had distilled the beer in which Famus was drownded, and was gwine to carry it to the May muster to sell." This report produced a powerful sensation in the community, and was the only topic of conversation. All appeared to believe it, and there was a general determination "not to drink one drap uv Hamp's nasty old Famus licker."

The auspicious muster-day arrives, and the people collect from Stewart's Creek, Ring's Creek, Beaver Dam, Big Fisher's and Little Fisher's Rivers, from the "Hollow," "the Foot uv the Mounting" — from the Dan to the Beersheba of that whole country. I, too, was there — though but a lad, deeply interested in the action of that important day — to see who would triumph, Hamp and Famus, or an indignant community.

As soon as they collect they meet in little squads to debate the grave question. The old "Revolutioners" are there, and their sage counsels decide all questions. "They fout for our liberties, and they must be hearn." "Uncle Jimmy Smith," a leading man among them, particularly on "licker questions," makes a speech to the crowd just

before Cap'en Moore tells the "orderly sargint" to "form ranks." Uncle
Jimmy lisps, but he is clearly understood by his waiting and attentive
audience. They are "spellbound" by his nervous and patriotic eloquence. What if he has a slight impediment in his speech? his eloquence is in his subject. Hear him:

"Now, boyith, I'm an old man — wath at the storming uv Stony
Pint, under old 'Mad Anthony Wayne,' ath we boyith allers called
him; and I've marched and countermarched through thick and thin;
hath fout, bled, and died nairly for seven long years; I hath theen many
outrages, but thith Famus business caps the stack and saves the
grain. Jist think uv thith feller, Hamp Hudson, to 'still the beer uv
that mash-tub that Famus — that nathty, stinkin', mangy dog — was
drownded in; and fur to think fur to bring it here fur to thell the
nathty, stinkin' whisky to hith neighbors, Cap'en Moore and company,
and to the old sogers, what fout for yer libertith. I tell you, boyith,
you can do ath you pleath, but old Jimmy Smith — old Stony Pint —
ain't a-gwine to tech it!"

"Nur I!" "Nur I, Uncle Jimmy!" shouted hundreds.

The voice of the sergeant is now heard like a Blue Ridge cataract:

"O-yis! o-yis! The hour of muster have arrove! O-yis! All uv ye
what b'longs to Cap'en Moore's company, parade here! Fall inter
ranks right smart, and straight as a gun-bar'l, and dress to the right
and left, accordin' to the militeer tacktucks laid down by Duane in his
cilebrated work on that fust of all subjecks."

They fall into ranks with precision, order, dignity, and gravity,
prompted by their patriotism. Besides, the old "'Lutionary sogers"
are looking at them.

Cap'en Moore now appears in his old-fashioned uniform, worn probably by some "'Lutionary cap'en" in many a bloody fight. 'Tis an
odd-looking affair; the collar of it repulses his "ossifer hat" from the
top of his "hade"; the tail, long and forked, striking his hams at every
step, and two great rusty epaulets on his shoulders — enough to weigh
down a man of less patriotic spirit, and on a less patriotic occasion.

Thus equipped, "as the law directs," he commences the "drill accordin' to Duane."

I had seen every muster on that patriotic spot from the time I was
able to get there and to eat a "gingy cake," but never had I seen as
poor a one as that was. There was no spirit nor life in the "militeer."
Instead of following Duane, they were whispering and talking about
Hamp and Famus. Indeed, they greatly needed the inspiration of
Hamp's barrel. Cap'en Moore bawled till he was hoarse; his "leftenant"
and "sargint" were exhausted, but it all did no good. They performed
no "revolutions" according to Duane, Steuben, nor any other author

extant. The old "Revolutioners" could render them no assistance, and in despair the "capting" dismissed them, in deep mortification.

But where are Hamp and Famus all this time? Yonder he sits, under the shade of a large apple-tree, solitary and alone, astride of his whisky-barrel.

It is now one o'clock P.M., and his chances look bad; his whisky-barrel has not been tapped, nor has any man dared to approach his condemned head-quarters. "Old Nigger Josh Easley" has sold all his "gingy cakes," and is showing his big white teeth, rejoicing at his unparalleled success. Josh is the only joyful man on the "grit." The rest are all melancholy, standing or sitting in little squads, debating the mash-tub question. Hamp is quite composed, and his looks say, "Never mind, gentlemen, I'll sell you every drap uv my licker yit."

Two o'clock arrives, and no one approaches Hamp's apple-tree. His prospects are growing worse. But look yonder! The crowd has collected around Uncle Jimmy Smith. Let us approach and hear him:

"Well, boyith, I don't know tho well about thith matter. Maybe we've accused thith feller, Hamp, wrongfully. He hath allers been a clever feller, and ith a pity ef he ith innercent uv thith charge. The fact ith, boyith, it's mighty dull, dry times; nuthin's a-gwine on right. Boyith, you are free men. I fout for your freedom. I thay, boyith, you can do ath you pleath, but ath fur me, old Stony Pint Jimmy Smith, *Famus or no Famus, I must take a little.*"

The speech of Uncle Jimmy was satisfactory and moving. His audience was not "spell-bound," for they moved up to Hamp's head-quarters with a "double-quick step"; the "bar'l" was tapped, "Famus or no Famus," by the generous Hamp, who never reproached them for their severe accusations. Soon the condemned barrel was emptied, the money was in Hamp's pocket, and he was merry as "Gingy-cake Josh."

Uncle Jimmy soon began to sing his Revolutionary ditties, spin his yarns, and was happy enough. Cap'en Moore, "leftenant" and "sargint," soon forgot their hard day's work. The "Litia" and others fell to discussing questions of great moment; but the whole affair ended in skinned noses, gouged eyes, and bruised heads. That was a *Famus* day in the annals of "Shipp's Muster-Ground."

Larkin Snow, the Miller

Larkin Snow was doomed to be a miller. I have ever believed that a man will fill the station for which he was designed by the Sovereign Master Overseer of mankind. Though Providence designs a man for a certain position, natural causes and agencies operate also, and, ere he is aware of it, he is fulfilling his destiny. But I will not moralize; my business is with facts.

Larkin Snow was a graduate — an old stager — in milling when I was a mill-boy; and the last time I heard of him, and no doubt at this present time of writing, he is grinding away at somebody's tub-mill, for he never owned a mill — not he. Over a quarter of a century ago I was a jolly, singing, hoop-pee mill-boy, and carried many a "grice" to William Easley's tub-mill on "Little Fish River," kept by my old friend Larkin Snow. But where am I wandering?

After all, the reader must indulge me a little while I pay a tribute of respect to the numerous tub-mills of my native country, for it does me good to think of them and of my mill-boy days. Who has not been a romping mill-boy?

Well, I love tub-mills, and ever shall, for my grandfather was the father of them in that section.

"But who is your grandfather?"

Never mind. Go and ask Larkin Snow, for he knows every man that ever built a mill, or ever kept one in that mountain territory. His memory is a perfect genealogy of mills and millers. Uncle Billy Lewis built a tub-mill on nearly every mountain branch (and they were numerous) where he could get two or three customers. Uncle Davy Lane, who figures largely in this volume, had a tub-mill on "Moore's Fork," as lazy and slow in its movements as its owner. The truth is, Uncle Davy had the advantage, for "sarpunts" could move him to the speed of electricity, but a "good head of water" made but little difference with his mill. His son "Dave" kept it (said Dave was his daddy's own son), and he and I used to bake "johnny-cakes" to keep from starving while it was grinding my "grice." We ate nearly as fast as it could grind. But my old neighbor, William Easley, had the fastest tub-mill in all that country, on Little Fisher's River, and Larkin Snow was his faithful miller.

Every man has ambition of some kind, and Larkin, though nothing but a humble miller who gloried in his calling, had his share, and a good one too, of ambition. His ambition consisted in being the best miller in the land, and in being *number one* in big story-telling. He had several competitors, as may be seen from these sketches, but he held his own with them all, even with Uncle Davy Lane. The reader will judge best, however, when he reads the stories given as samples of Larkin's gift in that line. Larkin must pardon us, should he ever see these pages, for giving but two of his fine stories, that of the eels and the fox-dog. These stories will do him ample justice.

Larkin Snow was a patient, kind, forbearing-looking man, of

ordinary size. His eyes squinted, and so did his sallow features. His dress was plain: tow and cotton shirt, summer and winter; striped cotton pants in summer, and dressed buckskin ones in winter; no coat in summer, a linsey hunting-shirt in winter. His hat was wool, turned up all round, gummed up with meal, and so was his entire suit. His looks were wholly unambitious — strange that he should ever strive to excel in big story-telling. But looks sometimes deceive one, and we will let Larkin speak for himself in the

STORY OF THE EELS.

"Now, you see, while I were keepin' Mr. Easley's mill," said Larkin, squinting his eyes and features, showing the remains of his little round teeth, nearly worn to the gums chewing tobacco, "I planted me a track patch near the bank uv the river, jist below the mill-dam. I knowed I could work it at odd spells, while the water were low and the mill ran slow, and I jist filled it with all sorts o' things and notions. But as all on us, the old Quilt (his wife), childering, and all, was mighty fond o' peas, I were mighty pertic'ler to plant a mighty good share uv them; and to make a bully crap o' Crowders and all other sorts o' peas uver hearn on, I pitched them in the best spot uv the little bit uv yeth near the river, clost on the bank.

"We, the old Quilt and I, spilt sevrul galluns uv humin grease workin' on 'um, and they growed monstus nice. We was a-congratterlatin' ourselves on the monstus crap we'd make, when we seed suthin kept crappin' 'um, pertic'ler right on the bank uv the river. Uvry mornin' it was wuss and wuss. I soon seen the thing would be out wi' my peas ef thar warn't a stop put to it, fur thar wouldn't a bin a Crowder to sweeten our teeth with. I kept watchin' and watchin', but couldn't make the least 'scuvry. The fence were allers up good, the gate shot, and not the track of varmunts could be seen nur smelt, har nur hide. I were mighty low down in the mouth, I tell you. Starvation huv in sight; my sallet were meltin' away mighty fast.

"I were so mightily taken down 'bout it I couldn't sleep a wink; so I thort I mout as well watch. I sneaked along down to the bank uv the river through my pea-patch.

"The moon were shinin' mighty bright, and what do you think I seen? I seen 'bout five hundred big maulbustin eels dart into the river out'n my pea-patch. I soon seen through the dreadful 'vastation uv my black-eyed Crowders; the pesky eels had done it."

"Dang it, Larkin," said Dick Snow, "whar did sich a gullbustin chance uv eels cum from?"

"Eels, you see," continued Larkin, "ef you knowed the natur on 'um, are mighty creeturs to travel, and they'd cum up — a host on 'um —

fur as the mill-dam, and couldn't git no furder. They had to live, and they'd cotched uvry minner, and had eat up uvry thing in the river about thar, and they moseyed out on my pea-patch.

"Now I warn't fur from lettin' them eat up my crap, so I put on my studyin' cap to find out the best plan to make a smash uv the whole bilin' on 'um. I soon hit the nail on the head, and fixed on the plan.

"You see thar were but one place whar they could git out'n the river inter my patch uv Crowders, and that were a narrer place, 'bout three foot wide, that crossed the river. I knowed it warn't wuth while to try to hold the creeters, they was so slickery; so, you see, I sot a big, whoppin bar'l near the river whar they cum out, near thar path. I told the old Quilt to fill it full uv dry ashes durin' the day while I were grindin', which she done, fur the old creetur thought a mighty sight uv her pea-patch.

"Now when night cum on, and a dark one too — a good night fur eels to graze, and when I thort all on 'um was out a-grazin', I sneaked along by the bank uv the river, mighty sly, I tell you, till I got to the bar'l. I then listened, and hearn 'um makin' the peas wake; so I jist turned the bar'l over right smack in thar path, and filled it chug full uv the dry ashes fur ten steps, I reckon. I then went up in the patch above 'um, gin a keen holler, and away they went, scootin' fur the river. You nuver hearn sich a rippin' and clatteration afore, I reckon. I knowed I had 'um; so, you see, I called fur a torchlight to see my luck. Now when the old Quilt and the childering brought the light, hallaluyer! what a sight. Sich a pile on 'um, all workin' up together in the dry ashes, like maggits in carron. The ashes were the very thing fur 'um, fur they soon gin up the ghost.

"I soon, you see, 'cided what to do with 'um. We went to work and tuck out'n the ashes five hundred and forty-nine, some uv 'um master eels. All the next day we was a-skinnin', cleanin', and barrelin' on 'um up. They'd got fat out'n my peas, but we got good pay out'n 'um fur it. The fryin-pan stunk fur months with fat eels, and we all got fat and sassy. So I were troubled no more with eels that year; fur I think, you see, we shucked out the whole river." . . .

Ham Rachel, of Alabama

Eufaula, Barbour County, Alabama, is a beautiful city, on the banks of the deep-channeled and rapid Chattahoochee, and in 1845, the time of the incidents of my story, was the mart of commerce for

Barbour, Pike, Coffee, Dale, and Henry counties in Alabama, and of several counties contiguous in Georgia.

These Alabama counties were mostly settled by a poor, plain, hardy, robust, and honest people, many of them wholly uneducated. All they cared for was "to make buckle and tongue meet" by raising stock, a few bales of cotton, and a little corn for bread. Stock — cow stock — being the chief commodity, they were denominated "cow counties."

Now, mind, these were the *first* settlers. Eufaula was a great city with them, like Paris, London, and New York to most folks. When a "squatter," as some naughtily called them, carried his one, two, or three bales to market in Eufaula, the "ole 'omun" must needs go, and maybe one or two of the "childering," to see the "big town." Hence you could see the ox-carts coming in, the "ole man" driving, and the "ole 'omun" sitting on the top of the one, two, or three bales, and the "childering" walking. The "ole 'omun" has brought with her several extra matters for sale: butter, eggs, socks, etc. Then for shopping after the "cotting" was sold. Hundreds of little notions must be bought, not forgetting a jug, at least, of the "good critter," for "ailments and sich things."

Of course Eufaula exerted a great influence over these counties in all things, particularly in politics. As the town went in politics, so did the country. Their favorite merchants were their oracles in these matters.

To illustrate:

I was in Eufaula in 1848, shortly after the candidates for the presidency, Cass and Taylor, were nominated. I was in the storehouse of Mr. G——, a Whig, when there came in one of the "sovereigns," a Democrat, a tall, stoop-shouldered, sallow-faced, meek, quiet, teachable-looking man, with copperas "britches" (no mistake), and a home-made cotton shirt, constituting his entire dress. His copperas was "gallused" up as high as his fork would admit, which nearly lifted him off the ground. His rustic looks and movements would have attracted the attention of the most unobserving man on earth. Mr. G. gave him a seat, which he accepted, and sat down characteristically. When seated, he looked to Mr. G. with looks indicating, "Speak, for thy servant heareth. I am as a young bird; cram anything down me you choose."

After drawing a long breath or two in a peculiar way, he said,

"What do the people say about here in regard of the nomination for pres*ident*, Mr. G.?"

Mr. G. We are all for Taylor; we know him; he has fought our battles; he is one of the people; if he were to come to your cabin, he would be at home, drink buttermilk, eat bread and butter and yam potatoes with you. As to General Cass, he's been doing nothing all his life but scooting canoes up and down the Western waters, and knows nothing about statesmanship. Taylor is the man for the people; he'll be elected sure.

COPPERAS. Yes, I've hearn ov Ginral Taylor; he has fout the Maxicans, and licked 'um all up, like a cow licks up salt, and has kivered the nation with glory, like a bedquilt kivers a bed; but as to this man, Cass, I nuver hearn ov him afore. I didn't know thar was sich a man treadin' sole-leather.

If Mr. Copperas did not see a merchant who was a Democrat before he left, he certainly voted for Taylor.

These things premised, it was my "manifest destiny" to spend a night in Barbour County in 1845, I believe — a night never to be forgotten. It was on the main road between Clayton, the county seat, and Eufaula, the mart of commerce. A little while before sundown I called at a very good-looking house, and requested to stay all night as a traveler. Permission was granted by the lady of the house. I saw no man. I soon learned that John M'D—— resided there, who had gone that day to Eufaula, and would soon return. I congratulated myself on my good fortune in getting to a quiet, good house, where I could take a refreshing night's rest. But alas! to moralize a little, how soon are our best, most sanguine hopes blasted! A man knoweth not what a *night* may bring forth, as well as a day.

I seated myself in the portico facing the public road, got hold of an old newspaper, almanac, or something of the kind, with which to amuse myself a little, but it was not long before I saw some half dozen wagons coming from toward Eufaula. They halted at the gate, came in with great freedom and boldness, drew water from the well, and watered their teams, as though it belonged to them, interspersing their labors with waggish remarks and blasphemy, not even respecting the presence of the lady, Mrs. M'D——. They then commenced popping their whips about in the yard loud enough to shock the nerves of nervous people, and then asked the lady if she "mout have some chickens fur sale. We hain't bin eatin' nothin' but dried beef so long we've wore ur corn-grinders down to the gums, and we want suthin' else by way of change."

"We've none for sale," replied Mrs. M'D——.

"No chickens!" said they. "Thar goes a durned old rooster, old as Mathuzlum, yit we'll buy him ruther than wear out ur teeth on dried beef. Won't you sell him? You've sartinly got uther roosters to sarve and take keer ov yer hens, hain't you?"

How the conference ended I can not tell, for I left, and retreated to another part of the house; but one thing I *do know:* those wagoners camped in the lane near the house.

As night came on I saw that the uneasiness of Mrs. M'D—— increased. She would go to the door and look toward Eufaula, uttering many nervous sighs. I suspected the cause, though I did not know that her husband loved "sperrits." Some time during the night I heard a crowd coming in at the gate. One peculiar voice, in short sentences, kept up a continual din, upbraiding and cursing "ole John fur gittin so *on*gentlemanly dog drunk." Soon as the lady heard *that,* she understood it, and covered her face in her hands and sighed deeply. Then came the clambering of five or six men in at the door, no one speaking but that reproachful sententious voice.

I left and went into another room. Soon that tormenting voice, which I soon learned was Ham Rachel's, sang out,

"Here, boys, put the ole drunkard fool in the bed. Ef Ham Rachel hadn't a brought him home, he'd a now a bin a-lyin' in the streets ov Eufauly, ur lyin' along the road, a-keepin' company with hogs. The ole cuss, he nuver can go to Eufauly 'thout gittin' full as a bee on chamber-lye, though Ham Rachel is allers 'zortin' him like a preacher not to fill his cussed guts so full. Here, Mrs. M'D——," addressing himself to the lady, "here is yer old, poor, unfortinate husband, which Ham Rachel has had the goodness to fetch home so offen agin and agin. The Lord on'y knows how offen Ham will have ter fetch him home yit. Some ov these times, when Ham Rachel ain't about, ole Nick will git him, and will pour hot lead down his cussed throat instid o' liquor. Ham won't go down to ole Nick's deadnin to see ter him," etc., etc.

Thus went on Ham Rachel almost endlessly. All the difference I could see was "ole John" was "a few" the drunkest "Injun" in the crowd that accompanied him home.

I saw I was caught in a bad box, and resolved to make the best of it. My course was soon determined upon; I would have nothing to do with the crowd, and would have nothing to say to them; I would keep my own room. With this resolution I went to the table. "Ole John's" attendants *must* have their suppers; they were entitled to it, for they had brought the old man home. Ham Rachel, being "chief cook and bottle-washer" of the crowd, must, of course, have his supper.

After grace was said, "God bless us and ur vittuls," Ham acting parson, being all hungry, we attacked the table with great energy. At the first assault there was no politeness displayed in helping each other. Ham generalized thus:

"Ev'ry man fur hisself, and God for all. Help yerself, stranger; you look like you mout be a man what can weed yer own row, clean at that. I dun-no whar yer live, but down here in these piny woods uvry man waits on hisself."

Nothing more was said till the edge of our appetites was blunted; but Ham all the time kept casting his inquisitive, restless eyes upon me, trying to read me like a book. At last he grew a little polite, and handed me a plate of fried yam potatoes.

"Take some 'taters, stranger; mighty plenty down here in these sand-hills. The on'y adjections Ham Rachel has to 'um, they make him a little too cholicified; but a little number six will bring the wind from you with a dreadful racket. My old 'omun allers uses yerbs, but yerbs ain't strong enough fur Ham Rachel."

On we went with our heavy assaults upon the table, demolishing whole dishes, "smitin' them with the aige ov the soord," as Ham expressed it.

"Stranger," said Ham, "take some butter; that's half ur livin' in this cattle country. It would be mighty tight times with us here ef it warn't fur milk and butter, cow-peas and yam 'taters. We'd look like the peaked eend uv nothin'; though the murrin's bin mighty bad among cattle lately; but Ham Rachel has great reasons to be thankful, fur he hain't lost more'n twenty-five ur thirty head, big and little."

We "swept the platter," and supper ended. I went to my room, determined to maintain my dignity and secrecy, hard as Ham was trying to read me. Ham followed, determined to take me prisoner, read my history, and get my whereabouts, latitude and longitude. We sat down; I purposely looked mum and dignified. Ham's curiosity was aroused; he could bear it no longer.

"Stranger," said he, "you're too durned stiff and pertic'ler. Ham Rachel loves fur a man to be as plain as an old shoe, and as thick as cow-peas in thar hull. I've got to know suthin' about yer. When Ham Rachel (I wish you knowed him) begins a thing, he carries it through, ur breaks the swingletree."

This was prefatory; here comes the main attack:

HAM. Ef I mout be so bold, whar do you live, stranger?

STRANGER. I "mout" live in New York, New Orleans, Mobile, or Montgomery, or anywhere else. *That's my business.*

HAM. By golly! that's durned smart. But, stranger, that answer don't co-robber-rate to yer looks. That ain't you. Ham Rachel won't answer a stranger that a-way. But I'll try yer agin, sence ye'r so ding snappish on that pint. Ef I mout be so bold, what sort o' biz'ness do yer foller, stranger?

STRANGER. That's too bold; but since you must know, it is my "biz'ness" to follow my nose — a pretty long one at that, you see.

HAM. Wusser and wusser. Durn it, I'll drap you. You're as snappish as a par o' sheep-shears.

Ham left, and went to the camp of the wagoners, who all the time had kept up every variety of noise, laughter, and vulgar witticisms. He had gone but a few minutes when "ole John" became very sick, and commenced throwing up his "rot-gut whisky." The throes were terribly painful; a human Vesuvius was in dreadful volcanic action. At every throe the lava would fall upon the floor like a dashing cataract, accompanied with deep-toned groans. As the action in the crater went on in rapid succession, it deepened and widened, and the streams of lava became more overwhelming and noisy. The bed creaked loudly, and every eruption looked as if it would throw him head foremost out of his resting-place.

Ham heard the noise of the volcano, and thought he would now lead the stranger out in conversation. He came running into my room with gestures the most wild and frantic, and burst forth:

"Stranger! stranger! do yer hear that ole devil pukin' out his innards? I wouldn't keer a dried-apple durn ef he would puke hisself inside outurds. He nuver will listen ter Ham Rachel, which nuver was cotch in sich a fix. Ham drinks his dram and pays his bob in all licker crowds, but he allers travels and keeps what he 'posits in his innards. He loves licker too well to be throwin' it away like ole John; besides, he's too savin' a man ter be wastin' his vittuls in that a-way. He may puke up his stockin's afore I'll go a-near him. Poor Miss M'D——! She'd no biz'ness a-marryin' — a 'omun ov her age — marryin' sich a dried-up ole cracklin'."

I still maintained my gravity, and Ham left and went to the noisy wagoners, who kept up their infernal din. The rest of the company — four — who came home with "ole John" and Ham, had lain down on pallets, and were running against each other in the snoring line as if some great prize were staked. No renowned artist, graphic pen, nor gifted music composer can describe the struggles and contests of these four rival snorers; of course, I shall not attempt it.

Before Ham left he gave them a blast thus:

"What the devil are you arter here? a-sawin' gourds, grindin' coffee, filin' saws, beatin' tin pans, blowin' horns, beatin' drums, blowin' fifes, shootin' pistols, and so forth, and so forth, breakin' the stranger ov his rest? I'd have a little breedin'."

I lay down about midnight, exposed to the cross-fire of three discordant batteries — the snorers, the wagoners, and the groanings of "ole John" — my nerves being none the better for the contiguity. I dozed a little, but was soon roused by a new sound. It was at the

wagoners' camp. It was the voice, tones, and intonations of a Hard-
shell Baptist preacher. The old "heavenly tone" rang loudly "in the
stilly night." It had the suck-in and the blow-out of the breath, the
uh! and the *ah!*

What! thought I, has some Greatheart of a preacher found those
scapegraces and commenced a thundering sermon upon them? "Give
it to them thick and heavy," said I to myself.

I was not long in suspense, for here came Ham running into the
room (a dim light was burning), puffing and blowing, with eyes and
hands upturned toward heaven with holy horror and indignation.

"Stranger! stranger! O stranger!" he shouted, "do you hear that?
That's no preacher, stranger; they're on'y a-mockin' preachin'.
They're mockin' old Eldridge, who used ter hold forth in these
deadnins, but ran away and went to Texas. Afore he run away
he baptized these very rascals who is a-mockin' him. Ham Rachel
seen it with these peepers o' his, and what he sees he sees. I've
hearn 'um shout, sing hymns and sperritul songs with ole Eldridge. Durn ole Eldridge! (Lord forgive Ham!), he's no better nur
them, but that's no reason fur them to make fun o' religion. Ham
Rachel (poor devil!) is no better nur he ought to be; but, thanks ter
Jubiter, he nuver made fun o' religion. Lord a massy on us,
stranger! do yer hear 'um at it yit? I'm afeered the yeth will open
her bow*ills* and swaller 'um up, like it done Korum, Datum, and
Byhum in the willerness. Ham Rachel's not a-gwine a-near 'um
agin this night. Ham don't intend to be revolved in thar drefful
catistrough; he'll fly up to roost right here."

Down he lay on one of the pallets, and was soon contending for the
prize among the snorers. About this time the preacher at the camp
ended his services, and all went to sleep and to snoring except "ole
John" and myself. "Ole John" kept up a groaning all night.

In the morning we were all a stupid set — scarcely had energy to
wash dirty hands and faces — until the jugs were resorted to. "Ole
John" and I fared the worst: he was too sick to drink, and I was
a rigid teetotaller.

Breakfast came on. The attack on the table was feeble compared
with the assault the evening before. On leaving, all were "dead-
heads" except myself. The rest had paid their way by bringing "ole
John" home. I paid my "fare" and left, but not alone. Not I. It has
ever been my destiny, if there is a bore in reach, he will find *me,*
and cling to me like one's shadow.

While paying my bill, Ham shouldered his two jugs and prepared
for traveling.

"Stranger," he said, "the roads forks jist down yender; one goes to Eufauly, and t'other by Ham Rachel's. As Ham's a-gwine home, he'll go that fur with yer, and show yer the right road."

Suiting action to words, off he "piked" for the gate. I mounted my horse, which had fared better than his master, and on we went, Ham all the way letting fly a diarrhoea of words and sentences, till we arrived at the "fork" of Ham's road. Ham halted. I then took a good parting look at him. There he stood, a lean, gaunt-looking specimen of freakish humanity, about five feet eight inches high, stoop-shouldered, long-armed, and knock-kneed, with a peaked dish face, little black restless eyes, long keen nose, and big ears. His dress was cotton pants, dyed black with copperas and maple bark, a coarse cotton shirt, collar large and open, no vest, coat, nor socks. His hat was old, broad-brimmed, and slouched down over his shoulders behind, and turned up before. His pants were "gallused" to their utmost capacity, leaving considerable space between his knees and the tops of his old brogan shoes; not having on "drawers," of course the skin was exposed. His two jugs were part of his dress. They hung across his shoulders, before and behind, suspended to a wide black greasy leather strap, nearly down to his knees before and his calves behind. Thus this strange figure stood before me, independent as a wood-sawyer, and made his parting speech:

"Stranger," said Ham, "that's the Eufauly road. But listen" (pointing down the road). "Do yer hear that cow-bell? Thar ain't less nur two hundred cattle arter that bell. That's Ham Rachel's cow-bell, and them's his cattle" (giving me a significant look and wink). "Stranger, give out yer Eufauly trip to-day, and go home with Ham Rachel, and stay a long week. He can treat yer like a king on the best these deadnins affords. Do yer see these jugs? then thar's more in Eufauly. Thar's plenty ov fiddles, gals, and boys 'bout here. I don't know whether ye'r married ur not: no odds; yer wife won't know it, and the gals won't keer a durn. You may sing, pray, dance, drink, ur do any thing else at Ham Rachel's. He's none ov yer hide-bound, long-faced cattle, which strains at gnats and swallers camels, as ole Eldridge — durn him! — allers said in his preachin'. Come, stranger, the world wasn't made in a day — took six, I think — come go wi' me."

"I thank you kindly, sir," I replied. "Your generosity is great; but my business is quite pressing, and I must be going. Good-morning to you, sir; I am much obliged."

"Good-by, stranger," replied Ham. "The Lord be wi' you. You'll find but few sich men in yer travils as Ham Rachel."

Ham took his road and I took mine, and that is the last I have seen or heard of him.

William C. Hall

(c. 1819-c. 1865)

🐾 A native of Yazoo County, Mississippi, William C. Hall attended Transylvania University and then worked on newspapers in New Orleans. His five "Yazoo Sketches" about Mike Hooter appeared first in the New Orleans *Delta* in 1849-1850 and then in the New York *Spirit of the Times.* Hall's Mike Hooter and Henry Clay Lewis's Mik-hootah of "The Indefatigable Bear-Hunter" were both based on the same man, a well-known cotton planter and devout Methodist of Yazoo County. Through the sketches of Hall and Lewis the wealthy and eccentric Michael Hooter of real life became a legendary backwoodsman. In Hall's stories he hunts, drinks, brags, preaches, and swears with extraordinary vitality, but at times he is a comic domestic coward, fearing that his wife "might raise pertickler hell" if he does not get home in time for supper.

TEXT: "How Mike Hooter Came Very Near 'Wolloping' Arch Coony" and "How Sally Hooter Got Snake-Bit" from *Polly Peablossom's Wedding,* ed. T. A. Burke (Philadelphia, 1851).

How Mike Hooter Came Very Near "Wolloping" Arch Coony

In the Yazoo hills, near the town of Satartia, in the good state of Mississippi, there lived, at no distant date, one Mike Hooter, whose hunting and preaching adventures became famous in all the land. Besides being a great bear-hunter, and hard to beat at preaching, Mike professed to be "considerable" of a fighter, and in a regular knock-down-and-drag-out row, was hard to beat.

In order that the world may not remain in darkness as to his doings in this last behalf, and fearing lest there may be no one who entertains for him that particularly warm regard which animates us towards him, we have thought it incumbent on us in evidence of our attachment for the reverend hero, to jot down an incident that lingers in our memory respecting him — bequeathing it as a rich legacy to remotest time. Entertaining such partiality, we may be pardoned for following Mike in one of his most stirring adventures, related in his peculiar and expressive vernacular.

I'm one of the peaceblest fellers, said Mike, that ever trotted on hind legs, and rather than git into er fuss 'bout nothin', I'd let er chap spit on me; but when it comes to rubbin' it in, I always in gen'rally kinder r'ars up an' won't stan' it.

But thar's some fellers up in Yazoo what would rather git into er scrimmage than eat. An' I've seen er few up thar what war so hungry for er fight that they fell away an' got so poor an' thin they had to lean up agin er saplin' to cuss!

That chap Arch Coony, was er few in that line! He was the durndest, rantankerous hoss-fly that ever clum er tree! I tell you what, ef I hadn't er bin thar I wouldn't er b'leeved it. I seed him one day in Satartia, git up from er jug of whiskey when he hadn't drunk morn'n half of it, and leave t'other half to spile, an' go an' pitch into er privit 'spute 'twene two Injuns, (when he didn't care er durn cent which wolloped t'other), an' lamin both on um out'n ther mockasins!

Well, you see, Arch was mighty fond of them kinder tricks, an' ef he seed er feller he thought he could lamm without no danger, he wouldn't make no bones, but he'd jest go up to the chap and make faces at him, and harry his feelings er bit, an' ef the feller showed spunky-like, he'd let him alone, an' ax him to take er drink; but ef he sorter tried to sidle out of it, Arch would git as mad as all wrath, an' sw'ar, an' cuss, an' r'ar, an' charge like er ram at er gate-post, and the fust thing you know'd he'd shuck off his coat, an' when the feller warn't 'spectin' nuthin', Arch would fetch him er side-wipe on the head, and knock him into the middle o' next week!

You see I ln't like them sorter doins much, me, myself, I didn't, an' I all'ays cr ever I got er chance at Arch I'd let him down er button-hole er two. He was gettin' too high up in the pictures enny how, an' sez I, one day, in er crowd; sez I, "ef that feller Arch Coony don't mind which side of his bread's buttered, I'll git hold of him one of these days, an' I'll make him see sites!" Well, you see, thar was two or three sheep-stealin' chaps listenin' to what I sed, an' they goes an' tells Arch the fust chance I got, I was gwine to larrup him. Well, that riled him like all fury, an' soon as he hearn it, he begin er cussin' like wrath, and sez he, "dod rot that ole Mike Hooter! — he pertend to be er preacher! — his preachin' ain't nuthin' but loud hollerin' no how!" So you see, them same chaps, they comes an' tells me what Arch had sed, an' I got mad, too, an' we had the durndest rumpus in the neighbourhood you ever hearn!

I didn't see nuthin' of Arch from that time till about er month.

Every time I went down to Satartia to buy enything — er barrel of whiskey, or backer, or such like truck, for privit use — I looked for Arch, and Arch he looked for me, but, somehow or 'tother, he never crossed my path. At last, one day I sent him word I believed he was skeer'd of me, and the fust chance I got I'd take the starch out'n him as sure as shooting; and he sent word back to me that was a game two could play at, and when I wanted to try it, he'd see if he couldn't help me.

Well, things went on that way for er long time, and I didn't see nothin' of Arch; so I begin to forget all about him. At last, one day, when me and two or three other chaps was gwine down to Big Black River, to go bar hunting on t'other side of it, I hearn the darndest clatter-wacking and noise in the road behind us, and when I turned round to see what in the name of thunder it was, thar was Arch an' er whole lot of fellers cummin' down the road, er galloping full tilt right up to us, an' er gwine bar huntin' too.

When I seed him, I was so mad I thought I should er burst right wide open! I was hot, I tell you, and sez I to myself, Now Mr. Arch, I've got you, and if you don't keep your eye skin'd, I'll lick you till your hide won't hold shucks.

Toreckly, Arch he cum up along side, and looked me right plum in the face as savage as er meet axe! and, sez he, "Good mornin', ole Preach! — give us your paw!"

I see thar was hell in him as big as er meetin' house, and I 'termined to give him as good as he sent; so I looked at him sorter servagerous like, and, sez I, "Look here, hoss, how can you have the face to talk to me, arter saying what you sed?"

"Why," sez he, "Uncle Mike, didn't you begin it?"

"No," sez I, "an' ef you sez I begun it, I'll larrup you in er inch of your life!"

Sez he, "You eternal ole cuss, ef you want to larrup me, just larrup away as soon as you darn please, and we'll see which 'ell git the wust of it!"

"Now," sez I, "I likes you, Arch, 'cause I all'ays thought you was a fust-rate feller; but ain't you been 'busin' me every war fur evry thing you could think of?"

"Yes," sez he, "but didn't you say you'd git holt of me one of these days and make me see sites?"

"No," sez I, "I didn't; but this here's what I sed," sez I, "ef that feller Arch Coony *don't mind which side of his bread's buttered,* I'll git holt of him one of these day and make him see sites!"

"Well," sez he, "Uncle Mike, you knows I'm the most peaceablest feller living, and always minds which side of my bread's buttered, and ef that is all you sed 'taint nothin' — so let's take er drink!"

Then he tuck out er tickler of whisky, and arter he'd tuck three er four swallers out'n it, sez he, "Uncle Mike, obleege me by taking er horn!"

"No," sez I, "I won't do no sich er dog on thing, for when I likes a chap I likes him, and when I don't like him, I don't like him; but if you wants to fight, I'm your man."

You oughter seen Arch then! I think he was the most maddest man that ever wobbled on two 'hind legs! He r'ard an' pitched, and cussed, an' swore, 'tell you'd er thought the day of judgmen' was at hand!

When I see him cuttin up that way, I commence' getting mad, too, an' my knees, they begin to shake, sorter like I had er chill; an' —— Skeer'd — no, sir! — an' I sposed thar was gwine to be the devil to pay! I give you my word. I ain't bin so wrathy afore but once since, an' that was t'other day when Mat Cain, the blacksmith, drunk up my last bottle of "ball-face," an' when I 'tacked him 'bout it, sed he thought it was milk.

But that ain't neither here nor thar. As I was a sayin', Arch, he cussed at me, an' I cussed at him, an' the fellers what was along with me sed I beat him all holler!

Toreckly I begin to get tired of jawin' away so much, an' sez I, "Arch, what's the use of makin sich er allfired racket 'bout nothin'? Spose we make it up!"

"Good as wheat," sez he.

"Well," sez I, "give us your paw," sez I, "but," sez I, "thar's one thing you sed what sorter sticks in my craw yit, an' ef you don't pollogise, I'll wollop you for it right now!"

"What does yow mean?" sez he.

Sez I, "Didn't you sed one day that my preachin' warn't nuthin' but loud hollerin'?"

"Yes," sez he, "but didn't you send me word one time that you b'lieved I was skeered of you, an' the fust chance you got, you'd take the starch out'n me as sure as er gun?"

Sez I, "Yes, but what does that signify?"

"Well," sez he, "ef you'll take back what you sed, I'll take back what I sed."

Then I begin to get as mad as all wrath; an' sez I, "You eternal sheep-stealin', whisky-drinkin', nigger-lammin', bow-legged, taller-faced son of er —— never mind what — does you want me to tell er lie by chawin up my own words? Ef that's what's you're arter, jest come on, an' I'll larrup you tell your mammy won't know you from a pile of sassage meat."

So we kep er ridin' on an' er cussin one another worse than two

Choctaw Injuns, an' toreckly we cum to the ferry-boat whar we had to cross the river. Soon as we got thar, Arch he hopped down off'n his ole hoss, an' commenced shuckin' his self fur er fight, an' I jumped down, too. I see the devil was in him as big as er bull, so I begin grittin' my teeth, an' lookin' at him as spunky as er Dominicker rooster; an' now, sez I, "Mister Arch Coony, I sed I'd make you see sites, an' the fust thing you know, I'll show em to you!" Then I pulled off my ole Sunday-go-to-meetin' coat, an' slammed it down on er stump, an', sez I, "Lay thar, ole Methodist, till I learn this coon some sense!"

I soon see thar was gwine to be the bustinest fight that ever was; so I rolled up my sleeves, an' Arch rolled up his'n, and we was gwine at it reg'lar.

"Now," sez he, "ole pra'r meet'n, pitch in!"

Well, I jist begin sidelin' up, an he begin sidelin' up, an soon as I got close nuff to him, so as I could hit him a jo-darter, sez he, "Hole on er minit — this ground's too rooty — wait till I clear the sticks away from here, so as I can have a far chance to give it to you good!"

"Don't holler till you're out'n the woods," says I, "p'raps when I'm done with you, you won't say my preachin' ain't nuthin but loud hollerin', I *spec!*"

When he'd done scrapin' off the groun', it looked jest like two bulls had bin thar, pawin' up the dirt — I give you my word it did.

Well, as I sed before, he sidled up and I sidled up, "an' now," sez I, "look out for your bread-basket, ole stud, fur ef I happen to give you er jolt thar, p'raps it'll turn your stomach."

So thar we stood, head and tale up, jest like two chicken cocks in layin' time; an', sez I to him, "Arch, I'm gwine to maul you tell you won't know yerself!"

Soon as we got close 'nuff, an' I see he was erbout to make er lunge at me, sez I, "Hole on, dod drot you! wait till I unbutton my gallowses, an' may-be-so, then I'll show you them sites what we was talkin' 'bout!"

Well, all the fellers was stanin' roun' ready to take sides in the fight, an' toreckly the chap what kep the ferry, he 'gin to get tired of keepin' the ferry-boat waitin', an sez he, "Cuss your pictures, I'm not gwine to keep this here boat waitin' no longer, an' people on t'other side waitin' to get over; so, ef you wants to fight, you come over on t'other side an' fight thar!"

"Good as ole wheat," sez I; "ennything to keep peace away — ef you say so; lets get in the boat and settle it over thar." Well, they all agreed to that without sayin' er word, an' Arch, he got into the ferry-boat, and all the fellers they follered. When the boat was 'bout pushin' off, I jumped into the eend of it, an' was gwine to lead my hoss on too, but the all-fired critter was skeer'd to jump on to it, and sez I to the man what kept the ferry, sez I, "Why in the h—ll don't you wait till I gets this durned four-legged critter into the boat?" He didn't wait to say er word, but kep shovein' the boat out, and toreckly my hoss begin pullin' back with the bridle, an' I er holein on to it, an' the fust thing I know'd I went kerswash into the drink! So you see, in er bout er minit thar was I, on this side of the river, an' thar was Arch on t'other side, an' no chance for me to git at him. I tell you what, I was hot then! — an' what was worser, Arch he holler'd out an' sed he b'lieved I'd skeer'd the hoss an' made him pull back on purpose to git out'n the scrape. When I hearn him say that, I was so mad I farly biled!

Hows'ever, I soon see 'twarn't no use raisin' er racket 'bout what couldn't be helped, so I 'cluded I'd have my satisfaction out'n him enny way, an' I begin shakin' my fist at him, an' er cussin' him. Sez I, "You eternal, yaller-faced, pisen-mouthed, suck-egg son of er ——! what is it you ain't mean 'nuff for me to call you?" I tell you what (an' I hope to be forgive for swarin') I cussed him blue!

Well, I was so outdone I didn't wait for the boat to come back, for it was gittin' most night, an' too late for bar huntin' that day — 'sides, my wife she would be 'spectin' me at the house, an' might raise pertickler h—ll if I didn't git thar in time; so I jumped on my ole hoss an' put for home. But the way I cussed and 'bused Arch when I got on that hoss, was er sin! — an' the further I got away from him the louder I hollered! I pledge you my word, you might er hearn me er mile!

To make a long story short, the last word I sed to him, sez I, "Arch, you've 'scaped me this time by er axident, but the next time you cross my path, I'll larrup you worse nor the devil beatin' tan-bark! — I will, by hokey!"

Whew! whistled Mike, drawing a long breath. I tell you what, I come the nearest wollopin' that feller, not to do it, that ever you saw!

At this point Mike donned his coon-skin cap, and giving it a terrific *slam,* that brought it over his eyes, vanished!

How Sally Hooter Got Snake-Bit

Our old acquaintance, Mike Hooter, made another visit to town last week, and being, as he supposed, beyond the hearing of his brethren in the church, (for be it remembered, that Mike is of pious inclining, and a ruling elder in the denomination of Methodists), concluded that he would go on a "bust." Having sold his crop of cotton and fobbed the "tin," forth sallied Mike with a "pocket full of rocks," and bent on a bit of a spree. After patronizing all the groceries, and getting rather mellow, he grew garrulous in the extreme, and forthwith began to expatiate on his wonderful exploits. After running through with a number of "Pant'er and Bar fights," and several "wolf disputes," he finally subsided into the recital of events more nearly appertaining to members of his family. "That Yazoo," said Mike, "is the durndest hole that ever came along. If it ain't the next place to no whar, you can take my head for er drinkin gourd — you can, an' as for that ar devil's camp ground, what they calls Satartia, if this world was er kitchen, it would be the slop hole, an' er mighty stinkin one at that! I pledge you my word, it comes closer bein' the jumpin off place than any I ever hearn tell on. Talk about Texas. It ain't nothin' to them Yazoo hills. The etarnalest out-of-the-way place for bar, an' panters, an' wolfs, an' possums, an' coons, an' skeeters, an' nats, an' hoss flies, an' cheegers, an' lizzards, an' frogs, an' mean fellers, an' drinkin' whiskey, an' stealin' one-anothers' hogs, an' gittin' corned, an' swappin' hosses, an' playin' h—ll generally, that ever you did see! Pledge you my word, 'nuff to sink it. An' as for snakes! whew! don't talk! I've hearn tell of the Boa Constructor, an' the Annagander, an' all that kind er ruptile what swollers er he-goat whole, an' don't care er switch uv his tail for his horns; an' I see the preacher tell 'bout Aaron's walkin' stick what turned itself into er sarpent, an' swoller'd up ever-so many other sticks, an' rods, an' bean poles, an' chunks o' wood, an' was hungry yet — an' all that kinder hellerbelloo, but that's all moonshine. Jist wait er minit till you've hearn 'bout the snakes what flourishes up 'bout my stompin' ground, an' how one uv um come precious nigh chawin' up my datter Sal, an' if you don't forgit evrything you ever know'd, then Mike Hooter's the durndest liar that ever straddled a fence rail. Jeeminy, criminy! Jest to see him, one uv them ar great big, rusty rattlesnakes, an' hear him shake that ar tale uv hizzen! I tell you what, if you didn't think all the peas in my corn field was er spillin in the floor, thar ain't no 'simmons! Talk about

the clouds burstin an' the hail rattling down in er tin pan! Why 'taint
er patchin to it! Cracky! its worse nor er young earthquake — beats
h—ll!

"Now, I don't valley er snake no more nor er she bar in suckin
time — 'specially er rattlesnake, cause you see it's er vurmin what
always rattles his tail 'fore he strikes, an' gives you time to scoot out'n
the way, but the wimmin folks an' my gal Sally is always, in generally,
the skeerdest in the world uv' em. I never seed but one woman what
wouldn't cut up when er snake was 'bout, an' that was ole Misses
Lemay, an' she didn't care er dog on bit for all the sarpints that ever
cum er 'long. That old gal was er hoss! Pledge you my word I
b'leeve she was pizen! — couldn't be no other way. Didn't never hear
how that ole petticoat bit the snake? Well, I'll tell you.

"She went out one day an' was er squattin' down, pickin' up
chips, an' the first thing she know'd she got onto the whappinest,
biggest, rustiest yaller moccasin that ever you shuck er stick at, an'
bein' as how she was kinder deaf, she didn't hear him when he 'gin
to puff an' blow, and hiss like. The fust thing she knowed he bit
her, *slap* — the all-firedest, biggest kinder lick! You orter seen that
old gal, how she fell down, an' rolled, an' waller'd, an' tumbled 'bout
and holler'd nuff, an' screamed, an' prayed, an' tried to sing er sam,
and played h—ll generally! You'd er thought the very yearth was
er cummin to an eend! Then she begin hollerin' for help. Sez she,
Misses Hooter, cum here an' kill this here snake! Well, my wife
run out and fotch the old 'oman in the house an' gin her some
whiskey, an' she tuk it like milk. Torectly she sorter cum to herself,
and sez my wife to her — sez she to Misses Lemay, sez she — 'Misses
Lemay, what hurts you?'

" 'Snake-bit!' sez she.

" 'Whar 'bouts?' sez I.

" 'Never mind,' sez she — 'snake bit!'

" 'But Misses Lemay!' sez I, 'tell me whar he bit you, so as we
may put somethin' to it.'

"Sez she, lookin' kinder glum, and turnin' red in the face — sez
she to me, 'It don't want nuthin' to it: I'm snake-bit, an' taint none
er your bizziness whar!'

"With that I smelt a mice, and commenced larfin. You orter hearn
me holler! If I didn't think I'd er bust my biler, I wish I may never
see Christmas! I ain't larfed so much since the time John Potter got
on the bar's back without no knife, an' rode him 'round, like er hoss,
and was skeer'd to get off! I give you my word I farly rolled!

"Soon as the ole 'oman 'gin to open her eyes, an' I see thar warnt
nuthin' much the matter with her, my wife she grabbed up the tongs

an' went out to kill the snake, an' I follered. When I see the reptile, sez I to my wife, 'jest wait er minit,' sez I. ' 'Taint no use killin' him — he's past prayin' for!' I pledge you my word he was as dead as Billy-be-d—d! 'What made him die?' sez my wife to me. 'Don't know,' sez I — ' 'spose he couldn't stand it.' Toreckly Mat Read he cum up, an, when he hearn what had been goin' on, he was so full er larf his face turned wrong side out'ards, and sez he — 'Poisoned, by golly!'

"That ole 'oman ain't been skeer'd uv er snake sense, an' goes out huntin 'em reglar. I told her one day, sez I, 'Misses Lemay,' sez I, 'I'll give you the best bunch of hog's bristles I've got to brush your teeth with, if you'll tell me how not to git skeer'd uv er snake!' She didn't say nare a word, but she turned 'round an' took me kerbim right 'tween the eyes! I tell you what, it made me see stars. I ain't sed snake to her since.

"Howsever, that ain't tellin' you how the sarpint kinder chawed up my darter Sal. I'll tell you how 'twas. You see there was gwine to be a mity big camp meetin' down at Hickory Grove, an' we all fixed up to go down an' stay er week, an' my wife, she looked up everything 'bout the house, an' all sorts of good things — bacon, an' possum fat, an' ash cake, an' a great big sausenger, 'bout as big as your arm, an' long enuff to eat er week — 'cause, she said Parson Dilly loved sausengers the best in the world. Well, when we got there, I went to the basket what had the vittals in it, to git somethin' to eat, but the sausenger wasn't thar, an' sez I to my darter, sez I, 'Sally, gal, what's 'come er that ar sausenger?' Then she turned red in the face, an' sez she, 'Never mind — it's all right.' I smelt that thar war somethin' gwine on wrong — for you see the wimmin folks 'bout where I lives, is h—ll fur new fashions, an' one day one uv them ar all-fired yankee pedlars come er long with er outlandish kind uv er jigamaree to make the wimmin's coat sorter stick out in the t'other eend, an' the she's, they all put on one, case they 'sposed the he's would love to see it. Well, my Sal, she got monsous stuck up 'bout it, an' axed me to giv her one; but I told her she had no more use for one, nor er sittin' hen had for a midwife, an' I wouldn't do no such er thing, case how she was big enough thar at first.

"Well, as I was er sayin', camp meetin' day it came, an' we was all thar, an' the she-folks they was fixed up in er inch uv their lives, an' thar she was er fijjittin, an' er twistin' an' er wriglin about with er new calico coat on, all stuck up at the hind eend, an' as proud as er hee lizzard with two tails! Tell you what — she made more fuss nor er settin' hen with one chicken! I was 'stonished what to make uv that whoppin big lump on behind. Howsever, it was 'simmon time, an' she'd bin eatin er powerful sight uv um, an' I 'sposed she was gittin fat — so I shut up my fly trap, an' lay low an' kep dark! Toreckly the preachin' it begin, an' Parson James, he was up on er log er preachin', an' er goin' it 'hark from the tomb!' I tell you what Brother James was loud that day! Thar he was, with the Bible on er board — stickin 'twene two saplins, an' he was er cummin' down on it with his two fists worse nor maulin rails; an' er stompin his feet, an' er slobberin' at the mouth, an' er cuttin up shines worse nor er bob-tail bull in fly time! I tell you what, ef he *didn't* go it boots that time, I don't know! Torectly I spy the heatherns they commence takin' on, and the sperit it begin to move um, for true — for brother Sturtevant's ole nigger Cain, an' all uv um, they 'gin to kinder groan an' whine, an' feel erbout like er corn stalk in er storm, an brother Gridle, he begin er rubbin his hands an slappin' um together, an' scramblin' about on his knees, an' er cuttin' up like mad! In about er minit, I hearn the all-firedst to do, down 'mongst the wimmin, that ever cum along, and when I kinder cast my eye over that way, I spy my Sal er rarein' and er pitchin', er rippen' an' er tarein' and er shoutin' like flinders! When brother James see that, he thought she'd done got good, an' he cum down off the log, an' sez he, 'Pray on sister!' — an' the she's they all got round her, an' cotch hold uv her, and tried to make her hold still. But 'twarnt no use. The more they told her to 'don't' the more she hollered. Toreckl' I diskiver she'd done got 'ligious, an' I was so glad, it kinder lift me off'n the ground — an' sez I, 'go it Sal! — them's the licks! — blessed am them what seeks, for them's um what shall find!' Then the wimmin they all cotch holt of her by the har, an' commence wollerin' her 'bout in the straw, an' sez I, 'that's right, sisters — beat the Devil out'n her.' And they *did* too! I tell you what — the way they did hustle her about mongst the straw and shucks was forked! In about er minit I 'gin to get tired and disgustified, an' tried to make her shet up, but she wouldn't, but kep a hollerin worser and worser, an' she kinder keeled up like a possum when he makes 'ten he's dead! Toreckly she sorter cum to herself so she could talk, an' sez I, 'Sal, what ails you, gal?' The fust word she sed, sez she, 'Snake!'

" 'Whar 'bouts?' sez I.

" 'Snake,' says she agin — 'sarpent! take it off, or he'll chaw me up be g—d!'

" 'Well!' sez my wife; 'that's cussin!'

" 'Whar's enny snake?' sez I.

" 'Snake!' sez she; 'snake! snake!!' an' then she put her han' on the outside of her coat, an' cotch hold uv somethin, and squeezed it tight as er vice!

"When I seed that, I knowed it was er snake sure nuff, what had crawled up under her coat; an' I see she'd put her hand on the outside uv her clothes, an' cotch it by the head. Soon as I see'd that, I knowed he couldn't bite her, for she helt onto him like grim death to a dead nigger; and I 'cluded 'twarn't no use bein' in too big er hurry; so I told John Potter not to be skeer'd an' go an' grab the sarpent by the tail, and sling him h—llwards! Well, Potter he went and sorter felt uv him on the outside uv her coat, an' I pledge you my word, he was the whappinest biggist reptile that ever scooted across er road! — I tell *you* if he warn't as big as my arm, Mike Hooter is as big er liar as ole Dave Lemay — and you know he's a few in that line! Well, when Potter diskiver that she helt the snake fast, he begin feelin' up for the reptile's tail, sorter like he didn't like to do it at fust, an' then sorter like he did. When it come to that, Sal she kinder turned red in the face and squirmed er bit, but 'twarn' no time for puttin' on quality airs then, and she stood it like er hoss! Well, Potter he kep er feelin' up, an' feelin' an' er feelin' up, sorter easy like, an' toreckly he felt somethin' in his han'. 'I've got him,' sez Potter, 'well I have, by jingo!' 'Hole on to him, Sal,' sez I, 'and don't you do nothin, Mr. Potter, till I give the word, and when I say "go!" then, Sal, you let go uv the varmint's head; and Potter — you give the all-firedest kind on er jerk, and sling him to h—ll and gone!'

"I tell you what, them was squally times! and I vise you, the next time you go up to Yazoo, jest ax enny body, and if they don't say the snakes up in them parts beats creation, then Mike Hooter'll knock under."

At this point of the narration we ventured to ask Mike what became of the snake.

"As I was er sayin'," continued he, "thar was my Sal er holein the sarpent by the head, and John Potter he had him by the tail, and Sal she was er hollerin' and er screamin', an' the wimmin, they was all stannin' round, skeered into er fit, and the durndest row you ever hearn — 'hole on to him, Sal,' sez I; 'and you, John Potter, don't you move er peg till I give the word; and when I say "jerk!" then you sling him into the middle of next week.' I tell you what, we had the orfullest time that ever I see! Let's liquor!

"That's the best red eye I've swallered in er coon's age," said the speaker, after bolting a caulker. "But, how did you manage at last?" asked a listener.

"Well, you see," said he, "thar was my Sal, an' thar was all the folks, and thar was the snake, an' John Potter holein' him by the tail, skeer'd out'n his senses, and h—ll to pay! I was gettin' sorter weak in the knees, I tell you, an' brother James' eyes looked like they'd pop out'n his head, an' sez I to John Potter, sez I to him, sez I, 'John Potter, don't you budge tell I say go! and when I gives the word, then you give him er jerk, and send him kerslap up agin that tree, and perhaps you'll gin him er headache. Now John Potter,' sez I, 'is you ready?' sez I. 'I is,' sez he, 'Now look at me,' sez I, 'and when I drap this handkercher,' sez I, 'then you jerk like flujuns,' sez I. 'Yes,' sez he. Then I turned round to Miss Lester, and sez I, 'Miss Lester, bein' as how I haint got no handkercher, 'spose you let me have that koon-skin cape uv yourn.' Sez she, 'Uncle Mike, you can have enny thing I is got.' ' 'Bliged to you,' sez I, 'and now John Potter,' sez I, 'when I drops this koon-skin cape, then you pull!' 'Yes,' sez he. 'Now,' sez I, 'keep your eye skinned, and look me right plum in the face, and when you see me drap this, then you wallum the sarpent out. Is you ready?' sez I. 'Yes,' sez he. 'Good,' sez I, 'jerk!' an' when I said jerk, he gin the *whoppinest* pull, and sent him kerwhop! about er mile an er feet! I pledge you my word, I thought he'd er pulled the tail of the varmint clean off!''

Here Mike took a quid of tobacco, and proceeded — "I've bin in er heap er scrapes, and seen some of the all-firedest cantakerous snakes that ever cum erlong, but that time beats all!"

"What kind of a snake was it," asked a listener. "I'll tell you," said he — " 'twarnt nuthin more'n I 'spected. Sal thought she'd look big like, an' when she was shoutin' and dancin' er bout, that sausenger what she'd put on for er bustle, got loose round her ankle, and she thought 'twas er snake crawlin' up her clothes!"

Mike left in a hurry.

Francis James Robinson

(c. 1820-c. 1870)

Country doctor, newspaper writer, Georgia county clerk, and humorist, Francis James Robinson led a varied and apparently somewhat troubled existence. Details of his life are few but revealing. His extant letters and his collection of humorous sketches, *Kups of Kauphy* (Athens, Ga., 1853), reflect a restless and fiery personality. Prewar Northern comments on Southern life and institutions so enraged him that he concluded his book with an impassioned plea to be spared further interference: "We claim as a right, guaranteed by the Constitution, to be let alone!" After the war he supported the Republican Party in Georgia, writing for the short-lived Augusta *Daily National Republican,* which helped elect Rufus Bullock governor. Ambitious to become editor and unhappy because some of his more fervid articles had been rejected, he gave vent to his anger in a letter to Bullock in 1868: "I have written article after article that has been suppressed while the mamby-pambyism of Jim Ellis and his plagiarisms go into the paper to fill up space." After explaining that he had been "connected with types and newspapers since . . . a boy of 17," he requested Bullock's support for the editorship. His requests and tempestuous complaints went for nothing, however, and the next year he found himself back in Lexington, Georgia, where he had been elected Ordinary for Oglethorpe County. Even there he encountered difficulties, for the previous ordinary refused to surrender his office to Robinson. More fiery letters went to the governor before the argument was settled.

Robinson's volume of sketches, *Kups of Kauphy,* is a little-known but unusually representative book of Old Southwest humor. In seven stories, Robinson ranges from the tall tale to the Negro humor of "Old Jack C." A professed admirer of Longstreet and Thompson, he recognized the artistic value of the vernacular, explaining in his preface: "Wherever it has been possible we have let our characters use their own language in portraying their *individuality!*" Dialogue thus abounds in most of his sketches. Like other Southern humorists he sought to portray manners realistically and sometimes based his characters on actual people. "Old Jack C." was a famous waiter in Madison, Georgia, and the title of Robinson's book was probably meant to suggest one of the most eccentric and amusing heroes of Oglethorpe County, Governor George Matthews. According to one contemporary writer Governor Matthews always read aloud "with the confidence which accompanied the consciousness of doing a thing very well. He pronounced fully the *l* in *would, should,* and *ed* at the termination of words with a long drawling accent. He spelled coffee thus, *Kauphy.*"

In the two sketches included here Dr. Robinson's medical training is evident. Both include medical terms and doctors or pseudo-doctors. Rance, one of the most accomplished liars in Southern humor, can perform a delicate bone operation involving brilliant surgical innovations. Or he can shoot deer at better than 600 yards with a Colt pistol and then kill twelve Comanche Indians with six bullets. He is one of the first of the Texas braggarts in literature. Lije Benadix is a typical dirt eater, a member of the lowest poor white class. His laziness and gluttony make him fair game. Lije's temporary illness, which so frustrates the attending physician, again illustrates the Southwestern humorist's lack of usual restraints and his tendency to link bodily discomfort with humor.

TEXT: "Lije Benadix" and "Rance Bore-'em" from *Kups of Kauphy: A Georgia Book in Warp and Woof* (Athens, Ga., 1853).

Lije Benadix

In the year 18— there vegetated a specimen of the *genus homo,* in the county of K—— in the glorious old junior State of the original thirteen, about whom we propose to say a few words, and as a description of his *tout ensemble,* manners, etc. will the better elucidate our tale, we will proceed to give our readers a pen and ink sketch of our friend and hero, *Mr. Lije Benadix.* He was, we suppose, some forty years of age — married, and, as a natural consequence, his table was surrounded with many "olive branches." To feed all these mouths, required from *Lije,* pretty hard scratching; though the principal *feeder* seemed to be Lije himself. He was, withal, incorrigibly *lazy* — now with plenty to satisfy the appetite — again without a dust of meal in his larder. In fruit season, he could manage to get his fill of fruits; and when plums and cherries became ripe in May, then Lije, cormorant-like, would gulp them down in large quantities, bolting then *en masse!* It is fair to presume that with his lazy habits, enormous appetite and a generous diet, Lije would have soon become a second Falstaff, but as he did not have the good fortune to possess the last named very important accompaniment, he was gaunt as a grey hound, his skin yellow and wrinkled, features shrunken and extremities diminutive! Upon the whole, an observer would at once pronounce him to be a man unused to a diet sufficiently healthy and nutritive: for upon *ordinary* occasions, with his "copperas mixed" clothes hanging upon him as upon a drying line, the conclusion would also be pretty certainly arrived at, that Lije was either "drying" up, preparatory to flying away, or had his garments made amply large for *extra-ordinary* occasions too. As often as he became possessed of a bushel of meal, in pay for "splitting rails," (the only species of work of any kind he seemed to fancy,) he would lie at home, and himself and family would cook and eat continuously until the last "hoe cake was baked" and eaten; then, perhaps, he would stir around for another job of work. Sometimes the opportunity was afforded him to "provision his ship," as for instance when called to the county seat during the session of the Superior Court. On these occasions "landlord, cook and waiters" suffered; for his usual allowance, to give a specimen, *was thirteen cups of coffee* and other provisions in the same proportion. Once he ventured to call for the *"fourteenth"* cup, when his host could stand it no longer, and ordered him peremptorily to leave the house, telling him he was welcome to what he had eaten.

"Why, Landlord, do let a fellow finish eatin — I aint nigh done yit!" protested Lije.

"Get out of my house, I tell you; for I'd as soon undertake to feed a caravan of animals, with a circus thrown in!"

And poor Lije, *still hungry,* as he protested, and ready to pay for all he ate, was obliged to *vamoose.*

At one time Lije became possessed, by some means, of a large turkey, which he took to a neighboring county seat during the session of the Court there. — This bird he *sold* to the hotel keeper, and as we shall see, also *sold* the purchaser. Lije received, in cash, one dollar, and was to have his dinner in the bargain! The fowl was duly spitted, *secundem artem,* and our host congratulated himself upon this accession to his ordinary supplied table, and thus being able to give his boarders a treat. In the meantime, Lije hung around the hotel, noticing from time to time, the clock, and peering into the dining room to make his observations. Just before the dinner hour he slipped into the dining hall, called a waiter, told him he was in a hurry to go home, and as his master had promised him his dinner, he wanted some of the "Old Gobler." It was set before him, and he attacked it bravely. Not a long while after Court adjourned, and the landlord took occasion to announce a fine fat turkey for dinner, setting all who heard him on the *qui vive.* As soon as the bell rung all rushed to the table; anxious eyes wandered up and down it — while every one called for *turkey!* The landlord, hearing a report of "there's none, massa, lef," pricked up his ears and called out,

"Waiter! what does this mean? Where's that turkey?"

"Him eat up, sir, all but de bone!"

"The d—l! who done it, you rascal? Tell me, or I'll break every bone in your skin!"

"Dat man you bot um from, sir, I spec, for he come a little while ago and tell me you promise 'im his dinner — he was in hurry — and wanted de *turkey!* Dat all I know 'bout um, massa."

"Bring me the dish, sir!"

The dish was brought, and upon it reposed as nice a skeleton as one would wish to see; not a particle left upon the bones that was eatable. At this "visible explanation," the whole table was set in a roar, and the joke being so good a one, each one good-humoredly forgot his disappointment and made the most of the "common doins" before them.

With these specimens of "Lije's" prowess in the eating line, we shall again introduce him to you in another, as the cap-stone of all. There poor Lije lies, stretched on his back, swollen to three times his natural size and laboring under not only indigestion, but the most desperate state of constipation, perhaps, ever attempted to be removed by the medical faculty. It was in the midst of plum and cherry time, and in default of more digestible food, Lije had supplied his larder with a quantity, and had attacked them with his usual voracity and disregard of consequences. Hence his situation; for, like the Anaconda, who upon bolting his occasional meal becomes inert, so Lije had gorged himself until he had become helpless. Contrary to his expectations, his digestive apparatus was insufficient to accomplish the Herculean task thus imposed, and he was placed thereby, completely *hors du combat*, exhibiting a kind of inanimate existence, only. At this particular stage of his case he called in a physician, who, after exerting his skill for some time, gave him up, with the conviction that there was not yet made known in the Pharmacopiæ of Medicine any *emetic* or *purgative* sufficiently powerful to be brought to bear successfully upon the truly appalling case under his care. He, therefore, retreated from the field, leaving poor Lije in the hands of his Creator and to his own natural powers, satisfied that all human means having failed, nothing short of a miraculous intervention would ever restore poor Lije to active life and to the helpless and dependant family around him. His condition was noised abroad and many of Lije's neighbors had called to see him, and among them was a *"Yerb Dokter,"* as he called himself, named *Lobelia,* with the prefix, of course, of "Dockter." This professional gentleman had, however, no idea of trying his skill, not he! but proposed that a messenger should be sent some fifteen miles to an adjoining county to procure the services of a practitioner of extensive practice and long experience

in medicine; who, by the way, was well known in that region, his
practice even extending there usually. As Dr. Lobelia made the
proposition, he was selected as the messenger to Dr. W——, and
there might have been seen the very unusual sight of a "yerb" doctor's
going for an allopathic physician! However, we must charitably suppose that Dr. L—— was actuated by sympathy for suffering humanity, and for once laid aside all his professional prejudice and antipathy
so notoriously known to exist between the one and the other. He
found Dr. W—— worn down with fatigue and unable to return with
him that evening, but received the prescription of a dose of *calomel*
and the promise of a visit next morning. Now, it is very well known
that a mad-dog has no greater antipathy to water than has a "yerb"
doctor to *calomel,* the medicine prescribed; and Dr. Lobelia took
occasion to express his disbelief in its use, and a want of confidence
in it any way!

"Give it to him, sir, as I direct," said Dr. W——, "and it will do
him as much *good* as if *you* had every confidence in it!"

Dr. L—— returned to Lije's that evening, but remaining in the
"same opinion still" in regard to the calomel, did *not* administer the
dose as directed.

The next morning (Monday) by 10 A.M. Dr. W. arrived at the
place. There he found a large number of Lije's neighbors, men and
women, collected in the house and about the yard, discussing his
case pro and con; for it had excited the curiosity of every one, besides interesting many who had kind feelings for him and his family.
Dr. W. entered the house, a small, contracted affair, built of round
logs and covered with oak boards. In *the* room, for we believe the
house contained but a single apartment, on a bed Lije was stretched
on his back, an uninterested witness of all that might be said and
done. The doctor approached his bedside and made the inquiry,

"How do you feel to-day, Mr. Benadix?"

"V-e-r-y p-o-o-r-l-y, d-o-c-t-o-r," replied Lije.

The doctor then proceeded to examine him, and found his symptoms to be these: "pulse slow and rather feeble, without fever, skin
rather cooler than natural, vomiting about every half hour, ejecting
a half pint of a morbid secretion accumulated between the intervals
of vomiting, abdomen enormously distended and as tight as a drum-
head, and tongue but slightly coated." After this examination of the
case was concluded he asked,

"Well, Mr. Benadix, how many plums and cherries have you eaten?"

"Not — very — many — doctor!" replied Lije, in a slow and drawling tone of voice.

"Yes, you did," spoke up his wife quickly, "you eat nearly or quite two pecks, and you eat hulls, stones and all — you did."

"Ah! indeed," remarked Dr. W., "it is very strange that a man of your age, Mr. Benadix, should eat such a quantity of plums and cherries, stones and all! — Now, sir, if you had been an old turkey gobler, you might, with some show of reason, have ate those articles, because, then you would have had a *gizzard* with which to have *ground up* such an indigestible mass!"

His wife hearing this and thinking it necessary that "the truth, the whole truth" of the affair should be made known to the doctor, again spoke up and said,

"Yes, an' you eat a pan full of honey-comb on top of 'em too — you did."

"I-n-d-e-e-d!" remarked the doctor, somewhat tartly, "if you had only ate the pan full of *rich soil* instead of the *honey-comb*, you might very soon have had an orchard and nursery very convenient!"

The doctor was somewhat vexed at the unprecedented imprudence of his patient, and in anticipation of the trouble he would have in consequence; but having received all the information he could, he at once determined to attempt to relieve him if possible. Before leaving home, he had provided himself with all the emetic and purgative medicines, from the simplest to the most powerful known; and, on his way, passing a store, procured a pound or so of tobacco (for enemas) as a *corps de reserve*. He asked and obtained the gratuitous services of a gentleman present as assistant; and to work they both went; commencing with purgatives, they gave him during the day, Castor Oil, Salts and Senna, Salts and Magnesia, Jalap and C. Tartar, Rhubarb and Aloes, Gamboge and Scammony, and Calomel to no purpose, for the stomach would not retain any of them longer than from a half to one hour. *Croton Oil* and a very strong *infusion of Tobacco,* were reserved until towards evening. Continually embarrassed by the ejection of the medicines, but determining not to be backed out, as fast as one dose was ejected another was given, with little regard to quantity, varying the matter occasionally by a simple *enema.* After the day was well nigh spent, and the patient being, (as he very frequently and invariably would say, when asked how he felt) *"about as usual,"* the doctor determined to "charge the enemy" with the "advance guard" of his "reserve forces" in the shape of *Croton Oil* — informing his assistant before he did so, "that it was a powerful drug, and if it could be retained in the stomach one hour he would be hopeful of giving his patient relief, and he would be able to tell in that time what it was capable of accomplishing." So Lije swallowed *two drops!* and the doctor, watch in hand, sat by his bedside to count the moments as they flew, asking his patient at intervals how he felt, and receiving the same unsatisfactory answer of *"about as usual."*

"Do you not feel any effect from the last medicine you have taken?" asked the doctor, Lije being unaware of its name or quality.

"It — burnt — my — throat — a — little!" answered Lije.

The hour passed — an additional half hour — no effect was produced by the Croton Oil — the patient seeming to be *"about as usual!"* Finding the enemy so well fortified, the doctor informed his assistant "that the potent and all powerful 'reserve' must now be resorted to — that tobacco enemas must be used — that the remedy seldom failed to overcome the most obstinate constipation; that at the same time it produced such a relaxation of the system as to give one the appearance of being about to die, and that he (the assistant) must not get alarmed if this should prove to be the fact in Lije's case!" The tobacco had been infused for six hours, and was necessarily very strong; but upon using the *enema* even longer than usual in such cases, the disheartening result was the same as with all the other remedies. For Lije remained still *"about as usual!"* Baffled at all points, the doctor rested awhile from his labors, only, however, to continue the onset with renewed vigor! The sun was now nearly set, and the doctor, before leaving for home, put up a large number of powders, consisting wholly of calomel, about three grains in each, with directions for one to be administered every three hours, day and night, until he saw the case again on the following Wednesday. Before taking his departure, the doctor went to the bedside of his patient to bid him "good-bye," and to speak a few words of hope and encouragement. As he turned towards the door and before reaching it, Lije drawled out the question of

"D-o-c-t-o-r, w-h-a-t s-h-a-l-l I e-a-t?"

Now this was a little more than human nature could put up with, and the doctor turned towards him instinctively and replied,

"Eat! Eat, the d—l! Get what's in you out first, then it will be time enough for you to eat more, sir!" and left him.

Wednesday came and found the doctor, according to promise, at Lije's bed-side, who, he found, upon making inquiry, *"about as usual"* — no better and no worse. He had regularly taken the powders day and night. They were continued, and in addition about the same routine was pursued as on the Monday previous; and after a day's labor with the same result, sundown again finding Lije "about as usual," a large supply of the powders were then made and the same directions given. On this visit the doctor found several of the neighbors at the house, and they were very inquisitive as to the situation of the patient as well as to the kind of "physic" given him. To all the questions put, the doctor cheerfully responded, and was very much amused at the commentaries made. Those who swore at all, swore "he would die in the fix he was in any how, and that if the disease did not *kill* him, the doctor would with all that *calomel!*" Said they: "Why, dod-rot it, he'll be salivated so badly, all his teeth will *drap* out and his jaws be eat off, so ef he does git over it, he never kin eat nothin'. He'd e'nymost be dead, for if Lije loves ennything at all, it's eatin."

"Oh! there's no danger," replied the doctor, "the secretions are all suspended, and he cannot be salivated in the situation he is now in!"

"Dun know so well about that nuther, for Dr. Lobelia sez there's many a man's leg bones full of *quicksilver!*"

"Pooh! pooh! what nonsense — all stuff!" answered the doctor, as he turned away to prepare for his departure.

But they continued the discussion, and one might hear an exclamation occasionally of, "Poor fellow! ef the plums don't kill him, the *doctor* and his *calomy* will!" Upon the doctor asking Lije again how he felt, he gave the invariable reply of *"about as usual."* He left him, and did not repeat his visits, though he heard from time to time how his patient was progressing. The calomel powders were continued regularly up to the *following Saturday evening.*

Four weeks after exactly, the doctor, being on a professional visit in the same region of country, observed in the road ahead of him, not very far from a mill and near the stream upon which it was situated, a thin, tall, gaunt man, who at the distance was not a familiar form to him. The man bore some resemblance to "Lije," but the portly aldermanic rotundity he possessed when lying on his back a few weeks before had all disappeared, and instead, he had become shrivelled and shrunken, lank and lean as usual. On a nearer approach, however, the doctor at once recognized his old patient, and accosted him with,

"How are you, to-day, Mr. Benadix?"

"A-b-o-u-t a-s u-s-u-a-l, d-o-c-t-o-r," replied Lije.

"I am very glad, indeed, sir, to see you about, Mr. Benadix, for at one time, we all thought you were not long for this world, sir! I presume after all our labor and pains, the medicine was effective and relieved you at last, sir?" continued the doctor.

"O, yes, doctor, it commenced about sundown on Saturday evening arter you was thar, and it 'taint done till yit!" answered Lije, as the doctor, unable to contain himself, he was so full of laughter, made off. His resurrected patient lived many years after, and though he still retained the same *"love of eatin',"* he was careful not to try again the powers of his *digestive* apparatus by bolting such another lot of plums and cherries, "seeds, hulls and all!"

Rance Bore-'em

No pent-up *Bar room* could contract his powers,
Nor time nor place — mattered it to *Rance;*
Start *Bore-'em* once, and talk he would for hours!
Awake, asleep, and may be in a trance;
Deeds of great prowess, would he oft relate —
Himself the *Hero* of the battle ground —
The place was Texas: newly made a State! —
And hence, this *second Baron* had been found. — MACHINE.

"Gentlemen, speaking of hunting, when I was in Texas, a parcel of us went out after *deer* one day; some armed with rifles, some with U. S. *yagers,* carrying ounce balls, which would kill at 400 yards — I had a "Colt" only. We soon scared up a flock, and off they went over the prairie — pop went the *rifles* and *yagers,* but not a single deer dropped. I told 'em to stand back and let me try my luck; and if you believe me, gentlemen, *I killed one of 'em* with every barrel, going at full speed! *Six* of 'em fell, and that's not all, I had the curiosity to measure the distance, and I found the nearest to have been just 444 yards off from me, and the farthest one just 600 yards 1 foot and 3 inches! Yes, and when I could get my *mustang* stopped so far as to come up to the slain deer, there I saw a panther to each deer, endeavoring to carry them off. There were six panthers and six deer, and nobody but me about, so I loaded up and every fire down came a panther! When I had finished my work, as I thought, I looked around and about a dozen Camanche Indians were coming towards me at full speed. Thar I was, solitary and alone! You'd better believe I loaded it up quick — but I had only a *six shooter,* and there were twelve Indians! So I waited for 'em, and as they came yelling towards me, I let two of 'em get into a line and *every fire I emptied two saddles!* Phew! but I done some work that morning. Well, I waited awhile for my comrades, but as I found out afterwards, they had got scared at the state of things and ran back to town! So I turned to and caught the six horses first and lassoed them together, then I skinned the deer and panthers, hanging the *peltries* to my saddle horn, and lashed the venison carcases to the horses, wheeled the whole into line and marched them safely home. When I got into town I found ready sale for my booty, pocketed the money, treated the crowd all 'round, and they elected me captain of the beat right away!"

"Yes, I can tell you, gentlemen, a better ice-cream story than that; for when I was in Texas, I once went up to the mountains there, and I found one day in a small cove a cow, and feeling a little dry, I thought I'd get a little milk, so I out with my drinking cup and I assure you, upon the honor of a gentleman, when I tasted it, *I found it was ice-cream already sweetened, and flavor'd with lemon juice!* Fact, every word of it, but I was more astonished when informed by the Texians, that that was no unusual thing in that luxurious country, for the cow had lived upon *snow* upon the mountains all her life, and that it was strongly impregnated with *Lemon,* which, added to the saccharine matter known to exist naturally in *milk,* produced the result I had thus become acquainted with! Considering this cow as a valuable acquisition to a *bar-room,* I went as soon as I could to town; there went into a partnership with a man in the "wet grocery" line, and we hired men and teams to bring the cow and some *snow* for her to feed on, down to town, and there I have no doubt the *same cow is still!* I sold out after a few months, having made money enough from the business! But I heard from the cow not long since, and every morning she gave *"Ice Milk Punch,"* and every evening *"Ice-cream!"* Ah, gentlemen, Texas is a great country — a wonderful country — a magnificent country!"

"Were you speaking of *fishing,* sir? Well, gentlemen, I had some experience in the "art of hooking" when I was in Texas, which I must tell you. Expecting to find large *fish* in the waters of the great State of Texas, as I passed through New Orleans, I had made to order some extra large hooks and a supply of *lines,* such as vessels use in anchoring! The place at which I stopped was near a large river, and the sport promised to be excellent; but it far exceeded my expectations, for we often had to send home for several yoke of oxen to pull out some of the *fish* we hung, and it was sometimes hard work at that! This is a fact, gentlemen, I could get twenty men to testify to — but this is nothing to one *haul* we made, which, if I hadn't seen, no man on earth could have made me believe a moment. We made up a party and prepared a large quantity of *bait* and provision for a several days fish. When we reached the banks of the river, we put in our hooks — those same big ones I had had made in New Orleans — and I think there were *ten* of us fishing close together! All at once we had a bite, every hook was swallowed, and away we pulled, but couldn't move whatever it was; so we carried our lines out and made them fast to a *few small trees* — I suppose none of them *more* than *twenty feet in diameter* — until we could get help. So we sent after and procured *twenty yoke of oxen* — hitched *two yoke to each line,* and with a long pull and a strong pull of men and oxen, up and out came one of the largest kind of Catfish — his mouth being at least ten feet across — out of him we made *fifty barrels of oil,* for which, in N. Orleans, we obtained thirty dollars each, thus making the pretty little sum of fifteen hundred dollars — a nice morning's work, gentlemen. Ah! Texas is a great — a glorious — a grand country to live in — everything *grows* in such plenty and profusion!"

"I am reminded, gentlemen, by what you have just been discussing, of a surgical performance of my own, *when I was in Texas;* and, with your permission, I will relate it to you. I was travelling once from —— to —— and stopped at night at a solitary cabin in the broad and open prairie — there I found a distressed family. The man had been a *Ranger* once, but from exposure and battles with the Indians he had become diseased and almost a perfect wreck. Situated as he was, so far from a medical man, he was unable to get relief. The main lower bone of his right leg and the upper bone of his left arm, from some constitutional cause, I suppose, had become diseased with what the doctors call "caries of the bones." Now, you all know, gentlemen, that that is a disease, which, when it attacks the bones, they become *dead,* and nature endeavors to relieve herself of the incumbrance by throwing them out in scales! I told him I was no doctor, but would warrant a cure in *three days!* He agreed that I should try my skill upon him — so next morning I procured a piece of *young green white oak,* from the nearest woods, some ten miles off, with which I returned to the cabin. I had no tools to work with, save *an old hatchet* and my "Arkansas tooth-pick." Not discouraged or cast down, I went to work, and by night had "fashioned out" my *wooden substitutes* to my entire satisfaction — making as nice a *Humerus* and *Tibia* as one would wish to see, and awaiting but the return of daylight to *extract* the useless and deadened bones and insert them instead! From my knowledge of *anatomy,* gathered from a hasty perusal of a work upon that subject, I was enabled to give the proper *shape* to the body and *articulating* ends of my wooden bones so that there could be no difficulty for want of a perfect fit. After breakfast next day — having given my *"tooth pick"* a preparatory sharpening — I caused the patient to lie down on his back — having given him a pretty stiff horn of "buck-eye" — and baring his left arm, proceeded at once to make a *deep incision,* ranging from the *scapular* to the articulation of the *ulna* and *radius;* having thus laid bare the *bone,* I dissected off the *insertions* of the *tendons* and *muscles,* and with my thumb and index finger easily removed the remaining portions of the bone. You would suppose that considerable blood would flow, but it was not the case; a few small *vessels* were ruptured only, for I had been particularly careful not to damage the larger ones. I then anointed the wooden *substitute* with *bears' grease* — from my own supply of the genuine article made from *bears* of my own killing — inserted it, carefully replacing the ligaments to their proper places, brought the edges of the flesh and skin together, took a few *stitches* with *pack thread,* bathed the parts in Mustang Liniment, which I had sent expressly to the city of Mexico for, bandaged up the limb, *secundem artem,* and allowed the patient a few hours rest! His only exclamation during the whole operation was — *"D—n it, how dull your old knife is!"* Finding that my patient did not evince any symptom of debility, after a due allowance of repose, I proceeded in the same way to treat the *Tibia,* and by sundown my patient was so far easy and comfortable that I consented, upon his application for something to eat, that he might eat a *"corn pone"* and some *"fried bacon"* for his supper — this he did heartily enough. Next morning, after a fine night's rest, he was able to walk about, experiencing no bad effects from my operations the day previous, and only complaining of a *feeling of stiffness* in the *joints,* which wore off as soon as he exercised sufficiently, so as to produce a general warmth over the system. On the *third* day after my successful manipulations, he pronounced himself *"as good as new"* — and I left him in the midst of his protestations of gratitude, the only coin he possessed with which to pay his doctor's bill! I would have *reported* this wonderful result of the application of science, to some *Medical Journal* — but not being a member of the *Faculty* — tho' the case itself should have brought me a diploma — and thus having impinged upon their domain — a fear that my motives might be impugned or my tale disbelieved, has hitherto prevented me from making my success known to the world! Now, gentlemen, I flatter myself, that since the day of Galen and Hippocrates, nothing has been accomplished in the science of medicine and surgery so transcendently brilliant or so unapproachably successful! and while I have, I think, good reason to exult over the wonderful results just related, I love science too well, not to believe that there are within the ranks of the men who love science — worship her and follow her teachings — many who could have performed the operation as well as I did; but none of them have ever done so, and therefore, I must claim — as a matter of right and justice — the pre-eminence.

"The sequel to this extraordinary case is not less astonishing than true; for after a year's sojourn in the State of Texas, and occasional interviews with my patient, I have the happiness to inform you, that no difference whatever, could be observed by himself or others, between the action and service of the limbs which I had in a manner renewed, and those *put up* by dame Nature herself.

"Really, gentlemen, that is a pretty good *turkey* story our friend X. has just related; but *when I was in Texas,* I had a small hunt, that I must relate to you. I received intelligence one evening, that a flock of *wild turkies* were in a wood not very far from the village I was living in. I made immediate preparations for an early before-day-start next morning; and were I to say, gentlemen, that the woods for miles, were literally covered and piled up with them — you would hardly believe me — but it was even so! You have all seen "crow conventions" and "wild pigeon" mass meetings, but the largest you ever saw multiplied by one hundred, would hardly compute the number I suppose to have been in this flock of *wild turkies!* Congratulating myself upon the prospect of fine sport, I commenced discharging and loading my "double-barrel" as fast as I could — paying no regard to aim — but firing at the lump. Down they dropped, *three, four, five* at a time; I suppose I followed this amusement for an hour, when thinking that I had killed as many as ought to satisfy any reasonable man, and fearing too, that I might overload myself, I ceased the carnage and set about gathering up the *"meat"* — upon the honor of a gentleman, I never found the first *whole bird* on the ground; they were so fat, that on falling *they had burst all to pieces,* and nothing was to be seen but a mass of *feathers, bones* and *flesh,* all mixed up together! This result I did not anticipate, and I was really vexed at my disappointment; for there I left, as nice a pile of turkey meat as was ever seen at one time, a prey to the hogs and wild varmints! Many persons were on the ground who can testify to the facts I have just given you; for curiosity had led crowds of the people to the spot. Ah! gentlemen, Texas is a game country — a deer and turkey country — that can't be beat!"

And now, kind reader, if you have followed us thus far in our report of the words of our friend Rance Bore-'em, you have, no doubt, arrived at the conclusion that for lying he certainly possessed a *genius;* and when we tell you that he claimed to be a *universal genius,* you will, perhaps, think him a prodigy, if *equalling himself,* as here shown you, in all other departments. But this of course he could not do; though if you discussed the subject of Theology, no learned Divine, not excepting Dr. Buck, had dived as deep as he into the mysteries of Revelation. So with Geology, Natural Philosophy, History, Medicine and Surgery, (he has given you a specimen of the latter) Anatomy, Physiology, etc., through the whole list of the natural and physical sciences. From the works of Creation itself to the construction of a bird trap; from the mechanism of a steam engine to the building of a toy wagon; from the chemical analysis of a drop of water to the geography of the moon, the fellow would endeavor to make you believe they were as household words to him. He was particularly fond of *Poetry,* and could on occasion repeat the *oft quoted trite* selections from Shakespeare, spin off large portions of Byron, and (from a wonderful affinity no doubt) delighted to revel in the riches of Hudibras. *Music* too received his *critical* attention; though it is a matter of doubt, if he ever knew a note upon the gamut or could sing a bar of *Old Hundred!* Rance had a good *memory,* a necessary qualification; he possessed *brassy pretension* and *shallowness,* and these combined with an inordinate love of the marvellous, and a wonderful *self-esteem* went far towards producing the *"bundle of inconsistencies,"* he really was! He was too, in addition, a most admirable specimen of that universally detested *genus,* the *"Loafer Bore,"* those business-less excrescences upon society, who are such a nuisance and such a curse; and he never lost an opportunity, in season or out of season, to bestow his attention upon the business of others. Thus vegetated friend Bore-'em, in a small village until by the general consent of its inhabitants, he was invited to "take up his bed and walk" away, for fear that a worse thing should come upon him! He may have returned, for aught we know to the contrary, to his beloved Texas, there again to re-enact the scenes of his former glory, mayhap. At any rate, for the peace and quiet of any town, it should be the daily petition of its inhabitants, *"from such,"* Good Lord! deliver us! So mote it be, amen.

Henry Clay Lewis

(1825-1850)

Of French and Italian Jewish descent, Henry Clay Lewis was born in Charleston, South Carolina. His father, David, came to America in 1777 with Lafayette, served in the Revolution, married the daughter of a surgeon, and kept a furniture store. He was a merchant in Cincinnati by 1831, when his wife died; and Henry, then six years old, went to live with the family of his oldest brother. The boy's situation was unhappy. In 1835 he stowed away on a river steamer bound for New Orleans. He was taken on as a cook's assistant, became a cabin boy, and for a time worked on boats on the Ohio, Mississippi, and Yazoo rivers. At Yazoo City, Mississippi, there lived another brother, a prosperous merchant and cotton planter, and for the next five years Henry helped him raise cotton in a region only slightly removed from the frontier wilderness. In 1841 he was apprenticed to a physician in Yazoo City, and in 1844 he entered the Louisville, Kentucky, Medical Institute, from which he received his degree in 1846.

Lewis's experiences as a medical student provided the basis for his first and most frequently reprinted sketch, "Cupping on the Sternum," published in the *Spirit of the Times* of August 16, 1845. His use of personal experience, often grisly and grotesque, became a characteristic of his writing, which when collected in 1850 as *Odd Leaves from the Life of a Louisiana "Swamp Doctor"* bore a title suggestive of its autobiographical origins.

Young Doctor Lewis's inability to obtain a practice in Yazoo City led him to explore the possibilities of a small settlement in Madison Parish, in northeastern Louisiana, where the Tensas River joins Bayou Despair. The country supplied him with a good living, the pseudonym "Madison Tensas," and literary source material in the form of the customs, pleasures, pastimes, and medical histories of the fever-ridden inhabitants. Here among prosperous plantation owners and "swampers," backwoodsmen and squatters whose holdings among the canebrakes and cypress jungles were subject to frequent flooding, he assumed the role of "swamp doctor." For a year he put aside his citified habits, clothed himself in mud boots, "swamp broadcloth," and a coonskin cap, and went to live in a log cabin. He seems to have enjoyed himself immensely and to have met with professional and financial success. He recounts his life in the bayou country with gusto but always, just beneath the surface, lies the dark, pestilential presence of the swamp. He was drowned in the summer of 1850 while returning through the swamp from the bedside of a patient.

Though possessed of a great capacity for enjoyment, Lewis was by descent, profession, and personality something of an outsider. Standing apart, he could see the element of cruelty and degradation which is the underside of comedy, a perception which he shared with George Washington Harris without sharing Harris's satiric turn of mind. In his lighter moments Lewis could poke fun at the excesses of his own prose style or find satisfaction in outwitting a rascal; but this is not the same as excoriating mankind in the hope that a cure will result. The young swamp doctor knew too much of sores and fevers to hold such expectations.

TEXT: "Cupping on the Sternum" from *Spirit of the Times,* Aug. 16, 1845; "A Tight Race Considerin'" and "The Indefatigable Bear-Hunter" from *Odd Leaves from the Life of a Louisiana "Swamp Doctor"* (Philadelphia, 1858).

Cupping on the Sternum

I had been a student of medicine about three weeks, and had got as far as cupping, cathartics, and castor oil, in the noble science of physic, when, as I was sitting in the office, investigating by induction the medicinal properties of a jar of tamarinds, I received a note from my preceptor which ran thus: —

Mr. L. — You will please take the large cups and scarificator, together with a large blister, up to Mr. J., and cup his Negro girl Chaney very freely over the *sternum;* after you have cupped her, apply the blister over the same, as she has inflammation of the lungs.

In anatomy, the "sternum" is that portion of the osseous system known in common parlance as the "breast bone," but at that time I was ignorant of the fact. I had not studied anatomy, and in my ignorance and simplicity of heart, imagined that the doctor wanted her to be cupped and blistered "a posteriori," or in other words, over the "seat," and that he had put "um" to the "stern" in the note, merely for sport, or, it might have been the latin termination of the word "stern." Filled with a sense of the delicacy and momentous import of my duty, I provided myself with the necessaries, and proceeded to cup Chaney on the *sternum.*

By way of parenthesis, let me create an idea of my patient, so that you may appreciate the field of my operation. Just imagine a butcher's block five feet long and four feet through at the butt, converted into a fat bouncing Negro wench, with smaller blocks appended

for limbs, and you will have a faint conception of the figure and proportion of the delectable portion of humanity upon whom my curative
capabilities were to be exhibited.

"How are you to-day, Chaney?" said I, as, entering the cabin of
my patient I stood before her.

"Oh, Massa young Doctor," said she. "I does feel 'mazing bad —
the mis'ry in my bosom, almost broke my heart; I can scasely per-
spire," (*re-spire,* I suppose she meant, as, judging from the big drops
which, like ebony beads, chased each other down her gleaming neck,
I thought that she perspired beautifully.)

"I am very sorry to hear it, Chaney; the Doctor has sent me up
here to cup and blister you, and I hope it will relieve you entirely."

"Well, the Lord's will and the Doctor's be done; this anguished sister
be's ready" — and she proceeded to divest her bosom of its conceal-
ments, thinking that she had to be cupped over the seat of the pain.
But it was a different *seat* than that which my cups were destined to
exhaust the atmosphere from.

"Stop, Chaney. I was not told to cup you on the breast, but on the
sternum, so you'll have to turn over!"

"What!" shrieked she, rising straight up in the bed, a great deal
whiter in the face than she had been for many a day. "you cup
me on de *starn!* You make de cussed 'cisions in my frame on *dem*
parts! Massa young Doctor, *tell* me, for de lub of prostituted 'manity,
is you in airnest? Oh no, cartainly, you is just joking — just making
'musement of de 'stresses of dis female!"

"No, Chaney, there is no mistake. The doctor says you must be
cupped there, and it must and shall be done, so get ready."

"Oh, Massa Doctor, you must be mistaken — you must indeed!
De pain no dere, but in my breast! How cupping dere goin cure pain
in de breast, eh? Tell me dat!"

"Well, Chaney, I don't know that I can do that, exactly, but I suppose it will be by sympathy. You know the stern and the bosom
are not many feet apart. Anyhow, I am going to cup you there, if
I have to call in help, so you had better consent."

Chaney, seeing that there was no retreat, agreed at last to the operation. Click! click! went the scarificator, and amidst the shouts of
the patient and my awful solicitude for fear I might cut an artery,
the "deed was did." But no blood flowed, nothing but grease, which
trickled out slowly like molasses out of a worm hole. I saw that the
cups were too in*fat*uated to draw blood from that quarter. I removed
them and applied the blister, and I expect fly ointment was in demand
about that time.

When the Doctor returned, after an absence of several hours, he found the patient *entirely relieved,* and a blister drawn with about a tubful of water in its interior. I reckon she used chairs mighty little for a few weeks, and she hated the idea of the operation so bad that she burnt up a brand new dress just because it was *bum*bazine and reminded her, by the first syllable of the *seat* of "Cupping on the Sternum."

A Tight Race Considerin'

During my medical studies, passed in a small village in Mississippi, I became acquainted with a family named Hibbs (a *nom de plume* of course), residing a few miles in the country. The family consisted of Mr. and Mrs. Hibbs and son. They were plain, unlettered people, honest in intent and deed, but overflowing with that which amply made up for all their deficiencies of education, namely, warm-hearted hospitality, the distinguishing trait of southern character. They were originally from Virginia, from whence they had emigrated in quest of a clime more genial, and a soil more productive than that in which their fathers toiled. The search had been rewarded, their expectations realized, and now, in their old age, though not wealthy in the "Astorian" sense, still they had sufficient to keep the "wolf from the door," and drop something more substantial than condolence and tears in the hat that poverty hands round for the kind offerings of humanity.

The old man was like the generality of old planters, men whose ambition is embraced by the family or social circle, and whose thoughts turn more on the relative value of "Sea Island" and "Mastodon," and the improvement of their plantations, than the "glorious victories of Whiggery in Kentucky," or the "triumphs of democracy in Arkansas."

The old lady was a shrewd, active dame, kind-hearted and long-tongued, benevolent and impartial, making her coffee as strong for the poor pedestrian, with his all upon his back, as the broadcloth sojourner, with his "up-country pacer." She was a member of the church, as well as the daughter of a man who had once owned a race-horse: and these circumstances gave her an indisputable right, she thought, to "let on all she knew," when religion or horse-flesh was the theme. At one moment she would be heard discussing whether the new "circus rider," (as she always called him), was as affecting in Timothy as the old one was pathetic in Paul, and anon (not anonymous, for the old lady did everything above board, except rubbing her corns at supper), protecting dad's horse from the invidious comparisons of some visitor, who, having heard, perhaps, that such horses as Fashion and Boston existed, thought himself qualified to doubt the old lady's assertion that her father's horse "Shumach" had run a mile on one particular occasion. "Don't tell *me,*" was her never failing reply to their doubts, "Don't tell *me* 'bout Fashun or Bosting, or any other beating 'Shumach' a fair race, for the thing was unfeasible; didn't he run a mile a minute by Squire Dim's watch, which always stopt 'zactly at twelve, and didn't he start a minute afore, and git out, jes as the long hand war givin' its last quiver on ketchin' the short leg of the watch? And didn't he beat everything in Virginny 'cept once? Dad and the folks said he'd beat then, if young Mr. Spotswood hadn't give 'old Swaga,' Shumach's rider, some of that 'Croton water,' (that them Yorkers is makin' sich a fuss over as bein' so good, when gracious knows, nothin' but what the doctors call interconception could git me to take a dose) and jis 'fore the race Swage or Shumach, I don't 'stinctly 'member which, but one of them had to 'let down,' and so dad's hoss got beat."

The son I will describe in few words. Imbibing his parents' contempt for letters, he was very illiterate, and as he had not enjoyed the equivalent of travel, was extremely ignorant on all matters not relating to hunting or plantation duties. He was a stout, active fellow, with a merry twinkling of the eye, indicative of humour, and partiality for practical joking. We had become very intimate, he instructing me in "forest lore," and I, in return, giving amusing stories or, what was as much to his liking, occasional introductions to my hunting-flask.

Now that I have introduced the "Dramatis Personae," I will proceed with my story. By way of relaxation, and to relieve the tedium incident more or less to a student's life, I would take my gun, walk out to old Hibbs's, spend a day or two, and return refreshed to my books.

One fine afternoon I started upon such an excursion, and as I had upon a previous occasion missed killing a fine buck, owing to my having nothing but squirrel shot, I determined to go this time for the "antlered monarch," by loading one barrel with fifteen "blue whistlers," reserving the other for small game.

At the near end of the plantation was a fine spring, and adjacent, a small cave, the entrance artfully or naturally concealed, save to one acquainted with its locality. The cave was nothing but one of those subterraneous washes so common in the west and south, and called "sink holes." It was known only to young H. and myself, and we, for peculiar reasons, kept secret, having put it in requisition as the depository of a jug of "old Bourbon," which we favoured, and as the old folks abominated drinking, we had found convenient to keep there, whither we would repair to get our drinks, and return to the house to hear them descant on the evils of drinking, and "vow no 'drap,' 'cept in doctor's truck, should ever come on their plantation." Feeling very thirsty, I took my way by the spring that evening. As I descended the hill o'ertopping it, I beheld the hind parts of a bear slowly being drawn into the cave. My heart bounded at the idea of killing a bear, and my plans were formed in a second. I had no dogs — the house was distant — and the bear becoming "small by degrees, and beautifully less." Every hunter knows, if you shoot a squirrel in the head when it's sticking out of a hole, ten to one he'll jump out; and I reasoned that if this were true regarding squirrels, might not the operation of the same principle extract a bear, applying it low down in the back.

Quick as thought I levelled my gun and fired, intending to give him the buckshot when his body appeared; but what was my surprise and horror, when, instead of a bear rolling out, the parts were jerked nervously in, and the well-known voice of young H. reached my ears. "Murder! Hingins! h—l and kuckle-burs! Oh! Lordy! 'nuff! — 'nuff! — take him off! Jis let me off this wunst, dad, and I'll never run mam's colt again! Oh! Lordy! Lordy! *all my brains blowed clean out!* Snakes! snakes!" yelled he, in a shriller tone, if possible, "H—l on the outside and snakes in the sink-hole! I'll die a Christian, anyhow, and if I die before I wake," and out scrambled poor H., pursued by a large black-snake.

If my life had depended on it, I could not have restrained my laughter. Down fell the gun, and down dropped I shrieking convulsively. The hill was steep, and over and over I went, until my head striking against a stump at the bottom, stopped me, half senseless. On recovering somewhat from the stunning blow, I found Hibbs upon me, taking satisfaction from me for having blowed out his brains. A contest ensued, and H. finally relinquished his hold, but I saw from the knitting of his brows, that the bear-storm, instead of being over, was just brewing. "Mr. Tensas," he said with awful dignity, "I'm sorry I put into you 'fore you cum to, but you're at yourself now, and as you've tuck a shot at me, it's no more than far I should have a chance 'fore the hunt's up."

It was with the greatest difficulty I could get H. to bear with me until I explained the mistake; but as soon as he learned it, he broke out in a huge laugh. "Oh, Dod busted! that's 'nuff; you has my pardon. I ought to know'd you didn't 'tend it; 'sides, you jis scraped the skin. I war wus skeered than hurt, and if you'll go to the house and beg me off from the old folks, I'll never let on you cuddent tell copperas breeches from bar-skin."

Promising that I would use my influence, I proposed taking a drink, and that he should tell me how he had incurred his parent's anger. He assented, and after we had inspected the cave, and seen that it held no other serpent than the one we craved, we entered its cool recess, and H. commenced.

"You see, Doc, I'd heerd so much from mam 'bout her dad's Shumach and his nigger Swage, and the mile a minute, and the Croton water what was gin him, and how she bleved that if it warn't for bettin', and the cussin' and fightin', running race-hosses warn't the sin folks said it war; and if they war anything to make her 'gret gettin' religion and jinin' the church, it war cos she couldn't 'tend races, and have a race-colt of her own to comfort her 'clinin' years, sich as her daddy had afore her, till she got me; so I couldn't rest for wantin' to see a hoss-race, and go shares, p'raps, in the colt she war wishin' for. And then I'd think what sort of a hoss I'd want him to be — a quarter nag, a mile critter, or a hoss wot could run (fur all mam says it can't be did) a whole four mile at a stretch. Sometimes I think I'd rather own a quarter nag, for the suspense wouldn't long be hung, and then we could run up the road to old Nick Bamer's cow-pen, and Sally is almost allers out thar in the cool of the evenin'; and in course we wouldn't be so cruel as to run the poor critter in the heat of the day. But then agin, I'd think I'd rather have a miler, — for the 'citement would be greater, and we could run down the road to old Wither's orchard, an' his gal Miry is frightfully fond of sunnin' herself thar, when she 'spects me 'long, and she'd hear of the race, certain; but then thar war the four miler for my thinkin', and I'd knew'd in such case the 'citement would be greatest of all, and you know, too, from dad's stable to the grocery is jist four miles, an' in case of any 'spute, all hands would be willin' to run over, even if it had to be tried a dozen times. So I never could 'cide on which sort of a colt to wish for. It was fust one, then t'others, till I was nearly 'stracted, and when mam, makin' me religious, told me one night to say grace, I jes shut my eyes, looked pious, and yelled out, 'D—n it, go!' and in 'bout five minutes arter, came near kickin' dad's stumak off, under the table, thinkin' I war spurrin' my critter in a tight place. So I found the best way was to get the hoss fust, and then 'termine whether it should be Sally Bamers, and the cow-pen; Miry Withers, and the peach orchard; or Spillman's grocery, with the bald face.

"You've seed my black colt, that one that dad's father gin me in his will when he died, and I 'spect the reason he wrote that will war, that he might have wun then, for it's more then he had when he was alive, for granma war a monstrus overbearin' woman. The colt would cum up in my mind, every time I'd think whar I was to git a hoss.

'Git out!' said I at fust — *he* never could run, and 'sides if he could, mam rides him now, an he's too old for anything, 'cept totin her and bein' called mine; for you see, though he war named Colt, yet for the old lady to call him old, would bin like the bar 'fecting contempt for the rabbit, on account of the shortness of his tail.

"Well, thought I, it does look sorter unpromisin', but its Colt or none; so I 'termined to put him in trainin' the fust chance. Last Saturday, who should cum ridin' up but the new cirkut preacher, a long-legged, weakly, sickly, never-contented-onless-the-best-on-the-plantation-war-cooked-fur-him sort of a man; but I didn't look at him twice, his hoss was the critter that took my eye; for the minute I looked at him, I knew him to be the same hoss as Sam Spooner used to win all his splurgin' dimes with, the folks said, and wot he used to ride past our house so fine on. The hoss war a heap the wuss for age and change of masters; for preachers, though they're mity 'ticular 'bout thar own comfort, seldom tends to thar hosses, for one is privit property and 'tother generally borried. I seed from the way the preacher rid, that he didn't know the animal he war straddlin'; but I did, and I 'termined I wouldn't lose sich a chance of trainin' Colt by the side of a hoss wot had run real races. So that night, arter prayers and the folks was abed, I and Nigger Bill tuck the hosses and carried them down to the pastur'. It war a forty-aker lot, and consequently jist a quarter across — for I thought it best to promote Colt, by degrees, to a four-miler. When we got thar, the preacher's hoss showed he war willin'; but Colt, dang him! commenced nibblin' a fodder-stack over the fence. I nearly cried for vexment, but an idea struck me; I hitched the critter, and told Bill to get on Colt and stick tight wen I giv' the word. Bill got reddy, and unbeknownst to him I pulled up a ' ch of nettles, and, as I clapped them under Colt's tail, yelled, 'Go!' Down shut his graceful like a steel-trap, and away he shot so quick an' fast that he jumpt clean out from under Bill, and got nearly to the end of the quarter 'fore the nigger toch the ground: he lit on his head, and in course warn't hurt — so we cotched Colt, an' I mounted him.

"The next time I said 'go' he showed that age hadn't spiled his legs or memory. Bill 'an me 'greed we could run him now, so Bill mounted Preacher and we got ready. Thar war a narrer part of the track 'tween two oaks, but as it war near the end of the quarter, I 'spected to pass Preacher 'fore we got thar, so I warn't afraid of barkin' my shins.

"We tuck a fair start, and off we went like a peeled ingun, an' I soon 'scovered that it warn't such an easy matter to pass Preacher, though Colt dun delightful; we got nigh the trees, and Preacher warn't past yet, an' I 'gan to get skeered, for it warn't more than wide enuf for a horse and a half; so I hollered to Bill to hold up, but the imperdent nigger turned his ugly pictur, and said, 'he'd be cussed if he warn't goin' to play his han' out.' I gin him to understand he'd better fix for a foot-race when we stopt, and tried to hold up Colt, but he wouldn't stop. We reached the oaks, Colt tried to pass Preacher, Preacher tried to pass Colt, and cowollop, crosh, cochunk! we all cum down like 'simmons arter frost. Colt got up and won the race; Preacher tried hard to rise, but one hind leg had got threw the stirrup, an' tother in the head stall, an' he had to lay still, doubled up like a long nigger in a short bed. I lit on my feet, but Nigger Bill war gone entire. I looked up in the fork of one of the oaks, and thar he war sittin', lookin' very composed on surroundin' nature. I couldn't git him down till I promised not to hurt him for disobeyin' orders, when he slid down. We'd 'nuff racin' for that night, so we put up the hosses and went to bed.

"Next morning the folks got ready for church, when it was dis-kivered that the hosses had got out. I an' Bill started off to look for them; we found them cleer off in the field, tryin' to git in the pastur' to run the last night's race over, old Blaze, the reverlushunary mule, bein' along to act as judge.

"By the time we got to the house it war nigh on to meetin' hour; and dad had started to the preachin', to tell the folks to sing on, as preacher and mam would be 'long bimeby. As the passun war in a hurry, and had been complainin' that his creetur war dull, I 'suaded him to put on uncle Jim's spurs what he fotch from Mexico. I saddled the passun's hoss, takin' 'ticular pains to let the saddle-blanket come down low in the flank. By the time these fixins war threw, mam war 'head nigh on to a quarter. 'We must ride on, passun', I said, 'or the folks'll think we is lost.' So I whipt up the mule I rid, the passun chirrupt and chuct to make his crittur gallop, but the animal didn't mind him a pic. I 'gan to snicker, an' the passun 'gan to git vext; sudden he thought of his spurs, so he ris up, an' drove them *vim* in his hoss's flanx, till they went through his saddle-blanket, and like to bored his nag to the holler. By gosh! but it war a quickener — the hoss kickt till the passun had to hug him round the neck to keep from pitchin' him over his head. He next jumpt up 'bout as high as a rail fence, passun holdin' on and tryin' to git his spurs — but they war lockt — his breeches split plum across with the strain, and the piece of wearin' truck wot's next the skin made a monstrous putty flag as the old hoss, like drunkards to a barbacue, streakt it up the road.

"Mam war ridin' slowly along, thinkin' how sorry she was, cos

Chary Dolin, who always led her off, had sich a bad cold, an' wouldn't be able to 'sist her singin' to-day. She war practisin' the hymns, and had got as far as whar it says, 'I have a race to run,' when the passun huv in sight, an' in 'bout the dodgin' of a diedapper, she found thar war truth in the words, for the colt, hearin' the hoss cumin' up behind, began to show symptoms of runnin'; but when he heard the passun holler 'wo! wo!' to his hoss, he thought it war me shoutin' 'go!' and sure 'nuff off they started jis as the passun got up even; so it war a fair race. Whoop! git out, but it war egsitin' — the dust flew, and the rail-fence appeered strate as a rifle. Thar war the passun, his legs fast to the critter's flanx, arms lockt round his neck, face as pale as a rabbit's belly, and the white flag streemin' far behind — and thar war mam, fust on one side, then on t'other, her new caliker swelled up round her like a bear with the dropsy, the old lady so much surprized she cuddent ride steddy, an' tryin' to stop her colt, but he war too well trained to stop while he heard 'go!' Mam got 'sited at last, and her eyes 'gan to glimmer like she seen her daddy's ghost axin' 'if he ever trained up a child or a race-hoss to be 'fraid of a small brush on a Sunday,' she commenced ridin' beautiful; she braced herself up in the saddle, and began to make calkerlations how she war to win the race, for it war nose and nose, and she saw the passun spurrin' his critter every jump. She tuk off her shoe, and the way a number ten go-to-meetin' brogan commenced givin' a hoss particular Moses, were a caution to hoss-flesh — but still it kept nose and nose. She found she war carryin' too much weight for Colt, so she 'gan to throw off plunder, till nuthin' was left but her saddle and close, and the spurs kept tellin' still. The old woman commenced strippin' to lighten, till it wouldn't bin the clean thing for her to have taken off one dud more; an' then when she found it war no use while the spurs lasted, she got cantankerous. 'Passun,' said she, 'I'll be cust if it's fair or gentlemanly for you, a preacher of the gospel, to take advantage of an old woman this way, usin' spurs when you know *she* can't wear 'em — 'taint Christian-like nuther,' and she burst into cryin'. 'Wo! Miss Hibbs! Wo! Stop! Madam! Wo! Your son!' — he attempted to say, when the old woman tuck him on the back of the head, and fillin' his mouth with right smart of a saddle-horn, and stoppin' the talk, as far as his share went for the present.

"By this time they'd got nigh on to the meetin'-house, and the folks were harkin' away on 'Old Hundred,' and wonderin' what could have become of the passun and mam Hibbs. One sister in a long beard axt another brethren in church, if she'd heered anything 'bout that New York preacher runnin' way with a woman old enough to be his muther. The brethrens gin a long sigh an' groaned 'it ain't possible! marciful heavens! you don't 'spicion?' wen the sound of the hosses comin', roused them up like a touch of the agur, an' broke off their sarpent-talk. Dad run out to see what was to pay, but when he seed the hosses so close together, the passun spurrin', and mam ridin' like close war skase whar she cum, he knew her fix in a second, and 'tarmined to help her; so clinchin' a saplin', he hid 'hind a stump 'bout ten steps off, and held on for the hosses. On they went in beautiful style, the passun's spurs tellin' terrible, and mam's shoe operatin' 'no small pile of punkins,' — passun stretched out the length of two hosses, while mam sot as stiff and strate as a bull yearling in his fust fight, hittin' her nag, fust on one side, next on t'other, and the third for the passun, who had chawed the horn till little of the saddle, and less of his teeth war left, and his voice sounded as holler as a jackass-nicker in an old saw-mill.

"The hosses war nose and nose, jam up together so close that mam's last kiverin' and passun's flag had got lockt, an' 'tween bleached domestic and striped linsey made a beautiful banner for the pious racers.

"On they went like a small arthquake, an' it seemed like it war goin' to be a draun race; but dad, when they got to him, let down with all his might on Colt, scarin' him so bad that he jumpt clean ahead of passun, beatin' him by a neck, buttin' his own head agin the meetin'-house, an' pitchin' mam, like a lam for the sacryfise, plum through the winder 'mongst the mourners, leavin' her only garment flutterin' on a nail in the sash. The men shot their eyes and scrambled outen the house, an' the women gin mam so much of their close that they like to put themselves in the same fix.

"The passun quit the circuit, and I haven't been home yet."

The Indefatigable Bear-Hunter

In my round of practice, I occasionally meet with men whose peculiarities stamp them as belonging to a class composed only of themselves. So different are they in appearance, habits, taste, from the majority of mankind, that it is impossible to classify them, and you have therefore to set them down as queer birds "of a feather," that none resemble sufficiently to associate with.

I had a patient once who was one of these queer ones; gigantic in stature, uneducated, fearless of real danger, yet timorous as a child of superstitious perils, born literally in the woods, never having been in a city in his life, and his idea of one being that it was a place where people met together to make whiskey, and form plans for swindling country folks. To view him at one time, you would think him only a whiskey-drinking, bear-fat-loving mortal; at other moments, he would give vent to ideas, proving that beneath his rough exterior there ran a fiery current of high enthusiastic ambition.

It is a favourite theory of mine, and one that I am fond of consoling myself with, for my own insignificance, that there is no man born who is not capable of attaining distinction, and no occupation that does not contain a path leading to fame. To bide our time is all that is necessary. I had expressed this view in the hearing of Mik-hoo-tah, for so was the subject of this sketch called, and it seemed to chime in with his feelings exactly. Born in the woods, and losing his parents early, he had forgotten his real name, and the bent of his genius inclining him to the slaying of bears, he had been given, even when a youth, the name of Mik-hoo-tah, signifying "the grave of bears," by his Indian associates and admirers.

To glance in and around his cabin, you would have thought that the place had been selected for ages past by the bear tribe to yield up their spirits in, so numerous were the relics. Little chance, I ween, had the cold air to whistle through that hut, so thickly was it tap-estried with the soft, downy hides, the darkness of the surface relieved occasionally by the skin of a tender fawn, or the short-haired irascible panther. From the joists depended bear-hams and tongues innumer-able, and the ground outside was literally white with bones. Av̄ ̄̄ was a bear-hunter, in its most comprehensive sen̄̄̄ ̄̄ ̄̄ ̄̄̄ ̄̄ ̄̄̄ ̄̄ ̄̄ ̄̄ of that vigorous band, whose occupa̅ ̄ ̄̄ ̄̄ ̄̄̄ gone — crushed beneath the advancing stride̅ ̄̄̄ ̄̄ romance-destroying civilization. When his horn sounded — so tradition ran — the bears began to draw lots to see who should die that day, for painful experience had told them the uselessness of all endeavouring to escape. The "Big Bear of Arkansas" would not have given him an hour's extra work, or raised a fresh wrinkle on his already care-corrugated brow. But, though almost daily imbruing his hands in the blood of Bruin, Mik-hoo-tah had not become an impious or cruel-hearted man. Such was his piety, that he never killed a bear without getting down on his knees — to skin it — and praying to be d—ned if it warn't a buster; and such his softness of heart, that he often wept, when he, by mistake, had killed a suckling bear — depriving her poor offspring of a mother's care — and found her too poor to be eaten. So indefatigable had he become in his pursuit, that the bears bid fair to disappear from the face of the swamp, and be known to posterity only through the one mentioned in Scripture, that assisted Elisha to punish the impertinent children, when an accident occurred to the hunter, which raised their hopes of not being entirely exterminated.

One day, Mik happened to come unfortunately in contact with a stray grizzly fellow, who, doubtless in the indulgence of an adventurous spirit, had wandered away from the Rocky Mountains, and formed a league for mutual protection with his black and more effeminate brethren of the swamp. Mik saluted him, as he approached, with an ounce ball in the forehead, to avenge half a dozen of his best dogs, who lay in fragments around; the bullet flattened upon his impenetrable skull, merely infuriating the monster; and before Mik could reload, it was upon him. Seizing him by the leg, it bore him to the ground, and ground the limb to atoms. But before it could attack a more vital part, the knife of the dauntless hunter had cloven its heart, and it dropped dead upon the bleeding form of its slayer, in which condition they were shortly found by Mik's comrades. Making a litter of branches, they placed Mik upon it, and proceeded with all haste to their camp, sending one of the company by a near cut for me, as I was the nearest physician. When I reached their temporary shelter I found Mik doing better than I could have expected, with the exception of his wounded leg, and that, from its crushed and mutilated condition, I saw would have to be amputated immediately, of which I informed Mik. As I expected, he opposed it vehemently; but I convinced him of the impossibility of saving it, assuring him if it were not amputated, he would certainly die, and appealed to his good sense to grant permission, which he did at last. The next difficulty was to procure amputating instruments, the rarity of surgical operations, and the generally slender purse of the "Swamp Doctor," not justifying him in purchasing expensive instruments. A couple of bowie-knives, one ingeniously hacked and filed into a saw — a tourniquet made of a belt and piece of stick — a gun-screw converted for the time into a tenaculum — and some buckskin slips for ligatures, completed my case of instruments for amputation. The city physician may smile at this recital, but I assure him many a more difficult operation than the amputation of a leg, has been performed by his humble brother in the "swamp," with far more simple means than those I have mentioned. The preparations being completed, Mik refused to have his arms bound, and commenced singing a bear song; and throughout the whole operation, which was necessarily tedious, he never uttered a groan, or missed a single stave. The next day, I had him conveyed by easy stages to his pre-emption; and tending assiduously, in the course of a few weeks, he had recovered sufficiently for me to cease attentions. I made him a wooden leg, which answered a good purpose; and with a sigh of regret for the spoiling of such a good hunter, I struck him from my list of patients.

A few months passed over and I heard nothing more of him. Newer, but not brighter, stars were in the ascendant, filling with their deeds the clanging trump of bear-killing fame, and, but for the quantity of bear-blankets in the neighboring cabins, and the painful absence of his usual present of bear-hams, Mik-hoo-tah bid fair to suffer that fate most terrible to aspiring ambitionists — forgetfulness during life. The sun, in despair at the stern necessity which compelled him to yield up his tender offspring, day, to the gloomy grave of darkness, had stretched forth his long arms, and, with the tenacity of a drowning man clinging to a straw, had clutched the tender whispering straw-like topmost branches of the trees — in other words it was near sunset — when I arrived at home from a long wearisome semi-ride-and-swim through the swamp. Receiving a negative to my inquiry whether there were any new calls, I was felicitating myself upon a quiet night beside my tidy bachelor hearth, undisturbed by crying children, babbling women, or amorous cats — the usual accompaniments of married life — when, like a poor henpecked Benedick crying for peace when there is no peace, I was doomed to disappointment. Hearing the splash of a paddle in the bayou running before the door, I turned my head towards the bank, and soon beheld, first the tail of a coon, next his body, a human face, and, the top of the bank being gained, a full-proportioned form clad in the garments which, better than any printed label, wrote him down raftsman, trapper, bear-hunter. He was a messenger from the indefatigable bear-hunter, Mik-hoo-tah. Asking him what was the matter, as soon as he could get the knots untied which two-thirds drunkenness had made in his tongue, he informed me, to my sincere regret, that Mik went out that morning on a bear-hunt, and in a fight with one, had got his leg broke all to flinders, if possible worse than the other, and that he wanted me to come quickly. Getting into the canoe, which awaited me, I wrapped myself in my blanket, and yielding to my fatigue, was soon fast asleep. I did not awaken until the canoe striking against the bank, as it landed at Mik's pre-emption, nearly threw me in the bayou, and entirely succeeded with regard to my half-drunken paddler, who — like the sailor who circumnavigated the world and then was drowned in a puddle-hole in his own garden — had escaped all the perils of the tortuous bayou to be pitched overboard when there was nothing to do but step out and tie the dug-out. Assisting him out of the water, we proceeded to the house, when, to my indignation,

I learnt that the drunken messenger had given me the long trip for nothing, Mik only wanting me to make him a new wooden leg, the old one having been completely demolished that morning.

Relieving myself by a satisfactory oath, I would have returned that night, but the distance was too great for one fatigued as I was, so I had to content myself with such accommodations as Mik's cabin afforded, which, to one blessed like myself with the happy faculty of ready adaptation to circumstances, was not a very difficult task.

I was surprised to perceive the change in Mik's appearance. From nearly a giant, he had wasted to a mere huge bony frame-work; the skin of his face clung tightly to the bones, and showed nothing of those laughter-moving features that were wont to adorn his visage; only his eye remained unchanged, and it had lost none of its brilliancy — the flint had lost none of its fire.

"What on earth is the matter with you, Mik? I have never seen any one fall off so fast; you have wasted to a skeleton — surely you must have the consumption."

"Do you think so, Doc? I'll soon show you whether the old bellows has lost any of its force!" and hopping to the door, which he threw wide open, he gave a death-hug rally to his dogs, in such a loud and piercing tone, that I imagined a steam whistle was being discharged in my ear, and for several moments could hear nothing distinctly.

"That will do! stop!" I yelled, as I saw Mik drawing in his breath preparatory to another effort of his vocal strength; "I am satisfied you have not got consumption; but what has wasted you so, Mik? Surely, you ain't in love?"

"Love! h—ll! you don't suppose, Doc, even if I was 'tarmined to make a cussed fool of myself, that there is any gal in the swamp that could stand that hug, do you?" and catching up a huge bull-dog, who lay basking himself by the fire, he gave him such a squeeze that the animal yelled with pain, and for a few moments appeared dead. "No, Doc, it's grief, pure sorrur, sorrur, Doc! when I looks at what I is now and what I used to be! Jes think, Doc, of the fust hunter in the swamp having his sport spilte, like bar-meat in summer without salt! Jes think of a man standin' up one day and blessing old Master for having put bar in creation, and the next cussing high heaven and low h—ll 'cause he couldn't 'sist in puttin' them out! Warn't it enough to bring tears to the eyes of an Injun tater, much less take the fat off a bar-hunter? Doc, I fell off like 'simmons arter frost, and folks as doubted me, needn't had asked whether I war 'ceitful or not, for they could have seed plum threw me! The bar and painter got so saucy that they'd cum to the tother side of the bayou and see which could talk the impudentest! 'Don't you want some bar-meat or painter blanket?' they'd ask; 'bars is monstrous fat, and painter's hide is mighty warm!' Oh! Doc, I was a miserable man! The sky warn't blue for me, the sun war always cloudy, and the shade-trees gin no shade for me. Even the dogs forgot me, and the little children quit coming and asking, 'Please, Mr. Bar-Grave, cotch me a young bar or a painter kitten.' Doc, the tears would cum in my eyes and the hot blood would cum biling up from my heart, when I'd hobble out of a sundown and hear the boys tell, as they went by, of the sport they'd had that day, and how the bar fit 'fore he was killed, and how fat he war arter he was slayed. Long arter they was gone, and the whip-poor-will had eat up their voices, I would sit out there on the old stump, and think of the things that used to hold the biggest place in my mind when I was a boy, and p'raps sense I've bin a man.

"I'd heard tell of distinction and fame, and people's names never dying, and how Washington and Franklin, and Clay and Jackson, and a heap of political dicshunary-folks, would live when their big hearts had crumbled down to a rifle-charge of dust; and I begun, too, to think, Doc, what a pleasant thing it would be to know folks a million years off would talk of me like them, and it made me 'tarmine to 'stinguish myself, and have my name put in a book with a yaller kiver. I warn't a genus, Doc, I nude that, nor I warn't dicshunary; so I detarmined to strike out in a new track for glory, and 'title myself to be called the 'bear-hunter of Ameriky.' Doc, my heart jumpt up, and I belted my hunting-shirt tighter for fear it would lepe out when I fust spoke them words out loud.

"'The bar-hunter of Ameriky!' Doc, you know whether I war ernin' the name when I war ruined. There is not a child, white, black, Injun, or nigger, from the Arkansas line to Trinity, but what has heard of me, and I were happy when" — here a tremor of his voice and a tear glistening in the glare of the fire told the old fellow's emotion — "when — but les take a drink — Doc, I found I was dying — I war gettin' weaker and weaker — I nude your truck warn't what I needed, or I'd sent for you. A bar-hunt war the medsin that my systum re-quired, a fust class bar-hunt, the music of the dogs, the fellers a screaming, the cane poppin', the rifles crackin', the bar growlin', the fight hand to hand, slap goes his paw, and a dog's hide hangs on one cane and his body on another, the knife glistenin' and then goin' plump up to the handle in his heart! — Oh! Doc, this was what I needed, and I swore, since death were huggin' me, anyhow, I mite as well feel his last grip in a bar-hunt.

"I seed the boys goin' long one day, and haled them to wait awhile, as I believed I would go along too. I war frade if I kept out of a hunt much longer I wood get outen practis. They laughed at me, thinkin' I war jokin'; for wat cood a sick, old, one-legged man do in a bar-hunt? how cood he get threw the swamp, and vines, and canes, and backwater? and s'pose he mist the bar, how war he to get outen the way?

"But I war 'tarmined on goin'; my dander was up, and I swore I wood go, tellin' them if I coodent travel 'bout much, I could take a stand. Seein' it war no use tryin' to 'swade me, they saddled my poney, and off we started. I felt better right off. I knew I cuddent do much in the chase, so I told the fellers I would go to the cross-path stand, and wate for the bar, as he would be sarten to cum by thar. You have never seed the cross-path stand, Doc. It's the singularest place in the swamp. It's rite in the middle of a canebrake, thicker than har on a bar-hide, down in a deep sink, that looks like the devil had cummenst diggin' a skylite for his pre-emption. I knew it war a dangersome place for a well man to go in, much less a one-leg cripple; but I war 'tarmined that time to give a deal on the dead wood, and play my hand out. The boys gin me time to get to the stand, and then cummenst the drive. The bar seemed 'tarmined on disappinting me, for the fust thing I heard of the dogs and bar, they was outen hearing. Everything got quiet, and I got so wrathy at not being able to foller up the chase, that I cust till the trees cummenst shedding their leaves and small branches, when I herd them lumbrin back, and I nude they war makin' to me. I primed old 'bar death' fresh, and rubbed the frizin, for it war no time for rifle to get to snappin'. Thinks I, if I happen to miss, I'll try what virtue there is in a knife — when, Doc, my knife war gone. H—ll! bar, for God's sake have a soft head, and die easy, for I *can't* run!

"Doc, you've hearn a bar bustin' threw a cane-brake, and know how near to a harrycane it is. I almost cummenst dodgin' the trees, thinkin' it war the best in the shop one a comin', for it beat the loudest thunder ever I heard; that ole bar did, comin' to get his death from an ole, one-legged cripple, what had slayed more of his brethren than his nigger foot had ever made trax in the mud. Doc, he heerd a *monstrus long ways ahead of the dogs.* I warn't skeered, but I must own, as I had but one shot, an' no knife, I wud have prefurd they had been closer. But here he cum! he bar — big as a bull — boys off h—ll-wards — dogs nowhar — no knife — but one shot — *and only one leg that cood run!*

"The bar 'peered s'prised to see me standin' ready for him in the openin'; for it war currently reported 'mong his brethren that I war either dead, or no use for bar. I thought fust he war skeered; and, Doc, I b'leve he war, till he cotch a sight of my wooden leg, and that toch his pride, for he knew he would be hist outen every she bear's company, ef he run from a poor, sickly, one-legged cripple, so on he cum, a small river of slobber pourin from his mouth, and the blue smoke curlin outen his ears. I tuck good aim at his left, and let drive. The ball struck him on the eyebrow, and glanced off, only stunnin' him for a moment, jes givin' me time to club my rifle, an' on he kum, as fierce as old grizzly. As he got in reach, I gin him a lick 'cross the temples, brakin' the stock in fifty pieces, an' knockin' him senseless. I struv to foller up the lick, when, Doc, I war fast — my timber toe had run inter the ground, and I cuddent git out, though I jerked hard enuf almost to bring my thigh out of joint. I stuped to unscrew the infurnal thing, when the bar cum too, and cum at me agen. Vim! I tuck him over the head, and, cochunk, he keeled over. H—ll! but I cavorted and pitched. Thar war my wust enemy, watin' for me to giv him a finisher, an' *I cuddent* git at him. I'd cummense unscrewin' leg — here cum bar — vim — cochunk — he'd fall out of reach — and, Doc, *I cuddent git to him.* I kept workin' my body round, so as to unscrew the leg, and keep the bar off till I cood 'complish it, when jes as I tuck the last turn, and got loose from the d—d thing, here cum bar, more venimous than ever, and I nude thar war death to one out, and comin' shortly. I let him get close, an' then cum down with a perfect tornado on his head, as I thought; but the old villin had learnt the dodge — the barrel jes struck him on the side of the head, and glanst off, slinging itself out of my hands bout twenty feet 'mongst the thick cane, and thar I war in a fix sure. Bar but little hurt — no gun — no knife — no dogs — no frens — no chance to climb — *an' only one leg that cood run.* Doc, I jes cummenst makin' 'pologies to ole Master, when an idee struck me. Doc, did you ever see a piney woods nigger pulling at a sassafras root? or a suckin' pig in a tater patch arter the big yams? You has! Well, you can 'magin how I jurkt at that wudden leg, for it war the last of pea-time with me, sure, if I didn't rise 'fore bar did. At last, they both cum up, bout the same time, and I braced myself for a death struggle.

"We fit all round that holler! Fust I'd foller bar, and then bar would chase me! I'd make a lick, he'd fend off, and showin' a set of teeth that no doctor, 'cept natur, had ever wurkt at, cum tearin' at me! We both 'gan to git tired, I heard the boys and dogs cumin', so did bar, and we were both anxshus to bring the thing to a close 'fore they cum up, though I wuddent thought they were intrudin' ef they had cum up some time afore.

"I'd worn the old leg pretty well off to the second jint, when, jest 'fore I made a lick, the noise of the boys and the dogs cummin' sorter confused bar, and he made a stumble, and bein' off his guard I got a fair lick! The way that bar's flesh giv in to the soft impresshuns of that leg war an honor to the mederkal perfeshun for having invented sich a weepun! I hollered — but you have heered me holler an' I won't describe it — I had whipped a bar in a fair hand to hand fight — me, an old sickly one-legged bar-hunter! The boys cum up, and, when they seed the ground we had fit over, they swore they would hav thought, 'stead of a bar-fight, that I had been cuttin' cane and deadenin' timber for a corn-patch, the sile war so worked up, they then handed me a knife to finish the work.

"Doc, les licker, it's a dry talk — when will you make me another leg? for bar-meat is not over plenty in the cabin, and I feel like tryin' another!"

William Penn Brannan

(1825-1866)

William Penn Brannan, author of widely popular burlesque sermons, was an itinerant artist and writer for newspapers who used the pseudonyms "Bill Easel" and "Vandyke Brown." He was born in Cincinnati and painted portraits there in the 1840's, exhibited at the National Academy of Design in 1847, was an engraver in Chicago, and worked in river towns down the Mississippi to New Orleans. He was an associate editor of the Cincinnati *Daily Union* in 1865 but moved to New York where he published a volume of verse, *Vagaries of Vandyke Brown*, the same year.

Thomas Bangs Thorpe compared the steadfast in faith to the clinging opossum in his somewhat rambling essay, "Opossums and 'Possum Hunting." A frontier preacher warns the faithful that "The world, the flesh, the devil compose the wind that is trying to blow you off the gospel tree. But don't let go of it, hold on to it as a 'possum would in a hurricane. If the forelegs of your passions get loose, hold on by your hind legs of conscientiousness; and if they get loose, hold on eternally by your tail, which is the promise that the saints shall persevere unto the end."

"The Harp of a Thousand Strings" was the specialty of Alf Burnett, a comedian who became famous as an entertainer in Union Army camps.

TEXT: "The Harp of a Thousand Strings" from *Spirit of the Times,* Sept. 29, 1855; "Where the Lion Roareth and the Wang-doodle Mourneth" from *The Harp of a Thousand Strings,* ed. S. P. Avery (New York, 1858), in which it appears without attribution of authorship.

The Harp of a Thousand Strings

I may say to you, my brethring, that I am not an educated man, an' I am not one of them as believes that education is necessary for a Gospel minister, for I believe the Lord educates his preachers just as he wants 'em to be educated; an' although I say it that oughtn't to say it, yet, in the State of Indianny, whar I live, thar's no man as gits a bigger congregation nor what I gits.

Thar may be some here to-day, my brethring, as don't know what persuasion I am uv. Well, I must say to you, my brethring, that I'm a Hard Shell Baptist. Thar's some folks as don't like the Hard Shell Baptists, but I'd rather have a hard shell as no shell at all. You see me here to-day, my brethring, dressed up in fine clothes; you mou't think I was proud, but I am not proud, my brethring, an' although I've been a preacher of the gospel for twenty years, an' although I'm capting of the flatboat that lies at your landing, I'm not proud, my brethring.

I am not gwine to tell edzactly whar my tex may be found; suffice to say, it's in the leds of the Bible, and you'll find it somewhar between the first chapter of the book of Generations, and the last chapter of the book of Revolutions, and ef you'll go and search the Scriptures, you'll not only find my tex thar, but a great many other texes as will do you good to read, and my tex, when you shall find it, you shall find it to read thus: —

"And he played on a harp uv a thousand strings — sperits of jest men made perfeck."

My tex, my brethring, leads me to speak of sperits. Now, thar's a great many kinds of sperits in the world — in the fuss place, thar's the sperits as some folks call ghosts, and thar's the sperits of tur-pentine, and thar's the sperits as some folks call liquor, an' I've got as good an artikel of them kind of sperits on my flatboat as ever was fotch down the Mississippi river; but thar's a great many other kinds of sperits for the tex says, "He played on a harp uv a *t-h-o-u-s*-and strings, sperits of jest men made perfeck."

But I'll tell you the kind uv sperits as is meant in the tex, is FIRE. That's the kind uv sperits as is meant in the tex, my breth-ring. Now thar's a great many kinds of fire in the world. In the fuss place thar's the common sort of fire you light your cigar or pipe with, and then thar's foxfire and camphire, fire before you're ready and fire and fall back, and many other kinds uv fire, for the tex says, "He played on a harp uv a *thous*and strings, sperits uv jest men made perfeck."

But I'll tell you the kind of fire as is meant in the tex, my brethring — it's HELL FIRE! an that's the kind uv fire as a great many uv you'll come to, ef you don't do better nor what you have been doin' — for "He played on a harp uv a *thous*and strings, sperits of jest man made perfeck."

Now, the different sorts uv fire in the world may be likened unto the different persuasions uv Christians in the world. In the fuss place, we have the Piscapalions, an' they are a high sailin' and high-falutin' set, an they may be likened unto a turkey buzzard, that flies up into the air, an' he goes up, and up, and up, till he looks no bigger than your finger nail, and the fuss thing you know, he cums down, and down, and down, and is a fillin' himself on the carkiss of a dead hoss by the side of the road, and "He played on a harp of a *thous*and strings, sperits uv jest men made perfeck."

And then thar's the Methodis, and they may be likened unto the squirrel runnin' up into a tree, for the Methodis beleeves in gwine on from one degree of grace to another, and finally on to perfection, and the squirrel goes up and up, and up and up, and he jumps from limb to limb, and branch to branch, and the fuss thing you know he falls and down he cums kerflumix, and that's like the Methodis, for they is allers fallen from grace, ah! and "He played on a harp uv a *thous*and strings, sperits uv jest men made perfeck."

And then, my brethring, thar's the Baptist, ah! and they have been likened unto a possum on a 'simmon tree, and thunders may roll and the earth may quake, but that possum clings thar still, ah! and you may shake one foot loose, and the other's thar, and you may shake all feet loose, and he laps his tail around the limb, and clings and he clings furever, for "He played on a harp uv a *thous*and strings, sperits uv jest men made perfeck."

Where the Lion Roareth and the Wang-doodle Mourneth

MY BELOVED BRETHERING: I am a unlarnt Hard Shell Baptist preacher, of whom you've no doubt hearn afore, and I now appear here to expound the scripters and pint out the narrow way which leads from a vain world to the streets of Jaroosalem; and my tex which I shall choose for the occasion is in the leds of the Bible, somewhar between the Second Chronik-ills and the last chapter of Timothytitus; and when you find it, you'll find it in these words: "And they shall gnaw a file, and flee unto the mountains of Hepsidam, where the lion roareth and wang-doodle mourneth for his first born."

Now, my brethering, as I have before told you, I am an oneddicated man, and know nothing about grammar talk and collidge highfalutin, but I am a plane unlarnt preacher of the Gospil, what's been foreordaned and called to prepare a pervarse generashun for the day of wrath — ah! "For they shall gnaw a file, and flee unto the mountains of Hepsidam, whar the lion roareth and the wang-doodle mourneth for his first born" — ah!

My beloved brethering, the tex says they shall gnaw a file. It does not say they *may*, but shall. Now, there is more than one kind of file. There's the hand-saw file, the rat-tail file, the single file, the double file, and profile; but the kind spoken of here isn't one of them kind nayther, bekaws it's a figger of speech, and means going it alone and getting ukered, "for they shall gnaw a file, and flee unto the mountains of Hepsidam, whar the lion roareth and the wang-doodle mourneth for its first-born — ah!"

And now there be some here with fine close on thar backs, brass rings on thar fingers, and lard on thar har, what goes it while they're yung; and thar be others here what, as long as thar constitooshins and forty-cent whiskey last, goes it blind. Thar be sisters here what, when they gets sixteen years old, cut thar tiller-ropes and goes it with a rush. But I say, my dear brethering, take care you don't find, when Gabriel blows his last trump, your hands played out, and you've got ukered — ah! "For they shall gnaw a file, and flee unto the mountains of Hepsidam, whar the lion roareth and the wang-doodle mourneth for his first born."

Now, my brethering, "they shall flee unto the mountains of Hepsidam"; but thar's more dams than Hepsidam. Thar's Rotter-dam, Haddam, Amster-dam, and "Don't-care-a-dam" — the last of which, my brethering, is the worst of all, and reminds me of a sirkumstans I onst knowed in the state of Illenoy. There was a man what built him a mill on the north fork of Ager Crick, and it was a good mill and ground a sight of grain; but the man what built it was a miserable sinner, and never give anything to the church; and, my dear brethering, one night there came a dreadful storm of wind and rain, and the mountains of the great deep was broke up, and the waters rushed down and swept that man's mill-dam to kingdom cum, and when he woke up he found that he wasn't worth a dam — ah! "For they shall gnaw a file, and flee unto the mountains of Hepsidam, whar the lion roareth and the wang-doodle mourneth for his first-born — ah!"

I hope I don't hear anybody larfin; do I?

Now, "whar the lion roareth and the wang-doodle mourneth for his first-born" — ah! This part of my tex, my beseaching brethering, is not to be taken as it says. It don't mean the howling wilderness, whar John the Hard Shell Baptist fed on locusts and wild asses, but it means, my brethering, the city of New Y'Orleans, the mother of harlots and hard lots, whar corn is wuth six bits a bushel one day and nary a red the nex; whar niggers are as thick as black bugs in spiled bacon ham, and gamblers, thieves, and pickpockets goes skiting about the streets like weasels in a barn-yard; whar honest men are scarcer than hen's teeth; and whar a strange woman once took in your beluved teacher, and bamboozled him out of two hundred and twenty-seven dollars in the twinkling of a sheep's-tail; but she *can't* do it again! Hallelujah — ah! "For they shall gnaw a file, and flee unto the mountains of Hepsidam, whar the lion roareth and the wang-doodle mourneth for his first-born — ah!"

My brethering, I am the captain of that flat-boat you see tied up thar, and have got aboard of her flour, bacon, taters, and as good Monongahela whiskey as ever was drunk, and am mighty apt to get a big price for them all; but what, my dear brethering, would it all be wuth if I hadn't got religion? Thar's nothing like religion, my brethering: it's better nor silver or gold gimcracks; and you can no more get to heaven without it, than a jay-bird can fly without a tail — ah! Thank the Lord! I'm an oneddicated man, my brethering; but I've sarched the Scripters from Dan to Beersheba, and found Zion right side up, and hard shell religion the best kind of religion — ah! 'Tis not like the Methodists, what specks to get to heaven by hollerin' hell-fire; nor like the Univarsalists, that get on the broad gage and goes the hull hog — ah; nor like the Yewnited Brethering, that takes each other by the slack of thar breeches and hists themselves in; nor like the Katherliks, that buys threw tickets from their priests; but it may be likened unto a man what has to cross the river — ah! — and the ferry-boat was gone; so he tucked up his breeches and waded acrost — ah! "For they shall gnaw a file, and flee unto the mountains of Hepsidam, whar the lion roareth and the wang-doodle mourneth for his first-born!"

Pass the hat, Brother Flint, and let every Hard Shell Baptist shell out.

Kittrell J. Warren

(1829-1889)

Kittrell J. Warren was one of the last of the Southwestern humorists. Born in Alabama, he came to Georgia as a youth. He studied law and actively engaged in politics as a state legislator and county judge. He was also a newspaper writer and editor. In 1861 he enlisted in the Confederate Army as a private. From his experiences in the army came three books: *Ups and Downs of Wife Hunting* in 1861, a brief jokebook for soldiers; *History of the Eleventh Georgia Vols . . .* in 1863, an account of the activities of his own military unit; and *Life and Public Services of an Army Straggler* in 1865.

The *Army Straggler,* unlike most contemporary treatments of the Civil War, avoids moralizing and patriotic outbursts. The hero, Billy Fishback, is in fact that most despised of human creatures, the army deserter. A clever scavenger, he follows in the wake of battle and destruction, and like Simon Suggs capitalizes on other people's greed, stupidity, or misfortune. Occasionally he is joined by Captain Slaughter, whose easy facility with big words aids Billy considerably in his machinations. Together, they prefigure the Duke and the Dauphin of Mark Twain's *Huckleberry Finn.*

TEXT: Chapter 5 of *Life and Public Services of an Army Straggler* (Macon, Ga., 1865).

The Courtship of Billy Fishback, Army Straggler

A day or two after the occurrences related in the last chapter, Lee's army moved off in the direction of Culpepper, and our hero having previously hired an adept in the writing business, to prepare some papers for him, started back in the direction from which he had traveled in the commencement of his public career. Don't understand me as saying that he went off on those vulgar vehicles, his feet.

While official chargers were in every part of the army, he would have been untrue to the first law of nature had he condescended to take the people's line. On the contrary, when it was announced over night that the forces would move out by day-light next morning, he and

Dick Ellis retired to a log and set their wits in motion to work out some plan by which they might both mount themselves and effect their escape without apprehension. Ellis had a brother in the Federal service at Yorktown, and thither he determined to go. Fishback consented to bear him company, yet had no idea of doing so. It was not a part of his programme thus to sleep off the golden dreams that were flitting before his mind. But no common mortal like Ellis was permitted to peep into the sanctum of his intentions. Well, each took an oath never to reveal a word that passed between them in this conference, and then they set to planning. Major Holmes had one of the finest horses in the army. Fishback knowing that the better the animal, the greater would be the efforts to re-secure him, kindly proffered to aid in stealing *that horse* for Dick. Dick was to leave about midnight in the direction of West Point. Two hours afterwards Fishback would go to the Major, inform him of the theft, state that he had tried to stop the rogue but being afoot could not, that if he only had a horse he would certainly catch him, for he knew precisely which way he had gone. If the Major refused to send him he was to give wrong directions to whoever was sent in pursuit, and steal off the best he could; if, however, as was not doubted, he would mount Fishback and start him, they could get together and jog along as leisurely as they desired, having no one at all on their trail. About four miles from camp, and along a dim, unfrequented thorough-way, Dick was to wait until our hero came up, when they were to make for the Federal lines at Bottom's bridge.

Sure enough, about two o'clock, A. M., Fishback rushed into the Major's tent breathless with running and excitement, and began to shake him. "Majer, Majer!" "What the dickens do you want?" "Somebody's stold yore hoss, and rid him off. I met him when I was a cummin off uv guard jest now and tried to stop him; he's gwine a toards Beaver Dam. I know jest whar he's gone." "Well, well, well, I'm sorry for that. Fishback, can't you go after him for me? Wake up Adjutant, I want to borrow your horse to send after mine; some scoundrel's stolen him. Fishback, Capt. Smith thinks you can do any thing you put your hand to: catch my horse and I'll entertain the same opinion, besides giving you a round hundred dollars; and here, take my pistol and kill the villain wherever you lay eyes on him." This pistol business presented a new idea to the mind of our hero, who thereupon suggested that as there were several roads, it would be well enough to send some one with him. Fishback and Jack Wilcox were, therefore, properly instructed, "armed to the teeth," in the stirrups and off at a lope in less time than a stuttering man could have told about it. "Don't come back without my horse," bawled out

Holmes, as the riders disappeared. They had not gone far before
Fishback came to a sudden halt, and bending as far down as possible,
looked intently on the ground. "Here's hosses tracks," said he, "this
rode's mity dim, but goze into tother one about five miles from here,
and *hit* cuts off a little. I gess he's gone it. You go thru and I'll
go round. The Major's told us to kill him when we cetch him, and
we're ableeged to do it. I dont luv to kill fokes, you'r a heap danger-
ouser man than I am, you take *hit*." This well seasoned morsel of
flattery had the desired effect. "Yes," observed Jack, "I'll follow
him, and if he gets overhauled by me his infernal skull will leak shucks
after this."

Thus they parted, the one congratulating himself that "dead men
tell no tales" and the other burning with a murderous and revenge-
ful spirit.

From the difficulty of inquiring the direction to the place he was
aiming for, Fishback lost considerable distance and took a number of
wrong roads.

About noon of the second day after his departure, he was traveling
slowly along, his head down and mind buried in deep study. "Yes,
I'll fool him like I did about the Rufe Bates letter and the pocket-book
and all, taint no trouble to fool him. I'll jest tell how sum feller tride
to teck my hoss away, and we fout, and how he nockt me down
and crippled me so I never walkt a step in two munths, and then
jumpt a straddle o' my hoss and gallopt off. Never shall furgit the
Majer's last words, 'don't cum back thout my hoss,' nor I haint.
Capn Smith's a thinkin o' me rite now, he luves his 'brave, onest
Billy.' Dick Ellis aint a guine to pester about tellin nothin. That fool
Jack's dun turned him over to the tender mersez uv the carron
croze. That's a good joke I've got on Dick, maniged to get his branes
shot out thout my tellin a word." He was just raising his head to
enjoy a good laugh over this pleasant and amusing little incident,
when he found himself immediately before the cabin of his old friend
Mrs. Lane. It was several miles to the next house; he felt hungry
and weary. The prospects of being identified, (considering the number
of soldiers who had passed at various times, and the situation of the
"widder," during his former visit), were very small, and then too,
the cheering reflection that "widders don't hurt," constituted argument
sufficient to control his decision on the question whether he would
stop for dinner. But first, our wary Fishback asked a child he saw
playing in the yard, whether its "mammy" had married again, and
having received a negative reply, threw his bridle over the gatepost,
walked in, engaged dinner, dashed himself into a seat and was again

lost in the delightful revery his arrival had so abruptly interrupted.

Directly, a grim, surly looking man, wearing heavy, black, whiskers, badly pock-marked, and carrying the remains of a deep scar in his right cheek, passed through the room, giving our hero, as *he* thought, a very indelicate stare. This circumstance not only broke up his meditations but opened the eyes of Fishback to a number of remarkable truths. The stranger passed into the apartment he had slept in; he saw the old shanty had given place to a neat shed-room opening in the rear upon a snug row of negro houses. His quick perception immediately convinced him that "the child had fooled him on purpose, and the widder *was marred* again."

We will here explain for the benefit of the reader, that Mrs. Lane *never did* suspect our hero of having stolen Bones or the blankets. The events of the morning were of such a character that that antiquated animal had not been thought of until near noon, when he was found quietly occupying the lot to which he had returned. It is true, he had on a saddle and bridle and the gate was open, but Col. Lane merely set him to rights, and (his mind being engrossed with other matters) did not think to mention it. The missing blankets were charged to the roguery of an innocent man, and one of the children *distinctly saw* the soldier, (meaning Fishback) leave about day-light, and "directly after papa came home." Mrs. Lane was a little afraid her neglect had wounded his feelings. But after all, on that happy morning there was no room in the minds of the Lane family to be occupied by a strange soldier, so even our hero was cared for, and thought of no more. Col. Lane regained a portion of his property, left his wife comfortable and went back to the army.

On the day of Fishback's return, a neighbor had agreed with Mrs. Lane, to call over at noon and superintend the killing of a beef, in which they were both interested. That neighbor was the man whose presence so unmercifully disquieted our hero. After some stirring round he and Mrs. Lane took a stand near the room door, (the former holding in his hand a huge butcher-knife) and began to converse in an under tone, each eyeing him in a way he fancied exhibited no great sociability. The children too, stared at him in a most uncomfortable manner. He wanted to leave but was afraid the butcher knife would be inserted into his corpus the moment he made the break. At this juncture he looked out and saw his horse's tail disappearing behind the lot gate, and shrunk back trembling, sweating and rolling his eyes as the "brave Billy" had never done before. Occasionally his ear would catch disjointed fragments of sentences uttered by the sotto voce talkers such as "skin him," "butcher him," &c., either of which were sufficiently diaphoretic in its effects to put him into what the doctors call "a fine perspiration." But his suspense, although it seemed an age, did not last long. Presently the man in the whiskers remarked — as our hero thought — in an alarmingly vehement manner, "I'll get the gun and shoot him now," accompanying the words with a brisk movement into the room he was occupying. Fishback didn't stay to the shooting. Having sprung out at the door, he wrenched open the gate and ran for dear life, allowing his horse to eat "at will" and leaving the astonished family a striking example of the uncertainty of human nature and mortal legs.

Having measured the distance of five miles with such rapidity as to quite exhaust his wind and strength, Fishback crept into a thicket and sat down to rest.

"Well, now haint I done it," said he. "Lost my hoss and all my clene close by jest not having no sense. Mite a node it wont safe to stop thar, but I wus so hungry and wornt afeard o' wimmin, and jest nately wonted to see how the widder wus a gittin on starvin. That husband o' hern's a everlastin fool, jest a gwine to shute a feller thout sayin peze to him. Them vittles they was a fetchin in did smell monstrous invitin. Ding it all I'me a hongry, hit's raal mean not to feed a feller whats fitin fur the country. When *I fit* I fit fur the country so's to make the country fit fur me, and this is the ways its all turned out. Well reckon I'll git sum more cloze by then I retch old man Graveses and these passes I've got and them'l last me twell more cums in. Hit's a most too clost by to be a pickin up a nuther hoss."

Without any further adventure of a noteworthy character, our hero marched on, and late in the evening of the next day, reached Major Graves'.

He reminded the family of having called there before, but so many soldiers had stopped in passing that the Major could not recollect him until he referred to the then recent death of his father and the unsettled condition of the estate. "Oh yes, sir, yes sir," said he, "I remember you well, you are often pleasantly mentioned in my family. It is so strange my old eyes would not at first assist me to identify you. Well, sir, to what fortunate circumstance are we indebted for your present visit? Have a seat, sir, let me take your hat."

"Mammy was a lyin at the pint uv death and sent me word to cum home and stay with her twell she died. So atter the fites round Richmond, I got a discharge and jest as I was a gwine to start home I got a letter sayin she was dead" — here he shook his head mournfully and winked fast, as if to dissipate an intruding tear. "So I bought me a hoss and started back to the army — my hoss lay down and died yisteddy. I'm a gwine to the front, hit's the only place for me, a poor olphin, to go to — must start mighty soon in the mornin." One of the young ladies suggested, that as he was evidently very much wearied by hard marching, and the weather so oppressively warm, it would perhaps be an economy of time in the long run, for him to stop over a day or two. "Ah gal," said he, speaking very seriously, "I'd like to stay monstrous well, but my bleedin country axes me with tears in hit's eyes, to come up to the scratch, and thar I mean to come, so help me Jerediah Moss."

This stirring and patriotic speech was rewarded by an immediate invitation to supper. Soon after eating, he pled weariness and retired; not, however, until he had given Miss "Calline" several ingenuous manifestations of tender feeling, which only served as a source of amusement to her.

Next morning, Fishback was a bed-ridden, and badly tortured victim of rheumatism. Major Graves came in to see him, and prescribed a perfect diarrhœa of remedies. "No use projickin with medicines when I'm this way," said Fishback — "hit don't do narry speck o' good, this nasty, stinkin rumatism's allers a pesterin me, and the Docter says pills and draps makes it a sight wuss. Here Majer, retch thar in my pocket and git my pocket-book, and carry hit to Miss Graves, and tell her to keep it for me twel I git well, and not to let nobody open it; hit's a holdin secrets I'd hate mighty bad for *any boddy* to find out."

The wise Fishback had placed a proper estimate on female curiosity. He knew that after his injunction was announced the "gals" would "move heaven and earth" to pry into the mysteries of the pocket-book. Sure enough, they watched where their mother deposited it and as soon as her back was turned, stole it out, went to their own room, locked the door and began to hunt the *forbidden* secrets. The pocket-book was found to contain eleven hundred and thirty dollars, a discharge "granted William Fishback to return home and superintend the large agricultural interests of his mother, Mrs. Prissy Fishback," and also a letter, which read as follows:

Isabella, July 2d, 1862.

Mr. William Fishback,

Honored Sir: — It becomes my melancholy duty to inform you that your excellent mother is now no more. She died on the night of the 22nd ult., from congestion of the brain, superinduced, as you know, by a combination of pre-existing diseases.

During her last illness she spoke of you often, and expressed great anxiety to see you. I know you have been long anticipating this sad event, but it will, of course, cast a gloom over your feelings, as it has over those of all her friends. I never knew a woman so universally beloved, nor one so unceasingly kind, attentive and charitable to the suffering and needy. But, waiving these sorrowful suggestions, I must give you some information with reference to the situation of the estate, which now belongs solely to you. As there were a good many outstanding matters that required immediate attention, I have, at the urgent solicitation of your overseer, taken out temporary letters of administration. I sincerely hope you will be allowed to come home and manage the business yourself. I have too many matters of my own to look after, just now, to be well able to assume such additional and weighty responsibilities with justice to myself. I had the appraisement yesterday, your negroes and real estate were valued at $98,503.89; Bank and railroad stock $16,336.04; ready money and Sterling Exchange, $16,944.00; notes and accounts $18,620.00; making a total of $148,404.93. The whole of this estimate made on a gold and silver basis. The stock and household and kitchen furniture, including the piano and the two sofas, were not embraced in this appraisement, as it was understood that they belonged to you individually. There were a good many other things left out which it was not thought necessary to appraise. I understand the indebtedness of the estate is less than $1,800. The present crop promises well, and will pay that amount easily. The overseer informs me that the prospect was never so good at this season of the year, before.

Capt. Anderson, our representative, was killed, (as you know) at Port Republic, and there is great anxiety among the citizens generally, for you to be elected to fill his vacancy. There is a flying report in circulation here that you have been consulted on the subject and declined the candidacy. I hope and believe this rumor is without foundation, since it is certainly true that you are the only man in Worth County who could be elected without opposition. This is peculiarly a time when everything like political feeling and election excitement should be avoided, and as it is in your power so easily to harmonize all conflicting elements by representing Worth, I earnestly hope you will not refuse to do so. And in addition to this you won't consider it flattery in an old and intimate friend, and one who you know appreciates you, to say that your force of character, your patriotic energy and earnestness in behalf of the cause, your strength and vigor of mind, and above all, the unspotted purity of your whole life, eminently entitle you to a seat in the Georgia Legislature, and give earnest of the useful manner in which you will honor and dignify the position. Under all the circumstances, I really think, my dear sir, that you can serve the country more effectually in that way than any other.

Hoping soon to receive an answer giving me permission to place your name before the citizens of Worth,

I am, respected sir, with much esteem,

Your very sincere friend,

JOEL T. OLIVER.

Although, as we have stated, this inspection was conducted in secret session and with closed doors, yet no sooner was it completed than the whole group rushed into the presence of the old people and made a full revelation of all their discoveries. This, of course, resulted in a long family chat. The Major concluded that "although Fishback was illiterate, *he* had not been mistaken in regarding the young man as a solid, reliable, high-toned youth and one that would work his passage through life."

Mrs. Graves thought "he was yet quite young and could undoubtedly get the rust rubbed off by mixing a little with the world, representing his county in a few sessions of the Georgia Legislature, and marrying an educated girl." In making this last remark, her eyes fell, by the purest accident, on Caroline, who blushed deeply and replied that she "didn't believe Mr. Fishback wanted to marry anybody."

"Wife," remarked the Major, "I think he is rather pleased with Caroline. Go, my daughter, and comb your hair and button on your collar; it's eleven o'clock, and he thinks he'll be well enough to come down to dinner. Children, be particular, and don't let him have any reason to suspect that you have opened his pocket-book. What laudable modesty, to thus shrink from an examination of papers that stamp his character with the impress of Honor! Go Caroline, and fix yourself up."

"Ma," said little Ellen, "when sis Carline and Mr. Fishback marries mayn't I go to Georgy wid em and be dare baby?" This observation was followed by a loud laugh on the part of the young ladies, a scolding from Mrs. Graves and an adjournment of the convention.

The Misses Graves were now wholly forgetful of the fact that they had ever giggled at the comical chat and gawkish manners of our hero. There was nothing gawkish or comical about him. *He was such a nice gentleman — so original and unaffected — deported himself in such an artless and independent manner, and might be so appropriately said to draw the language in which he conversed, from Nature's pure, unwrought well-spring.* When dinner was announced, Fishback, supported by the Major, hobbled down stairs, and made his way to the table.

By one of those thoroughly intentional *accidents* that are "fixed aforehand," his chair and that of Miss Caroline were next to each other. "I hope," said she, "you are improving, Mr. Fishback."

"Yes, I'm a bundance better, but I can't bear no weight on my left leg yet. Miss Calline, I thought o' you a heap since I was here that time; seems to me like you git purtier and purtier."

"Oh, Mr. Fishback, you are *such* a flatterer — how many young ladies have you spoken to in the same manner since you were last here?"

"Narry one, dad fetched ef I have. I never makes game o' no umurn — allers says what I think, and think jest what I say — nigger fetch me one o' them thar flitters"; (this remark had reference to some fritters Mrs. Graves had prepared for dessert, and were placed on a table in the corner of the room, but which our unposted hero proposed to mix with the large supply of meat and greens to which he had been helped).

"Of course, you gentlemen never fail in bringing to bear a sufficient amount of plausibility to demonstrate your own sincerity." This sentence smelt a little too strong of the dictionary for Fishback to quite understand its signification; so, rather than venture a reply that might be inappropriate, he merely observed, "that's what *you* say."

"Yes indeed, and it's so. Now, Mr. Fishback, I appeal to your candor — isn't it?"

"You aint heard me say it was — fetch me a flitter, nigger, can't you hear nothin? — niggers is a mighty pester."

Thus they went on chatting and eating, until our hero made the scholarly announcement that he was "chock full," and the rest felt the force of the same interesting truth.

Fishback now became a lame convalescent, limping about the house and occasionally a short distance up the road. His appearance among the young ladies was a signal for all to retire excepting "Calline." With her, and in fact with the whole family, he had now no equal.

Brother Jack was informed by letter, that "sister Caroline was going to marry a gentleman of immense wealth and a member of the Georgia Legislature." His fame was noised through the settlement, and ladies were constantly dropping in "just to make a pop-call, see if the family were well and hear the news"; but with no other real object than that of catching a glimpse of the newly discovered prodigy. Each carried home her opinion, and dealt it out like a faithful commissary. Mrs. Brown "considered him a barbarian, monster; he couldn't begin to roost round her; she'd bet he'd give all the Graveses the itch." Kate Henry "knew *he* was no member of the Legislature; she'd bet he couldn't find the way there." Jennie Lee "was really surprised at Caroline Graves for reading that letter to everybody until it was nearly worn out by finger-marks — had a great mind to tell her it was an arrant forgery, and he nothing more nor less than a deserter. Why he smelt *so offensive,* with the tobacco juice running out at both corners of his mouth, he was absolutely hideous; she had no doubt he was at home a penniless and unprincipled vagabond." Miss Sallie Davis "thought he ought to be named Count D'Orsay Chesterfield, he was such a model man in dress and manners; oh, he did converse so charmingly about his 'mammy' and his 'crap,' his 'taters, water-millions' etc.; *he* was a honey." Thus did envious neighbors berate the lordly lover of the fortunate Caroline. But she lived in blissful ignorance of their denunciations. Indeed, since scarcely a lady called without threatening to steal him from her or passing some other such compliment, she entertained no doubt that he was an object of general admiration. Gilbert Van, a young man of limited means, but fine attainments and decided promise, who had been paying court to her, now saw his orb pass into total eclipse behind the rising splendors of the illustrious Fishback. Minnows must clear the track when whales are afloat. Our hero's object now was to marry Caroline and induce the Major to sell his real property, crop and all, for the purpose of settling on his (Fishback's) unoccupied lands in Georgia. After the marriage and sale should be accomplished, he would take his wife, the negroes and most of the money, and leave for Georgia, letting the Major remain behind with his family a few weeks until he could get fixed up for him. At some convenient point on the route, he intended selling the negroes, leaving his wife (as he had no use for one), and traveling to parts unknown. But he properly suspected that before trusting him so implicitly, the Major would want a little more evidence on the subject of his wealth and standing at home. For the purpose of supplying this deficiency, he frequently sat for hours by the road side waiting to find among the passing stragglers a suitable accomplice. While Fishback was planning for the future, however, and the neighbors comparing his claims to respectability, time was rolling on, and the shy, modest Caroline growing impatient to get courted. Our hero, who still remembered the admonition of Squalls, was too humane to allow her suspense to continue. So, one evening, as they sat in the piazza together, he drew his chair close to hers and remarked, "I swear pine blank, Calline, I luv you better'n any young umurn I ever seed."

"Ah, Mr. Fishback, you know you're just flattering me."

"No, I'll be dad blasted ef I am. I luved you the first time I ever seed you, and ef you'd jest marry me, no trouble shan't never bother you no more. Say yes, that's a purty gal?" With a woman's disposition to evade giving the answer, she dreads, and yet longs to make, Miss Caroline replied in an affectionate and entreating manner: "Why don't you let them elect you to the Legis—— there, now."

"Run me for what? been into that pocket-book o' mine, ah?"

"Now, Mr. Fishback," speaking excitedly, "let me tell you exactly how it happened —" "No you needn't, hunny, its all right, but I was *mighty* in hopes no body wouldn't see them papers; say, what you're gwine to do about havin me?"

"You're not in earnest; you want some of those charming Georgia girls." "Drat the infernal Georgy gals, they ain't fit to tote guts to a bar! Say, answer the question; won't you marry me?"

Miss Caroline laughed, grew red, and finally subsiding into seriousness, replied: "It is an important matter, and you must allow me a day or two to reflect and make up my mind." "Well, hunny," said he, looking at her affectionately, and speaking as gently as he could, "all right, but don't keep me in expense longer as you can help it, for I shall be mighty worried twel you let me know."

The young ladies were now summoned to the parlor, (and in going for them Caroline told all that passed, with incredible rapidity), and the evening was shortened by mirth and music. Time thus killed, dies a chloroform death. It glides away bearing a blissful, sweet unconsciousness that it is passing. But I have no *time* for digression.

About sunset a soldier came to the yard gate and hailed. Fishback usually acted the porter familiar, on such occasions, but now appearing to feel so intensely happy in his present position, he waited for Major Graves to answer the summons. "Can I stay here to-night?" spoke the man, as the Major opened the door. — "Stop," said Fishback, to the ladies. "I've hearn that voice — stop your blasted pyanner, and lemme listen." "Not well," replied the Major, "we are poorly prepared for company, at this time, two miles ahead you will find a good house to stop at." "Well, but my dear sir, I am so egregeously fatigued ——," our hero listened no further; rushing through the door, he ran out, and the two friends met and shook hands in the most "transporting, rapturous" manner; — "How de Isick, how de do old feller, come in a hepe." Having introduced Mr. Slaughter, — for such was the name borne by that individual — to the family, he made him lift off his harness and seat himself among the family.

"Well, Billy," said he, "it has been some time since we met before, and both of us have doubtless passed through a fearful ordeal during the eventful and sanguinary interiem." "You heerd my horn blow, big sis," was the appropriate and forcible reply of the quick-witted Fishback.

"But the lowering future is yet ominous of events in which we, perchance, will be integerals of a most belligrent aggregation." "That's jest *my* notions." "And perhaps we may become the doomed victims of a cruel, relentless and crucifying bellicosity." "That's the very thing I was gwine to a sed."

"But, though we should fall, it is consoling to reflect that the liberty for which we have struggled, is progressive, diffusive and eternal." "Them's the same words I've been thinkin about, right-smart while — when did you hear from Georgy?" "I left home two weeks ago, to-day." "Oh, yes," speaking sorrowfully, "I hearn o' that." "Well, I believe there's nothing else in the way of news; yes, I received a telegraphic dispatch during my sojourn in Richmond, last Monday, stating that you had been unanimously elected to a seat in the Georgia House of Representatives, from our county." "Won't have it, can't stand it, ain't a gwine to be pestered with no such." "Yes, you must," whispered a female voice, accompanying its words with a look of melting tenderness. "No, but I'll be dinged if I do; my country in the bog and me a sittin primpt up, like I was a havin my dod-drotted picter tuck; gal, you don't know what you'r talkin about — how's my crap a gittin on." "Very well, indeed, very well; a more productive harvest has never been garnered on the premises than that which is at present ripening. Your estate has been appraised at near one hundred and fifty thousand dollars (according to the gold and silver basis) and it is reported that the outstanding liabilities amount to less than fifteen hundred dollars; really, my dear Fishback, you have enough to commence life comfortably, with your economy and good financiering qualities, a large fortune will certainly be accumulated."

"Yes, I've got enough to scrouge along with ef I can only git a good, savin wife." At this he ogled Caroline, who let her eyes drop, and looked, for all the world, like she meant to try and make a "savin wife."

"You might add considerably to your capital stock by effecting a union with the rich and literary heiress, Miss Julia Evans. It is reported that she's in the incipient stages of dementation, on your account." "She be darnd; Jule Ivins' been tryin to git me a mighty long time." "But she can't do it, can she?" tenderly whispered a soft voice. "No, indeed, mam," said Slaughter, replying to the question; "although she is wealthy, intelligent and justly accounted a star of the first magnitude among the queenly luminaries of that refulgent clime, yet I venture to say that our friend Fishback is peculiarly the proprietor of his own heart, which will never be bartered for gold or splendor."

"I commend Mr. Fishback for that," said she, "for of all unpardonable violations of the laws of our being, I regard mercenary love the most unpardonable. It is like selling, not our brother Joseph, but our very selves into perpetual bondage." "You are correct. It is indeed, an imitation of Judas — bartering immortality for a sum of money. We are not the owners of the soul, and have no right to vend it — that eternal element has been entrusted to us as custodians only; a truth which we find beautifully illustrated in the parable of the talents — if we bury it in the cumbrous rubbish of filthy lucre, how fearful will be the ulterior consequences?"

"If I can but have true affection in an humble home, I'll never be willing to exchange it for all the pompous wretchedness wealth can purchase."

"I endorse that sentiment most cordially. Bribe the needle to play truant to the pole — train the untrameled wind to blow not 'where it listeth' — teach the thirsty sun-beam to leave undrunk the dews of heaven, but this heart must revolve in its allotted periphery, or cease to move."

Although, so far as we know, our hero was wholly unacquainted with any foreign language, he had caught the gist of this conversation, and now ventured his own sentiments on the subject, in the following laconic style: "I'll be dad blasted ef I hadn't ruther try to set on a dozen rotten eggs twel I hatcht the last one uv 'em, as to marry a umurn jest for her munny, and spect to git along; thar aint narry bit o' use a tryin. Hit's like cetchin a jack-a-ma-lantern; it looks powerful easy, but hit haint no go. I shant marry for nuthin but love" — looking significantly at Caroline — "dad blasted ef I do."

The conversation continued for some time, Slaughter occasionally "piling the agony" on Fishback who manifested the most dignified indifference to worldly honors. It is said that our hero was several times embarrassed by forgetting the name of his *intimate friend,* which he explained away in a satisfactory manner by saying his "Mammy had whipt him so much when he was little, about callin folks by thar names he'd got so he couldn't recollect nobody's name." This rumor, however, is so variant from the character of our hero that we pronounce it a flagrant slander. The two friends occupied the same bed that night, and both rose early next morning. "You must pay me *Fifty* dollars for my services, Fishback," remarked Slaughter.

"Why, you said you'd tend to it for ten dollars and lodgin."

"I know I did, but I've reconsidered; certainly a man should have the privilege of changing his mind. I have managed your case so successfully that I am satisfied fifty dollars will be but a paltry remuneration. "Can't pay you but ten." "Very well, I'll settle my own bill, unsay all I have said, and we'll separate as we met. That, of course, will be satisfactory, since the terms of settlement can't be agreed upon."

"I'll give you twenty-five: ain't got narry nuther cent ef I had to be hung." "That's all satisfactory, perfectly so; we'll just rue the trade and leave the matter where it stood before I came; this can be accomplished pleasantly enough by just telling what passed between us up the road yesterday. As for taking less than *fifty*, I couldn't entertain such an idea. My price or the original status, are the only alternatives I can accept, and either will be entirely agreeable to me." "Ef I borry the fifty for you will you put in some more o' them jodarters about me bein a good egg?" "Yes, I'll branch out on the subject of your disposition, at the breakfast table, and make a few additional remarks on points already canvassed, if the fifty is in hand; but as you haven't got the money convenient, I have no objections to canceling the contract; don't, I conjure you, don't raise the money just for my accommodation. I'd prefer to rescind."

It is needless to say, the spondulics were forthcoming. Breakfast and the purchased praises having been faithfully completed, Slaughter's haversack was filled, and he passed on.

Fishback's character was now established by concurring testimony, in which there could have been no collusion, and Caroline found herself urged by the family and her *ardent affection*, to consummate the proposed marriage, with the least possible delay. The Major readily consented to offer his real property for sale, — move from the borders to the Georgia interior, and settle on the rich wire-grass lands of his future son-in-law. Our hero, likewise, after much persuasion, finally yielded a reluctant consent to pull loose from the warm embra of "grim-visaged war," and "caper nimbly" in the Legislature. Whereupon, Thursday, the twelfth day of October, was fixed upon as the happy, nuptial day. The Major was so anxiously urged by every member of his family, present and prospective, to sell out on any terms, that in less than one week after his lands were put upon the market, he had passed a title, and received as the whole purchase money, a sum so inadequate as, only for the bright prospect ahead, would have made him feel ruined. But Fishback knew where better lands could be procured for half the amount; he (Fishback) had consented to take the money and thus invest it, and the Major felt so happy that the trade had been completed, that he almost made a boy of himself.

Time moved on, and the wedding day, for which our hero longed most monstrously, drew near. Invitations went in every direction, and the Graveses and their neighbors, were all astir. The ladies in the settlement, including Mrs. Brown and Misses Lee, Henry and Davis gave active aid in preparing for the great event. One of Caroline's dresses — a jaconet muslin — underwent slight repairs, and was set apart for the wedding night, and a fine, flowered silk, for the day succeeding. Fishback had obtained, the day before his arrival, all the necessary equipments to make a very respectable marriage suit; the pants, it is true, not having been cut for him, were rather short and a little too tight around the ankle, or rather, above it, for they didn't reach quite that far down. But that was a matter of no consequence. Cakes and sweet things of every variety and in great profusion were undergoing the process of preparation. The Major stated that "this was to be, not only a wedding, but a farewell supper, in which he intended his friends should feast to fullness." The truth is he had never been so elated at any event of his life, as the prospect of a wealthy son-in-law and a body of rich Georgia lands, and therefore, felt like it was his time to stand treat.

The evening before the wedding day, one of the young ladies ran into our hero's room and resting her hand on his shoulder, began: "Oh, I'm so happy, I've just got a letter from brother Jack, and he'll be here to-morrow; now, won't you help us persuade him to move to Georgia — won't you, my good brother, William?" "Yes, we'll take him along — how much land's he got?" "About four hundred acres, papa says." "Let him sell out at half price, and I'll take his money and buy twist as much land in Georgy, and hit clerd and fenst, and better'n his'n." "Now, if you'l only manage to make brother understand that, and get him to go with us, I promise to be *the best sister.*" "All right, I'll fix that pint."

It seemed now that riches were actually crowding themselves upon the fortunate Fishback. In three days he was to start for the South with the Major's money, daughter and negroes, leaving the Major himself to sell a small remnant of his crop, which was yet undisposed of, (while the remainder of the family paid a few parting visits), and bring them on afterwards. Now, he determined that the credulous Jack should let *his* lands, negroes and produce drift into the same channel. Charmed with the pleasing prospect, he felt that he could hardly wait for the slow motioned Time, and again did he rehearse in two minutes, the weighty arguments he would wield on that occasion; the earnestness and force with which he would urge immediate action, in view of another invasion, and the persuasive influence that might be expected from the family. The theme was thrillingly delightful, and he dwelt on it with the rapture of an enthusiast.

The morning of the twelfth at length came on, and was clear, pleasant, and marked by no jostling variation from the steady progress with which events were ripening, except that, perhaps, Miss Caroline felt a greater flutter in the region of her heart, than she had before experienced, and the Major's stove-pipe hat was somewhat slicker than usual. The hour of one o'clock came, dinner was ready, and was about to be commenced — several visiting ladies present, among whom were Misses Lee and Henry, were "up to their eyes" in business, and our hero with his affianced sat in the parlor, their hands locked together, and their eyes and voices expressing infinite happiness; when suddenly the cry arose, "brother Jack's come! brother Jack's come!" and the female Graveses charged "the big gate," and swarmed around him. Each began at the same time, and in the most impatient manner to herald the praises of their inchoate husband and brother. "I know you'll love him, brother Jack," said Caroline, "he's so good and so noble." "Yes, and he's fine looking," remarked another; "and pa thinks," observed a third, "that he's a gentleman of great solidity of character, the first order of business talents and remarkably good judgment." Thus they moved on slowly, each trying to out talk the rest.

Fishback sat at the window, straining his eyes to catch a glimpse of the notorious Jack, who was yet hid by the intervening grove; he felt great anxiety to see whether that gentleman possessed a persuadable physiognomy. Presently his anxious eyes were rewarded by the coveted sight. Having passed from behind some paradise trees in about ten steps of the house, he came in full view, and oh! terrific truth, that brother was none other than the black-whiskered, pockmarked man who had behaved in such blood-thirsty manner at Mrs. Lane's. There was no time to be lost. He sprang out at the window with a violence that disturbed his equilibrium. "La," said one of the young ladies vhat a frightful fall Mr. Fishback's got!" "I'm afraid it hurt him," observed the sympathetic Caroline, starting herself to his relief. But the hero of our story was a goner. Having rushed through the back yard, he soon became lost to view in the neighboring woods, leaving his hat, pocket-book and washing to be attended to by the Graveses; his adorable "Calline" to be commended for her discernment and sagacity, by the firm of Mrs. Brown & Co., and the wedding guests to play a long, pleasant and interesting game of Criticism.

Anonymous

♨ "A Sleep-Walking Incident" depicts a recurrent situation in Southwestern tales: a dignified visitor in need of lodging is forced to spend the night in the shack of a backwoodsman whose family consists mainly of ripe young daughters (cf. Field's "Honey Run"). The chief event in such sketches is usually the visitor's attempt to disrobe for bed without the girls seeing him. This story, however, is far superior to most of its counterparts both in humorous situation and in character development. The old man is a stern individualist who lives by a code as rigid as his ancient back. His role is comic, but he commands interest for his pride, his relationship with his family, and his perfectly formulated rules for killing undesirable guests.

The anonymous author of "Where Joe Meriweather Went To" subtitled his sketch "A Kentucky Yarn," but it might have come from any place in the Old Southwest. Its characters are typical: a gullible listener who is extremely eager for news of the outside world, and a robust and highly imaginative visitor who never loses the opportunity to relate a "stretcher." Bill Meriweather can effectively manufacture a domestic tall tale, such as his account of the tobacco-spitting Chawback, or create a yarn of cosmic proportions.

TEXT: "A Sleep-Walking Incident" and "Where Joe Meriweather Went To" from *Polly Peablossom's Wedding,* ed. T. A. Burke (Philadelphia, 1851).

A Sleep-Walking Incident *

Many, very many years have taken their turn in making me older, if not more wise, since the sunny days of youth, when there was not a sallow leaf on life's tree — when all was light and glow, and I felt but the present, the past unheeded, and the future unknown. Oh, joyous fifteen, that green isle now dimly seen over life's waste of waters, how we look and long to tread thy shores again! But our bark of life is speeding away. Small — smaller still. The dim eye of age can see thee no more — *thou* art "the past."

Soon after this hour in life's morning, I was sent into the upper counties of this State, on a trip of business, and which I contrived to make a trip of pleasure, save the "scrape" about to be narrated.

Night had overtaken me some miles short of my intended stopping-

---

* The author of this sketch (who signed himself "Sugartail") was actually George Washington Harris. It was first published in the *Spirit of the Times,* 16 (September 12, 1846), 343. Our thanks to M. Thomas Inge for calling this to our attention. HC and WBD.

place, so I hailed the first house that I came to — a large square cabin sort of a house, with but one apartment, which served as "parlour, hall, kitchen and all," — to know if I could obtain shelter for myself and horse? A stout, iron-looking little old man answered the summons, and after resting his arms and chin on the gate for some seconds, he said, rather deliberately, that he "didn't adzactly know, seeing as how his house was small, and he had company; but seeing as how I was a benighted boy, he reckoned I mought jist lite." I did so, and found the house "full of gals." First, there was the "old oman," of course, all tidiness and check apron, then three blooming daughters, all shyness and blushing, a married daughter and her yearling child, (these were the "company" alluded to,) and *then* there was that everlasting, long-legged, ubiquitous, eighteen-year-old boy, who is to be seen at all houses in the country, with that everlasting tight roundabout, strained across his shoulder blade, which seems to belong inherently to all chaps of his class, and he patronized mixed socks and low-quartered shoes. That specimen of the class "green boy" deserves more than a passing notice at my hands, if I had the talent and room, but I must content myself by merely saying that his name was Tewalt, and that I will never forget him, or the service he rendered me in my "hour of great peril," although for a time he annoyed me not a few; and I may hazard the assertion, that if he remembers all that was gleaned from me that night, and all that occurred next morning, he is a perfect locomotive encyclopædia of useful knowledge.

Supper passed off, during which, and the interval preceding bed-time, I was subjected to a categorical examination on matters in general, and my business in particular, the old lady acting as principal inquisitor, prompted in whispers by the girls. They listened and giggled, the married daughter nursed and tried to look matronly, the dog lay at the corner of the hearth, and dreamed perhaps of his last rabbit chase; the cat washed her face, as all well-ordered cats will do, after a hearty saucer of milk, and I, poor I, wished it well over. I counted the minutes as indicated by a twenty-four-hour Yankee clock, which, nailed against the log wall, ticked off the time most methodically; and surveyed the prospect for bed *room,* with deep interest. I counted the beds (three, all in a row, across the back of the house,) over and again; then I counted noses, and found an awful disproportion between them and the beds. I resolved divers arithmetical problems of position in my mind, to ascertain if possible how to class said noses, so as to violate no known and acknowledged law of usage and propriety, in sleeping matters made and provided. But all in vain. I was beginning to entertain serious thoughts in relation to the stable-loft, when the old lady opened the first act by peremptorily ordering Tewalt off to one bed, then with the help of the girls she metamorphosed another into a gigantic "shake-down" before the fire; she managed to increase its dimensions prodigiously, until it attained at least the size of an ordinary onion-bed. This encampment, as I said, was spread before the fire, and was for the benefit of the girls, married and single, rank and file. Now my mind was at rest; they (the girls), baby and all, were safely disposed of, and the horrid suspicion had passed away that I might have to sleep "spoon fashion" with perhaps three, and that fat baby at the foot. I now saw as clearly through the old lady's sagacious arrangements as if they had been the result of the aforesaid abortive mathematical calculations. Tewalt and myself were to have one bed, and the old folks the other; to my unsophisticated boyhood, this arrangement was the best that possibly could be made under the circumstances. The old lady, considerate old soul, hung a quilt over two chairs, as a kind of battery for me to undress behind, and cautioning the two girls in an undertone not to *look,* she told me I might go to bed as soon as I liked. I, nothing loth, obeyed the intimation, and in spite of the stray eyeshots fired at me from the region of the fire-place, got safely to bed, and was soon in the land of dreams.

The first thing I remember, I felt some one inflicting furious digs in my side; it struck my dreaming imagination that it was the aforesaid Tewalt, who wanted some incomprehensible point in the evening's conversation elucidated, so I moved not. Soon I saw him standing over me, his legs at least sixty feet long, and kicking me in the ribs at a smashing rate, with a foot about the size of a steamboat's yawl. Then he changed and had on petticoats of the proportions of a circus tent, with a huge gig-top on for a night-cap, and nursing the Yankee clock for a baby, and every blow it struck resembled a blast from a pair of infantile lungs highly inflated! Anon, he became a gigantic pair of fire-tongs, with red-hot feet, and he pinched me on the arm until it *scizzed* again! This awoke me, sure enough, and I found the pinching still going on at about the rate of 120 to the minute.

"Hello, old fellow!" says I, "that'll do. What in the name of the Lunatic Asylum *do* you want?"

"It aint no *old* feller, an you may thank gracious goodness that it aint; but you jist git rite up an mosey, afore I calls the old feller!"

This was spoken close to one ear in a good round whisper, while a suppressed sort of giggling appeared to originate about a foot from the other. I lay perfectly still, and tried to arouse my faculties as to the cause of all this rumpus. I then ventured to raise my head a fraction and saw that the fire was not in the same place that it occupied when I went to bed. Had Tewalt turned my bed round by the furious kicks above named? No, that must have been a dream, and I was awake *now* — as wide as ever you saw a cat, with all the dogs in the neighbourhood at the foot of the apple-tree, and she on the first limb. I listened, and the blessed old clock had moved towards another point of the compass, and was boxing away as if nothing had occurred to disturb its equanimity; the old man's snoring, too, had partaken of this general first-day-of-May excitement, and, like the clock and the fire, had changed its quarters. Strange, that, but may be I had only heard the echo on the wall. But the old man being sedate, it was not presumable that he would patronize other than a becoming and sedate snore, and would tolerate no other, however sonorous, nor be guilty of playing such fantastic tricks before — a stranger! And the heavy breathing of Tewalt, too, had retired to a respectful distance in the rear, but it *was* his breathing, and no mistake; I was familiar with the sound. Well, what was the matter? Was I tight? No, I had drank nothing. Was I crazy? No, for I was fully aware of everything, save that my ideas of relative position had become confoundedly mystified.

"I say, cuss your *sassey* little picter, are you gwine to leave afore I calls dad, for he'll jist give you goss in a minit, little hoss, and we gals couldn't save your cussed ternal scalp if we wanted tu! Say, ar ye gwine, *durn* yer imperdence!"

Oh, my stars! the awful truth flashed on my mind in an instant. I had got in bed with the girls, and would soon be a lost boy, barrin' better luck than John Tyler ever had. But my presence of mind came to my aid, so I replied to this whispered tirade by giving a heavy groaning sort of snore, and turning over from my tormentor, I reconnoitred my location by throwing out first an arm and then a leg. The arm lit across the heaving warm breast of *somebody* with considerable muscular energy, for quick as light it was seized, and no rocket ever flew with more of a "vim," than it did from its soft resting place, and lit smack across the face of my pinching friend, the married daughter, who was unmasked by this move of her sister, for in its descent it chanced also to hit the "yearling" a wipe in the neighbourhood of the nose, and such a yell as followed, or rather such a series of yells, I never before heard. My leg, I suppose, had lit upon forbidden ground also, for it followed the arm with no bad consequences, only a wicked sort of a dig in my side, which I thought might be inflicted with the naked elbow; this was intended as a kind of interest on the operation, given in "have-the-last-lick" spirit of mind.

Well, after calculating the probable location of my own bed, I made one bound, which cleared me of the enemy's camp, and I lit alongside of Tewalt.

"Well, durn your carcass," says he, "you wanted to sleep *warm*, did you, so you jist goes atween the gals! They warmed ye, didn't they? drat your picter! Ha! ha! ha! Well, now, if that aint hot, I'm d-a-r-n-e-d!"

A running-fire of conversation was kept up between the shake-down and the old folks' bed for some time, but as it was not of a *very* complimentary nature, so far as I was concerned, I will not inflict on the reader what both pained and scared me. After rolling about for some time in a rather perturbed state of mind, I fell asleep, and was awoke by the old lady to come to breakfast. Tewalt was gone, I knew not where, the shake-down had vanished, and things looked tidy and clean.

When we set up to breakfast I felt like a criminal, and I know that I looked like one; the girls blushed, the married one was serious, the old lady seemed pious, and the old man looked devilish; so you may guess how I relished my breakfast. Not a word did I say that I could help, and the old lady's disposition of the previous evening to ask questions seemed to have vanished, so I was not interrupted in my taciturnity.

The meal over, I asked the old man the amount of my bill. "I don't charge ye a cent!" This was said in a tone and manner that I neither liked nor understood; so as my horse was at the gate, with Tewalt holding the bridle, I turned round to bid the girls "good morning," and there they were, holding up the log that served for a mantle-board with their foreheads, and seemed to be in tears. This mystified me more than ever; the old man had taken down an old black snakish-looking rifle, and was changing the priming. I inquired if he was going to hunt? "Y-a-s," he drawled out; "I'm agwine to kill a mink what's been among my pullets!" Well, I didn't like *that* either; so, without more ceremony, I started to the horse, and as I left the door, I heard one of the girls (a sweet, blue-eyed damsel she was, too), and the one who had converted my arm into a projectile with such dire effect the night before, say, "Oh, daddy, now don't; we all know he *was* asleep, poor little fellow! Don't, daddy, don't!"

The old scoundrel growled a reply which I did not hear, and followed me.

When I reached my horse, I mounted, and Tewalt, who stood beyond the horse, drew from the leg of his breeches, a long, keen hickory, and stealthily gave it to me, saying:

"Don't hold it so, dad'll see it, and when ye *get the word*, jist gin that horse of yourn hot darnation about his tail, or may be you won't ride long if ye don't."

He was cut short in his charitable speech by the approach of the old
he shark, *gun* in hand.

"Now, sir," says he, "ye come here benighted, didn't ye?"

"Yes, sir," said I, submissively.

"I took ye in like a gentle*man*, didn't I?"

"Yes, sir, you did, and I am ———"

"Stop! that ain't the pint. I fed you an your horse on the best I
had, didn't I?"

"Yes, sir," replied I, "and I am willing ———"

"Stop! *that* ain't the pint. I give you a *good* bed to sleep on, didn't
I?"

"Yes, sir," I said, "you did all ———"

"Stop! *that ain't the pint.* Ye got your breakfast, didn't ye?"

I nodded assent.

"My boy and gals treated you like a gentle*man*, didn't they?"

I nodded again.

"Well, I've refused yer money, hain't I?"

"Yes, sir, and I wish you would ———"

"Stop! that ain't the pint; *but this is the pint!*" and the fire sim-
mered in his eyes like molten iron in glass globes; all his forced calm-
ness had left him, and he was an old Tiger *all over.* "You've eat my
bread — yer hoss eat my corn — ye smoked my pipe — ye had my
bed, an all fur nuthin — and then ye wanted to circumve nt, not one,
but all my gals, married and single, at one bite, darn yer little snakish
gizzard; and now we'll settle, *or I can't draw a bead!* I never vierlates
the law of horspitality at this house, nur on my grit, so you see that
crossfence, down *thar?*" (it was about one hundred and fifty yards
off.)

I barely nodded my head, and in looking, my eye caught the form
of Tewalt and the girl with the blue eyes, behind the stable, busily
enacting a piece of pantomime, evidently for my benefit. Tewalt
gave an imaginary horse an awful imaginary thrashing, leaning forward,
and occasionally stealing a look over his shoulder, as if he expected
to see the devil. She took very deliberate aim at him with a corn stalk,
and then poked him between the shoulder-blades with it, in no very
slight manner.

"Well," continued the *old he,* "when I give you the word, you may
start, an if ye start too soon, I'll spile yer hide with my own grit, an
I don't want to do *that!* I say, when I give the word you may go, an
perhaps you'd use them long boot heels of yourn *some,* fur when you
start *so do I,* an when *I* gets to that fence — mind, it's *my line,* then
we are off my grit; *I'm jist agwine to shute you, jist like a cussed mink*

fur getting among my hens! I'll only spile ye with two holes, one behind, an t'other before, jist sixty-three to the pound, adzactly, and yer kin can't say I hurt ye on my land!"

He began to hitch up his breeches with his disengaged hand, and laid off his hat, so I ventured to ask — more dead than alive — what the "word" would be?

"It'll be 'the old quarter tackey word.' I'll ax ye if yer ready, an when ye ar, jist say 'go!' If ye ain't, say 'no,' but mind yer dont *balk often,* or I mite git to ravin an fittin, and go off afore you want me to, and then ye'll be *dead* beat sartin!"

During this preliminary I was gently plying my horse on the off side with my heel and hickory, to stir him up a little. I had ridden a few quarter races in my time, and was pretty well up to the dodge. The old villain asked, between his set teeth, "ar ye ready?" I shouted "go!" and away we went. My hickory now fell ten times faster on the real horse than Tewalt's did on the imaginary one, and as soon as the old cuss heard it he bawled out to his boy, "Oh, dat rat yer heart, I say; I'll bore a hole in *you,* when I get to ye!"

I ventured to turn my head and take a look at him; he had foamed at the mouth until it adorned each corner like a pair of whiskers, made of whipped eggs, and he was running *some,* I tell *you!* My horse, perfectly astounded at such unusual treatment, fairly flew; the panels of fence looked like a continuous stripe along the road, and the wind whistled a merry jig in my listening ears. *Spang!* whiz — phit! the ball had sped, and it had *missed!* I saw it tear the bark from a hickory, a few yards ahead. Oh, how fresh and warm the blood rushed back around my heart! I felt safe, mischievous, and glad, and began to rein up my horse. When I succeeded in doing so, I wheeled him in the road to reconnoitre. There stood the old Tiger, leaning on the muzzle of his gun, as if in a brown study; so I resolved to give him a parting "blizzard." I shouted, "Hello, old cock; you have good victuals and a fine family, your galls in particular; but I would not give a button for your gun or your temper! You can't shoot for sour owl bait! Tell the girls 'good-bye,' and the same to you, you old scatter-gun!"

He began to re-load furiously, so I whistled to my horse, and left those parts — forever, I hope. I have often wondered since, what he *did* do to poor Tewalt, for smuggling the hickory which enabled me to tell this story.

Where Joe Meriweather Went To

"I do believe that's Bill Meriweather," said the old lady hostess of the "Sign of the Buck" tavern, as, attracted by the noise of a horse's hoofs, she raised her eyes from her occupation of stringing dried slips of pumpkin, and descried, this side of the first bend in the road, a traveller riding a jaded horse towards the mansion. "I do believe that's Bill Meriweather. It's about time fur him to be round agin a buyin' shoats. But whar's Joe? Phillisy Ann," continued Mrs. Harris, raising her voice, "catch a couple of young chickens, and get supper ready as soon as you can, you dratted lazy wench you, for here comes Bill Meriweather. But whar's Joe? How do you do, Mr. Meriweather?" concluded the old lady, as the stranger arrived in front of the porch.

"Lively," replied that individual, as he proceeded to dismount and tie his horse. "How do you come on yourself, old 'oman?"

"Pretty well, Bill; how's craps down in your parts?"

"Bad, uncommon bad," replied Bill. "There's a new varmint come around in our county, that's got a mortal likin' for the tobaker crap. They looks a good deal like a fox, but are as big as a thr'e year old nigger, and can climb a tree like a squirrel, and they steals a dozen or so 'hands' every night, and next mornin' ef you notice, you'll see all the tops of the pinoaks around the plantation kivered with them a-dryin', and the infernal Chawbacks — that's what we call 'em — a settin' up in a crotch, a chawin' what is cured, and squirtin' ambeer all over the country. Got any on em' up here yet?"

"The goodness, Lord ha' mercy, no, Bill! But whar's Joe?"

Up to this time Mr. Meriweather had been as pleasant and jovial a looking Green River man, as you might find in a week's ride along the southern border of Kentucky, and had finished his lecture on the natural history of the Chawback, and the unsaddling of his horse at the same time; but no sooner had the old lady asked the question, "Whar's Joe?" than he instantaneously dropped on the bench alongside the questioner, gave her an imploring look of pity and despair, let his head fall into his open palms, and bending down both until they nearly touched his knees, he uttered such a sigh as might a Louisville and New Orleans eight-boiler steam-packet in the last stage of collapsed flues.

"Goodness gracious, Bill! what's the matter?" cried the old lady, letting her stringing apparatus fall. "Hev you got the cramps? Phillisy

Ann, bring that bottle here out'n the cupboard, quick, and the pepper-pods."

"Ah-h!" sighed the sufferer, not changing his position, but mournfully shaking his head, "I ain't got no cramps, ah-h!"

However, Phillisy Ann arriving in "no time" with the article of household furniture called for, that gentleman, utterly disregarding the pepper pods, proceeded to pour into a tumbler, preparatory to drinking, a sufficient quantity of amber-coloured fluid to utterly exterminate any cramps that might, by any possibility, be secretly lingering in his system, or fortify and barricade himself against any known number that might attack him in the distant future; and having finished, immediately assumed his former position, and went into most surprisingly exact imitations of a wheezy locomotive on a foggy morning.

"Merciful powers! what can the matter be?" exclaimed the widow, now thoroughly excited, as Meriweather appeared to be getting no better fast, but was rocking himself up and down "like a man who is sawing marble," groaning and muttering inarticulate sounds, as if in the last extremity of bodily anguish. But Mr. Meriweather was for some time unable to make any reply that could be understood, until at length, at the conclusion of a very fierce paroxysm, she could catch the words, "Poor Joe!"

"Is there anything the matter with Joe?" asked the old lady.

If it were possible for any *one* man to feel and suffer as far as appearance went, all the agony and misery that a half dozen of the most miserable and unfortunate of the human race ever have felt and suffered, and yet live, Mr. Meriweather certainly was that individual, for he immediately went off into such a state of sighs, groans, and lamentations, of "Poor Joe!" "Poor brother Joe!" that the widow, aroused to the highest state of sympathy and pity, could do nothing but wipe her eyes with her apron, and repeat the question —

"Where is Joe, Mr. Meriweather? Is he sick?"

"Oh-h, no!" groaned the mourning brother.

"Is he dead, then? Poor Joe!" faintly inquired the old lady.

"The Lord ha' mercy on our sinful souls! then *whar* is he?" cried the widow, breaking out afresh, "is he away to Orleans — or gone to Californy? Yes, that's it! an' the poor boy'll be eaten up by them 'diggers' that they say goes rootin' round that outlandish country, like a set of mean stinkin' ground hogs. Poor Joe! he was a fine little fellow, an't was only the other day last year when you was on your rounds, that he eat all my little be——"

"No, he ain't gone to Californy as I know," interrupted his brother.

"Then, for mercy's sake, do tell a body what's become on him!" rather tartly inquired the old lady.

"Why, you see, Mrs. Harris," replied Mr. Meriweather, still keeping the same position, and interrupting the narrative with sundry bursts of grief — which we'll leave out — "you see, Mrs. Harris, Joe and I went up airly in the spring to get a boat load of rock from Boone County, to put up the foundation of the new house we're building, fur there ain't no rock down in them rich sily bottoms in our parts. Well, we got along pretty considerable, fur we had five kegs ov blast along, and that with the hire of some niggers, we managed to get our boat loaded, and started fur home in about three weeks. You never did see anything rain like it did the fust day when we was a floatin' down, but we worked like a cornfield nigger ov a Christmas week, and pretty near sundown we'd made a matter of nigh twenty mile afore we were ashore and tied up. Well, as we didn't have any shelter on the flat, we raised a rousin' big fire on the bank, close to whar she was tied up, and cooked some grub, and I'd eaten a matter of two pounds of side, and half ov a possum, and was a sittin' on a log, smokin' a Kaintuck regaly, and a talkin' to brother Joe, who was a standin' chock up agin the fire with his back to it. You recollex, Mrs. Harris, brother Joe, who allers was a dressy sort of a chap, fond of the brass buttons he had on his coat, and the flairin'est kind ov red neckerchers; and this time he had on a pair of buckskin breeches with straps under his boots. Well, when I was a talkin' to him ov the prospect for the next day, all of a sudden I thought the little feller was a growin' oncommon tall; till I diskivered that the buckskin breeches, that were as wet as a young rooster in a spring rain, wur beginnin to smoke an' draw up kinder, and wur a liftin' brother Joe off the ground!"

"Brother Joe," sez I, "you're a going up."

"Brother," sez he, "I ain't a doing anything else!"

And he scrunched down mighty hard, but it warnt ov no use, for afore long he wur a matter of some fifteen feet up in the air!"

"Merciful powers!" interrupted the widow.

"Brother Joe!" sez I.

"I'm here," sez he.

"Catch hold ov the top ov that black jack," sez I.

"Talk!" sez brother Joe, and he sorter leaned over and grabbed the saplin like as maybe you've seen a squirrel haul in an elm switch ov a June mornin'. But it warn't ov no use, fur, old 'oman, ef you'll believe me, it gradually began to giv' way at the roots, and afore he'd got five foot higher, it just split out'n the ground, as easy as you'd pull up a spring raddish.

"Brother Joe!" sez I.

"I'm list'nin," sez he.

"Cut your straps!" sez I, fur I seed it was his last chance.

"Talk!" sez brother Joe, tho' he looked sort a reproachful at me, for broachin' such a subject, but arter apparently considering awhile, he outs with his jack-knife, and leanin' over sideways, made a rip at the sole of his left boot. There was a considerable degree of cracklin fur a second or two, then a crash sorter like as if a wagon-load ov cord wood had bruk down, and the fust thing I knowed, the t'other leg shot up like, started him, and the last thing I seed ov brother Joe, he was *whirlin' round like a four-spoked wheel with the rim off, away down clost toward sun-down!"*

Samuel Langhorne Clemens
["Mark Twain"]

(1835-1910)

❧ In terms of the history of the movement and on the basis of literary artistry, Mark Twain's works are the culmination of Southwestern humor. Not only did he derive raw material for his novels, stories, and lectures from this literary tradition but also narrative techniques and his orientation toward realism. This is not surprising in view of his early life and formative years as a writer.

Samuel Langhorne Clemens was born in the frontier village of Florida, Missouri, at the forks of the proverbial Salt River, to which his father, a Virginia lawyer, had come after a sojourn in Kentucky. Four years later the family moved to Hannibal on the western bank of the Mississippi, a sheltered rural community that Twain was later to idealize but one in which he saw incidents of violence and inhumanity and, by way of the river traffic, vistas of the outside world. When his father died in 1847, Twain, like his older brother Orion, was apprenticed to a printer. By 1850 Orion had his own newspaper, the Hannibal *Journal,* and Mark went to work for him first as a printer and then as a writer as well. The newspapers which arrived as exchanges were filled with Southwestern frontier sketches, in many instances simply versions of stories Twain had grown up knowing. It was almost inevitable that he should try his hand at something of this kind. On May 1, 1852, "The Dandy Frightening the Squatter," signed "S.L.C.," appeared in the *Carpet-Bag,* published by the humorist Benjamin P. Shillaber in Boston. Except for the pieces he had written for Orion's newspaper, this was Mark Twain's first literary work.

In 1853 Mark Twain left Hannibal to become a journeyman printer. A period of wandering followed. Among other places, he worked in New York, Philadelphia, St. Louis, and Cincinnati, usually as a printer and often supplying special correspondence to midwestern newspapers. By April, 1857, his wanderlust had reached such extremes that he was on a steamboat bound for New Orleans with vague plans to go to South America. Along the way he decided to become a river pilot instead.

As a pilot on the Mississippi from 1857 to 1861 when the Civil War closed the river, Twain added another dimension to his Southwestern experience. Although he did little writing, he contributed a burlesque prediction of weather and flood conditions on the Mississippi River which was well within the Southwestern vein to the New Orleans *Daily Crescent.* In June 1861 he returned to Hannibal where he joined a Confederate militia unit, serving casually and ingloriously for about a month. Then, at the urging of his brother Orion, newly appointed Territorial Secretary of Nevada, he traveled to the West where he remained until the end of 1866. By turns he became a miner and prospector, a newspaper reporter for the frontier *Virginia City Territorial Enterprise,* and a writer for San Francisco newspapers and literary magazines, a special correspondent on a tour of Hawaii for the Sacramento *Union,* and a lecturer. He also came to know other writers, including the humorist Artemus Ward and the local colorist Bret Harte. When he returned to New York in January 1867, he was a seasoned professional.

One effect of his years in the West was to re-enforce the influences of the Southwest which he knew so well. "The Celebrated Jumping Frog," the "Blue-Jay Yarn," and the "Old Ram" are Southwestern yarns once removed: it is geography, time, and technical competence which sets them apart. For the remainder of his literary career, whenever Twain wrote realistically and utilized an American setting, his work reveals traces of the Old Southwestern tradition.

Text: "The Dandy Frightening the Squatter" from *Carpet-Bag,* May 1, 1852; "The Celebrated Jumping Frog of Calaveras County" from *The Celebrated Jumping Frog of Calaveras County and Other Sketches* (New York, 1867); "A Wonderful Buffalo Hunt" and "Jim Blaine and His Grandfather's Old Ram" from *Roughing It* (Hartford, 1872); "Baker's Blue-Jay Yarn" from *A Tramp Abroad* (Hartford, 1880); "Frescoes from the Past" from *Life on the Mississippi* (Boston, 1883).

The Dandy Frightening the Squatter

About thirteen years ago, when the now flourishing young city of Hannibal, on the Mississippi River, was but a "wood-yard," surrounded by a few huts, belonging to some hardy *"squatters,"* and such a thing as a steamboat was considered quite a sight, the following incident occurred:

A tall, brawny woodsman stood leaning against a tree which stood upon the bank of the river, gazing at some approaching object, which our readers would easily have discovered to be a steamboat.

About half an hour elapsed, and the boat was moored, and the hands busily engaged in taking on wood.

Now among the many passengers on this boat, both male and

female, was a spruce young dandy, with a killing moustache, &c., who seemed bent on making an impression upon the hearts of the young ladies on board, and to do this, he thought he must perform some heroic deed. Observing our squatter friend, he imagined this to be a fine opportunity to bring himself into notice; so, stepping into the cabin, he said:

"Ladies, if you wish to enjoy a good laugh, step out on the guards. I intend to frighten that gentleman into fits who stands on the bank."

The ladies complied with the request, and our dandy drew from his bosom a formidable looking bowie-knife, and thrust it into his belt; then, taking a large horse-pistol in each hand, he seemed satisfied that all was right. Thus equipped, he strode on shore, with an air which seemed to say — "The hopes of a nation depend on me." Marching up to the woodsman, he exclaimed:

"Found you at last, have I? You are the very man I've been looking for these three weeks! Say your prayers!" he continued, presenting his pistols, "you'll make a capital barn door, and I shall drill the key-hole myself!"

The squatter calmly surveyed him a moment, and then, drawing back a step, he planted his huge fist directly between the eyes of his astonished antagonist, who, in a moment, was floundering in the turbid waters of the Mississippi.

Every passenger on the boat had by this time collected on the guards, and the shout that now went up from the crowd speedily restored the crest-fallen hero to his senses, and, as he was sneaking off towards the boat, was thus accosted by his conqueror:

"I say, yeou, next time yeou come around drillin' key-holes, don't forget yer old acquaintances!"

The ladies unanimously voted the knife and pistols to the victor.

The Celebrated Jumping Frog of Calaveras County

In compliance with the request of a friend of mine, who wrote me from the East, I called on good-natured, garrulous old Simon Wheeler, and inquired after my friend's friend, *Leonidas W.* Smiley, as requested to do, and I hereunto append the result. I have a lurking suspicion that *Leonidas W.* Smiley is a myth; that my friend never knew such a personage; and that he only conjectured that, if I asked old Wheeler about him, it would remind him of his infamous *Jim*

Smiley, and he would go to work and bore me nearly to death with some infernal reminiscence of him as long and tedious as it should be useless to me. If that was the design, it certainly succeeded.

I found Simon Wheeler dozing comfortably by the bar-room stove of the old, dilapidated tavern in the ancient mining camp of Angel's, and I noticed that he was fat and bald-headed, and had an expression of winning gentleness and simplicity upon his tranquil countenance. He roused up and gave me good-day. I told him a friend of mine had commissioned me to make some inquiries about a cherished companion of his boyhood named *Leonidas W.* Smiley — *Rev. Leonidas W.* Smiley — a young minister of the Gospel, who he had heard was at one time a resident of Angel's Camp. I added that, if Mr. Wheeler could tell me any thing about this Rev. Leonidas W. Smiley, I would feel under many obligations to him.

Simon Wheeler backed me into a corner and blockaded me there with his chair, and then sat me down and reeled off the monotonous narrative which follows this paragraph. He never smiled, he never frowned, he never changed his voice from the gentle-flowing key to which he tuned the initial sentence, he never betrayed the slightest suspicion of enthusiasm; but all through the interminable narrative there ran a vein of impressive earnestness and sincerity, which showed me plainly that, so far from his imagining that there was any thing ridiculous or funny about his story, he regarded it as a really important matter, and admired its two heroes as men of transcendent genius in *finesse*. To me, the spectacle of a man drifting serenely along through such a queer yarn without ever smiling, was exquisitely absurd. As I said before, I asked him to tell me what he knew of Rev. Leonidas W. Smiley, and he replied as follows. I let him go on in his own way, and never interrupted him once:

There was a feller here once by the name of *Jim* Smiley, in the winter of '49 — or may be it was the spring of '50 — I don't recollect exactly, somehow, though what makes me think it was one or the other is because I remember the big flume wasn't finished when he first came to the camp; but any way, he was the curiosest man about always betting on any thing that turned up you ever see, if he could get any body to bet on the other side; and if he couldn't, he'd change sides. Any way that suited the other man would suit him — any way just so's he got a bet, *he* was satisfied. But still he was lucky, uncommon lucky; he most always come out winner. He was always ready and laying for a chance; there couldn't be no solit'ry thing mentioned but that feller'd offer to bet on it, and take any side you please, as I was just telling you. If there was a horse-race, you'd find him flush, or you'd find him busted at the end of it; if there was a dog-fight, he'd bet on it; if there was a cat-fight, he'd bet on it; if there was a chicken-fight, he'd bet on it; why, if there was two birds setting on a fence, he would bet you which one would fly first; or if there was a camp-meeting, he would be there reg'lar, to bet on Parson Walker, which he judged to be the best exhorter about here, and so he was, too, and a good man. If he even seen a straddle-bug start to go anywheres, he would bet you how long it would take him to get wherever he was going to, and if you took him up, he would foller that straddle-bug to Mexico but what he would find out where he was bound for and how long he was on the road. Lots of the boys here has seen that Smiley, and can tell you about him. Why, it never made no difference to *him* — he would bet on *any* thing — the dangdest feller. Parson Walker's wife laid very sick once, for a good while, and it seemed as if they warn't going to save her; but one morning he come in, and Smiley asked how she was, and he said she was considerable better — thank the Lord for his inf'nit mercy — and coming on so smart that, with the blessing of Prov'dence, she'd get well yet; and Smiley, before he thought, says, "Well, I'll risk two-and-a-half that she don't, any way."

Thish-yer Smiley had a mare — the boys called her the fifteen-minute nag, but that was only in fun, you know, because, of course, she was faster than that — and he used to win money on that horse, for all she was so slow and always had the asthma, or the distemper, or the consumption, or something of that kind. They used to give her two or three hundred yards start, and then pass her under way; but always at the fag-end of the race she'd get excited and desperate-like, and come cavorting and straddling up, and scattering her legs around limber, sometimes in the air, and sometimes out to one side amongst the fences, and kicking up m-o-r-e dust, and raising m-o-r-e racket with her coughing and sneezing and blowing her nose — and always fetch up at the stand just about a neck ahead, as near as you could cipher it down.

And he had a little small bull pup, that to look at him you'd think he wan't worth a cent, but to set around and look ornery, and lay for a chance to steal something. But as soon as money was up on him, he was a different dog; his under-jaw'd begin to stick out like the fo'castle of a steamboat, and his teeth would uncover, and shine savage like the furnaces. And a dog might tackle him, and bully-rag him, and bite him, and throw him over his shoulder two or three times, and Andrew Jackson — which was the name of the pup — Andrew Jackson would never let on but what *he* was satisfied, and hadn't expected nothing else — and the bets being doubled and doubled on the other side all the time, till the money was all up; and then all of a sudden he would grab that other dog jest by the j'int of his hind leg and freeze on it — not chaw, you understand, but only jest grip and hang on till they throwed up the sponge, if it was a year. Smiley always come out winner on that pup, till he harnessed a dog once that didn't have no hind legs, because they'd been sawed off by a circular saw, and when the thing had gone along far enough, and the money was all up, and he come to make a snatch for his pet holt, he saw in a minute how he'd been imposed on, and how the other dog had him in the door, so to speak, and he 'peared surprised, and then he looked sorter discouraged-like, and didn't try no more to win the fight, and so he got shucked out bad. He give Smiley a look, as much as to say his heart was broke, and it was *his* fault, for putting up a dog that hadn't no hind legs for him to take holt of, which was his main dependence in a fight, and then he limped off a piece and laid down and died. It was a good pup, was that Andrew Jackson, and would have made a name for hisself if he'd lived, for the stuff was in him, and he had genius — I know it, because he hadn't had no opportunities to speak of, and it don't stand to reason that a dog could make such a fight as he could under them circumstances, if he hadn't no talent. It always makes me feel sorry when I think of that last fight of his'n, and the way it turned out.

Well, thish-yer Smiley had rat-tarriers, and chicken cocks, and tom-cats, and all of them kind of things, till you couldn't rest, and you couldn't fetch nothing for him to bet on but he'd match you. He ketched a frog one day, and took him home, and said he cal'klated to edercate him; and so he never done nothing for three months but set in his back yard and learn that frog to jump. And you bet you he *did* learn him, too. He'd give him a little punch behind, and the next minute you'd see that frog whirling in the air like a doughnut — see him turn one summerset, or may be a couple, if he got a good start, and come down flat-footed and all right, like a cat. He got him up so in the matter of catching flies, and kept him in practice so constant, that he'd nail a fly every time as far as he could see him. Smiley said all a frog wanted was education, and he could do most any thing — and I believe him. Why, I've seen him set Dan'l Webster down here on this floor — Dan'l Webster was the name of the frog — and sing out, "Flies, Dan'l, flies!" and quicker'n you could wink, he'd spring straight up, and snake a fly off'n the counter there, and flop down on the floor again as solid as a gob of mud, and fall to scratching the side of his head with his hind foot as indifferent as if he hadn't no idea he'd been doin' any more'n any frog might do. You never see a frog so modest and straightfor'ard as he was, for all he was so gifted. And when it come to fair and square jumping on a dead level, he could get over more ground at one straddle than any animal of his breed you ever see. Jumping on a dead level was his strong suit, you understand; and when it come to that, Smiley would ante up money on him as long as he had a red. Smiley was monstrous proud of his frog, and well he might be, for fellers that had traveled and been everywheres, all said he laid over any frog that ever *they* see.

Well, Smiley kept the beast in a little lattice box, and he used to fetch him down town sometimes and lay for a bet. One day a feller — a stranger in the camp, he was — come across him with his box, and says:

"What might it be that you've got in the box?"

And Smiley says, sorter indifferent like, "It might be a parrot, or it might be a canary, may be, but it an't — it's only just a frog."

And the feller took it, and looked at it careful, and turned it round this way and that, and says, "H'm — so 'tis. Well, what's *he* good for?"

"Well," Smiley says, easy and careless, "He's good enough for *one* thing, I should judge — he can outjump ary frog in Calaveras county."

The feller took the box again, and took another long, particular look, and give it back to Smiley, and says, very deliberate, "Well, I don't see no p'ints about that frog that's any better'n any other frog."

"May be you don't," Smiley says. "May be you understand frogs, and may be you don't understand 'em; may be you've had experience, and may be you an't only a amature, as it were. Anyways, I've got *my* opinion, and I'll risk forty dollars that he can outjump any frog in Calaveras county."

And the feller studied a minute, and then says, kinder sad like, "Well, I'm only a stranger here, and I an't got no frog; but if I had a frog, I'd bet you."

And then Smiley says, "That's all right — that's all right — if you'll hold my box a minute, I'll go and get you a frog." And so the feller took the box, and put up his forty dollars along with Smiley's, and set down to wait.

So he set there a good while thinking and thinking to hisself, and then he got the frog out and prized his mouth open and took a teaspoon and filled him full of quail shot — filled him pretty near up to his chin — and set him on the floor. Smiley he went to the swamp and slopped around in the mud for a long time, and finally he ketched a frog, and fetched him in, and give him to this feller, and says:

"Now, if you're ready, set him alongside of Dan'l, with his forepaws just even with Dan'l, and I'll give the word." Then he says, "One — two — three — jump!" and him and the feller touched up the frogs from behind, and the new frog hopped off, but Dan'l give a heave, and hysted up his shoulders — so — like a Frenchman, but it wan't no use — he couldn't budge; he was planted as solid as an anvil, and he couldn't no more stir than if he was anchored out. Smiley was a good deal surprised, and he was disgusted too, but he didn't have no idea what the matter was, of course.

The feller took the money and started away; and when he was going out at the door, he sorter jerked his thumb over his shoulders — this way — at Dan'l, and says again, very deliberate, "Well, *I* don't see no p'ints about that frog that's any better'n any other frog."

Smiley he stood scratching his head and looking down at Dan'l a long time, and at last he says, "I do wonder what in the nation that frog throw'd off for — I wonder if there an't something the matter with him — he 'pears to look mighty baggy, somehow." And he ketched Dan'l by the nap of the neck, and lifted him up and says, "Why, blame my cats, if he don't weigh five pound!" and turned him upside down, and he belched out a double handful of shot. And then he see how it was, and he was the maddest man — he set the frog down and took out after that feller, but he never ketchd him. And——

[Here Simon Wheeler heard his name called from the front yard, and got up to see what was wanted.] And turning to me as he moved away, he said: "Just set where you are, stranger, and rest easy — I an't going to be gone a second."

But, by your leave, I did not think that a continuation of the history of the enterprising vagabond *Jim* Smiley would be likely to afford me much information concerning the Rev. *Leonidas W*. Smiley, and so I started away.

At the door I met the sociable Wheeler returning, and he button-holed me and recommenced:

"Well, thish-yer Smiley had a yaller one-eyed cow that didn't have no tail, only jest a short stump like a bannanner, and ——"

"Oh! hang Smiley and his afflicted cow!" I muttered, good-naturedly, and bidding the old gentleman good-day, I departed.

A Wonderful Buffalo Hunt

.   .   .   .

Next morning, just before dawn, when about five hundred and fifty miles from St. Joseph, our mud-wagon broke down. We were to be delayed five or six hours, and therefore we took horses, by invitation, and joined a party who were just starting on a buffalo hunt. It was noble sport galloping over the plain in the dewy freshness of the morning, but our part of the hunt ended in disaster and disgrace, for a wounded buffalo bull chased the passenger Bemis nearly two miles, and then he forsook his horse and took to a lone tree. He was very sullen about the matter for some twenty-four hours, but at last he began to soften little by little, and finally he said:

"Well, it was not funny, and there was no sense in those gawks making themselves so facetious over it. I tell you I was angry in earnest for awhile. I should have shot that long gangly lubber they called Hank, if I could have done it without crippling six or seven other people — but of course I couldn't, the old 'Allen's' so confounded comprehensive. I wish those loafers had been up in the tree; they wouldn't have wanted to laugh so. If I had had a horse worth a cent — but no, the minute he saw that buffalo bull wheel on him and give a bellow, he raised straight up in the air and stood on his heels. The saddle began to slip, and I took him around the neck and laid close to him, and began to pray. Then he came down and stood up on the other end awhile, and the bull actually stopped pawing sand and bellowing to contemplate the inhuman spectacle. Then the bull made a pass at him and uttered a bellow that sounded perfectly frightful, it was so close to me, and that seemed to literally prostrate my horse's reason, and make a raving distracted maniac of him, and I wish I may die if he didn't stand on his head for a quarter of a minute and shed tears. He was absolutely out of his mind — he was, as sure as truth itself, and he really didn't know what he was doing. Then the bull came charging at us, and my horse dropped down on all fours and took a fresh start — and then for the next ten minutes he would actually throw one hand-spring after another so fast that the bull began to get unsettled, too, and didn't know where to start in — and so he stood there sneezing, and shovelling dust over his back, and bellowing every now and then, and thinking he had got a fifteen-hundred dollar circus horse for breakfast, certain. Well, I was first out on his neck — the horse's, not the bull's — and then underneath, and next on his rump, and sometimes head up, and sometimes heels — but I tell you it seemed solemn and awful to be ripping and tearing and carrying on so in the presence of death, as you might say. Pretty soon the bull made a snatch for us and brought away some of my horse's tail (I suppose, but do not know, being pretty busy at the time), but *something* made him hungry for solitude and suggested to him to get up and hunt for it. And then you ought to have seen that spider-legged old skeleton go! and you ought to have seen the bull cut out after him, too — head down, tongue out, tail up, bellowing like everything, and actually mowing down the weeds, and tearing up the earth, and boosting up the sand like a whirlwind! By George, it was a hot race! I and the saddle were back on the rump, and I had the bridle in my teeth and holding on to the pommel with both hands. First we left the dogs behind; then we passed a jackass rabbit; then we overtook a cayote, and were gaining on an antelope when the rotten girth let go and threw me about thirty yards off to the left, and as the saddle went down over the horse's rump he gave it a lift with his heels that sent it more than four hundred yards up in the air, I wish I may die in a minute if he didn't. I fell at the foot of the only solitary tree there was in nine counties adjacent (as any creature could see with the naked eye), and the next second I had hold of the bark with four sets of nails and my teeth, and the next second after that I was astraddle of the main limb and blaspheming my luck in a way that made my breath smell of brimstone. I *had* the bull, now, if he did not think of *one* thing. But that one thing I dreaded. I dreaded it very seriously. There was a possibility that the bull might not think of it, but there were greater chances that he would. I made up my mind what I would do in case he did. It was a little over forty feet to the ground from where I sat. I cautiously unwound the lariat from the pommel of my saddle —"

"Your *saddle?* Did you take your saddle up in the tree with you?"

"Take it up in the tree with me? Why, how you talk. Of course I didn't. No man could do that. It *fell* in the tree when it came down."

"Oh — exactly."

"Certainly. I unwound the lariat, and fastened one end of it to the limb. It was the very best green raw-hide, and capable of sustaining tons. I made a slip-noose in the other end, and then hung it down to see the length. It reached down twenty-two feet — half way to the ground. I then loaded every barrel of the Allen with a double charge. I felt satisfied. I said to myself, if he never thinks of that one thing that I dread, all right — but if he does, all right anyhow — I am fixed for him. But don't you know that the very thing a man dreads is the thing that always happens? Indeed it is so. I watched the bull, now, with anxiety — anxiety which no one can conceive of who has not been in such a situation and felt that at any moment death might come. Presently a thought came into the bull's eye. I knew it! said I — if my nerve fails now, I am lost. Sure enough, it was just as I had dreaded, he started in to climb the tree —"

"What, the bull?"

"Of course — who else?"

"But a bull can't climb a tree."

"He can't, can't he? Since you know so much about it, did you ever see a bull try?"

"No! I never dreamt of such a thing."

"Well, then, what is the use of your talking that way, then? Because you never saw a thing done, is that any reason why it can't be done?"

"Well, all right — go on. What did you do?"

"The bull started up, and got along well for about ten feet, then slipped and slid back. I breathed easier. He tried it again — got up a little higher — slipped again. But he came at it once more, and this time he was careful. He got gradually higher and higher, and my spirits went down more and more. Up he came — an inch at a time — with his eyes hot, and his tongue hanging out. Higher and higher — hitched his foot over the stump of a limb, and looked up, as much as to say, 'You are my meat, friend.' Up again — higher and higher, and getting more excited the closer he got. He was within ten feet of me! I took a long breath, — and then said I, 'It is now or never.' I had the coil of the lariat all ready; I paid it out slowly, till it hung right over his head; all of a sudden I let go of the slack, and the slip-noose fell fairly round his neck! Quicker than lightning I out with the Allen and let him have it in the face. It was an awful roar, and must have scared the bull out of his senses. When the smoke cleared away, there he was, dangling in the air, twenty foot from the ground, and going out of one convulsion into another faster than you could count! I didn't stop to count, anyhow — I shinned down the tree and shot for home."

"Bemis, is all that true, just as you have stated it?"

"I wish I may rot in my tracks and die the death of a dog if it isn't."

"Well, we can't refuse to believe it, and we don't. But if there were some proofs —"

"Proofs! Did I bring back my lariat?"

"No."

"Did I bring back my horse?"

"No."

"Did you ever see the bull again?"

"No."

"Well, then, what more do you want? I never saw anybody as particular as you are about a little thing like that." . . .

Jim Blaine and His Grandfather's Old Ram

Every now and then, in those days, the boys used to tell me I ought to get one Jim Blaine to tell me the stirring story of his grandfather's old ram — but they always added that I must not mention the matter unless Jim was drunk at the time — just comfortably and sociably drunk. They kept this up until my curiosity was on the rack to hear the story. I got to haunting Blaine; but it was of no use, the boys always found fault with his condition; he was often moderately but never satisfactorily drunk. I never watched a man's condition with such absorbing interest, such anxious solicitude; I never so pined to see a man uncompromisingly drunk before. At last, one evening I hurried to his cabin, for I learned that this time his situation was such that even the most fastidious could find no fault with it — he was tranquilly, serenely, symmetrically drunk — not a hiccup to mar his voice, not a cloud upon his brain thick enough to obscure his memory. As I entered, he was sitting upon an empty powder-keg, with a clay pipe in one hand and the other raised to command silence. His face was round, red, and very serious; his throat was bare and his hair tumbled; in general appearance and costume he was a stalwart miner of the period. On the pine table stood a candle, and its dim light revealed "the boys" sitting here and there on bunks, candle-boxes, powder-kegs, etc. They said:

"Sh —! Don't speak — he's going to commence."

THE STORY OF THE OLD RAM.

I found a seat at once, and Blaine said:

"I don't reckon them times will ever come again. There never was a more bullier old ram than what he was. Grandfather fetched him from Illinois — got him of a man by the name of Yates — Bill Yates — maybe you might have heard of him; his father was a deacon — Baptist — and he was a rustler, too; a man had to get up ruther early to get the start of old Thankful Yates; it was him that put the Greens up to jining teams with my grandfather when he moved west. Seth Green was prob'ly the pick of the flock; he married a Wilkerson — Sarah Wilkerson — good cretur, she was — one of the likeliest heifers that was ever raised in old Stoddard, everybody said that knowed her. She could heft a bar'l of flour as easy as I can flirt a flapjack. And spin? Don't mention it! Independent? Humph! When Sile Hawkins come a browsing around her, she let him know

that for all his tin he couldn't trot in harness alongside of *her.* You
see, Sile Hawkins was — no, it warn't Sile Hawkins, after all — it
was a galoot by the name of Filkins — I disremember his first name;
but he *was* a stump — come into pra'r meeting drunk, one night,
hooraying for Nixon, becuz he thought it was a primary; and old
deacon Ferguson up and scooted him through the window and he lit
on old Miss Jefferson's head, poor old filly. She was a good soul —
had a glass eye and used to lend it to old Miss Wagner, that hadn't
any, to receive company in; it warn't big enough, and when Miss
Wagner warn't noticing, it would get twisted around in the socket, and
look up, maybe, or out to one side, and every which way, while
t' other one was looking as straight ahead as a spy-glass. Grown
people didn't mind it, but it most always made the children cry, it
was so sort of scary. She tried packing it in raw cotton, but it
wouldn't work, somehow — the cotton would get loose and stick out
and look so kind of awful that the children couldn't stand it no way.
She was always dropping it out, and turning up her old dead-light
on the company empty, and making them oncomfortable, becuz *she*
never could tell when it hopped out, being blind on that side, you
see. So somebody would have to hunch her and say, 'Your game
eye has fetched loose, Miss Wagner dear' — and then all of them
would have to sit and wait till she jammed it in again — wrong side
before, as a general thing, and green as a bird's egg, being a bashful
cretur and easy sot back before company. But being wrong side before
warn't much difference, anyway, becuz her own eye was sky-blue and
the glass one was yaller on the front side, so whichever way she
turned it it didn't match nohow. Old Miss Wagner was considerable
on the borrow, she was. When she had a quilting, or Dorcas S'iety
at her house she gen'ally borrowed Miss Higgins's wooden leg to
stump around on; it was considerable shorter than her other pin, but
much *she* minded that. She said she couldn't abide crutches when
she had company, becuz they were so slow; said when she had company and things had to be done, she wanted to get up and hump
herself. She was as bald as a jug, and so she used to borrow Miss
Jacops's wig — Miss Jacops was the coffin-peddler's wife — a ratty old
buzzard, he was, that used to go roosting around where people was
sick, waiting for 'em; and there that old rip would sit all day, in
the shade, on a coffin that he judged would fit the can'idate; and if
it was a slow customer and kind of uncertain, he'd fetch his rations
and a blanket along and sleep in the coffin nights. He was anchored
out that way, in frosty weather, for about three weeks, once, before
old Robbins's place, waiting for him; and after that, for as much as
two years, Jacops was not on speaking terms with the old man, on

account of his disapp'inting him. He got one of his feet froze, and lost money, too, becuz old Robbins took a favorable turn and got well. The next time Robbins got sick, Jacops tried to make up with him, and varnished up the same old coffin and fetched it along; but old Robbins was too many for him; he had him in, and 'peared to be powerful weak; he bought the coffin for ten dollars and Jacops was to pay it back and twenty-five more besides if Robbins didn't like the coffin after he'd tried it. And then Robbins died, and at the funeral he bursted off the lid and riz up in his shroud and told the parson to let up on the performances, becuz he could *not* stand such a coffin as that. You see he had been in a trance once before, when he was young, and he took the chances on another, cal'lating that if he made the trip it was money in his pocket, and if he missed fire he couldn't lose a cent. And by George he sued Jacops for the rhino and got jedgment; and he set up the coffin in his back parlor and said he 'lowed to take his time, now. It was always an aggravation to Jacops, the way that miserable old thing acted. He moved back to Indiany pretty soon — went to Wellsville — Wellsville was the place the Hogadorns was from. Mighty fine family. Old Maryland stock. Old Squire Hogadorn could carry around more mixed licker, and cuss better than most any man I ever see. His second wife was the widder Billings — she that was Becky Martin; her dam was deacon Dunlap's first wife. Her oldest child, Maria, married a missionary and died in grace — et up by the savages. They et *him,* too, poor feller — biled him. It warn't the custom, so they say, but they explained to friends of his'n that went down there to bring away his things, that they'd tried missionaries every other way and never could get any good out of 'em — and so it annoyed all his relations to find out that that man's life was fooled away just out of a dern'd experiment, so to speak. But mind you, there ain't anything ever reely lost; everything that people can't understand and don't see the reason of does good if you only hold on and give it a fair shake; Prov'dence don't fire no blank ca'tridges, boys. That there missionary's substance, unbeknowns to himself, actu'ly converted every last one of them heathens that took a chance at the barbacue. Nothing ever fetched them but that. Don't tell *me* it was an accident that he was biled. There ain't no such a thing as an accident. When my uncle Lem was leaning up agin a scaffolding once, sick, or drunk, or suthin, an Irishman with a hod full of bricks fell on him out of the third story and broke the old man's back in two places. People said it was an accident. Much accident there was about that. He didn't know what he was there for, but he was there for a good object. If he hadn't been there the Irishman would have been killed. Nobody can ever make me believe anything different from that. Uncle Lem's dog was there. Why didn't the Irishman fall on the dog? Becuz the dog would a seen him a coming and stood from under. That's the reason the dog warn't appinted. A dog can't be depended on to carry out a special providence. Mark my words it was a put-up thing. Accidents don't happen, boys. Uncle Lem's dog — I wish you could a seen that dog. He was a reglar shepherd — or rather he was part bull and part shepherd — splendid animal; belonged to parson Hagar before Uncle Lem got him. Parson Hagar belonged to the Western Reserve Hagars; prime family; his mother was a Watson; one of his sisters married a Wheeler; they settled in Morgan county, and he got nipped by the machinery in a carpet factory and went through in less than a quarter of a minute; his widder bought the piece of carpet that had his remains wove in, and people come a hundred mile to 'tend the funeral. There was fourteen yards in the piece. She wouldn't let them roll him up, but planted him just so — full length. The church was middling small where they preached the funeral, and they had to let one end of the coffin stick out of the window. They didn't bury him — they planted one end, and let him stand up, same as a monument. And they nailed a sign on it and put — put on — put on it — sacred to — the m-e-m-o-r-y — of fourteen y-a-r-d-s — of three-ply — car - - - pet — containing all that was — m-o-r-t-a-l — of — of — W-i-l-l-i-a-m — W-h-e —"

Jim Blaine had been growing gradually drowsy and drowsier — his head nodded, once, twice, three times — dropped peacefully upon his breast, and he fell tranquilly asleep. The tears were running down the boys' cheeks — they were suffocating with suppressed laughter — and had been from the start, though I had never noticed it. I perceived that I was "sold." I learned then that Jim Blaine's peculiarity was that whenever he reached a certain stage of intoxication, no human power could keep him from setting out, with impressive unction, to tell about a wonderful adventure which he had once had with his grandfather's old ram — and the mention of the ram in the first sentence was as far as any man had ever heard him get, concerning it. He always maundered off, interminably, from one thing to another, till his whisky got the best of him and he fell asleep. What the thing was that happened to him and his grandfather's old ram is a dark mystery to this day, for nobody has ever yet found out.

Baker's Blue-Jay Yarn

.   .   .   .

Animals talk to each other, of course. There can be no question
about that; but I suppose there are very few people who can understand them. I never knew but one man who could. I knew he could,
however, because he told me so himself. He was a middle-aged,
simple-hearted miner, who had lived in a lonely corner of California,
among the woods and mountains, a good many years, and had studied
the ways of his only neighbors, the beasts and the birds, until he
believed he could accurately translate any remark which they made.
This was Jim Baker. According to Jim Baker, some animals have only
a limited education, and use only very simple words, and scarcely
ever a comparison or a flowery figure; whereas, certain other animals
have a large vocabulary, a fine command of language and a ready and
fluent delivery; consequently these latter talk a great deal; they like it;
they are conscious of their talent, and they enjoy "showing off." Baker
said, that after long and careful observation, he had come to the
conclusion that the blue-jays were the best talkers he had found
among birds and beasts. Said he: —

"There's more *to* a blue-jay than any other creature. He has got
more moods and more different kinds of feelings than other creatures;
and mind you, whatever a blue-jay feels, he can put into language.
And no mere commonplace language, either, but rattling, out-and-
out book-talk — and bristling with metaphor, too — just bristling!
And as for command of language — why *you* never see a blue-jay
stuck for a word. No man ever did. They just boil out of him! And
another thing: I've noticed a good deal, and there's no bird, or cow,
or anything that uses as good grammar as a blue-jay. You may say
a cat uses good grammar. Well, a cat does — but you let a cat get
excited, once; you let a cat get to pulling fur with another cat on a
shed, nights, and you'll hear grammar that will give you the lockjaw.
Ignorant people think it's the *noise* which fighting cats make that is
so aggravating, but it ain't so, it's the sickening grammar they use.
Now I've never heard a jay use bad grammar but very seldom; and
when they do, they are as ashamed as a human; they shut right down
and leave.

"You may call a jay a bird. Well, so he is, in a measure — because
he's got feathers on him, and don't belong to no church, perhaps; but
otherwise he is just as much a human as you be. And I'll tell you for

why. A jay's gifts, and instincts, and feelings, and interests, cover the whole ground. A jay hasn't got any more principle than a Congressman. A jay will lie, a jay will steal, a jay will deceive, a jay will betray; and four times out of five, a jay will go back on his solemnest promise. The sacredness of an obligation is a thing which you can't cram into no blue-jay's head. Now on top of all this, there's another thing: a jay can out-swear any gentleman in the mines. You think a cat can swear. Well, a cat can; but you give a blue-jay a subject that calls for his reserve-powers, and where is your cat? Don't talk to *me* — I know too much about this thing. And there's yet another thing: in the one little particular of scolding — just good, clean, out-and-out scolding — a blue-jay can lay over anything, human or divine. Yes, sir, a jay is everything that a man is. A jay can cry, a jay can laugh, a jay can feel shame, a jay can reason and plan and discuss, a jay likes gossip and scandal, a jay has got a sense of humor, a jay knows when he is an ass just as well as you do — maybe better. If a jay ain't human, he better take in his sign, that's all. Now I'm going to tell you a perfectly true fact about some blue-jays.

"When I first begun to understand jay language correctly, there was a little incident happened here. Seven years ago, the last man in this region but me, moved away. There stands his house, — been empty ever since; a log house, with a plank roof — just one big room, and no more; no ceiling — nothing between the rafters and the floor. Well, one Sunday morning I was sitting out here in front of my cabin, with my cat, taking the sun, and looking at the blue hills, and listening to the leaves rustling so lonely in the trees, and thinking of the home away yonder in the States, that I hadn't heard from in thirteen years, when a blue-jay lit on that house, with an acorn in his mouth, and says, 'Hello, I reckon I've struck something!' When he spoke, the acorn dropped out of his mouth and rolled down the roof, of course, but he didn't care; his mind was all on the thing he had struck. It was a knot-hole in the roof. He cocked his head to one side, shut one eye and put the other one to the hole, like a 'possum looking down a jug; then he glanced up with his bright eyes, gave a wink or two with his wings — which signifies gratification, you understand — and says, 'It looks like a hole, it's located like a hole — blamed if I don't believe it *is* a hole!'

"Then he cocked his head down and took another look; he glances up perfectly joyful, this time; winks his wings and his tail both, and says, 'Oh, no, this ain't no fat thing, I reckon! If I ain't in luck! — why it's a perfectly elegant hole!' So he flew down and got that acorn, and fetched it up and dropped it in, and was just tilting his head back with the heavenliest smile on his face, when all of a sudden he was paralyzed into a listening attitude, and that smile faded gradually out of his countenance like breath off'n a razor, and the queerest look of surprise took its place. Then he says, 'Why I didn't hear it fall!' He cocked his eye at the hole again, and took a long look; raised up and shook his head; stepped around to the other side of the hole and took another look from that side; shook his head again. He studied a while, then he just went into the *de*tails — walked round and round the hole, and spied into it from every point of the compass. No use. Now he took a thinking attitude on the comb of the roof and scratched the back of his head with his right foot a minute, and finally says, "Well, it's too many for *me,* that's certain; must be a mighty long hole; however, I ain't got no time to fool around here, I got to 'tend to business; I reckon it's all right — chance it, anyway!'

"So he flew off and fetched another acorn and dropped it in, and tried to flirt his eye to the hole quick enough to see what become of it, but he was too late. He held his eye there as much as a minute; then he raised up and sighed, and says, 'Consound it, I don't seem to understand this thing, no way; however, I'll tackle her again.' He fetched another acorn and done his level best to see what become of it, but he couldn't. He says, 'Well, *I* never struck no such a hole as this before; I'm of the opinion it's a totally new kind of hole.' Then he begun to get mad. He held in for a spell, walking up and down the comb of the roof, and shaking his head and muttering to himself; but his feelings got the upper hand of him presently, and he broke loose and cussed himself black in the face. I never see a bird take on so about a little thing. When he got through he walks to the hole and looks in again for half a minute; then he says, 'Well, you're a long hole, and a deep hole, and a mighty singular hole altogether — but I've started to fill you, and I'm d—d if I *don't* fill you, if it takes a hundred years!'

"And with that, away he went. You never see a bird work so since you was born. He laid into his work like a nigger, and the way he hove acorns into that hole for about two hours and a half was one of the most exciting and astonishing spectacles I ever struck. He never stopped to take a look any more — he just hove 'em in, and went for more. Well, at last he could hardly flop his wings, he was so tuckered out. He comes a-drooping down, once more, sweating like an ice-pitcher, drops his acorn in and says, '*Now* I guess I've got the bulge on you by this time!' So he bent down for a look. If you'll believe me, when his head come up again he was just pale with rage. He says, 'I've shoveled acorns enough in there to keep the family thirty years, and if I can see a sign of one of 'em, I wish I may land in a museum with a belly full of sawdust in two minutes!'

"He just had strength enough to crawl up on to the comb and lean his back agin the chimbly, and then he collected his impressions and begun to free his mind. I see in a second that what I had mistook for profanity in the mines was only just the rudiments, as you may say.

"Another jay was going by, and heard him doing his devotions, and stops to inquire what was up. The sufferer told him the whole circumstances, and says, 'Now yonder's the hole, and if you don't believe me, go and look for yourself.' So this fellow went and looked, and comes back and says, 'How many did you say you put in there?' 'Not any less than two tons,' says the sufferer. The other jay went and looked again. He couldn't seem to make it out, so he raised a yell, and three more jays come. They all examined the hole, they all made the sufferer tell it over again, then they all discussed it, and got off as many leather-headed opinions about it as an average crowd of humans could have done.

"They called in more jays; then more and more, till pretty soon this whole region 'peared to have a blue flush about it. There must have been five thousand of them; and such another jawing and disputing and ripping and cussing, you never heard. Every jay in the whole lot put his eye to the hole, and delivered a more chuckled-headed opinion about the mystery than the jay that went there before him. They examined the house all over, too. The door was standing half-open, and at last one old jay happened to go and light on it and look in. Of course that knocked the mystery galley-west in a second. There lay the acorns, scattered all over the floor. He flopped his wings and raised a whoop. 'Come here!' he says, 'Come here, everybody; hang'd if this fool hasn't been trying to fill up a house with acorns!' They all came a-swooping down like a blue cloud, and as each fellow lit on the door and took a glance, the whole absurdity of the contract that the first jay had tackled hit him home and he fell over backwards suffocating with laughter, and the next jay took his place and done the same.

"Well, sir, they roosted around here on the house-top and the trees for an hour, and guffawed over that thing like human beings. It ain't any use to tell me a blue-jay hasn't got a sense of humor, because I know better. And memory too. They brought jays here from all over the United States to look down that hole, every summer for three years. Other birds too. And they could all see the point, except an owl that came from Nova Scotia to visit the Yo Semite, and he took this thing in on his way back. He said he couldn't see anything funny in it. But then, he was a good deal disappointed about Yo Semite, too."

Frescoes from the Past

By way of illustrating keelboat talk and manners, and that now-departed and hardly-remembered raft-life, I will throw in, in this place, a chapter from a book which I have been working at, by fits and starts, during the past five or six years, and may possibly finish in the course of five or six more. The book is a story which details some passages in the life of an ignorant village boy, Huck Finn, son of the town drunkard of my time out West, there. He has run away from his persecuting father, and from a persecuting good widow who wishes to make a nice, truth-telling, respectable boy of him; and with him a slave of the widow's has also escaped. They have found a fragment of a lumber raft (it is high water and dead summer time), and are floating down the river by night, and hiding in the willows by day, — bound for Cairo whence the negro will seek freedom in the heart of the free States. But in a fog, they pass Cairo without knowing it. By and by they begin to suspect the truth, and Huck Finn is persuaded to end the dismal suspense by swimming down to a huge raft which they have seen in the distance ahead of them, creeping aboard under cover of the darkness, and gathering the needed information by eavesdropping: —

But you know a young person can't wait very well when he is impatient to find a thing out. We talked it over, and by and by Jim said it was such a black night, now, that it wouldn't be no risk to swim down to the big raft and crawl aboard and listen, — they would talk about Cairo, because they would be calculating to go ashore there for a spree, maybe, or anyway they would send boats ashore to buy whiskey or fresh meat or something. Jim had a wonderful level head, for a nigger: he could most always start a good plan when you wanted one.

I stood up and shook my rags off and jumped into the river, and struck out for the raft's light. By and by, when I got down nearly to her, I eased up and went slow and cautious. But everything was all right — nobody at the sweeps. So I swum down along the raft till I was most abreast the camp fire in the middle, then I crawled aboard and inched along and got in among some bundles of shingles on the weather side of the fire. There was thirteen men there — they was the watch on deck of course. And a mighty rough-looking lot, too. They had a jug, and tin cups, and they kept the jug moving. One man was singing — roaring, you may say; and it wasn't a nice song — for a parlor anyway. He roared through his nose, and strung out the last word of every line very long. When he was done they all fetched a kind of Injun war-whoop, and then another was sung. It begun: —

> "There was a woman in our towdn,
> In our towdn did dwed'l (dwell,)
> She loved her husband dear-i-lee,
> But another man twyste as wed'l.
>
> Singing too, riloo, riloo, riloo,
> Ri-too, riloo, rilay - - - e,
> She loved her husband dear-i-lee,
> But another man twyste as wed'l."

And so on — fourteen verses. It was kind of poor, and when he was going to start on the next verse one of them said it was the tune the old cow died on; and another one said: "Oh, give us a rest." And another one told him to take a walk. They made fun of him till he got mad and jumped up and begun to cuss the crowd, and said he could lam any thief in the lot.

They was all about to make a break for him, but the biggest man there jumped up and says: —

"Set whar you are, gentlemen. Leave him to me; he's my meat."

Then he jumped up in the air three times and cracked his heels together every time. He flung off a buckskin coat that was all hung with fringes, and says, "You lay thar tell the chawin-up's done," and flung his hat down, which was all over ribbons, and says, "You lay thar tell his sufferin's is over."

Then he jumped up in the air and cracked his heels together again, and shouted out: —

"Whoo-oop! I'm the old original iron-jawed, brass-mounted, copper-bellied corpse-maker from the wilds of Arkansaw! — Look at me! I'm the man they call Sudden Death and General Desolation! Sired by a hurricane, dam'd by an earthquake, half-brother to the cholera, nearly related to the small-pox on the mother's side! Look at me! I take nineteen alligators and a bar'l of whiskey for breakfast when I'm in robust health, and a bushel of rattlesnakes and a dead body when I'm ailing! I split the everlasting rocks with my glance, and I squench the thunder when I speak! Whoo-oop! Stand back and give me room according to my strength! Blood's my natural drink, and the wails of the dying is music to my ear! Cast your eye on me, gentlemen! — and lay low and hold your breath, for I'm bout to turn myself loose!"

All the time he was getting this off, he was shaking his head and looking fierce, and kind of swelling around in a little circle, tucking up his wrist-bands, and now and then straightening up and beating his breast with his fist, saying, "Look at me, gentlemen!" When he got through, he jumped up and cracked his heels together three times, and let off a roaring "whoo-oop! I'm the bloodiest son of a wildcat that lives!"

Then the man that had started the row tilted his old slouch hat down over his right eye; then he bent stooping forward, with his back sagged and his south end sticking out far, and his fists a-shoving out and drawing in in front of him, and so went around in a little circle about three times, swelling himself up and breathing hard. Then he straightened, and jumped up and cracked his heels together three times before he lit again (that made them cheer), and he began to shout like this:

"Whoo-oop! bow your neck and spread, for the kingdom of sorrow's a-coming! Hold me down to the earth, for I feel my powers a-working! whoo-oop! I'm a child of sin, *don't* let me get a start! Smoked glass, here, for all! Don't attempt to look at me with the naked eye, gentlemen! When I'm playful I use the meridians of longitude and parallels of latitude for a seine, and drag the Atlantic Ocean for whales! I scratch my head with the lightning and purr myself to sleep with the thunder! When I'm cold, I bile the Gulf of Mexico and bathe in it; when I'm hot I fan myself with an equinoctial storm; when I'm thirsty I reach up and suck a cloud dry like a sponge: when I range the earth hungry, famine follows in my tracks! Whoo-oop! Bow your neck and spread! I put my hand on the sun's face and make it night in the earth; I bite a piece out of the moon and hurry the seasons; I shake myself and crumble the mountains! Contemplate me through leather — *don't* use the naked eye! I'm the man with a petrified heart and biler-iron bowels! The massacre of isolated communities is the pastime of my idle moments, the destruction of nationalities the serious business of my life! The boundless vastness of the great American desert is my enclosed property, and I bury my dead on my own premises!" He jumped up and cracked his heels together three times before he lit (they cheered him again), and as he come down he shouted out: "Whoo-oop! bow your neck and spread, for the pet child of calamity's a-coming!"

Then the other one went to swelling around and blowing again — the first one — the one they called Bob; next, the Child of Calamity chipped in again, bigger than ever; then they both got at it at the same time, swelling round and round each other and punching their fists most into each other's faces, and whooping and jawing like Injuns;

then Bob called the Child names, and the Child called him names back again: next, Bob called him a heap rougher names, and the Child come back at him with the very worst kind of language; next, Bob knocked the Child's hat off, and the Child picked it up and kicked Bob's ribbony hat about six foot; Bob went and got it and said never mind, this warn't going to be the last of this thing, because he was a man that never forgot and never forgive, and so the Child better look out, for there was a time a-coming, just as sure as he was a living man, that he would have to answer to him with the best blood in his body. The Child said no man was willinger than he for that time to come, and he would give Bob fair warning, *now*, never to cross his path again, for he could never rest till he had waded in his blood, for such was his nature, though he was sparing him now on account of his family, if he had one.

Both of them was edging away in different directions, growling and shaking their heads and going on about what they was going to do; but a little black-whiskered chap skipped up and says: —

"Come back here, you couple of chicken-livered cowards, and I'll thrash the two of ye!"

And he done it, too. He snatched them, he jerked them this way and that, he booted them around, he knocked them sprawling faster than they could get up. Why, it warn't two minutes till they begged like dogs — and how the other lot did yell and laugh and clap their hands all the way through, and shout "Sail in, Corpse-Maker!" "Hi! at him again, Child of Calamity!" "Bully for you, little Davy!" Well, it was a perfect pow-wow for a while. Bob and the Child had red noses and black eyes when they got through. Little Davy made them own up that they was sneaks and cowards and not fit to eat with a dog or drink with a nigger; then Bob and the Child shook hands with each other, very solemn, and said they had always respected each other and was willing to let bygones be bygones. So then they washed their faces in the river; and just then there was a loud order to stand by for a crossing, and some of them went forward to man the sweeps there, and the rest went aft to handle the after-sweeps.

I laid still and waited for fifteen minutes, and had a smoke out of a pipe that one of them left in reach; then the crossing was finished, and they stumped back and had a drink around and went to talking and singing again. Next they got out an old fiddle, and one played, and another patted juba, and the rest turned themselves loose on a regular old-fashioned keel-boat breakdown. They couldn't keep that up very long without getting winded, so by and by they settled around the jug again.

They sung "jolly, jolly raftsman's the life for me," with a rousing chorus, and then they got to talking about differences betwixt hogs, and their different kind of habits; and next about women and their different ways; and next about the best ways to put out houses that was afire; and next about what ought to be done with the Injuns; and next about what a king had to do, and how much he got; and next about how to make cats fight; and next about what to do when a man has fits; and next about differences betwixt clear-water rivers and muddy-water ones. The man they called Ed said the muddy Mississippi water was wholesomer to drink than the clear water of the Ohio; he said if you let a pint of this yaller Mississippi water settle, you would have about a half to three-quarters of an inch of mud in the bottom, according to the stage of the river, and then it warn't no better than Ohio water — what you wanted to do was to keep it stirred up — and when the river was low, keep mud on hand to put in and thicken the water up the way it ought to be.

The Child of Calamity said that was so; he said there was nutritiousness in the mud, and a man that drunk Mississippi water could grow corn in his stomach if he wanted to. He says: —

"You look at the graveyards; that tells the tale. Trees won't grow worth shucks in a Cincinnati graveyard, but in a Sent Louis graveyard they grow upwards of eight hundred foot high. It's all on account of the water the people drunk before they laid up. A Cincinnati corpse don't richen a soil any."

And they talked about how Ohio water didn't like to mix with Mississippi water. Ed said if you take the Mississippi on a rise when the Ohio is low, you'll find a wide band of clear water all the way down the east side of the Mississippi for a hundred mile or more, and the minute you get out a quarter of a mile from shore and pass the line, it is all thick and yaller the rest of the way across. Then they talked about how to keep tobacco from getting mouldy, and from that they went into ghosts and told about a lot that other folks had seen. . . .

BIBLIOGRAPHY

BIBLIOGRAPHY

The following selected bibliography is divided into "General Studies" of Southwestern humor and books and articles on "Individual Authors." Since these categories overlap considerably, both should be consulted for information on either single authors or the broader aspects of Old Southwest humor. Works by authors who appear in this collection are mentioned in the various headnotes, and the most important early anthologies are named passim in the information on the "Text" which follows the headnotes.

General Studies and Critical Anthologies

Alderman, Edwin Anderson, and Joel Chandler Harris, eds. *Library of Southern Literature.* 15 vols. Atlanta, 1907.

Anderson, John Q. "Scholarship in Southwestern Humor—Past and Present," *Mississippi Quarterly,* 17 (1964), 67-86.

————. *With the Bark On.* Nashville, 1967.

Avery, S. P., ed. *The Harp of a Thousand Strings; or, Laughter for a Lifetime.* New York, 1858.

Bettersworth, John K. "The Humor of the Old Southwest: Yesterday and Today," *Mississippi Quarterly,* 17 (1964), 87-94.

Bier, Jesse. *The Rise and Fall of American Humor.* New York, 1968, pp. 52-76.

Blair, Walter. *Horse Sense in American Humor.* Chicago, 1942.

————. *Native American Humor, 1800-1900.* New York, 1937.

————. "The Popularity of Nineteenth-Century American Humorists," *American Literature,* 3 (1931), 175-194.

————. "Traditions in Southern Humor," *American Quarterly,* 5 (1953), 132-142.

Blanck, Jacob. *Bibliography of American Literature.* New Haven, 1955-.

Boatright, Mody C. "The Art of Tall Lying," *Southwest Review,* 34 (1949), 357-363.

————. *Folk Laughter on the American Frontier.* New York, 1942.

Bolton, Theodore. "The Book Illustrations of Felix Octavius Carr

Darley," *Proceedings of the American Antiquarian Society,* 61 (1951), 137-182.

Bradley, Sculley. "Our Native Humor," *North American Review,* 242 (1937), 351-362.

Budd, Louis J. "Gentlemanly Humorists of the Old South," *Southern Folklore Quarterly,* 17 (1953), 232-240.

Chittick, V. L. O. "Ring-Tailed Roarers," *Frontier,* 13, (1933), 257-263.

_____. *Thomas Chandler Haliburton ("Sam Slick"): A Study in Provincial Toryism.* New York, 1924.

Clark, Thomas D. "Humor in the Stream of Southern History," *Mississippi Quarterly,* 13 (1960), 176-188.

_____. *The Rampaging Frontier: Manners and Humors of Pioneer Days in the South and the Middle West.* New York, 1939.

Clemens, Samuel Langhorne, comp. *Mark Twain's Library of Humor.* New York, 1888. Reprinted, New York, 1969.

Collins, Carvel. "Faulkner and Certain Earlier Southern Fiction," *College English,* 16 (1954), 92-97.

Colville, Derek. "History and Humor: The Tall Tale in New Orleans," *Louisiana Historical Quarterly,* 39 (1956), 153-167.

Costerus: Essays in English and American Language and Literature, n.s., special supplementary volume 2 (Southern and Southwestern Backwoods Humor), in press.

Covici, Pascal, Jr. *Mark Twain's Humor: The Image of a World.* Dallas, 1962.

Cox, James M. "Humor of the Old Southwest," in *The Comic Imagination in American Literature,* ed. Louis D. Rubin, Jr. New Brunswick, 1973, pp. 101-112.

Current-Garcia, Eugene. "Alabama Writers in the *Spirit,*" *Alabama Review,* 10 (1957), 243-269.

_____. "Newspaper Humorists in the Old South, 1835-1855," *Alabama Review,* 2 (1949), 102-121.

Davis, Charles E., and Martha B. Hudson. "Humor of the Old Southwest: A Checklist of Criticism," *Mississippi Quarterly,* 27 (1974), 179-199.

DeVoto, Bernard. *Mark Twain's America.* Boston, 1932.

Dillingham, William B. "Days of the Tall Tale," *Southern Review,* 4 (1968), 569-577.

Dondore, Dorothy A. "Big Talk! The Flyting, the Gabe, and the Frontier Boast," *American Speech,* 6 (1930), 45-55.

_____. *The Prairie and the Making of Middle America: Four Centuries of Description.* Cedar Rapids, 1926.

Dorson, Richard M. "The Identification of Folklore in American Literature," *Journal of American Folklore*, 70 (1957), 1-8.

------------. *American Folklore*. Chicago, 1959, pp. 49-69.

Eaton, Clement. "The Humor of the Southern Yeoman," *Sewanee Review*, 49 (1941), 173-183.

------------. "The Southern Yeoman: The Humorists' View," in *The Mind of the Old South*. Baton Rouge, 1964, pp. 101-118. Reprinted in *The Civilization of the Old South*, ed. Albert D. Kirwan. Lexington, 1968, pp. 57-77.

Eby, Cecil D. "Faulkner and the Southwestern Humorists," *Shenandoah*, 11 (1959), 13-21.

Ferguson, J. DeLancey. "The Roots of American Humor," *American Scholar*, 4 (1935), 41-49.

Flanders, B. H. "Humor in Ante-Bellum Georgia," *Emory University Quarterly*, 1 (1945), 149-156.

Haliburton, T. C. *The Americans at Home; or Byeways, Backwoods, and Prairies*. 3 vols. London, 1854.

------------. *Traits of American Humor by Native Authors*. 3 vols. London, 1852.

Hansen, Arlen J. "Entropy and Transformation: Two Types of American Humor," *American Scholar*, 43 (1974), 405-421.

Hauck, Richard Boyd. *A Cheerful Nihilism: Confidence and "the Absurd" in American Humorous Fiction*. Bloomingtor 1971, pp. 40-76.

Hill, Hamlin. "Modern American Humor: The Janus Laugh," *College English*, 24 (1963), 171-176.

Hoffman, Daniel G. *Form and Fable in American Fiction*. New York, 1961.

------------. *Paul Bunyan: Last of the Frontier Demigods*. Philadelphia, 1952.

Hubbell, Jay B. *The South in American Literature 1607-1900*. Durham, 1954.

Hudson, Arthur Palmer, ed. *Humor of the Old Deep South*. New York, 1936.

Hyde, Stuart W. "The Ring-Tailed Roarer in American Drama," *Southern Folklore Quarterly*, 19 (1955), 171-178.

Inge, M. Thomas. "Literary Humor of the Old Southwest: A Brief Overview," *Louisiana Studies*, 7 (1968), 132-143.

Johnston, Charles. "Old Funny Stories of the South and West," *Harper's Weekly*, 67 (4 January 1913), 21.

Jordan, Philip D. "Humor of the Backwoods, 1820-1840," *Mississippi Valley Historical Review*, 25 (1938), 25-38.

Kuhlmann, Susan. *Knave, Fool, and Genius: The Confidence Man as He Appears in Nineteenth-Century American Fiction.* Chapel Hill, 1973.

Link, Samuel A. "Southern Humorists: Longstreet, Baldwin, Hooper, W. T. Thompson, Davy Crockett, and Others," in *Pioneers of Southern Literature.* Vol. 2. Nashville, 1900, pp. 465-545.

Lynn, Kenneth S. *Mark Twain and Southwestern Humor.* Boston, 1959.

McIlwaine, Shields. *The Southern Poor-White, from Lubberland to Tobacco Road.* Norman, 1939.

Masterson, James R. *Tall Tales of Arkansaw.* Boston, 1942.

Meine, Franklin J. "American Folk Literature," *Amateur Book Collector,* 1 (1951), 3-4.

_____. *Tall Tales of the Southwest.* New York, 1930.

Moore, Arthur K. "Specimens of the Folktales from Some Antebellum Newspapers of Louisiana," *Louisiana Historical Quarterly,* 32 (1949), 723-758.

Moses, Montrose J. *The Literature of the South.* New York, 1910.

Parks, Edd Winfield. *Ante-Bellum Southern Literary Critics.* Athens, Ga., 1962, pp. 60-65.

_____. "The Intent of the Antebellum Southern Humorists," *Mississippi Quarterly,* 13 (1960), 163-168.

_____. "The Three Streams of Southern Humor," *Georgia Review,* 9 (1955), 147-159.

Parrington, V. L. *Main Currents in American Thought,* vol. 2: *The Romantic Revolution in America, 1800-1860.* New York, 1927.

Pearce, James T. "Folk Tales of the Southern Poor-Whites, 1820-1860," *Journal of American Folklore,* 63 (1950), 398-412.

Penrod, James H. "Characteristic Endings of Southwestern Yarns," *Mississippi Quarterly,* 11 (1961-1962), 27-35.

_____. "The Folk Hero as Prankster in the Old Southwestern Yarns," *Kentucky Folklore Record,* 2 (1956), 5-12.

_____. "The Folk Mind in Early Southwestern Humor," *Tennessee Folklore Society Bulletin,* 18 (1952), 49-54.

_____. "Folk Motifs in Old Southwestern Humor, *Southern Folklore Quarterly,* 19 (1955), 117-124.

_____. "Minority Groups in Old Southern Humor," *Southern Folklore Quarterly,* 22 (1958), 121-128.

_____. "Teachers and Preachers in the Old Southwestern Yarns," *Tennessee Folklore Society Bulletin,* 18 (1952), 91-96.

_____. "Two Types of Incongruity in Old Southwest Humor," *Kentucky Folklore Record,* 4 (1958), 163-173.

Richardson, H. Edward. "Faulkner, Anderson, and Their Tall Tale," *American Literature,* 34 (1962), 287-291.

Rickels, Milton. "The Humorists of the Old Southwest in the London *Bentley's Miscellany,*" *American Literature,* 27 (1956), 557-560.

Rideout, Walter B., and James B. Meriwether. "On the Collaboration of Faulkner and Anderson," *American Literature,* 35 (1963), 85-87.

Rourke, Constance. *American Humor: A Study of the National Character.* New York, 1931.

Rubin, Louis D., ed. *A Bibliographical Guide to the Study of Southern Literature.* Baton Rouge, 1969.

Sederberg, Nancy B. "Antebellum Southern Humor in the *Camden Journal:* 1826-1840," *Mississippi Quarterly,* 27 (1973-1974), 41-74.

Simpson, Lewis P. "The Humor of the Old Southwest," *Mississippi Quarterly,* 17 (1964), 63-66.

Skaggs, Merrill Maguire. *The Folk in Southern Fiction.* Athens, Ga., 1972, pp. 25-35.

Stewart, Randall. "Tidewater and Frontier," *Georgia Review,* 13 (1959), 296-307.

Tandy, Jennette. *Crackerbox Philosophers in American Humor and Satire.* New York, 1925.

Thompson, William F. "Frontier Tall Talk," *American Speech,* 9 (1934), 187-199.

Thorp, Willard. *American Humorists.* University of Minnesota Pamphlets on American Writers, no. 42. Minneapolis, 1964.

Turner, Arlin. "Realism and Fantasy in Southern Humor," *Georgia Review,* 12 (1958), 451-457.

――――. "Seeds of Literary Revolt in the Humor of the Old Southwest," *Louisiana Historical Quarterly,* 39 (1956), 143-151.

――――. ed. *Southern Stories.* New York, 1960, pp. xii-xviii.

Watterson, Henry. *The Compromises of Life.* New York, 1903, pp. 59-101.

――――, ed. *Oddities in Southern Life and Character.* Boston, 1883.

Weber, Brom. "American Humor and American Culture," *American Quarterly,* 14 (1962), 503-507.

West, James L. W., III. "Early Backwoods Humor in the Greenville *Mountaineer,* 1826-1840," *Mississippi Quarterly,* 25 (1971), 69-82.

Yates, Norris W. "Antebellum Southern Humor as a Vehicle of Class Expression," *Bulletin of Central Mississippi Valley American Studies Association,* 1 (1958), 1-6.

INDIVIDUAL AUTHORS

Joseph Glover Baldwin

Amacher, Richard E., and George W. Polhemus, eds. *The Flush Times of California.* Athens, Ga., 1966.

Braswell, William. "An Unpublished Letter of Joseph Glover Baldwin," *American Literature,* 2 (1935), 292-294.

Current-Garcia, Eugene. "Joseph Glover Baldwin: Humorist or Moralist?" *Alabama Review,* 5 (1952), 122-141.

Farish, H. D. "An Overlooked Personality in Southern Life," *North Carolina Historical Review,* 12 (1935), 341-353.

McDermott, John Francis. "Baldwin's 'Flush Times of Alabama and Mississippi'—A Bibliographical Note," *Papers of the Bibliographical Society of America,* 45 (1951), 251-256.

McMillan, Malcolm C., ed. "Joseph Glover Baldwin Reports on the Whig National Convention of 1848," *Journal of Southern History,* 25 (1959), 366-382.

Mellen, George F. "Joseph G. Baldwin and the 'Flush Times,'" *Sewanee Review,* 9 (1901), 171-184.

Wetmore, T. B. "Joseph Glover Baldwin," *Transactions of the Alabama Historical Society, 1897-1898,* 2 (1898), 67-73.

William Penn Brannan

Kummer, George. "Who Wrote 'The Harp of a Thousand Strings'?" *Ohio Historical Quarterly,* 67 (1958), 221-231.

Samuel Langhorne Clemens

Babcock, C. Merton. "Mark Twain, Mencken and 'The Higher Goofyism,'" *American Quarterly,* 16 (1964), 587-594.

Baender, Paul. "The 'Jumping Frog' as a Comedian's First Virtue," *Modern Philology,* 60 (1963), 192-200.

Bellamy, Gladys Carmen. *Mark Twain as a Literary Artist.* Norman, 1950.

Blodgett, Harold. "A Note on Mark Twain's Library of Humor," *American Literature,* 10 (1938), 78-80.

Branch, Edgar Marquess. *The Literary Apprenticeship of Mark Twain.* Urbana, 1950.

―――――. "'My Voice is Still for Setchell': A Background Study of 'Jim Smiley and His Jumping Frog,'" *PMLA,* 82 (1967), 591-601.

Cohen, Hennig. "Mark Twain's Sut Lovingood," *The Lovingood Papers,* 1962, pp. 19-24.

―――――. "Twain's Jumping Frog: Folktale to Literature to Folktale," *Western Folklore,* 22 (1963), 17-18.

Cox, James M. *Mark Twain: The Fate of Humor.* Princeton, 1966.

DeVoto, Bernard. "The Matrix of Mark Twain's Humor," *Bookman,* 74 (1931), 172-178.

Gerber, John C. "Mark Twain's Use of the Comic Pose," *PMLA,* 77 (1962), 297-304.

Havard, William C. "Mark Twain and the Political Ambivalence of Southwestern Humor," *Mississippi Quarterly,* 17 (1964), 95-106.

Krause, S. J. "The Art and Satire of Twain's 'Jumping Frog' Story," *American Quarterly,* 16 (1964), 562-576.

Leisy, Ernest E. "Mark Twain and Isaiah Sellers," *American Literature,* 13 (1942), 398-405.

Long, E. Hudson. "Sut Lovingood and Mark Twain's *Joan of Arc,*" *Modern Language Notes,* 64 (1949), 37-39.

Lorch, Fred W. "A Source for Mark Twain's 'The Dandy Frightening the Squatter,'" *American Literature,* 3 (1931), 309-313.

McKeithan, D. M. "Bull Rides Described by 'Scroggins,' G. W. Harris, and Mark Twain," *Southern Folklore Quarterly,* 17 (1953), 241-243.

————. "Mark Twain's Story of the Bulls and the Bees," *Tennessee Historical Quarterly,* 11 (1952), 246-253.

Rodgers, Paul C., Jr. "Artemus Ward and Mark Twain's 'Jumping Frog,'" *Nineteenth-Century Fiction,* 28 (1973), 273-286.

Spengemann, William C. *Mark Twain and the Backwoods Angel: The Matter of Innocence in the Works of Samuel L. Clemens.* Kent, Ohio, 1966.

Stein, Allen F. "Return to Phelps Farm: *Huckleberry Finn* and the Old Southwestern Framing Device," *Mississippi Quarterly,* 24 (1971), 111-116.

David Crockett

Blair, Walter. "Six Davy Crocketts," *Southwest Review,* 25 (1939-1940), 443-462.

Bright, Verne. "Davy Crockett Legend and Tales in the Oregon Country," *Oregon Historical Quarterly,* 51 (1950), 207-215.

Davis, Curtis Carroll. "A Legend at Full-Length," *Proceedings of the American Antiquarian Society,* 69 (1959), 155-174.

Dorson, Richard M. *Davy Crockett: American Comic Legend.* New York, 1939.

Hoffman, Daniel G. "The Deaths and Three Resurrections of Davy Crockett," *Antioch Review,* 21 (1961), 5-13.

Leach, Joseph. "Crockett's Almanacs and the Typical Texan," *Southwest Review,* 35 (1950), 88-95.

Miles, Guy S. "David Crockett Evolves, 1821-1824," *American Quarterly*, 8 (1956), 53-60.

Rourke, Constance M. *Davy Crockett*. New York, 1934.

_____. "Davy Crockett: Forgotten Facts and Legends," *Southwest Review*, 19 (1933-1934), 149-161.

Shackford, James Atkins. *David Crockett, the Man and the Legend*. Chapel Hill, 1956.

_____, and Stanley J. Folmsbee, eds. *A Narrative of the Life of David Crockett of the State of Tennessee*. Knoxville, 1973.

Joseph M. Field

Smith, Sol. *Theatrical Management in the West and South*. New York, 1868.

Spotts, Carle Brooks. "The Development of Fiction on the Missouri Frontier," *Missouri Historical Review*, 29, pts. 4-6 (1935), 100-108, 186-194, 279-294.

William C. Hall

Anderson, John Q. "Mike Hooter: The Making of a Myth," *Southern Folklore Quarterly*, 19 (1955), 90-100.

George Washington Harris

Bass, W. W. "Sut Lovingood's Reflections on his Contemporaries," *Carson-Newman College Faculty Studies*, 1 (1964), 33-48.

Blair, Walter. "Sut Lovingood," *Saturday Review of Literature*, 15 (7 November 1936), 3-4, 16.

Boykin, Carol. "Sut's Speech: The Dialect of a 'Nat'ral Borned' Mountaineer," *The Lovingood Papers*, 1965, pp. 36-42.

Bridgman, Richard. *The Colloquial Style in America*. New York, 1966, pp. 23-31.

Bungert, Hans. "Re: Stark Young's Sut Lovingood," *The Lovingood Papers*, 1965, pp. 53-54.

Current-Garcia, Eugene. "Sut Lovingood's Rare Ripe Southern Garden," *Studies in Short Fiction*, 9 (1972), 117-129.

Day, Donald. "The Humorous Works of George W. Harris," *American Literature*, 14 (1943), 391-406.

_____. "The Life of George Washington Harris," *Tennessee Historical Quarterly*, 6 (1947), 3-38.

_____. "The Political Satires of George W. Harris," *Tennessee Historical Quarterly*, 4 (1945), 320-338.

_____. "Searching for Sut," *The Lovingood Papers*, 1965, pp. 9-15.

Eastman, Elbridge Gerry, and William Crutchfield, "Sut's Dedicatory," *The Lovingood Papers*, 1962, pp. 11-17.

Howell, Elmo. "Timon in Tennessee: The Moral Fervor of George Washington Harris," *Georgia Review,* 24 (1970), 311-319.

Inge, M. Thomas. "A Personal Encounter with George Washington Harris," *The Lovingood Papers,* 1963, pp. 9-12.

––––––, ed. "Early Appreciations of George W. Harris by George Frederick Mellen," *Tennessee Historical Quarterly,* 30 (1971), 190-204.

––––––. "George Washington Harris and Southern Poetry and Music," *Mississippi Quarterly,* 17 (1964), 36-44.

––––––, ed. *High Times and Hard Times: Sketches and Tales by George Washington Harris.* Nashville, 1967.

––––––. "The Satiric Artistry of George W. Harris," *Satire Newsletter,* 4 (1967), 63-72.

––––––. "Stark Young's Sut Lovingood," *The Lovingood Papers,* 1964, pp. 45-46.

––––––. "Sut and His Contemporary Reviewers," *The Lovingood Papers,* 1965, pp. 55-56.

––––––. "Sut and His Illustrators," *The Lovingood Papers,* 1965, pp. 26-35.

––––––. "Sut Lovingood: An Examination of the Nature of a 'Nat'ral Born Durn'd Fool,' " *Tennessee Historical Quarterly,* 19 (1960), 231-251.

––––––. "William Faulkner and George Washington Harris: In the Tradition of Southwestern Humor," *Tennessee Studies in Literature,* 7 (1962), 47-59.

Knight, Donald R. "Sut's Dog Imagery," *The Lovingood Papers,* 1965, pp. 59-60.

Leary, Lewis. *Southern Excursions: Essays on Mark Twain and Others.* Baton Rouge, 1971, pp. 111-130.

McClary, Ben Harris. "George and Sut: A Working Bibliography," *The Lovingood Papers,* 1962, pp. 5-9.

––––––. "On Quilts," *The Lovingood Papers,* 1965, pp. 61-62.

––––––. "The Real Sut," *American Literature,* 27 (1955), 105-106.

––––––. "Sut Lovingood Views 'Abe Linkhorn,' " *Lincoln Herald,* 56 (1954), 44-45.

––––––. "Sut Lovingood's Country," *Southern Observer,* 3 (1955), 5-7.

Matthiessen, F. O. *American Renaissance: Art and Expression in the Age of Emerson and Whitman.* New York, 1941, pp. 641-645.

Parks, Edd Winfield. "Sut Lovingood," in *Segments of Southern Thought.* Athens, Ga., 1938.

––––––. *Sut Lovingood's Travels with Old Abe Lincoln.* Chicago, 1937.

Penrod, James. "Folk Humor in Sut Lovingood's Yarns," *Tennessee Folklore Society Bulletin,* 16 (1950), 76-84.

Plater, Ormonde. "Before Sut: Folklore in the Early Works of George Washington Harris," *Southern Folklore Quarterly,* 34 (1970), 104-115.

Rickels, Milton. *George Washington Harris.* New York, 1965.

————. "The Imagery of George Washington Harris," *American Literature,* 31 (1959), 173-187.

Weber, Brom. "A Note on Edmund Wilson and George Washington Harris," *The Lovingood Papers,* 1962, pp. 47-53.

————, ed. *Sut Lovingood.* New York, 1954.

Wilson, Edmund. *Patriotic Gore.* New York, 1962, pp. 507-520.

————. "Poisoned!" *New Yorker,* 31 (7 May 1955), 150-159.

Johnson Jones Hooper

Hoole, W. Stanley. *Alias Simon Suggs: The Life and Times of Johnson Jones Hooper.* University, Ala., 1952.

Hopkins, Robert. "Simon Suggs: A Burlesque Campaign Biography," *American Quarterly,* 15 (1963), 459-463.

Inge, M. Thomas. "Simon Suggs Courts a Widow: A New Sketch," *Alabama Review,* 17 (1964), 148-151.

Smith, Winston. "Simon Suggs and the Satiric Tradition," in *Essays in Honor of Richebourg Gaillard McWilliams,* ed. Howard Creed. Birmingham, 1970, pp. 49-56.

Thorp, Willard. "Suggs and Sut in Modern Dress: The Latest Chapter in Southern Humor," *Mississippi Quarterly,* 13 (1960), 169-175.

Wellman, Manly Wade, ed. *Adventures of Captain Simon Suggs, Late of the Tallapoosa Volunteers.* Chapel Hill, 1969.

West, Harry C. "Simon Suggs and His Similes," *North Carolina Folklore Journal,* 16 (1968), 53-57.

George Wilkins Kendall

Brown, Harry James, ed. *Letters from a Texas Sheep Ranch.* Urbana, 1959.

Copeland, Fayette. *Kendall of the* Picayune. Norman, 1943.

Coulter, E. Merton, ed. *The Other Half of Old New Orleans: Sketches of Characters and Incidents from the Recorder's Court of New Orleans in the Eighteen Forties as Reported in the "Picayune."* Baton Rouge, 1939.

Kendall, John S. "George Wilkins Kendall and the Founding of the New Orleans *Picayune,*" *Louisiana Historical Quarterly,* 11 (1928), 261-285.

Thomas Kirkman

Owen, Thomas McAlory. "Samuel Kirkman," in *History of Alabama and Dictionary of Alabama Biography.* Vol. 3. Chicago, 1921.
"Samuel Kirkman," in *Northern Alabama: Historical and Biographical.* Birmingham, 1888, p. 313.

Henry Clay Lewis

Anderson, John Q. "Folklore in the Writings of 'Louisiana Swamp Doctor,' " *Southern Folklore Quarterly,* 19 (1955), 243-251.
―――――. "Henry Clay Lewis, Alias 'Madison Tensas,' M.D., The Louisiana Swamp Doctor," *Bulletin of the Medical Library Association,* 43 (1955), 58-73.
―――――. "Henry Clay Lewis, Louisville Medical Institute Student, 1844-1846," *Filson Club Historical Quarterly,* 32 (1958), 30-37.
―――――. *Louisiana Swamp Doctor.* Baton Rouge, 1962.
Rose, Alan H. "The Image of the Negro in the Writings of Henry Clay Lewis," *American Literature,* 41 (1969), 255-263.

Augustus Baldwin Longstreet

"An Unreprinted *Georgia Scene,*" *Emory University Quarterly,* 2 (1946), 100-101.
Fitzgerald, Oscar Penn. *Judge Longstreet: A Life Sketch.* Nashville, 1891.
Ford, Thomas W. "Ned Brace of *Georgia Scenes,*" *Southern Folklore Quarterly,* 29 (1965), 220-227.
Harkey, Joseph H. "A Note on Longstreet's Ransy Sniffle and Brackenridge's *Modern Chivalry,*" *The Western Pennsylvania Historical Magazine,* 52 (1969), 43-45.
Knight, Lucian Lamar. *Reminiscences of Famous Georgians.* Vol. 2. Atlanta, 1908, pp. 174-184.
McElderry, B. R., Jr., ed. *Georgia Scenes.* New York, 1957.
Poe, Edgar Allan. "Georgia Scenes," *Southern Literary Messenger,* 2 (1836), 287-292.
Silverman, Kenneth. "Longstreet's 'The Gander Pulling,' " *American Quarterly,* 18 (1966), 548-549.
Smith, Gerald J. "Augustus Baldwin Longstreet and John Wade's 'Cousin Lucius,' " *Georgia Historical Quarterly,* 61 (1972), 276-281.
Wade, John Donald. "Augustus Baldwin Longstreet, A Southern Cultural Type," in *Southern Pioneers in Social Interpretation,* ed. Howard W. Odum. Chapel Hill, 1925, pp. 119-140.
―――――. *Augustus Baldwin Longstreet: A Study of the Development of Culture in the South,* ed. M. Thomas Inge. Athens, Ga., 1969.

_____. "Old Books: *Georgia Scenes,*" *Georgia Review,* 14 (1960), 444-447.

Alexander G. McNutt

Davis, Reuben. *Recollections of Mississippi and Mississippians.* Boston, 1889, pp. 83-85.

Foote, Henry S. *Casket of Reminiscences.* Washington, 1874, pp. 198-215.

Lowry, Robert, and William H. McCardle. "The Administration of Governor McNutt," in *A History of Mississippi.* Jackson, 1891, p. 298.

Charles F. M. Noland

Masterson, James. "An Arkansaw Colonel" and "Col. Pete Whetstone," in *Tall Tales of Arkansaw.* Boston, 1943, pp. 29-54.

Shinn, Josiah H. "The Life and Public Service of Charles Fenton Mercer Noland," *Publications of the Arkansas Historical Association,* 1 (1904), 330-343.

Worley, Ted R., and Eugene A. Nolte, eds. *Pete Whetstone of Devil's Fork: Letters to the* Spirit of the Times, *by Charles F. M. Noland.* Van Buren, Ark., 1957.

James Kirke Paulding

Aderman, Ralph M. "James K. Paulding on Literature and the West," *American Literature,* 27 (1955), 97-101.

Adkins, Nelson F. "James K. Paulding's Lion of the West," *American Literature,* 3 (1931), 249-258.

Conklin, Willet Titus. "Paulding's Prose Treatment of Types and Frontier Life Before Cooper," *University of Texas Studies in English.* 1939, pp. 163-171.

Henry, Joyce. "Five More Essays by James Kirke Paulding?" *Papers of the Bibliographical Society of America,* 66 (1972), 310-321.

Hodge, Francis. "Biography of a Lost Play: *Lion of the West,*" *The Theatre Annual,* 12 (1954), 48-61.

Mason, Melvin Rosser. " 'The Lion of the West': Satire on Davy Crockett and Frances Trollope," *The South Central Bulletin,* 29 (1969), 143-145.

Tidwell, James N., ed. *The Lion of the West.* Stanford, 1954.

Turner, Arlin. "James K. Paulding and Timothy Flint," *Mississippi Valley Historical Review,* 34 (1947), 105-111.

Watkins, Floyd C. "James Kirke Paulding and the South," *American Quarterly,* 5 (1953), 219-230.

----------. "James Kirke Paulding's Early Ring-Tailed Roarer," *Southern Folklore Quarterly,* 15 (1951), 183-187.

William T. Porter

Betts, John R. "Sporting Journalism in Nineteenth-Century America," *American Quarterly,* 5 (1953), 39-56.

Brinley, Francis. *Life of William T. Porter.* New York, 1860.

Collins, Carvel. "The Spirit of the Times," *Papers of the Bibliographical Society of America,* 40 (1946), 164-168.

Current-Garcia, Eugene. " 'Mr. Spirit' and *The Big Bear of Arkansas,*" *American Literature,* 27 (1955), 332.

----------. " 'York's Tall Son' and his Southern Correspondents," *American Quarterly,* 7 (1955), 374-375.

Hauck, Richard Boyd. "Predicting a Native Literature: William T. Porter's First Issue of *The Spirit of the Times,*" *Mississippi Quarterly,* 22 (1968-1969), 77-84.

Yates, Norris W. *William T. Porter and the* Spirit of the Times: *A Study of the Big Bear School of Humor.* Baton Rouge, 1957.

John S. Robb

McDermott, John Francis, ed. *Streaks of Squatter Life, and Far-West Scenes.* Gainesville, 1962.

----------. "Gold Fever: The Letters of 'Solitaire,' Goldrush Correspondent of '49," *Missouri Historical Society Bulletin,* 5 (1949), 115-126, 211-223, 316-331; 6 (1949), 34-43.

Spotts, Carle Brooks. "The Development of Fiction on the Missouri Frontier," *Missouri Historical Review,* 29, pt. 4 (1935), 100-108.

Solomon Franklin Smith

Spotts, Carle Brooks. "The Development of Fiction on the Missouri Frontier," *Missouri Historical Review,* 29, pts. 4-5 (1935), 100-108, 186-194.

Harden E. Taliaferro

Boggs, Ralph S. "North Carolina Folktales Current in the 1820's," *Journal of American Folklore,* 47 (1934), 269-288.

Coffin, Tristram P. "Harden E. Taliaferro and the Use of Folklore by American Literary Figures," *South Atlantic Quarterly,* 64 (1965), 241-246.

Ginther, James E. "Harden E. Taliaferro, a Sketch," *Mark Twain Quarterly,* 9 (1953), 13-15, 20.

Guernsey, A. H. "Surry County, North Carolina," *Harper's New Monthly Magazine,* 25 (1862), 178-185.

Jackson, David K., ed. *Carolina Humor: Sketches by Harden E. Taliaferro.* Richmond, 1938.

Penrod, James H. "Harden Taliaferro, Folk Humorist of North Carolina," *Midwest Folklore,* 6 (1956), 147-153.

Whiting, B. J. "Proverbial Sayings from Fisher's River, North Carolina," *Southern Folklore Quarterly,* 11 (1947), 173-185.

Williams, Cratis D. "Mountain Customs, Social Life, and Folk Yarns in Taliaferro's *Fisher's River Scenes and Characters,*" *North Carolina Folklore Journal,* 16 (1968), 143-152.

William Tappan Thompson

Ellison, George R. "William Tappan Thompson and the *Southern Miscellany,* 1842-1844," *Mississippi Quarterly,* 23 (1970), 155-168.

Hubbell, Jay B. "William Tappan Thompson," in *The South in American Literature 1607-1900.* Durham, 1954, pp. 669-672.

McKeithan, D. M. "Mark Twain's Letters of Thomas Jefferson Snodgrass," *Philological Quarterly,* 32 (1953), 353-365.

Miller, Henry Prentice. "The Background and Significance of *Major Jones's Courtship,*" *Georgia Historical Quarterly,* 25 (1946), 267-296.

Thompson, Maurice. "An Old Southern Humorist," *Independent,* 50 (1898), 1103-1105.

Thomas Bangs Thorpe

Blair, Walter. "The Technique of the Big Bear of Arkansas," *Southwest Review,* 28 (1943), 426-435.

Current-Garcia, Eugene. "Thomas Bangs Thorpe and the Literature of the Ante-Bellum Southwestern Frontier," *Louisiana Historical Quarterly,* 39 (1956), 199-222.

McDermott, John Francis. "T. B. Thorpe's Burlesque of Far West Sporting Travel," *American Quarterly,* 10 (1958), 175-180.

Rickels, Milton. "A Bibliography of the Writings of Thomas Bangs Thorpe," *American Literature,* 29 (1957-1958), 171-179.

———. *Thomas Bangs Thorpe: Humorist of the Old Southwest.* Baton Rouge, 1962.

———. "Thomas Bangs Thorpe in the Felicianas, 1836-1842," *Louisiana Historical Quarterly,* 39 (1956), 169-197.

Simoneaux, Katherine G. "Symbolism in Thorpe's 'The Big Bear of Arkansas,'" *The Arkansas Historical Quarterly,* 25 (1966), 240-247.

Kittrell J. Warren

Watkins, Floyd C. "A Tale of the Civil War," *Emory University Quarterly,* 13 (1957), 48.

⸺, ed. *Life and Public Services of an Army Straggler.* Athens, Ga., 1961.

⸺, ed. *Ups and Downs of Wife Hunting.* Emory University, Ga., 1957.

Mason Locke Weems

Purcell, James S., Jr. "A Book Pedlar's Progress in North Carolina," *North Carolina Historical Review,* 29 (1952), 8-23.

Salley, Alexander S. "Horry's Notes to Weem's Life of Marion," *South Carolina Historical Magazine,* 60 (1959), 119-122.

Skeel, Emily E. F., ed. *Mason Locke Weems: His Works and Ways.* New York, 1929.

⸺, ed. *Three Discourses.* New York, 1929.

Van Tassel, David D. "The Legend Maker," *American Heritage,* 13 (February 1962), 58-59, 89-94.

Wroth, Lawrence C. *Parson Weems: A Biographical and Critical Study.* Baltimore, 1911.